Cary Grant, the Making of a Hollywood Legend

OXFORD CULTURAL BIOGRAPHIES

Gary Giddins, Series Editor

A Generous Vision: The Creative Life of Elaine de Kooning
Cathy Curtis

Straighten Up and Fly Right: The Life and Music of Nat King Cole
Will Friedwald

Music by Max Steiner: The Epic Life of Hollywood's Most Influential Composer
Steven C. Smith

Cary Grant, the Making of a Hollywood Legend
Mark Glancy

Cary Grant, the Making of a Hollywood Legend

MARK GLANCY

UNIVERSITY PRESS

OXFORD
UNIVERSITY PRESS

Oxford University Press is a department of the University of Oxford. It furthers the University's objective of excellence in research, scholarship, and education by publishing worldwide. Oxford is a registered trade mark of Oxford University Press in the UK and certain other countries.

Published in the United States of America by Oxford University Press
198 Madison Avenue, New York, NY 10016, United States of America.

Library of Congress Control Number: 2020943043
ISBN 978–0–19–005313–0

1 3 5 7 9 8 6 4 2

Printed by Sheridan Books, Inc., United States of America

For
Roger Law

Contents

List of Illustrations   ix
Foreword by Gary Giddins   xiii
Acknowledgments   xvii

Introduction   1

PART ONE: ARCHIE LEACH, 1904 TO 1927

Chapter 1   9

Chapter 2   21

Chapter 3   31

Chapter 4   45

PART TWO: MATINEE IDOL, 1927 TO 1936

Chapter 5   57

Chapter 6   72

Chapter 7   84

Chapter 8   95

Chapter 9   106

Chapter 10   119

Chapter 11   128

Chapter 12   140

PART THREE: STARDOM, 1937 TO 1950

Chapter 13   155

Chapter 14   172

Chapter 15   187

Chapter 16   201

Chapter 17   217

Chapter 18   232

Chapter 19   246

Chapter 20   263

Chapter 21   280

Chapter 22   295

PART FOUR: TRUTH SEEKER, 1951 TO 1962

Chapter 23   313

Chapter 24   327

Chapter 25   343

Chapter 26   358

Chapter 27   376

PART FIVE: LEGEND, 1962 TO 1986

Chapter 28   395

Chapter 29   413

Notes   425
Sources: Abbreviations   487
Select Bibliography   489
Filmography   501
Index   541

List of Illustrations

1.1   Archie Leach in 1904   10
Source: The Cary Grant Papers, courtesy of the Margaret Herrick Library

1.2   Archie's birthplace: the house on Hughenden Road, Bristol   11
Source: author's own collection

1.3   Elias James Leach, circa 1900   14
Source: The Cary Grant Papers, courtesy of the Margaret Herrick Library

1.4   Elsie Maria Leach, circa 1900   15
Source: The Cary Grant Papers, courtesy of the Margaret Herrick Library

1.5   Archie Leach, circa 1910   16
Source: The Cary Grant Papers, courtesy of the Margaret Herrick Library

2.6   The former Bristol Lunatic Asylum, now a part of the University of the West of England, Glenside Campus   23
Source: author's own collection

2.7   Archie Leach (front row, at the far left) in a Boy Scouts parade in November 1916   26
Source: The Cary Grant Papers, courtesy of the Margaret Herrick Library

3.8   The Pender Troupe, circa 1918, with Archie seated in the front row at the far right   35
Source: The Cary Grant Papers, courtesy of the Margaret Herrick Library

3.9   The Pender Troupe in New York, circa 1920, with Archie on the far left   39
Source: The Cary Grant Papers, courtesy of the Margaret Herrick Library

3.10   Archie looking sharp in a suit, with a tie-pin and a pocket square, circa 1920   40
Source: The Cary Grant Papers, courtesy of the Margaret Herrick Library

5.11   Seven-year-old Eric Leach with his father, Elias James Leach, and his mother, Mabel Johnson Bass, in 1929   63
Source: The Cary Grant Papers, courtesy of the Margaret Herrick Library

5.12   Archie and his father in Bristol, 1929   64
Source: The Cary Grant Papers, courtesy of the Margaret Herrick Library

5.13   Archie's first film, the short *Singapore Sue* (Paramount Pictures, 1931), with Anna Chang   68
Source: author's screen capture

5.14   Archie in St. Louis during the summer of 1931   70
Source: The Cary Grant Papers, courtesy of the Margaret Herrick Library

6.15   In the first scene of his first feature film, *This Is the Night* (Paramount Pictures, 1932), Cary Grant is applauded by Charles Ruggles.   80
Source: author's screen capture

6.16   Cary Grant and Tallulah Bankhead in *Devil and the Deep* (Paramount Pictures, 1932), one of his many tuxedoed "mannequin" roles, where he was required to do little other than look handsome   82
Source: author's screen capture

7.17   Cary Grant and Marlene Dietrich in *Blonde Venus* (Paramount Pictures, 1932). Director Josef von Sternberg restyled Cary's hair, giving him the parting that became integral to his appearance.   88
Source: author's screen capture

7.18   Cary Grant and Sylvia Sidney in *Madame Butterfly* (Paramount Pictures, 1932). Decades later, Sidney admired his intense performance in this scene.   93
Source: author's screen capture

8.19   Cary with Mae West in *She Done Him Wrong* (Paramount Pictures, 1933). She insisted that her costumes ensure that audiences' eyes would be on her.   99
Source: author's screen capture

9.20   Cary Grant and Virginia Cherrill on November 25, 1933, soon after his arrival in Britain   112
Source: The Cary Grant Papers, courtesy of the Margaret Herrick Library

11.21 Katharine Hepburn, masquerading as a boy in *Sylvia Scarlett* (Paramount Pictures, 1935), rejects Monkley's suggestion that they keep warm by sleeping in the same bed.   136
Source: author's screen capture

12.22 Cary Grant and Randolph Scott are "Batching It" in the fan magazine *Modern Screen* (September 1937).   143
Source: author's own collection

13.23 Cary found his métier playing a relaxed, informal American gentleman in *The Awful Truth* (Columbia Pictures, 1937). Here, he questions his wife Lucy (Irene Dunne) and her vocal instructor (Alexander D'Arcy).   162
Source: author's screen capture

13.24 In *Bringing Up Baby* (RKO Radio Pictures, 1938), David is covered in feathers, one of the many affronts to his clothing, which gradually break his composure.   166
Source: author's screen capture

13.25 As David seethes, Susan (Katharine Hepburn) explains to her aunt (May Robson) why he "just went gay all of the sudden" in *Bringing Up Baby*.   169
Source: author's screen capture

14.26 After her release from the asylum, Elsie Leach sent her son several
       photographs showing her looking stylish and well-groomed.   173
       Source: The Cary Grant Papers, courtesy of the Margaret Herrick Library

14.27 Phyllis Brooks and a very tanned Cary Grant at his Santa Monica beach
       house, circa 1938   176
       Source: The Cary Grant Papers, courtesy of the Margaret Herrick Library

15.28 In *His Girl Friday* (Columbia Pictures, 1940), Cary and Rosalind Russell's
       verbal fireworks distract from the drab settings.   197
       Source: author's screen capture

17.29 *Suspicion* (RKO Radio Pictures, 1941) begins as a light romantic comedy,
       with only a hint of shadow behind Joan Fontaine and Cary.   224
       Source: author's screen capture

17.30 By the end of *Suspicion*, Johnny is in full shadow as he brings
       Lina a glass of milk.   225
       Source: author's screen capture

17.31 Cary threw himself into the broad comedy of *Arsenic and Old Lace*
       (Warner Bros., 1944) but he was embarrassed by his performance.   229
       Source: author's screen capture

18.32 Elsie Leach with her "little doggy," circa 1942.   244
       Source: The Cary Grant Papers, courtesy of the Margaret Herrick Library

19.33 In *Destination Tokyo* (Warner Bros., 1943), Cary initially looks very sharp
       in uniform, but, as in his comedies, circumstances conspire to undo his
       composure.   249
       Source: author's screen capture

19.34 In wartime, Barbara Hutton and Cary Grant posed for this publicity photo,
       showing their quiet home life at Westridge. In fact, she entertained lavishly
       and often.   253
       Source: The Cary Grant Papers, courtesy of the Margaret Herrick Library

19.35 Cary's recollections of working-class life informed *None but the Lonely Heart*
       (RKO Radio Pictures, 1944). Here, Ernie Mott argues with his mother (Ethel
       Barrymore).   257
       Source: author's screen capture

20.36 Awkward to film but perfect on screen: the long, intimate kissing scene in
       Notorious (RKO Radio Pictures, 1946)   271
       Source: author's screen capture

20.37 Friends and co-workers: Cary, Ingrid Bergman, and Alfred Hitchcock
       during the making of *Notorious*   273
       Source: The Cary Grant Papers, courtesy of the Margaret Herrick Library

22.38 Betsy Drake in *Every Girl Should Be Married* (RKO Radio Pictures, 1948)
has the look and manner of Katharine Hepburn, but she is interested only in
becoming a wife and mother.   298
Source: author's screen capture

22.39 Cary is a surprisingly lumbering and unattractive "war bride." With Ann
Sheridan in *I Was a Male War Bride* (Twentieth Century-Fox, 1949).   303
Source: author's screen capture

24.40 The gilded cage; Cary Grant and Alfred Hitchcock, making his cameo
in *To Catch a Thief* (Paramount Pictures, 1955)   330
Source: author's screen capture

24.41 Cary, Grace Kelly, and Alma and Alfred Hitchcock on the set
of *To Catch a Thief*   334
Source: The Cary Grant Papers, courtesy of the Margaret Herrick Library

25.42 Cary Grant and Sophia Loren felt awkward filming the appropriately solemn
wedding scene of *Houseboat* (Paramount Pictures, 1958).   349
Source: author's screen capture

25.43 In *Indiscreet* (Warner Bros., 1958), a split screen allows Cary Grant and
Ingrid Bergman to perform a love scene together but in different beds.   353
Source: author's screen capture

26.44 Cary as Roger Thornhill, one of the "Mad Men," dictating to his secretary
(Doreen Lang) as he walks up Madison Avenue in *North by Northwest*
(MGM, 1959)   362
Source: author's screen capture

26.45 In one of the most famous scenes in film history, Roger Thornhill
is attacked in fields far from Madison Avenue.   365
Source: author's screen capture

26.46 Thornhill "puts his body into his work" when Eve (Eva Marie Saint)
shoots him with blanks.   368
Source: author's screen capture

26.47 Despite some tensions while making *North by Northwest*, Cary and
"Hitch" appear amicable.   371
Source: The Cary Grant Papers, courtesy of the Margaret Herrick Library

28.48 Audrey Hepburn flirts with Cary Grant in *Charade* (Universal, 1963). 398
Source: author's screen capture

28.49 In *Walk, Don't Run* (Columbia Pictures, 1966), Cary waves a misty-eyed
farewell in the last scene of his last film.   410
Source: author's screen capture

29.50 Barbara and Cary on their wedding day, with Jennifer, on the terrace of their
Beverly Grove home.   422
Source: The Cary Grant Papers, courtesy of the Margaret Herrick Library

Foreword

Since Plutarch, cultural biography has too often lent itself to the extremes of hagiography and demonization: biography not as fact-based narrative with a critical point of view, but as testimony of slavish devotion or blunt disdain. A particularly toxic mode of disdain, fueled by gossip and amplified by outrage, focuses on artists once regarded with veneration and later found to be imperfect. Cary Grant was among those who got it in the neck. Some of the early accounts of his life were so intent on portraying a bitterly disturbed and miserly closet-case that readers unfamiliar with his uniquely creative luminosity on screen (if any such readers exist) might wonder why he merited a full-dress biography at all. Mark Glancy puts artist and art in perspective, and finds much to admire in both.

Grant was born for the screen. One suspects he would have been amusing but diminished on stage. Of course, he came from the stage, but, significantly, not the stage of Shakespeare and Shaw. Rather, like Keaton and Chaplin, he served his apprenticeship in variety—the theater of pratfalls, sketches, blackouts, beer drinking songs, and stilt-walking, the last his specialty when he toured under his birth name, Archie Leach. He remade himself onscreen, mastering the tools of the more intimate medium, including the close-up; the mutable mise en scène on which to impose his graceful angularity; and the microphone, which caught the nuances of his much-imitated but finally inimitable voice. "Nobody talks like that!" the Jack Lemmon character challenges the Tony Curtis character, who does a spot-on Grant impression in *Some Like It Hot*, invariably getting a raucous laugh because no one did speak like that during Prohibition, when that film takes place, or after, except for Cary Grant.

In *Cary Grant, the Making of a Hollywood Legend*, Glancy examines his accent as a fusion of Bristol, where he was born, and Brixton, where he worked, with his methodical attempt to sound American, resulting in an agile mid-Atlantic concoction entirely sui generis. Glancy, a British film historian who has focused on the cinematic connections between two countries separated by a common language, gives us a thorough and knowing account of his life and career, not least the difficult years of his childhood. (Even Freud might have blanched at the Oedipal snags arising from his father telling young Archie that his mother was dead when, in fact, he committed her to a mental asylum three miles away so that he could live with another woman.) One primary research source was the "thirty-nine linear feet of boxes," filled with papers that Grant had amassed and preserved for posterity's sake. They were available to previous biographers who evidently perused them superficially or not at all.

Glancy excels in detailing the extraordinary discipline with which Grant averted a bleak future to remake himself into one of the most adored figures of his time—a character as solidly imagined as any fictional prototype, but with a twist. He remained flexible enough to prevail for three decades as a resourceful actor while retaining an essential, consistent core that justified his much-quoted quip, "Everyone wants to be Cary Grant. Even I want to be Cary Grant." The transformation of Archie into Cary involved years of dedication.

In examining each of seventy-two films that Grant made in thirty-four years (he left the business at the height of his popularity at age sixty-two), Glancy provides an enlightening step-by-step account of the intelligence and effort required to mount a career in the studio era. Learning how to act for the camera was relatively straightforward compared to achieving and holding on to stardom. Grant's masters at Paramount, the first studio to take him on, saw him merely as a tall, handsome fellow with a snazzy wardrobe who could squire its leading ladies if Gary Cooper or Fredric March weren't available. Apparently, not even Mae West, who plucked him from obscurity for two pictures, saw how funny he could be. Grant studied filmmaking and film acting assiduously, and after his 1937 breakthrough in *The Awful Truth*, he worked even harder to show his diversity and maintain his place as a box-office favorite. He read countless scripts, prevaricating over his choices, demanding rewrites, selecting co-stars and directors, managing the business end as well as or better than his agent, all the while respecting the expectations of a growing audience. He made it all look so easy. That was part of the genius of Cary Grant: everything looked easy, even climbing Mount Rushmore while ducking bullets. He proved that one could do almost anything in a smartly tailored tuxedo and that, gray hairs notwithstanding, there would always be a twenty-something beauty to chase after him.

Glancy does not paper over Grant's failings. He could be rude, shifty, disaffected, fickle, and even a cad (on first meeting Sophia Loren, with whom he soon fell in love, he asked, "How do you do, Miss Lolloloren, or is it Miss

Lorenigida?"). He made mistakes in romance and in assessing his work: he tried to get out of *The Awful Truth*, which established his persona and stardom, and complained angrily that *North by Northwest*, which canonized both, was an incomprehensible mess—until he saw the finished film and salaamed his apologies to its director, Alfred Hitchcock, whose favorite actor Grant was. Mark Glancy does full justice to a complex man and his abiding art, which looks so effortless any one of us could do it in our dreams.

Gary Giddins, Series Editor

Acknowledgments

When Cary Grant *finally* won his first and only Academy Award in 1970, he accepted in a typically gracious and generous manner, naming the directors and writers who had contributed to his films and his career. "Ours is a collaborative medium," he said of filmmaking, thanking them for collaborating with him. Writing books is also a collaborative process, although it is not often discussed in this way. Even when a book has a single author there can be many people involved in the book's research, writing, and publication, playing a vital part in all three areas. That is certainly the case with this book, and so I must thank my many collaborators, who have guided, informed, and inspired me along the way.

Research in film industry archives is central to this book, and so I will begin by thanking the Los Angeles–based archivists with whom I have worked. At the Margaret Herrick Library, Jenny Romero guided me through the Cary Grant Papers, with Faye Thompson and Kristine Krueger providing patient assistance with the collection's photographs. In the Performing Arts section of the UCLA Library's Special Collections, Peggy Alexander, Julie Graham, and Julianna Jenkins steered me through the RKO Radio Pictures Studio Records. At the University of Southern California's Cinematic Arts Library, I worked my way through a number of different collections with the assistance of Sandra Garcia-Myers, Brett Service, and the ever-generous Ned Comstock. In all of these archives, I was lucky to have stellar archival research assistance from Barbara Hall, and I am grateful to her for sharing her expertise with me.

While writing the book, I became involved (as editorial consultant) with the making of the documentary *Becoming Cary Grant* (2017), and I benefited from working with the producer, Nick Ware, and the director, Mark Kidel. They opened many doors for me, and gave me access to research materials I would not otherwise have had. They also put me in touch with Cary Grant's widow, Barbara Jaynes, who very graciously invited me to lunch at his former home, where she still lives, and talked to me about his career and their life together. I am grateful to her for this, and for allowing my unusual request to see the vault where Cary Grant kept his own personal archive. She agreed without raising an eyebrow at the odd things that interest historians.

While writing, I also became involved with the wonderful Cary Grant Festival, also known as Cary Grant Comes Home for the Weekend, which was founded in Bristol in 2014 and has been held biennially since then. Dr. Charlotte Crofts, the tireless festival director, brings together experts and enthusiasts from around the world for these festivals. I have learned a great deal from attending them and from giving talks alongside Kathrina Glitre and Andrew Spicer. I owe particular thanks to Stella Man of the Glenside Hospital Museum, and to Dr. Paul Tobia, who wrote a doctoral thesis on the Bristol Lunatic Asylum, for discussing the history of the asylum with me, and guiding my thinking in this area.

Closer to home, I owe many thanks to the School of History at Queen Mary University of London, for the research funding and periods of sabbatical leave that enabled me to write this book. Julian Jackson, the head of the school for many years, was an especially supportive and enthusiastic advocate of my research. I have long enjoyed exchanging opinions and ideas with him and also with my very keen colleagues James Ellison and Mark White. I am indebted to another colleague, Dan Peart, for pointing me toward funding provided by the Isobel Thornley Trust. I am grateful to the Isobel Thornley Trust and its trustees for a grant supporting the publication costs of this book.

Thanks also to Charles Barr, Eileen and Milton Brener, James Chapman, Peter Evans, Adrian Garvey, Elisabetta Girelli, Helen Glancy, Luke and Cynthia Glancy, Hannah Graves, Sue Harper, Anna Knight, Devan Pailet, Jeffrey Richards, Kiki Sarna, Martin Shingler, Jennifer Smyth, Sarah Street, and Kathleen Walsh for encouragement, ideas, and information, and to Philippa Brewster, Gary Giddins and Norm Hirschy for their support with bringing this book to publication. Matt Jacobsen has my special thanks for offering me distractions and inspiration in just the right measures and whenever needed. Wan Ching Yee has my special thanks for many reasons, including pointing out to me, all those years ago, where Archie Leach went to school.

Finally, Roger Law has been my enthusiastic co-researcher, film-finder, film watcher, editor, and so much more, from our first trip to the archive to the last edit of the manuscript. This book is dedicated to him with gratitude and love.

Introduction

"I definitely don't trust biographies," Cary Grant said in 1984. "I've had some hatchet jobs done on me."[1] He was speaking on stage and in his one-man show, *A Conversation with Cary Grant*. Although he had retired from the screen two decades earlier, audiences were thrilled to be in the presence of this legendary Hollywood star, and he relished the opportunity to speak directly to his fans, setting the record straight and telling his own story. Of course the evening included a reel of clips from some of his best-known films. Always a romantic leading man, these showed him in intimate situations with three generations of leading ladies, including Marlene Dietrich, Irene Dunne, Katharine Hepburn, Ingrid Bergman, Grace Kelly, Deborah Kerr, Eva Marie Saint, and Audrey Hepburn. Often a clown, they also showed him falling on his face, performing cartwheels, and getting slapped, sprayed, tripped up, and tickled by these same co-stars. For most of the evening, though, he took questions about his personal and professional life and offered frank answers with his characteristic charm and humor.[2]

His distrust of biographies was fed by a steady stream of unauthorized accounts of his life. Half a dozen of these books were published in his lifetime, most of them insisting that although he personified effortless elegance, grace, and good manners on-screen, he was actually a deeply flawed and unhappy man off-screen. "They're all absolute nonsense," he commented.[3] He knew that there would be worse to come after his death, when libel laws would no longer protect him. He was appalled to see this happen to others of his generation, including his friend Alfred Hitchcock. Hence, he told his wife Barbara and his daughter Jennifer to brace themselves for the "onslaught" of books and articles that would be published after his death, telling his life story in the most unflattering terms.[4] He was right to warn them. All too often, biographies of Cary Grant have taken the form of exposés, with gossip, hearsay, and invention serving as their primary sources.

Long before he died, he developed his own form of defense against the lies and misconceptions that were written about him. He had a fireproof vault built into his home in Beverly Hills: a steel-reinforced, walk-in vault of a kind normally used by banks or jewelers. He had no intention of storing cash or jewels in this room-sized safe. Instead, he filled the drawers and lined the shelves with memorabilia from every stage of his life. Many of the items are personal. His teenage diary, letters from his mother and father, birth and marriage certificates, and photographs document his childhood in Bristol, England. Many more concern his long and surprisingly varied career in show business: scrapbooks, scripts, correspondence, and contracts that document his years in music hall and vaudeville, on the Broadway stage, and his four decades in Hollywood. The vault served as his own personal archive, and one filled with material that reveals the real circumstances, challenges, and achievements of his extraordinary life.[5]

There were practical reasons for installing the vault. During the Second World War, many of his British friends and members of his family lost their homes during the Blitz on Bristol, and the bombs destroyed their photographs and mementoes as well as their houses. He was determined to protect his own past from California's wildfires and mudslides. There is no doubt, however, that he was also creating his own archive. He saved not only the letters he received but carbon copies of the replies he sent, and when he clipped articles about his life and career from newspapers and magazines, he wrote corrective notes in the margins ("Nonsense!" was a frequent entry) or attached a typed sheet to them, listing their inaccuracies before filing the articles away. Even in retirement, he was a steadfast archivist, meticulously saving his press clippings and correspondence.[6]

There were also more personal reasons for creating the archive. At the end of his life he was an extraordinarily wealthy man, living very near the top of Beverly Hills, in a house that had views stretching from downtown Los Angeles to the Pacific Ocean. Yet the fame and fortune he achieved as a film star, and his debonair screen image, masked his origins as Archie Leach, a working-class Bristol boy who endured an unusually tough childhood and a long struggle to establish himself in show business. The memorabilia that he put in the vault connected one side of his life with the other, documenting the long process through which Archie Leach became Cary Grant. After his death, Barbara Grant donated the contents of the vault to the Margaret Herrick Library in Beverly Hills. The Cary Grant Papers, as the collection is now known, consists of 39 linear feet of boxes containing documents, photographs, and ephemera from every period of his professional and personal life.[7]

The Cary Grant Papers are the starting point for this book. When I first looked through the papers, I was astonished by what I found—not only because the collection illuminates so many aspects of his life that are murky or misunderstood, but also because it is clear that previous biographers made little (if any) use of them. I went through the collection systematically and, convinced that they offered scope for a much more substantive, fully sourced biography, I went on to conduct further research in a range of other archives. The Bristol City Records Office was a particularly important source of information about his family and his childhood, while film industry archives offered extensive information about his film career, including the records of film studios (MGM, Paramount, RKO, Twentieth Century-Fox, and Warner Bros.), and the papers of directors (George Cukor, Alfred Hitchcock, George Stevens) and producers (Arthur Freed, Hal Roach, Jerry Wald) who played an important role in his career. In the midst of this research, I contributed to the documentary *Becoming Cary Grant* (2017) and in that capacity I was able to view hours of his home movies (filmed mainly in the 1930s and 1940s) and thus to see the world through his eyes, or at least his lens.

Throughout this research, my aim has been to write neither an exposé nor an uncritical celebration of Cary Grant's life and career. Rather, I want to tell a more intimate, sympathetic, and accurate account of how Archie Leach became Cary Grant, and how Cary Grant sustained his success and reputation across many decades. On-screen, his ability to embody a host of seemingly contradictory qualities—that is, to be both British and American, working class and upper class, masculine and feminine, elegant and comical—lies at the core of his appeal across many decades, but it is important to consider, too, how he tailored his image to specific moments, contexts, and film genres. He first emerged as a distinctive and popular film star in the zaniest of Depression-era screwball comedies, *The Awful Truth* (1937), and he made this genre his own over the next few years with films such as *Bringing Up Baby* (1938), *His Girl Friday* (1940), and *The Philadelphia Story* (1940). Yet the screen persona he created was pliable enough to suit the tear-jerker *Penny Serenade* (1941), the war drama *Destination Tokyo* (1943), the gothic thriller *Notorious* (1946), the lush romantic melodramas *An Affair to Remember* (1957) and *Indiscreet* (1958), and the stylish spy stories *North by Northwest* (1959) and *Charade* (1963).

His distinctive screen image did not fully emerge until he was in his thirties, but it was nevertheless informed by his troubled childhood in Bristol. One of the most poignant aspects of my research has been exploring his relationship with his mother. It is now well known that Elsie Leach was committed to the Bristol Lunatic Asylum when he was a boy, and that he did not see her again for nearly twenty years. However, reading her medical records, her many letters to her son, and other family documents allows me to shed new light on the circumstances of her commitment to the asylum, the impact that this had on him, and the struggle that mother and son went through to rebuild their relationship years later.

The long journey that Archie Leach made from Bristol to Hollywood, beginning when he ran away from home to join an acrobatic troupe at the age of fourteen and ending when he made his first film at the age of twenty-eight, is another fascinating dimension to this story. He left Bristol without finishing school and with no professional training of any kind. Yet he remade himself as the most debonair of men on the screen. Exploring this transformation is a key part of the life story that is told in the pages that follow, with emphasis on the questions of how and when he developed the accent, manners, grooming, and performance skills of a star who came to define worldly sophistication.

Throughout much of his film career, Cary Grant was considered a delightful entertainer but also a star who simply "played himself" on-screen. It was only after he retired (and presumably because he was so missed once he stopped making new films) that he began to be recognized as an incomparable talent. Ten years after his retirement, this reassessment was driven by two of the most esteemed American film critics. Pauline Kael's lengthy analysis of his career, "The Man From Dream City," was published in the venerable *New Yorker*, while David Thomson's declaration that he was "the best and most important actor in the history of cinema" was made in his highly regarded *Biographical Dictionary of Film*.[8] Subsequent appraisals of his talent have often assumed that his trademarks as a performer—an athletic grace and precision—stemmed from his teenage training as a music hall acrobat, but anyone who has seen his earliest films can observe that the transition from stage to screen was not a straightforward one for him. He was an uncertain actor initially, and he learned his craft through dedication and careful scrutiny of his own performances.

His dedication ultimately enabled him to make some of the best-known films of the twentieth century, and to work with some of Hollywood's greatest directors. One of the pleasures of writing this book has been investigating the making of his classic films as well as his near-misses and total flops. It is fascinating to see the new perspectives that directors such as George Cukor, Leo McCarey, Howard Hawks, George Stevens, and Alfred Hitchcock brought to the Cary Grant screen persona, as well as his own contributions to the films he made with these and other directors. From the late 1930s onward, he was usually involved in every step of the filmmaking process, from scripting to casting to editing. He brought a fastidious perfectionism to inspecting sets and costumes and everything else that appeared on-screen. In Hollywood's studio era, it was very unusual for a star to have the control, power, and influence that Cary Grant enjoyed, but he was a trailblazer, breaking down barriers by becoming a "freelance" star in 1937 and asserting his authority thereafter. He inspired many other stars to follow his example.

As the title of this book indicates, I am interested in every aspect of the making of this Hollywood legend. This includes his private life—how it was reported, to what extent the reports were true or false, and how it has been remembered. Here, I must declare my stance on an issue that has proved to be remarkably contentious. Biographies of Cary Grant can be divided between those that take for granted that he was heterosexual and those that insist that he was a closeted gay man whose most important romantic relationships were with male partners. I approached this issue with an open mind, but I have not found any evidence to support the idea that he was secretly gay. He married five times, and when he was not married to a woman, he was usually romantically attached to one. Several of his wives and girlfriends have attested to his sexual interest in women and dismissed the rumors about him, not least his third wife, Betsy Drake. "Why would I believe Cary was homosexual," Drake asked, "when we were busy fucking?"[9] No biographer can prove or disprove all aspects of their subject's sexuality, and it is impossible for me to say whether or not Cary Grant had any attraction to, or sexual experiences with, men. However, I can make the case that he was predominantly—and enthusiastically—heterosexual, and I can offer a new perspective on how and why rumors about his sexuality developed and intensified over the years.

Chronicling the making of a legend entails acknowledging early byways and dead ends on the road to creating and sustaining his most distinctive and attractive persona. "Everyone wants to be Cary Grant. Even I want to be Cary Grant," he famously said. It is a characteristically self-deprecating statement, and one that belies the fact that Cary Grant was the careful, determined invention of a man born as Archie Leach. In the pages that follow, my starting point is that his invention was a work of genius, the product of decades of determined hard work, and it deserves a faithful, reliable accounting.

PART ONE
ARCHIE LEACH, 1904 TO 1927

1

Cary Grant's very first memory was of his mother bathing him in a portable enamel bathtub in front of the fire at his grandmother's house, and feeling ashamed of being put on naked display in that way. He was, he recalled, "a squirming mass of protesting flesh" as he was dunked and washed.[1] Ironically, the films he made decades later often used similar scenes for comedy. He would be robbed of his clothes while showering, or made to shower in his clothes or in icy water—all situations that provoked howls of protests and whinnies of frustration from the otherwise debonair, well-mannered characters he played. His earliest memory, however, had no comedy. It served as a reminder that, although on-screen he came to personify twentieth-century affluence and sophistication, he was born into a world that had not yet fully emerged from the Victorian era.

His recollections of his childhood in Bristol, England, highlight the privations of working-class life in the early 1900s. Bristol had long been a prosperous port city. Situated in the southwest of England, on the River Avon, it was an embarkation point for exploring the Americas in the fifteenth century. In the centuries that followed, it became a major port for slaves and tobacco, trades that brought wealth to the city. Sometimes termed "the San Francisco of Britain," Bristol is a picturesque city built on steep hills affording wide views, and its wealthiest neighborhood, Clifton, has streets lined with elegant Regency terraces. The stunning Clifton Suspension Bridge, spanning the Avon Gorge, is not as vast as Golden Gate Bridge, but it has a majesty all its own. Most of Bristol's population did not live in Clifton, of course, but in the more crowded working-class districts closer to the city center.

At the beginning of the twentieth century, Bristol grew rapidly (the population leaped from 222,000 in 1891 to 357,000 in 1911) and it became a thriving center for manufacturing and trade.[2] New streets were springing up along Gloucester Road, the high street that extends northward out of the city, with houses built for the city's working classes. Cary Grant's first home was in one of these new streets near Gloucester Road. The gray stone terraced house at 8 Hughenden Road (now renumbered as number 15) was one of twenty small, identical houses built at the turn of the century on what used to be farmland in Horfield, a parish previously separate

Photograph 1.1 Archie Leach in 1904

Source: The Cary Grant Papers, courtesy of the Margaret Herrick Library

from, but now incorporated into, Bristol's expanding boundaries. Like all of the streets in this working-class district of the city, Hughenden Road is a narrow street with tightly-packed-together terraced houses, but because it was built at the very edge of the expanding city, back in 1904 there were fields and open spaces just beyond it (some still remaining today as Horfield Common).[3]

This house was, in his memory, "only one step ahead of freezing," because it was heated only by small fireplaces, in which coal fires were lit sparingly.[4] There was no electricity, and thus no refrigerator or washing machine. Baths were taken in portable tubs brought into the kitchen specially for the occasion and filled with water by hand. Toilets were outside, in the "privy" just beyond the back door, and chamber pots were kept under the bed for nighttime relief. Clothing and shoes were tended with care as they were expensive and difficult to clean. Most children left school at the age of twelve or very shortly

Photograph 1.2 Archie's birthplace: the house on Hughenden Road, Bristol
Source: author's own collection

thereafter, to begin a lifetime of work. There was no radio or television, and a weekly trip to the music hall or the cinema was a treat relished by many.

Archie was born at home, as most babies were at the time, and he arrived in the early morning hours of January 18, 1904. His parents, Elias and Elsie Leach, named him Archibald Alec Leach.[5] They had been married nearly six years earlier, on May 30, 1898, in a church, St. Matthias on the Weir, in central Bristol.[6] What young Archie did not know, and Cary Grant would find out only in middle age, was that he was his parents' second child. Their first, John

William Elias Leach, was born five years before him and just nine months after his parents' marriage. When the firstborn baby was just eleven months old, he became ill. Some accounts say that Elsie accidentally shut a door on his tiny finger, which then became infected.[7] Other accounts, including the baby's death certificate, say that he died from convulsions arising from tubercular meningitis.[8] All accounts agree that Elsie was sick with worry during his illness, and that she sat beside his cot night and day, without sleep, until a doctor ordered her to rest. It was while she was sleeping, in the evening of February 7, 1900, that he died. She never forgave herself and, it seems, she was never fully able to let go of her grief.[9]

Elsie Maria Kingdon Leach was born on February 8, 1877, and so she was just one day shy of her twenty-third birthday on the day her firstborn died. By all indications, she had a troubled childhood. She always maintained that she was born in Clifton, and it is true that she was born on the edge of this smart neighborhood, at 2 Berkeley Place. However, her family's home was on an inelegant street leading down the hill from Clifton to the docks along the River Avon at Hotwells.[10] When she was four years old, her family was living at the bottom of this hill, in a small house fronting the Poor House Steps.[11] The poorhouse itself was long gone, but the address, on a steep alleyway connecting Mardyke Wharf with Church Lane, was a marker of the family's hard times.

Elsie's Bristol-born father, William Kingdon, and her Welsh-born mother, Elizabeth Morgan Kingdon, had twelve children, and they struggled to make ends meet. Her father was a shipwright who worked on the docks, building and maintaining ships, until he fell on hard times and went into the Stapleton Workhouse as a pauper. In 1887, he died there at the age of fifty-three.[12] Elsie's mother was left to support five children between the ages of three and twelve, including ten-year-old Elsie, by working as a laundress. Elsie's older sister, Alice Kingdon, was also working as a laundress, but in 1891 she too was declared a pauper and went into the workhouse at Barton Regis. This was very much against her will. She cried loudly at night, expressed suicidal thoughts, and protested against the cold by dropping hot coals down her garments, burning herself. A few weeks after her admission to the workhouse, the authorities there declared her "unmanageable" and transferred her to the Bristol Lunatic Asylum, where she would remain for twenty-seven years.[13] Meanwhile, one of Elsie's brothers, twelve-year-old Charles, was placed "under detention" aboard HMS *Formidable*, a former Royal Navy warship that now served as a form of floating borstal, housing 350 "wayward boys" off the coast of Portishead (near Bristol).[14]

Elsie's other siblings had menial and semi-skilled jobs—laundress, domestic servant, and slaughterman—but Elsie herself fared somewhat better. She went to live with her older sister Emmaline, who had married a traveling salesman and was living at 7 Raglan Place, just off Gloucester Road.[15] By the age of fourteen, Elsie had left school but it is not clear what she did in the years before she married Elias Leach at age twenty-one. What is clear is that she emerged from her impoverished childhood with a determination to move up in the world, far above the Poor House Steps, and to have a more stable, respectable family of her own with Elias Leach.

Elias James Leach was born on June 29, 1872, the fourth of John and Elizabeth Leach's nine children.[16] John Leach was born in the rural village of Frocester, Gloucestershire. Originally, his family name was Bristow, but he changed it to Leach when he moved to Bristol to become a potter.[17] His wife was born Elizabeth Leaf in Poole, Dorset, and she too moved to Bristol with her family as a child.[18] She worked as a tailoress before her marriage, and when John died at the age of forty-seven, leaving her with four children under the age of twelve, she went to work as a milliner (hatmaker). The widowed Elizabeth Leach kept her family close. Most of her children followed in her footsteps, taking up work in clothing trades. They were milliners, bootmakers, a tailor's cutter, and in his father's case, a tailor's presser in a factory. When they left home, many of her children lived near to her in the tightly packed streets of St. Paul's, a working-class neighborhood adjacent to the city center.[19]

It is easy to see the pride that Elias Leach took with his appearance as a young man. A portrait of him, carefully posed and taken in a photographer's studio, reveals a dapper dresser. His hair is carefully styled and his moustache is neatly trimmed. His clothing—a wide-lapeled suit with a boutonnière, wing-tipped collar, and bow tie—shows him styled as a gentleman rather than a factory worker. Years later, he would tell his son Archie that it is better to have one superior suit rather than several inferior suits, and this probably explains how he could afford to look so fashionable on a factory worker's wages.

A portrait of Elsie, taken in the same studio and most likely on the same day, reveals a similarly elegant dresser. Her floor-length dress shows a corseted, hourglass figure, while her elaborate lace collar and brooch, and her carefully arranged pompadour hairstyle, suggest refinement. Her stance

Photograph 1.3 Elias James Leach, circa 1900
Source: The Cary Grant Papers, courtesy of the Margaret Herrick Library

demonstrates an almost regal bearing. Throughout her life, Elsie would stand straight and proud for photos, as though demonstrating her respectability through her upright posture.

In these photographs, at least, we can see the common ground between Elsie and Elias. They were a strikingly good-looking couple—Elsie an olive-skinned and dark-eyed beauty, Elias a little fairer but with a similarly refined, handsome appearance—and they clearly aspired to enjoy the finer things in life. In their youth, they were each said to enjoy doing (separate) party turns mimicking the style of popular music hall singers.[20] They were also conventionally religious in an understated, Church of England manner. They faithfully attended Horfield Parish Church, just across the common from Hughenden Road, and they had Archie baptized there three weeks after his birth, on February 8, 1904, which also happened to be Elsie's twenty-seventh birthday.[21]

Photograph 1.4 Elsie Maria Leach, circa 1900
Source: The Cary Grant Papers, courtesy of the Margaret Herrick Library

It is worth looking for common ground and happy times for Elsie and
Elias because, in their son's memories, they had a miserable marriage.[22]
A portrait of young Archie, taken in the same photographer's studio when
Archie was five or six, shows that he is as well dressed and carefully posed
as his parents, but the downcast, slightly apprehensive look on his face fits
with his recollection of an unhappy home life. His parents fought constantly,
he recalled, and almost always about money. Elias worked at the Todd's
clothing factory, opposite Temple Meads railway station. His wages were

good by working-class standards but they did not allow for the middle-class lifestyle that Elsie sought.[23]

Elsie had dreams of getting ahead in life, or at least enabling her son to get ahead in life. She put Archie into the local Bishop Road School a year early, at the age of four, because she was convinced he was brighter than other children. She insisted that he must have piano lessons and took pride that, by the age of seven, he played fluently. She instilled good manners in him, taking tuppence out of his meager pocket money if he spilled food on the tablecloth that she brought out for Sunday dinner. She took him to the Picture House on Clare Street, a movie house in the city center that was so refined that it had a tearoom. It was here that Elsie first introduced Archie to using a pastry fork.[24] Decades later, he scoffed at these pretensions, but there can be little doubt that his mother's concern for decorum and propriety planted the seeds of his polished screen image.

Photograph 1.5 Archie Leach, circa 1910
Source: The Cary Grant Papers, courtesy of the Margaret Herrick Library

Elias Leach, in his son's opinion, was beaten down by his dull life. He spent five weekdays plus Saturday mornings at his repetitive work—pressing jackets, trousers, and waistcoats before they left the factory. Elsie's disappointment in their modest circumstances did not help him. Elias took to drinking, sometimes heavily. Cary Grant's second earliest memory was being awakened in the middle of the night by his father, who was carousing with friends in the living room after an evening in the pub. His father brought him downstairs, carrying him on his shoulders and insisting that he recite a poem he had memorized, all while still sitting atop his swaying father's shoulders. His mother and father had terrible rows when he came home in this condition, rows that lasted for hours (or so it seemed to a child).[25]

There were happy times between father and son. His father took him to the Metropole Cinema in St. Paul's, a much less expensive neighborhood movie house, where there was no tearoom and no need for a boy to be on his best behavior. Saturdays at midday, when his father walked home from work, Archie would run to meet him and rummage through his coat pockets to see if he had bought him sweets or, better yet, chocolates. His father rarely disappointed him. The happy times between his mother and father, however, were so few and far between that only a few fond moments stood out in their son's memory. He recalled an evening when his parents stood together before a window, with their arms around one another, watching a lightning storm. On another occasion, he recalled them consoling one another over the death of King Edward VII in 1910. They also threw a children's party for him and his friends—with his father conducting a magic lantern show with a sheet for a screen, and Elsie supplying paper hats, noisemakers, lemonade, cake, and blancmange—that was so wonderful he never forgot it.[26]

The vast majority of working-class families rented rather than owned their own homes, and so they moved house if rents went up or better opportunities arose elsewhere, but the Leach family moved more than most. When Archie was three years old, they moved to 50 Berkeley Road, another street off Gloucester Road that led into farmland and fields.[27] The new house was only slightly larger than the house on Hughenden Road, but the back garden was particularly long. Archie's father put a swing up for him, fixing it to an apple tree, and happily tended to a vegetable patch.[28] Two years later, the family moved again, this time to a flat above a shop at 132 Cheltenham Road, a far less respectable address on a busy thoroughfare, and one unlikely to have a garden. Archie had to leave Bishop Road School and go to a school closer to home, the North Street Wesleyan

School.[29] The reasons for this move are unknown, but a move from a house to a flat suggests that his father could no longer afford the rent at the house, a problem that could only have exacerbated tensions between him and his wife.

Within six months, a solution of sorts was found in tragic circumstances. Elsie's older sister Charlotte was thirteen years her senior and had married well. Her husband, Walter Monk, was a solicitor's clerk and, together with their son and four daughters, they were living in a newly developed, lower-middle-class neighborhood of Bristol, on the border between Bishopston and Ashley Down. By 1910, Charlotte developed breast cancer and, after, a long and painful illness, she died in the autumn.[30] Elsie and Elias moved to a house just around the corner from the Monks and took in the three eldest daughters as boarders: Lillian, a twenty-two-year-old domestic nurse; Dora, an eighteen-year-old office clerk; and Josephine, a fifteen-year-old office clerk. The rent that these three young women paid enabled Elsie and Elias to afford a three-bedroom terraced house at 5 Seymour Avenue, and, because this was not far from Bishop Road, Archie was able to return to his old school.[31]

Under Elsie's watchful eye, Archie thrived at school. His one surviving report card was probably saved because it was his best, but it is nevertheless a sign that Elsie's belief in him was deserved. He really was exceptional. The report card dated May 1913, when he was nine years old, states that he ranked first in his class of forty-one pupils. He had perfect marks for reading, arithmetic, writing, and drawing, and near-perfect marks for dictation (earning 19 out of 20 marks) and conduct (18 out of 20).[32] He recalled that his parents carefully scrutinized his report cards, and that they made him mind his manners carefully with adults, including obeying the dictates that he should speak only when spoken to and sit still.[33]

In the summer of 1913, the family and its three boarders moved to a larger house at 137 Cotham Brow. This was not a fashionable neighborhood. The house was within a stone's throw of the railway arches that cross the busy Cheltenham Road. It was, however, the family's largest and most imposing home. The mid-nineteenth-century terraced building, with its four-story stone façade, large windows, and Dutch trimmings along the roof, had a bit of high Victorian style. It also had eight rooms, allowing Archie's three cousins a separate living space of their own. He generally took little interest in these cousins, but when one of them had a new boyfriend who owned what was then termed a "motorcar," Archie was thrilled to be invited for a drive. He sat proudly in the back seat of the open-top vehicle, hoping that one of his friends would spot him on this first-ever ride in a car.[34]

A major benefit of the Cotham Brow house, as far as Archie was concerned, was that it was just around the corner from the Scala Cinema, a cheap neighborhood movie house. When he returned to Bristol twenty-five years later, he revisited this old haunt and filmed it with his own 16mm movie camera. As a boy, he was delighted to spend Saturday afternoons there in the on-screen company of cowboy star "Broncho Billy" Anderson, and comedians Charlie Chaplin and "Fatty" Arbuckle. The Scala aside, the Cotham Brow house was a mixed blessing, because in order to afford it, his father had to leave the Todd's factory and take a job in Southampton, some 80 miles from Bristol, where there was better-paid work in a factory making khaki uniforms for the army.[35]

For his parents, the new job appealed on very different grounds. Elsie got the more impressive house she had always hoped for, while Elias got to sow his wild oats far from home. When Archie briefly visited him in Southampton later in that summer of 1913, without Elsie, he was surprised to find his father appeared younger "and rather sporty looking too." He knew his mother would disapprove. His father's Southampton adventure ended when he found that his new wages were not stretching to support both his Bristol family and his sporty lifestyle. He came home in the autumn of 1913, embarrassed to take up his old job at Todd's again.[36]

After his father's return, the family stayed together for just over a year. Then one day in February 1915, two weeks after Archie's eleventh birthday and when he was in his last year at Bishop Road elementary school, he came home to find that Elsie was not there to greet him as usual. His cousins told him that she had gone to a local seaside resort—probably Clevedon or Weston-Super-Mare—for a rest. Archie found this peculiar and a little annoying, because he thought his mother could have taken him with her. When he pressed his father for information, his father implied that he was in touch with his mother, and she sent her love, but he offered no more specific information than that. As the days passed, the increasingly bewildered Archie began to think that his exacting mother had left him deliberately. He lay awake at nights wondering what he had done to make her so angry that she abandoned him.[37]

After two weeks, one of his cousins decided to put an end to his questions. "Archie, I have to give you some unhappy news," she told him. "Your mother is dead."[38] It is not clear whether he believed this or recognized that it was a falsehood designed to silence all discussion about his mother. Without a funeral and a grave to visit, it is likely that his uncertainty persisted, and that the combination of all of his feelings—abandonment, grief, mistrust—became an indistinguishable burden. The experience was so confusing for him that, later in life, he could not place it correctly in time. He variously stated that at the time of his mother's disappearance he was nine, ten, or twelve, but never the correct age of eleven. His feelings were so deeply buried that he could not access them, and yet they would always stay with him. He would have difficulty sustaining his romantic relationships with women. He would have difficulty especially with trust, fearing that any woman he got close to would leave him. And he would spend much of his life, or at least his much of his professional career, trying to live up to the aspirations that his mother had set for him before she disappeared.

2

Elsie Leach was not dead. Archie did not know it, but his mother was just 3 miles from home, a patient at the Bristol Lunatic Asylum in Fishponds (on the outskirts of Bristol). His father had taken her there and had her committed. Decades down the line, when Cary Grant recalled the terrible day that he came home from school to find her gone, he never remembered noticing that she was mentally unwell prior to her disappearance. He recalled that she had some peculiarities: when he was an infant, she kept him in baby clothes far too long, and when he was a young boy, she kept him in short pants far too long.[1] He also spoke privately about an incident when, as a child, he got separated from her while shopping in a Marks and Spencer department store. He could not find her and as he grew increasingly anxious, his mother suddenly seized him. "You see how it is, Archie?" she asked angrily. "Who looks out for you? Who came to save you? Me, that's who! I'm the only one in the whole world who cares about you, and you better not forget it."[2] It was an unpleasant memory but, like the reluctance to dress him in age-appropriate clothing, it points more toward maternal possessiveness than mental illness.

Looking back, he thought that the loss of her first child was the most likely explanation for Elsie's "breakdown," which he described as a "retreat within herself" and a "withdrawal from the world."[3] However, this was not the diagnosis she was given when she was admitted to the asylum on February 3, 1915. Her admission record shows that Elias Leach stated that his wife had been "queer in her head" for four months. "She thinks that several women are concealed in the house and that they put poison in her food. She hears voices through the wall and thinks [she is] being watched." Elsie insisted that her fears were real. She took out a folded piece of paper with two hairs in it, apparently as evidence of the women hiding in her house, and said that she found white powder around the house and thought it was poison.[4]

The doctor did not believe her. Finding her "talkative and excited" and assuming her suspicions were "delusions," he diagnosed her with "mania." This was one of the three "forms of insanity" most commonly diagnosed at the asylum. The vast majority of patients were said to be suffering from dementia, melancholia, or mania. Dementia was the diagnosis most often used with elderly women. Melancholia was ascribed to those who seemed depressed. And mania was used for women who were, like Elsie, "hysterical, at times laughing at others crying" (as she was described on the day of her admission).[5] Because the term "mania" does not correspond directly with any modern psychiatric diagnosis, it is difficult to gauge what—if anything—was actually wrong with Elsie.[6] Given that she was deemed to be a danger neither to herself nor to others, it seems reasonable to question whether her commitment was really necessary. Given that Elsie and Elias were so unhappy together, and divorce was so difficult to obtain in this era, it also seems reasonable to question whether Elias was committing Elsie as a means of extricating himself from their marriage.

Two factors suggest that both Elias Leach and the doctor at the asylum genuinely believed that Elsie was mentally ill. One is that the asylum was in no position to accept patients who were not truly in need of care. The care and treatment of patients was funded by local government, which scrutinized the asylum's records and policies to ensure against waste. Furthermore, in February 1915, the asylum was running out of beds. It had a record number of patients—449 men and 516 women—and over the prior six months many of its staff had been called up for service in the First World War. New patients could be admitted only when there was a clear and pressing need.[7] The second factor is that Elsie's older sister, Alice Kingdon, had been a patient at the asylum for over twenty years, and Alice was also diagnosed with "mania."[8] As Elsie's admission record noted, her sister's illness was considered a "predisposing cause" of Elsie's own illness, the assumption being that this form of mental illness ran in the family.[9]

The more likely cause of Elsie's illness was the tension in her marriage. Her anxieties—about other women and the threat of harm in her own home—may have been amplified in her mind but they were not entirely irrational. Elias Leach took the opportunity to institutionalize her even though she was not a danger to herself or to others, and he demonstrated little sympathy for, or interest in, Elsie from this day forward. He forgot to write to her while she was in the asylum, and he started a new family in her absence. Her confinement was his freedom, and he seized it.

The Bristol Lunatic Asylum was not a Bedlam-like madhouse or "snake pit" that forced lobotomies or electro-shock therapy on its patients. The greystone buildings look austere and imposing from the outside, but they were built in the spirit of Victorian paternalism. The asylum's patients were treated by removing them from the life circumstances that were making them ill, and allowing them to recuperate in a clean, orderly environment.

Photograph 2.6 The former Bristol Lunatic Asylum, now a part of the University of the West of England, Glenside Campus
Source: author's own collection

They were fed a carefully measured but nutritious diet. They were encouraged to take fresh air and exercise, and to also work in some capacity in the hospital—as seamstresses, in the laundry or kitchen, or sweeping floors. They had a library, weekly concerts, and a weekly dance (the only occasion on which men and women mixed).[10]

Yet for all of its order and benevolence, the asylum allowed patients no privacy or autonomy. They slept in large rooms with dozens of beds lined up side-by-side in rows. They were allowed visitors just once a week, and they were seldom allowed off the asylum's grounds. Indeed, the local newspaper referred to them as "inmates" rather than patients. Perhaps worst of all for Elsie was that, within two months of her arrival, the asylum was turned over to the Red Cross. It became Beaufort War Hospital, a military hospital for wounded soldiers, and all of the asylum's patients were transferred to eight other asylums spread throughout southwest England. It is not known where Elsie was sent, but leaving Bristol, and the possibility of family visits, must have been heartbreaking for her.[11]

She returned to the Bristol asylum when the war was over. From that point onward, as her nephew Ernest Kingdon recalled, Elsie's siblings visited her regularly, presumably visiting Alice Kingdon as well. It is not known whether Elsie and Alice were on the same ward, and thus able to see one another, while they were both in the asylum. Alice was seventeen years older than Elsie, and she had been committed when Elsie was fourteen years old, and so they may not have had a particularly strong familial bond. It is known that Elsie asked for her dancing shoes to be sent to her (presumably to attend the weekly dances), and that she regularly asked why she could not be released.[12] The answer to that question seems to be that her husband had no interest in facilitating her release.

When Elsie was committed, Elias and Archie moved out of the big Cotham Brow house and separated from the three cousins (from Elsie's side of the family) who had been their lodgers. Father and son moved to the rougher and tougher neighborhood of St. Paul's, where they lived nearer to the Leach family. Elias's brothers John and Alfred lived nearby with their families (at 9 Dean Street and 3 Brighton Road, respectively).[13] Elias took rooms at 12 Campbell Street, a house divided into three separate dwellings, because his mother already had rooms there, and Elias hoped that she would look after Archie.[14] However, Elizabeth Leach had married again in 1908, to a dock laborer named Arthur Palmer.[15] She drank too much and took little interest in her grandson. Archie found her to be "a cold woman" and saw little of her.[16]

Elsie's influence over Archie persisted insofar as his high marks at Bishop Road elementary school ensured that he was able to continue his education at Fairfield secondary school, with a scholarship from the local authority paying his fees.[17] Fairfield was just up the hill from St. Paul's, in the neighboring district of Montpelier, and its four-year program was designed to educate the working-class student who was unlikely to go on to university but might work in an office—as a clerk, for example—rather than on a factory floor. There were approximately 350 students studying in this highly structured, authoritarian environment, in which caning students was a routine punishment even for mild misconduct.[18]

Archie's life at home, by contrast, was completely unstructured. He was tall for his age, but "scrawny" and "untidy."[19] His father worked long hours, and he no longer had Elsie preventing him from carousing outside of work. Archie was left to fend for himself, "scrounging around in the kitchen or the stone larder," trying to find food to make his own meals. He was often "alone and unsettled" in the cold, lonely rooms on Campbell Street, and he looked for any activity to take him away. He got part-time jobs, taking tickets at a fun fair on Redland Green and later at a chemist's shop on Stokes Croft, and he was relieved to get out of the house.[20]

He needed the money for school. His scholarship did not extend to school uniforms, gym clothes, books, and other items he struggled to afford. When he first started at Fairfield, he had dreams of going on to university, but he slowly realized that he would not be able to afford it.[21] He could not even afford to see a dentist. When he slipped and fell on the ice outside Fairfield, breaking one of his upper front teeth in half, he had to go to a local dental school, where the broken tooth could be extracted free of charge.[22] He was left with a gaping hole in his smile, but over time this proved to be a stroke of luck. Gradually, the gap closed and the loss of this tooth left him with the kind of evenly spaced, straight teeth usually only achieved with orthodontic intervention.

He found a sense of camaraderie and belonging in the Boy Scouts. During the First World War, the Boy Scouts thrived as a patriotic, quasi-military organization that allowed boys too young to join up to wear uniforms, march, conduct drills, and carry out some wartime duties.[23] Archie was thrilled to be given the role of junior air raid warden, responsible for extinguishing the gas-lit streetlamps in the event of an air raid. He kept his uniform neatly folded by his bedside, ready to put it on and dash out if the alarm sounded. It was almost disappointing to him that the raids did not reach as far as Bristol. Then, in the summer of 1915, the Scouts enabled him to leave Campbell Street altogether. He got a summer posting on the docks in Southampton, where the troops departed by sea to France and the front line. This could be harrowing work. One of his tasks was to hand out life jackets as the soldiers boarded the transport ships, unsure whether their ship would make it across the English Channel or be sunk by a German U-boat. But he also found it wonderfully exciting to be away from home, to meet new people, and to have a useful role to play. His wanderlust was awakened that summer and it would stay with him the rest of his life.[24]

Back in Bristol, he continued in the Boy Scouts at least through the autumn of 1916, when he was photographed, proudly beaming for the camera, in a military-style parade through the streets of Bristol. Many years later, Elsie would see the photo and scold him for being the only boy with his sleeves rolled up.[25] It was perhaps an early sign that the Scouts were not for him. He began looking for any means of escape from his life. He was fascinated with the steamships and schooners that came up the River Avon, docking at the wharves in the city's "floating harbor" (where sea-gates retain the water of high tide). He applied to be a cabin boy on board one of the ships, but at the age of twelve, he was too young for the job.[26]

A few months later, after he'd turned thirteen, he had a fateful encounter. Chemistry was one of his favorite subjects at Fairfield, and an assistant chemistry teacher also worked as an electrician, including working on the lighting system at the Hippodrome Theatre. Perhaps recognizing Archie's loneliness, the teacher offered to show him the lighting system at the theater. Designed in the ornate baroque style of the smartest Edwardian theaters, the Hippodrome was a local wonder, but it was not the architecture that impressed Archie. Crucially, the teacher instructed Archie to come to the Hippodrome's stage door rather than its public entrance. Backstage at the Saturday matinee, Archie found himself, as he put it, "in a dazzling land of smiling, jostling people wearing and not wearing all sorts of costumes and doing all sorts of clever things."[27] It was a mesmerizing epiphany for him. "And that's when I knew! What other life could there be but that of an actor? They happily traveled and toured. They were classless, cheerful, and carefree. They gaily laughed, lived, and loved."[28]

Photograph 2.7 Archie Leach (front row, at the far left) in a Boy Scouts parade in November 1916

Source: The Cary Grant Papers, courtesy of the Margaret Herrick Library

He wrote this many years later, when he had time to reflect on why, from the moment he entered the Hippodrome, he lost interest in other aspects of life and centered all his energy and attention on music hall. The backstage bonhomie was one part of the theater's appeal (and it was certainly something he did not find at home). The opportunity to leave home and tour the country, if not the world, also had a strong pull for him. His references to costumes and classlessness point to the appeal of escaping the limitations of his family circumstances and working-class life more generally. Young Archie learned that entertainers had a language and standards and customs of their own, and that they valued talent and earning power over class and family background. This was a world he wanted to be a part of, and one that promised a very different future to anything his family or school had led him to believe was possible.[29]

He was not mesmerized by "the Theater"—that is, the kind of dramatic arts performed at Bristol's oldest theater, the Theatre Royal, where works by Shakespeare, Ibsen, and Shaw were staged. He was mesmerized by that much more popular form of entertainment, music hall, which typically included a whole range of acts within one show. These might include acrobats, animal acts, comedians, dancers, dramatic and comic vignettes, magicians, musical bands, singers, and all sorts of "novelty acts" that are not so easily categorized. Speed and variety were the hallmarks of music hall. The acts were typically on stage for 10 to 20 minutes (although headliners got more time), and the program was repeated twice each night, and more on Saturdays, for a week or half-week. Then the performers moved on to the next city and the next engagement.[30] It was a life of constant motion, which, initially at least, looked attractive to a boy filled with wanderlust.

By his own admission, he was "obsessed" with the Hippodrome, and also Bristol's other major music hall, the Empire, across town in Old Market, where his electrician-teacher also serviced the lighting. After hanging around for weeks, Archie finally met the Empire's manager, who hired him as a lighting assistant in the first instance. "This became my home away from home," he recalled. "I had a place to be. And people let me be there." In November 1917, one of the most famous magicians, "The Great David Devant," was the headline act, and Archie was in the balcony, helping an experienced lighting man to operate the heavy arc lights. Archie was tasked with holding his light steady, keeping the beam focused on Devant, but he became so spellbound by the act that he allowed his beam to trail downward and reveal the hidden

mirrors that created the magical illusion, ruining Devant's act. It was an inauspicious beginning to a long show business career.[31]

Decades later, he recalled that after this fiasco, he was no longer welcome
at the Empire.[32] His diary from the time, however, shows that this was not
the case. He was taken off the lights, but he continued to work at the Empire
as a backstage runner, doing errands and other odd jobs for the performers,
for months after the lighting fiasco. He kept a careful track of his earnings in
the back of the diary, recording his regular pay of two shillings and sixpence,
as well as the tips—up to ten shillings in a week—that he received from the
performers. He also recorded an amazing stroke of luck. On November 24,
he was on Denmark Street, the side-street location of the Hippodrome's stage
door, when he spotted a crisp, clean five-pound note on the pavement. This
was a huge sum (the equivalent of nearly four hundred pounds in 2020), and
it is easy to imagine his glee at finding it. When he proudly showed it to his
father, Elias made him follow the letter of the law, turning the note into the
police and then waiting three months to see if anyone claimed it. Archie obe-
diently turned the note in at Bridewell Street police station, but he also carefully recorded its serial number and went back to the station every Saturday
to see if it had been claimed. His diary counts down the weeks until he received his windfall. On February 24, he was finally able to collect it. He gave
the "fiver" to his father, who in turn gave him increased pocket money.[33]

Archie's diary was not the kind used for writing lengthy or reflective
thoughts. It was a Boy Scout diary, for the school year 1917–18, and boys
were meant to record their progress in all manner of scouting activities, including tests passed and badges earned. The printed portions of the diary are
filled with instructions on how to tie knots, send smoke signals, use Morse
code, read a compass, and other practical skills. Yet Archie's handwritten
entries show absolutely no interest in these matters. He used the diary to record all of his show business activities. He saw films two or three times a
week, sometimes recording only the name of the theater he went to (most
often the King's Cinema near Old Market), but sometimes—presumably
when he was particularly impressed—the title of the film, too. He returned
to see several chapters of the twenty-part American serial *Gloria's Romance*
(1916), with his future *Topper* (1937) co-star, Billie Burke, playing a girl lost
in the Everglades. He also recorded that he went to the People's Palace, on
Baldwin Street, to see *Auld Lang Syne* (1917), a British film marking the
screen debut of Jack Buchanan, a debonair actor Cary Grant would cite as
one of his key influences.[34]

Most of the diary entries refer to what was happening at the Empire, including the good or bad tips he received, the backstage arguments, and the acts that impressed him. He admired a "good comedy cyclist named Lotto," a "jolly good" French dancing troupe called Entre Nous, and he was initially impressed by Captain de Villier's "Zeppelin Destroyer," a 20-foot wireless balloon that flew through the auditorium, but then, three days later, he noted that the balloon "got out of control and went on people [seated] in the circle." He left the Empire in February 1918 to work at the upscale Prince's Theatre, on Park Row in Clifton. The Prince's had just one show while he worked there, the pantomime *Old King Cole*, and so he referred to the theater as "the Panto." Just three weeks later, he left the Panto because he got a "good job at the Hippo"—his nickname for the Hippodrome.[35]

One of the biggest music hall stars of the period, the male impersonator Vesta Tilley, was currently headlining at the Hippo with her revue, *Six Days' Leave*. "Vesta Tilley was there," a star-struck Archie noted in his diary the day he got the job, and, a few days later, "Miss Tilley gave me an autograph." He was enthralled by her as well as by the many other performers. In the back of the Boy Scout diary, there are pages entitled "My Friends," where the scout is meant to fill in the names of his fellow scouting pals. Archie, however, listed the names and addresses of the performers he had befriended: Bart and Bart Comedy Acrobats, Charlie Harvey of the Heave O! Revue, George Cornwall of the "Where's the Chicken Co.," and so on.[36]

There are few signs of his home life in the diary. He noted that on his fourteenth birthday, January 18, it snowed and he received "a new suit, a new pair of shoes, and a new cap" as presents, presumably from his father. A few weeks later he commented that his grandmother was so ill that he had to send for the doctor. But otherwise, his family is notable only for their absence from this account of his life, which lists everything from what he ate ("had second fish and chips") to the letters he received and sent, to the occasions he walked home with Cissie Hillier (who worked at the Empire). Of course, not many fourteen-year-olds would record their family life in their diary, but there is a strong sense throughout these months that he had been all but abandoned. While his afternoons and evenings were taken up with his work at the theaters, his days were often empty and formless.[37]

"Late for school in the morning," and "got up late in the morning," were frequent entries, and he recorded that he "stayed away from school" so many times that he eventually shortened this to "stayed away." His days outside of school were apparently spent wandering the streets of Bristol, and seeing films whenever he had money to spare. He often wrote "roamed about" or "roamed about all day" as his summary for the daytime, before noting that he worked at the Empire, Panto, or Hippo in the evening. School activities are scarcely mentioned, except for one day in February when "Maps" (the geography teacher's nickname) "gave me a hiding in his lesson," with the result that Archie "bunked out of school and stayed away in the afternoon."[38]

This was no way for a scholarship boy to behave. Even when he was at school, he had never done his homework, and he sat in the back row of the classroom, daydreaming.[39] His days at Fairfield were numbered, and on March 13, 1918, for his last diary entry, he wrote only "SSC" (Secondary School Certificate). He was in the midst of the third year of a four-year program, and so this was not a diploma but only a certificate showing that he had attended secondary school. His Fairfield record ends with an ignoble "U. Remove" signaling that it was an unclassified certificate and that he was expelled.[40] There are differing accounts on why this happened. In later years, he always maintained that he was caught spying through a window into the girl's lavatory.[41] In another account, recalled by a local friend long after Cary Grant's death, Archie was caught masturbating in the boy's lavatory.[42]

Whatever offense he committed, his expulsion was carried out in the most humiliating way. The day after his offense, an unsuspecting Archie attended the school's morning assembly, where the usually mild-mannered headmaster, Augustus "Gussie" Smith, called him to the podium to reprimand him. Archie was so dazed by the experience that he took in only a few scattered words, "inattentive . . . irresponsible . . . incorrigible . . . a discredit to the school" before he realized that he was being very publicly expelled. With his upper lip quivering, and his head hanging in shame, he walked out of the hall and left the school—never to return as a pupil. The shame of it was enormous, and so too was his fear of telling his father about his disgrace.[43] Whether he feared for himself and for his future was another matter. At the age of fourteen, he already knew that what his mother had told him was true. He had to look after himself; no one else would. He also knew that show business offered him the most adventurous, exciting means of doing this.

3

"I am very sorry that I have not written to you before," Elias Leach wrote to his wife; "you must excuse me once again." This letter, the only one from Elias to Elsie in the Cary Grant Papers, was written in early May 1918. "I am very pleased to say that Archie is going along alright and also that he is in the very best of health and that he is enjoying himself alright," he reassured her, without revealing to her that Archie had been expelled from school seven weeks earlier. He did say that Archie saw his cousins often, and that he sent Elsie "love and kisses," thereby giving her the impression that her son knew where she was.[1] In fact, Archie did not know if his mother was alive or dead, and he certainly did not know that his father was writing to her.

Elias's neglect of Elsie would increase as time passed. The law did not allow him to divorce her, but in her absence he started a new family. Mabel Johnson Bass was a widow twenty years younger than Elias. She, too, worked as a tailor's presser in a Bristol clothing factory, although it is not known if she worked at Todd's with him.[2] By 1921, they were living together in Bristol and in September of that year they had a child, Archie's half-brother, Eric Leach.[3] Back in May 1918, it is not clear what drove Archie to run away from home. It may have been his father's new relationship, the loneliness of life on Campbell Street, the shame of his expulsion from Fairfield, or some combination of these factors. Whatever the reason was, it led him, in mid-May, to leave Bristol without telling anyone where he was going. He departed at dawn, after a sleepless night of worry, tiptoeing out of the house before anyone else was awake, and then walking to Temple Meads railway station, where he boarded the first train to London, and from there another train to Norwich.[4]

He was heading for a job interview with Bob Pender, the leader of the Pender Troupe of "knockabout comedians" who performed at Bristol's Empire or Hippodrome once a year or so. Backstage gossip had alerted Archie to Pender's difficulty maintaining his full troupe because the younger men were being called up for wartime service. Archie wrote to him, pretending to be Elias Leach, and suggesting that his son could join the troupe. Then he watched the letter box at home, waiting to see if Pender wrote back. When he did, Archie managed to intercept the letter before his father saw it. He was astonished that Pender not only expressed an interest in him, but also enclosed rail fare to pay for his trip to Norwich, where the Pender Troupe was currently performing at that city's Hippodrome Theatre.[5]

After the four-hour journey from Bristol, Archie arrived at the Norwich Hippodrome by mid-morning, and he found the troupe starting their limbering-up exercises.[6] Bob Pender was the stage name of Robert Lomas, a stocky, solid, forty-six-year-old music hall veteran. He had made his name playing in pantomimes, that peculiarly British form of Christmas show that stages fairy tales and folk tales as musical comedies filled with slapstick humor, sly double entendres, and audience participation. Lomas and his troupe always found work in the eight-week pantomime season in midwinter, including many seasons at London's famed Theatre Royal, Drury Lane, playing in pantomimes such as *Dick Whittington*, *Jack and the Beanstalk*, and *Puss in Boots*. Outside of pantomime season, they toured the world's music halls with a high-energy act that delighted audiences with its humor and athletic feats.[7]

Archie may have seen the Pender Troupe at the Bristol Empire. They played there as recently as July 1917, and their 20-minute act was likely to delight adolescent boys in particular.[8] The nine-member troupe, billed as "The Nippy Nine," performed a range of stunts and displays: "whirlwind" dancing, gymnastics (somersaults, back flips, human pyramids), "animal impersonations" (with the troupe wearing giant papier mâché masks as they moved about the stage), and a stilt-walking routine known as "The March of the Giants." In the latter, their most distinctive piece, the nine performers emerged on stage in a line, starting with the shortest boy on the lowest stilts and gradually working up to the tallest boy on the highest stilts. They performed comic routines on the stilts that required courage as well as skill. It was a long way to fall from the stilts to the hard stage floor.[9]

When Archie arrived backstage at the Norwich Hippodrome, Bob Pender was likely to have regarded this lanky fourteen-year-old as a potential "tallest boy" in the not too distant future. Archie was interviewed by Pender and his wife Margaret. She was formerly a well-known pantomime ballerina named Maggie Bowman, and now she traveled with and looked after the troupe.[10] Archie met their teenaged daughter, Doris, and Bob's younger brother, Tommy, both of whom were in the troupe. The vagaries of show business meant that other members came and went, but the war caused particular problems. The younger men were drafted, and if they tried to evade military service, as two in the Pender Troupe had recently done, Pender himself was fined. Hence, Pender readily employed Archie, recognizing that he needed training but also that he was very keen to learn and had a few years before he could be drafted.[11]

The troupe was currently touring with a new show, *Getting Ready for Pantomime*, that allowed them to perform their usual range of stunts under the umbrella of a storyline centering on a pantomime rehearsal that goes comically wrong. In April, they launched the tour with a week in Camden (north London), and then they moved on to a different city each week through the end of the year.[12] After Norwich, Archie accompanied the troupe when it moved 40 miles down the road to Ipswich.[13] There, at the Ipswich Hippodrome, he met the zany American comedian Don Barclay, who was playing on the headline act that week. Barclay was twelve years older than Archie, but he took an interest in Archie when he saw some of the Pender boys pretending to teach this inexperienced kid how to apply stage makeup, but actually making up his face like a clown. Barclay intervened and offered to teach Archie properly. He was charmed to find that this runaway boy "was so polite, such a little gentleman." When Archie addressed him as "Sir" or as "Mr. Barclay," he said, "Call me Don." But Archie, who had been taught by his mother always to call older men "Sir," could only manage to call his new friend, "Don, Sir." In later years, after they met again many times, Cary Grant never forgot Barclay's kindness to him, and occasionally when he called him, and Barclay answered the phone, he would ask, "Is that you, Don, Sir?"[14]

One evening in Ipswich the stage manager knocked on the door of the troupe's dressing room and announced that a man who said he was Archie's father was at the stage door, asking to see his son.[15] In the future, Cary Grant would often tell the story of how his father pursued him all the way from Bristol to Ipswich (on England's eastern coast). In his version, his father insisted that he must come home and resume his studies, and Archie obeyed him, and then on his return to Fairfield he was expelled for spying on the girl's loos.[16] This version of the story paints a portrait of a devoted father, but it does not hold up to scrutiny: Archie was expelled from school in March, and the Penders were not in Norwich and Ipswich until May. However, Elias Leach really did track down his son, and when he found him, he insisted that Archie must have a written contract with Bob Pender. Originally dated June 18, 1918 (and later inexplicably amended to August 3 and August 9 of the same year), the contract guaranteed his salary of ten shillings a week plus room and board, and it stipulated that his pay would increase as he "improved" as a performer. The contract lasted nearly four years, until Archie turned eighteen, and it could be terminated only with six months' notice.[17] When it was signed, his father left him to his new life as an apprentice in the Pender Troupe.

Archie was thrilled to have a contract, a career, and a future in show business as a performer rather than a backstage runner.[18] The troupe's near constant touring also fed his wanderlust. Through the summer and autumn of 1918, *Getting Ready for Pantomime* played in major British cities such as Liverpool, Leeds, and Manchester, as well as smaller towns ranging from Devonport in southwestern England to Aberdeen in northeastern Scotland.[19] On tour, they stayed in what they called "digs," shared rooms in theatrical boarding houses paid for by Pender. Archie preferred it when they were in London, performing at venues in and around the city (week-long stints in Camberwell, Canning Town, Hammersmith, Kingston upon Thames, Rotherhithe, and Woolwich were included in this tour). He was enthralled by the vast capital city, and in his spare time he rode trams and buses in every direction, taking in the sights by riding double-decker buses, and sitting in the upper-front seat to get the best view.[20]

The weeks spent in London also offered a more stable home life. He and the other young members of the troupe lived with the Penders in their four-story terraced home at 247 Brixton Road. Brixton, a neighborhood in south London, was noted for its large community of music hall performers, and Archie was thrilled to learn that that Vesta Tilley lived nearby. The Pender house had dormitory-style sleeping arrangements, and Bob Pender imposed a rigid schedule that kept the boys in line. They had to be "up, washed, dressed, and downstairs for breakfast at seven-thirty," then they had an hour for reading or recreation before limbering-up exercises began, followed by training and rehearsing. If it was a show night, they would be at the theater for their two shows, usually beginning at 6:30 and 8:30, and then home and straight to bed. If they were between shows, lights went out at 10:00 sharp.[21]

The training was rigorous. As the new boy, Archie was initially daunted to find himself in the company of the "Nippy Nine," who were so strong and able. As a left-handed boy, he was accustomed to feeling clumsy, but this was intensified by being in the presence of the well-trained, muscular Pender troupers. A photograph of the Pender Troupe, likely taken soon after Archie's arrival, shows him to be a rather young and slight fourteen-year-old. Seated at the very edge of the group, and not wearing a suit and tie like the other members, he also looks like a civilian posing alongside soldiers. He would not feel as though he belonged to the troupe until he was fully trained and ready to perform.

He learned to walk on stilts in the Penders' back garden, where the lowest stilts were strapped to his feet, giving him greater stability, and walking back and forth until his steadiness improved. Then he moved on to higher and higher stilts. When the high stilts were mastered, he learned to walk on the stilts with his head cloaked in a large papier mâché mask. By contrast, the gymnastic feats were comparatively easy to learn. These, too, were practiced in the garden, weather permitting, or in the front room of the house, which was given over to rehearsal space.[22]

There was no dialogue in the act, and so Archie's voice did not figure in his training. His Bristol accent gradually softened after he left the city, and some Brixton tones—the south London variant of a cockney accent— seeped into his speech during his teen years, but this was not by design. His training was entirely physical, and he described the performance skills

Photograph 3.8 The Pender Troupe, circa 1918, with Archie seated in the front row at the far right

Source: The Cary Grant Papers, courtesy of the Margaret Herrick Library

that he learned in two ways. One was to refer to himself as a "tumbler" rather than an acrobat, a term that emphasized the gymnastic elements of Pender's music hall act and distinguished it from flying trapeze artists at the circus.[23] The other was to refer to "the fine art of mime"; that is, communicating with an audience through precise movement and expression alone. He had long appreciated silent comedy, whether in the form of Lotto the Cyclist on stage or Charlie Chaplin on the screen, but learning to do this himself took time. Bob Pender gave him "expert tuition," but he also learned by standing in the wings, watching the best acts on stage and carefully studying their technique and timing.[24] This training would serve him well in Hollywood, where—eventually—he became the master not only of comic timing but also using the smallest of gestures and expressions to the greatest effect.

Two months after Archie left home, the *Getting Ready for Pantomime* tour reached Bristol, where the troupe played the Empire Theatre for a week in late July 1918. He was thrilled to return to his hometown, performing in the very first theater that employed him. He had only a minor role in the act in these early days, but he was proud to be on stage at all, especially when his father came to watch a performance. Archie stayed with his father on Campbell Street that week, and years later he still recalled fondly that he and his father walked home together after the show. "We hardly spoke," he wrote, "but I felt so proud of his pleasure and so much pleasure in his pride. And I happily recall that we held hands for part of that walk."[25] Then the Penders moved on, and on again, to further cities.

On Armistice Day—November 11, 1918—the troupe was in Preston (in the northwest of England). Archie never forgot the day, the reverential atmosphere, and the sense of loss. When the announcement was made at 11:00 a.m., schools sent their pupils home, and the local mills and factories let their employees have the rest of the day off. Crowds filled the streets, and a brass band played in the town square as people milled through the streets, commemorating rather than celebrating the end of a war that had lasted for four years and cost so many lives. The Hippodrome was nearly empty that night, but the show went on, and by the end of the week the local paper observed that the Penders had drawn "screams of laughter" with their "irresistible" humor.[26] They played Dumbarton, Scotland, the following week, and then moved on to Glasgow, and one of the city's leading theaters, the Alhambra, where the troupe joined the cast of *Jack and the Beanstalk* for a twelve-week run of this popular pantomime.[27] If Archie was homesick during his first

Christmas away from home, he was perhaps distracted by being in the midst of this vast, spectacular show.

In March 1919, the pantomime season ended, and the troupe began touring again, with weeks in Birmingham, Weymouth, Manchester, Salisbury, Rotherham, Smethwick, Salford, Liverpool, Dundee, St. Helens, Morecambe, and Eccles before another week at the Bristol Empire in September. By this time, Bob Pender had re-employed so many returning servicemen—the former troupers who had gone to war and now returned to civilian life—that he was able to form two Pender troupes and send them on separate tours. A ten-member troupe continued touring with *Getting Ready for Pantomime*, which included the stilt-walking act (now billed as "The Walk of the Giants") that thrilled audiences most. And a six-member troupe was touring with *After the Show*, which featured "singing, acrobatting, eccentric and Russian dancing" performed by "the most talented young people in vaudeville."[28]

Pender may have overstretched himself. He was soon placing advertisements in the trade weekly *The Stage*, listing weeks that both troupes were "at liberty" and available for bookings.[29] He also created some anxiety among the younger performers. Archie was assigned to the *After the Show* tour, and he suspected that this was the inferior troupe. This was confirmed when the two groups were given different bookings for the 1919–20 pantomime season. The older, more experienced troupe would join the cast of *Jack in the Beanstalk* at the grand Liverpool Olympia theater, while the younger group was relegated to a production of *Dick Whittington* at the smaller, quieter Pier and Pavilion on Colwyn Bay in North Wales.[30]

In *Dick Whittington*, Archie found himself "walking the next-to-highest stilts in a graduated line of other stilt walkers, with my head inside a huge papier mâché mask on which sat a large, white, limp lady's bonnet with a frill around it, and my elongated body and long legs encased in a great calico dress that had frilled collar and cuffs to match the hat." He could laugh about the costuming. What he really minded was that, while the other troupe was enjoying the bright lights of the big city of Liverpool, his troupe was spending the winter season on a seaside pier in a small town. The cold winds off the Irish Sea made the pier a distinctly chilly venue.[31]

When the pantomime season ended, Bob Pender revealed big news to the troupe. He had secured a lengthy booking in New York City, starting in the summer of 1920. It is hard to imagine now, in the age of jet travel, how exciting this would have been back then. Transatlantic journeys were the reserve of the wealthy. For ordinary people—unless they were in the military or worked on ocean liners—this kind of travel was impossible. For Archie, it would be a dream come true, but there was just one catch. Pender would only be taking eight performers with him. Half the troupe would go to New York, while the other half would stay behind, continuing to tour British music halls. Archie's anxiety about his status in the troupe was at fever pitch until he was chosen for New York—and the biggest adventure of his life so far.[32]

He gave one of his last performances in Britain at the Finsbury Park Empire, a big venue situated in one of the roughest neighborhoods in London.[33] It was the sort of neighborhood where even the police walked in twos, and the sort of theater where the performers feared leaving their valuables in their dressing rooms.[34] What a contrast when the troupe took the train to Southampton and boarded the ocean liner RMS *Olympic*, setting sail on July 21, 1920, for a seven-night journey to New York City via Cherbourg, France. Bob Pender bought the troupe second-class tickets, allowing them to travel in comfort rather than in the cramped quarters of third class.[35]

As if the journey was not exciting enough, the ship was abuzz with the news that two of Hollywood's biggest stars were on board. Douglas Fairbanks and Mary Pickford were returning to the United States after honeymooning in Europe. Seeing them on the ship's deck gave Archie his first opportunity to observe the public adulation of film stars. He watched as Fairbanks and Pickford were continually asked for their autographs, and asked to pose for photos, by the other passengers. This kind of intrusion would be the bane of his own existence in later years. Autograph-seekers, in particular, drove him to despair. But as a sixteen-year-old, he was thrilled to be able to meet Fairbanks and tell him how much he admired him. The handsome star, known for his athletic grace, was a likely hero for a young acrobat and, in person, Archie admired his gentlemanly manners and his deep tan.[36] These became the markers of film stardom that Archie himself would adopt when he became a Hollywood star.

Archie and his fellow troupers could scarcely sleep on the last night of the crossing because they did not want to miss their early morning arrival in New York. The Manhattan skyline was unlike anything in Britain (London's tallest building was St. Paul's Cathedral), but it was familiar to filmgoers like Archie, and he wanted to see it in person. He was at the ship's railings on the clear, surprisingly cool morning of July 28, 1920, when the skyline came into view. The tallest building in New York at that time was the seventy-story Woolworth Building, and as Archie stood on the deck, awestruck by this and

Photograph 3.9 The Pender Troupe in New York, circa 1920, with Archie on the far left

Source: The Cary Grant Papers, courtesy of the Margaret Herrick Library

many other skyscrapers, he could scarcely imagine that he would one day marry the heir to the Woolworth fortune.[37]

He was not yet the dashing figure he would eventually become. The immigration official who took his details noted that he had the dark brown eyes and black hair, but also that he was as yet only 5 feet, 9 inches in height and that he had a "sallow" complexion.[38] A photograph taken of the troupe, soon after they arrived in New York, shows that at sixteen he was still a slight boy compared to the other members, and suggests that he had a shy demeanor. Another photo from the same period, taken on his own, reveals more confidence and considerable pride in his appearance.

Archie marveled at New York City: everything was faster and bigger. Except, it turned out, the stage of the theater that booked them. When the nine members of the Pender Troupe arrived at the Globe Theater on 46th Street and began their rehearsal, they found that the stage was not deep enough or high enough for the stilt-walking finale of their act. They did not have enough room to move about on the shallow stage, and the audience would not be able to see the heads of the highest stilt-walkers. For a moment, this seemed to threaten the troupe's future in New York, but the Globe

Photograph 3.10 Archie looking sharp in a suit, with a tie-pin and a pocket square, circa 1920
Source: The Cary Grant Papers, courtesy of the Margaret Herrick Library

was owned by the same company that owned the much larger Hippodrome Theater, which was currently preparing a show with a cast of hundreds. The troupe was sent for an audition there.[39]

New York's vast Hippodrome was a legendary venue among vaudevillians. Located on 6th Avenue, it took up the entire block between 43rd and 44th streets, and had over five thousand seats. Its stage had plenty of room for stilt-walkers: it was 148 feet wide, 96 feet deep, and had a proscenium arch that was 60 feet high. The theater's most distinctive feature was a glass pool, so large that it took nearly a million gallons of water to fill it, that rose up from beneath the stage.[40] This was a theater for circuses and spectacular shows, and in July 1920, one of the biggest shows ever staged was about to open. *Good Times* was a show in three acts, with no discernible story but a progression of epic set pieces, ranging from elephant tricks to high-divers plunging from the rafters into the pool and emerging as statuesque "nymphs."[41]

The Pender Troupe auditioned and got a spot in the middle of the second act, in the "Toy Store" scene that featured dolls coming to life to sing and dance. As this scene unfolded, the Penders appeared, on their stilts and with their papier-mâché masks, to perform a comedy sketch in which the tallest in the group—some 12 feet tall on stilts—drops his hat, and the shortest retrieves it and passes it up the line to its owner. Their appearance went over so well that it drew comment in the most prominent reviews of this "monster pageant" of a show. Hence, the show's director, R. H. Burnside, gave them an additional appearance in Act Three's circus scene, performing what was described as "their quaint animal impersonations."[42]

Good Times was a good break for the Pender Troupe. They featured in the most talked-about, celebrated show of the year, which played to packed houses from August 13, 1920, to May 1, 1921.[43] However, the troupe was just one act within a vast show, boasting a cast of one thousand performers. They were not stars and they were not living a life of luxury. Bob and Margaret Pender rented a small apartment on 46th Street and 8th Avenue (Cary Grant recalled the rooms as being like a set of narrow railway carriages), and there the three teenage members of the troupe lived under the Penders' watchful eyes. In addition to sixteen-year-old Archie, there was sixteen-year-old Leslie Brooks (the shortest member of the troupe at only 4 feet, 10 inches) and eighteen-year-old Henry Hart. There was little privacy in this cramped apartment. At night the boys lined up to wash their socks and handkerchiefs in a kitchen tub. They lined up to use the ironing board. They took turns buying and cooking food (Archie relying on beef stew as his specialty), washing dishes, and doing other household chores.[44]

If the domestic routine on 46th Street was humdrum, there were also two shows to perform—at 2:15 and 8:15—every day except Sundays. In his free time, Archie took to New York as he had taken to London, fascinated by its size, its sights, and the variety of its neighborhoods. The double-decker buses with open-air tops that went up Fifth Avenue from Washington Square and then across town to Riverside Drive were a particular favorite of his. He was thankful that movie theaters were open on his only day off (Sunday screenings were not allowed in Britain), and he delighted in the varieties of ice creams available and the huge portion sizes (the "banana split" was unknown in Britain).[45]

When *Good Times* finished in May 1921, Archie experienced his first bout of end-of-show blues. The performers who had worked together for ten months, forming friendships and romances, were disbanding, and many would not see each other again. It was a scenario he would become accustomed to when he moved on to Broadway shows and film shoots.[46] The Pender Troupe itself did not disband, or even return to Britain, but instead went on a tour of the American East Coast and Midwest. The troupe's success at the Hippodrome had enabled Bob Pender to secure a full year of dates on the prestigious B. F. Keith Vaudeville Circuit, beginning inauspiciously in Wilkes-Barre, Pennsylvania, and then continuing with half-week or week-long engagements in just about every medium- to large-sized city east of St. Louis and north of the Mason-Dixon Line, as well as a few dates in Canada.[47]

The act that the Pender Troupe took on the road was a 13-minute run-through of their best-known, most crowd-pleasing routines: eccentric dancing, gymnastics, and stilt-walking. There were some high points to the tour. In September, when they played Washington, DC, the troupe was very excited to learn that former president Woodrow Wilson was in the audience, and even more excited when they were lined up to meet him after the show. Wilson was a giant on the world stage, famous for negotiating the Versailles Treaty, and Archie could scarcely believe it when he heard Wilson saying how much he enjoyed the troupe's performance.[48] In October, another high point was playing New York's Palace Theatre. Located at Broadway and 47th Street, this was considered the finest vaudeville theater in the country and the flagship of the Keith's circuit.[49] The Pender Troupe was at the bottom of the bill, but they earned two curtain calls from the appreciative audience.[50]

There were some low points, too. In December, they played Boston, and a reviewer noted that a long bout of dreary, drizzly weather meant that the theater was half-empty and the audience was unenthused. The troupe was "saved from a flop" only by their stilt-walking finale.[51] They moved on to Syracuse, Montreal, Toronto, Hamilton, and Detroit before arriving in Rochester, New York. There, Archie came down with rheumatic fever, and he was laid up in bed for two weeks. The troupe had to move on to their next date, leaving him alone in a boarding house for his eighteenth birthday on January 18, 1922. One of the performers on the same program in Rochester, the actress Jean Adair, heard about this lonely, sick English boy, and went to visit him, returning with cake when he told her it was his birthday. It was a kindness he would never forget, and he would remind her of it when they met again on the set of *Arsenic and Old Lace* in 1941.[52]

Archie's eighteenth birthday marked the end of the contract that his father had signed for him nearly four years earlier, and he told Bob Pender that he would be leaving the troupe after he had served his six months' notice. Pender tried to talk him out of it, offering to raise his pay to $35 a week, but Archie was adamant that he had decided to return to Britain. Two years earlier, Pender had promised all the troupe members he would pay their return fare if and when they decided they wanted to go home. Archie was calling him on this promise, insisting that he was leaving the troupe and the United States. Both Bob and Margaret Pender tried to convince him to stay, but to no avail.[53]

Finally, an exasperated Bob Pender bought Archie's return ticket, on a ship sailing from New York to Southampton on May 29, and then he wrote a letter to Elias Leach, explaining Archie's departure from the troupe. Pender had been a boss, a teacher, and a surrogate father to Archie for four years, and some affection for him is apparent in the words he wrote to his father. "He has been a good boy since he has been with me," Pender observed, "and I think he is throwing away a good chance but he does not think so." Some frustration with Archie is apparent in the letter, too. "I must tell you he is most extravagant and wants to stay at the best hotels and live altogether beyond his means," Pender wrote disapprovingly. "He has very big ideas for a boy his age."[54]

Archie did have big ideas. He had observed the Penders' lives and decided that he wanted more. Although the troupe was considered successful, their work entailed staying in boarding houses, working relentlessly, and watching every penny that they earned. There was an incident in Chicago, just before Archie left, that probably convinced him that he was making the right decision. On stage, in the midst of the stilt-walking routine, Bob Pender lost his balance and went crashing down to the stage floor, bruising his face and his body. Yet the forty-eight-year-old returned for the next show and performed despite his painful injuries.[55] This was hardly a life to aspire to, and Archie was ready to move on.

He had no intention of returning to Britain, but instead cashed in the ticket that Pender purchased for him. He would stay in New York, trying his hand at vaudeville on his own. Pender, of course, learned of Archie's deceit, and he was annoyed and hurt by it. As the years went by, he was hurt, too, that Archie never contacted him again. In the 1930s, when the movie star Cary Grant spoke in interviews about his early days in the Pender Troupe, reporters would occasionally seek out Bob Pender. They found him retired from the stage and running a novelty shop in Southend-on-Sea. In 1938, the year before he died, Pender told one reporter that he had written to Cary Grant several times, asking to see him on his next trip to London, but he never received a reply.[56] It was later in life that Cary became sentimental about his days with Bob and Margaret Pender, realizing how much he owed them and regretting the way he left them.[57] As a young man, however, he was too restless to linger on sentiment and regrets. He was looking forward rather than back, and toward a career of his own.

4

In the summer of 1922, Archie used the money that he got from Bob Pender—supposedly for his return fare to Britain—to go back to New York City and seek work on his own. He rented a room for just $11 per month in a boarding house on 46th Street near Ninth Avenue. This put him in the infamous slum known as "Hell's Kitchen," but it was also near the edge of the theater district and the two spots he visited most. One, on 8th Avenue at 46th Street, was a sleek art deco diner ironically named Ye Eat Shoppe, where out-of-work performers lingered over cheap meals. Archie calculated that he could feed himself there on just 50 cents a day, while keeping an ear out for work. The other, just around the corner on 46th Street, was the National Vaudeville Artists Club (the NVA), which provided a restaurant, a lounge, and a billiards room for members at a rate of just $10 per year. There, he could mix with other newcomers and unknowns, as well as the well-known theatrical and vaudeville figures who visited the club after their shows.[1]

The NVA offered a friendly environment, but he found most of the newcomers were struggling just as much as he was. As his money dwindled, he realized that gaining a new foothold in show business was going to be more difficult than he imagined. He had performed in hundreds of theaters over the previous four years, and yet his own name had never appeared on the bill. He was simply a member of the Pender Troupe. Another problem was that he never had a speaking part on stage. Thus, when agents asked him, "What experience have you had?" and "Have you ever spoken lines?" his answers meant that he was quickly shown the door. His aim was to appear on stage under his own name and without a papier-mâché mask or high stilts preventing the audience from getting a good look at him.[2]

His greatest asset was his appearance. At the age of eighteen, as his height reached nearly 6 feet, 2 inches, he was slowly but surely becoming a strikingly handsome adult. He kept himself well groomed and, although he could not afford an extensive wardrobe, he remembered his father's advice and spent his money on one superior suit rather than several inferior ones. "People should notice you first, not the clothes," his father had advised him. "The best clothes are always graciously understated. Good clothes never call attention to themselves."[3] He admitted succumbing to just one fashion trend that he later regretted, wearing a "jazz age" bow-tie. He was proudly sporting this when he visited Don Barclay backstage after a show. Barclay did not have to say anything. He simply pulled the bowtie forward and let it snap back against Archie's neck. They both laughed, and Archie realized his fashion *faux pas*.[4]

His good looks, good manners, and English accent made him a charming fellow, too, and he was not short of invitations to dinners and parties. On one particularly august occasion he was asked to escort the famed Metropolitan Opera star Lucrezia Bori to a dinner party. He was delighted, and also relieved when she suggested they walk to and from the party, thus saving him the taxi fare that he could not afford. Another guest at the party was George Tilyou, the founder of Steeplechase Park, an amusement park off the boardwalk on Coney Island. Archie told Tilyou about his past in vaudeville, including his stilt-walking, and somehow—with some clever maneuvring by Archie—the conversation turned into a job offer. Archie would advertise Steeplechase Park by walking along the boardwalk on his high stilts, wearing the garish red and green uniform of its doormen and inviting passersby to come in and purchase a ticket.[5]

Cary Grant told this tale often in interviews. Once he was a movie star, it served as a wry anecdote about his past, and one that conveyed just how far he had come in show business. He liked to boast that he negotiated double pay on weekends, demanding the extra money because when children were on the boardwalk they made a game of trying to knock him off his stilts. He boasted, too, that he set up deals with the hotdog and ice cream vendors on the boardwalk, getting free food in return for drawing attention to them by eating a hotdog or having an ice cream cone while on stilts.[6] Anecdotes aside, there can be no doubt that this was a career nadir for him. He left the Pender Troupe to get off his stilts, but now he was stilt-walking on a boardwalk rather than a stage.

He was not on the boardwalk for long. He met up with some of his fellow Pender troupers, who told him that the production team behind *Good Times* was putting together another spectacular show at New York's Hippodrome. They each auditioned individually rather than as a troupe, and Archie got two minor parts in the new show.[7] *Better Times*, as it was called, was another extravaganza designed to take advantage of the Hippodrome's vast stage. One act featured eleven dancing elephants, while another had sixteen show-jumping horses. Others were elaborate pageants featuring scores of performers. Archie was in a musical comedy number, "I Dreamt I Went to the Grand Opera Ball," that was staged as a parade of fifty characters from famous operas. He was one of the four "meistersingers" from Wagner's *Die Meistersinger von Nürnberg*. He also featured in "The Land of Mystery," as one of a "multitude of skeletons" who come to life and dance, glowing white against a black backdrop.[8]

Intriguingly, the latter scene featured three of his fellow Pender troupers. Tommy Lomas and Billy Smith were billed as "The Gloomy Boys" in this scene, while Archie and Jack Notman were billed as "The Joyful Girls." It isn't clear whether this means that Archie was in drag, but the billing is important for another reason. This was the first time that his name was included in a cast list, and when the show was reviewed in *Variety*, with full credits listed, his name appeared in the weekly "bible of show business" for the very first time. Even if it was one of dozens of names, this was a definite step up in his career. The show's long run, beginning in September 1922 and lasting eight months, gave him steady work at last, with the familiar schedule of two shows daily and Sundays off.[9]

By the time *Better Times* closed in April 1923, Archie had joined Tommy Lomas, Jack Notman, and Billy Smith—all originally Pender troupers—to form the Lomas Troupe (presumably named for Lomas because he was the eldest and most experienced member). Six additional members were auditioned and hired over the next month.[10] Bob Pender was furious when he heard about this. Assuming that they were going to replicate his own act, he threatened legal action from Britain. Archie hurriedly wrote home to his father, telling him to be wary of any contact from Pender, and enclosing a ten-shilling note as a sign of his own success. His father replied to him immediately, agreeing not to correspond with Pender. He praised Archie for having the "pluck" to stay in the United States rather than return to Britain. A new father at the age of fifty, Elias also thanked him for the cash. "It only shows me how much you must think of us in sending us the money," he wrote. His signature, "your ever loving Dad," was surrounded by a circle of kisses marked with the letter x.[11]

Pender could not stop the Lomas Troupe from reviving the most popular routine from his act. The troupe's show, entitled *From the Bottom to the Top*, climaxed with the graduated line of masked stilt-walkers—with the shortest going on stage first and the tallest last—that always amused audiences. However, the 14-minute act was different from Pender's act in at least one very important respect: it had dialogue. The show's opening was a comic turn in which two English "toffs" and two "rubes" get into an argument that leads to a frenzied chase around the stage, complete with a horse-and-wagon chase (not a real horse, but two members of the troupe dressed as a horse). Archie was one of the toffs: a "dapperly dressed fop carrying a cane." Thus, the act mixed physical comedy with some dialogue, and for the time being at least, Archie was putting on a British rather than an American accent.[12]

The troupe tried out *From the Bottom to the Top* several times, honing it with well-received appearances on the East Coast, before they embarked on a tour of the Pantages Theater circuit in late July 1923.[13] The Pantages theaters were not as large or as high-toned as the Keith's theaters that the Pender Troupe had played, but it was an extensive circuit and it kept the Lomas Troupe on the road for many months.[14] Beginning in the Pacific Northwest, the tour took Archie to parts of the United States and Canada that he had not yet seen, including week-long dates in Vancouver, Tacoma, Spokane, Seattle, and Portland, before moving down to southern California in late October 1923. The warm, sunny climate made a big impression on him. Even before he arrived in Los Angeles, Archie was marveling at the palm trees, orange groves, and vineyards from the train window.[15]

He fell in love with Los Angeles at a time when it was a smog-less city, and there were still empty lots along the broad tree-lined boulevards that led to Hollywood. The Hollywood sign—then the "Hollywoodland" sign—had been erected earlier that year to advertise a new subdivision of houses on the fringe of Hollywood, which had become the film industry's capital over the previous ten years. When Douglas Fairbanks invited the troupe to visit the Pickford-Fairbanks Studios, they got a chance to visit Hollywood and see a film being made.

Archie's first time in a film studio was watching his hero, Douglas Fairbanks, making what turned out to be one of his most popular films, *The Thief of Bagdad* (1924). The film's director, Raoul Walsh, would one day direct Cary Grant in *Big Brown Eyes* (1936). Amid the excitement of this visit, the nineteen-year-old Archie must have looked upon the film studio and the sunny city, and imagined a future for himself there. He must have recognized that movies were slowly squeezing vaudeville out of theaters.[16] On the Lomas Troupe's tour of the Pantages circuit, they were often at the top of a bill that included four or five other acts, but the rest of the "evening's entertainment" was a feature film. It was a bad sign for the Lomas Troupe, and the future of vaudeville, that the films were often more prominently advertised than the live acts.[17]

They had another week in southern California, in Long Beach, before moving on to Salt Lake City, and then continuing on to the West, the Midwest, and the South, working their way eastward in a roundabout manner. In New Orleans, Archie discovered the all-American sport of baseball for the first time. He had been walking around the city "flat pocket," as he put it—that is, without any money—when some of the stagehands at the theater challenged the performers to a game. Bored and restless, he joined in even though he had never even watched a game. He had played cricket back in Bristol, and so he at least knew how to use a bat as a left-hander, and he hit the first ball pitched to him. He did not realize that the rules did not allow him to have another pitch (as they did in cricket). Hence, as he stood at home plate, his teammates shouted "Run! Run!" at him. He soon learned the rules, and he came to admire them. "I love the strategy of baseball—the steal, the bunt, the hit and run, the squeeze play," he explained in later years, after he had enjoyed many games, although mainly as a spectator and not a player.[18]

By March 1924, after ten months of touring, the troupe had exhausted the Pantages circuit, but they remained on the road for another eight months, picking up dates in the East and the Midwest. Many of these were in the high-toned Keith's theaters, but they were placed at the bottom of the bill.[19] In the summer, they also spent weeks playing state fairs in Virginia and Wisconsin, and the Central Canada Exhibition in Ottawa.[20] Looking back on this period of his life, Cary Grant recalled that life as a vaudevillian was "as tough as anything." The troupe played as many as six performances a day, and in their spare time they scouted for meals and a means of washing their clothes. If possible, they took an overnight train to the next city to avoid having to pay for a room for the night. "On the night trains," he remembered, "I'd look into the windows of the houses along the way and see people living ordinary lives. That was my goal. To live in my own house."[21]

The near-constant touring satiated his wanderlust, at least temporarily. Tensions within the troupe were running high—hardly surprising, given the amount of time they spent on the road and in cramped quarters—but they kept going as long as they could because the money was good. Archie was making $50 per week, which was a middle-class income at the time.[22] By the autumn of 1924, though, Archie had saved enough to return to New York and start looking for a new act. The rest of the troupe would soon reunite and hit the road again, but Archie did not join them.[23]

In December 1924, his career turned a very significant corner when he auditioned for *The Woman Pays*. This comedy playlet was developed by Jean

Dalrymple, a young writer who had become a small-scale vaudeville producer, writing scripts and casting performers before selling the "package" to booking agents. For *The Woman Pays*, she had already cast two established vaudeville performers, Constance Robinson and Jack Janis, to play an engaged couple on a date in a smart restaurant. The woman is lively and pretty, while the man is affable but dull. When the bill comes, he is mortified to find he does not have enough money to pay it, and they get into an argument about her extravagant menu choices. Hurt, she leaves the table, and at the door of the restaurant she meets the most handsome, charming fellow she has ever seen, who offers to pay their bill for them. Her fiancé won't allow it, and in the ending it is, as the title indicates, the woman who pays, but not before she dances with her handsome new friend and sings a song about him.[24]

Dalrymple put out a casting call for the handsome charmer, but she was frustrated when agents sent her a stream of "Rudolph Valentino types," as she put it. When she insisted that she wanted a more American man, they sent her "dull looking farm boys." Finally, Archie walked through the door, and she was dazzled by him. "He was absolute perfection," she recalled. He fit the bill of "somebody I could fall for, someone women in the audience would be crazy about." Her partner, Don Jarrett, sat in on the casting sessions and he was not so impressed. He thought Archie was too inexperienced and his accent was too odd. Dalrymple, however, saw something in the handsome newcomer. She was impressed by his good looks of course, but also that he seemed to find the show genuinely funny, giggling when he read the lines for the first time.[25] Archie got the job, his first role as a handsome charmer.

The Woman Pays was booked into smaller theaters on the Keith's, Orpheum, and Proctor's circuits.[26] In December 1924, the tour started auspiciously enough at a Proctor's house on 58th Street in New York City, and then it went through seemingly every small city in the Midwest, from Oshkosh, Wisconsin, to Davenport, Iowa. The first performance in New York drew a prominent review in *Billboard*, which complained that Constance Robinson and Jack Janis delivered their lines like "sledgehammer blows." The description of Archie, only as a "man who played a bit," may have stemmed from the rather ungenerous billing, which referred to the performers as "Robinson, Janis and Company."[27] Other reviews of the show indicated that it was a very slight comedy, but as the tour progressed the cast seems to have loosened up and had some fun with their lines. Midway through the tour, the billing changed to "Robinson, Janis and Leach," suggesting that Archie was doing well with his part.[28]

In February 1926, after 14 months on the road, the tour ended in Chattanooga, Tennessee. By this time—after three cross-country tours over the prior five years—Archie felt as though he had walked down every Main Street in the United States, and he eagerly returned to New York City. He rented a "small but clean and pleasant" room at the NVA, where, as he put it, he was "permitted to run up bills while trying to run down jobs." At twenty-two, he was old enough and experienced enough to be considered a safe pair of hands, and he formed a number of temporary partnerships with different comedians, typically playing dates in and around New York City at weekends, when movie theaters often added live performances to their programs.[29]

Cary Grant recalled this period, when he was working with a number of different partners in vaudeville, as the time when he learned the most about audiences and how to make them laugh. He recalled learning how to time jokes—when to move, when to handle a prop, how long the gap should be afterward—by trying different things out and studying audience responses. These were skills that would serve him well in films. He also found that his forte was playing the "straight man" in comic duos—that is, the one who feeds lines to a comedian who then responds with a joke. The "straight man" serves as a kind of surrogate for the audience, reacting to the comedian's jokes in tandem with them, although with more exaggerated gestures such as widened eyes or a double take.[30] Archie worked well in this role not only because he honed his comic skills, but also because audiences liked having such a handsome fellow as their surrogate. This was a dynamic that would serve him well in films, too.

As much as he enjoyed this work, there was not enough of it, and it did not pay well enough to sustain him. Eventually, the NVA or another landlord must have evicted him, because one day in 1926 Archie turned up at Jack Kelly's flat on Commerce Street in Greenwich Village, having been thrown out of his own room elsewhere. It is not clear how Archie and "Kelly," as he was known, first met, but Kelly was a struggling actor, too, and so they may have met at an audition, or at Ye Eat Shoppe, or the NVA. They would have taken an interest in each other because, although Kelly was from Australia, they were both considered "Britishers" in the United States. They both came from working-class backgrounds, their fathers were both tailors, they were both in their twenties, and they were both very ambitious. Kelly had recently decided that he would never make it as an actor, and that he would aim to be a set designer instead, but they both dedicated themselves to pursuing careers in show business.[31]

Kelly would eventually become the Hollywood costume designer known as Orry-Kelly, and he would win three Academy Awards over the course of his long and very successful career. He was also known to be gay, and so in retrospect the relationship between Archie and Kelly has attracted speculation, particularly from Cary Grant's previous biographers, some of whom assumed that the two men were lovers.[32] In 2016, however, Orry-Kelly's long-lost autobiography surfaced. It was discovered in a relative's attic, tucked inside a pillowcase, where, presumably, it had been ever since Kelly died more than fifty years earlier.[33] *Women I've Undressed*, as the book's title suggests, is mainly about his career as a costume designer, but it also recalls Kelly's years in New York and his close, although often volatile, friendship with Archie Leach.

In his book, Kelly does not address the issue of sexuality directly. A gay man of his generation, writing in the early 1960s, would not have been able to discuss his homosexuality openly. But he does make it very clear that Archie was attracted to women and especially to blonde women (as he was later in life). "He fell in and out of love with many blondes, all of them beautiful," Kelly wrote, adding that by and large they found him irresistible too. He suggests Archie was more than ready to use his looks to get ahead and recalls a time Archie put his regular girlfriend, the chorus girl Doreen Glover, on hold to date another blonde, Minnie, who could get him a screen test at Warner Bros. When the screen test did not turn out well, he forgot about Minnie and went back to Doreen.[34]

Gillian Armstrong's documentary about Kelly, *Women He's Undressed* (2015), strongly suggests that Archie and Kelly were lovers, and not least when the film quotes Kelly as saying that while Archie had many girlfriends, "he always came home to *me*." But this line (or any similar line) is not in Kelly's autobiography. Far from giving the impression that he and Archie were lovers, he paints a picture of their relationship as often difficult and at times combative. In his eyes, Archie is ridiculously vain, and Kelly enjoys taking him down a peg or two, which makes Archie's temper flare. Kelly finds Archie overly tight with his money and eager to cover up his humble social origins, and he gives the impression that Archie had bad taste in clothing until he gave him some useful pointers.[35]

Always one step away from hunger or eviction, or both, Archie and Kelly shared schemes for keeping the wolf from the door. Archie occasionally—and reluctantly—spent weeks at Coney Island, and on stilts, in order to pay the rent. Kelly painted murals on the walls of speakeasies. His specialty was decorating them with what he described as "naughty red monkeys" and "jade green frogs," both of which looked like "licentious old men."[36] He also hand-painted silk ties, selling them to shops, friends, and acquaintances. Archie got in on the action, helping out with both the mural and tie painting (although the more detailed work on the ties was left to Kelly). More importantly, Archie began hawking them to anyone and everyone he thought able to afford them, including his own doctor. With Archie as the salesman, and his charm turned on, turnover rose considerably.[37]

Archie and Kelly moved in the same social circle of up-and-coming performers—including comedians George Burns and Gracie Allen, and writers Lester Cole and Moss Hart—who met in Ye Eat Shoppe as well as any speakeasy that they could find.[38] New York was in the midst of the "Jazz Age" and the Prohibition laws were flouted. The speakeasies in and around the theater district were not only thriving but also bringing together a diverse array of people: gangsters and socialites, the famous and the unknown in show business, as well as gay and straight drinkers.[39] Thus, one night in the spring of 1927, when Archie went to the midtown nightclub of the sultry torch singer Helen Morgan, he was casually introduced to Reginald ("Reggie") Hammerstein, a young Broadway director who was the brother of the musical composer Oscar Hammerstein II and the nephew of the theatrical impresario Arthur Hammerstein.

Between sets, Archie told Reggie about his career struggles in vaudeville. Work was so thin lately that he had taken a job as an extra in a Metropolitan Opera House production of *Electra*—not a speaking part, and certainly not a singing part, but he was at least on the stage.[40] As Reggie listened to Archie's woes, he could not help but wonder why this handsome young man was so keen to succeed in the rough-and-tumble world of vaudeville. Now twenty-three years old, Archie looked like a potential leading man and a likely matinee idol. Wouldn't he be better suited, Reggie asked, to the more sophisticated and glamorous world of Broadway shows, and particularly the light musical comedies that were the specialty of his own family? Archie had to process this suggestion. His ambitions had focused on vaudeville for so long that it was difficult to imagine another career route. But when Reggie offered to introduce him to his uncle Arthur, and then when Arthur Hammerstein offered him a small part in his next Broadway show, Archie's ambitions—and his fortunes—changed dramatically.[41]

PART TWO

MATINEE IDOL, 1927 TO 1936

5

When Reggie Hammerstein introduced Archie to his uncle Arthur, Broadway was enjoying its biggest ever season. A record 264 new shows opened in 1927–28.[1] One of the biggest was Arthur Hammerstein's operetta *Golden Dawn*. Hammerstein hired Archie, paying him $75 per week, to play an Australian character named Anzac in *Golden Dawn*.[2] The casting points to one reason Reggie was so keen to give Archie an audition. Americans often could not place Archie's odd accent, mistaking its blend of working class Bristol and Brixton tones for an Australian accent.[3] It's likely that Reggie not only saw a potential matinee idol in Archie, but also heard an "Anzac."

Rehearsals for *Golden Dawn* started on August 22, 1927, and a month later the show previewed for a week in Wilmington, Delaware, before moving on to previews in Pittsburgh for a week, Detroit for two weeks, Philadelphia for two weeks, and then opening on Broadway on November 30.[4] This round of cities—all major stops for touring shows—would become very familiar to Archie over the next few years. Broadway players were not quite as itinerant as vaudevillians, but their shows often did not begin or end in Manhattan, and they frequently received a warmer welcome on the road. Archie enjoyed getting to know these cities, exploring their sights, and detecting the distinctions between their audiences. Snobby Wilmington audiences, he learned, did not laugh so long or so loudly as they did 35 miles up the road in Philadelphia, and he adjusted his timing accordingly.[5]

Golden Dawn did well, commercially and critically, during its out-of-town previews.[6] When it reached New York, however, it found a less welcoming reception. The opening night was also the opening of the newly built Hammerstein Theater (now the Ed Sullivan Theater), on Broadway near 53rd Street, and the new venue got far better notices than the show. New York critics praised the leads, Metropolitan Opera star Louise Hunter and Broadway baritone Paul Gregory, and they liked the musical score, but they were not impressed by the story. The comic-book melodrama centers on Dawn, a young white woman living happily with an African tribe whose members "worship her as a goddess" until she meets a group of white prisoners of war released from a nearby camp. When she falls in love with one of prisoners, the tribe turns on her, and she is saved from their wrath only just before the curtain falls.[7]

Staged as a spectacular and exotic story set "in the deepest heart of Africa," the show featured white actors in blackface performing "voodoo conga dances."[8] The New York critics did not address the racist tropes directly, but instead complained about the formulaic, plodding, empty storyline. Their criticism hurt at the box office, but Arthur Hammerstein let the show run for 184 performances, until May 5, 1928, because he did not want the first show at his new theater to be labeled as a flop. Tickets were heavily discounted but nevertheless by the end of the run *Golden Dawn* was playing to "rows upon rows of empty seats."[9] Archie's role, as one of the prisoners of war, was too small to be noticed by critics. He also served as the understudy to the leading man, Paul Gregory, and throughout the run of the show, he was terrified that Gregory would fall ill and he would have to take his place. One afternoon, when Gregory got to the theater with just a few minutes to spare, Archie was already costumed and ready to go on in his place. He was "quaking with fright" at the prospect, and he begged Gregory never to do this to him again.[10]

Arthur Hammerstein had more confidence in Archie than he had in himself. During the run of *Golden Dawn,* he raised his salary from $75 to $200 per week, a leap that signaled his intention to groom Archie as a musical theater star. A new contract also stipulated that to "further and improve your talents," Archie would work with a "vocal instructor," to be paid for by Hammerstein.[11] It is not clear whether this referred to his speaking or singing voice, but it is likely that he had some training for both. His singing voice would prove to be a major limitation to his Broadway career. His speaking voice, meanwhile, may have suited the role of Anzac but it would have to be Americanized and stage-trained for further roles. Archie's accent would slowly become a mix of Bristol, Brixton, and Broadway. The Broadway training can be heard especially in the distinctly staccato quality of his speech, which emphasizes consonants for the sake of clarity.

His new and lucrative contract enabled him to leave behind his many years of living in boarding houses, shared apartments, and the NVA. Now he could rent an apartment of his own at 325 East 80th Street, on the not-so-smart side of Manhattan's Upper East Side, and he could buy an automobile, a luxury he had aspired to since his first ride back in Bristol. Having never actually driven before, he had to learn to drive in his new Packard Phaeton, a sporty four-seater with a detachable roof. He loved this car—a public display of his new success—and by his own admission, he "doted" on it, cleaning and polishing it, and of course taking it out for long drives, at every opportunity.[12]

In the summer of 1928, he often drove out to the tip of Long Island, where Don Barclay had rented a beach cottage. Together, they developed a vaudeville act that they performed in theaters a few weeks later (out of the theatrical "season," when he was not paid by the Hammersteins, he could work in vaudeville but not on Broadway).[13] Their act, entitled *Oh! I Did Not*, included one routine in which Archie was an earnest mind-reader and Barclay moved through the audience, seeking questions for him. Barclay would relay audience questions to Archie on stage, such as, "Where is this man's father?" Archie would concentrate for a moment and reply, "In Denver, Colorado!" Then the man in the audience would respond with something along the lines of, "No, he's not. He's in Memphis," to which Archie would reply, "You're wrong. Your mother's husband is in Memphis, but your father is in Denver." Archie thought the joke was in bad taste, but it always got a big laugh.[14]

In later years, Cary Grant often recalled these vaudeville days, with their silly routines and audience participation, with fond nostalgia. He had few, if any, fond memories of his time in Broadway musicals.[15] His uncertainty about his singing voice made the shows difficult for him. Hence, the news that Hammerstein was casting him in one of the lead roles in *Polly*, a new musical version of a popular romantic comedy *Polly with a Past*, filled him with trepidation. This was a small-scale show compared to *Golden Dawn*, with just a dozen cast members, and Archie had a much more prominent part in it. Starting on October 2, he had four weeks of rehearsals to master it. Previews began in Wilmington in November, with further preview weeks scheduled for Philadelphia and Detroit, prior to a Broadway opening in January 1929.[16]

Archie was cast as Rex Van Zile, a wealthy, shy young man who asks Polly, a maid, to help him in his efforts to win the affection of a high-society girl. Then he finds himself falling for Polly instead. Polly was played by the dainty British actress known simply as June. She had starred in several musical comedies in London's West End, as well as Alfred Hitchcock's early film thriller, *The Lodger* (1926), but she was unknown to American audiences. Arthur Hammerstein brought her to New York for *Polly*, aiming to establish her as a Broadway star.[17] A duet between June and Archie, on the song "Sweet Liar," was considered a standout moment in the show, with June's "sweet soprano" adding character to Archie's baritone. However, it was the comedian Fred Allen, doing a comic turn as a reporter, who received the best notices.[18]

On opening night in Wilmington, Archie's first night jitters apparently got the better of him. The critic for the local *Morning News* observed that he was much "better and more likeable" in the second act than he was in the first, suggesting that he managed to loosen up midway through the evening.[19] The critic for the *News Journal* was delighted by his appearance: "He is more than six feet tall, lean, brown, and athletically hard, and his fine cut features, gleaming teeth and curly black hair are well calculated to draw forth feminine adoration." But the same critic was not so delighted by his singing, describing it only as "above average for a male lead in a musical comedy."[20] The following week, the critic for the *Philadelphia Inquirer* made a similar, though more cutting point: "Archie Leach made a fine and manly figure as the lover and danced with skill but did seem to fail to bring out the musical beauty of the score."[21]

Arthur Hammerstein evidently agreed. *Polly* was scheduled to run for four weeks in Philadelphia, but Hammerstein closed the show at the end of the second week, and he replaced Archie before it opened again in Detroit and New York.[22] Archie may have taken some solace when *Polly* lasted for only fifteen performances on Broadway—the problem clearly was not him alone—but by that time he was already in another show and working for a different company. To his dismay, Hammerstein sold his contract to the rival Shubert Organization, one of the biggest companies in the business, and the executive J. J. Shubert sent him straight back to Wilmington. There, just a few weeks after *Polly* closed, Archie appeared in the previews of what promised to be one of the biggest shows of the 1928–29 season.[23]   .

Boom Boom aimed to be a thoroughly modern musical comedy—full of spectacularly staged song-and-dance numbers, and with humor spiced by risqué innuendo and double entendres. The plot centered on a portly, aging "rake," played by popular comedian Frank McIntyre, who leers at young women and makes suggestive jokes about them. He somehow finds himself engaged to his son's attractive girlfriend, Jean, played by the trilling soprano Jeanette MacDonald. Archie played the son's treacherous friend, Reggie Phipps, and he had one big number with MacDonald, in which they danced the tango and sang "Nina," a song about a Spanish siren.[24] Archie wisely decided to deliver lines such as *She kissed with such pash/she'd scorch your mustache* in a tongue-in-cheek style.[25] Apparently this masked the limitations of his singing voice; he drew some of his best reviews for *Boom Boom*. One Wilmington critic remembered him from *Polly* and commented that he was "fully twice as good in *Boom Boom* as he was in the previous show."[26]

There were further previews in Atlantic City, Philadelphia, Baltimore, and Newark before *Boom Boom* opened at Broadway's Casino Theater on January 28, 1929. Like *Golden Dawn*, it failed to win over New York critics and audiences, although few despaired as deeply as the future screenwriter Charles Brackett, who was then a theater critic for the *New Yorker*. Brackett told his readers that as he watched this vulgar, garish show, he could not help but wonder, "Wouldn't it be better if civilization ended?"[27] Other critics reported that the opening night audience was so unimpressed with the show that, when a celebrated naval captain arrived ten minutes late, and tried to take his seat quietly, the audience turned from the stage and gave him a standing ovation. The applause for the captain lasted so long that the orchestra conductor abandoned the show's score to play "The Star-Spangled Banner" in his honor. The show resumed but at the intermission audience members were overheard joking that even the Navy could not save this show.[28]

Jeanette MacDonald loathed *Boom Boom*. She pleaded with J. J. Shubert to release her from her contract and when he refused, she lost her temper and shouted, "This is the rottenest show I've ever been in!"[29] Shubert struggled to keep *Boom Boom* running on Broadway, with cut-price tickets sustaining it for just seventy-two performances. When it closed on March 30, the show went on the road for three months, traveling to Pittsburgh, Cincinnati, Chicago, and Boston. On tour, the box-office takings remained weak but the reviews were better, and Archie's status as an up-and-coming matinee idol was confirmed by observations such as "Archie Leach is almost too handsome."[30]

He was noticed in *Boom Boom*. During the Broadway run, Fox Films asked him to make a screen test, together with Jeanette MacDonald, in a local film studio. Delighted, they performed "Nina" for the camera and then waited eagerly for the studio's verdict. Cary Grant would long insist that the studio rejected him because he was bowlegged and his neck was too thick, but MacDonald recalled a more polite response. "We feel neither of these people has a screen personality" was the verdict.[31] She and Archie would have the last laugh, of course, but she was able to laugh much sooner than he was. MacDonald escaped from *Boom Boom* before the end of the tour (as soon as her contract allowed), and she went directly to Hollywood. She made films first at Paramount and then at MGM, where she became the undisputed queen of screen operettas for the next decade.

The *Boom Boom* tour finished in June 1929, and Archie briefly returned to New York. He had reason to be pleased: the Shuberts had renewed his contract, raising his weekly salary from $200 to $300, and guaranteeing him at least twenty-five paid weeks in the year.[32] He went to see Kelly, who was now running a speakeasy on 49th Street. Kelly had rented an empty shop, painted his trademark lecherous frogs on the walls, and found a bootlegger, he later claimed, through "one of Archie's many girlfriends." He had a fine time until the bootleggers—"two of the toughest characters I've ever seen"—demanded more money from him. An unsuspecting Archie arrived at Kelly's just in time for the showdown, when the heavies arrived to collect $750 or do some irreparable harm to Kelly. At gunpoint, Archie placated them with the $250 he had in his wallet. Then he and Kelly fled, fearing the gunmen would return for more.[33]

After the trouble with Kelly, Archie was less flush with cash, but he was still able to carry out his summer plans. On the morning of July 22, 1929—almost nine years to the day since he had left Britain—he arrived in Liverpool on the SS *Adriatic*.[34] He was twenty-five years old and he had not seen his family or set foot in his home country since he was sixteen. Yet he still identified strongly as a Brit, with a preference for tea over coffee, a penchant for fish and chips, and a longing to see his father and Bristol again.[35] There he found his father living with Mabel Bass and their eight-year-old son, Eric. Archie met his half-brother for the first time, and the surviving photographs suggest it was a happy occasion. One shot has Elias, Mabel, and Eric Leach sitting on a bench, smiling and looking very relaxed, while another shows Archie and his father looking dapper on a motorbike. Archie also spent time in London, staying at the Regent's Palace Hotel, off Piccadilly Circus and very handy for the West End theater district. Then, after four weeks in Britain, he departed for New York on August 17, traveling in second class (as he had on the journey over) on the SS *Arabic*.[36]

He returned to begin rehearsals for *A Wonderful Night*. This was another lavish Shubert show, complete with a revolving stage and a cast of over one hundred performers. It was a more respectable show than *Boom Boom*. Based on Johann Strauss's operetta *Die Fledermaus* (1874), *A Wonderful Night* combined Strauss's music and story with some updated 1920s humor. Archie was cast as the dashing Max de Grunewald, the philandering husband at the center of this tale of mistaken identity and masked balls among Vienna's upper classes. For most other aspiring actors, this would have been

Photograph 5.11 Seven-year-old Eric Leach with his father, Elias James Leach, and his mother, Mabel Johnson Bass, in 1929

Source: The Cary Grant Papers, courtesy of the Margaret Herrick Library

a plum role, but from the beginning, Archie was anxious about his singing voice, worrying that "*A Wonderful Night* wasn't going to be so wonderful."[37]

The first night, on October 31, 1929, arrived amid the panic of the Wall Street Crash. The stock market had been plummeting for several days, but as Archie walked to the Majestic Theater that afternoon, he was more worried about his performance and the revolving stage that kept breaking down during rehearsals. On the street, he ran into Fred Allen, his co-star from *Polly*, and he confided his fears. "Hmmm, my boy, suppose you come with me," Allen said, leading him downtown to the observatory at the top of the Woolworth Building. There, they looked down on a city that suddenly looked small and much less frightening. Archie's anxiety did not vanish altogether, but it diminished, and this lesson in perspective was one he remembered, and shared with other first-nighters, for many years to come.[38]

A Wonderful Night did moderately well at the box office, lasting for 125 performances on Broadway, until February 15, 1930. This was no small achievement given the deepening economic gloom and the show's mixed reviews. Many critics did not like the modern humor of the story but they

Photograph 5.12 Archie and his father in Bristol, 1929
Source: The Cary Grant Papers, courtesy of the Margaret Herrick Library

admitted that Strauss's melodies were a saving grace.[39] Archie, however, received the worst reviews of his Broadway career. Critics complained that he was out of place in the upper-class, continental milieu. The critic for *Billboard* put it most bluntly by stating that he "does not belong in a Johann Strauss operetta."[40] This was echoed by others: he was "woefully miscast" and "his acting has a vaudeville quality" (*Brooklyn Daily Times*); he "managed to miss the proper tone entirely" (*New York Sun*); and he came across as "a mixture of John Barrymore and cockney" (*Brooklyn Eagle*).[41]

This was the first time since he left vaudeville that critics suggested that he did not have enough class to be a Broadway lead, and the first time that his accent (rather than his singing voice) was criticized. The barbs continued as the tour moved on to Philadelphia, Detroit, Boston, Cleveland, and Chicago. He grew accustomed to reading criticisms along the lines of "Archie Leach is a trifle minus of voice" (*Philadelphia Inquirer*), but criticism of his comic performance—and references to his "nancified antics" (*Chicago Daily News*)—must have stung him.[42] Remarkably, many of these the reviews went into his first scrapbook of press clippings, and they have remained there ever since, testifying to the rocky path that led him to Hollywood.

The Shuberts did not lose faith in him. During the run of *A Wonderful Night* they raised his salary from $300 to $400 per week.[43] But they did not have a new show for him during the 1930–31 season. The company was hard hit by the economic downturn and, as it teetered on the brink of bankruptcy, its performers took a "voluntary" pay cut. Archie's salary dropped to $275 per week, and he was assigned to a touring show that had already finished its Broadway run.[44] This was quite the comedown, but he liked the show and its star, and so he swallowed his pride and joined the cast of *The Street Singer* in September 1930. He started in Philadelphia and continued to Detroit, Pittsburgh, Hartford, Boston, and Toronto, before finishing in Montreal in January 1931.[45]

The Street Singer owed a heavy debt to George Bernard Shaw's *Pygmalion*. Archie played George, a young American millionaire in Paris, who bets his wife that he can make a great lady out of any waif on the streets. Former ballerina turned musical star Queenie Smith played the waif, a street-singing flower girl with whom George gradually falls in love. A bright and breezy musical comedy, *The Street Singer* drew mostly admiring reviews. Archie suffered the usual round of cutting comments about his voice. "The handsome Mr. Leach is distinguished by his good looks and uncommonly bad singing," the critic for the *Detroit News* jibed.[46] But his performance as an American millionaire brought some interesting praise. One critic observed that he had "a drawing-room ease" (*Philadelphia Public Ledger*), while another wrote that he "rivals only Jack Buchanan in the way he wears clothes."[47] Both comments suggest that this contemporary, sophisticated comedy allowed him to take a step toward realizing the kind of characters he might play and the kind of image he might pursue in Hollywood.

Archie would have been particularly flattered by the comparison with the debonair Buchanan, an actor he had admired ever since he saw *Auld*

Lang Syne back in Bristol. When a role called for sophistication, he imitated Buchanan, along with two other well-dressed, smooth British actors, Sir Gerald Du Maurier and A. E. Matthews. However, he had a kind of awakening when he saw Noel Coward in *Private Lives*.[48] Then thirty-one years old and already a major figure, Coward wrote and starred in this sharp, chic marital comedy, which was a landmark success in London's West End before it arrived on Broadway in January 1931. He represented a new breed of English gentleman—refined and self-assured as ever, but with an insouciant playfulness and a lack of pretension, quite modern too. Like many of his other plays, *Private Lives* manages simultaneously to ridicule and glamorize the upper classes, and to bring a measure of fun to sophistication. This was the kind of story, character, and image that Archie would pursue for himself—with a more American flavor—when he got the chance. For the moment, he watched and learned, becoming a fan and then a friend of Coward's.

He began trying to craft a public image for himself. While touring with shows, he accepted invitations to charity events and other public functions, attending as a celebrity guest. He gave interviews to local newspapers and was always ready with the right words. In an interview with the *Boston Globe*, he flattered the locals by explaining why he preferred American over British musical theater, leading the reporter to conclude, "There is something thoroughly likeable and charming about this tall Englishman."[49] He also felt free to invent many elements of his life story when speaking with reporters. As a matinee idol—that is, a man to be admired for his polished good looks—he sometimes felt compelled to describe his background in stridently masculine terms.[50] He was originally a prizefighter, he said, a "dangerous heavyweight," no less, and he got into acting because a "girl reporter" convinced him that he was "much too good-looking to be in the ring."[51]

More often, he invented a life story designed to appeal to American stereotypes of Britain and the theater. He told some reporters that his father was "a London tailor who caters exclusively to royalty," or, on other occasions, "a Bristol clothing manufacturer."[52] His grandfather, he said, was Percival Leach, "the greatest Shakespearian actor of his generation." Archie carried this fib so far that on one occasion, an item appeared in *Billboard* stating that the great Percival Leach was arriving in New York to spend the holidays with his grandson, Archie.[53] He said that his mother's family also had a theatrical background—they were in a well-known troupe of actors known as "The Sidney Teppers."[54] His own real experience with the Pender Troupe was recast as the brief, eccentric rebellion of a boy born with the theater in his blood, which came to an end when he attended "Fairfield College" or, in other versions of the story, "Clifton University."[55] Afterward, he claimed that he belonged to a British theater company and appeared on the West End stage until Arthur Hammerstein saw him there and brought him to New York.[56]

This reinvention of himself, and the determination to mask the harsher truths of his past, marks him as a figure similar to Jimmie Gatz in F. Scott Fitzgerald's *The Great Gatsby* (1925). Gatz, too, denied the realities of his rough background and he used style, accent, and manners (as well as his wealth) to reinvent himself as the dashing Jay Gatsby.[57] In his early days in Hollywood, Archie went even further with his deceptions, recasting one of the more humiliating episodes of his life, when he ruined the Great David Devant's magic act at the Bristol Empire, as a triumph. He told reporters that he started in show business as a fourteen-year-old working the lights at the Empire, and insisted that he soon invented a new theatrical lighting technique that has been in use ever since.[58] He never specified exactly what this technique was.

This type of deception can easily turn into self-deception, but there are no signs that Archie began to believe his fabrications. Indeed, he seems to have kept his sense of humor about it all. The first dog that he owned in Hollywood, after he changed his name to Cary Grant, was a Sealyham terrier that he named Archibald. Once he achieved some fame, he gradually said less and less about his family, and Percival Leach vanished as suddenly as he had appeared in his life story. It would be decades, though, before he was able to reveal to the public anything approaching the truths of his childhood and family background.

Orry-Kelly recalled that Archie was desperate for publicity in this period. When their friend Belle Livingstone was released from a Harlem jail in March 1931, they went to greet her. She had been jailed for running a notorious speakeasy, and so press photographers were there to greet her too. In the newspapers, Archie was pictured at her side, but he was not named in the accompanying reports. According to Kelly, he "threw a fit" over this, disappointed that he had missed the opportunity for some press coverage.[59]

He had reason to be disappointed. He had not worked since *The Street Singer* tour ended in January, and this dry spell lasted until May, when he was cast in *Singapore Sue*, a ten-minute short film made at Paramount's Astoria Studio on Long Island. He was paid $150 for a six-day shoot, a rate far below his Shubert salary, but this was a chance for him to be seen by Paramount producers in Hollywood, and he grabbed it.[60] *Singapore Sue*, however, turned out to be an excruciatingly bad showcase for him. Admittedly, the script is terrible, but playing a macho American sailor in Singapore, trying to pick up the eponymous hostess of a seedy basement bar, is far outside his range. His performance demonstrates that he had yet to develop an understanding of acting for the camera. He performs as though he is on stage, projecting to the back row of the upper circle. His mannerisms are exaggerated, his facial expressions are too broad, and, despite his Broadway training, his accent still shows traces of Bristol and Brixton.

Even his handsome appearance—the one thing the harshest stage critics admired him for—is undermined by unflattering makeup, flat lighting, and an ill-fitting costume. His skin tone and teeth look bad, and the sailor's suit reveals the "thick neck" mentioned when Fox rejected him. Paramount certainly wasn't impressed. Neither Anna Chang (who plays Sue) nor Archie was offered a studio contract on the basis of *Singapore Sue*, and the film was shelved until August 1932, when Cary Grant's career momentum started to build.[61] He loathed the film. When he won his Lifetime Achievement

Photograph 5.13 Archie's first film, the short *Singapore Sue* (Paramount Pictures, 1931), with Anna Chang
Source: author's screen capture

Academy Award, the Academy put together a reel of film clips representing every phase of his career, and asked him to approve it. His only request was that they remove a brief bit of *Singapore Sue*. Nearly forty years afterward, his performance still embarrassed him.[62]

When filming finished in mid-May, 1931, Archie got in his Packard and embarked for St. Louis, Missouri, where J. J. Shubert was producing a repertory season of musicals for the Municipal Opera Company, to be performed in the open-air theater in Forest Park. In his autobiography, Orry-Kelly claims that he got this job for Archie. Kelly was working for the Shubert Company as a costume designer, and while preparing the costumes for the St. Louis shows, he asked J. J. Shubert's nephew, Milton Shubert, if he would give the out-of-work Archie a few parts in the shows. "But he's such a lousy actor," Shubert supposedly replied before agreeing to cast Archie. Kelly's version of events is clearly not true. Archie went to St. Louis because he was under contract to the Shuberts, and two of the shows he had toured with, *The Street Singer* and *A Wonderful Night*, were being performed there. He had star billing in these and several other shows, and he was treated as a local celebrity throughout his three months in St. Louis.[63]

The summer started badly. Archie's companion on the road journey was Billy Smith, one of the older Pender Troupe members who came over to New York with Archie in 1920, and later joined him in the Lomas Troupe. They remained friends, and Smith came along for the ride, hoping he could find work with the Shuberts. On the road, he kept telling Archie that he was driving too fast, until Archie finally lost control of the car and it overturned. They were able to get the car fixed, but when Smith didn't find work in St. Louis, he sued Archie for damages, and the friendship came to an end.[64] In St. Louis, he was among other old friends, including Don Barclay and former co-stars from various Shubert shows. He lived humbly, sharing an apartment with comedian Jack Goode over a Walgreen's drugstore near Forest Park. Goode remembered that they spent the summer carousing and "chasing girls," but there were also six shows a week to perform, with a different show each week, and Archie had leading roles in seven of these.[65] Never one to shirk from hard work, he always recalled this summer fondly.[66]

Returning to New York in late August, he auditioned for a new show, *Nikki*. He was so keen on this that, when he got the part, he asked to be released from his long-term Shubert contract. Shubert, in increasingly dire financial straits, let him go, and Archie signed a one-show contract with producer Harrison Hall that paid $375 per week.[67] *Nikki* was a musical adaptation of

Photograph 5.14 Archie in St. Louis during the summer of 1931
Source: The Cary Grant Papers, courtesy of the Margaret Herrick Library

John Monk Saunders's *Nikki and Her War Birds*, a set of "lost generation" short stories about five American fliers in Paris after the war, trying to come to terms with their mental and physical scars. When they meet the breezy, delightful Nikki in a café, they all fall in love with her, but she falls in love with the most dashing of them all, Cary Lockwood, who would of course be played by Archie.

Saunders wrote the stage adaptation and helped to fund the play because he was intrigued to see *Nikki* turned into a musical, or at least a drama with songs, and because his wife, the Hollywood star Fay Wray, would play the title role. Wray would find her greatest fame playing the delicate, blonde beauty loved by the giant ape of *King Kong* (1933), but for the moment she was seeking credibility on the Broadway stage. She was nervous about this and about her unhappy marriage to Saunders. He was an alcoholic and, anxious about his investment in *Nikki*, he criticized her performance at length. From the very first rehearsal, she found relief and comfort in the eager attention that Archie paid to her. A frisson developed between them and it distracted her from all of her worries.[68]

She could not help but notice that Archie seemed to light up when she spoke. She saw his thoughts in his eyes: "I love what you have to say. I like you. Say what you said again. I love hearing it. That is fascinating." In turn, he felt confident around her. "He was sure of himself, happy to be in a theater," she recalled, remembering him as "a person simply enjoying what he was doing, a person in the right milieu, a person who belonged." The only thing she did not like about him was his name. How could someone so debonair be called Archibald, she wondered. She took to calling him "Cary," his character's name in the play, and he responded by calling her "Nikki."[69]

When the show opened on September 29, 1931, she found that he was a generous performer, moving downstage when she spoke so that the audience's eyes would be on her, a selflessness rare among actors. The show received mixed reviews and from the beginning the box office was not strong, but they both enjoyed their short time together in it.[70] He had developed a crush on her that would last for many years, and playing "Cary" to her "Nikki" at least allowed him to act out his feelings during the eight shows each week.[71] *Nikki* was the sweetest moment of his Broadway career. It was also the moment that led him away from Broadway, and to his own future as Cary Grant.

6

Throughout his career, when Cary Grant explained how he made the leap from stage to screen, he would say that he went to Hollywood on an impromptu vacation (a "tramp road trip," as he put it). He wasn't seeking film work. He didn't intend to stay long. He just went to see some friends and, while he was there, he just happened to come to the attention of film producers, and they just happened to offer him an irresistibly lucrative contract. The story was typical of the tales he told about his own life, in which a breezy outlook and a lot of luck brought him incredible success.[1] The truth is not necessarily more mundane, but it suggests that he was cannier and more ambitious than he liked to admit. He strived for his success, even as he made it look effortless.

Archie Leach actually had few other options when he left New York for Hollywood in mid-November 1931. *Nikki* closed on October 31 after running for just five weeks. The producers moved the play from the Long Acre to the George M. Cohan Theater, and lowered ticket prices in a bid to attract audiences, but still *Nikki* played to half-empty houses.[2] It was one of many shows that failed that autumn. Two years after the Wall Street Crash, as unemployment climbed and banks failed, the bright lights of Broadway were going dark. Over half of the theater district's sixty theaters closed, and most of those that remained open did a meager business.[3] Thus, as *Nikki* stalled, and Archie looked around for a new show, he realized that his prospects were bleak. The theatrical giants who had once fostered his stage career, the Hammersteins and the Shuberts, were on the verge of bankruptcy. Casting calls were few and far between, and although he had been well paid for *Nikki*, the money would not last forever.

Hollywood offered a ray of hope amid this gloom. The Depression was hitting the film industry too, but the industry responded by offering audiences two films for the price of one. Double features became the norm, along with raffles and lotteries and giveaways—anything that would stem the decline of ticket sales. Hollywood was down but not out. Producers were still looking for new stars, and an experienced stage actor with matinee idol looks stood a good chance of getting a screen test at least.

Still, he was not entirely certain about Hollywood. He had been rejected after screen tests with Warner Bros. and Fox, and he must have realized by now that (the still unreleased) *Singapore Sue* sparked no interest at Paramount. He did not want to travel across the country, risking weeks if not months without pay, only to find more rejection and disinterest. His friends urged him to go. Fay Wray insisted he would do well in films.[4] Jack Kelly was already in Hollywood—after St. Louis he headed west rather than returning to New York—and he could help Archie learn the lay of the land. William Grady, his New York agent, offered him a letter of introduction to Walter Herzbrun, a well-connected Hollywood agent. Phil Charig, who had composed the music for both *Polly* and *Nikki*, was keen to try his luck in films too, and Phil suggested that they travel across the country together.[5]

Archie wavered until he saw Fay Wray a few days after *Nikki* closed. On the last night, they shared a tender moment. In the play's closing moment, they stood in an embrace, with the spotlight on their heads, and then the light went out and the curtain fell. On the closing night, when the light went out, he kissed her on the forehead and said, "God bless you, Nikki," as the final curtain fell. They were both sorry to see their time together end. She wanted to host a closing night party, but John Monk Saunders—moody and troubled at the best of times—had taken the play's closing as a personal failure. "Please! *No*" was his response to his wife's proposed party.[6]

"Nikki" and her besotted "Cary" were reunited a few nights after the play closed, when they both attended the opening night gala for a Broadway comedy, *Here Comes the Bride*. The party was held at the newly opened Waldorf-Astoria Hotel, a colossal art deco palace that had been designed before the Wall Street Crash and now looked like a monument to a lost era of ostentatious wealth and luxury. The show, too, seemed to belong to that lost era. Everyone could tell that it was doomed to fail (as it did after just six performances). An evening that was planned as a sparkling celebration thus fizzled out quickly.[7]

Amid the downbeat chatter, Fay told Archie that she and John were leaving for Hollywood. John's screenplay for *The Dawn Patrol* (1931) was nominated for an Academy Award, and he wanted to attend the ceremony in Los Angeles. Fay could see that the news of her departure hit Archie hard. As she left the party, climbing the grand stairway of the hotel's banquet room, she turned to see that he was still standing where she had left him, watching her leave while everyone else at their table was seated. At the top of the stairs, she turned again and he was still there, standing and watching her. She could not help but admire how handsome he looked in white tie and tails, and she could not help but feel flattered by how despondent he looked.[8]

Irene Mayer Selznick, the daughter of MGM studio boss Louis B. Mayer, was sitting next to Archie and recalled that "he had only two things on his mind that night: whether he should go to Hollywood and Fay Wray. He was very stuck on her."[9] Overnight, Archie decided that if "Nikki" was going to Hollywood, "Cary" would too. He phoned Fay the next day to announce that he and Phil Charig would leave within a week. Phil, a "quiet" and "amusing" fellow, according to Archie, made a good companion for the long journey.[10] They crossed the country in Archie's Packard Phaeton. Interstate highways did not exist yet and so, far from being a breezy vacation, they spent a week on the 3,000-mile journey from coast to coast, traveling through the snow and ice of the Midwest and then down the many dry and dusty miles of Route 66 to Los Angeles. In some places the roads were still unpaved, and roadhouses were few and far between.

It was Archie's infatuation with Fay that finally pushed him to make this long, uncertain journey. Even though he knew that their relationship was unlikely to progress beyond yearning and sublimated desire, he wanted to be near her. He also knew that he liked the city. During the two weeks he spent in Los Angeles with the Lomas Troupe in 1923, he had marveled at the palm trees and wide boulevards of the sunny, spacious, up-and-coming city. Eight years later, Los Angeles had nearly doubled in size, and the open fields he had seen on the fringes of Hollywood were paved over. Around the world, the very name Hollywood had become synonymous not only with filmmaking but also with glamour, beauty, and wealth. It could be disappointing, then, to arrive and find—as Jack Kelly did a few months before Archie—that the famed corner of Hollywood and Vine looked "like the corner of any two streets in any small town."[11]

Kelly had not yet found steady employment when Archie and Phil arrived in late November. He was staying at the Warner-Kelton, a large residential hotel just a few blocks down from Hollywood and Vine, where rooms could be rented cheaply by the week. Built in the Spanish Colonial style so popular in California in the 1920s, the hotel boasted a palm court and swimming pool, but despite its luxurious aspirations it had become a slightly disreputable place. There was a speakeasy in the basement and, with rooms costing just $10 per week, the residents included the film industry's down-and-out as well its up-and-coming. Archie was in the latter category, but he wanted better digs than the Warner-Kelton. He stayed there for just one night before renting an apartment in a quieter building a mile away on North Kingsley Drive.[12]

Over the coming weeks, he and Kelly saw each other almost every day, meeting up for 65-cent meals in diners and driving out to the beach at weekends. Yet Kelly still enjoyed taking his handsome friend down a peg or two, making fun of his accent and questioning his taste in clothes. Now that Archie's ambitions were aiming higher than ever, he resented Kelly's jibes all the more. Too often, Archie took the bait and lost his cool, but their stormy friendship—and what Kelly called their "silly brawls"—continued during these first few months in Hollywood.[13]

Archie, meanwhile, pursued his key contact in the film industry, the agent Walter Herzbrun, who agreed to help the tall, dark, and handsome new arrival. Herzbrun arranged for him to be invited to a dinner party at the home of B. P. Schulberg, the powerful head of production at Paramount Pictures. Another guest that night, the Paramount director Marion Gering, was impressed enough to offer him a screen test—of sorts. The screen test, or tests, were not for Archie. Instead, he was paid to appear in tests for actresses. He stood at the edge of the frame, feeding them lines. He was not lit and only the back of his head was meant to be in view. But when Gering and Schulberg watched the tests, they were struck by his screen presence. In silhouette, his height, his athletic frame, and his thick black hair gave him a sturdy, masculine screen presence that was complemented by his more elegant profile, including—if he managed to turn just slightly to camera—the gently curving dimple in his chin. Archie must have managed to turn slightly to camera, because afterward he was offered his own screen test. This test has not survived, but it is likely that Gering invested some time and effort into it, making sure Archie was costumed, made up, and lit in a more flattering manner than he had been in *Singapore Sue*.[14]

The new test impressed Schulberg and other Paramount executives. "We've got another Gable!" they exclaimed in unison.[15] Or so the legend goes. Hollywood legends have many of these "Eureka!" moments. Nevertheless, it is clear that B. P. Schulberg really did believe in Archie's star potential. On December 11, 1931, Archie signed a contract with Paramount that gave him a salary of $450 a week.[16] This was three or four times what other new contract players were paid at Paramount, and it signaled that the studio had plans for Archie; that he was regarded as a potential star.

Crucially, although the contract bound Archie to Paramount for five years, the studio had the option to cancel or renew the contract every six months.

This was a standard feature of the long-term contracts that stars signed. All of the power rested with the studio. The actors had no say in which films they made, who wrote and directed them, or who they would co-star with. They could be sent on a "loan-out" to another studio. If they refused to make a film, they could be put on "suspension" without pay and they could not work for any other company. It was an arrangement that many frustrated actors compared to indentured servitude, but it was very well-paid servitude and it had huge benefits. Studios invested in the stars they believed in, building them up through films and publicity, and raising their salaries if everything went well.[17]

The first demand Paramount put to Archie was that he must change his name. Schulberg and Gering told him that audiences would not pay to see someone named Archie Leach. The name was too old-fashioned and too drab for a movie star. Archie was neither indignant nor insulted by this. He was intrigued by the possibilities. That evening, he joined Fay Wray and John Monk Saunders for dinner, celebrating Saunders's win at the Academy Awards, but Archie's name change became the topic of the evening. The trio agreed that Archie should take the name of the character who had set him on the path to Hollywood, Cary Lockwood. But when Archie met with the studio executives the next day, they rejected this. "Cary" was fine, Schulberg explained to him, but there was already a film actor named Harold Lockwood, and at any rate long, elaborate names like Rudolph Valentino and Richard Barthelmess belonged to the frivolous 1920s. The hard times of the 1930s called for simpler, blunter names. A ready-made list of approved names was produced, and they all stopped at "Grant," asking "Grant? Cary *Grant*?" It was another "Eureka!" moment, and not least because the initials C and G matched those of the two leading stars of the moment, Clark Gable and, turned around, Gary Cooper. And so, just three weeks after leaving New York, Archie Leach had a new name, a new career, and a new professional home at Hollywood's most powerful studio.[18]

Cary never expressed an iota of hesitancy or regret about changing his name. Down the line, the story he always told was about *how* he chose his new name. It was not about *why* he agreed so readily to change it, or why he chose to use his new name both professionally and personally. The fact that he told this story so often was unusual. Fred Astaire (real name: Frederick Austerlitz), John Wayne (Marion Morrison), Carole Lombard (Jane Peters), and Mickey Rooney (Joseph Yule), to name a few, did not draw attention to their earlier identities so frequently. But the transformation of Archie Leach into Cary Grant was a key part of his image from the beginning of his film career. It was an affirmation of Hollywood's glamour, and it showed that this foreign-born young man was living the American Dream of upward mobility and personal fulfillment.[19]

Publicity aside, he eagerly accepted the new name and the movie-star identity that went with it. From the time he signed his contract with Paramount, everyone he met in Hollywood—friends, co-workers, and lovers—would know him as Cary rather than Archie. His eager acceptance of his new identity was not a form of deception or denial but a means of stepping up to the enormous challenge that he faced during these early months in Hollywood. He was staking a claim to film stardom even though he had very little experience with films. Every morning, when he passed through Paramount's grand studio gates, he knew he had to embrace this opportunity fully—becoming Cary Grant and believing in Cary Grant—or risk losing it altogether.

The Paramount studio lot was like a vast walled city within Hollywood. The 26-acre site had fourteen sound stages and a backlot for outdoor filming. There was every form of office, dressing room, workshop, and rehearsal space for the thousands of people who worked on the lot every day. They included the producers, directors, screenwriters, engineers, art designers, construction crew, makeup artists, musicians, and actors directly involved in filmmaking, as well as ancillary staff. The studio produced between fifty and sixty films each year, ranging from million-dollar prestige films to run-of-the-mill "programmers" made for double features. A steady stream of films was needed for the chain of movie theaters that Paramount owned. The chain extended to 1,400 movie houses in the United States alone, plus an international distribution network on top of that.

Whether they were prestige films or programmers, films were all that anyone talked about within the studio walls. The studio chatter was about which films would be made next, who would be cast in them, whose reputation was going up or down, and who was easy or difficult to work with. There were no newsstands or grocery stores to distract from the business at hand. The world outside the studio did not matter, unless the talk was about box-office grosses and which films were proving to be hits or misses.[20] This was the environment in which Archie Leach became Cary Grant. He accepted its all-encompassing nature and, during the early years of his contract, he thrived within it.

Paramount was home to some of the most popular stars of the era. The Marx Brothers reinvented screen comedy at the studio with their wonderfully anarchic *Animal Crackers* (1930), *Monkey Business* (1931), and *Duck Soup* (1933). Maurice Chevalier brought his droll romantic charm to playful musicals such as *Love Me Tonight* (1932) and *One Hour with You* (1932). The studio's one true siren was Marlene Dietrich, the German-born star who was transformed into an exotic fantasy figure by her Svengali-like director, Josef von Sternberg, in the films *Morocco* (1930), *Dishonoured* (1931), and *Shanghai Express* (1932). Of the studio's leading men, Fredric March was considered to be the most serious actor, especially when he won the Academy Award for his performance in *Dr. Jekyll and Mr. Hyde* (1931). The most popular of Paramount's leading men, however, was unquestionably Gary Cooper, the tall, laconic star who made his name as the cowboy hero of *The Virginian* (1929) and quickly proved a master of many genres, starring alongside Dietrich in the melodrama *Morocco*, with Sylvia Sidney in the gangster film *City Streets* (1931), and with Carole Lombard in the comedy *I Take This Woman* (1931).[21]

Cooper's career at Paramount might have served as a cautionary tale for Cary. The studio was so eager to cash in on his popularity after *The Virginian* that Cooper was cast in five or six films each year over a two-year period. The continuous filming left him exhausted, depressed, and ill. Suffering from anemia and jaundice, he lost 30 pounds from his already slim frame. In May 1931, he walked out of the studio and embarked on a long vacation. He traveled through Europe and Africa, not returning to Hollywood until April 1932. While he was away, the studio encouraged speculation that Cary might be Cooper's replacement, and after Cooper returned, this encouraged a rivalry between the two stars.[22] Articles planted in the film fan magazines— including one entitled "Cary Versus Gary"—made it seem as though they were interchangeable.[23] Pitted against one another, they never became friends.

Although both men were tall and handsome, the idea that they were similar in appearance or personality is easily exaggerated. Cooper's Western drawl and shy hesitancy made him the ideal cowboy. He personified an American archetype, and his popularity and reputation never wavered. Cary, by contrast, had the polish and glamour of a matinee idol, but it was not at all clear how he could be transformed into an intriguing screen personality. What sort of image and film roles would suit such a suave man? He was British but his voice and demeanor did not fit with Hollywood's stereotype of the refined English gentleman. He did not have the experience or gravitas to take on the "serious" roles Fredric March played. Most of his experience was in musicals but no one thought he should continue along that path. While the name Cary Grant had been easy to agree upon, it soon became apparent that no one at Paramount knew exactly who Cary Grant would—or could—be on-screen.

New contract players reported each morning to the studio's Talent Department. They were assigned to stylists who would test them with different makeup, hairstyles, and clothing. They had photographs taken—indoors, outdoors, and in a variety of scenarios. They met with publicists who planned stories about them for the fan magazines and newspaper gossip columns.[24] They also spent four hours each day in a dramatic training school with studio director Stuart Walker as their teacher. The training aimed to teach stage actors the techniques of screen acting. Cary studied alongside fellow new arrivals at the studio, including Adrienne Ames, Sari Maritza, and George Raft. A few weeks later, another new arrival, Randolph Scott, joined the classes. Walker used a standing set on one of the soundstages—a living room with a hallway and staircase—to take his class through a scene. They would play the scene once as though they were acting in a theater, and then again as though acting for the camera, with Walker emphasizing the distinctions between stage and screen acting craft.[25]

Cary's first day of filming filled him with dread. It arrived on January 19, 1932, the day after his twenty-eighth birthday, when he reported to the set of his first Paramount film, *This Is the Night*. He would always suffer first-day nerves on the set, but this was different. Where other newcomers were initially given small roles in modest films, he had a co-starring role in a prominent film, alongside a director and cast who were all established professionals. It did not help that, when he was told that he would be playing an Olympic javelin thrower, he eagerly bought javelins and went to Griffith Park to practice with them, only to find later that there were no javelin-throwing scenes in the film.[26] Far from it: *This Is the Night* is a stagey comedy set in penthouse apartments and five-star hotels in swanky European locales. Cary's character is Stephen Mathewson, an American athlete living abroad. He returns from a competition unexpectedly and finds his wife (Thelma Todd) planning a holiday in Venice with her Parisian lover (Roland Young). A highly-strung friend (Charles Ruggles) gives the couple an alibi by inventing a wife (Lily Damita) for the lover. Somehow they all embark for Venice, where adjoining hotel rooms ensure a stream of farcical shenanigans.

The story was, in the words of *Variety*, a "Frenchy bedroom chase."[27] Paramount was known for this kind of sophisticated comedy. The studio's top director, Ernst Lubitsch, could bring a shimmering gleam to the most worn bedroom chase stories. The director of *This Is the Night*, Frank Tuttle, was not quite so magical, but he did give Cary a momentous dramatic entrance in his first scene. Cary is heard crooning a ballad off-screen before he strides into the frame. If this was a reference to Archie Leach's stage career, his singing voice—a deep but dull baritone—confirms his limitations as a musical star. Yet when he appears on-screen, he looks every inch the movie star: tall, handsome, and full of charming exuberance. He also looks perfectly at home in the sleekly modern art deco design of his Paris apartment. He has come a long way away from the basement bar of *Singapore Sue* and, for a moment at least, it seems as though his Noel Coward mannerisms will allow him to stride elegantly through his first feature film.

Unfortunately, though, his breezy confidence does not last long. Throughout the rest of the film it is all too obvious that he is straining to appear casual. It does not help that his character is under-written. Why would this strapping athlete merely stand by while his wife is having an affair? And why would his wife prefer the effete, middle-aged Roland Young to her own very handsome husband? We are meant to be so amused by the story that

Photograph 6.15 In the first scene of his first feature film, *This Is the Night* (Paramount Pictures, 1932), Cary Grant is applauded by Charles Ruggles.
Source: author's screen capture

we do not ask these questions, but none of the actors appears to be enjoying this frothy confection, and Cary especially looks uncomfortable. His role as the suspicious-yet-puzzled husband is the kind that Ralph Bellamy would play so well a few years down the line in *The Awful Truth* and *His Girl Friday*. Bellamy would bring a comical, stalwart solidity to these roles and Cary, playing the more confident and sophisticated lover, would bounce off him with perfect light comic timing. None of these qualities is apparent in *This Is the Night*. Cary places his hands in his pockets in nearly every one of his scenes, as though he does not know what else to do with them. His facial expressions lack subtlety and they are held for too long. His voice is strangely inexpressive. The fusion of accents—Bristol, Brixton, and Broadway—is unmistakably his, but there is no shading or nuance in his speech. Today, watching him in *This Is the Night* is a rather uncanny experience. He looks and sounds like Cary Grant but he is not yet *the* Cary Grant.

He was riddled with anxiety during the filming. "I tried to imitate those who put their hands in their pockets with a certain amount of ease and non-chalance," he recalled, "but at times when I put my hand in my trouser pocket I couldn't get the blinking thing out again because it dripped with nervous perspiration."[28] Seeing himself on-screen was also excruciating. Actors were generally discouraged from joining the producer and director in the screening room to watch the "rushes" (the footage filmed each day), but Cary could not stay away. "I watched the initial rushes and sank with fear. I was desperate to succeed but I couldn't act at all," he recalled.[29] He would have to learn to act while the cameras rolled, watching the rushes to learn his craft, realizing what worked and what did not on-screen. His Paramount years would be marked by steady progress as well as many frustrations.

When *This Is the Night* was released in April 1932, it did a modest business at the box office and met with mixed reviews.[30] Cary's own scrapbooks reveal the tepid responses to his debut. At best, his performance was described as "efficient" (*New York Times*), "pleasantly adequate" (*New York Post*), while at worst, it was observed that he appeared "a bit ill at ease" in the film (*Los Angeles Examiner*).[31] Reviews in the film industry trade papers were important because they were the most likely to be noticed by Paramount's executives. With his contract up for renewal—or cancellation—in May, a positive response could be crucial. *Variety* mentioned him but got his name wrong. "It's hard to tell about Gary Grant due to the limitations of his role," the critic observed, adding that "He looks like a potential femme rave."[32] This was the best that could be said for Cary Grant's film debut.

It was also all that Paramount expected from him. His next few films required him only to be handsome. He appears just briefly in both *Sinners in the Sun* (1932) and *Merrily We Go to Hell* (1932). As the moralistic titles suggest, these are Depression-era fables about ordinary people who get caught up in fast living before realizing the error of their ways. In both films, Cary is a lounge lizard, drinking in high-toned speakeasies, looking rakishly handsome in a white tie and tails, and wooing married women. "Don't you know I'm *mad* about you?" he asks Carole Lombard, the star of *Sinners in the Sun,* but Lombard brushes him off in favor of the married man *she* is pursuing. In *Merrily We Go to Hell*, his character is so louche that, as the champagne flows freely, he makes a joke of introducing his date to her own husband. He disappears from the film when the married couple, played by stars Sylvia Sidney and Fredric March, reconcile.

He is very handsome, too, in *Devil and the Deep* (1932), playing a naïve young naval lieutenant who is punished for showing some kindness to his

Photograph 6.16 Cary Grant and Tallulah Bankhead in *Devil and the Deep* (Paramount Pictures, 1932), one of his many tuxedoed "mannequin" roles, where he was required to do little other than look handsome
Source: author's screen capture

commander's wife. There is not much to his role, and the film's esteemed stars overshadow him. Charles Laughton plays the insanely jealous commander with a maniacal glee, but Tallulah Bankhead steals nearly every scene from Laughton with a contrasting performance of blasé desperation. In the midst of these dynamic star turns, and with a subordinate role, Cary can only look dashing in his perfectly tailored uniform. The director Marion Gering, his earliest supporter, clearly favors him with some flattering close-ups, but within 15 minutes his character is out of the story. The commander has the naïve lieutenant transferred, and Gary Cooper arrives as his replacement (in a far more substantive role). It was clear that Cary was never going to win the "Cary versus Gary" battle. At Paramount, Cooper would always overshadow him.

Orry-Kelly recalled that Cary fretted constantly about whether the studio would renew his option after the guaranteed period of six months.[33] Cary himself later admitted that he was "petrified" during these early months in Hollywood, uncertain of both his ability and his image on-screen.[34] These uncertainties led him to start investing his paychecks in his own men's clothing store, called Neale, Smart Men's Apparel. The store was meant to be his insurance policy, a fallback position if Paramount dropped him. The store was named after the man he hired to run it for him, Lester Neale, and Cary's own involvement was kept quiet. It opened on Wilshire Boulevard, near downtown Los Angeles, in May 1932, and for two months it did a good business and Cary enjoyed popping in, sometimes with friends from the studio, to see the latest stock. Then Cary discovered that Lester Neale was pocketing all of the shop's earnings and paying none of its bills. Even the electricity bill had not been paid. The shop—and his fallback career—quickly came to a bad end.[35]

By the time the store closed in July, his immediate worries about his film career could be put on hold. Paramount renewed his contract. His pay remained the same at $450 per week, but the studio revealed ambitious plans for him.[36] He would make six films in rapid succession over the next twelve months. His roles would be more significant, at least insofar as he would not be limited to one or two scenes. And, if he was stuck playing a matinee idol, he would at least be a matinee idol in service to the studio's most glamorous star, Marlene Dietrich, and in the most anticipated film of the year, *Blonde Venus*.

Not everyone who journeyed to Hollywood found the film industry as easy to crack as Cary did. Phil Charig could not find work and returned to New York within six months. Jack Kelly had a tough first few months but stuck it out, once again taking occasional work painting murals on the walls of nightclubs as a way of making ends meet. When that work ran out, and he couldn't pay his rent, he ended up on Cary's sofa for a night, before Cary loaned him the money for new lodgings.[1] Finally, he got a job at Warner Bros., took Orry-Kelly as his professional name, and soon became known as one of the top costume designers in Hollywood. Yet no matter how successful he became, Kelly would never match Cary's success, or the income, grace, and favor that came with being a star.

Their friendship foundered as Cary eagerly embraced the lifestyle Hollywood offered him. "The woman I marry is going to already own a mink coat and a diamond bracelet," Cary told him one day, daydreaming aloud about his future. Kelly disapproved. "Grant was taking over Leach," he concluded. Kelly understood all too well that the business of Hollywood was creating glamour. His trademark as a designer was to "design for distraction"—that is, he created clothes that diverted the eye from a star's physical imperfections and accentuated their more attractive qualities. In his private life, however, he was a down-to-earth Aussie and proud of it. "The Kid from Kiama," as he liked to call himself, would never forget or try to rise above his true origins.[2] Cary, by contrast, was the boy who left Bristol and wanted to move up in the world. The friends Cary made during his first years in Hollywood were not just glamorous. They had class and wealth and style as well.

First among his new friends was Randolph Scott, who joined Paramount two months after Cary. The two up-and-coming stars might have seen each other as rivals, but they were so different in looks and image that they did not feel competitive. Although they were both 6 feet, 2 inches tall and leanly built, Randy (as he was known to his friends) had blonde hair and blue eyes, and a square-jawed, wholesome demeanor. The slight drawl of his accent, his polite manners, and his upright bearing were redolent of what Southerners called "good breeding" and "old money," and in fact he did come from a wealthy

North Carolina family. He had been to prep school and would have gone on to university, but he was six years older than Cary and the First World War had interrupted his education. In the army, he trained in both horsemanship and marksmanship, skills that served him well when he went to Hollywood and began making Westerns. While Cary's early films saw him donning tuxedos and drinking champagne in nightclubs, Randy's early films—and many of his later ones too—had him riding the range.[3]

The matinee idol and the cowboy met early in the spring of 1932 while attending Stuart Walker's drama class at Paramount. Soon after meeting, while having lunch in the studio commissary, they agreed that they should try sharing a house rather than renting separate apartments. This was partly a matter of affording a larger place but also a strategy for sharing the costs of the staff required for a Hollywood star's lifestyle, which included a butler, a cook, a cleaner, and a gardener.[4] Cary's salary of $450 per week was much higher than Randy's $115 per week, but Cary had the financial mess at the Neale store to clear up.[5] This may explain why the first house they shared, at 217 South Canon Drive in Beverly Hills, was relatively modest by movie-star standards. The Spanish-style bungalow had just six rooms. Six months later, in the autumn of 1932, they moved to a much larger house at 2285 West Live Oak Drive in the Hollywood Hills and then moved again in 1933 to a high-walled mansion at 1975 De Mille Drive in nearby Laughlin Park.[6] Each house was bigger than its predecessor, and the last two had the essential requirements of movie-star living: sprawling rooms, a swimming pool, and views overlooking the city.

Cary had shared lodgings with show business pals ever since he left Bristol and found his alternative family in show business. This was his preferred way of living. His friendship with Randy was strengthened by their shared career ambitions. Both men were driven to succeed and neither had any pretentions about this. They didn't think of themselves as serious actors but instead as aspiring film stars intent upon learning the craft of acting for the camera. They understood that their careers depended in no small part on their appearance, and they dedicated themselves to daily workouts and weigh-ins. They both worked on their accents, Cary trying to Americanize what remained of his British accent and Randy trying to pick up the pace of his Southern drawl.[7]

It must have been reassuring for both of them to find an ally as they embarked on new lives in a city and an industry that was far removed from anything either man had known before. Fay Wray observed that Cary and Randy shared confidences. Soon after the two men moved in together, she met Randy at a party. They danced together, and as they did, Randy took the opportunity to lean in and tell her, "Cary is *so* in love with you."[8] Others observed that Randy's sunny, easygoing disposition had a steadying effect on the more highly-strung Cary. During this first year in Hollywood, in particular, Cary had moments of extraordinary self-doubt about his ability as an actor. He wondered if he should flee from Paramount before he was inevitably fired. The calmer and cooler Randy was able to talk Cary out of some of his insecure, impetuous impulses.[9]

Cary was intrigued by Randy's wealthy background and social connections. Eager to invest his new earnings, he learned about stocks and bonds from Randy, who was often observed reading the *Wall Street Journal* between takes on the film set. He met Randy's friend, the millionaire Howard Hughes, who had inherited one of the world's largest fortunes. Later in life, Hughes would become a paranoid recluse, but in the 1930s he was a cocky young adventurer, with interests in both filmmaking and aviation. His company, the Hughes Aircraft Corporation, designed planes for speed and Hughes tested the new aircraft himself. Sometimes Cary joined him, blazing across the skies of southern California as Hughes sought to break all speed records.[10] At moments such as these it must have occurred to Cary, too, that "Grant was taking over Leach," but it is likely that he welcomed the transformation.

Cary's rising fortunes came as Paramount sank into a deepening financial crisis over the course of 1932. As the Depression worsened and ticket sales plummeted, the studio found it increasingly difficult to produce hit films. *Blonde Venus*, it was hoped, would be an exception. When the film was in production, director Josef von Sternberg and star Marlene Dietrich were at the top of their game in box-office terms, but the studio boss B. P. Schulberg fought with them about the script, which he disliked, and the film was delayed during the spring of 1932. Dietrich backed up von Sternberg as he refused to follow Schulberg's orders.[11] They were powerful enough figures that the conflict led to Schulberg being pushed out of his post as chief of production at the studio. He became a mere producer, working beneath the new studio boss Emmanuel "Manny" Cohen.[12]

When filming started on May 30, 1932, von Sternberg was able to make *Blonde Venus* exactly as he had planned it. He boasted to the press that he had chosen each and every member of the cast, from the leading players to the extras. "One player who is out of the mood of a scene . . . can make the entire scene out of key," he asserted.[13] Cary met with his approval. He was cast as Nick Townsend, a gangster-ish tough guy who falls madly in love with Dietrich's Helen Faraday. It was a big part: he was third-billed behind Dietrich and the gentlemanly English actor playing her husband, Herbert Marshall. This was a huge step up for Cary's career, but working with von Sternberg and Dietrich placed him in the middle of one of the most creative and tempestuous relationships in Hollywood. In later years, he would become friends with both of them, separately, but at this early stage in his career he was wary of both the hot-tempered director and the pampered star.

Von Sternberg approached filmmaking with the understanding that films could be deeply suggestive and tap into erotic fantasies and desires. Seen through his lens, Dietrich was a mysterious, radiant, and luminously alluring woman. Whether he surrounded her with fog, smoke, or veils, she seemed to embody all that was ambiguous and unknowable in sexuality. Androgyny was a key part of her image. Although she was actually a slight and delicate woman, she looked elegantly statuesque wearing a man's top hat and tails. Dietrich herself gave ample credit to von Sternberg for her success and she refused to work with any other director, but she also taunted him. They had both left their spouses in Berlin so that they could live and work together in Hollywood, and von Sternberg became bitterly jealous if Dietrich looked at another man, including her co-stars. During the making of *Morocco*, when it was rumored that Dietrich and co-star Gary Cooper were having an affair, von Sternberg became so jealous of Cooper that he took to shouting instructions at him in German.[14] Cooper refused to work with the director again.

Cary was happy to take the opportunity to work with Dietrich and von Sternberg, but their odd relationship created an unusually tense set. Dietrich flirted with Cary, and then assumed that he must be gay when he did not respond to her advances.[15] He observed the peculiar dynamic between the star and the director. "I could see what they were up to," Cary recalled, "and I wasn't going to get mixed up in that."[16] Instead, he stood back and watched as von Sternberg directed his terrible temper at Dietrich. "He yelled at her all the time," Cary said decades later, apparently still bewildered by their relationship.[17] Cary was not the only one to complain. The technician's union protested that the director was a slave driver who kept the crew working until 9:30 in the evening without breaks for meals.[18]

Von Sternberg took enough interest in Cary to make one crucial change to his appearance. When *Blonde Venus* was made, Cary still looked boyish— as boyish as a 6-foot, 2-inch, twenty-eight-year-old man could be—and the trade papers described him as a "juvenile lead." His youthful appearance was

Photograph 7.17 Cary Grant and Marlene Dietrich in *Blonde Venus*
(Paramount Pictures, 1932). Director Josef von Sternberg restyled Cary's hair,
giving him the parting that became integral to his appearance.
Source: author's screen capture

mainly due to his thick, black, wavy hair, which he combed straight back
from his forehead, accentuating his widow's peak and the roundness of his
face. Von Sternberg wanted Nick Townsend to appear tougher and more
mature. Hence, on the first day of filming he took a long look at Cary, and
then demanded a comb and began to restyle his hair. He gave him a prominent parting on the right side of his head, the razor-sharp, straight-as-an-
arrow line that became a defining feature of his appearance.[19] Suddenly, Cary
looked leaner, more masculine, and less boyish. It was an early yet crucial
step in his advancement from fresh-faced matinee idol to intriguing leading
man. He would keep his hair styled this way for the rest of his career, and he
would always urge directors to favor his sharp-edged right side.

In letters to her husband back in Berlin, Dietrich observed that her
"young, handsome, cockney" co-star was selling shirts on the set. Most likely,
he was trying to unload the leftover stock from Neale's apparel shop. After
hawking ties on the streets of New York, Cary was apparently unembarrassed

by this. Dietrich found him odd but also amusing. "He's so charming," she wrote, "that people come from all over the lot to buy them from him."[20] Von Sternberg, meanwhile, struggled to get Cary to convey his charm on screen. Throughout the filming, as Cary remembered it, the director "bemoaned, berated and beseeched" him to relax.[21] To von Sternberg's credit, he also gave Cary direction that allowed him to do something more than stuff his hands into his pockets. In *Blonde Venus*, his eyes are always trained on Dietrich, and his entire body seems to extend toward her, as though he cannot resist her sexual allure. His performance is better than anything else he did during his first year in films, and it suited a film designed as a showcase for her.

The paper-thin story was conceived as a means of broadening the range of roles Dietrich played beyond the world-weary *femme fatale*. In *Blonde Venus*, Dietrich's Helen Faraday is a devoted wife and mother who returns to the stage as a nightclub singer because her husband becomes ill and needs expensive medical treatment. The hitherto quietly domestic woman is transformed into a brazen performer, striding onto the nightclub stage wearing a gorilla costume and teasing the audience with ape-like aggression. When she strips out of the costume, she reveals a tiny form-fitting outfit of sequins and feathers, and sings "Hot Voodoo" as a chorus line, costumed as scantily clad African tribal dancers, sways behind her. It is an astonishing spectacle, and it leaves her nightclub audience, including Cary's Nick Townsend, completely bewitched.

With all of the emphasis on Dietrich, Cary's role is thinly sketched. Initially, it seems like Nick Townsend might be a gangster. He is first seen breaking up a nightclub argument by throwing a punch that floors an aggressive drunk. Then in later scenes he is referred to as both a politician and a millionaire. His character's only real purpose is to declare his desire for Dietrich. "I'm *crazy* about you," he tells her in one scene, and in another he kisses her and says, "If this is a dream, I hope I never wake up." He pays for her husband's operation and supports her and her child in style. Ultimately, though, she rejects him in favor of her recuperating husband. Once again, as in *This Is the Night*, Cary competes with a much older and less handsome star for the leading lady, and once again he loses. These humiliations would become unthinkable in his later career, but in the early years they were commonplace.

Paramount's studio executives were so delighted with his performance in *Blonde Venus* that they raised his salary from $450 to $750 per week.[22] Yet his success in the film was a mixed blessing. Producers saw that he looked good on the arm of a leading lady, and, more importantly for them, they saw that their leading ladies looked better with him on their arm. This meant that there would be many more of these parts, and they would distract from attempts to find a more distinctive screen image for him.

One idea was that he could star in "talkie" remakes of Rudolph Valentino's silent films. In May 1932 these plans were far enough along that a remake of Valentino's *Blood and Sand* (1923) was announced in the trade papers, with Cary playing the rags-to-riches bullfighter and Tallulah Bankhead as the seductress who ruins him.[23] When Cary discussed the proposal with newspaper reporters, he was understandably wary of following in Valentino's footsteps.[24] The silent star had died at the height of his fame six years earlier, and his still ardent admirers were unlikely to welcome an imitator. Equally, Valentino's image—as an object of lust for women—appealed to his fans but was considered to be contemptible by many others. His masculinity had been questioned and his talent mocked.[25] Cary could only have been relieved when plans for *Blood and Sand* were quietly dropped.

Another idea, stemming from the moment Paramount executives saw his screen test, was to build him up as a rival to Clark Gable. Early publicity followed this line none too subtly. A profile in the British fan magazine *Film Pictorial* plainly stated that Cary was "just like Clark Gable—another likeable rough guy of the screen."[26] Similarly, the syndicated American gossip columnist Louella Parsons described him as "the husky type who gets his woman and that, after all, seems to be the popular screen hero now."[27] Many of his early film roles fit this Gable mold. Like Gable, Cary would play contemporary, confident American city slickers. Free of Victorian constraints about sex and manners, these characters express themselves directly and often aggressively, coming on to women and (when necessary) throwing punches at men.

In *Hot Saturday* (1932), his first film after *Blonde Venus*, Cary played the kind of callous, flashy character that Gable often played. Romer Sheffield is a millionaire who uses his money to attract women and then to discard them with a payoff when he tires of them. In Cary's hands, however, the character took on a dandy-ish quality that Gable never had. In his first scene, he emerges from a chauffeur-driven cream convertible wearing a perfectly tailored white suit. He is later seen lounging in jodhpurs (presumably after an afternoon of riding). Still later, at a party, he boasts a flamboyant cravat. At bedtime he wears a long, flowing, Japanese-styled robe. Cary made Sheffield a man to be looked at and desired, in the style of Valentino, while also playing him as a Gable-styled tough guy.

Cary liked his co-star, Nancy Carroll, recalling her as a "feisty Irish girl" who had been one of the studio's leading stars a few years before *Hot Saturday* was made. But he also recognized that her combative relationship with Paramount's executives meant that she was "fading fast" at the studio. In fact, she was fading so fast that Cary was given top billing for the first time in *Hot Saturday*.[28] The billing certainly does not reflect the story, which centers squarely on Carroll's character. She is a small-town girl whose reputation is ruined when she spends a hot Saturday evening at the lakeside vacation home of Cary's wealthy playboy. When she turns for support to a wholesome family friend, played by Randolph Scott, Cary all but disappears from the film. He and Randy share just one brief and unremarkable scene.

The director, William A. Seiter, makes the most of Cary's flashy wardrobe, and the story's stultifying small-town values are enhanced by some location filming (near Lake Arrowhead), but otherwise *Hot Saturday* is a strictly routine melodrama. It is the type of film that Paramount produced by the dozen in the early 1930s, when the popularity of double features put pressure on the studio to feed its vast cinema chain with an increasing number of films. These "programmers" or "B films" were produced quickly (just three weeks for *Hot Saturday*), at modest costs (approximately $250,000), and with brief running times (71 minutes) so that they could fit on a double bill.[29] A review in *Variety* defined *Hot Saturday* as a programmer and informed exhibitors that this "banal," "familiar," and "conventional" film should be placed on the lower half of the double bill, but the reviewer at least admired Cary's performance, noting that he demonstrated "extreme restraint" as an actor.[30]

Madame Butterfly (1932) was a more ambitious film. A five-week shooting schedule and a production cost of just over $400,000 indicate that Paramount intended this to be more than a programmer.[31] Based on the same story as Puccini's opera, the film stars the Bronx-born Sylvia Sidney as Cho-cho San, the devoted geisha who falls deeply in love with the American naval officer Lieutenant Pinkerton. When Pinkerton is transferred to the United States, she does not tell him that she is pregnant but waits faithfully for his promised return. Years later, when he finally comes back, he is accompanied by his American wife, and a devastated Cho-cho San commits suicide.

Gary Cooper was meant to play Pinkerton, but Cooper's most recent contract gave him story approval (effectively the right to choose which films he made), and Cooper did not approve of playing the dull and unsympathetic Pinkerton. When *Madame Butterfly* was already in pre-production in July 1932, he flatly refused to do it. This threatened to derail the film completely.

It had been conceived as an intimate love story that would be played against a background of spectacular and exotic scenery, and a second unit had already filmed location footage in Japan, using doubles who resembled Sidney and Cooper. Without Cooper—or a figure very similar to Cooper—the location footage would have to be discarded. Cary was cast primarily because his height and frame were similar to Cooper's. Importantly, though, the story was revised to suit him.[32]

When Cooper dropped out, producer B. P. Schulberg commissioned an entirely new script. Schulberg told the writers that the film should serve the studio's broader purpose of building Cary into "a substantial bet" (that is, a major star). He thought that Cary was not the right actor to play Pinkerton as a "heel," as Cooper would have played him, and he asked for a rewrite that would allow audiences, and not just Cho-cho San, to fall in love with the character. Pinkerton was thus given a more charming and romantic manner in the new script.[33] *Madame Butterfly* marked the first time, and certainly not the last time, that a character would be revised to suit Cary Grant's screen image, and specifically the audience's predisposition to want to like such a handsome figure.

Marion Gering, who had already done so much to advance Cary's career, directed *Madame Butterfly*, and once again Gering gave him some very effective close-ups. Especially in his final scene, when Pinkerton says goodbye to Cho-cho San, Cary registers Pinkerton's shame and remorse with admirable subtlety. Co-star Sylvia Sidney recalled that no one took Cary seriously as an actor at the time the film was made, but decades later, when she saw *Madame Butterfly* in a retrospective devoted to her own career, the goodbye scene struck her as a powerful demonstration of his talent. "It was such good acting, such internal acting, the look in his eyes . . . There was something about what he did in that close-up that was shattering," she commented.[34]

Making Pinkerton into a more romantic figure also entailed having him sing a love song, "My Flower of Japan," to Cho-cho San. This was not a good idea. Cary's voice betrays all of the limitations noted by stage critics in previous years, and now even a film fan magazine took aim at his singing. The reviewer for *Motion Picture* complained that he "drones" rather than sings the song, and advised the studio to cut the scene from the film, while the review in *Variety* said that he was "not so hot" as a singer.[35] Singing aside, many reviewers thought that the story did not quite work as melodrama. As one put it, the film is "an opera denuded of operatics" (*Los Angeles Times*).[36] The box-office returns were modest.[37]

Photograph 7.18 Cary Grant and Sylvia Sidney in *Madame Butterfly* (Paramount Pictures, 1932). Decades later, Sidney admired his intense performance in this scene.
Source: author's screen capture

Madame Butterfly was one of many Paramount films that failed to attract audiences during the winter of 1932–33, when the Depression reached its deepest point. *Blonde Venus* in particular fell short of expectations, and contributed to studio's downward spiral toward bankruptcy.[38] Von Sternberg had been allowed to let production costs soar, as he indulged in extensive re-takes, right up to the film's release date (prints had to be flown from Hollywood to New York at the last minute).[39] Critics then took aim at a film they were eager to characterize as a self-indulgent, immoral mess, but Cary was by and large spared the critical drubbing that von Sternberg and Dietrich took.[40]

If *Blonde Venus* was not quite as significant for Cary as it was meant to be, the night of its premiere in Los Angeles proved to be a fateful one for him. This was the night he met Virginia Cherrill. It was October 6, 1932. Virginia was a beautiful, twenty-four-year-old actress still basking in the glow of her success as Charlie Chaplin's leading lady in *City Lights* (1931). She went to the

Blonde Venus premiere with a group of friends. They walked the red carpet in their finery, and then went to the Brown Derby for a late dinner. Afterward, in the parking lot, they came across another foursome leaving the restaurant. One of Virginia's friends knew Randolph Scott and introductions were made. Virginia later recalled being impressed that Scott's date was a famous heiress, Doris Duke. She could not recall the name of Cary's date, but she remembered being charmed by Cary and flattered by his attentiveness to her. He took an opportunity to light her cigarette. She told him that she liked the film, and he made an offhand joke that started both of them laughing.[41] So began a high-profile relationship that would have many laughs as well as many arguments, one that ultimately led to their marriage as well as a very messy and public divorce.

Cary would have recognized Virginia Cherrill from her role as the blind flower girl in *City Lights*, and part of his attraction to her is likely to have been her connection with Chaplin. He had admired Chaplin ever since he spent his Saturday afternoons at the Scala Cinema back in Bristol, and *City Lights* was widely regarded as another career peak for the acclaimed filmmaker. For Cary to be dating Chaplin's leading lady—the woman Chaplin longed for within the film—was a marker of just how far the former Archie Leach had traveled since his days at the Scala.

There are some remarkable parallels in the humble, early lives of Charlie Chaplin and Archie Leach. Both came from unstable, working-class British families, with absent fathers and mothers who assumed "middle class airs" amid increasing poverty and hardship.[1] Chaplin's mother, too, was committed to an asylum (in London), and both Charlie and Archie found an escape from their unhappy family lives in music hall. Their backgrounds, however, informed their careers in very different ways. Chaplin's impoverished childhood served as the basis for his portrayal of "The Tramp," the scrappy fellow in an ill-fitting suit and bowler hat who is comically out of place in the respectable bourgeois world. Cary's image was much more aspirational. He became famous for being perfectly dressed, and for looking as though he belonged among the wealthy and stylish.

By the end of Cary's career, Pauline Kael would be able to observe that his "romantic elegance is wrapped around the resilient, tough core of a mutt, and Americans dream of thoroughbreds while identifying with mutts."[2] At the beginning of his career, though, he was slow to reveal the "mutt." In the early 1930s especially, he was doing his best to perfect his image as a thoroughbred. This was a trait that he shared with Virginia Cherrill. She was well mannered and beautiful: a slim blonde, with big blue eyes, delicate features, and a porcelain complexion. Yet her father was something of a scoundrel, by her own account, and when Virginia was five years old, her mother left him and returned to her parents' farm in Carthage, Illinois.[3]

Henceforth, Blanche Cherrill worked to ensure that her daughter would marry well. She took a post as a matron at a convent school in return for reduced tuition fees for Virginia. Mother and daughter thus went to live at the boarding school together. Later Blanche took a job as a secretary in Chicago, scrimping and sacrificing in order to send Virginia to a private college, where she could mix with high-society girls. Virginia clearly understood what was expected of her: at the age of eighteen, she married into a wealthy Chicago family. The marriage was short-lived, but it gave her the opportunity to travel to Los Angeles, where she was spotted by Charlie Chaplin. She had no experience in films, but Chaplin was so smitten by her that he cast her in *City Lights*.[4]

Overnight, she became a movie star and gained an entrée to the highest social circle in Hollywood. That is, she became close friends with the film star Marion Davies, a lavish hostess and also the mistress of publishing magnate William Randolph Hearst. Virginia often spent weekends at the Hearst mansion, San Simeon, on the coast between Los Angeles and San Francisco. There, at this colossal folly of an estate, the publisher and his mistress played host to film stars, writers, politicians, and other notable people. Hearst laid down strict rules for the guests. Unmarried couples could not share a bedroom, and all guests were limited to just one cocktail each night, but otherwise a weekend at San Simeon was like visiting a private and very fashionable resort. Guests were encouraged to swim, play tennis, ride horses, enjoy screenings of the latest films, and admire Hearst's vast collection of art and antiquities.[5]

Virginia was regarded as the "prettiest girl in Hollywood" and she had her choice of suitors. At the time she met Cary, she was dating the musical composer and humorist Oscar Levant, but their relationship was not serious. Cary, according to Virginia, was *very* serious. After their first meeting in the parking lot of the Brown Derby, he was so eager that he phoned her several times before she arrived home. Her mother answered the phone. Blanche had followed her daughter to Los Angeles, and she still had high hopes that Virginia would marry well, but she thought that there was something odd about this very sudden, very ardent admirer. She told Virginia as much as soon as she arrived home, but Virginia took Cary's next phone call and agreed to go to dinner with him the very next night. There was just one catch: mother would be coming along as a chaperone.[6]

Blanche Cherrill never softened her hard appraisal of Cary, but after that first dinner she at least stopped accompanying the couple on their dates. They were seen everywhere that mattered—film premieres, balls at the best hotels, dancing at the hottest nightclubs—and they enjoyed weekends at San Simeon too. Gossip columnists reported their every move and photographs of them together appeared regularly in newspapers and magazines. The beautiful young couple seemed to be living a fantasy life far removed from the Depression, which was reaching its deepest, darkest point during that winter of 1932–33. Millions of people had lost their jobs, their savings, and their homes, and there was no end to the misery in sight. Films and gossip about film stars served as a distraction from the disastrous economic news, and Cary and Virginia quickly became one of the most glamorous and talked-about couples in Hollywood.[7]

Paramount's answer to the Depression was to make increasingly risqué films, as the titles of some of Cary's earliest films suggest (*Sinners in the Sun, Merrily We Go to Hell, Hot Saturday*). However, the strategy did not really work as planned. The films did not fully deliver on the promise of their titles, and audiences stayed away. Until, that is, Paramount's new head of production, Manny Cohen, recruited Mae West as the studio's latest contract star. There was nothing diminutive or gentle about Mae West. A few years earlier, her plays—*Sex* (1926), *Pleasure Man* (1928), and *Diamond Lil* (1928)—had brought the bawdy humor of burlesque to the Broadway stage. In jokes and in songs, she acknowledged aspects of sexuality, including homosexuality and women's sexual desire, that were previously unspeakable on Broadway, yet her campy, ribald delivery made it seem as though she was merely speaking obvious, unvarnished truths.

Mae West was controversial enough in the big city. *Sex* had been raided by the New York police and West was jailed for ten days on an obscenity charge. It was almost unthinkable that Hollywood would put her on the screens of every small town movie house in the United States, but these were desperate times. Cohen cast her first as George Raft's mistress in the gangster film *Night After Night* (1932), and her scene-stealing performance in that film convinced him to allow her to star in an adaptation of her own play, *Diamond Lil*. Renamed *She Done Him Wrong* (1933), the film went into production on November 28, 1932, and Cary was cast as her co-star.[8]

In later years, West took credit for "discovering" Cary Grant. She claimed that she was in a producer's office on the Paramount lot, talking about casting the leading man for *She Done Him Wrong*, when she spotted Cary walking past the window and immediately said, "That's the best looking guy in Hollywood. If that guy can talk, I'll take him!"[9] Cary hated the story for its implication that he owed his career to Mae West, and he eagerly pointed out its inaccuracies. He actually met West months earlier at Hollywood's American Legion Stadium, where many stars and filmmakers attended the

Friday night fights. *She Done Him Wrong* was not his first but his eighth film. And director Lowell Sherman told Cary that he chose him for *She Done Him Wrong* because he admired his performance in *Blonde Venus*.[10] This last point seems likely. The two films are very different but they both require a leading man whose handsome appearance would flatter but not distract from a formidable leading lady.

"I was window dressing," Cary complained, and it is true that he has very little to do in *She Done Him Wrong*.[11] Set in New York's Bowery in the 1890s, the film centers entirely on the saloon singer Lady Lou. She is the quintessential Mae West character. With her ample hourglass figure pressed into the tightest and most elaborate of gowns, she struts through her scenes, confident of her own desirability and dismissive of any moral code that might disempower her. When a character refers to her as a "fine woman," she replies, "I'm the finest woman who ever walked the streets." And when a younger woman expresses concern for her own reputation, she advises her, "When women go wrong, men go right after them." She wants only two things from men, diamonds and sexual satisfaction. Her songs—"I Wonder Where My Easy Rider's Gone" and "I Like a Guy What Takes His Time"—express her desire in terms so plain that it is hard to imagine how they made it past Hollywood's censors at the Hays Office.

Cary plays the one man who does not melt in her presence. He is introduced as Captain Cummings, a Salvation Army officer trying to save souls at the saloon. West eyes him hungrily. Standing at the foot of a staircase leading to her bedroom, she issues what would become Hollywood's most legendary come-on, "Why don't you come up sometime—an' see me?" (often misquoted as "Come up and see me sometime"). He declines, insisting that he will be attending to his duties at the Salvation Army mission, but she continues to treat him like a cat toying with a mouse. "Don't be afraid," she teases, "I won't tell." When he still resists, she dismisses his moral stance with the knowing comeback, "You can be *had*." Of course, no man can remain impervious to Mae West in a Mae West film. In the ending, Cummings is revealed to be an undercover policeman investigating a crime ring in the saloon. He arrests most of the other characters but, rather than placing handcuffs on her wrists, he places a wedding ring on her finger. It is only then, as the film fades out, that they finally kiss.

Cary's role is pivotal to the story, but he has surprisingly little time on-screen and most of it is spent deflecting West's come-ons. She effectively turned the tables on Hollywood's gender bias, insisting that she should appraise and admire men, who were there to be looked at by her. At the same time, she insisted that she must be the center of attention in every scene. She instructed the costume designer Edith Head that her wardrobe should be so distracting that all eyes would remain on her no matter what was happening in the scene.[12] Thus, even when Lady Lou casts her lascivious gaze over Captain Cummings, the contrast between her sparkling, sequined, low-cut gown and his plain black uniform ensures that the audience is transfixed by her rather than him.

She Done Him Wrong was filmed in just three weeks, and at the modest cost of $200,000, but it was a box-office sensation when it was released in January 1933.[13] It was not a film that made the industry proud. A review in *The Hollywood Reporter* commented that "Some folks may object to this one on the ground that the 'garbage has been piled too high,' but it is plenty funny."[14] Many "folks" did object to the film. The clamor for greater censorship of films intensified, and the Hays Office came under fire for allowing

Photograph 8.19 Cary with Mae West in *She Done Him Wrong* (Paramount Pictures, 1933). She insisted that her costumes ensure that audiences' eyes would be on her.

Source: author's screen capture

Mae West to appear in movie houses everywhere.[15] Nevertheless, the trade papers suggest that the industry as a whole—and not just Paramount—was relieved to see that the Depression had not killed interest in films altogether. Audiences would still turn out *en masse* for the right film. In 1933, that film was *She Done Him Wrong*. It was Paramount's biggest hit in ten years, earning $2.3 million in North America box-office rentals.[16] No single film could save Paramount from its dire financial situation, but this one bolstered its balance sheet at a crucial juncture.

For Cary, it was the best of films and the worst of films. At last, he had a hit film, and he would benefit from all of the accompanying publicity. In interviews, he dutifully paid tribute to West. "She is more than an actress— even more than a first-rate actress," he told *Screenland* magazine, "She's a creative artist as well."[17] It was only later in life that he revealed how much he disliked her. He was taken aback by her crude manner of speaking. When she was called to the set, he remembered, she would yell, "I ain't ready!" He also found her unattractive, observing that "She was not at all svelte. She had a flabby belly which always wiggled when she walked."[18] But what really made him "shudder," as he put it, was her heavy makeup and costuming. "She wore so much makeup, and that figure and those tall high heels. You couldn't find Mae in there. I'm not attracted to artificiality. I'm not attracted to makeup. And certainly Mae wore more of it than anyone I've ever seen in my life." She was, he noted disapprovingly, "an absolute fake."[19]

Cary was a "fake" of sorts too, but his screen image was designed to appear genuine and to be wholly convincing. The care he took with his clothing and appearance, for example, strived for understated elegance. His goal was to appear natural when he wore fine clothes and not as though he was costumed. He hated wearing makeup on the set. Pancake and eyeliner were still the norm for men, but he discovered that he could keep it to a minimum if he kept himself well tanned. His healthy glow was real, even if it did require many hours of sunbathing to maintain. Mae West, by contrast, made a display of her fakery, revealing rather than denying the artifice necessary for on-screen sex appeal.

It is notable, too, that West's vulgarity—her crude speech and her overt sexuality—went against the good manners that Elsie Leach had been so keen to instill in her son. West's persona was essentially an assault on Victorian values, especially as they applied to women and sexuality. She mocked the sense of propriety and respectability that was such a key part of Cary's distant memories of his mother, and now such a key part of what he found attractive in women. He was attracted to women who were petite, refined, and elegant; women who, if they were not exactly *like* his mother, would at least have been approved of by his mother.

Virginia Cherrill fit the bill. When Kelly met Cary and Virginia at a party, he immediately saw that Cary had found the mink-coat-and-diamond-bracelet girl he had once described to Kelly as his ideal bride.[20] Virginia not only had an air of refinement but she was also young and slim, and—to please Cary—she wore little makeup. Virginia herself suspected that Cary's intense interest in her was fueled by his dislike of West. He became increasingly "obsessive" toward her during the making of *She Done Him Wrong*, she remembered.[21] One evening, while she was still seeing Oscar Levant, Cary arrived at her door in a rage. He had recognized Levant's car in her driveway and he wanted to confront Levant, or Virginia, or both of them. They decided not to answer the door. At that point, according to Virginia, Cary got into his car and began to drive it into Levant's car repeatedly, "hammering it as if he meant to kill somebody." Cary eventually drove off into the night, and Virginia later agreed to stop seeing Levant, but his jealous rage that night was an early warning that his romantic intensity could transform quickly into irrational behavior.[22]

Virginia observed that Cary did not like to speak about his past, but she got an unexpected glimpse into his earlier life when they attended a white-tie ball at the Biltmore Hotel in downtown Los Angeles. A man approached Cary and said that he remembered seeing him on stage with either the Pender or the Lomas troupe. In the midst of a formal evening, there was something patronizing in the man's tone, and not least in the observation that Cary had been the best acrobat the man had seen "outside of a circus." He challenged Cary to perform the stunts he had mastered as a teenager, betting him $50 that he was not up to it. Cary took the bet. He removed his jacket and tie, and asked the bandleader for a drum roll. To the amazement of everyone in the ballroom, he then performed a back flip with a full-body twist in the middle, landing perfectly on his feet again. He won the $50 bet as well as a round of applause from the entire ballroom. Virginia was awestruck; at once full of admiration for his ability and bravado, and wary of the mysteries that lay behind his handsome façade.[23]

She admired his drive and ambition too. Virginia was not planning on a long-term career. Making films was an unexpected and temporary windfall for her. By contrast, she observed that Cary "never lost sight of his goal" to become a star. He studied his scripts, obsessed over his performance, watched the daily rushes, and maintained a rigorous diet and fitness regimen.[24] He also endured Paramount's punishing schedule, which had him on the studio lot for ten hours a day, six days a week. Sunday was the only day off, and the studio's conveyor belt filmmaking brought him a new role every eight weeks. This was nearly twice the workload of contemporaries such as Gary Cooper and Clark Gable. Frustratingly, none of these films was written with him in mind. He was still a generic leading man who could be assigned to whatever script came along.

They came along quickly. After the rushed filming of *She Done Him Wrong*, he went directly into his next film in the week before Christmas, 1932.[25] It proved to be one of the strangest in his career. *The Woman Accused* (1933) begins on familiar enough ground. Nancy Carroll (from *Hot Saturday*) is once again his co-star. Cary plays a millionaire playboy and she is a flapper. When he proposes marriage, she warily confesses that she has had a previous lover, but he assures her that he wants to marry her anyway. Up to this point, the film is a modern romance with some fashionable mores and chic art deco settings. But the script was based on a magazine serial written by ten popular authors, each writing an installment in succession and according to their own outlook and disposition. The story therefore veers wildly in tone, careering from one genre to another over its 73-minute running time.[26]

In the ending, *The Woman Accused* becomes an urban crime film. Carroll's character is accused of murdering her previous lover, and the evidence rests on the testimony of a gangster's henchman (Jack LaRue). Cary, now assuming the role of her rough and tough defender, sneeringly refers to the Italian American henchman as "one of these wets" (an ethnic slur), and he horsewhips him until he agrees to retract his testimony. The frenzied whipping scene is as violent as any to appear in a Hollywood film in this period, and it is a nasty ending to an incoherent, messy film. Not surprisingly, *The Woman Accused* was dismissed by critics and ignored by audiences.[27]

It was during this period that Cary realized that Paramount's executives had no particular vision or plan for his career. When the rival Fox studio asked to borrow Cary for *The Warrior's Husband* (1933)—meaning Fox would pay his salary as well as a surcharge to Paramount—Manny Cohen was eager to agree to the deal. But Cary balked at this, insisting that he should have an overdue break from filming rather than go on a loan-out to another studio. It was dangerous for him to refuse assignments because the studio could suspend him without pay, but luckily the matter was diffused when Gary Cooper dropped out of *The Eagle and the Hawk* (1933). Rather than going to Fox on a loan-out, Cary would once again fill in for Cooper, taking a role he rejected.[28]

Cooper's objections to *The Eagle and the Hawk* were not recorded, but it is likely that he saw too many similarities between this John Monk Saunders story and Saunders's earlier First World War aviation stories, including *Wings* (1927) and *The Dawn Patrol* (1930). Cooper may also have decided, as he did with *Madame Butterfly*, that his character was unsympathetic and dull. Certainly, Fredric March has the better role in *The Eagle and the Hawk*. March plays an altruistic hero who is admired by everyone in his squadron but cracks under the pressure of seeing so many young fliers die in action. This left Cary to play another tough guy role—the callous, less able flier who alienates everyone in his squadron. He throws two punches within the first five minutes of the film, and he is humorless and cold throughout it. In one scene, a bomb hits the barracks and brings the ceiling and rafters down on the fliers. This was filmed with real explosives, and Cary was apparently too close to them. He was hit in the head by a falling plank, which left him with a bruised face and a gash across his scalp. The injuries were not serious but they won him some time away from the studio. Unable to film for two weeks, he was able to step off the relentless conveyor belt of film production at Paramount.[29] By this point, in March 1933, he had appeared in ten films over the previous fourteen months.

He returned to the studio to finish his remaining scenes for *The Eagle and the Hawk*, and then moved quickly on to his next film. This was another hand-me-down role. George Raft was originally set to play the seasoned gangster who wants to "go straight" in *Gambling Ship* (1933), and when he was unavailable, Paramount sought William Powell to replace him.[30] Powell, too, had scheduling conflicts. It was only then that Cary was cast in this "machine gun melodrama."[31] With a streak of gray in his hair and a cigarette hanging from his lips, he almost looked like a gangster, but he could never convey genuine street-tough ruthlessness. He was far more convincing in the romantic scenes with another gangster's moll (played by Benita Hume). Not that many people noticed. *Gambling Ship* was another "programmer," shot over just four weeks in April and May of 1933.[32] On release in June, *The Hollywood Reporter* slated it, warning that audiences would be "unimpressed by the plot, directing [and] acting."[33] When it was released in June it hardly caused a ripple.[34]

After a string of weak films, Cary may have been relieved to return to Mae West for her second star vehicle, *I'm No Angel* (1933). He was not an aviator, a gangster, an undercover policeman, or even a Salvation Army officer in *I'm No Angel*. He was a handsome Park Avenue millionaire, with perfect manners and easygoing charm. His role, as a high-society lawyer who is seduced by Mae West's social-climbing circus performer, was as thin as any he ever played. He was required only to pay tribute to West's beauty and to speak the lines that set up her jokes. "I could be your slave," he tells her. "That could be arranged," she retorts. After one of her performances in the ring, he tells her, "You were very good tonight," and she replies, "When I'm good, I'm very good, but when I'm bad, I'm better."

He is only one of several men she seduces. In fact, he does not appear in the film until its midway point, and initially it looks as though he may have returned to the stiffness of his earliest films, with his hands kept firmly in his pockets. It soon becomes clear, though, that his reserve is warranted by her man-eating demeanor, and he loosens up and becomes convincingly affectionate toward her as the film proceeds. By contrast with *She Done Him Wrong*, he appears more at ease with their repartee in *I'm No Angel*.

Filmed between July and September 1933, *I'm No Angel* was rushed into cinemas for an October release.[35] The Los Angeles premiere was held at Grauman's Chinese Theater, and the festivities began with West having her handprints cast in cement in the theater's famous forecourt. The crowd roared their approval at the star, whose money-spinning success defied the downward spiral of the Depression. A live stage show preceded the film and much to Cary's surprise, the Lomas Troupe was among several other acts booked to reflect the film's circus setting. Cary was delighted to see Tommy Lomas and the others backstage. When Sid Grauman introduced Cary to the audience, he took the opportunity to praise the troupe and recall his own days as a "tumbler" with them.[36]

It had been nine years since he left the Lomas Troupe behind, and on this night, amid the hoopla of the premiere, there could be no doubt of the distance he had traveled since then. Everyone knew that *I'm No Angel* would be a huge success and another financial lifeline to Paramount. In fact, its box-office earnings nearly matched those of *She Done Him Wrong*, reaching $2.2 million in North America.[37] This meant that Cary co-starred in two of the biggest box-office hits of the decade, and yet he was completely overshadowed by the films' true star. "The picture is all Mae West," *The*

Hollywood Reporter observed in its review of *I'm No Angel*, adding that "the attractive Cary Grant has a few lines."[38] His role was not quite *that* small, but it is telling that when Noel Coward visited Hollywood in 1933, he gave Cary the sheet music to his song "Bitter Sweet" and he autographed it, "To Cary— In Memory of Mae West."[39]

"We Can't Afford a Hollywood Marriage!" Beneath this headline in *Hollywood* magazine, Cary and Randy were pictured whistling as they did the dishes together at the kitchen sink and singing happily at the piano in their living room. In the accompanying interview, they admitted that they earned high salaries by ordinary American standards. Yet even as Hollywood enriched them, the stars claimed that it shackled them with unwanted burdens and restrictions. "If I were a young doctor or lawyer in some other place, drawing the same salary, I could afford to marry easily," Cary purportedly said. "It's what Hollywood demands of a motion picture personage that hurts. It's a car and driver, a house in Beverly Hills and a beach house in Malibu. It's the front you've got to put up." Randy chimed in, saying, "Yeah, and if I were married it would be trips to Europe and trips to Palm Springs and Lord knows where else—all first class. What Cary and I want to do is to hop a tramp steamer for the South Sea islands and can you imagine a woman coming along on a trip like that?"[1]

This was typical fan magazine fluff. The 1930s was the "golden age" of the Hollywood fan magazine. In the United States, there were a dozen major titles and they were read by millions of people. These magazines were not owned directly by the studios, but the studios supplied them with press releases and images that were designed to build and sustain a star's image and popularity.[2] Glamour was the key attraction for the magazines' readers, who were mostly women and wanted to read about the private lives of the stars. Hollywood stardom was portrayed in escapist terms, as a lifestyle free of ordinary responsibilities and conventions but also one with its own pitfalls.[3] Cary and Randy therefore did not discuss acting or their careers, and they were not photographed in rehearsals or on the set. They discussed their status as Hollywood's most eligible bachelors, and they were photographed at home, in the house that Paramount publicists dubbed "Bachelor Hall."[4]

For the studio's publicists, the "Bachelor Hall" publicity angle was an opportunity to promote two up-and-coming stars at once. The *Hollywood* magazine article was published in October 1933, the month that *I'm No Angel* reached American movie theaters. It was part of a campaign to reinforce Cary's new fame and extend some of his good fortune to Randy, who had not yet scored a hit. The sight of these "strapping he-men," as they were described in *Hollywood* magazine, doing dishes and living in "an Eve-less Eden," was intended to highlight both their availability for marriage and the idea that they were desperate for a woman's help and care. In the same month, they featured in the "Modern Hostess" recipe column of *Modern Screen*. They spoke about their favorite seafood dishes (crab and asparagus salad for Cary, baked lobster for Randy) and the magazine supplied the recipes so that readers could dine like the stars.[5] The publicity campaign also extended to radio. Billed once again as Hollywood's most eligible bachelors, they featured in a nationally broadcast advertisement for Betty Crocker prepared foods, speaking about how useful instant food products were to men who had no wives to cook for them. *Variety* noted that the ad was a "grand plug" for both the products and the stars.[6]

From a modern perspective, the photographs of Cary and Randy at home are easily misconstrued. The pictures of them dining, washing dishes, making coffee, and collecting mail from their mailbox together suggest that they are an inseparable, very happy, gay couple. Many contemporary observers assume that these photos are candid snapshots of their private life together. Some of Cary's biographers argue that the photos prove that Cary and Randy were not just friends but lovers whose relationship was an open secret in Hollywood.[7] These writers also assume that the publication of the photos was a leak or mistake. Marc Eliot, for example, writes that the photos "somehow found their way into the newspapers" in the 1930s.[8] Other writers argue that the images are evidence of Hollywood's hidden gay history.[9]

There is no doubt that Hollywood has a hidden gay history, but these photos do not figure in it. Paramount's archives reveal that the photos were commissioned by the studio's publicity department and taken by a professional photographer who carefully staged them.[10] Cary's own publicity scrapbooks, meanwhile, reveal that the photographs were not published by mistake. The scrapbooks from this period contain clippings from a wide range of film fan magazines, and page after page includes articles featuring these photos.[11] Far from trying to hide Cary and Randy's relationship, Paramount actively publicized it.

The idea that Cary and Randy were lovers has led some modern writers to suppose that Cary's marriage to Virginia Cherrill was a sham—that deception rather than genuine romance lay at the heart of their relationship.[12] In this line of thinking, the studio urged Cary firstly to date Virginia and then to marry her as a means of covering up his relationship with Randy.

Some writers also suppose that Virginia was looking to marry well, and that she played on Cary's insecurities in order to bring the reluctant groom to the altar. It is true that, when she was dating Cary, her film career was not going well. After her high-profile debut in *City Lights* she had short-term contracts first with Fox and then with MGM, but MGM dropped her in May 1933, and after that she was reduced to making low-budget films for "poverty row" producers.[13] Becoming Mrs. Cary Grant was, in this version of events, a means of maintaining her position in Hollywood's high society. However, as Cherrill's biographer, Miranda Seymour, points out, in 1933 it was far from clear that Cary's career would have any longevity. If Virginia was looking for wealth and status, she could have done better.[14]

What many of the modern accounts overlook is that, at the time, Cary and Virginia were pictured together more often than Cary and Randy, and they were the subject of intense interest and speculation. The questions of if and when they would marry began almost as soon as they were first seen together in public. They were a strikingly attractive couple, as Virginia's diminutive blonde beauty perfectly complemented Cary's dark and handsome stature. Often photographed in formal evening clothes—Cary in a tuxedo and Virginia in a ball gown—they could be mistaken for the bride and groom figurines atop a wedding cake. When pressed to comment about their plans, Cary was intriguingly evasive. "I'll let you know when I buy the ring," he would tell reporters, which was not quite a confirmation or a denial.[15]

In Virginia's own account of how and why she and Cary married, she unequivocally rejected the idea that he was gay. She gave very few interviews after she left Hollywood, but in the early 1990s a long-time family friend taped an interview with her in which she spoke frankly about her relationship with Cary. Recalling both Cary and Randy affectionately, she was very clear that the friendship between them was genuine, but the publicity suggesting that they shared every meal and then washed the dishes together was not. "They lived in the same house, and they got on well, but they didn't necessarily lead the same lives," she said. Like other women who had a sexual relationship with Cary, she said that he was an enthusiastic lover. "Cary was crazy about women," Virginia recalled. "He was great in bed and so funny. We'd sometimes roll out on to the floor we were laughing so much. And Randy . . . Randolph Scott was no more gay than Cary was. And he was *so* handsome, he had women falling all over him."[16]

Cary could be charming and funny, Virginia recalled, but he could also be intensely jealous and insecure. "He kept asking me to marry him, but I knew, deep down, that I could never be happy with a man who made me feel so trapped," she said, adding, "and yet I couldn't bear to think of living without him."[17] They were apart for six weeks in the summer of 1933, when Virginia went to Hawaii to film *White Heat* (1934) on location.[18] When she returned to Los Angeles, he was so eager to see her that he met her ship before it docked at Long Beach. He chartered a tug to take him out to the SS *Monterey* and then climbed aboard the liner on a rope ladder. It was a remarkably public display of affection but if it was intended to set the stage for a proposal of marriage, as the gossip columnists insisted, it was not successful.[19]

Virginia also spoke of his temper and the terrible arguments that they had. In October, he visited her on the set at Monogram, one of Hollywood's "poverty row" studios, while she was making *He Couldn't Take It* (1933). Over lunch in her dressing room, they got into an argument so heated that everyone on the set could hear them shouting. Once again, the gossip columns were abuzz with speculation.[20] No one knew exactly why they argued, but it was assumed that their wedding plans had gone awry. Later that month, they took a ten-day road trip through Arizona and New Mexico, and reporters dogged them at every stop. Were they engaged? Were they eloping? They smiled for the cameras but denied any immediate marriage plans.[21]

Around the same time, Cary began to tell reporters that he hoped to spend Christmas with his father in Bristol, and there was speculation that Virginia might go with him and that they might marry there.[22] There were rumors, too, that Randy and his girlfriend, the British actress Vivian Gaye, might join them on the trip and that they too might get married in England.[23] Yet somehow—for reasons that have never been clear—Virginia was alone when she set out for New York by train on November 7, and then sailed to Southampton on November 11. While she was en route to New York, Cary suddenly rushed to meet her by plane, arriving in time to say goodbye to her just before her ship sailed.[24] No, he did not have plans to follow her immediately, he told reporters on the deck of the SS *Champlain*, but yes, he still hoped to spend Christmas with his father. "I see no reason why actors should lie about their marriage plans, and if we were to be married, I should say so," he said, and then added, rather unconvincingly, "All of this is just a coincidence."[25]

Marriage concerns aside, the autumn of 1933 was an anxious time for Cary. His plans to spend Christmas in Bristol were prompted by a sudden and unexpected phone call from his father. They had been out of touch for so long that Elias Leach could only reach him by phoning Paramount and asking the switchboard operator to put him through to Cary Grant. Remarkably, he got through, and despite the crackling transatlantic phone line, Cary recognized his father's voice at once. His father told him that he wanted to see him—he had something to discuss that could not be said over the phone—and he asked Cary to come back to Bristol.[26] This was a considerable request, not only because of the expense of traveling to England but also the time that the journey took. It was at least a week of travel each way. Cary had to wait months before his schedule could be cleared, and in the meantime he could only wonder what his father wanted to talk to him about.[27]

Another source of anxiety—and frustration—was Paramount's haphazard management of his career. In October, as *I'm No Angel* broke box-office records around the country, Paramount loaned him to Twentieth Century Pictures (before the company merged with Fox) for *Born to Be Bad* (1934). "Loan-outs" were by and large a bad sign. Sometimes studios used them as a means of punishing a wayward star. More often, as in this case, they signaled that the studio had no pressing projects for a contract player, and so they were happy to let a rival studio pay the star's salary for a month or two. Certainly, this film offered nothing new or interesting for Cary. He would eventually have a good working relationship with Twentieth Century's executive producer, Darryl F. Zanuck, but *Born to Be Bad* was a modestly produced, formulaic woman's film, and his role was another that required him only to serve as the bland love interest for a much more formidable leading lady.[28]

In this case, however, the leading lady turned out to be not so formidable. Twentieth Century had planned to borrow Jean Harlow, MGM's very popular "blonde bombshell," to play the gold-digger who toys with the affections of an upstanding, wealthy, happily married man. Harlow might have brought some much needed sass and brass to *Born to Be Bad*, but the deal to borrow her fell through. In her place, Loretta Young was cast, and Cary had to deliver lines such as, "You're bad, bad all the way through. You're a beautiful bad girl!" to the doe-eyed twenty-year-old, who looked too sweet and vulnerable to be a hard-boiled home wrecker. Young knew that she was unsuited to her part and recalled "acting my head off and not getting any place" in *Born to Be Bad*. She found Cary to be distant and uncommunicative on the set, but she did not blame him for being downcast during the making of this "perfectly terrible" film.[29] Cary himself spoke in later years of the "sheer awfulness" of the film and disowned it.[30]

His frustration grew when his next assignment turned out to be another hand-me-down role. The film was an adaptation of the classic children's story *Alice in Wonderland* (1933), in which a wide array of Paramount stars would play the characters Alice encounters on her travels. Initially, Cary was not cast in the film, and Paramount wanted the crooner Bing Crosby to play the Mock Turtle, but negotiations between the studio and Crosby dragged on while the film was in production, and then they failed when it was nearly complete. It was only then, in early November and just six weeks before the film's release, that Cary was asked to don a turtle suit and sing "Beautiful Soup" to Alice.[31]

The best thing about his role in *Alice in Wonderland* is that it allowed him to shed his matinee idol image and do a music hall turn, sobbing as he sings and bouncing up and down with childish despair. But the film as a whole misfired. The young actress playing Alice, Charlotte Henry, was not up to the task, and Paramount did not seem to realize that packing a film with stars such as Gary Cooper, W. C. Fields, Jack Oakie, and many more would count for little if the costumes were so heavy that the stars were unrecognizable. *Alice in Wonderland* had a high-profile release over the holidays but it met with very mixed responses from both critics and the public.[32]

When he shed his turtle suit, Cary was finally free to leave for England. This promised to be a triumphant return. His fame ensured that he would be celebrated as a hometown hero in Bristol. Yet his father's ominous invitation meant that it was also a daunting journey to make. It is telling that he did not want to return alone. From the first time he mentioned the trip, he spoke about his wish to have Virginia with him, as well as Randy and Vivian Gaye if they were able to come.[33] In return, he promised his friends that he would show them a traditional English Christmas and give them a tour of the countryside. As it happened, when *Alice in Wonderland* finished, Virginia had already embarked for Britain and Vivian Gaye had decided not to join them.[34]

Cary and Randy embarked on the six-day journey from New York to Plymouth on November 17, and Paramount sent them off in style, with a first-class suite on the luxurious SS *Paris*. Marc Eliot claims that Cary was miserable aboard the *Paris*—that he locked himself in the suite and refused to get out of his pajamas.[35] A memento saved among Cary's personal papers tells a different story. On the last night of the voyage, Cary and Randy joined with another film star on board, David Manners, to throw a dinner party for a select few guests. They had an invitation printed and Cary saved one that he had his guests and co-hosts sign. The invitation mocked formality by saying, "Three licentious old men from Hollywood invite youse to dinner." The meal itself was nothing short of *haute cuisine*. The seven courses included turtle soup, caviar, sole, partridge, asparagus, foie gras, a selection of desserts, vintage wines, and Cordon Rouge champagne. The Broadway actress Ruth Draper simply signed her name on the menu. David Manners signed his name alongside a smiley face and the message "Hello Kid." The wealthy philanthropists Mr. and Mrs. W. L. Mellon Jr. signed with an eagerly scrawled, "Hurrah for Plymouth tomorrow!!!" Randy playfully signed, "To my spouse, Cary. Randy," suggesting that they were taking some ribbing about having no brides to accompany them on a journey that was widely reported as one that would end in marriage. The ship's commissaire signed with a pun—"A ship which did carry Grant is a happy ship"—which hardly supports the idea that he spent the voyage in glum isolation.[36]

The smiles continued on the next day, Thursday, November 23, when Virginia met the ship at Plymouth. Photographs show Cary and Virginia beaming, even as reporters once again grilled them about their wedding

Photograph 9.20 Cary Grant and Virginia Cherrill on November 25, 1933, soon after his arrival in Britain

Source: The Cary Grant Papers, courtesy of the Margaret Herrick Library

plans.[37] Still, they had no definite answer. "I am hopeful, but it is up to Miss Cherrill," Cary politely announced. "She is naturally the deciding factor."[38] They traveled together to London, where Paramount had arranged for Cary and Randy to share another suite, this time at the chic Savoy Hotel, overlooking the Thames. In return, the studio asked Cary to promote *I'm No Angel* when it was released in Britain at the end of the month, including making a personal appearance at the London premiere.[39]

In London, though, he could smile no more. He developed a fierce toothache, and when the pain continued to intensify, a dentist was summoned to the Savoy, and the dentist in turn summoned an anesthesiologist. Cary had developed an abscess beneath a tooth, which had to be removed there and then.[40] That first night at the Savoy was a miserable one, but on Friday morning he agreed to see reporters in his suite and for the first time he announced that he and Virginia would marry. It was not clear what had changed since the ship had docked, but he now spoke about his hope that they could be married in Bristol. He added that he was very eager to get there. "I haven't seen Dad for three and a half years," he told reporters, "and I am just longing to get back." On Saturday evening, Paramount arranged for Cary to be a guest on a popular radio program. He brought along Randy and Virginia, and introduced them on air, but the show was primarily about Cary and the journey he had made from a Bristol boyhood to Hollywood fame.[41]

Finally, on Sunday, he was able to travel to Bristol. He went without Randy and Virginia so that he might speak privately to his father, but first he faced a hero's welcome from his extended family. His father gave a party for him in his flat at 13 Victoria Walk in Cotham (not far from the Cotham Brow house that Elias, Elsie, and Archie lived in when Elsie was institutionalized). Aunts, uncles, and cousins from both the Kingdon and Leach families were invited to greet—and in some cases to meet for the first time—their rich and famous relative. The two families did not normally mix, and this was the first contact that the Kingdons had with Archie since he was a boy. "It was as though he had fallen off the face of the earth," his cousin Ernest Kingdon recalled, but any lingering resentments were put aside.[42]

As the evening wore on, the small flat became crowded and stuffy with cigarette smoke. Brothers Ernest and David Kingdon, who were twenty-three and thirty-five years old, respectively, suggested to Cary that they step outside for some fresh air. They began to walk and, much to their surprise, their glamorous cousin said that he would like to get some fish and chips. They stopped at one of the local shops, and then continued walking, fish and chips in hand, through the cramped streets of the city, eating as they walked.[43] This would become a ritual for Cary. Going back to Bristol always entailed getting fish and chips and—despite being accustomed now to caviar and champagne—he always marveled at what a delight they were.[44]

During his two days in Bristol, he once again "roamed about" the city on foot, as he had done during his days as a schoolboy truant, revisiting his old haunts. Importantly, his roaming now took him to the offices of the local newspapers where he made a deal with the editors. On this and on future visits to the city, he would give each paper an interview and allow himself to be photographed if reporters would otherwise leave him and his family alone.[45] It was a canny strategy. The newspapers loved having the inside scoop on his visits and he always gave them some notable news. On this trip, the *Bristol Evening Post* was invited to accompany him on his return to Fairfield School, where he generated a lot of excitement. Cary was led from classroom to classroom by the head teacher, who introduced him to the class before he walked in and said an enthusiastic, "Hi, gang!" Over and over again, he met with cheers and requests for his autograph. It was a triumphant return to the school that had expelled him fifteen years earlier, and it was made sweeter by being pictured on the front page of the local newspaper.[46]

He found Bristol unchanged, he told reporters. "I have loved walking about the old streets, tripping over the same cobblestones." If he was disappointed to find that both the Empire and the Hippodrome had abandoned live music hall performances for films, he would have been delighted to see Fay Wray's name on the Empire marquee (starring in *Ann Carver's Profession*) and Randolph Scott's on the Hippodrome marquee (in *Man of the Forest*). The Prince's Theatre still had stage shows, and Cary was pleased to find an old friend from his Broadway days, the actress Vera Pearce, starring in the current production of *Wild Violets*. When her dresser announced that Cary Grant was asking to see her, she assumed that he was joking, and then she was thrilled when he put his head round the door. They chatted between scenes and at the interval, and he watched the show from the wings. Cary preferred to witness the excitement backstage—as he had in his younger days—rather than sit with the audience.[47]

Amid the hoopla surrounding his return to Bristol, there was still the worrying talk to be had with his father. Cary had not seen him since he visited Bristol four years earlier. Since then, Elias's partner, Mabel Johnson Bass, had died at the age of forty. She contracted pneumonia in the midst of a typically cold and damp Bristol winter, and within just a few weeks, she died at home in the flat they shared on Rosemary Street in central Bristol (the area now redeveloped as Broadmead).[48] The sixty-one-year-old Elias was left with their ten-year-old son, Eric, and a broken heart. Cary was shocked to see that this once handsome and robust man was a shadow of his former self. "I almost didn't recognize him," he told Dyan Cannon decades later. "He'd pretty much ruined himself with drinking. Jowls hanging, bloodshot eyes. He looked just like an old, broken down alcoholic."[49]

When he contacted Cary at Paramount, his father may have known that he, too, did not have much time left to live. This was the likely reason to tell Cary about his mother at last. It would be Cary, after all, who would take responsibility for Elsie when Elias Leach died, and yet Cary did not even know that Elsie was alive. His father asked him to meet him at a quiet pub and, once they got their pints of beer and sat awkwardly for a moment, he broke the news. "It's about your mother," he said, looking down at his glass. "She's not dead."

Cary could not believe that he was hearing his father correctly. They had not spoken about Elsie in eighteen years. He finally managed to ask, incredulously, "What is that supposed to mean?" The guilt that his father had been harboring for so many years spilled out. "I was trying to protect you," he insisted over and over again, as a bewildered Cary broke in to ask, "Are you telling me my mother is still alive?" His father told him the truth: that Elsie was in Fishponds and that she had been committed there eighteen years earlier.[50]

Cary knew Fishponds. Everyone in Bristol knew that Fishponds was where the asylum was (although it had been renamed the Bristol Mental Hospital after the war). It was the last place you would want to find your mother. "I had to put her away," his father insisted. Cary suddenly understood something about his life that he could not have known before. Through all the years that he had idolized his father, his father was lying to him. Through all the years that he felt betrayed by his mother, and angry with her for abandoning him, it was actually his mother who had been betrayed and abandoned. Through all the years that he had sought adventure and wealth and fame in the world, she had been locked away, alone and seemingly forgotten. As the full force of the realization hit him, he could only flee from the pub. "You should *thank* me!" he heard his father bellowing as he left. "I did it for *you*!"[51] But this was the worst thing he could tell Cary, who would spend the rest of his life coming to terms with what happened to Elsie.

Cary dropped from sight altogether. He was due back in London for the premiere of *I'm No Angel* on Wednesday, November 29, but he did not appear.[52] He no longer talked to reporters. Rumors about the wedding, and when and where it might happen, ceased. Randy suddenly sailed back to New York on December 6, some four weeks early, and without having been to Bristol or had his traditional English Christmas.[53] Nothing was seen or heard of Cary until December 14, when it was reported that he was recuperating in a London nursing home, having had emergency surgery.[54] A statement was issued to the press, saying that the surgery stemmed from an injury he had suffered on the set of *The Eagle and the Hawk* seven months earlier.[55] One previous biography speculates that he had a severe case of hemorrhoids—with bleeding so bad that he feared he had rectal cancer—and that he had an operation to remove them.[56] Another speculates that he may have had plastic surgery on his nose, although there was no discernible change in its appearance.[57] Forty years later, Cary reportedly told his girlfriend, Maureen Donaldson, that his father's revelation had sent him on a prolonged spell of drinking, and that he checked into a nursing home to dry out.[58]

No documents have survived to verify what actually happened, but there is no doubt that Cary was in the hospital. He was photographed sitting up in a hospital bed over Christmas, with a decorated tree in the background and Virginia at his side.[59] And when he and Virginia went to a Registry Office on January 7, he gave his address as Granard House, Arthur Street, in Fulham, which was a newly opened private hospital.[60] We may never know exactly why he went to the hospital, but the shocking news he received in Bristol could only have magnified whatever health problems he had. Taking to his bed may have been the only way he could deal with what he heard from his father.

Cary and Virginia's trip to the Registry Office, to marry at last, did not go well. The registrar refused to marry them until he could see Virginia's divorce papers. She sent for them, but it took weeks for them to arrive from Los Angeles.[61] In the meantime, while Cary remained in the hospital, Virginia decided to accept an offer of work. While he continued to recuperate, she co-starred in the low-budget film *Money Mad* (1934), made at Worton Hall Studios in Isleworth. A reporter visiting the set was completely charmed by her, and seemingly amazed to find that an actress could be both beautiful and knowledgeable about films. When the reporter turned the conversation to her marriage plans, she admitted that, "Everything seems to be conspiring against us. We seem to get all the bad luck, but it will be all right soon. If we don't get married here, we shall when we return to Hollywood."[62]

On January 18, Cary had his thirtieth birthday without fanfare. He was well enough to leave Granard House and join Virginia at a flat she had taken on Albemarle Street in Mayfair. A few days later, at the weekend, they traveled together to Bristol for her long-delayed first visit to the city. Cary made amends with his ailing father by buying him a top-of-the-line radio set, a luxury his father could never afford himself and one to comfort him in his old age.[63] He made amends with his wider family, who had been hoping for a Hollywood wedding on their doorstep, by inviting them to the city's posh Grand Hotel for a party. Virginia did not say much about this occasion in later years, but she did observe that Cary's father was "a nice old man, a worker type, very friendly."[64]

When they left Bristol later that week, Cary saw Virginia off at the main railway station, Temple Meads, but for his own journey he used the air taxi service based at the city's new Whitchurch Airport. He had the pilot chase and overtake her train, which had departed 30 minutes earlier, and then fly alongside it until he spotted her in a window and waved.[65] This flamboyant, romantic gesture was a sure sign that he was recovering. Back in London, he and Virginia dined with the actor Charles Laughton, and also with the Wimbledon tennis champion "Bunny" Austin and his wife, while they continued waiting for Virginia's divorce papers to arrive.[66]

Papers or no papers, they made plans to sail on the SS *Paris* to New York on February 9.[67] The departure date allowed Cary to see his mother on her birthday—February 8—a reunion he had longed for as a child and now dreaded as an adult. On that bright, frosty morning, he returned to Bristol and approached the bleak stone buildings of Fishponds with trepidation. Inside, a nurse showed him to a room where arrangements had been made for him to speak privately with Elsie. Cary could not help but anticipate seeing his mother as she had looked twenty years earlier, when she was in her late thirties. Back then, she had thick black hair and a smooth olive complexion, and she prided herself on looking neatly presented and respectable. He therefore scarcely recognized the woman he met at Fishponds.[68] Elsie was fifty-seven years old that day, but she was a prematurely wizened old woman, with white hair and missing teeth.[69]

"Who are you?" she asked him, because he bore so little resemblance to the eleven-year-old schoolboy she had last seen. "I'm your son," he replied, "I'm Archie." He attempted to bend down and kiss her on the cheek, but she pushed him away, not quite sure of him.[70] It was a rejection he would remember for the rest of his life. He was sure that his mother blamed him for leaving her there, for not finding out what had happened to her. She stared at him blankly as he tried to explain that he had not known, that he had only just discovered that she was still alive. She could not believe that this fully grown man—who told her that his name was now Cary Grant and that he was rich and famous and lived in America—was her Archie.[71]

He returned to London that evening, relieved that the visit was over and eager to see Virginia. When she announced that her divorce papers had at last arrived, Cary impulsively suggested that they should try to marry the next day, before they caught the boat train to Plymouth. Virginia assumed that this would be impossible; that at such short notice the registrar would have no openings. But first thing in the morning Cary went to Caxton Hall, a London registry office known for marrying wealthy and famous couples, and he found that there had been a cancellation. They could be married if they were ready within the next hour. Cary rang Virginia with the news and urged her to hurry down to the hall. She made it. Neither the bride nor the groom was dressed for a wedding—both wore their everyday clothes beneath heavy winter coats—but they looked genuinely happy when they emerged after the brief ceremony.[72]

Photographers and fans had gathered outside the hall, and they cheered the couple. "We're so happy!" Cary announced as Virginia smiled beside him. As they tried to make their way to a taxi, the crowd surged around them. A street harpist was jostled and knocked over but then recovered and began to serenade them once more. Cary managed to usher Virginia into a taxi, but in the confusion the taxi sped off without him, and he was left standing in the middle of the street without his bride. Looking stricken with doubt, he desperately hailed another taxi and urged the driver to speed after her.[73]

The wedding that had been the subject of so much prolonged anticipation and speculation thus turned out to be a quick and chaotic event. Their messy exit from Caxton Hall was like a scene from one of his later films. Indeed, their engagement and all of the twists and turns of their relationship could have been turned into a screwball comedy. But screwball comedies tend to finish just at the moment the couple reunites, and then the films fade out on a kiss that promises eternal happiness. Cary wanted to believe in this kind of happy ending. In Plymouth, just before the SS *Paris* sailed, he told reporters, "We're going back to Hollywood to live a simple, quiet life."[74] In reality, though, his married life with Virginia would have more melodrama than comedy, and it would be anything other than simple or quiet.

Virginia's happiest memories of her marriage to Cary centered on their honeymoon aboard the SS *Paris*, as they sailed from Plymouth to New York. The liner company was eager to publicize the glamorous couple's presence on board. They were asked to pose for photographs and to stroll the decks and smile at the other passengers, just as Douglas Fairbanks and Mary Pickford had done during Cary's very first transatlantic crossing back in 1920. In return, the Grants traveled for free and in luxury. "They gave us the biggest suite on the ship," Virginia fondly recalled, adding, "We spent a lot of time in our rooms."[1]

When the ship arrived in New York on February 15, they enjoyed a suite at the Algonquin Hotel, well known for attracting prominent theatrical and literary patrons. Paramount footed the bill this time, asking the couple in return to give a few interviews and to see a few Broadway shows and report back on them. Among the shows, appropriately, was a comedy entitled *The Pursuit of Happiness*.[2] Regarding their own happiness, Cary insisted that marriage should not stop Virginia pursuing her own career as long as she wanted to. "When a man starts to interfere with the things that give his wife happiness," he told reporters, "and vice versa, the marriage hits the rocks." His statement was so modern in 1934 that it made headlines.[3]

When pressed for more definite plans, including what would happen to Randolph Scott when the newlyweds returned home to the house that Cary and Randy had shared, it was Virginia's turn to be modern and unconventional. "Randy has been constantly with us," she told reporters, "and the three of us get on so well. . . ." Before she could finish, a reporter interjected with a joke. "You can have a design for living," the reporter said, referring to Noel Coward's recent comedy about a ménage à trois.[4] They were not quite *that* modern.

When they returned to Hollywood, the newlyweds rented a place of their own at La Ronda on Havenhurst Drive (in what is now West Hollywood). This fashionable Spanish Colonial–style apartment complex had courtyards and lush gardens, stocked with orange and lemon trees, that were hidden from the street, yet it was also near the nightlife on Sunset Boulevard and not far from Paramount.[5] Randy continued to live on his own at the DeMille

Drive mansion until another apartment came up for rent at La Ronda. He then became the Grants' neighbor.[6] They continued to go out together—to the fights on Friday nights, to parties, and to film industry dinners and benefits—but Randy was still seeing Vivian Gaye, and so the threesome was really a foursome on most occasions.[7]

Cary did not have a lot of time for nightlife in 1934. Paramount was working him hard to make up for the time lost during his three months away and to exploit the notoriety he achieved with *She Done Him Wrong* and *I'm No Angel*. In recognition of the success of these comedies, studio executives finally heeded his pleas to play comedy. His delayed return from England meant that he missed the first of the comedies designated for him, *Come On Marines* (1934). Richard Arlen took his place and Cary probably did not mind.[8] The film was another routine "programmer" that was quickly forgotten. Instead, just one day after arriving home in Los Angeles, he reported to the studio to make *Thirty Day Princess* (1934) with a friendly director, Marion Gering, and a familiar leading lady, Sylvia Sidney.[9] The trio that had previously made the somber *Madame Butterfly* now embarked on a frothy romantic comedy.

Thirty Day Princess is a Cinderella story set in Manhattan. Sylvia Sidney has two roles: she plays a European princess, visiting the United States to publicize a bond drive for her impoverished country, and she also plays a down-on-her-luck American actress hired to masquerade as the princess when the latter falls ill at the outset of the tour. Cary is Porter Madison III, a tough-talking newspaper editor who sets out to expose the princess but falls in love with her. Preston Sturges wrote the script while suffering frequent interference from producer B. P. Schulberg. The conflict between them led Sturges to insist in his memoir that not many of his ideas made it into the finished film.[10]

In fact, the story, pace, and tone of *Thirty Day Princess* are remarkably similar to Sturges's later films, including the classics *The Lady Eve* (1941) and *The Palm Beach Story* (1942). No one would claim that *Thirty Day Princess* is the equal of those films, but it does have some of their distinctive charms. For Sturges, the United States is a madcap country, at once brashly modern and materialistic but also all-too-easily impressed with Old World snobbery and status. In his gentle, good-natured satires, the romances are initiated by masquerade and deception but they prove to be genuine. *Thirty Day Princess* is no different. Cary himself later described the film as "quite lovely," although he rightly observed that Sylvia Sidney is its true star.[11]

Seen today, *Thirty Day Princess* seems like a forerunner of the much better-known *His Girl Friday* (1940). Cary's Porter Madison III, like Walter Burns in *His Girl Friday*, is a breezy yet cynical big-city newspaper editor. However, comparing the two films only highlights how much he developed as an actor in the six years between them. In *Thirty Day Princess*, he does not have the on-screen ease and confidence that would be his trademark by the time of *His Girl Friday*. Putting on an American accent intermittently brings out a nasal quality to his voice. At times, he holds his head in a way that, when seen in profile, forms a double chin, and occasionally when he speaks his upper lip forms a slight yet unattractive snarl. He was still learning his screen craft and studying his own performances to identify and overcome these inelegant imperfections.

In retrospect, it is remarkable too that Porter Madison III makes such ardent declarations of love to the princess. "I love you! Ever since the first night I met you!" he tells her. Cary was often required to proclaim his devotion to his Paramount co-stars, but in later films he was so seldom so earnest. It was so much more convincing when women pursued him, and so much more interesting when he expressed his affection and desire in wry, understated tones. Paramount gave him few opportunities to be wry. He was seen first and foremost as a supporting man for the studio's leading ladies, and this entailed passionate declarations of his love in almost every film.

When *Thirty Day Princess* was released in May 1934, Sylvia Sidney garnered most of the critics' attention for playing the dual roles of princess and pretender. He received some measured praise in *The Hollywood Reporter*, which observed that "Cary Grant has never put more genuine spirit and vitality into a part than he does here."[12] But the film's good reviews did not carry over into box-office returns. Sylvia Sidney did not have the star power to draw large audiences, and the charming *Thirty Day Princess* quickly sank into obscurity.[13]

Meanwhile, Cary's production marathon continued through the spring of 1934 with two more comedies. In *Kiss and Make-Up* and *Ladies Should Listen* he abandoned the American tough-guy image that the studio had pressed upon him ever since he played a javelin thrower in *This Is the Night*. Instead he was cast as an "art deco dandy." This was only a slightly better fit for him. He was too athletic and down-to-earth to register the true frivolity of the dandy. Nevertheless, like the archetypal Regency dandy, Beau Brummel, he was known for his impeccable style and fashion sense. And like Hollywood's other dandies—Robert Montgomery, Fred Astaire, and Melvyn Douglas—he had a classless and cosmopolitan quality. He seemed perfectly at home in swanky penthouses, cruise liners, and cocktail bars, but there was not a touch of snobbery about him.[14]

He certainly dresses with flair in *Kiss and Make-Up*. As a Parisian doctor making rounds in a clinic, he is fully suited in morning dress—complete with a flamboyant cravat, a carnation in his lapel, and a dapper pocket square. His attire is just about plausible because his character, Dr. Maurice Lamar, is a cosmetic surgeon and his *Temple de Beauté* clinic is nothing short of an art deco palace. The film's sets and costumes never disappoint. From the opening shot—showing Dr. Lamar's point of view as he arrives at his clinic and is greeted by adoring staff and patients—it is evident that visual style is the filmmakers' primary concern. Unfortunately, the storyline is too thin to sustain interest. The doctor is besotted with a vain patient (Genevieve Tobin) whose appearance he has perfected through many procedures, and he is slow to realize that his less glamorous secretary (Helen Mack) is his true love. The dialogue is a succession of one-line gags and, despite the response to his singing in *Madame Butterfly*, Cary is made to croon a love song ("Love Divided By Two") not once but twice, and with similarly lackluster results.

Kiss and Make-Up had a rocky production history. Genevieve Tobin was a replacement for Carole Lombard, a bigger and more appealing star who backed out of the film.[15] Unusually, the film had two directors, Harlan Thompson and Jean Negulesco (credited as the "associate director"), and an uncredited third director, Ralph Ceder, was added to shoot the film's finale, a slapstick chase scene that brings a very sudden shift in style and tone.[16] A preview screening prompted some cutting and some hurried re-takes, but the film could not be fixed.[17] When it was released in the summer of 1934, *Kiss and Make-Up* played to nearly empty movie theaters.[18]

Both *Kiss and Make-Up* and *Ladies Should Listen* were made on speedy four-week filming schedules. Hence, when *Kiss and Make-Up* failed to find an audience, *Ladies Should Listen* was already finished, and it was too late to abandon this similarly frothy, high-toned yet lightweight comedy. Once again, Cary plays a Parisian dandy caught up in comical romantic intrigue. His character, Julian de Lussac, is infatuated with the exotic and seductive Marguerite (Rosita Moreno), but she is a con woman intent on scamming him. He is pursued by lovestruck yet very plain Susie (Nydia Westman) and also by the more attractive and quietly smitten telephone operator Anna (Frances Drake), who eavesdrops on his conversations. In the film's best moments, Cary demonstrates considerable comic ability. In drawing-room repartee, his eyes dart and widen to good effect, and in the slapstick sequences he plays with zeal and dexterity. For the first time, his skills as a "tumbler" are fully apparent on-screen. That the film falls short of the zany, zippy fun that it aims for is the fault of its script, which is laden with flat gags and contrived situations.

These frivolous comedies were very different to his life at home. According to Virginia, he drank heavily during their marriage, and when he drank he grew angry and suspicious of her. Although he had encouraged her to resume her film career, whenever a potential job came up for her, he found fault with it. Their troubles deepened when Virginia suffered a miscarriage in the late spring. They were both distraught, and Cary drank even more heavily.[19] Near the end of filming *Ladies Should Listen* he reported ill for a week, one of the few times in his career when he was not ship-shape and perfectly punctual on set. He returned to finish the film, and afterward the studio allowed him to take three weeks of leave in June 1934.[20]

These three weeks provided a measure of relief for both Cary and Virginia. She was keen to visit her family in Illinois, and she knew that he loved a road trip, in his Packard and with the top down, and so in mid-June they set out on the long journey from Los Angeles to Chicago. He was especially keen to stop in St. Louis and show her the city that he had adopted as his American hometown. When they arrived, and met with reporters at the city's Park Plaza Hotel, the fair-skinned Virginia was sunburned from days on the road, and even he had to admit that the drive through Kansas had been hot and dusty. Otherwise, they were in a joking and affectionate mood. He was looking forward to seeing his friends at Forest Park, and attending that evening's open-air production of *Cyrano de Bergerac*. The city's zoo and a Cardinals baseball game also beckoned. After St. Louis, they drove on to Carthage, to see Virginia's family, and then to Chicago, where they visited the Chicago World's Fair before embarking on the long drive home.[21]

Cary had been told that when he returned to Paramount in July his next film would be either *The Lives of a Bengal Lancer* (1935) or *Enter Madame!* (1934).[22] *The Lives of a Bengal Lancer* was by far the bigger production: a lavishly mounted British Empire adventure film with Gary Cooper in the lead. It could only have been a disappointment, then, to find that he was instead assigned to support a fairly minor star, Elissa Landi, in the comedy *Enter Madame!* The story was adapted from a well-worn stage play about a young American opera fan who marries an Italian diva. Cary plays the wealthy, dashing American dandy Gerald Fitzgerald, who meets Landi's Lisa della

Robbia while following her concert tours across Europe. They fall in love and marry, but then he finds he has nothing to do but trail after her, taking care of her Pekingese dog and suffering her tantrums.

The role is typical of this period of his career: he wears white tie and tails through most of the film, and declares his love for her passionately ("You darling, you darling, you darling! Promise me you'll never leave me!"). Yet no matter how limited his roles were on the page, the improvement in his performance skills is apparent with each film. In *Enter Madame!* he demonstrates a new comic finesse, including the ability to convey the humor of the moment—whether it is his impatience or panic or disbelief—through facial expressions rather than through words. Elissa Landi, by contrast, was a dramatic rather than a comic actress, and her performance of scenes from the operas *Tosca* and *Cavalleria Rusticana* brings the comedy to a halt. Both stars appear to be out of place in some scenes. Cary has no purpose in a film dedicated to opera, and Landi does not belong in a screwball comedy.

While the film was being made, Virginia was keen to participate in the Hollywood social whirl. She and Cary went to parties at Marion Davies's colossal mansion on the beach at Santa Monica, to a fancy-dress ball at the Biltmore Hotel, and, with friends, for an overnight stay at the Agua Caliente Casino in Tijuana. They gave a party themselves at a newly opened roller skating rink in Culver City, renting the rink for the evening so that friends could skate without being accosted by fans. Cary was often dragged out reluctantly. Paramount's ten-hours-a-day, six-days-a-week filming schedule was exhausting for him.[23]

Virginia found that he was happiest either when traveling or at work. The man who had spent his youth on the road, longing for a home, a family, and some stability, was tormented when he finally had all three. Domestic life brought his fear of abandonment to the fore. At home, he continued to drink and to brood, and he became ever more intensely and irrationally jealous. Virginia found that he trusted her with his closest friends, Randolph Scott and Howard Hughes. She could chat with them at parties without sparking his suspicions. When she spoke with other men, however, he became convinced that she was plotting to have an affair with them.[24]

Their troubles remained concealed from the public until the very end of their marriage. In Virginia's account, the end came on September 29, 1934, when she and Cary joined three or four other couples for a Saturday night dinner at the Cocoanut Grove nightclub in Hollywood. Virginia was seated near the elderly British character actor Sir Guy Standing. As she chatted with him, she became aware that Cary was bristling with anger. Finally, he leaned across the table and warned Standing that he had better not make a pass at his wife. An argument ensued, baffling their friends, and then Cary insisted on leaving early. At home, thinking that he simply had too much to drink, Virginia went to bed without him. She woke in the middle of the night to find him sitting on the bed, glaring at her and with his hands pressed around her neck, as though he was going to strangle her. When she shouted, "You hate me enough to want me dead?" he backed away. She packed a suitcase and drove to her mother's apartment in Beverly Hills. Not quite eight months into the marriage, she decided that she could no longer live with him.[25]

By Sunday morning, the gossip columnist Louella Parsons had heard about the argument and reached Virginia by telephone at her mother's house. "It's true that we have had a quarrel," Virginia admitted. "Whether or not it is permanent or not is up to Cary. I will not discuss the reason for our trouble, but things have been going from bad to worse." Cary, who spent the day with Randy and other friends at the beach in Santa Monica, was taken aback to hear from Parsons later that afternoon. "It is silly to say that Virginia and I have separated," he insisted. "We have just had a quarrel. You know how it is. People argue and disagree, and then kiss and make up," he said, quoting the title of his recently released film. He assured Parsons that he and Virginia would reconcile, and that she would come home soon.[26]

But Virginia did not come home. Cary phoned her over and over again every day. An unsympathetic Blanche Cherrill often answered the telephone and informed Cary that her daughter did not want to speak with him.[27] It was bad timing that Randy had left town. He was usually able to steady Cary and prevent him from acting on impulse, but he had gone to New York City to visit his father, who had fallen ill there.[28] Cary continued drinking and trying to reach Virginia. Late Thursday night, he was very drunk when Virginia finally took one of his calls. Their conversation quickly became heated and he threatened to kill himself if she did not come home. She hung up on him, but later, feeling wary, she phoned back and asked the houseboy to check that Mr. Grant was okay. The houseboy found him on his bed, unconscious, and with a bottle marked as poison at his side.[29]

In his drunken state, Cary had decided not to kill himself, but to re-enact a scene from *Ladies Should Listen*, in which the lovesick Julian de Lussac stages his suicide while on the telephone with Marguerite, so that she will rush to his bedside. Cary's plan went horribly wrong when the houseboy rather than Virginia discovered him. The houseboy called an ambulance, and the semi-conscious Cary was taken to the emergency room of the Hollywood Receiving Hospital, where he had his stomach pumped despite telling the doctors that although he had a great deal to drink, he had only threatened and did not actually take the poison. Virginia arrived to see that he was okay and then promptly returned to her mother's house, telling friends that there was now "no chance" that they would reconcile.[30]

The next morning, October 5, 1934, newspapers around the world carried headlines such as "Cary Grant Found Poisoned: Actor Silent About Motive."[31] By the time the afternoon editions were published, he had explained to reporters that while he had been very drunk, he had not taken any poison. "Cary Grant Treated for Alcoholism" was typical of the next wave of headlines. The humiliation of these events must have been overwhelming for him, but in the glare of bad press—even this extraordinarily bad press— he used his showmanship as a form of resilience. "I don't think I'll ever take a drink again," he told reporters, adding for their amusement, "Please pass the tomato juice."[32]

At this point in his life, his public resilience was not matched by his emotional maturity. In a bid to force Virginia to come home, he emptied their joint bank account and refused to give her any money. He also plotted to make her jealous. Just two weeks after their separation, he was spotted with Gertrude Michael, one of his co-stars in *I'm No Angel*, dancing in a succession of Hollywood nightclubs, where they were bound to be seen by gossip columnists.[33] Virginia was not swayed. Instead, she pawned her jewelry, including her engagement ring, and hired a lawyer.[34] Through October and November, negotiations between their lawyers went nowhere, and on December 4 she went to court seeking a maintenance allowance during their separation.

In court, she painted a grim picture of marriage to a man previously celebrated as one of Hollywood's most eligible bachelors. She explained to the judge that her husband accused of her of being extravagant, although she insisted that she was not. He prevented her from working herself. In private and in public, she testified, he flew into rages and called her "vile and opprobrious names," embarrassing her in front of her friends. He drank heavily and abused her both emotionally and physically.[35] Cary appeared in court too. He denied the charges, and rather ungallantly told the judge that his wife worked to support herself before their marriage and that she could work to support herself again. The judge did not agree. Pending a final divorce agreement, Cary was ordered to give her an allowance of $725 each month and also to pay $2,500 toward her legal fees.[36]

There is no doubt that Virginia's testimony aimed to cause the maximum embarrassment to her husband. She could have predicted the headlines that followed, such as "She Says He's Stingy," accompanying articles that recounted her grievances. The coverage of his first divorce marked the beginning of his enduring reputation for taking a miserly care over matters of money.[37] Twenty-five years later, gossip columnist Hedda Hopper would sneer that "he still has the first five cents he ever made."[38] In 1934, he only had himself to blame for this. His refusal to give Virginia an allowance left her with no choice but to go public with her complaints.

Remarkably, her charges of physical abuse drew less attention in the press. It may have been taken for granted that "cruelty" charges were necessary in the 1930s, when the law required grounds for divorce. It should be noted, too, that Virginia dropped the abuse charges when she and Cary reached a financial settlement ahead of their final divorce hearing in March 1935.[39] Yet sixty years later she maintained that his jealousy could overwhelm him and drive him into an angry rage. Even for her, though, this was not his defining characteristic. "I was carrying a torch for Cary for years after we parted," she recalled. "I was *so* in love with him."[40]

For Cary, Virginia's departure was another abandonment. Decades later, he reflected on his first marriage with some sadness and insight. "I doubt if either of us was capable of relaxing sufficiently to trust the happiness we might have had," he wrote about Virginia. "My possessiveness and fear of losing her brought about the very condition it feared; the loss of her."[41] In the immediate aftermath of their separation, however, he could scarcely speak or think about her. While the pages of his personal scrapbooks display many good and bad critical reviews, and many articles about various aspects of his life, the stories about Virginia are few and far between. One scrapbook does contain a single press clipping that reports Virginia's third marriage, to the Earl of Jersey in 1937, but this is not displayed in the book along with the other clippings. Rather, it is folded within a closed envelope, which is itself tucked into the very back of the book.[42] Hidden, out of sight, buried away; for much of his life this was the only way Cary could deal with his feelings.

11

As his marriage ended amid a swirl of unflattering publicity, Cary could not take much solace in his professional life. A succession of box-office flops in 1934 raised doubts about the future of his career. The first of these was *Born to Be Bad*, the film he had made on loan to Twentieth Century Pictures before he went to England. It sat on the shelf for six months while the Hays Office deliberated about it, eventually insisting on cuts that reduced the story to its bare bones and pared the running time to a mere 59 minutes.[1] On release in May 1934, critics savaged it.[2] Although Cary was hardly to blame for its shortcomings, he was singled out by *Variety* for giving a "colorless, meaningless performance."[3] The films that followed—*Thirty Day Princess*, *Kiss and Make-Up*, *Ladies Should Listen*, and *Enter Madame!*—fared better with the critics but not with audiences. One theater owner was so disgruntled after screening both *Kiss and Make-Up* and *Ladies Should Listen* to empty houses that he publicly complained that "trying to make Cary Grant a comedian won't go over."[4] At the time, this was not as ill-judged a statement as it now seems.

Cary admitted to a reporter that "a jinx seems to be following me." He thought that the problem was that he had been typecast as a tall, dark, and handsome "clothes horse," and he urged the studio to let him play an unsympathetic role for a change.[5] Paramount obliged because it was struggling to cast the male lead in *Wings in the Dark* (1935).[6] Producer Arthur Hornblow Jr. had developed the script for his fiancée, Myrna Loy, a major star on loan from MGM. She would play Sheila Mason, an aviator loosely based on Amelia Earhart but very much in keeping with Loy's screen image as a calm, cool, confident modern woman.[7] It was not clear who would play Ken Gordon, a single-minded aviator who loses his sight and therefore his purpose in life. Embittered and angry, he rejects the people who try to help him, and in the ending he is prevented from committing suicide only by a last-minute plot twist.

Cary was cast in the role just days before his own reported suicide attempt in early October, and the film was shot in the month leading up to his court case with Virginia in December 1934.[8] Virginia visited the set several times to confer with Cary, apparently preferring to discuss their problems at the studio rather than alone at home.[9] Myrna Loy recalled in her memoirs that Cary was preoccupied by his marital problems throughout the shoot.[10] The film, however, demonstrates that he was able to channel his bitterness and despair into his portrayal of Ken Gordon. He plays this role with a sense of understated anger that is unlike anything he had done before. He even looks different: the dapper drawing-room dandy is gone and instead he is a slightly disheveled, tousle-haired flier.

This is not to suggest that *Wings in the Dark* is an overlooked gem of a film. Even in 1935, as reviews make clear, the story seemed ridiculously contrived. In the climax, Sheila is flying in a heavy fog. Unable to find an airport runway, and running out of fuel, she is saved only when Ken takes to the skies for a mid-air rescue. He is still blind, but he is guided by instruments he developed for flying through fog. As if this was not melodramatic enough, he insists that when they have safely landed, he will kill himself by immediately taking off again and crashing his plane. She prevents this by blocking his plane with her own on the runway. "Unconvincing and improbable" was the verdict in *Variety*, but the reviewer also said that the film benefited from "two stellar performances" by Loy and Grant, pacy direction by James Flood, and some spectacular aerial photography.[11] *The Hollywood Reporter* similarly observed that the story itself represented "a rank abuse of plausibility" but recognized the film had "entertainment and thrills" and that "Cary Grant gives a splendid performance as the tragic young flyer." The same reviewer predicted that *Wings in the Dark* would be "a nice little picture for the family trade." This proved to be correct.[12]

In February 1935, when it was released in the plush, big-city theaters that catered to metropolitan audiences, *Wings in the Dark* was a moderate success, but as its release spread to neighborhood and rural theaters, it found more enthusiastic audiences.[13] At last, Cary had a hit film that allowed him to be something more than the man on Mae West's arm. Paramount executives must have been impressed by his performance. In November 1934, while the film was in production and the daily rushes were being scrutinized, his contract came up for renewal. With several recent box-office flops and a scandalous divorce weighing on him, this might have been a moment for the studio to let him go, but instead he gained a significant salary increase, raising his weekly pay from $750 to $1,250. This was still a fraction of Gary Cooper's $5,000 weekly salary, but it was a sign that executives did not think his career would be damaged by the bad press he had received. He was also given a new, upgraded dressing room on the corridor known as "Star Row," furnished with a piano for him to play on his breaks, which confirmed that the studio was still backing him.[14]

When *Wings in the Dark* was completed in December 1934, Cary dropped off the radar. Having made five films within the previous ten months, and having seen his marriage disintegrate in a particularly public and humiliating way, he was ready for a hiatus from filmmaking and public life. He ceased attending the usual round of premieres, nightclubs, and balls, and vanished from public view almost entirely. He was eager to return to England to see his family but, harboring hopes that he and Virginia might reconcile, he stayed in Hollywood.[15] In January, when she got a small part in the touring company of the Broadway play *Merrily We Roll Along,* he attended the opening nights in both Santa Barbara and San Francisco. The unrelenting Louella Parsons spotted Cary and Virginia together and told her readers that a reconciliation looked likely.[16] It was not to be. In March, they met for their court hearing, and then Virginia left for London.

With all hopes for a reconciliation dashed, and news of the divorce out of the newspapers, he re-emerged in May 1935, when he flew to New York to perform in a radio play. The comedy *Adam and Eva,* co-starring Constance Cummings, was the first of his many appearances on the Lux Radio Theatre, in 50-minute plays that were usually adaptations of recent films. He enjoyed the intensity of the four-day rehearsal period followed immediately by a live broadcast. On this occasion, he liked the salary too. He had not worked since December and broadcasters paid film stars well.[17]

The day before he left for New York, he attended a private party for Fred Stone, a Broadway actor who had recently come to Hollywood. There, over cocktails, he spotted Betty Furness, a well-spoken, blonde and blue-eyed actress, who bore a striking resemblance to Virginia.[18] He immediately fell for her, and when he discovered that she, too, was leaving for New York the next day, but traveling by train, he impetuously invited her to join him on the plane. Thanks to Howard Hughes, Cary loved flying, but Furness had never flown before. Eager to get to know Cary, she agreed to join him on the eighteen-hour journey that included six refueling stops. The cabins were not pressurized, and so when the plane was not taking off or landing, it was bouncing along the tops of the clouds. She was sick several times along the way. "This was a marvelous way to get acquainted with someone," she laughed later.[19]

Cary was not put off. When they got to New York, he asked her out every evening. His tendency to fall quickly and deeply in love was tempered only by her youth. Although she had been in Hollywood and under contract at RKO for three years, she was only nineteen years old when they met. He was evidently embarrassed by the age difference. He insisted to reporters that they were not romantically involved, and that her mother had asked him to look after her during her trip to New York.[20] He had to drop this ruse when they returned to Hollywood and she brought him back on to the social scene. Many years later, her memories of him were very similar to Virginia's happiest memories of him. "We laughed and laughed and laughed," Furness recalled fondly. "We drove around a lot with the top down. We did silly things. Cary was a very sophisticated man, but a part of him wasn't that way at all." Speaking in the 1990s, she was also keen to say that their affair was genuine, and not—as some alleged in retrospect—a distraction staged by the studios for publicity purposes. "I would like to say that my relationship with Cary was a romance on both parts. It was not set up by anyone."[21]

After the New York trip, Cary returned to Paramount with a new determination to take charge of his career. He was thrilled to hear that Irving Thalberg, the leading producer in Hollywood, wanted to borrow him for MGM's production of *Mutiny on the Bounty* (1935). Clark Gable and Charles Laughton had the leading roles as Fletcher Christian and Captain Bligh, but Thalberg had Cary in mind for the third-billed role of Roger Byam. He was bitterly disappointed when Paramount refused to loan him, citing scheduling conflicts.[22] Cary himself sought the lead in Warner Bros.' swashbuckling adventure film *Captain Blood* (1935), but Warner Bros. instead cast a newcomer named Errol Flynn.[23] Perhaps most intriguingly, after seeing Emlyn Williams's play *Night Must Fall* (1935) on stage, he bid for the screen rights to the story. He was keen to play a handsome charmer who turns out to be a murderer, but he would have to wait until he met Alfred Hitchcock to fulfill that ambition. Williams went instead with MGM, which cast Robert Montgomery in the lead.[24]

He was taking the initiative because Paramount had so little for him. With its finances in crisis, the studio was undergoing another upheaval. During Cary's hiatus, production chief Manny Cohen was ousted and replaced by the director Ernst Lubitsch, but it soon became apparent that Lubitsch was less effective than Cohen at organizing the production of sixty films per year.[25] Lubitsch was at least keen to keep Cary happy. Another salary increase, up to $1,500 per week, was awarded in May, even though Cary had not made a film since his last salary increase.[26] But this proved to be a sweetener to a rather bitter pill. His first film under the Lubitsch regime was a disaster from start to finish.

The Last Outpost (1935) was put on the production roster after the success of *The Lives of a Bengal Lancer* initiated a cycle of British Empire adventure films at Paramount and other studios. The ambitions for *The Last Outpost* were modest. The director, Charles Barton, was known mainly for making "B" Westerns. Although the budget allowed for some location shooting in the desert near Palm Springs and at the Paramount ranch in the foothills of the San Bernadino Mountains (near Los Angeles), costs were set at a modest $350,000.[27] Filming with Charles Barton lasted for five weeks, from May 20 to June 26, at which point the film was eight shooting days over schedule and should have been finished. Instead, the script was being hastily rewritten, and director Louis Gasnier took over from Barton. The veteran Gasnier, who had co-directed Cary in *Gambling Ship*, struggled to make sense of the story and to maintain morale on the set. Filming went on for another three weeks, from July 25 and August 17, and then an additional two weeks from August 26 to September 9.[28] By this time, costs had ballooned from the budgeted $350,000 to $527,000, and the film had become a confused mess, known to its disgruntled cast and crew as "The Last Outhouse."[29]

The script that Barton filmed centered on a melodramatic love triangle. Cary's character, Michael Andrews, is a British army officer on the Eastern Front during the First World War. When captured by locals, he is saved from execution by a British intelligence officer, John Stevenson (Claude Rains). Unknowingly, he then falls in love with Stevenson's wife, Rosemary (Gertrude Michael). In the original script, Rosemary would die in a car accident, revealing her relationship with Andrews to her husband in her dying breaths. A vengeful Stevenson would then contemplate allowing Andrews to be slaughtered in battle, only changing his mind when the ghost of his dead wife appears before him and pleads with him to save the life of her lover.[30]

Gasnier was brought in to remake the film with less romance and more action. In the revised version, Rosemary disappears without explanation midway through the film, and in the last scene Stevenson is killed while reluctantly saving Andrews. The producers apparently hoped that scenery and spectacle would make this simplified storyline more interesting. Further filming was done on location in Guadalupe (Mexico) and Yuma (Arizona), but the producers also turned to stock footage—seemingly anything they could find in the cutting room—to add excitement to the film.[31] Thus, although the film is set in Kurdistan and Sudan, there are shots of snowy mountain peaks and dense jungles, as well as some wildly incongruous cutaways to baboons, elephants, hippos, and zebras; anything, it seems, to distract from the threadbare story.

"Friends told me *The Last Outpost* wasn't that bad," Cary recalled, "but it was."[32] His friends might have told him, more frankly, that the film is awful but his performance is not. Playing a British character for the first time, he adopted the pencil-thin moustache and slightly clipped accent of Ronald Colman, who was then the biggest British star working in Hollywood. Colman tended to underplay his action-adventure roles, and both Cary and his co-star, Claude Rains, adopted a similar style, not trying to compete with the baboons and zebras in *The Last Outpost*. They did not get along. Rains, too, came from a working-class British background, but he had a formidable theatrical pedigree. He was a veteran of the West End stage, and he had taught acting classes at the Royal Academy of Dramatic Art. In private correspondence, Rains scorned the acting ability of both Cary and Gertrude Michael, and alluded to high tensions on the set.[33] He and Cary would play romantic rivals again in *Notorious* (1946). At the time of *The Last Outpost*, each man could only have been relieved that the film vanished from cinemas too quickly to cause them any significant embarrassment.

The Last Outpost was the only film that Cary would make at Paramount in 1935. The studio's producers had nothing pressing for him, and his next two films were made on loan-outs to other studios. *Sylvia Scarlett* (1935), made at RKO, proved to be a landmark in his career. It was his first film with two very sympathetic collaborators, Katharine Hepburn and George Cukor. Of all of the women he co-starred with, Hepburn was the sharpest and spikiest. In 1935, she was by far the bigger star. Yet at a time when film stars were known for their glamour, Hepburn favored a natural and athletic look, and she rejected the elaborate gowns, hairstyles, and makeup typical of the era. Her brisk, intelligent manner defied the norms of diminutive femininity.

Audiences were clearly intrigued by her liberated and modern personality, but it is notable that in her most popular and acclaimed early films—*A Bill of Divorcement* (1932), *Little Women* (1933), and *Alice Adams* (1935)—she plays a girl still confined within a conventional family. She plays a girl in *Sylvia Scarlett* (1935) too, but in this most unconventional story she is a girl who dresses as a boy. Some sources say that it was Hepburn's idea to adapt Compton Mackenzie's novel, *The Early Life and Adventures of Sylvia Scarlett* (1918), for the screen, and it is easy to see that she relished playing a boy in the film.[34] Others say it was George Cukor's idea.[35] Cukor was gay, and many of his films center on masquerade and theatricality.[36] Regardless of who first thought of making the film, both the director and the star were excited by it and they had enough clout at RKO to get approval for the film. Studio executives set a generous budget of $657,000 for the film, placing it in the top class of RKO's productions.[37]

Everyone agrees that it was Cukor's idea to cast Cary in the film. Cukor had come to Hollywood from Broadway, and he was always more concerned with performance than he was with visual style and technique. He later admitted that, prior to *Sylvia Scarlett*, he thought Cary was merely "a rather handsome, rather wooden leading man." But Cukor had heard something about Cary's music hall past and he suspected that Cary understood the "raffish life," of getting by at the edges of respectability, that *Sylvia Scarlett* depicts.[38] He decided to take a chance, casting Cary as Jimmy Monkley, a British working-class blaggard who will do anything—from smuggling to con jobs to a bit of clowning on stage—if it keeps him from the daily grind of factory or clerical work. Monkley was the kind of man that young Archie Leach might have turned out to be if he had not immersed himself so completely in show business. "He saw something behind my smoothness," Cary recalled gratefully, adding, "I loved the part and George helped me to unwind."[39]

Filming began in mid-August and lasted for two months (interrupted, for Cary, by the reshoots for *The Last Outpost*). It was a happy shoot. "Every day was Christmas on the set," Cukor recalled.[40] Cukor and Hepburn had already made two films together (*A Bill of Divorcement* and *Little Women*) and they were close friends. When filming moved on to location, first in Laurel Canyon (northwest of Hollywood) and later at Trancas Beach (north of Malibu), they took turns having their personal staff prepare picnic lunches for the principal cast and crew. Photographs from the occasions reveal that these "picnics" had tablecloths, silverware, and serving bowls filled with summer soups and salads. The photographs also show the smiles and laughter befitting a film shoot with a large measure of good spirits.[41]

One day, when lunch was being served on a bluff overlooking Trancas Beach, everyone watched in awe as a twin-propeller plane landed on the beach. "That's my friend, Howard Hughes," Cary nonchalantly informed them. Hughes had come to join them for lunch—ostensibly to see Cary and show him the plane but also because he was keen to meet Hepburn. "I gave Cary a black look," Hepburn wrote in her memoir. She claimed that she disapproved of Hughes arriving uninvited at her picnic and that she refused to acknowledge him throughout the meal. But another photograph from the set shows Hepburn and Hughes chatting amiably while Cary inspects the plane. Whatever happened that day, in the months that followed, Hepburn and Hughes embarked on a long love affair.[42]

Throughout the filming, Cukor marveled at Cary's performance. "Suddenly during the shooting he felt all his talents come into being," he recalled. "He suddenly burst into bloom."[43] Cary plays Monkley as a cold and calculating chancer, always on the lookout for himself, overdressed yet completely inelegant, and quick to resort to his fists. Cary convincingly reproduced the cockney mannerisms of this type of man, jabbing with his finger to make a point, cupping his hand around his cigarette as he smokes, squinting his eyes when he concentrates. His even greater accomplishment was breathing life into what might otherwise have been a cardboard villain. When drunk, Monkley dances a high-kicking jig with infectious exuberance. When he and his companions form a stage group, the Pink Pierrots, his earnest singing and ridiculous costume make him endearingly pathetic. When Sylvia's father (Edmund Gwenn) disappears, Monkley comforts her with a surprisingly tender embrace.

Monkley's desire for Sylvia (even when she is in drag as Sylvester) softens some of his hard edges. Dressed as a boy, Hepburn-as-Sylvia stokes desire in everyone. When a cockney housemaid named Maude (Dennie Moore) joins the Pink Pierrots, she tries to give Sylvester kissing lessons. They meet a bohemian artist, Michael (Brian Aherne), who admits to Sylvester that he has "a queer feeling when I look at you." But it is Cary's Monkley who makes the warmest advances. When he and Sylvester are assigned to bunk together, Monkley undresses in front of him, urging him to "C'mon, get your pajamas, let's get curled up," adding, "It's a bit nippy tonight. You'll make a nice hot water bottle." By now shirtless, Monkley looks genuinely crestfallen when Sylvester runs away, yelling after him, "Hey, what's the matter with you? I took a bath last Saturday night!" Cary delivers this last line (not in the script but ad-libbed on set) in a perfectly deadpan manner.

The playful gender ambiguities and the nocturnal scenes set in open-air, pastoral locales lend *Sylvia Scarlett* a Shakespearian tone. For all of the film's charms, however, there is no denying that it sags in its second half. When Sylvia meets Michael, she is so enamored that she removes her drag and puts on a dress to please him, which puts an end to the fun. It is also unconvincing. All of the chemistry is between Sylvia/Sylvester and Monkley, and when their characters' relationship fizzles out, the film does as well.

Photograph 11.21 Katharine Hepburn, masquerading as a boy in *Sylvia Scarlett* (Paramount Pictures, 1935), rejects Monkley's suggestion that they keep warm by sleeping in the same bed.
Source: author's screen capture

Eventually, *Sylvia Scarlett* became a "queer classic." Its admirers regard it as one of the most sexually subversive films of the decade, a blow against the conservatism of the Hays Office and the timidity of film producers.[44] In the 1930s, the film was simply regarded as a disaster. RKO released it on Christmas Day, 1935. This was a bizarre miscalculation and the film faced a barrage of hostile reviews as well as disappointing box-office returns.[45] Yet for Cary it was anything but a flop. Reviews with headlines such as "Cary Grant Is a Cheap Crook" praised him and reserved their disapproval for Cukor and especially for Hepburn.[46] *The Hollywood Reporter* was typical in stating that Cary "steals the picture from under some very fine noses" and predicting that the film would have a profound effect on his career, putting him "right at the top of the heap in one brilliant jump."[47] There was similar praise in *Variety* ("Cary Grant steals the picture"), the *Los Angeles Times* ("The film really is a triumph for Mr. Grant"), the *New York Times* ("Cary Grant, whose previous work has too often been that of a charm merchant, turns actor in the role of the unpleasant cockney and is surprisingly good at it"), and many other papers.[48]

Cary was not in Hollywood to enjoy this round of glowing reviews. On November 1, 1935, a week after he finished the last re-takes on *Sylvia Scarlett*, he flew to New York, and a few days later he sailed on the *Aquitania* to England. Some speculated that this sudden trip was made to see Virginia, but they met just once in London, for a long talk and nothing more.[49] He went to England to see his family. Two years after the chaotic trip that he spent mostly in the hospital, he wanted to return and spend the holidays with his father and his half-brother Eric, and also begin to get to know his mother again.[50] He knew that his father was not well, and in order to spend a few months in the country, he got Paramount's permission to make a film there.

British film producers were keen to import Hollywood stars, but Cary's deal was not a good one. Other stars of his caliber went to work with Alexander Korda's London Films, which produced films on a scale akin to Hollywood, or with the up-and-coming Gaumont-British Pictures, which was making a name for itself with Alfred Hitchcock's spy thrillers. But Cary accepted an offer from a newly established production company, Garrett-Klement Pictures.[51] He may have been persuaded by the high salary of $65,000 for ten weeks of work.[52] He may have liked the script, adapted from E. Phillips Oppenheim's novel *The Amazing Quest of Mr. Ernest Bliss* (1919), about a British millionaire named Ernie Bliss who decides to give up his riches for a year and prove that he can support himself. He may also have been swayed because the company hired an American screenwriter with Hollywood experience, John Balderston, and an experienced German director, Alfred Zeisler, who had recently moved to England. It may simply have been a choice made in haste because he wanted to see his family.

Whatever his reasons were, making *The Amazing Quest* (1936), as the story was renamed, was a bad career move. Cary does not seem at home in the contemporary London settings. His accent and demeanor do not fit with either the millionaire's high-society friends or the ordinary working folk he encounters when he leaves his wealth behind. His co-star, the American actress Mary Brian, had been a successful silent film star, but her career was in a steep decline by the mid-1930s, and she apparently had little feeling for this role. She is nearly expressionless on-screen. The film also unfolds at a plodding pace. On first release in Britain, it was 79 minutes long, but many months passed before the film found a US distributor, and then it was the "B" film company Grand National, which cut the running time to 62 minutes and renamed the film *Romance and Riches*.[53] Even in this reduced form, as the reviewer for *The Hollywood Reporter* commented, it was suitable only for the lower half of a double bill.[54]

This bad career move proved to be very important to him personally.[55] He arrived in London on November 14, 1935, and he scarcely had time to settle into his plush new residence at 11 Park Lane, a rented house that he shared with fellow American actors abroad Otto Kruger and Robert Young, before he journeyed down to Bristol to visit his father over the weekend of November 16–17.[56] His father told him how important his films were to him—that he went to see them as a way of seeing him—and Cary left Bristol thinking that he would return for the holidays.

Back in London, he reported to Elstree Studios to begin work on *The Amazing Quest*. During the second week of filming, his father developed a strangulated hernia and had emergency surgery. At Elstree, producer Robert Klement could see that Cary was sick with worry. He urged him to take a break from filming and go to Bristol, but Cary insisted that they keep to the shooting schedule.[57] Then his father's condition suddenly worsened. He developed gangrene in his bowel, leading to septicemia. He was rushed into surgery but did not survive the operation. On December 1, 1935, and at the age of sixty-three, Elias Leach died at the Bristol Royal Infirmary.[58]

On December 4, Cary attended the funeral in Bristol, and then returned to Elstree and continued filming. His complicated relationship with his father ended in this curious way. All of his life, he sought his father's approval and also resented his wayward ways. Hence, he traveled thousands of miles to be near his father, and then used work as a pretext to keep him that last 100 miles away from Bristol. "He never discussed his father or his mother with me," Mary Brian commented.

Cary and his co-star began having dinners together while making *The Amazing Quest* and gradually their friendship deepened into a romance. She recalled that London put him in a nostalgic frame of mind. He was eager to see the sights and to see "every show in London." One of these was Noel Coward's *Tonight at 8:30*. When Cary found that the show was sold out, Coward invited them to watch from the wings, and he joined them for dinner afterward. Cary also took her to music halls, where Brian was surprised to see acrobats, pantomime, and drag acts. On January 28, 1936, they watched the funeral procession of King George V as it passed in front of the Park Lane house. Cary was evidently captivated by the pomp and spectacle. As they watched, he filmed the procession with his own camera. Still, he did not discuss his own father's death with her. "He just wasn't ready" for the conversation, she concluded.[59]

Decades later, when Cary was middle-aged, he reflected on his father's death in terms that were at once sympathetic and condescending toward a man who was born with little and died with little. "The cause of my father's death was recorded as extreme toxicity," he wrote, "but it was more probably the inevitable result of a slow-breaking heart, brought about by the inability to alter the circumstances of his life."[60] In Bristol, in the weeks following the funeral, Cary tried to address the circumstances of those affected by his father's life. He befriended his half-brother Eric, writing to him often over the next few years, sending him the American comic books that he loved, and making sure that the fourteen-year-old (who had lost his mother three years earlier) was looked after.[61] He also became his mother's legal guardian and, at the urging of his uncles David and Charles Kingdon, he began to plan for her release from the asylum.[62]

On July 26, 1936—eight months after her husband's death—Elsie was finally discharged. She was fifty-nine years old and had spent the last twenty-one years and seven months of her life there. Her release notes indicate that it had been twenty-one years and five months since her "last attack of mental illness," meaning that she had not had an "attack" since she arrived. The notes also indicated that she was now classified as having "recovered." Thus, it appears that her mental illness was caused, or at least exacerbated by, her suspicions of her husband and her anxiety about their failing marriage. Recovery, for Elsie, entailed living apart from Elias Leach. She was too loyal to admit this, and she would profess her loyalty to him for many more years, but it is an inescapable fact that her "recovery" neatly coincided with his death.

When she was released, Elsie went to stay with her younger brother, Charles Kingdon, who, as a young teenager, had been detained on the HMS *Formidable*. Now he was a respectable butcher living in the south London neighborhood of Plumstead.[63] She would begin her new life there and with him. By this time, Cary had been back in California for several months.[64] He would return to Bristol many times. He always enjoyed seeing the city, and over the years he would slowly rebuild his relationship with his mother. However, he would always maintain a certain distance from his family, preferring to embrace his new identity in Hollywood. Show business had enabled him to alter the circumstances of his own life, and, as a still aspiring film star, he was restless to fulfill his ambitions.

When *The Amazing Quest* was completed, and Cary returned to Hollywood in February 1936, he was disappointed to find that, despite the acclaim he received for *Sylvia Scarlett*, his home studio had no special plans for him. It offered him roles that any of its leading men could play, in films that held little commercial or critical promise. The train-bound comedy *Florida Special* (1936) and the Coast Guard drama *Border Flight* (1936) were typical of the dull "programmers" lined up for him, but he was replaced by Kent Taylor and John Howard, respectively, when he delayed his return. He stayed off salary in hopes that something better could be found, and he worried that his career was in a rut.[1]

Randy was in a similar position. He, too, was cast in Paramount "programmers," sent on loan-outs, and given co-starring roles in high-profile films, such as the Mae West comedy *Go West Young Man* (1936) and the Fred Astaire and Ginger Rogers musical *Follow the Fleet* (1936), but his career lacked upward momentum. In the industry's annual ranking of stars, the Quigley ranking "of money-making stars" (relating to their box-office drawing power), both Cary and Randy were at the bottom of a list of approximately one hundred names.[2] Paramount categorized them among its many "featured players" rather than ranking them among the studio's twenty fully-fledged stars. In their fourth year under contract, they could still be regarded as "up-and-coming," but it must have been frustrating for them to see more recent arrivals in Hollywood, such as Robert Taylor, Fred MacMurray, and Henry Fonda, moving up more quickly.[3]

Cary and Randy were much more firmly established members of the film industry's social scene. In August 1935, they left their apartments in La Ronda and moved some 12 miles west to Santa Monica. Still a small resort town in the 1930s, Santa Monica was known for its "pleasure pier" and a wide stretch of sand extending along the Pacific Ocean. The beachfront area north of the pier was known as the "Gold Coast" or "Rolls Royce Row" because many filmmakers had properties there. Marion Davies's mansion on the beach nearly rivaled San Simeon in grandeur, with a ballroom, a white marble swimming pool, and over one hundred rooms. Louis B. Mayer, the head of MGM, built a comparatively modest twenty-room villa on the beach.

Cary's childhood hero, Douglas Fairbanks Sr., lived at the beach after his divorce from Mary Pickford. Another silent film star, Constance Talmadge, owned a property at 1018 Ocean Front (now Parking Lot 5A on the Pacific Coast Highway), and this was the house that Cary and Randy rented. Their other neighbors along Ocean Front were the producer Hal Roach and actors Fay Bainter, George Bancroft, Merle Oberon, Gregory Ratoff, and Norma Shearer. A couple of years later, the English actors David Niven and Robert Coote rented a guesthouse from Marion Davies that Cary—together with Carole Lombard, Alice Faye, and Ida Lupino—dubbed Cirrhosis-by-the-sea because the parties were so constant. An exclusive beach club brought other stars and filmmakers to Santa Monica at weekends.[4]

The house at 1018 Ocean Front was a rather plain, three-story white Spanish Colonial. Like others on this stretch of road, it stood on a plot of sand between the ocean and the steep bluffs that led up to more solid ground. Its front door opened onto the street, but the back of the house had a broad, elevated terrace, perched 10 feet above the beach and looking out to sea. The terrace had room for a swimming pool, a handball court, and seating. Gated stairs led down to the beach, ensuring privacy from the public. Inside the house, the living room, dining room, and kitchen were modestly sized, but there was a large den with a built-in bar, backgammon tables, and a grand piano that Cary often played. Upstairs, the house was broad enough that both Cary and Randy had bedrooms facing the sea.[5] There was also a guest bedroom and living quarters for Cary's personal secretary, Frank Horn, who oversaw the household and its staff (a chauffeur, a cook, and a maid).[6]

Cary, Randy, and little Archibald, the Sealyham terrier, made this their home for the next five years—the longest period Cary had ever lived in one house. It was by all accounts a happy home. Cary loved being by the sea and in the sunshine. When he was between films, he worked on his tan on the terrace. When he was filming, he was at the studio six days a week from 7:00 a.m. until 6:00 p.m. on most days, but Sunday was reserved as a day for socializing. He and Randy often held an open house, inviting guests to drop by and enjoy the beach, the pool, the games, and the food and drink laid on by their staff. These were fun occasions, but hobnobbing also served them well in the industry, particularly when both men became freelance stars and relied heavily on networking to further their careers.[7]

Mary Brian was a regular guest at the Sunday parties in 1936. She and Cary continued seeing each other after they returned from London. She recalled that Douglas Fairbanks Jr., David Niven, and Reginald Gardiner were among the other regular Sunday guests who also came from the nearby beach club and from the house next door, where Constance Talmadge's husband, Townsend Netcher, entertained frequently.[8] Cary's own photographs and home movies include a few images of the parties, showing guests chatting in deck chairs, swimming, and playing ping-pong or backgammon in the sunshine. Some wear swimsuits and others wear casual clothes at these laid-back parties.

Cary filmed home movies on less social occasions too. He loved to film the sea, whether it was from the decks of the liners he traveled on or the terrace at the back of the beach house. Another of his favorite subjects was Archibald, who can be seen chasing balls, standing on the pool's edge snapping playfully at a toy float in the pool, and at one point falling in the water. Cary also filmed a succession of his girlfriends, who are seen posing for him in bathing suits, playing with Archibald, and sunbathing. Randy sometimes appears in these films, but Cary's camera does not linger so long or so appreciatively on him.

Life at the beach house was captured for the film fan magazines, too, but a very different impression is given by the professional photos. Paramount continued using Cary and Randy's friendship as a publicity angle in these magazines. When Cary was married to Virginia, a profile in *Modern Screen* pictured the two men together beside a headline that read, "Still Pals: Not Even a Wife Could Separate Randy and Cary—But Then, Virginia Wouldn't Want To."[9] A year later, when they moved to Santa Monica, the studio seized upon the opportunity to photograph them in their new home. The young, Yale-educated photographer Jerome Zerbe was commissioned for the job. Zerbe had a distinctive approach to photographing stars. He eschewed the carefully lit, studio-bound glamour photography that was the norm in 1930s Hollywood, preferring to capture stars in shots that appear spontaneous and unposed, and therefore more intimate and revealing.[10]

Zerbe's photographs of Cary and Randy perfectly exemplify his approach. The shots taken inside the beach house show them casually yet impeccably dressed as they eat dinner, feed the dog, make cocktails, play backgammon, and read together. The shots taken outside show them shirtless as they sunbathe on adjacent loungers, throw a handball, lift weights, jog on the beach, swim in the pool, and shower (separately) after swimming. The implication is that the two men spend every moment together, living lives of perpetual leisure. As many modern observers have noted, a sexual frisson can be seen in these photographs. Zerbe must have been aware of this. He was gay, and his images of Cary and Randy idealize both their relationship and their bodies.

Cary was certainly aware of this. Among Zerbe's collected photos, there is a particularly stunning print of Cary on the beach, wearing only a bathing suit and gazing into the distance, which he jokingly signed, "To Jerry, modestly, Cary."[11]

Paramount's publicists were aware of the sexual frisson in the photographs too, and in some instances they objected to it. In one shot, Zerbe framed Cary and Randy in silhouette on the deck, with the sun setting in the distance behind them, as Randy lit Cary's cigarette. In another, they were posed sitting closely together on the diving board in their bathing suits, with Randy's hands poised as if to nudge Cary into the water. The Paramount publicists marked these as "kill shots"; that is, photos that should not be published.[12] However, the studio was happy to distribute the other photographs, and to have them accompany articles with headlines such as "Movie Bachelors at Home" (in *Screenland*) and "Batching It" (in *Modern Screen*). These follow the pattern of previous articles. Although Cary was thirty-two and Randy was thirty-eight, they are referred to in the articles not only as bachelors but as "the boys" and "best friends"; terms that emphasize their eligibility for marriage and also contextualize the reader's gaze, suggesting that the photos

Photograph 12.22 Cary Grant and Randolph Scott are "Batching It" in the fan magazine *Modern Screen* (September 1937).
Source: author's own collection

can be admired in a motherly or sisterly manner rather than in an openly sexual manner.[13]

Over the years, neither Cary nor Randy ever commented on what they thought of this publicity angle, but there is no doubt that they were willing participants in it. For example, they also appeared together in MGM's short promotional film *Pirate Party on Catalina Isle* (1936), apparently vacationing together on the resort island. In truth, their short scene, like separate scenes with Errol Flynn, Lily Damita, and Mickey Rooney, was shot on MGM's backlot. Nevertheless, their appearance in the film suggests that they fully cooperated with the campaign to promote them as Hollywood's most famous best friends.[14]

One of Paramount's chief publicists, Julie Lang Hunt, wrote an article after she left the studio in which she revealed that she found Cary to be a charming man but a very difficult star to promote. He had a "phobia" about publicity, she wrote, and although he was always gracious with reporters, he hated talking with them about "anything less abstract than the Versailles Treaty." Hunt was baffled by his reticence, but she may not have realized just how much of his studio biography was fabricated. The stories about his grandfather (that great Shakespearian actor Percival Leach), his father's clothing manufacturing business, his education at "Clifton University," and the theatrical lighting device that he invented as a fourteen-year-old boy still survived in the clippings files of newspapers and press agencies. As his fame grew so too did the likelihood that these fabrications would be exposed.[15] For Cary, posing for photos with Randy may have been a means of keeping studio publicists happy while also avoiding the tangled web he had woven about his early life.

Randy, too, may have played along as a means of placating the studio's publicists. He was so publicity-shy that when he married in March 1936, he kept it a secret from both the studio and the press for six months. The marriage was unexpected. His father died from a sudden heart attack on March 4 in his hometown of Raleigh, North Carolina.[16] When he went home for the funeral, he renewed an old romance with the heiress Marion duPont. He stayed in North Carolina for several weeks, and before he went home they married as a form of promise that their relationship would endure even though he worked in Hollywood and she bred horses in Virginia. The secrecy was designed to keep the gossip columnists at bay while they decided how and where they would ultimately live together.[17]

Cary, meanwhile, finally agreed on his next film with Paramount. *Big Brown Eyes* (1936) may have seemed a better prospect than *Florida Special* and *Border Flight* because its producer, Walter Wanger, was a major figure in Hollywood and a recent arrival at Paramount, and Cary had admired its director, Raoul Walsh, ever since he had watched him directing Douglas Fairbanks in *The Thief of Bagdad* back in 1923. Still, he must have been disheartened to be cast in *Big Brown Eyes* only after scheduling complications caused Fred MacMurray to withdraw from the film.[18] As hard as it is to imagine now, MacMurray was regarded as the more promising star in 1936. He started at Paramount only a year earlier, but he quickly made a name for himself in the kind of light romantic comedies that would have suited Cary, supporting Claudette Colbert in Wesley Ruggles's *The Bride Comes Home* (1935) and Carole Lombard in Mitchell Leisen's *Hands Across The Table* (1935). Both Walter Wanger and the other star of *Big Brown Eyes*, Joan Bennett, were disappointed to see MacMurray replaced by Cary. "Nobody wanted him," Raoul Walsh recalled.[19]

Cary took top billing in the film, but Wanger was clearly intent on building up Joan Bennett, who was his contract star as well as his future wife. *Big Brown Eyes* centers on her character, a brassy, gum-chewing manicurist named Eve who becomes an ace reporter. Cary is Dan, her policeman boyfriend on the trail of jewel thieves in New York City. The story is the kind of wisecracking gangster drama that Warner Bros. might have filmed more convincingly with James Cagney and Joan Blondell in the leads. Cary is hardly at home in a tough-guy role that requires him to call women "dames" and to say "So long, Toots" to Eve when he departs. Raoul Walsh must have added one scene on Cary's behalf, because Dan impersonates Mae West, vamping it up in a scene that ends with Eve telling him to "Come up and see me sometime." But the routine, like everything else in the film, seems contrived and forced. On release, critics were unusually frank. The *New York Times* critic Frank S. Nugent, for example, called the film "a pain in the neck."[20] Audiences were completely indifferent to it. Wanger's financial ledgers reveal that *Big Brown Eyes* did not even recoup its modest production cost of $290,000.[21]

His next assignment took him to the most glamorous and profitable studio in Hollywood, MGM. Alas, this loan-out was not for a film as high-profile as *Mutiny on the Bounty*, but it was for an important role in the Jean Harlow star-vehicle *Suzy* (1936). In her memoirs, the MGM screenwriter Lenore Coffee recalled that Cary initially hated his character and wanted to walk away from *Suzy*. In a pre-production meeting, he bluntly told the film's producer that

"The part is completely wrong for me and I won't play it." He was then surprised to find that the producer urged him to explain his objections to Coffee and work with her on revising the character to his satisfaction. This was not how rebellious stars were handled at Paramount. At MGM, though, he and Coffee went through the script scene by scene, redeveloping his character and improvising variations on his scenes. Coffee recalled that while Cary began as a reluctant participant in this process, by the time they had revised the story, or at least his character, he was happy. "I think this is going to work," he told her when they were done.[22]

MGM's script files confirm the broad outline of Coffee's account. *Suzy* was always designed to showcase its star, Jean Harlow, and to shift her screen persona away from being a brassy sex siren and establish her as a more warm-hearted adventuress. Suzy is an American showgirl who finds herself entangled in a spy ring, initially in London and then in Paris, during the First World War. She also finds herself with two husbands. Terry, played in the film by Franchot Tone, is a rather dull but reliable inventor who is apparently killed by the Germans in London. Her second husband, Andre, is a wealthy Parisian, and this is the role assigned to Cary. In an early script by Herman Mankiewicz, Andre is described as a sensitive idealist who rejects his family's military traditions and espouses socialism and pacifism.[23] This is likely to have been the character Cary found to be "completely wrong" because in the revised story, co-written by Coffee, Andre became an aristocratic flying ace who breaks Suzy's heart.[24] This was a character that Cary could play with confidence.

The script was subsequently sharpened by writers Dorothy Parker and Alan Campbell, and Andre became a more charming and flirtatious figure.[25] His initial interest in Suzy is registered through offhand teasing of her, including a nightclub scene in which he sings her own song ("Did I Remember?") back to her. Andre has a touch of Noel Coward–style sophistication, to be sure, but Cary brings a more solidly masculine quality to the character. It does not seem too far-fetched that this rakish fellow could be a flying ace who has brought down fourteen German planes. His caddish behavior toward Suzy also makes him a bit darker than Coward's sophisticates. With *Suzy*, Cary moved a little bit closer to achieving his ambition to play a villain.[26]

Two other plot details also suggest Cary's hand in revising his character. When Andre's father scolds him for his sudden marriage to Suzy, he recalls that Andre was impulsive as a child, saying, "Your first brilliant act was running away from home to join a traveling circus." Another autobiographical point arises when Andre chases after Suzy as she leaves Paris for London. Andre follows her train in his plane, swooping over the train in a grand romantic gesture, just as Cary had done for Virginia as she departed Bristol by train in January 1934. These small incidents offer early examples of a much broader phenomenon in Cary's career: the boundary between his characters' identities and his own life would always be permeable, and elements of one would continually infuse the other.

Suzy is not *his* film. He is third-billed in the credits after Jean Harlow and Franchot Tone, and the publicity centered squarely on Harlow.[27] She was the reason MGM invested over $600,000 in production costs, and she was the reason audiences flocked to see the film in the summer of 1936.[28] *Suzy* was a major hit, earning $1.2 million in North America alone.[29] Critics rightly pointed out that the film tries to strike too many chords at once. It is at various points a comedy, a romantic melodrama, and a war film with aviation battles.[30] Even if it was unlikely to win any awards, its commercial success was important for Cary. After so many flops, he needed another hit film.

Leaving MGM, he found that Paramount had nothing interesting to offer him. One idea was that he and Randy would co-star in *Spawn of the North*, playing salmon fisherman who are rivals for the love of Carole Lombard. Paramount promised to make the film in Technicolor and on location in Alaska, but Cary made no secret of his disdain for the story, not to mention his reluctance to film on location in Alaska.[31] (The film was made two years later, with George Raft, Henry Fonda, and Dorothy Lamour starring.) A more routine proposal, and one that he eventually had to accept, was making *Wedding Present* (1936) for producer B. P. Schulberg. The studio's former production boss was now supervising just a few films each year, and this one demonstrated how far he had fallen.

Wedding Present once again teamed Cary and Joan Bennett. Although their previous film, *Big Brown Eyes*, had been a commercial and critical failure, the stars were put through very similar paces in this wisecracking comedy about city slickers in love and involved with gangsters. The setting for *Wedding Present* is Chicago, and they both play ace reporters. Cary is Charlie Mason, and Joan Bennett is his fiancée, "Rusty." Together they play practical jokes on the newspaper's editor (George Bancroft) until Charlie gets fired from his job. Then Rusty plays practical jokes on Charlie. At the frenzied climax, when Rusty is about to marry someone else, a drunken Charlie sends an array of emergency vehicles—the police, the fire department, ambulances—to disrupt her wedding day and succeeds in winning her back. The last shot reveals that Charlie and Rusty are riding in an ambulance from the insane asylum, a reference that could only have made Cary cringe.

In script form, some of the characters and situations are similar to those of *His Girl Friday*, yet there is nothing in the film that points toward the sharp humor and fast pace of the later film. In *Wedding Present*, the characters are so thinly conceived, and the situations piled on so thick and fast, that the film seems painfully strained. The critic for the *Chicago Tribune* defined the film as "baloney rendered most indigestible through lack of humor," while in New York's *Daily News* it was labeled "anything but funny."[32] *Variety* warned exhibitors that the film was "a complete void of entertainment" and that it was not strong enough to play at the top of a double bill.[33] When it was released in November 1936, it quickly sank into obscurity.[34]

In its own awful way, *Wedding Present* was a crucial film in Cary's career. In July 1936, when the filming started, Paramount exercised its right to renew his contract for six months and with a contingent salary increase to $2,000 per week.[35] This was the final "option" that the studio had. When this six-month term ended, he would be free to seek offers elsewhere. According to Cary, studio boss Adolph Zukor was keen to sign him to another five-year term and offered to raise his salary to $3,500 per week as a part of a new deal.[36] However, his recent run of Paramount films, including *Wedding Present*, convinced him that any new contract would have to have a "story approval" clause, allowing him to choose which films he made. Zukor refused this and negotiations stalled.[37]

Cary immediately signed with a newly established Hollywood agent, Frank W. Vincent, who had worked as a vaudeville booking agent on the Orpheum theater circuit. Their paths may have crossed during their vaudeville days—*The Woman Pays* toured the Orpheum circuit—or they may simply have found a connection in their shared affection for vaudeville. Whatever brought them together, they became close friends and Vincent helped Cary to find his way in a studio system stacked against stars. Cary's first instruction to his new agent was that any new contract must be non-exclusive. He insisted that his career would no longer be governed by studio executives.[38] He was going to take control by becoming a "freelance" star.

Some sources cite Cary's decision to leave the comfort and stability of a long-term studio contract as a milestone in Hollywood history, and credit him as the first star to brave independence, or freelance status, at the height of the studio system.[39] But this is not quite correct. Before Cary, other major stars worked outside of long-term, exclusive studio contracts. In 1930, both

Barbara Stanwyck and Irene Dunne arrived in Hollywood, having already enjoyed success on Broadway, and they signed non-exclusive, multi-film contracts that extended, over the years, to a number of different studios. Around the same time, former silent film stars Constance Bennett and Clara Bow signed lucrative deals with Warner Bros. and Fox, respectively, that were for two films only and gave them the right of approval over both the script and the director of their films. Beginning in 1933, Ronald Colman signed a succession of non-exclusive deals that gave him approval over the story and the director of his films, as well as a percentage of their gross earnings. All of these stars were willing to forgo the insurance a long-term contract afforded in return for the creative control they gained through non-exclusive contracts. As long as they retained their popularity, the studio had an incentive to treat them well, accede to their wishes, and hope that they returned to make additional films.[40]

Cary was not alone in wanting to free himself from Paramount's control. The studio was losing its stars at an alarming rate in the mid-1930s. Claudette Colbert had the clout to renegotiate her contract with the studio in 1933. She gained the right to make films at other studios, approval over the story and the director of the films she made at Paramount, and a percentage deal on the earnings of her films. Carole Lombard renegotiated her contract in 1937, gaining the right to make films with other studios. The studio's top star, Gary Cooper, refused to renew his exclusive contract in 1936 and signed parallel deals with both Paramount and the independent producer Samuel Goldwyn.[41] The difference for Cary was that Paramount executives valued Colbert, Lombard, and Cooper enough to give them what they wanted when their contracts were up for renewal. They were not willing to do this for Cary. They did not regard him as a star but as a second-string leading man, one who could step into the shoes of Cooper or even Fred MacMurray when they were unavailable. Giving him story approval would negate his purpose at the studio.

If Cary's decision to freelance was not as groundbreaking as some have said, it was truly remarkable in another light. The other stars were at the top of their careers when they decided to freelance, and they were certain to be in demand. Cary was not in that position in 1936. There was a sense of drift rather than an upward momentum to his career. He blamed Paramount for this, but leaving the studio was no guarantee that he would finally find more suitable roles. He risked unemployment or, more likely, a descent into poverty-row productions. He had seen Virginia Cherrill and Mary Brian go down that path and he did not want to follow them. Yet he quickly proved that Paramount really had been holding him back. It was only when he took control of his career that he became a top-ranked star, and this in itself was a blow to the logic of the studio system. His success demonstrated very clearly that the studio did not always know better or ensure the best future for its contracted talent.

During his last six months at Paramount, with his contract negotiations stalled, the studio sent him on two loan-outs that offered him little chance to shine. The first involved a swap with Columbia Pictures. Paramount wanted Columbia's star, Jean Arthur, to take the lead in Mitchell Leisen's *Easy Living* (1937) and in return they loaned Cary to Columbia for *When You're in Love* (1937).[42] In this musical comedy, he is second-billed to the opera singer Grace Moore, and much of the running time is given to her singing, but a thin storyline centers on a screwball romance. She plays Louise Fuller, an Australian opera star who becomes stranded in Mexico and urgently needs a visa to return to the United States. Cary is Jimmy Hudson, an American drifter in Mexico who disapproves of her wealthy lifestyle but agrees to marry her, thus granting her the visa, for a price.

The clash between her pampered refinement and his rough edges would be familiar to anyone who has seen *It Happened One Night* (1934), and with good reason: Robert Riskin wrote the screenplay for both films. But whereas Frank Capra had directed *It Happened One Night*, Riskin was given the chance to direct his own screenplay with *When You're In Love*, with his brother, Edward Riskin, producing the film. The result should have been predictable. The writer was unwilling to trim his own words, and the brother did not overrule him. The very slight story drags on for nearly two hours, and it strains to achieve what was known as the "Capra touch"; that is, moments that charm the audience with their homespun sentimentality.

Cary found himself in a familiar mode, playing a Clark Gable–style American everyman, and playing second string to the real star of the film, Grace Moore. In this case, he could not concoct any screen chemistry with the leading lady. There is not a spark between them. When it was released in February 1937, *When You're in Love* did well in some major cities, where there was an audience for opera, but it did not have a broad appeal.[43] Moore's film career soon waned and Riskin never directed again. Much later, Cary would disown both of his "opera films," *Enter Madame!* and *When You're In Love*. When they were shown on late-night television, he would tell friends, "That wasn't me! That was some other fellow!"[44]

His last assignment under the Paramount contract—another loan-out—proved to be a prolonged, chaotic affair. He was sent to RKO to make *The Toast of New York* (1937), a big-budget costume drama set during America's "gilded age."[45] The character actor Edward Arnold was given the starring role of Jim Fiske, a real Wall Street "robber baron" who amassed a fortune through manipulating financial markets. Frances Farmer co-stars as Fiske's mistress, Josie Mansfield. In his first historical role, Cary plays a fictional character, Nick Boyd, who is Fiske's friend and business partner, but the film really belongs to Edward Arnold. He portrays Fiske as a man of great charisma and cheer, even as he is cornering the market in gold for his own selfish purposes. It is surprising to see financial corruption treated so lightly in *The Toast of New York*, a perspective unlikely to appeal to audiences still living with the aftermath of the Wall Street Crash.

The production troubles began when director Alexander Hall became ill. He was replaced by Rowland V. Lee, who disliked the script and asked for scenes to be rewritten as filming progressed.[46] Tensions escalated further because Frances Farmer was not happy with the rewritten script and she made no secret of this. Farmer, whose battles with mental illness and against the strictures of the studio system would be dramatized in the film *Frances* (1982), recalled in her memoir that she was combative on the set. "I argued with the producer. I fought with the director, and I got into verbal knock-down drag-out battles with the writers," she wrote; "I made it extremely difficult for everyone on set by belittling the whole procedure." She observed that Cary was "polite but impersonal" toward her, and concluded that he was "undisturbed and unaffected by my outbursts."[47] This is highly unlikely. Cary hated any kind of tension or upset on the set, and throughout his career he tried to avoid working with anyone who had a reputation for being "difficult." The making of *The Toast of New York* was likely to have been a trial for him, and a long one at that. The eight-week shooting schedule extended to fifteen weeks, into April 1937, and thus far beyond the end of his Paramount contract. By the time it was completed, RKO had spent over $1 million on the film. Little of that investment was returned when the film quickly fizzled out at the box office.[48]

As his Paramount contract came to an end in January 1937, Cary attended a public party for the studio boss Adolph Zukor, who had handled his contract negotiations, and he was photographed smiling at Zukor's side.[49] He was right to be magnanimous. His five years at Paramount had served as an apprenticeship in film acting—a chance to learn its skills and techniques—and he had made the most of that chance. If not many of the films he had appeared in were popular or memorable, this was hardly the fault of a novice who had little if any control over his films. What was important was that he had progressed beyond being a tall, dark, and handsome leading man. He had developed a grace and ease on-screen, and an ability to convey his thoughts through finely nuanced facial expressions. What he needed at the outset of his freelance career was the right film to demonstrate his talents and prove himself with audiences at last. At the time of Zukor's party, it was not yet clear what that film might be, but it was very clear that he was not going to find it at Paramount.

PART THREE

STARDOM, 1937 TO 1950

13

By the time his five-year contract with Paramount ended in early 1937, Cary had made twenty-seven films—over a third of the films he would make during his entire career. Yet if he had chosen to retire at this juncture, he would now be all but forgotten. Like so many other middling leading men of the period (Richard Arlen, Chester Morris, Kent Taylor, Franchot Tone), he would have soon faded into obscurity. He might have been recalled for serving as a leading man to Marlene Dietrich and Mae West, and for doing such an unexpected turn in *Sylvia Scarlett*, but there would be no legend attached to his name. His legend really begins in his first year as a freelancer. It is was in this year—1937—that Cary Grant's stardom developed over the course of three remarkable films.

Initially, there were no offers from the major studios. They did not want to encourage their own contract stars to contemplate independence, and so they shunned him, and offers came only from minor studios and independent producers. Columbia Pictures was definitely in the minor league. It had long relied on "B" Westerns and serials for the bulk of its output, but in recent years it had scored a few mainstream successes, most notably with director Frank Capra's two landmark comedies *It Happened One Night* (1934), starring Clark Gable and Claudette Colbert, and *Mr. Deeds Goes to Town* (1936), starring Gary Cooper and Jean Arthur. But Gable, Colbert, and Cooper were only visiting Columbia. The studio had few big names under contract, apart from Jean Arthur and Capra himself. Physically, the studio lot in Hollywood was smaller and more cramped than Paramount's. There was no room for largesse at Columbia, and the head of production, Harry Cohn, was notorious as an autocratic, penny-pinching hothead.[1] "Poor Harry," Cary recalled many years later. "He was always in a dither about something. He had a bad temper and he had to blow off steam a lot."[2]

Cary knew the score at Columbia. In his last months under contract to Paramount, he was on a loan-out there, filming the ill-fated *When You're in Love*. On February 4, 1937, he signed a contract with Columbia that had a number of clauses designed to protect him from the studio's limitations. Most importantly, it was a non-exclusive deal that allowed him to make films at other studios. He would not be associated with Columbia alone. A minimum production cost for his films was set at $400,000, the threshold for an A-class feature film at this time, and each film would be made by "a director of first class reputation." His contract also stipulated that he would provide his own wardrobe, so long as the film was in modern dress. This ensured not only that he could maintain his own standards of fashion and tailoring, but also that his own clothes became tax deductible. This was a demand he would maintain throughout the rest of his career. So, too, was the right of approval he demanded over every publicity and "still" photograph released to the press.[3] It is notable that once Cary had this control over his own image, the "best friends" publicity angle that centered on his friendship with Randy came to an end.

His salary at Columbia was a big step upward. He had been making approximately $20,000 per film at Paramount, but the Columbia contract guaranteed him $50,000 per film for the first two films, and it had options (at the studio's discretion) for two more films at $75,000 each, and four more films at $100,000 each.[4] The only problem was that Columbia made only a handful of top-budget "A" films each year, and when he signed the contract, on February 4, 1937, the studio had nothing ready for him. He continued to look around for his first freelance film.

He nearly signed to make a film with the independent producer Sol Lesser, supporting the ten-year-old child star Bobby Breen in *Make a Wish* (1937).[5] He was saved from this ignoble fate when Hal Roach, his friend and neighbor on Ocean Front, made a better offer.[6] Roach was also an independent producer, whose small studio was known mainly for making short comedy films, and for launching the careers of Harold Lloyd, Laurel and Hardy, and Our Gang. More recently, Roach had decided to move into feature film production, and he secured a distribution deal with MGM for five films.[7] One of these was the charming, lightweight screwball comedy *Topper* (1937), which became Cary's first freelance film.

Cary was a latecomer to *Topper*. All of the other cast members were in place by the time he signed with Roach on March 4, 1937. It is not known what caused the delay, but it may have been a first instance of Cary's caution when it came to committing to films. He became notorious for being both picky and indecisive, and for considering films at length before eventually turning them down, or agreeing to them and then immediately trying to back out of the deal.[8] The power to choose his own films was a burden as well as a blessing. In this first instance, he may simply have held out for more money. His salary for *Topper* was a flat fee of $75,000, which was more than any other cast member was paid, and a significant portion of the film's $500,000 budget.[9]

There were reasons to be reluctant about *Topper*. The comedy involves a bit too much gimmickry. Cary and Constance Bennett play a married couple, George and Marion Kerby, who are at first a typically chic screwball couple, out on the town and making the rounds of nightclubs and bars. The twist comes when they are killed in a car accident on the way home. Their souls remain earthbound, and they realize that they must perform a good deed before they can ascend to heaven. They therefore set out to liven up the dull, hen-pecked existence of their banker, Cosmo Topper (Roland Young). As ghosts, George and Marion can make themselves visible or invisible at will, and much of the humor arises from the special effects rather than the performers' comic skills. There is also a subplot centered on Marion flirting with the uptight, repressed Topper (or "Toppy" as she calls him), and so Cary's George does not figure in a long stretch of the film.

Despite these limitations, *Topper* proved to be funnier than any of Cary's previous films. Where the Paramount comedies rely heavily on wisecracks and a rapid succession of forced antics, there is more room for gentle, wry humor in *Topper*. From the very first scene—George and Marion driving a convertible down a country lane—the pace is relaxed and Cary's on-screen presence is assured. He sits atop the back of the car seat while driving, steering with his feet rather than his hands, and humming absentmindedly to himself. He ignores Marion's questions about where they are going and what they are doing until finally he sings his response: "Ohhhh, we're going to Wall Street to see old man Topper/That moss-covered Topper. . . ." His playfulness sets exactly the right tone, signaling to the audience that, although a fatal car accident and ghosts will figure in the story, none of this is meant to be taken seriously.

The playful side to George Kerby is set out in the script, but director Norman Z. McLeod allowed Cary to enhance this through improvisation. A scene in which George is late for a board of directors' meeting at Topper's bank is described succinctly in the script: George "enters hurriedly" and "with a slide he slips into a chair." His only dialogue is, "Made it!" In the film, however, Cary throws open the door, slides across the room while saying, "Weather clear! Track fast!" with boyish glee, throwing one leg over the back of the chair as he takes his seat at the table. It is a delightfully dramatic, smooth entry, and a considerable enhancement of the script. Similarly, the script calls for him to be distracted during the meeting while Topper "drones on" with facts and figures, but Cary enhanced this through the playful movement of his eyes as he looks around the table, and later through slumping in his seat, with one foot resting on the table, as he continues humming to himself and intermittently issuing a jazzy, breathy "yeah."[10]

In moments such as these, he arrives at one of his trademarks as comic performer. He became a master of a kind of contrived nonchalance that allows him to be at once within the screwball world and at the same time outside of it, laughing with the audience at its absurdity. The mirth and mischief in his facial expressions nearly breaks the illusion of the fictional world. He was clearly eager to do this. In one scene, the popular songwriter Hoagy Carmichael makes an uncredited cameo, playing the piano and singing his own song, "Old Man Moon," in a bar. As George and Marion leave the bar, Cary ad-libbed, "Bye, Hoagy!" and the line was left in the film. It is, of course, only a short step from this to the many self-referential comments Cary would make in the films that followed. In this and other respects, *Topper* was an important launching pad for his freelance career.

Critics were not so impressed with *Topper* when it was released in July 1937. The complaints were not aimed at Cary in particular but at the film's irreverent treatment of the dead. This was deemed to be in bad taste.[11] Audiences, on the other hand, loved the film. It proved to be so popular that Roach immediately initiated a sequel, *Topper Takes a Trip* (1939), but by the time the script was ready, Cary had so many films lined up that he had to decline this one.[12] In the sequel, he appears only in a flashback to the first film.

Even before *Topper* was released, on the strength of preview screenings and word of mouth within the industry, Cary was suddenly fielding offers from the major studios. Warner Bros. sought him for the second lead in the Bette Davis melodrama *Jezebel* (1938), but the studio was aghast to discover that he would not compromise on a salary demand of $75,000, and the part went to Henry Fonda instead.[13] RKO pushed for a non-exclusive, multi-film deal but then balked at the same salary demand.[14] While the negotiations continued, he started on the first of his Columbia films, *The Awful Truth* (1937), on June 21, 1937.[15] The date is worth noting as one of the most significant in his career. *The Awful Truth* was his breakthrough, a delightful comedy in its own right and also one that established the screen personality that Cary would riff on for the rest of his career.

The director, Leo McCarey, was one of the best Cary would ever work with. Like Norman Z. McLeod, McCarey was a pioneer of silent film comedy. He, too, had worked for Hal Roach in the silent era, and he too had directed films for Laurel and Hardy and the Marx Brothers. At his best, McCarey was able to add warmth and humanity to the barbs and pratfalls of screwball comedy, and *The Awful Truth* is certainly one of his best. The film's top-billed star was Irene Dunne. In 1937, she was already well known for both musicals and for melodramas, but she had recently branched out to comedy with the hit *Theodora Goes Wild* (1936). Like all of Cary's preferred co-stars—Katharine Hepburn, Ingrid Bergman, Grace Kelly, and Deborah Kerr—Dunne had an elegant, well-spoken manner as well as a mischievous sense of humor. Indeed, Dunne's good manners and bearing could come across as regal and mature compared to Cary's playfulness. This was the first of three films they would make together, and in each of them he seems sillier and more boyish with her than he does with any of his other favorite co-stars, and she seems almost maternal rather than romantic toward him (she was six years older than him).

McCarey's version of *The Awful Truth* was based on a drawing-room comedy that had been a hit Broadway play in 1922, a silent film in 1925, and a talkie in 1929. In all of the staged and filmed versions, the story centers on a wealthy couple who separate due to suspicions of infidelity, then realize the awful truth that they still love one another and have to find some means of reconciling. In the three earlier versions of the story, the wife alone is suspected of infidelity, and much of the comedy arises from her subsequent engagement to a man who is obviously—and comically—unsuitable for her. It was McCarey's idea that both husband and wife should be suspected of infidelity, and that the husband too would have a comically unsuitable new partner. This would put the story on a more modern and equal footing, and it would open up the story's potential for screwball humor.[16]

McCarey commissioned a new script, notably seeking a woman, the popular novelist and screenwriter Viña Delmar, to add a more liberated, feminine perspective to the comedy.[17] But McCarey had no intention of following Delmar's script line by line. His working method was to give his actors an opening line or a situation and ask them to improvise the scene, with the idea that the humor arising between the actors will be fresher and livelier than the exact dialogue laid down by the writer. When the actors became stuck, or he had run out of ideas to throw at them, McCarey would play the piano—there was always a piano on his set—until inspiration struck.[18] This was a highly unusual method of filming during the studio era, when every minute on the set cost money and executives scrutinized the amount of footage shot each day. Only a director of McCarey's stature could get away with this and only so long as he turned out profitable films.

Cary did not object to a measure of improvisation. As his performance in *Topper* suggests, he was open to using the script as a starting point, and then expanding on it during rehearsals and filming. Discarding the script altogether was another matter. He had learned to deal with his on-the-set anxieties by studying his script closely, and memorizing and reviewing his lines right up to the point when the director called, "Action!" Even as late in his career as *North by Northwest* (1959), his co-star James Mason observed him on the set "clutching his script until the last moment" before stepping in front of the camera.[19] When making *The Awful Truth*, with no script to clutch, he became very anxious.[20]

Cary's unhappiness on the set of *The Awful Truth* has become an often-told tale about the film. His co-stars, Irene Dunne and Ralph Bellamy, recalled that he was bewildered by McCarey's approach to filmmaking.[21] McCarey arrived each morning with scraps of paper, on which he had scrawled starting points for scenes to be filmed that day, and he asked the actors to take it from there, working out routines and rehearsing them before the cameras rolled. Cary felt so lost that within a few days he was looking for a way out of the film. Bellamy recalled that Cary asked to swap roles with him, presumably so that Cary could have the smaller part in the fiasco unfolding before him. McCarey himself recalled that Cary wrote a lengthy memo entitled "What's Wrong with This Picture" and offered to pay the studio boss Harry Cohn $5,000 if he would release him from the film. McCarey claimed that he was so incensed when he heard about the offer that he replied to Cohn, "Well, if that isn't enough, I'll put in $5,000 too." Cohn refused both of their offers. The filming was "strained all the way through," according to McCarey.[22]

If these stories have been told often, and probably embellished along the way, it is because the film turned out to be so good. Tales about classic films that started as unhappy, chaotic productions are a staple of popular film histories. In this case, though, the tales also serve to explain why there is something discernibly new and different about Cary Grant in *The Awful Truth*. It is hard to imagine that a breakthrough this significant was achieved without a measure of tension and resistance. Yet the strain on the set must have eased at some point. The film was shot on schedule in just eight weeks, a remarkable feat given that it was rewritten as it was filmed. Furthermore, as Dunne and others have pointed out, McCarey himself served as a role model for Cary's new urbane, man-about-town image. Both the director and the star were tall, dark, and handsome, but McCarey was more open and extroverted than the often reserved and apprehensive Cary. The director had an "infectious zaniness"—a mischievous, light-hearted, flirtatious manner—which Cary mimicked for the role of Jerry Warriner in *The Awful Truth* and, over time, made his own.[23] This allowed him to develop a new character type, a suave leading man who is also a slapstick clown, taking pratfalls and making himself look ridiculous for the amusement of audiences.

McCarey saw Cary's polished charm and good looks as a surface, and he saw that puncturing this surface had great comic potential. If audiences could sense some of the turmoil that lay beneath his surface charm, if they could glimpse the frantic energy needed to maintain the polish, they would laugh with him as he struggled to keep his cool. Hence, each scene in *The Awful Truth* begins on a bright and breezy note, but before long a note of discord is heard and that note gradually builds—sometimes to a cacophony—until Cary must register and acknowledge it. The humor lies in watching him as he first tries to ignore the discordant note, then tries to accommodate it while maintaining an air of calm, cool dignity, and finally allows the pretense to collapse altogether.

Cary's metamorphosis is signaled at the start of the film. Jerry Warriner is first seen in a locker room, wearing only his shorts so that he can take a sunbath and appear tanned for his wife Lucy. The story point here is that Jerry is supposed to have been in Florida for the past week and he thinks Lucy will be suspicious if he comes home without a tan. On another level, though, the scene serves as means of stripping Cary down at the outset of the film so that we can observe him emerging anew in the next scene, not only fully clothed and tanned but also with a new assuredness and a dark edge to his comic persona.

When Jerry invites friends from the athletic club back to his home for drinks, they raise their eyebrows when Lucy is not there to greet him, but he pretends to be nonchalant and reassures them that she must be with her Aunt Patsy (Cecil Cunningham). As he is saying this, Aunt Patsy walks into the room behind him, ruining the excuse he is making. No sooner has he introduced Aunt Patsy to the guests than Lucy arrives, trailed by her handsome music instructor, Armand (Alexander D'Arcy), and explaining that on their way home from a recital their car broke down and they had to spend the previous night at an inn. Jerry remains calm throughout the scene, but his suspicions about what may have happened, and his hostility to Armand, play out in his eyes. They flash and dart nervously, almost as an aside to the audience, and too subtly to be picked up by the other characters. Similarly, when he pronounces certain words with added emphasis, there is a suggestion that the audience is hearing something the other characters may not. When Jerry offers Armand a glass of eggnog, he asks him if he wants the drink seasoned. "A little *nutmeg*?" he queries, emphasizing "nutmeg" in a manner that suggests he would have to be nuts to believe the story Armand and his wife are telling him.

Throughout the film, Jerry's easygoing manner is put to the test over and over again. After agreeing to a divorce, Jerry goes to Lucy's apartment to visit their dog, and he finds Lucy with a new suitor, the Oklahoma oil man Daniel Leeson (Ralph Bellamy). He makes polite but increasingly barbed conversation with them, and they all behave as though the situation is convivial rather than awkward. When he then turns to the dog, and the others try to ignore him, he plays the piano and encourages the dog to bark in time to the music. The dog, a wire fox terrier named Mr. Smith (played by the canine

Photograph 13.23 Cary found his métier playing a relaxed, informal American gentleman in *The Awful Truth* (Columbia Pictures, 1937). Here, he questions his wife Lucy (Irene Dunne) and her vocal instructor (Alexander D'Arcy).
Source: author's screen capture

star "Asta"), is more than up to the challenge, and the raucous duet between them becomes a moment of pure music hall fun. It ends with Jerry and Mr. Smith roughhousing on the floor and, as Lucy walks out in disgust, Jerry feigns a smile to her that transforms into a brief but detectable dog-like snarl. Beneath the polished surface, a measure of real jealousy and resentment can be detected.

For the most part, Jerry's hostility is wrapped up in humor. When he meets Lucy and Daniel in a smart nightclub, he can scarcely contain his sarcastic glee when hearing that, once married, they will live in Oklahoma City. "If it should get dull," he says to Lucy with a smirk, "you can always go over to *Tulsa* for the weekend." When he sees that Leeson is an embarrassingly bad dancer, Jerry tips the bandleader so that he can watch Lucy be humiliated all over again. His delight in her misfortune would be unattractive if it did not stem from his genuine love for her. This is apparent even when Jerry is engaged to marry the debutante Barbara Vance (Molly Lamont). Lucy unexpectedly attends a dinner party with Barbara's snooty family, introduces herself as Jerry's sister, and proceeds to embarrass him. She behaves outrageously, pretending to be an alcoholic and offhandedly suggesting that he is one too. "We call him 'Jerry the Nipper,'" she laughs as the assembled family looks on with stiff disdain. Yet Jerry seems to be embarrassed for her rather than by her.

He allows her to lead him away to Aunt Patsy's cabin in the woods, where all pretenses can be dropped at last, and they admit that they still want to be together just moments before their divorce becomes final. The protracted final scene—a long build-up to their reconciliation—has him wearing only an old-fashioned nightshirt. "Air-conditioned," he says to Lucy, hiking the garment like a skirt to demonstrate its antiquity. Stripped of his urbane and fashionably modern clothing, he is finally able to reconnect with her. "I've been a fool," he confesses to her while wearing this foolish garb. "So long as I'm different, don't you think things could be the same again?" he asks her. Lucy, seductively reclining in a double bed, apparently acquiesces, although the censorship strictures of the time prevented a more overt display of their reunion.

Throughout *The Awful Truth*, Cary plays his character with such ease that henceforth everyone assumed that this dapper, urbane, quick-witted, wry fellow was the real Cary Grant. It was an idea that would dog him through the rest of his career, as he built upon and played variations of this character. He was not really acting, it was assumed, but had somehow found a means of playing himself on-screen. *Variety*, for example, praised his performance in *The Awful Truth*, but also noted that the role of Jerry Warriner was "cut precisely to his measure."[24] It is notable, too, that the film received five Academy Award nominations (McCarey and Everett Riskin for outstanding production, McCarey for best director, Dunne for best actress, Bellamy for best supporting actor, and Delmar for best adaptation), and McCarey won for best director, but Cary was the only one of the film's major talents not to receive a nomination.

These frustrations aside, *The Awful Truth* was a runaway hit when it was released in October 1937, and it was a watershed in his career and in the public's understanding of him.[25] It still holds up today as a sophisticated and yet wonderfully silly comedy. One immediate sign of its success was that, after months of negotiations, RKO finally agreed to Cary's contract terms in September 1937. *The Awful Truth* had not yet been released, but previews and the industry buzz about the film convinced the studio that he was worth signing for a non-exclusive three-film deal at $75,000 per film.[26]

He was free to choose which films to make at RKO, and he immediately agreed to make the screwiest of screwball comedies, *Bringing Up Baby* (1938). Once again, Cary was a late arrival to the production. The film had been planned as a cure for the ailing career of Katharine Hepburn, who had suffered a number of flops since *Sylvia Scarlett* three years earlier. She made a spate of costume films—*Mary of Scotland* (1936), *A Woman Rebels* (1936), and *Quality Street* (1937)—that did not play well beyond metropolitan cities, and together they sealed her image as the haughty "Katharine of Arrogance."[27] Comedy, it was hoped, would make her more likeable.[28] In *Bringing Up Baby* she plays Susan Vance, a madcap heiress who embarks on all kinds of adventures to snare a man with whom she falls immediately and overwhelmingly in love.

Casting Hepburn's co-star was an afterthought by comparison. Even the dog was cast before Cary, with Asta once again playing the role of the charismatic, persistent terrier. Many names (Ronald Colman, Leslie Howard, Fredric March, Ray Milland, Robert Montgomery) had been suggested for the male lead during pre-production, but none was interested in playing a man who is pursued so relentlessly by a woman.[29] This did not concern Cary at all. Being pursued would make a welcome change of pace for him after his Paramount films, in which he had to pursue so many leading ladies and make such ardent declarations of love to them. He was concerned about playing a scientist—a paleontologist more interested in reconstructing a brontosaurus skeleton than in love or sex—and he was especially concerned about playing this dry fellow for laughs. He found one of his most sympathetic collaborators, however, in director Howard Hawks. For this first of their five films together, Hawks advised him to base the character on the nervous, fumbling, bespectacled figures played by the silent film comedian Harold Lloyd. When Cary got a pair of glasses identical to Lloyd's, the part of David Huxley suddenly came into focus for him.[30] Like Lloyd's characters, David tries to keep his nonchalance as circumstances around him grow chaotic. He is the "straight man," comically speaking, clinging to his rational outlook with ever-increasing desperation as Susan brings unruly desire and sexuality into his sterile world.

Susan puts David through a succession of mishaps as he pursues a million-dollar donation for his museum. When they first meet on a golf course, she takes his ball as her own, drives off in his car, and manages to dent its fender. When they meet again in a hotel bar, she drops an olive just as he is entering the room and he slips on it, falling onto his hat and crumpling it. She accidentally tears his dinner jacket. She conspires to make David help her transport a leopard ("Baby" of the title) from New York to her aunt's house in Connecticut. On the way she has a car accident with a farmer transporting ducks and geese, and so Baby gets a meal and David ends up covered in feathers. She steals his clothes while he is in the shower, and he is forced to wear her negligee. She allows her aunt's dog to steal his "intercostal clavicle"—the last bone he needs for his reconstruction of a dinosaur's skeleton—and then they must hunt through the night for both the dog and Baby, an escapade that allows her to break his glasses, burn his socks, and "accidentally" catch him in the butterfly net meant to catch Baby. She mistakes a vicious circus leopard for the gentler Baby and lets it loose. She and David end up in jail and, in the ending, Susan pursues him all the way back to the museum in New York, where she manages to destroy his brontosaurus skeleton.

As in *The Awful Truth*, much of the humor in *Bringing Up Baby* stems from chipping away at the polite and easygoing façade of Cary's character. Hawks, like McCarey before him, recognized that his façade was also a form of reserve; his perfection makes him unknowable and emotionally inaccessible. But in *Bringing Up Baby* the slapstick is more intense, and the indignities that he suffers are more frenzied. The key moment for Hawks, which would be repeated in many later films (and not just those directed by Hawks), is the removal of Cary's clothes, which serve as a form of armor for him, protecting his dignity and composure. When Susan steals David's clothes while he is

Photograph 13.24 In *Bringing Up Baby* (RKO Radio Pictures, 1938), David is covered in feathers, one of the many affronts to his clothing, which gradually break his composure.
Source: author's screen capture

showering, and he is reduced to wearing her frilly white negligee, he loses his cool completely. His explanation to Susan's Aunt Elizabeth—"I just went *gay* all of the sudden!"—is accompanied by a wonderfully indecorous leap in the air, with hands waving in mock glee.

The joy of *Bringing Up Baby* is that none of these indignities comes across as sadistic or emasculating for David. Susan is liberating him from the rigid, conventional life that has led him to contemplate a sexless marriage with his rather severe fiancée, Miss Swallow (Virginia Walker), who advocates all work and no play. While Susan's machinations result in David wearing a negligee, it is notable that he looks more masculine than ever when wearing it and he becomes even more attractive in the eyes of Susan. "You're *so* good looking without your glasses," she tells him not once but twice as he changes from the woman's negligee to an even more ridiculous man's fox-hunting outfit. The idea that both women's and men's clothes look like drag on him highlights his androgyny, and the idea that he needs to be saved from the straitjacket of a conventional marriage and career.

In the scenes that follow, he gradually softens toward her as she leads him on open-air adventures, tracking wild leopards in the Connecticut woods on a moonlit night, and singing "I Can't Give You Anything But Love, Baby" to placate the escaped animal. In the ending, he declares that the day he spent with Susan was the best day of his life and even goes so far as to say, "I think I may be in love with you." By this time, she has pursued him all the way to the museum, and at the moment of this declaration, she causes the brontosaurus skeleton that he has spent years reconstructing to collapse. Only then, when she has completely destroyed this monument to his rationality and materialism, do they kiss, and their very quick, very chaste kiss is seen only just before the fade-out. In *Bringing Up Baby*, the fun is all in the chase, and it is so much fun that everything that comes later is likely to be a let-down.

Cary and Katharine Hepburn loved making this film together. He was particularly impressed that she was willing to perform the stunt preceding their kiss in the last scene of the film. This called for her to climb atop the brontosaurus skeleton, and for him to catch her as the skeleton collapses, pulling her up to the platform he is standing on. Cary tutored her in acrobatics: "I trained Kate myself. She was fearless. There was no mattress on the floor. I had her let me grab her, not by the hands because her arms would pop out of their sockets. I grabbed her by the wrists and we were up there tossing back and forth as the skeleton crashes." It was, he added, the "scariest thing I've ever done, but Kate said it was wonderful."[31]

The only problem the film posed for him was working with two real leopards, "Nissa" and "Princess." Although their trainer stood nearby with a whip, ready to strike if they got out of line, they made him very nervous. In the film, it is not difficult to detect that a double or stand-in was used for Cary in many of the scenes he shares with them. Hepburn teased him about this by dropping a stuffed leopard through the vent in his dressing room while he rested. "Wow! He was out of there like lightning," she laughed.[32]

Hepburn thought that she and Cary "were very good together because it looked like we were having a great deal of fun together, which we were." Their fun included many departures from the script. "Cary and I worked out an awful lot of stuff together. We'd make up things to do on the screen—how to work out those laughs in *Bringing Up Baby*. That was all Cary and me."[33] Hawks did not object to their improvisation. He thought it was vital to the comedy. "On set you start changing things and fixing it so the stuff that you know the actors can do well is in there, and it becomes fun."[34] Having never worked before with either Cary or Hepburn, he encouraged them to develop the scenes. In the hotel barroom, when Susan's dress is torn and her backside exposed, the hilarious lockstep walk that they do was Cary's invention, based on a real experience he had in London. When she broke her heel in a scene set in the woods, he encouraged her to repeat "I was born on the side of a hill" while lopsidedly limping along in her broken shoe. In the jail scene, Hepburn invented a criminal name for herself, "Swinging Door Susie," and borrowed "Jerry the Nipper" from *The Awful Truth* for David. Cary immediately shot back with, "She's making all this up out of motion pictures she's seen!"[35]

Cary's line, "I just went gay all of the sudden," is the film's most famous bit of improvisation. The scene with the negligee was in the shooting script but not this particular bit of dialogue.[36] This has led to speculation about what he meant and why he said it. The word "gay" was not widely used to mean homosexual in the 1930s, although it was used that way within the gay sub-culture of the time.[37] Thus, some have supposed that, in his frilly negligee, he was making a coded statement about his own sexuality. It seems likely that Cary knew the meaning of the word. He had gay friends during his theater days in New York, and his personal secretary, Frank Horn, was gay.[38] Yet the in-joke hardly has to refer to his own sexuality. Rather, the idea that he could be gay "all of the sudden" is a step along the path away from David's rigid conformity and toward a world of other, less conventional opportunities.

The improvisation created many of the film's most delightful moments, but it also slowed the filming down to a barely perceptible crawl. Hawks blamed the animals ("That goddamned leopard—and then the dog running around with the bone") and he blamed the stars' silliness. Filming the scene in which Susan asks David about "the bone" took days, Hawks complained. "They were putting dirty connotations on it and then they'd go off on peals of laughter."[39] The daily reports from the set reveal just how slowly the film progressed. Day after day, delays were attributed to rewriting scenes and then working out the new staging, lighting, and camera angles needed to shoot them. The "I just went gay all of the sudden" scene, for example, was filmed over two full days on the studio floor, working from 9:00 a.m. to 6:00 p.m. On the first day, they spent 3½ hours revising this scene and shot only 29 seconds of film. On the next day, they spent 2½ hours making further revisions to the scene and shot only 95 seconds of film. This was the norm throughout the filming.[40] As Hepburn later boasted, "We wanted it to be as good as it could possibly be. Nothing was ever too much trouble."[41]

Photograph 13.25 As David seethes, Susan (Katharine Hepburn) explains to her aunt (May Robson) why he "just went gay all of the sudden" in *Bringing Up Baby*.
Source: author's screen capture

The studio leaned on Hawks to speed up, but he continued at his own pace.[42] Filming started on September 23 and it was scheduled to finish on November 20, but at that point they were only halfway there. The cast and crew took just one day for the Thanksgiving holiday, and then spent fifteen days filming the jail scenes. The daily reports from the set offered explanations such as "rewriting seven script pages" and "four hours rewriting scenes" to explain why as little as 24 seconds of film was shot in an entire day. Filming halted for Christmas Day and New Year's Day but otherwise continued through the holidays. Finally, on January 6, 1938, *Bringing Up Baby* was completed just before midnight.[43] By this time, the production costs had ballooned from the budgeted $768,000 to $1,073,000. Most of the extra money went to Hawks, Hepburn, and Grant. They were on weekly salaries, which meant that the extra time was very lucrative for them: Hawks's salary rose from a budgeted $88,000 to $202,5000, Hepburn's from $72,500 to $122,000, and Cary's from $75,000 to $123,000.[44]

The director and his stars were sure that the extra expense was worthwhile and that they would be vindicated when the film became a hit. Cary was so committed to *Bringing Up Baby* that he joined Hawks and the film editor George Hively in the cutting room and played an "important advisory role" in trimming the film to a lean 102 minutes.[45] On January 17, just eleven days after filming was completed, the film was rushed to preview audiences in the Inglewood and Huntington Park suburbs of Los Angeles. Everyone involved in making the film held their breath until the audience started laughing and then let out a huge sigh of relief when the laughs came thick and fast.[46] The trade papers raved about it too. *Bringing Up Baby* was deemed "hilarious" by *Variety*, and "easily the best comedy of the year" by *The Hollywood Reporter*, while the *Motion Picture Herald* described watching the film with a preview audience who "laughed until tears came, slapped their thighs, punched each other in the ribs, chuckled, chortled and howled."[47]

The film was released on the West Coast in mid-February, and it did excellent business in cities such as Los Angeles, San Francisco, and Portland.[48] Then something strange happened. The curmudgeonly *New York Times* critic, Frank S. Nugent, found the film's slapstick humor to be overly familiar and he advised readers that they would find the film funny only "if you've never been to the movies."[49] In the *New Yorker*, John C. Mosher was not quite so damning, but he diminished the film by calling it a "flibbertygibberty farce."[50] Other commentators piled in, complaining that the slapstick humor was old-fashioned and that Hepburn was not suited to "goofy comedy."[51] As a result, the all-important and closely monitored New York City release turned out to be a disaster. It was booked to play for two weeks in one of the city's biggest and best venues, Radio City Music Hall, but it had to be pulled after a slow first week.[52]

Bringing Up Baby was by no means an outright failure in 1938, but it suffered from hostile responses from two quite different corners: metropolitan audiences suspected that the film's slapstick was beneath them, while rural and "neighborhood" audiences continued to steer clear of Katharine Hepburn.[53] Hence, the film did not come close to covering its high production costs in 1938, and even a re-release in 1941, when it could ride on the coattails of *The Philadelphia Story*, did not bring it into profit.[54] Its reputation improved through repeated TV screenings from the 1950s onward, and also through screenings in repertory theaters in the 1960s and 1970s. By the 1970s, the film's combination of slapstick humor and sexual innuendo was regarded not only as hilariously funny but also slyly subversive. It became a vintage screwball classic, and it still stands today as one of the most popular and admired film comedies.[55]

This fine reputation was nowhere to be seen in 1938. When the film faltered at the box office, both Howard Hawks and Katharine Hepburn were booted out of RKO.[56] *Bringing Up Baby* was actually Cary's third loss-maker at RKO, after *Sylvia Scarlett* and *The Toast of New York*, but he emerged unscathed from every debacle. He was not held responsible for the high costs and modest returns in the same way that Hawks and Hepburn were, and, unlike them, he had two recent hit films to his credit. *Topper* and *The Awful Truth* were still in circulation when *Bringing Up Baby* was released. RKO wisely decided to maintain his contract, and he very quickly became the studio's biggest star.

If his first year as a freelancer ended badly for his colleagues, it was nothing short of a triumph for him personally. His income skyrocketed from $52,000 in 1936 to nearly $250,000 in 1937.[57] More importantly, the three films he made that year ensured that he would never be forgotten. With McCarey and Hawks guiding him, he developed a star personality that would serve him for the remainder of his career, and he realized that improvisation was needed to fuel his spontaneity on-screen. In later years, he compared improvisational acting to playing jazz, explaining that the scene starts with a "a central theme" and then the actors must improvise but "never lose sight of the original mood, key or rhythm, no matter how far out they go." He credited both McCarey and Hawks with allowing him to explore the parameters of improvisation.[58]

From Hawks's perspective, Cary Grant had simply found himself as an actor. Speaking in 1938, Hawks said that "he's doing things now, little gestures, facial expressions, that he wouldn't have dared to do when he first came to Hollywood, because he lacked confidence. Now he's got it. Confidence brings poise and polish and what I call 'style' to a player. Once a performer has it, his reading of his lines and his reactions take on a sparkle. Cary right now is hot."[59] Coming from a man who had just lost his job, this was a generous yet accurate appraisal of Cary's talent and his status. From this point onward, everyone in Hollywood wanted to work with him. It was unlikely that a screwball comedy would be made without the script being offered to him first, or at least having the male lead defined as a Cary Grant type. He found his métier, but he was still keen to experiment and to see just how far he could go without ever losing sight of the character and image he created.

14

"Just a line enclosing a few snaps," Elsie Leach wrote to her son, "Do you think they look anything like me, Archie?" The letter arrived in October 1937, while he was filming *Bringing Up Baby*, and the accompanying photographs showed that Elsie had been transformed since her release from the asylum fourteen months earlier. Her gray hair had been dyed brown and carefully cut and curled in the short, neat style of the period, and in each of the photographs she proudly models different dresses—all fashionably tailored—as well as matching hats, gloves, and handbags. Now sixty years old, Elsie was enjoying her new freedom and affluence. "I am still young old mother," she joked in the letter, taking pride in her smart and stylish appearance.[1]

After her release, she lived for a few months with her brother, Charles Kingdon, in south London, but she missed her hometown, and she wanted to live independently, and so it was agreed that as an interim step toward complete independence, she would live in a guest house in Clifton, the smart neighborhood that she was so proud to have been born in. A monthly allowance from Cary, paid through a firm of London solicitors, enabled her to afford this. The guest house, in a fine Georgian terrace on Whiteladies Road, had the additional attraction of being across the street from one of the city's newest picture houses, the Embassy, where she would watch her son's films, sometimes over and over again.[2]

Cary could be proud that he provided his mother with everything that she needed, but it was difficult for him to accept that he was what she wanted most. Her letters, from the first, pleaded with him to visit her. She longed to recover the family life that she lost twenty years earlier, and she did not express any anger or resentment toward the husband who had left her in the asylum for so long. "No man shall take the place of your father," she wrote in her first letter. She insisted that she would not reach a settlement regarding her husband's pension, or seek a home of her own, until Cary came to Bristol. To her Victorian mindset, these were men's affairs. "I am desperately longing waiting anxiously every day to hear from you. Do try and come over soon," she wrote. This first letter was sent in an envelope addressed in small, uncertain handwriting to "Mr A.A. Leach, Cary Grant, Actor, Paramount Studios,

Photograph 14.26 After her release from the asylum, Elsie Leach sent her son several photographs showing her looking stylish and well-groomed.
Source: The Cary Grant Papers, courtesy of the Margaret Herrick Library

Hollywood, California," indicating that she did not know her own son's private address, and she did not know that he had left Paramount eight months earlier.[3]

In later years, when Cary spoke about his renewed relationship with his mother, he always insisted that it was her choice to stay in Bristol, and that she would never have dreamed of visiting him, let alone coming to live with him, in faraway California.[4] Her letters, and Cary's own correspondence with the solicitors, indicate that this was not true. She frequently expressed her lone-liness and her longing to see him in plaintive terms: "I do my darling wish you were nearer. I could see you more often. And do for you."[5] Occasionally, she also suggested that she could visit him: "I wish darling I was over with you. I am vexed to think you are so far away."[6] Most of his replies were made in brief cablegram messages that always conveyed love and good wishes but never offered so much as a hint of an invitation to California.[7] His London solicitors were aware that he did not want his mother to visit him. When Cary instructed the solicitors to give her £20 as a Christmas gift, they advised against it because they had observed that she was already saving as much of her monthly allowance as she could "with a view to collecting enough money to pay for her fare to America." She received a silver serving tray instead of the money.[8]

As poignant as this situation seems, it is not hard to imagine Cary's re-luctance to bring his mother into his new life. He had grown up thinking that she had abandoned him, and suddenly, in his thirties, he was confronted with a mother who had been abandoned. This alone was difficult, but in addi-tion he had reinvented himself. No one called him Archie anymore—except his mother. She *always* addressed him as Archie, and he dutifully signed his letters to her with "Archie." Little wonder, then, that he did not want her in California. The only person in the world who still called him Archie, and made him call himself Archie, could not be allowed to intrude on his new life as Cary Grant.

It was a life lived among the wealthy and well connected. He was delighted by his own new wealth. His annual income in 1938, at $341,000, stood among the highest in Hollywood.[9] When he saw Fay Wray at a party, he was eager to tell her about it. "Nikki, I'm so *rich*," he said, and she could not help but notice that he made "rich" sound like it was all that he needed to be.[10] Publicly, he was more circumspect when discussing his income, turning the conversation into one about the extraordinary rate of income tax applied to his earnings.[11] This was a tactic he most likely learned from his many wealthy friends.

His closest friends remained Randolph Scott and Howard Hughes, and fi-nancial investing was one of their prime topics of conversation.[12] He had also become close friends with the Countess di Frasso, who had started life as the American heiress Dorothy Taylor and then married the elderly Carlo, Count Dentice di Frasso. The Count inherited a magnificent sixteenth-century es-tate overlooking the city of Rome, the Villa Madama, and his American wife supplied him with the money for its upkeep and renovation. But Dorothy di

Frasso found life among the Italian aristocracy a little dull, and so she spent much of her time in Beverly Hills. She had no interest in filmmaking but she enjoyed the lavish social occasions. A determinedly frivolous woman, she made Cary laugh and distracted him from his bouts of gloom and anxiety.[13]

Noel Coward, the doyen of café society, was another very stylish and well-connected friend with a penchant for frivolity. Coward loved the Ocean Front beach house, and it became a matter of routine that he stayed with Cary and Randy on his semi-annual trips to Hollywood.[14] Cary also maintained his friendship with Marion Davies and the Hearst family long after his divorce from Virginia. He was friends with both the seventy-five-year-old newspaper titan William Randolph Hearst Sr. and his son, thirty-year-old William Randolph Hearst Jr., and he often spent weekends with one or both of them at San Simeon. He became such a frequent guest at the palatial estate that he started requesting a different bedroom on each visit, aiming to achieve the distinction of spending the night in every one of the estate's many guest bedrooms.[15]

When Davies threw a huge circus-themed party over a weekend at San Simeon, Hollywood's high society costumed themselves appropriately. Tyrone Power and Sonja Henie came as clowns, Carole Lombard and Clark Gable were in Wild West gear, Bette Davis was the bearded lady, and Irene Dunne was a tightrope walker. But the most dramatic entrance was made by Cary and a large group of his friends: Randy, their neighbor Townsend Netcher, Hal Roach and his wife, Mervyn LeRoy and his wife, Harry Joe Brown and Sally Eilers, and Florence Lake. They came as the acrobatic troupe "The Flying San Simeons," costumed with pink silk shirts emblazoned with the troupe's name, white pantaloons with a frilled sash, and ballet slippers.[16] Cary had come a very long way from his own days as an acrobat.

The fan magazines and gossip columns characterized him as a "man about town" and a "bachelor at large."[17] This fit with his screen personality but there was also some truth to this characterization of his private life. His relationship with Mary Brian lasted for a year after they made *The Amazing Quest* together, but when she began to talk about marriage and children, he refused to commit and they parted.[18] Some supposed that his relationship with Countess di Frasso was a romantic one, and they did attend some public occasions together, including the premiere of *Topper*, but it is unlikely that he became romantically involved with a married woman sixteen years his senior.[19] He was attracted to young, refined, very slight, blonde women. One of them was Roberta Mullineaux Cooper, who was described by journalists as a "Pasadena debutante."[20] Another was RKO's top female star, Ginger Rogers. Cary was "head over heels in love" with Rogers while making *Topper*, according to Hal Roach, but Rogers insisted that she and Cary should be friends and not lovers.[21] Cary soon met another blonde actress, Phyllis Brooks, with whom he quickly became very serious.[22]

Phyllis Steiller had changed her last name to Brooks when she was signed by Universal Pictures in 1934. She had started working as a model when she was still in her teens because her upper-middle-class family had lost its money in the Wall Street Crash. She became the "Ipana Girl"—that is, the face of a brand of toothpaste—and it is easy to see why. She had a dazzlingly warm smile. Modeling quickly led to film work, and she was just twenty-two when she met Cary at a party at Marion Davies's beach house in the summer of 1937. He was there with Ginger Rogers, and Phyllis thought that they both looked slightly ridiculous. He was "so tanned he was almost

Photograph 14.27 Phyllis Brooks and a very tanned Cary Grant at his Santa Monica beach house, circa 1938.

Source: The Cary Grant Papers, courtesy of the Margaret Herrick Library

black" and Ginger was "lobster red." She thought nothing more of it until she met him again at the Mocambo nightclub a few nights later. He invited her to Ocean Front for a Sunday party and from there their relationship steadily developed to the point that everyone assumed they would marry, including Phyllis herself.[23] They were regularly photographed at premieres and spotted at fashionable nightclubs and restaurants: the Brown Derby, the Cocoanut Grove, and the Trocadero. Another, less public side to their relationship can be seen in Cary's home movies. He filmed her many times, the camera lingering on her as she sunbathed, played with the dog, and posed for him. Seen through his lens, their affection for one another is abundantly clear.

They both worked hard. Cary made four films back-to-back in his first year as a freelancer. Phyllis was under contract to Twentieth Century-Fox and had prominent roles in Shirley Temple's films and in the popular *Charlie Chan* detective series. When working, they often had quiet nights at home. She remembers that Cary was forever trying to learn to play "Rhapsody in Blue" on the piano, and that they played backgammon "all the time." They had dinners at home with Randy, whose hasty marriage to Marion duPont had lasted less than a year. He was now seeing Paramount's "jungle princess," Dorothy Lamour, who joined what Phyllis fondly recalled as "the nucleus" at the beach house.[24] Their other close friends were Hollywood's most reclusive couple, Katharine Hepburn and Howard Hughes. Phyllis observed that Hepburn and Hughes were "very much in love," and that they shared a paradoxical trait. They had both chosen to live public lives and yet they hated being seen in public. Phyllis had to find restaurants "with very dark corners" for their meals as a foursome.[25]

Cary's relationship with Hepburn continued to be strong on-screen as well as off. They went straight from making *Bringing Up Baby* at RKO to making the more sophisticated comedy *Holiday* (1938) at Columbia. Based on Philip Barry's 1928 Broadway play, *Holiday* was originally planned by the Columbia boss Harry Cohn as a film that would reunite the talent behind *The Awful Truth*, with Leo McCarey directing and Cary starring alongside Irene Dunne.[26] McCarey, however, did not want to return to such familiar ground so soon. He declined the offer, and Cohn turned to director George Cukor instead. Cukor then insisted that Hepburn rather than Dunne should play the lead. Cohn seldom yielded to the demands of his directors, but in January 1938, amid the initially rapturous responses to *Bringing Up Baby*, he agreed to borrow Hepburn from RKO.[27] Irene Dunne lost the part and, by her own admission, she was so devastated when she heard the news that she spent a weekend "crying her eyes out."[28]

Hepburn was the better choice. Dunne was a little too mature, at the age of thirty-nine, to play an heiress rebelling against her wealthy father's materialism and social snobbery. Hepburn was younger and feistier, and she had understudied the lead role of *Holiday* when the play was on Broadway ten years earlier. Over the course of its eight-month run, she had learned every nuance of the dialogue and humor while watching from the wings night after night.[29] She also had a unique on-screen chemistry with Cary that was just right for this film. He brought out something more playful and less prim in her, while she brought out something more down to earth and less glamorous in him. George Cukor encouraged this. Cukor was never interested in the debonair Cary Grant, but he was always interested in revealing at least some of the rough edges around Cary's smooth façade. In *Holiday* as in *Sylvia Scarlett*, he urged Cary to allow at least a bit of Archie Leach to seep into his performance.[30]

Cary's character, Johnny Case, is an ordinary fellow who finds himself caught up in the world of the extraordinarily wealthy, but rather than playing this as Cary Grant—a man who learned to be at home in that world—Cary plays it as an interloper. Johnny Case's suit is off the peg and slightly rumpled, his bow tie is unfashionable and slightly askew, and his hair is just a little unruly. When he speaks about his hard-luck childhood ("I've been working since I was ten"), a bit of Archie's background comes through. When he suddenly performs forward-flips and cartwheels, springing gleefully across the floor on his hands, Archie's former life as a "tumbler" is referenced more directly.

Johnny Case is an "everyman" role, and this was a welcome addition to Cary's repertoire. After playing the irresponsible millionaire of *Topper*, the wealthy playboy of *The Awful Truth*, and the highly-strung paleontologist of *Bringing Up Baby* (1938), it was time to play a less eccentric character.[31] In *Holiday*, he serves as a natural point of identification for audiences, who observe the lifestyle of the ostentatiously rich through Johnny's eyes. It is no surprise when Johnny sours on the idea of marrying the heiress he met on holiday, Julia Seton (Doris Nolan). She wants to polish him up, get him a job with her family's banking firm, and lead him into her Park Avenue lifestyle. But Johnny is unimpressed by the family's wealth ("I don't want too much money, more than I need to live by"), and he gradually falls for Julia's more idealistic and unconventional sister, Linda (Hepburn).

It is obvious from their first meeting that Johnny and Linda will fall in love but, as in *Bringing Up Baby*, their romance is surprisingly chaste. A single, brief kiss in the very last shot—just before the final fade-out—is all that we see. In the tradition of screwball comedy, Cukor signals their attraction to one other through childish mischief rather than adult sexuality. Johnny stays with Linda in the mansion's attic playroom when Julia insists that he attends the black-tie occasion in the formal rooms downstairs. It is the free-spirited Linda, not Julia, who admires Johnny's handsprings, and it is Linda who eagerly climbs on top of his shoulders to perform a double somersault with him. Once again, as in the finale of *Bringing Up Baby*, Hepburn performed this stunt herself and took lessons in the art of tumbling from Cary.[32] Or, at least, she performed part of it. She stands high on his shoulders, ready to tumble, but then stunt doubles perform the rest of the maneuver.

These hijinks aside, *Holiday* is a quieter film than *Bringing Up Baby*. Cukor was as interested in the family drama as he was in the wit and the clowning, and he achieved a satisfying balance between the two. He considered "opening up" the play, shooting a scene at a ski resort where Johnny and Julia are said to have met, but ultimately these outdoor scenes were discarded.[33] Instead, Cukor made a virtue of the story's staginess by focusing on the pitch-perfect performances of the cast. Edward Everett Horton (Cary's fey co-star in *Kiss and Make-Up* and *Ladies Should Listen*) and Jean Dixon play Johnny's bohemian friends. Lew Ayres is especially interesting as Julia and Linda's brother, whose alcoholism masks his own barely repressed resentments. Before filming began, Columbia announced that Ginger Rogers would play Julia, but it is not surprising that this did not pan out.[34] A major star would not want to play the rejected sister. Instead, the part went to the lesser-known Doris Nolan, who does not distract from Hepburn's sparky charisma.

Holiday delighted critics, with many admiring Cary's new "serious" side. It was also widely noted that, although the original play was first staged before the Wall Street Crash in 1928, ten years later the lingering Depression added weight to the story's critical stance toward bankers, elitism, and unfettered capitalism.[35] Katharine Hepburn's performance did not please everyone, including the *New York Times* critic Frank S. Nugent, who found her "very mannish" and "apt to grate on a man."[36] Hepburn's declining reputation may explain why so many writers have assumed that *Holiday* was a box-office flop. It is true that early in May 1938 she was branded as "box office poison" by an association of independent theater owners, and RKO promptly terminated her contract.[37] *Holiday*, however, was released later that month, and it proved to be very popular in the major metropolitan movie theaters. The *Motion Picture Herald* listed the film among eight "box-office champions" for the month of June, and the surveys published each week in *Variety* indicate strong receipts, including many holdover engagements, in most of the twenty big cities surveyed.[38] It was when *Holiday* went out to the cheaper rural and neighborhood theaters that it faltered. Reports from these much smaller, independent theaters are scattered and impressionistic, but they consistently refer to *Holiday* as a flop and point the finger of blame at Hepburn.[39]

Cary, once again proving immune to any criticism, was already preparing for his next role by the time *Holiday* was released. It was a form of preparation he always enjoyed: sunbathing. He decided that he needed an especially deep and dark tan to play a British soldier stationed on the northwest frontier of India in RKO's *Gunga Din* (1939). In May 1938, while he had a lull between films, he went to Hawaii for two weeks of sunbathing and sightseeing.[40] He took his movie camera, and the footage he shot once again demonstrates his fascination with ships going out to sea. Over and over again, on this trip and others, he filmed on deck as the ship moves out of the harbor, passing other ships and reaching the broad vista of the open sea. For a man who grew up in a busy port city, and longed as a boy to sail on the ships he saw in the harbor every day, filming these scenes was a way of recording wishes fulfilled many times over.

His wanderlust was probably the true reason for his two-week vacation. He did not really need to leave Ocean Front to work on his tan, and it is notable that he went to Hawaii without Phyllis Brooks. Nearly a year into their relationship, and with constant speculation in the press about whether or not they would marry, he may have been seeking time apart to think. If he was seeking solitude, he did not find it. Although many film stars visited the islands, Cary Grant's arrival was front-page news. The local paper not only reported that he was in town, but also informed readers that he was staying at the Royal Hawaiian Hotel on Waikiki Beach. This was an invitation to gawkers and autograph seekers. He had not yet come to the point where he loathed requests for his autograph so much that he often refused them. At this point, as the photographs in the local newspaper indicate, he was still smiling as he signed.[41]

Making *Gunga Din* offered another avenue of escape from domesticity and the pressure to marry. This big action-adventure comedy was filmed almost entirely on location, with the hills and mountains surrounding Lone Pine, California, standing in for India's northwest frontier. Lone Pine was a remote spot—six hours' drive from Los Angeles—and Cary spent most of the summer of 1938 there. A huge set was built—comprising an Indian town and an army camp—as well as living facilities for the six hundred people who worked and slept there, including two hundred extras on hand to populate the battle scenes. There were 220 horses, 32 mules, 6 goats, 4 elephants, and 3 dogs on location. It was a beautiful but harsh environment, and filming was halted by the frequent dust storms and occasional downpours, but the cast and crew worked every day, including Sundays, for two solid months at Lone Pine.[42]

Despite the hardships, Cary loved his summer on location. He had a small but private bungalow to live in, and his stand-in, Mel Merrihugh, probably suffered more time in the sun (as shots were lined up) than he did. For Cary, spending two months in the mountains and away from the studio grind was like going to summer camp. In all of the interviews he gave about the making of the film, over many years, he never had a bad word to say about it. "It was great fun," he remembered, "a lot of hard work but great fun."[43] Phyllis occasionally joined him at weekends but otherwise it was a very male environment. The few scenes involving the female lead, played by Joan Fontaine, were filmed mainly back at the studio. She spent just six days on location. Cary and the other leading stars, Douglas Fairbanks Jr. and Victor McLaglen, got into the boyish spirit of the film and enjoyed jokes and pranks with one another, but they could be competitive too. Their co-star, Sam Jaffe, recalled that if one of the three stars got a close-up, the other two would then insist that they should have a close-up of their own.[44]

The director, George Stevens, handled the stars' egos with care. This was the first of three films that Cary and Stevens made together, and it took Cary some time to discover that the director's softly spoken and vague demeanor masked a sharp, creative mind. Like all of Cary's favorite directors, Stevens did not shout orders or have bursts of temper. He maintained a quiet authority over the cast and crew while filming. And like all of Cary's favorite directors, Stevens treated his actors as collaborators and encouraged improvisation on the set.[45] He was another veteran of the Hal Roach Studios, where he worked with Laurel and Hardy and many other slapstick comedians.[46] On the set of *Gunga Din*, Cary found that Stevens did not act out scenes himself in the way that Leo McCarey did, demonstrating how they should be played, but Stevens did "come in with all sorts of gags, sight gags, wanting to try them out."[47] Douglas Fairbanks Jr. had similar memories. "George and Cary and myself would sit around most of the morning and try out the scene, rehearsing and making alterations, [then] send them in to be rewritten, [and then] revise them again. We wouldn't really get down to filming till after lunch."[48]

Gunga Din had originally been Howard Hawks's project, but after the delays and budget overruns on *Bringing Up Baby*, RKO no longer trusted Hawks with it.[49] The studio's new chief of production, Pandro Berman, aimed to make a spectacular, epic film. He therefore allowed an extraordinarily high budget of $1.3 million, which provided for star salaries as well as an unusually long shoot of 78 days, and he assigned the film to Stevens, who was considered to be the more efficient, trustworthy director. It is ironic, then, that Stevens—like Hawks on *Bringing Up Baby*—began rewriting and improvising scene after scene at Lone Pine, and waiting hours to get the right light, or halting filming for the day because of the wrong light. Back in Hollywood, Berman watched with dread as production costs ballooned to $1.9 million—the highest recorded at RKO at that time—and the shoot extended to 101 days.[50]

Berman found little comfort when he viewed the rushes that were sent from Lone Pine to Hollywood every day. Stevens was meant to be making a British Empire film akin to Paramount's *Lives of a Bengal Lancer* (1935), Twentieth Century-Fox's *Wee Willie Winkie* (1937), and Warner Bros.' *The Charge of the Light Brigade* (1937)—films that follow a line of earnest imperialism—but he was actually mixing high melodrama and broad comedy.[51] In his hands, *Gunga Din* became "a mad satire," as Cary described the film in later years.[52] Berman was so mystified by this approach that he considered shutting the film down. The investment was too big to write off, though, and so he allowed Stevens to continue but implored him to complete the film as soon as possible.[53]

Stevens insisted on rewriting the script that Howard Hawks had prepared with screenwriters Ben Hecht and Charles MacArthur.[54] Their script was partly based on the Rudyard Kipling poem, "Gunga Din," about an Indian *bhisti*, or water boy, who faithfully serves a British regiment even though the soldiers are callous and abusive toward him. Hecht and MacArthur also incorporated the characters from Kipling's *Soldiers Three* stories: a trio of rambunctious British soldiers stationed in India. To this mix, they added a touch of their own play, *The Front Page*, and its story about a Chicago newspaper reporter who wants to get married and move to New York but is stymied by the machinations of an editor who doesn't want to lose him. Hence, in *Gunga Din*, the tight-knit friendship of a trio of soldiers is threatened when one announces that he intends to marry and leave the army, but the other two plot and scheme to undermine his plans and make him re-enlist.[55]

The British character actor Victor McLaglen was cast as the elder Sergeant MacChesney. A former pugilist, McLaglen was perfect for the role of this gruff and tough career army man. Douglas Fairbanks Jr. was cast as the softly spoken and romantic Sergeant Ballantine, who wants to leave the army and marry Emmy Stubbins (Joan Fontaine). In later years, Fairbanks liked to tell the tale that he and Cary flipped a coin to determine who would play Ballantine and who would play the third soldier, the excitable and mischievous cockney Sergeant Cutter.[56] This made a good showbiz anecdote, but Pandro Berman recalled the casting in more realistic terms. Berman said that he asked Cary to play Ballantine, but Cary adamantly refused and insisted that he should play Cutter instead. Berman was impressed by his choice. "He knew what he was doing," Berman recalled. "He hated the straight part. It was a dull part and he knew that he could get something wonderful out of the other one."[57]

He did get something wonderful out of the part. Cary brought a boyish glee to the role of Cutter, a fun-loving, impulsive lad who is eager for adventures. It was the first leading role in his film career that did not involve a romance, and the first since *Sylvia Scarlett* to take him out of drawing rooms. Once again, he was a cockney, and although his character was identified only as "Cutter" in the script, in the film he is given the first name "Archibald" as a nod to Cary's own working-class origins. His vaudeville training is evident in his perfectly timed, wide-eyed double takes and expressions of surprise. One of the funniest scenes, when Cutter and MacChesney spike a bowl of punch at Ballantine's engagement party, is performed silently, and Cary's training in "the fine art of mime" is ably demonstrated.

His voice, too, is a perfectly honed comic instrument. His cockney accent has a boyish quality that makes the character endearingly unworldly. He whinnies with excitement and growls with anger. When he challenges MacChesney to a fistfight, he jabs and dances around him in a ridiculously overwrought manner. It is a marvelous comic performance, and it is remarkable that, no matter how outlandishly he behaves, he remains as attractive as ever on-screen. His shorter-than-usual haircut, trimmer physique, and dark tan made him unusually dashing in *Gunga Din*. He achieves the rare combination of being both absurd and strikingly handsome.

The problem with the film, at least for modern audiences, is its colonial perspective. Stevens and his scriptwriters, Fred Guiol and Joel Sayre, tempered this in some important respects. They cut the overtly racist language that was in Hecht and MacArthur's script, which had the British soldiers referring to the character Gunga Din as "black scum," an "ape," a "baboon," a "chimp," and a "monkey." They cut MacChesney's repeated physical abuse of the character, which included kicking him, shoving him, dragging him by the ear, and "shaking him as if he were a rag."[58] And they introduced slapstick humor as a means of deflating the pompous tone that was common to British Empire films of this era.[59] However, the Stevens-Guiol-Sayre script introduced new racist elements to the story, including making the villains the "Thuggee," a cult of bloodthirsty natives who oppose British rule.[60] Stevens also cast white actors in the Indian roles, using brownface to disguise them. Even the role of the heroic Indian water boy, Gunga Din himself, was given to the American actor Sam Jaffe, who darkened his skin and assumed an exaggeratedly servile manner for the film.

None of this caused much concern when the film was released in the United States in January 1939.[61] Otis Ferguson, writing in the *New Republic*, was the only prominent critic to condemn the film as "irresponsible and wrong" and to point out that the title character was an Uncle Tom figure.[62] Otherwise, critics praised *Gunga Din* for its brilliant cinematography, spectacular scenery, exciting battle scenes, and humor.[63] Audiences concurred. RKO held four preview screenings two months before the release, testing audience responses, and the comment cards demonstrate almost unanimous enthusiasm for the film.[64] It became a box-office smash—one of the biggest hits of Hollywood's "golden year" of 1939—and it played to packed movie theaters for many weeks.[65] It eventually earned over $2 million in North America and another $2 million in foreign markets, which meant that it recouped its extraordinary production costs and turned a profit.[66] Predictably, it was a big hit in Britain, where it was released in the months leading up to the outbreak of the Second World War, but it was banned in parts of India, where British Empire films often caused offense.[67]

Gunga Din was an important film for Cary. He was the top-billed star in one of the biggest box-office hits of the era, confirming his new status as one of the most bankable stars in Hollywood. It was also a further demonstration of his range as an actor, and proof of his appeal beyond the high-toned settings of screwball comedy. *The Hollywood Reporter* highlighted this in its review of *Gunga Din*: "There seems to be no end to the lad's ingenuity in thinking up new characterizations for himself and making them stick. He's grand."[68]

Henceforth, he was in greater demand. He was offered just about every leading film role that a man between the ages of twenty and sixty could play, but his ongoing obligations to both Columbia and RKO meant that he missed out on some films that he was keen to do. MGM's *Ninotchka* (1939) was one of these. Ernst Lubitsch was directing Greta Garbo in her first comedy, and Cary had long admired the reclusive star.[69] "I'm so happy you met me," he spluttered nervously at her when their mutual friend Noel Coward arranged a casual introduction at the Ocean Front house.[70] When scheduling difficulties prevented him from making the film, the role went to Melvyn Douglas instead.

Filming *Gunga Din* continued into October 1938, and afterward Cary took time off to visit Elsie in Bristol. During his summer at Lone Pine, he had been slow to respond to her letters, and she became increasingly anxious about when she would see him. Back in Los Angeles, he had a commitment to do a radio play of *Wings in the Dark* with Phyllis as his co-star, but then he departed—on his own—for New York and on to Southampton on the SS *Conte de Savoi*. This was his first visit with Elsie since she left the asylum, and he found it difficult. He was unaccustomed to the demands of family life, and he had a very extended family in Bristol. He complained after this trip that "aunts and cousins suffer hurt feelings when you call on other aunts and cousins."[71] It is likely that family tensions arose because he knew the Leach side of the family so much better than his mother's Kingdon side. Since his father's death, Cary listed his uncle John Leach as his next of kin on travel documents, and back in Santa Monica it was "Uncle John" and "Aunt Ro" (John Leach's wife, Rose) that he wrote to—rather than his Kingdon aunts and uncles—to ask about what he referred to as his mother's "condition."[72]

There were also tensions with Elsie. When he returned from the trip, a very emotional letter from her had already arrived, in which she expressed her surprise at hearing him on the BBC comedy series *Band Waggon* a few days after he had said goodbye to her in Bristol. She thought he had already left the country, and she was puzzled and hurt to hear him on the radio days later. She worried that she had "displeased" him in some way and she implored him to return "home"—to Bristol—as soon as he could.[73] A few weeks later another apologetic letter arrived. Again, her words suggest that their reunion had not gone well. "I felt ever so confused after so many years you have grown such a man," she wrote, adding, "I am more than delighted you have done so well." She thanked him for the brief cablegram she received from him that morning, and she ended her letter with her usual flurry of sentiments ("Your affectionate mother fondest love wishing you all the best").[74] This proved to be their pattern for many years. They were warm and sentimental at a distance and thrown off balance when together. They bewildered one another. As Elsie told him in her letters, she had nothing else to live for but him and wanted to see him whenever possible. Cary, on the other hand, dutifully looked after her financially and visited her whenever possible, but he was always eager to get away to the new life that he had made for himself.

15

His return to Hollywood began with a chilly mid-November crossing from Southampton to New York. These crossings, he had come to realize, were an opportunity to catch up with old friends and to make new ones. On this trip, Cary discovered Marlene Dietrich, Gracie Fields, and Jack Warner among his fellow passengers on the SS *Normandie*. He had become friendlier with Dietrich as the memory of making *Blonde Venus* faded, and because they had a mutual friend in Noel Coward. Although he did not know Fields, he was keen to share memories of music hall days with the stage veteran who was now a top film star in her native Britain. Warner was the powerful head of Warner Bros., and he would be an important friend for Cary in the future.[1]

When the *Normandie* docked in New York on Thanksgiving Day, 1938, Phyllis was waiting at the gangplank when he disembarked.[2] She had flown across the country to enjoy a week on the town with him. Their time in New York began well, with a few evenings of dancing and trips to the theater, including the frenetic hit comedy *Hellzapoppin'*, which Cary especially enjoyed.[3] Their New York holiday took a turn for the worse when Cary was suddenly subpoenaed to testify before a New York grand jury investigating an investment swindle involving Philippine bonds. A dozen Hollywood stars were targeted by the swindlers, including Cary, but he had not invested in the bonds and he had never met the accused swindler. This did not stop the city's tabloid newspaper, the *Daily News*, from snapping his picture as he left the courthouse and printing it beneath a headline labeling him a "Sucker."[4]

Much worse was to come. Phyllis thought she had caught a cold in New York, but she had developed bronchial pneumonia, a life-threatening illness even to the young at this time before penicillin was available. Cary and Phyllis stayed a few extra days in New York, hoping to return to Los Angeles when she got better, but after a week they decided to go ahead and make the cross-country journey with a nurse hired to look after her on the train. En route, her fever began spiking up to 105 degrees Fahrenheit. By the time they reached Los Angeles, she was unconscious and Cary had to carry her in his arms from the train to an ambulance waiting to take her to the hospital. For days, her life hung in the balance. Cary did his best to be cheerful with her, but he broke down in tears when he told friends about her condition. Finally, as Christmas approached, she began to improve, but she spent the holidays in bed and did not fully recover for another month.[5]

Phyllis lived with her mother, Daisy Steiller. Like Blanche Cherrill, Daisy Steiller did not like Cary Grant one bit. According to Phyllis, her mother was "a strict Victorian" and she was ashamed and embarrassed by her daughter's "open relationship" with Hollywood's most famous bachelor.[6] In fact, Cary and Phyllis did not openly live together. The morality clauses in studio contracts, as well as the mores of the times, prevented that, but Phyllis spent many nights and weekends at Ocean Front, and they were seen traveling together. This was enough to set her mother against him. The promise that they would someday be married carried no weight because a date had not been set. The disapproving Mrs. Steiller was therefore unimpressed when Cary bought Phyllis a mink coat for Christmas, and Cary was distinctly uncomfortable visiting his fiancée while she was recuperating in her mother's house.[7]

Under these tense circumstances, it was fitting that he returned to Los Angeles to make a somber, emotionally restrained film. *Only Angels Have Wings* (1939) was Howard Hawks's first film for Columbia, where he found refuge after falling out with RKO over *Bringing Up Baby*. Columbia's more limited resources are apparent in the film's small-scale reproduction of its setting. There was no budget for location shooting or big sets in the style of *Gunga Din*. Instead, the (fictional) South American port city of Barranca is seen only at night, with fog and rain ensuring that scenes can be contained within tight sets. Hawks, no doubt eager to demonstrate that he could keep costs down, used these limitations well. The dark, claustrophobic atmosphere is entirely in keeping with the story.

Cary plays Geoff Carter, the hard-bitten, cynical boss of an aviation firm that sends its pilots to carry airmail over steep mountains and in all weathers, despite the risk to their lives. Geoff is tough, steady, and cool under this pressure, and so too are his pilots (a wonderful ensemble cast including Thomas Mitchell and Richard Barthelmess). The men bond over their shared sense of duty and fate, and shut out their fears and anguish. When one of the younger pilots, Joe (Noah Beery Jr.), is killed in a crash landing, the others show no emotion. "Who's Joe?" they all ask when a newcomer insists that they should mourn him.

The newcomer is a Brooklyn showgirl named Bonnie Lee (Jean Arthur), who has been touring South America and is now on her way home. She is angry at the men's apparent callousness over Joe, but she is also drawn to Geoff Carter, and she stays on in the dismal port city to see if she can warm his cold heart. Bonnie almost pleads with him to show some emotion or express some interest in her. "I'm hard to get," she tells him; "All you have to do is ask!" Cary had come a long way from his Paramount films. All of those earnest declarations of love ("I'm *mad* about you") were now a thing of the past. As a freelance star, his characters were not always as hard-hearted and inaccessible as Geoff Carter, but they would almost always be the object of desire, eagerly sought after by his formidable co-stars.

Jean Arthur had established herself as a major star in Frank Capra's films, typically playing smart working women, such as a reporter in *Mr. Deeds Goes to Town* (1936) and a stenographer in *You Can't Take It With You* (1938). Arthur was shy and did not participate in the Hollywood social scene. She and Cary had never met prior to *Only Angels Have Wings*, but he admired her acting and looked forward to working with her.[8] When filming began, however, he was surprised to find that she was riddled with self-doubt and could not hide her anxiety on the set (as he at least tried to do). She, in turn, was put off by the bonhomie evident between Cary and Howard Hawks. She accused Cary of trying to steal scenes from her and she accused Hawks of letting him do it.[9] "We just never got along," Cary recalled years later, still dismayed that she caused such a fuss on the set and that she refused to take direction from Hawks.[10]

He and Arthur have some good moments together in the film. When she shows off to him by playing the Cuban jazz song "Peanut Vendor" on the piano, he responds by bellowing the lyric—"pea---nuts"—with perfect timing. They share a passionate kiss and a few tender scenes that lend some complexity to his hard-hearted role. Off-screen, however, there was discord. The tension arose because Hawks wanted her to adopt a more suggestive manner. She flatly refused, telling him, "I can't do that kind of stuff."[11] She insisted on delivering her lines in the wholesome Midwestern tones better suited to a Capra film, which meant that she did not sound anything like a showgirl wandering through South America. She did not look the part, either. Wearing a blazer and a high-collared blouse, she appears to be dressed for office work rather than the rowdy barrooms of South America. Cary, by contrast, wears a gaucho's hat, a low-slung gun holster, an aviator's leather jacket, and cowboy boots. This rather exotic outfit suggests his character is in Barranca to stay.

To be fair to Jean Arthur, Hawks also made the only other woman in the film very nervous. The twenty-year-old Rita Hayworth had her first major role in *Only Angels Have Wings*, playing Judy, the woman who once broke

Geoff Carter's heart. Midway through the film, she turns up married to another flier (Richard Barthelmess). Hawks wanted Hayworth to be show-stoppingly sensuous—the audience needed to understand why she would have had such an impact on Geoff—but he had difficulty directing her.[12] She found Hawks cold and patronizing, and she was very grateful when Cary stepped in to help. "Cary Grant was so lovely and kind to me," she recalled. "Mr. Hawks asked me to do certain things that I was very unhappy about, but between Cary and Hawks I did it. Cary is more genteel about these things."[13]

Hayworth's role was not a major one, but she made quite an impact. Playing Judy set her on the path to stardom and, strangely, it also led to one of the most famous lines in Cary's career. He does not actually say "Judy, Judy, Judy" in the film, but comedians could not resist imitating his staccato pronunciation of "*Ju*-dey" and they found that saying it three times in rapid succession—"*Ju*-dey, *Ju*-dey, *Ju*-dey"—was particularly evocative and funny. It became the most famous line he never said.[14]

Only Angels Have Wings is now acclaimed as a classic film, but it received good rather than great reviews when it was released in May 1939. Many critics considered it an aviation film first and foremost, and although they thought it was a fine aviation film, they also thought the formula was a little tired.[15] Initially, audiences seem to have agreed because, although it was a box-office success, it was not a big hit.[16] It was over the next few years that its reputation steadily grew as a result of repeated revivals. During the war years, especially, the film never seems to have gone out of circulation. Its moody atmosphere, the camaraderie of the men, and the ever-present threat of death made it a more timely film in wartime than it had been in peacetime.

It is not as well known as Michael Curtiz's *Casablanca* (1942) but in many respects *Only Angels Have Wings* influenced *Casablanca*, not only in its exotic setting and dark visual design, but also in its lead character. Like Geoff Carter, *Casablanca*'s Rick refuses to commit to anybody or anything, and his tough exterior conceals a deeply repressed emotional vulnerability. Hawks cast Humphrey Bogart and John Wayne in these hard-bitten roles too, and he reflected in later years that he had to temper each star's approach to revealing the hard-bitten character's vulnerable side. Getting this right was like walking a tightrope, he said, commenting that John Wayne could easily get "corny" and Humphrey Bogart could be "insensitive." With Cary, Hawks said, the concern was that he could be "oversensitive" and reveal too much of the character's vulnerability.[17] In *Only Angels Have Wings*, though, Cary gets it just right. It is the eventual revelation of his sensitivity—in the romantic scenes with Arthur and with Hayworth, and when he quietly and stoically sheds a tear over the death of Thomas Mitchell's character—that brings the character of Geoff Carter to life.

Few actors could have played both the boyish, happy-go-lucky Archibald Cutter of *Gunga Din* and the tough, repressed Geoff Carter of *Only Angels Have Wings*, and few stars would play such different characters within the space of a single year. Cary, however, was determined not be typecast, and now that he could choose his own films, he aimed to play a wide range of roles. Diversity, he had decided, was the key to a long-lasting career.[18] As soon as he had he finished making Hawks's very male melodrama at Columbia, he began working on a "woman's film" at RKO.

In Name Only (1939) was based on a popular romantic novel, *Memory of Love* (1935) by Bessie Breuer. It was an unlikely vehicle for Carole Lombard, who was best known as the zany heroine of screwball comedies, but Lombard also wanted to avoid typecasting, and she embraced this "weepie" as a welcome change of pace. She and Cary had known each other since his early days in Hollywood, when they were both under contract to Paramount. Although she was then a much better-established star, they moved in the same social circles and became friends. They shared two credits at Paramount, *Sinners in the Sun* (1932) and *The Eagle and the Hawk* (1933), but their characters' paths hardly crossed in these films. In 1936, Cary's growing resolve to leave Paramount was probably bolstered by Lombard's own decision to strike out freelance just a few months before him. While his freelance career swiftly ascended, hers was uneven, and by 1939 his recent box-office track record was significantly better than hers. Nevertheless, her savvy wheeling and dealing as a freelance star meant that for *In Name Only* she earned a salary of $100,000 and also had a clause in her contract giving her a bonus of $50,000 if the film's earnings surpassed $1.3 million.[19] Cary, who earned only a salary of $75,000, took note. A few months later, when he renegotiated his own RKO contract, he sought similar terms.

In late January 1939, Phyllis Brooks's first social outing since recovering from pneumonia was accompanying Cary to dinner at the home that Lombard shared with Clark Gable.[20] Cary was still only considering *In Name Only* at this stage, and the conversation inevitably turned to the story that would have a particular resonance for each of them.[21] For Lombard, this marital melodrama was a kind of public apologia for her relationship with Clark Gable. She and Gable had fallen in love a few years earlier, when Gable was separated from but still married to his second wife, Maria Langham, and over the next three years their affair became Hollywood's worst-kept secret. Langham held out for a significant financial settlement, and it was not until December 1938 that she agreed to a divorce.[22] It was in that same month that Lombard signed on to make *In Name Only*, a film that gave her the opportunity to portray the "other woman" not as a "home wrecker" but as the savior of a man trapped in an unhappy marriage by his cold and manipulative wife.[23]

Cary plays the husband, Alec Walker, who realizes that his wife, Maida (Kay Francis), married him only for his family's wealth and social position. Maida refuses to divorce him, and Alec seems resigned to a dismal life until he meets a lovely widow, Julie Eden (Lombard), and her young daughter, Ellen (Peggy Ann Garner). Maida schemes to make both her husband and his mistress look bad to friends and family, but when Alec becomes ill with pneumonia, Maida's treachery is finally revealed. Alex and Julie are reunited in a tearful hospital scene that had parallels in Cary's own response to Phyllis's recent bout with pneumonia. In the film's final fade-out, Alex is near to death and Julie swears to him that they can be together at last if only he can recover.

As many critics noted when *In Name Only* was released in August 1939, the film's story was a soap opera from start to finish, but the stars and John Cromwell's direction rendered it a compelling soap opera. Cary drew particular praise for a performance that begins with his usual debonair personality and then progresses through romantic ardor, bitter regrets, and, in the ending, a feverish sickbed scene that he plays like a delirious, bewildered child. Lombard, it was noted, completely abandoned her screwball personality and played Julie with intelligence and fragility.[24] In the *New York Times*, Kay Francis was also admired for playing the villainous wife as a "cat" with a "suave, superior and relentless" demeanor. Cromwell, known as a "tasteful" director, was recognized for handling the story in a "restrained" and "adult" manner.[25] Critical praise aside, though, the film was only a modest box-office hit by the standards of Cary Grant and Carole Lombard.[26] Audiences who enjoyed a soap opera may have found the film a little *too* tasteful for their liking, while fans of the two leads may have wished that they had made a screwball comedy together instead.

While Cary was filming *In Name Only*, Phyllis's health gradually improved, but when she was ready to return to work, Twentieth Century-Fox informed her that it was dropping her.[27] She announced to the press that she would freelance in future, but her career had never really taken off, and her options were limited. She found, like Virginia Cherrill, Mary Brian, and many other fading Hollywood stars before her, that the most lucrative offers came from British film producers eager to add some small measure of Hollywood glamour to their films. In late April, she embarked for London, where she would make two films at Elstree Studios.[28] Cary followed her as soon as *In Name Only* finished in June. Columnists were quick to speculate that they would be married there, but Cary denied this in his characteristically wry and roundabout way. He said that he was joining Phyllis in London "because it costs too much to telephone her every day from Hollywood."[29]

He was also eager to see his mother again. Since he last saw her in the autumn of 1938, Elsie had sent him a parcel for Christmas, a cigarette case for his birthday in January, a card for Valentine's Day, and ornamental eggs at Easter.[30] He was not good at writing back to her, and he did not remember her birthday in February. In March, she told him how eager she was to see him. "Well darling," she wrote, "I have been anxiously waiting to hear from you. But Mr. Davies [his London solicitor] tells me you are very busy. Archie darling don't work so hard. I would do anything you wish not for you to work so hard. I do wish you where [*sic*] nearer. I could see you more often. You are never out of my thoughts every minute of the day." Referring obliquely to the tension between them on his last visit, she wrote, "I shall feel more prepared to see you next time," and "If there is anything you disapprove of I am willing to be told."[31]

Cary sailed from New York to Britain on June 14, 1939, once again on the SS *Normandie*. When he reached London a week later, Phyllis was still busy filming, and so he spent most of his time with Elsie in Bristol. She was clearly doing well. She had a new, rented home of her own on Whiteladies Road, not far from the guest house she had been staying in, and she was able to live independently. When Cary arrived at Temple Meads train station, he enjoyed taking the bus up the hill from the station to her flat, imagining—for a moment at least—that he was still an ordinary Bristolian. Elsie was delighted to make one of his favorite dishes from childhood, a cottage pie, for him, and to have him at her table once again.[32]

He stayed at Bristol's Grand Hotel some nights, and on other nights he stayed with Phyllis in London and traveled down to Bristol for the day. His mission on this trip was to urge Elsie to move to a country cottage. With war on the horizon, and cities expected to be targeted in air raids, he hoped that she would agree to move further out of Bristol. Hence, he took her on long drives out of the city to see the surrounding towns and countryside. One day, they visited Clevedon, a nearby Victorian seaside resort, and on another day they drove through the beautiful Cheddar Gorge, 10 miles south of the city.[33] Cary's own home movies show his affection for Bristol and the rolling green countryside around the city. He focused his camera on familiar sights from childhood, filming Bishopston School, Fairfield School, the traffic coming down the very steep Park Street, the docks and warehouses that lined the city's harbor, and his old favorite, the Scala Cinema near Cotham Brow. For Phyllis's benefit, he also filmed a poster with her name on it, advertising the arrival of *Charlie Chan in Honolulu* (1939) in a local movie house.

He did not manage to convince Elsie to move to a country cottage, but eventually they reached a compromise. He bought a detached house for her on Howard Road in Westbury Park, a suburb of Bristol that was not likely to be high on the Luftwaffe's list of targets.[34] When he left Bristol for the last time on this trip, Elsie and a companion (probably his Aunt Rose Leach) saw him off at Temple Meads train station. He filmed them as they stood on the platform. Elsie giggles, as anyone might when a camera is pointed at them, but otherwise she looks sharp and fully in command of herself. In later years, this footage of them waving to him as the train departs, just two months before the outbreak of war, became particularly poignant. The war would prevent Elsie from seeing her son for more than six years, and "Aunt Ro" would be killed in the Blitz.

Signs of the impending war were everywhere in London during the summer of 1939. Cary's films show monuments such as the Marble Arch and Nelson's Column covered in placards that exhort the public to sign up for national service. The streets are full of people already in uniform, and, to fend off the anticipated air raids, barrage balloons hover over the city. It was an odd moment for a long European holiday, but this was the other reason for Cary's trip. Once Cary had seen Elsie, and Phyllis finished at Elstree, Cary and Phyllis set off for a four-week tour of the continent.

They traveled from Paris to Cannes and Monte Carlo (where Cary would later make *To Catch a Thief*), and then on to Rome, Naples, and Venice. In Rome, they stayed with the Countess di Frasso at her husband's family home, the palatial Villa Madama.[35] In Venice, they joined Hollywood friends Tyrone Power and Annabella, who were on an extended honeymoon.[36] Everywhere they went, Cary filmed not just the scenery, but also Phyllis, who sometimes mugs for the camera and always looks relaxed, beautiful, and deeply in love.

Their month together—far from the pressures and tensions of home— culminated with Cary asking Phyllis to marry him. They announced their engagement when they reached New York on August 8, having sailed from

Le Havre on the SS *Île de France*. The only proviso was that Cary did not want to marry until he had finished his next film. Columbia had summoned him home to start work on a new film with Howard Hawks. Working with Hawks was always a happy prospect for him, but the proposed starting date of August 15 left little time to arrange a wedding.[37]

The film was *His Girl Friday*, and it was Hawks's second reworking of *The Front Page*. This time he was not going so far as transplanting the story to India, as he did when developing the *Gunga Din* script, but he was making one very fundamental change. In Hecht and MacArthur's original story, the conniving newspaper editor Walter Burns wants to stop his best male reporter, Hildy Johnson, from marrying because marriage will entail Hildy leaving town and thus leaving his job. In *His Girl Friday*, however, Hawks turned the character of Hildy into a woman, and invented a back story in which Walter and Hildy were once married but now divorced. Hence, at the beginning of *His Girl Friday*, Hildy announces that she is remarrying and leaving town, and the sharpest of all screwball comedies is set in motion.

Hawks conceived of *His Girl Friday* with Cary in mind for the role of Walter Burns. Casting Hildy was more difficult. Jean Arthur was the obvious choice: she was under contract at Columbia, and her forte was playing spirited professional women like Hildy.[38] The problem was that after making *Only Angels Have Wings* Jean Arthur and Howard Hawks did not want to work together again.[39] Irene Dunne was the second choice, and studio boss Harry Cohn was keen to team her with Cary again. Dunne was not so sure. She prided herself on her ladylike image and found the character of Hildy too hard-bitten.[40] The start of filming was held up while the script was revised to accommodate her, but the role could not be softened to her satisfaction, and she backed out of the film in early September. Claudette Colbert, Joan Crawford, and Ginger Rogers reportedly turned down the role for the same reason.[41]

With filming now delayed by three weeks, Cohn arranged to borrow Rosalind Russell from MGM.[42] She was the perfect choice. As her comic turn in *The Women* (1939) had recently demonstrated, Russell had no qualms about appearing unladylike, and yet she was also attractive enough to be plausible as Cary Grant's ex-wife. She had the sharp tongue and quick wit needed to play Hildy, a reporter who can be "one of the boys" in the newsroom but is actually better than the boys at her job. When filming finally got underway on September 27, Russell (like Rita Hayworth and Jean Arthur before her) was uncomfortable with Hawks. She knew that she was not his first choice (or his second or third choice) to play Hildy and she found his quiet, icy manner unnerving. After a few days of work, she asked him if she was laying the comic banter on too thick. He assured her that she was not. "Keep doing what you're doing. Keep pushing Cary Grant around all you can," he instructed her.[43]

Cary and "Ross," as he called her, hit it off immediately. They came to understand that what the film lacked in terms of spectacle (it is set mainly in a few drab newsrooms and offices) would be made up for in their rapid-fire dialogue, banter, and barbs. Hawks encouraged them to improvise on the set, and to keep up a fast pace by overlapping their dialogue, talking over one another as people (and especially couples) often do. They had a fine time pushing each other around. When Cary was comfortable on a set, he could be full of jokes and pranks. "I loved working with him," Rosalind Russell said. She recalled that he played an entire scene with her, when she is typing and has her back to him, fully dressed from the waist up but without his trousers. When he walked across the room, she suddenly saw that he was in his underwear. It was "just a gag" and they "had to cut and start all over," but it matched the tone of irreverant, spontaneous fun that drives this film.[44]

Russell also observed that "Cary loved to ad-lib," and that "he could immediately go off into a spin and become any character that was called for." A friendly form of competition grew between them to see who could come up with the sharpest new material. Russell, who was new to this style of working, hired her own writer to help her match Cary's ad-libs. He then grew apprehensive about her contributions. "What have you got today?" he asked her warily each morning. One of her surprises was to throw her handbag at him in the middle of a scene. He ducked and, without losing a beat, he quipped, "Say, you're losing your eye. You used to pitch better than that!"[45]

As Walter and Hildy, they banter with one another so nimbly, and intertwine their barbs with such dexterity, that their antagonism toward one another comes across as a form of intimacy. Everything he says and does is wrapped up in cynicism. He dismisses their divorce ("Divorce doesn't mean anything these days"). He uses the Earl Williams news story—about the murder of an African American policeman—as just another means of manipulating Hildy. He dismisses the war news with an irreverence that was seldom heard in the films of this time ("Take Hitler and stick him on the funny page!"). Yet his confidence is momentarily knocked when Hildy tells him that she is going to marry another man. He slows down for a moment, looks contemplative, fidgets with his tie, and rubs his hands together

Photograph 15.28 In *His Girl Friday* (Columbia Pictures, 1940), Cary and Rosalind Russell's verbal fireworks distract from the drab settings.
Source: author's screen capture

absentmindedly. Only the darting of his eyes suggests that he is hatching a plan for his next move. When he places a carnation in his lapel—a vain, confident gesture—it is clear that he has his strategy in place and that he will do anything to get Hildy back.

If audiences go along with this, rooting for Walter's quest to prevent Hildy's impending marriage, it is partly attributable to her new fiancé. Ralph Bellamy plays Bruce Baldwin in the same slow-witted and laconic manner that he played the Oklahoma rancher engaged to Irene Dunne in *The Awful Truth*. In *His Girl Friday*, when Bruce tells Walter that he and Hildy are going to live in Albany with his mother, Walter says, "Oh that *will* be nice. A home in Albany—and with mother too," in the same smirking way that Grant spoke about Dunne moving to Oklahoma in *The Awful Truth*. These are the alternatives in screwball comedies: a stultifyingly dull life of maturity and responsibility or a whirlwind of playful but exhausting adventure.

Playfulness is essential to *His Girl Friday*. Walter is an unabashedly malevolent, manipulative, and self-centered character, and yet Cary brings a wry sense of fun to his performance, suggesting he is a caricature to be enjoyed rather than a believable villain. When he sends out stooges to get Bruce arrested, the situation is lightened when one of them asks what Bruce looks like. "Like that fellow in the movies," Cary ad-libbed, "you know—Ralph Bellamy." Better yet, when Walter is caught aiding and abetting an escaped murderer, and the police chief tells him that he is "through," Walter replies, "Listen, the last man who said that to me was Archie Leach just a week before he cut his throat." This, too, was ad-libbed on the set. Harry Cohn was furious when he first heard these lines, but they were left in the film, and Hawks was surprised to find how much audiences enjoyed them.[46] The lines did not break the fourth wall so much as treat the audience as a clever, knowing confidante.

Throughout the film, Cary alternatively keeps his cool, whinnies with frustration, and rants with anger. It is a remarkable performance, as funny as anything he had done before and yet shaded considerably darker. He maintains this duality to the very end. In the final scene, Hildy agrees to remarry Walter only to find that he wants to spend their honeymoon covering a strike in Albany. "Maybe Bruce can put us up," he says as he strides out the door, with Hildy struggling to keep up with him because she is carrying her own suitcase. Thus, right up to the fade-out, His Girl Friday refuses to give in to expectations of a happy ending. It is a determinedly unsentimental film, and one that seems remarkable for suggesting, in 1940, that a woman may find greater fulfillment in a career than in raising a family.

Hawks was so proud of the film's speed that he claims to have counted the words spoken per minute and established that His Girl Friday has twice as many as the average film.[47] He also recognized that audiences needed relief from the comic frenzy that he and his casts worked so hard to achieve. The fault with Bringing Up Baby, he reflected, was that every character is crazy and the comedy is unrelenting. In His Girl Friday, he made sure that the film quietens when Hildy is on the job as a reporter, speaking almost in a whisper to a man facing execution, and talking coolly and calmly to rival reporters. This, Hawks thought, explained why Bringing Up Baby petered out at the box office while His Girl Friday proved to be a solid hit when it was released in January 1940.[48]

Critics were divided between those who found the fast-paced overlapping dialogue to be "wearing," and those who found it hilarious.[49] Remarkably, no one seems to have realized in 1940 that His Girl Friday would become a classic, landmark film. It was not nominated for a single Academy Award that year. The director, the stars, and even the sound engineer (who had to capture all of the overlapping dialogue) were overlooked. Its accolades came much later, including recognition as one of the top twenty "funniest American movies of all time" by the American Film Institute in 2000.[50]

Filming *His Girl Friday* took just eight weeks, finishing on November 21, 1939, and when it was done Cary and Phyllis had planned to marry. There is no doubt that they were serious about their engagement. Early in October, he purchased a house for them to move into as soon as they married. The house, at 1038 Ocean Front, was just a few doors down from the beach house that he and Randy had been sharing for five years, and it too was built on the sand and looked out to sea. Built for the silent film star Norma Talmadge (the sister of Constance Talmadge), the house was larger and more elegant than the rented house, with a peculiarly Californian combination of English Tudor and French Normandy styles. It was big enough for raising a family, which Cary and Phyllis agreed was what they wanted to do, and it allowed Cary to stay in his favorite spot—right on the beach.[51]

Yet Phyllis never moved into the house. Daisy Steiller could not forgive Cary for going on a European tour with Phyllis while they were not married. Their travels had been covered in newspapers throughout the world, and Daisy was shamed by her daughter's public display of immorality. When they returned to Los Angeles, Daisy could no longer feign civility with Cary and she urged Phyllis not to marry him. Phyllis suspected that her mother's disapproval also may have stemmed from financial concerns. Phyllis's salary sustained the Steiller family finances. If Phyllis quit working to raise a family, the Steillers would no longer be able to live in the style to which they had become accustomed.[52]

The matter came to a head during the filming of *His Girl Friday*. Cary asked Phyllis to sign a prenuptial agreement stipulating that her mother would never be invited into their home. This was a tit-for-tat situation: since Cary was barred from the Steiller home by Daisy, he would bar Daisy from his own home. He may also have been concerned that if the Steillers could not support themselves, they would expect to live at 1038 Ocean Front. He had no intention of living with a disapproving mother-in-law. Phyllis understood Cary's concerns, but she refused to sign the agreement and the wedding was called off. "We were enormously happy together," she recalled many years later, "It was a joyous time . . . and it disintegrated into something awful."[53]

Cary never spoke about this situation, but it is not hard to imagine why he thought that his proposed prenuptial agreement was reasonable. He was maintaining a distance from his own mother—a clear separation with some limited moments of contact—and he was asking Phyllis to take the same approach to her mother. Phyllis was only twenty-four years old and had never lived apart from her mother, but Cary expected her to follow his example. He had yet to face up to just how unusual and unsettling his childhood had been, and the effect that his mother's disappearance had on him.

When Britain declared war on Germany in September 1939, Cary was thirty-five years old and he had been living in the United States for nineteen years. He had considered applying for American citizenship, and a year earlier he had gone to the federal building in Los Angeles to get the necessary forms, but the press picked up on this—nothing he did went without notice and comment now—and he found himself in a bind. If he became an American citizen, the British press would accuse him of deserting his country in its hour of need. If he did not follow through with his application, the American press would question why not. "I find myself torn between allegiances—one to my country of birth, towards which I have a great sentimental attachment, and the other to the country which gave me an opportunity for which I am indeed grateful," he carefully explained.[1]

When the war started, he had to wait and see whether men his age would be conscripted for military service in Britain. David Niven, a younger man at twenty-nine, voluntarily left his film career behind and went back to Britain to join the army. Cary went to Niven's farewell party in October 1939.[2] Along with many other prominent British actors in Hollywood (Brian Aherne, Ronald Colman, Robert Coote, Herbert Marshall, Basil Rathbone, George Sanders, and Reginald Gardiner) he toasted Niven and admired his sense of duty and patriotism, even as he worried that Niven was setting an example that others—himself included—would be expected to follow. The British press certainly thought that all of the "Hollywood Britons," as they were called, should follow Niven's example. A campaign to shame them began in 1939 and ran until the United States joined the war in 1941. British film fan magazines joined in. An article in *Picturegoer* featured a large photo of Cary in military uniform (his costume in *Suzy*), beneath the headline "Should the Boys Be Embarrassed?"[3]

There is no doubt that he saw these articles—the clippings are pasted into his personal scrapbooks—and there is no doubt that he really was embarrassed.[4] In July 1940, he joined a delegation (along with actors Laurence Olivier and Cedric Hardwicke, and the director Herbert Wilcox) that traveled to Washington, DC, to meet with the British ambassador, Lord Lothian. They wanted the ambassador to make it clear that they were not shirkers, hiding from military service in Hollywood. Lothian complied with a public declaration that only men between the ages of eighteen and thirty-one were required for war service. He also privately urged all of the Hollywood Britons to keep doing the work they were doing—that is, "flying the flag for Britain" in Hollywood—by making films based on British literature and history, and thus promoting British culture in the many neutral countries that showed Hollywood films, including the United States.[5]

Lothian's private directive was more of a stretch for Cary than the others. Personally and professionally, many of the Hollywood Britons defined themselves by their ties to the home country in a way that Cary never did. Cary did not join their cricket team, or read the *Times* of London, or insist on afternoon tea breaks on the set, as they were known to do. It is notable, too, that most of the Hollywood Britons came from upper-middle- or middle-class backgrounds, and they were ready and willing to play the officers and gentleman of historical films and literary adaptations. Cary, by contrast, seldom played British characters, and when he did he tended to play rough-and-ready cockneys such as Jimmy Monkley in *Sylvia Scarlett* and Archibald Cutter in *Gunga Din*. He was more closely identified with the character type he had done so much to establish: the modern, urbane American characters he played in screwball comedies. It was not clear exactly how he could "fly the flag for Britain" in Hollywood.

His contribution to the war effort would take some time to figure out. In the meantime, he could only continue to do what he did best. He made seven films over the next two years, beginning with *My Favorite Wife* (1940). This was the much-anticipated reunion of *The Awful Truth* team: Cary and Irene Dunne starring in a screwball comedy made under the auspices of Leo McCarey. The film was made at RKO rather than Columbia because McCarey now had a production deal at RKO, and for financial reasons he chose to produce rather than direct *My Favorite Wife*.[6] McCarey selected Garson Kanin as the film's director. The twenty-seven-year-old Kanin had recently directed one of RKO's biggest hits, the Ginger Rogers comedy *Bachelor Mother* (1939). He was gaining a reputation as the studio's "boy wonder," but he was also young enough to take orders and follow McCarey's lead.[7]

Cary approved of this set-up. Kanin, too, had a background in vaudeville comedy, and they had moved in some of the same circles in New York. He and "Gar," as Cary called him, became fast friends, and initially it looked as though this light and frothy comedy would be a pleasure to make. Then, on November 27, just two days before filming was due to begin, McCarey had a near-fatal car accident while driving home from a working weekend at Lake Arrowhead with the screenwriter Gene Fowler. Rescuers found their overturned car near Azusa, California. Fowler was lightly injured, but McCarey was pinned beneath the car with a fractured skull, a leg broken in several places, and a badly damaged arm and hand. His life hung in the balance, and it was clear that, if he did survive, he faced a long recovery.[8] Making *My Favorite Wife* would have to proceed without him: the sets were built and the cast and crew were ready to go. On December 6, a week later than planned, filming began under these gloomy circumstances.[9]

The script for *My Favorite Wife* was well prepared. This was not a film, like *The Awful Truth*, that McCarey intended to develop on the set and on a day-by-day basis. He had written the script with a husband-and-wife team of screenwriters, Sam and Bella Spewack, who brought a distinctively tender and affectionate spirit to this marital comedy.[10] Otherwise, there is little that is new in *My Favorite Wife*. Cary and Irene Dunne play characters almost identical to their characters in *The Awful Truth*, and many of their jokes and routines echo the earlier film as well. The story is a reworking of Tennyson's *Enoch Arden*—that is, the well-worn tale about the husband who is shipwrecked on a desert island and believed dead but returns many years later to find that his wife is happily remarried. The writers acknowledged Tennyson's story by naming Grant and Dunne's characters Nick and Ellen Arden, and they added the twist that it is Ellen who has been shipwrecked for seven years and presumed dead, while Nick has been left to raise their two children. The story begins as Nick marries his new bride, the gorgeous yet dragon-like Bianca (Gail Patrick), just as Ellen unexpectedly returns home.

Nick and Ellen's initial reunion—a long, passionate kiss in a hotel bar—is one of the few serious moments in the film. From that point onward, there is no doubt about who Nick's "favorite wife" might be, and no doubt that a happy ending will see Nick and Ellen reunited as husband and wife. In the meantime, the comedy rests in how far they will allow themselves to be embarrassed and humiliated in the cause of winning each other back. There are many fun moments, including incidental ones, such as when Nick is in a hotel elevator, on his way to the honeymoon suite with Bianca, when he sees Ellen for the first time since her return. He cannot quite believe his eyes, and his entire body slides sideways in sync with the closing elevator door. It is one of those perfect Cary Grant moments, when he expresses his alarm with equal measures of vaudeville slapstick and acrobatic grace.

In another scene, Nick is so desperate to escape from his honeymoon with Bianca that he calls her from the hotel lobby, telling her that he has already departed by plane on an impromptu business trip. When she protests, he makes a racket by putting his pen into a spinning fan and shouting, "The propellers! Can't hear you!" What neither realizes is that they are in adjoining phone booths, and there is a delightfully farcical moment when they collide into one another as they leave the booths. The script's weakness is that it does not allow the bewildered Bianca a single moment of sympathy. When she sits in the honeymoon suite alone, wearing a leopard-print robe she bought for this occasion, with Nick's matching robe empty beside her, her frustrated desire is played entirely for laughs. Gail Patrick hoped to breathe a bit more life into the role, but neither Kanin nor McCarey was interested in her ideas.[11] In her performance, Patrick at least suggests that there are hidden depths of ferocity to her character, but she is limited by a script that allows Bianca to be only an embarrassment to Nick.

Ellen is not jealous of Bianca but laughs at Nick for thinking that he could love a woman who would buy matching his-and-her leopard-print robes. Ellen, in turn, is embarrassed by Stephen, a carrot-munching vegetarian fitness enthusiast who was stranded with her on the desert island. Stephen's hyper-masculine athletic displays—he performs gymnastic stunts on the diving board of a hotel swimming pool—make Nick mop his brow and gasp in awe, but as soon as Stephen speaks, it is clear that he is too vacuous to be a genuine rival for Ellen's affections.

All of this is familiar to anyone who has seen *The Awful Truth*. Leo McCarey correctly predicted that audiences enjoyed the earlier film so much that they would happily watch its stars go through some of the same routines again.[12] But McCarey had also learned a thing or two from Howard Hawks and *Bringing Up Baby* (a debt he acknowledges with the leopard-print robes referring back to the leopards of Hawks's film). In *My Favorite Wife*, as in *Bringing Up Baby*, Cary becomes caught up in a whirlwind of feminine desire that is initially unnerving and ultimately overwhelming. Through various plot complications, Nick ends up modeling Ellen's dresses (albeit holding them up to his body rather than actually wearing them) and trying to match them with her hats. "They're for a friend of mine," he says to the psychiatrist Bianca has hired to observe him; "He's waiting downstairs."

If this is not quite as daring as the cross-dressing, "I just went gay all of the sudden" declaration in *Bringing Up Baby*, it is worth noting that the friend waiting downstairs is Stephen Birkett, and Birkett is played by Randolph

Scott. Some of Cary's biographers have suggested that the casting of Randy in this role and the scenes showing Nick mesmerized by Birkett's athletic display on a diving board are an in-joke acknowledging Cary and Randy's sexual relationship.[13] If there is an in-joke here, for Cary it was more likely to be one referring back to the reams of publicity that depicted Cary and Randy's poolside workouts; the publicity angle that ended as soon as he left Paramount and took control of his career. McCarey offered another explanation. He said that the scene was inspired by his own feelings of inferiority when he saw Hal Roach's well-toned physique at a swimming pool.[14]

Cary's home movies also tell a very different story from the one put forth by his biographers. He took his camera with him when the pool scene was shot on location at the Vista Del Arroyo Hotel in Pasadena. Between takes, he shot some vivid color footage. Randy does appear briefly, smiling for the camera, and Garson Kanin playfully mouths "Fuck you!" when Cary pointed the camera at him, but Cary mostly focuses on the women (presumably extras) sitting around the pool in bathing suits, and his lens lingers on their legs as they pose for him.

According to Kanin, Cary did suggest Randy for the role of Stephen Birkett.[15] After watching Cary's freelance career take off, Randy left Paramount too, but he had not yet found as much success as Cary had. It was a good turn on Cary's part to suggest him for a significant role in this high-profile film, paying him $30,000 for just two weeks of filming. There may have been a more sentimental reason too. Making a film together was also a way of marking the end of an era—living together for most of their first eight years in Hollywood—before Cary began his married life. When the casting decisions were made in October 1939, Cary had just purchased the beach house at 1038 Ocean Front and was planning to move into it the following month, after he and Phyllis married.[16] Alas, the marriage was called off and he remained at 1018 Ocean Front, but this was not foreseen when Randy was offered the part.

Filming was scheduled to last seven weeks, ending January 22, but in mid-January Leo McCarey was discharged from the hospital. He still had one leg in a cast and one arm in a sling, but he was determined to take charge of the film. He watched the rushes and insisted that several scenes had to be rewritten and refilmed, including the poolside scenes with Cary and Randy.[17] By mid-February, McCarey was able to assemble a rough cut of the film, but he still was not happy with it. Then he had the idea for an additional scene. The film's first scene is set in courtroom, where a grouchy judge declares Ellen legally dead and then marries Nick and Bianca. McCarey, impressed with Granville Bates's performance as the judge, wanted another scene with him, and so toward the end of the film Nick and Bianca return to court accompanied by Ellen and Stephen. The scene ties up some of the story's loose ends, and it allows the judge to make a few more jibes about the characters and their predicament. Cary was so amused by Bates that he had difficulty not cracking up during the filming (and he can be seen stifling laughs during the scene).[18]

When the re-takes were finished in mid-March and the film was finally completed, the shooting schedule had grown from a planned forty-one to sixty-two days, and the production costs rose from the budgeted $768,000 to $921,000.[19] If RKO executives were nervous about another screwball comedy with a bloated budget, a preview screening quickly assured them that they had a solid hit.[20] *My Favorite Wife* earned nearly $1.5 million in North America alone, and another $500,000 from foreign markets.[21] For the first time, Cary had a very direct stake in the takings. He had taken a salary cut in his new RKO contract—from $75,000 to $50,000 per film—in return for receiving 2.5 percent of the film's box-office earnings.[22] This was a canny move. When his salary and his percentage of the $2 million box-office gross were combined, he earned just over $100,000 from *My Favorite Wife*, and this was only the beginning of the earnings stream. He effectively owned 2.5 percent of the film in perpetuity, and he and his heirs would continue to collect royalty payments from television screenings as well as VHS, DVD, Blu-ray, and streaming sales (from this film and the subsequent films made under this contract).

When it was first released in May 1940, few imagined that *My Favorite Wife* would endure for so long after its initial popularity. It drew mixed responses from critics. In the midst of increasingly bleak war news, at least one high-profile review declared the film to be "altogether delightful" and "a little island of joy" in worrying times (*New York Times*).[23] Others were quick to sniff at the similarities with *The Awful Truth*.[24] It was the first time since Cary had become a freelance star that critics complained he was repeating himself, or sticking too closely to type, but this was not a criticism that stuck for long.

His next film was not only a departure from screwball comedy but also a strikingly odd choice of film for a British film actor in 1940. In the historical drama *The Howards of Virginia*, Cary plays a backwoods American patriot rebelling against the tyranny of British rule and fighting in the Revolutionary War. This surely was not what Lord Lothian had in mind when he urged

Cary to "fly the flag for Britain" in Hollywood, but there were some mitigating circumstances. One was that the film was planned long before the
war began. Columbia bought the rights to Elizabeth Page's bestselling novel,
The Tree of Liberty, in February 1939, and Frank Lloyd was hired to produce
and direct the film in the same month.[25] Lloyd, best known for *Mutiny on
the Bounty* (1935), wanted to make this film on a similarly lavish scale. He
sought a budget of $1.3 million, a sum that made studio boss Harry Cohn
very nervous.[26] Cohn insisted that Lloyd should set up his own production company and bring in outside investors to co-produce the film with
Columbia. This delayed the project.[27] The other mitigating circumstance
was that Lloyd too was British, and he and Cary set out to make a film that
portrays the American Revolution as a fight between two sets of English
settlers—snobbish Tories and egalitarian rebels—rather than a fight between
the American and British people.

After missing out on *Mutiny on the Bounty*, Cary jumped at the chance
to work with Lloyd on *The Howards of Virginia*. He signed a letter Lloyd
drafted for potential investors, promising that he would star in the film. He
liked Lloyd's idea of filming on location in Colonial Williamsburg, and he
shared with Lloyd a sense that historical films tended to be overly stuffy and
theatrical. "Maybe you've noticed what happens to actors when they put on
costumes and wigs," Cary remarked disapprovingly to a reporter, "They go
in for flourishes—wide flourishes." He aimed to play his character, a fictional
eighteenth-century Virginian tobacco farmer named Matthew Howard, in
a more down-to-earth style. For the sake of authenticity, he learned to use
a scythe, to plow a field, and to fell a tree. "I nearly killed myself trying to
chop down that tree," he laughed.[28] He adopted the dialect of an uneducated
yokel, donned a period wig (with long hair gathered in a ponytail), wore
grubby buckskins, and allowed himself to appear haggard and gray as his
character ages.

This was the furthest he had departed from his image as the debonair
modern gentleman of screwball comedy. Both Cary and Frank Lloyd were
nervous that audiences would resent being deprived of the star they expected to see, and so they added an early scene that aimed to appease his
fans.[29] When Howard arrives in Williamsburg from his backwoods farm, he
is wearing his dirty buckskins. His oldest friend—Thomas Jefferson no less—
urges him to take a bath and change into the sophisticated finery of a city
gentleman. Howard agrees to the bath, but insists he will not wear the fine
clothes. Jefferson waits until he is in the bath and then sends his buckskins

out to be cleaned, leaving him no choice but to wear the gentleman's suit. Standing naked but for a bath towel draped around him, he protests as vigorously as he did when Katharine Hepburn stole his clothing in *Bringing Up Baby*, but once again to no avail. In the next scene, he is uncomfortably dressed as a gentleman.

Screwball comedy fans were unlikely to find the rest of the film as pleasing. Like many other Hollywood films about the American Revolution, the film is so reverent toward the historical events that it portrays that it comes across as a historical pageant rather than a compelling drama.[30] The love story between the earthy Matt Howard and his well-to-do bride, Jane Peyton, is underwritten. It is not surprising that Joan Fontaine refused to play the role, backing out at the very last moment.[31] In her place, the young and relatively inexperienced Martha Scott was cast after filming had begun. Like many other novices who worked with Cary, Scott found him to be a generous co-star and mentor, one who took particular care with her lighting. "Cary wanted it to be right for me," she recalled decades later. "Working with him was such a happy experience."[32]

It was a long shoot, lasting from April to July 1940, with two weeks filming in Williamsburg, one week on location in Santa Cruz, California (for scenes set on the Peyton plantation), one week on location in Kernville, California (for scenes set at the Albemarle farm), and the other weeks on the Columbia studio lot in Hollywood.[33] On release in September 1940, critics dutifully admired the film's patriotic spirit but also noted that it was overly long (with a running time of nearly two hours). There were mixed notices for the fresh spirit Cary tried to bring to the historical film. Some found him "bumptious" and "distinctly annoying" (*New York Times*), while others found him "curious but vital" (*Los Angeles Times*) and "robust [and] convincing" (*Variety*).[34] Many took aim at his accent, and not without cause. While trying to speak as a backwoodsman, his accent wanders from Irish to West Country English to cockney and back to normal Cary Grant. This was a curious weak spot in his acting skills. Although his voice was a nuanced, sensitive instrument when he spoke in his own accent, he had difficulty adopting and sustaining accents other than his own.

Columbia's publicists knew that audiences did not go to see Cary Grant films for a history lesson, and so they promoted the film by releasing a still photograph from the bathing scene, showing Cary, apparently naked, in a small wooden tub.[35] Initially, this helped to draw large audiences. Early box-office reports were strong and "Cary Grant appeal" was cited as the primary draw.[36] The crowds diminished quickly, though, and the film was ultimately regarded as a flop.[37] Even the Academy Awards, which so often favored historical films, had little regard for this one. It was nominated only for best score and best sound, and it lost in both categories. It would be a long time before Cary made another historical drama.

Gossip columnists noticed that, during the filming of *The Howards of Virginia*, Cary seemed to have vanished from Hollywood's social scene. He could usually be spotted around town: at a film premiere, on a date at a restaurant, dancing in a nightclub, or at the Friday night fights. But in the spring of 1940, he was lying low. Then in late May the story broke. He was spotted on a date, dining and "cooing" in one of the darker corner booths of Chasen's restaurant in Beverly Hills. Cary Grant dating *anyone* was news. Cary Grant dating the heiress Barbara Hutton was like catnip to the columnists— bringing together Hollywood celebrity and high society—and they could not leave it alone.[38] From this point forward, every move the couple made, and every rumor about every move they might make, was reported.

Cary and Barbara first met nearly a year earlier, in June 1939, when they both sailed on the *Normandie* from New York to Plymouth and Le Havre. Cary was traveling on his own (to join Phyllis Brooks in London) and so too was Barbara, who was estranged from her second husband. They were seated together at dinner and Cary turned on his charm, telling her stories about Hollywood and talking about their mutual friend Dorothy di Frasso. They dined together on subsequent nights but went their separate ways when the *Normandie* reached Plymouth. A few months later, Barbara closed up her palatial London home and moved back to the United States for the duration of the war. She spent a restless few months traveling from New York to Palm Beach to Hawaii before she accepted an invitation to stay with di Frasso in Los Angeles. As she must have known, she was sure to see Cary again and, as everyone knew, he was now a single man.[39]

They were an unlikely match. Her grandfather was F. W. Woolworth, who amassed a fortune from his chain of five-and-dime stores. When she turned twenty-one in 1933, she inherited a sum estimated to be somewhere between $25 million and $42 million, making her the wealthiest woman in the world.[40] Although she was an American, she was drawn to the circles of the European aristocracy and the idle rich. Her first husband was Prince Alexis Mdivani of Georgia. Her second husband was Count von Haugwitz-Reventlow of Denmark. Both lived off her money and took a huge settlement from her when the marriages ended. She had a son, Lance Reventlow, with her second husband, and Lance became part of her wandering entourage of servants and hangers-on, making the rounds of luxury hotels, exclusive resorts, and private estates in a never-ending quest to find something or someone to amuse her.[41]

What could the former Archie Leach, who worked for every penny he ever had, have seen in such a pampered and self-indulgent woman? Barbara was not considered beautiful, but she had the delicate physique and refined facial features that Cary found attractive in women. She also had the finishing-school manners and etiquette that he admired, and he was impressed by her knowledge of the arts, and her impeccable taste in clothing, jewelry, and décor. And, for all their differences, their backgrounds were similar in one important way. Barbara's mother died when she was five years old and her father left her in the care of governesses, servants, and boarding schools. In this respect at least, the vast differences in their circumstances did not matter. There was a common ground in the sense of abandonment they felt as children, and the impact that the loss of their mothers had on the rest of their lives.[42]

They shared another significant trait: they were two of the most famous people in the world and their lives were picked apart and scrutinized in the press on a daily basis. Cary was admired for his achievements, but Barbara was known only for being rich, and this made her a figure for popular contempt. From the time she inherited the Woolworth fortune, she was mocked as a "poor little rich girl" and "the five-and-ten-cent heiress." Many Americans also scorned her for renouncing her United States citizenship in order to become the Countess Barbara von Haugwitz-Reventlow.[43]

Cary fell into infatuation very quickly. Although he did his best to keep their relationship out of the public eye, in private he made no secret of his adoration of her. A few dates into their relationship, he and Barbara went to a tea party given by Douglas Fairbanks Jr. and his wife at their new home, Westridge, in Pacific Palisades. Fairbanks noted that Cary "could not take his eyes off her" and she was "swept off her feet" by his attentive interest in her. A framed photograph of Barbara took pride of place in Cary's living room. "What a lady," he would say admiringly when friends asked about it. Martha Scott, observing his devotion, came to suspect that she had been cast in *The Howards of Virginia* primarily because she looked like Barbara.[44]

Barbara's class and manners were a key part of his attraction to her. She tutored him in matters of taste, especially where the arts were concerned.

It was with her guidance that he began collecting paintings by French masters such as Eugène Boudin and Maurice Utrillo, and, more eclectically, the Mexican artist Diego Rivera. He also allowed her to redecorate the dining room of his new home at 1038 Ocean Front, modeling it on the art nouveau décor of her favorite restaurant, Maxim's of Paris, a haunt of the rich and fashionable before the war.[45]

While he admired her taste, he also felt protective toward her, and thought that he could help her improve her public image. His first advice was that, at this moment of world crisis, while war was raging in Europe and the Far East, they should keep their relationship as quiet as possible. Not wanting to appear frivolous or unconcerned by the war, they mostly dined and entertained at home, going out only when they thought they could avoid paparazzi. He also advised her to avoid any ostentatious displays of wealth. On this point, she was not so cooperative. When she decided to establish her own local residence, she took a lease on one of the most opulent mansions in Beverly Hills: a thirty-room "renaissance villa" that had been built in the 1920s by the silent film star Buster Keaton as a vast monument to his own success.[46]

Cary, meanwhile, moved from 1018 to 1038 Ocean Front in June 1940. It was a move he had put off since breaking up with Phyllis Brooks seven months earlier, but one that would suit his deepening relationship with Barbara. The new house was more formal than the one that had become famous for "batching it," and so it was more likely to appeal to Barbara's tastes.[47] At any rate, the Woolworth heiress was not one to date a man who shared a house. Cary and Randy's relationship as roommates came to an end eight years after they first moved in together. Some biographers claim that this was a "break up" and that the two men no longer had any contact.[48] Actually, they remained friends as well as neighbors over the next few years, attending each other's birthday parties and film premieres, and working together for wartime causes. They would drift apart after the war, when Randy and his second wife had two children, but there were never any signs of acrimony between them.

Cary continued to hold Sunday gatherings, now at 1038 Ocean Front. He had become very good friends with Rosalind Russell. They performed duets at parties, singing old music hall songs, and he set her up with Freddie Brisson, a London agent who recently moved to Hollywood. "Ross" and Freddie were often there on Sundays, along with other good friends such as Johnny Maschio (a Hollywood agent), his wife Constance Moore, Douglas Fairbanks Jr., Marlene Dietrich, Reginald Gardiner, James Stewart,

Alexander Korda, and Merle Oberon. They gradually got to know Barbara but found her rather aloof and formal by Hollywood standards.[49]

Although the Hollywood social scene had its own hierarchies and snobberies, it was very different from the high-society circles that Barbara was accustomed to in one important respect. In Hollywood, just about everyone worked, or was married to someone who worked, in films. It was an industry town, and one dominated by the six-days-a-week shooting schedules. Barbara was distinctly out of place among these hard-working, career-oriented, and mostly self-made people. "What have you done with your life?" Charlie Chaplin asked her at a dinner party given by Jack Warner and his wife, Ann. It was not a question that she was used to, and, as she looked blankly back at him, he persisted. "You should really do something," Chaplin told her. "No one can be idle and be happy."[50]

It was entirely a coincidence that Cary's next film centered on a snooty high society heiress. He was a late and somewhat reluctant addition to the cast of *The Philadelphia Story*. This was another film that belonged to Katharine Hepburn first and foremost. The playwright Philip Barry, the author of the play *Holiday*, wrote *The Philadelphia Story* with Hepburn in mind. The new play was another sophisticated comedy of manners set among the very rich, but this time Hepburn's free spirits and fierce intelligence are recast as selfishness and snobbery. Barry suspected that the public would like to see her taken down a peg or two, and Hepburn apparently concurred. She had played the role of the imperious heiress Tracy Lord for over a year on Broadway before the film was made.[51]

The play was a big success, and Hepburn shrewdly bought the screen rights early in its run. Seeing this as her chance to return to Hollywood and prove that she was not "box office poison," she insisted that she would sell the rights only to a studio that agreed to star her in the film and to give her approval over the choice of director and co-stars. MGM's Louis B. Mayer agreed to her conditions. There was no difficulty over her choice of director: George Cukor was the recognized master of this kind of smart comedy. For her co-stars, Hepburn wanted the two biggest stars on the MGM lot, Clark Gable and Spencer Tracy, to ensure that her return to filmmaking was a box-office smash. When they both refused, she accepted James Stewart for one of the roles, but they struggled to find the second male lead until Mayer authorized Hepburn to search beyond MGM's studio gates. It was at this point that she turned to Cary and asked him to join her, playing Tracy Lord's ex-husband, C. K. Dexter Haven, in *The Philadelphia Story*.[52]

Cary fretted over this one more than most. In late June 1940 he started work on another comedy, *Passport to Life*, at RKO, with Garson Kanin directing and Irene Dunne co-starring. Scripting problems led them to delay filming *Passport to Life* until mid-August, when it was restarted and then abandoned again.[53] In between these dates, Cary knew that he could squeeze in four weeks of filming for *The Philadelphia Story*, but therein lay one cause of concern. He wasn't sure that the role he was offered in *The Philadelphia Story* was big enough, or important enough, for a star of his standing, and he thought he might prefer James Stewart's role instead.[54] He prevaricated until the very last moment.[55] MGM and Hepburn swayed him by offering him a salary of $125,000 for just four weeks of filming (by far his highest salary yet), and offering him top billing over Hepburn.[56] This clinched it for him. He reported to the set on July 8, 1940, and he never regretted his decision. In later years, he cited *The Philadelphia Story* as the film he most enjoyed making, and of course it turned out to be one of the finest and most memorable of all the films he made.[57]

The script was immediately revised to accommodate him.[58] This was not just a matter of beefing up his role. That had been done in the very earliest scripts as a means of accommodating either Clark Gable or Spencer Tracy.[59] When Cary was cast, the script was revised in a manner that drew on his screen history with Hepburn. George Cukor introduced a first scene showing the break-up of Tracy Lord and C. K. Dexter Haven's marriage.[60] Dexter strides out of their home, suitcases in hand, and Tracy follows him, carrying his bag of golf clubs. For a moment, it looks as though she may be helping him, but then she takes out one of the clubs and defiantly breaks it over her knee. He follows her back to the front door, pauses with his fist in the air, and instead opts to push her backward through the doorway into the house, where she lands with a thud. Everything about the scene—the music, the performances, and the well-heeled setting—cues the audience to understand it as a screwball scenario. It could be a coda to *Bringing Up Baby*, showing us that Susan and David's marriage was no less fraught than their courtship.

From this first scene onward, however, Dexter is not a particularly comical character. This is not a film in which Cary has his clothes stolen, or does a pratfall, or succumbs to a frenzy of frustration. Dexter is a character apart from the others. He returns to see Tracy marry for the second time, this time to the dull George Kittredge (John Howard), not out of malice or with hope of engineering a reconciliation, but in a protective role, with a plan to save the family from an exposé in a scandal sheet. Dexter does not squabble or make wisecracks as the other characters do. Instead, he is an observer, one who intervenes only when necessary and to push the other characters toward their own happy endings. Cary inflects some of Dexter's lines wryly. "You don't think I'd miss your *wedding*, do you?" he asks Tracy when he unexpectedly turns up the day before the event. For the most part, though, he serves as an all-seeing, all-knowing figure who is above the comic fray. This was surely director George Cukor's design. Once again, as in *Sylvia Scarlett* and *Holiday*, Cukor was not interested in the ready-made glamorous and funny Cary Grant, but sought out something more serious and challenging. Cary rose to the occasion, playing Dexter with a gravitas he had never shown before.

The on-screen chemistry between Cary and Katharine Hepburn was never better than in *The Philadelphia Story*. When Dexter tells Tracy that during their marriage he felt compelled to play the "high priest" to her "virgin goddess," she rises up to him, hands on hips and head held high, with the defensive retort, "Stop using those foul words." In this and other scenes, they treat one another as equals—a rare dynamic between a man and a woman in films of this era—and the charge between them is palpable. It is a shame, then, that this proved to be their last film together. Spencer Tracy co-starred in her next film, *Woman of the Year* (1942), and she apparently preferred him; it was the first of nine films they made together. Yet as Pauline Kael observed, Spencer Tracy is a stodgier and more dominant partner for Hepburn. In their films together he dampens her fiery temperament. In the films with Cary, by contrast, he is attracted to her precisely because of her fiery temperament.[61]

The Philadelphia Story is notable, too, as the only film that Cary made with James Stewart. If it seems as though their paths should have crossed more often, it is because they both went on to make four films with Alfred Hitchcock, a connection that makes their careers seem more interconnected than they actually were. Hitchcock, however, turned to Stewart when he needed an American everyman and to Grant when he needed a more cosmopolitan and modern gentleman. Despite their differences—in acting style and in image—they play off each other beautifully in *The Philadelphia Story*. Stewart's Mike Connors is a salt-of-the-earth reporter who initially sneers at the high-society wedding he is forced to cover, but then over the course of a bacchanalian evening falls in love with Tracy Lord. When Mike is very drunk, Stewart delivers his line, "Doggone it, C. K. Dexter Haven, either I am going to sock you or you are going to sock me," with his trademark Midwestern drawl, only for Cary to reply, in his own wry tone, "Shall we toss a coin?"

The moonlit tryst between Mike and Tracy is so cozy that it raises some question—rare in a romantic comedy—about which couple is destined for a happy ending. It is entirely implausible that Tracy will marry her fiancé, the priggish George Kittredge, but it is just about plausible that she could choose Mike Connors over C. K. Dexter Haven. In the ending, only the presence of Mike's wisecracking sidekick, Liz (Ruth Hussey), seems to prevent this. When Dexter and Tracy are finally reunited, their suddenly reignited ardor is far more intense than anything seen in *Bringing Up Baby* or *Holiday*. As Cukor's biographer, Patrick McGilligan, points out, there is a feeling of genuine spontaneity to the scene. In this film about romantic possibilities, the characters themselves seem surprised that it turns out this way.[62]

From its first screening, everyone loved *The Philadelphia Story*. The producer, Joseph Mankiewicz, was so confident about the film that he invited the waspish gossip columnist Hedda Hopper to attend the first preview screening, in Pomona, California, in September 1940. As expected, Hopper loved the film and reported the "constant laughter and the applause of the audience."[63] The American box-office tally, at over $2.3 million, made the film one of the five biggest hits of the year.[64] Critics fawned over Hepburn.[65] They praised James Stewart and the child actress Virginia Weidler (who plays Tracy's younger sister), and they admired the glamorous sheen that MGM's best designers and technicians brought to the film.[66] Yet amid all the praise, Cary's performance received so little attention that Mankiewicz felt compelled to write to him, three weeks into the film's release, and acknowledge his contribution to *The Philadelphia Story*:

> Whatever success the picture is having—and it is a simply enormous smash—is due, in my opinion, to you in far greater proportions than anyone has seen fit to shout about. . . . Your presence as Dexter and particularly your sensitive and brilliant playing of the role contribute what I consider the backbone and basis of practically every emotional value in the piece. I can think of no one who could have done as well, or have given as much.[67]

Mankiewicz's letter, saved among Cary's personal papers, was perhaps some comfort the following month, when all the film's major talents were nominated for Academy Awards apart from Cary: Mankiewicz for outstanding production, Cukor for best director, James Stewart for best actor, Katharine Hepburn for best actress, Ruth Hussey for best supporting actress, and Donald Ogden Stewart for best screenplay (adaptation). It was not the first or last time that Cary found that making a performance look effortless wins little critical fanfare. As frustrating as this must have been for him, he was magnanimous in praising and congratulating Stewart when he won the Best Actor award.[68]

The Philadelphia Story did lead to Cary winning one award, although not for his performance. He donated his salary for the film to the American Red Cross and the British Relief Fund (in equal amounts). Or, to be more accurate, MGM made the donations on his behalf, so that the money was not subject to income tax.[69] These donations, and donations the following year arising from his salary for *Arsenic and Old Lace*, led to him being awarded the King's Medal for Service in the Cause of Freedom in Britain after the war had ended. This was not an award given for espionage services, as some biographers have claimed.[70] It was a medal given to civilians in allied and neutral countries for their role in wartime fundraising. Cary's award specifically stated that it was made for "outstanding service to British War Relief Society," an organization that provided humanitarian aid to the British people during the war.[71]

The unverified claim that he was a spy stems from his friendship with Noel Coward, who is said to have recruited Cary to work for the British spymaster William Stephenson. Long after the war was over, Coward revealed that, because he was touring the world with his shows, and often meeting highly placed officials backstage and at functions, Stephenson asked him to keep his eyes and ears open, and to report back on the views expressed in neutral countries. It may be that Cary was also recruited to work for Stephenson, but he did not travel abroad as much as Coward did and, unlike Coward, he never claimed to serve in this capacity. This is not to say that Cary did not want to do more on behalf of the war effort. As we shall see, he wanted to make his wartime contribution on behalf of the United States, and throughout 1940 and 1941, he was biding his time until he could do that without being accused of betraying Britain.

17

The Philadelphia Story marked the apex of the smart, sophisticated brand of comedy that Cary had reinvented and made his own in the late 1930s. It also marked the beginning of the end of that cycle of comedies. With the war news growing ever darker in Europe, films that laughed at the foibles of the wealthy began to look old-fashioned. Cary recognized this and looked for ways to expand his repertoire. "I read fifteen to twenty scripts for every one film that I make," he commented in 1941.[1] Because he had ongoing and yet open deals with both Columbia and RKO, he could play these two studios off one another, pushing them to come up with stories, co-stars, and production teams that met his exacting standards. Because he was able to make deals with other studios too, he was offered just about everything. Even Paramount asked him to return. The studio's top producer-director, Cecil B. DeMille, wanted him for the historical film *Reap the Wild Wind* (1942).[2] Tempting as it may have been to make a triumphant return to Paramount, historical films were also high on his list of films to avoid. Ray Milland got the part instead.

Columbia tried to appeal to him by pitching films with Rosalind Russell as his co-star. A succession of comedies was proposed for them: *Bedtime Story* (1941), which was made instead with Fredric March and Loretta Young; *Our Wife* (1941), which was made with Melvyn Douglas and Ruth Hussey; and *This Thing Called Love* (1941), which Russell made with Melvyn Douglas.[3] As keen as Cary was to work again with "Ross," he was determined not to be confined to screwball comedy. By this time, there were a number of actors who served as second-string Cary Grants. Stars such as Fredric March, Melvyn Douglas, Ray Milland, and David Niven (before he joined the British army) picked up the roles Cary refused, just as Cary had once picked up the roles Gary Cooper refused.

George Stevens, who had directed *Gunga Din* at RKO but now had a production deal at Columbia, shared the sense that it was time for Cary to move in a new direction. "I didn't want to do gag pictures with Cary Grant," he recalled of this period. "He was doing nothing but comedies then, so I wanted to do something slightly different."[4] That something turned out to be the sentimental melodrama *Penny Serenade*, co-starring Irene Dunne. Both stars were nervous about this, assuming that after *The Awful Truth* and *My Favorite*

Wife audiences would expect them to provide laughs rather than tears.[5] Yet they pressed ahead with a story that has no comic escapades, and one in which their characters, Roger Adams and Julie Gardiner, are not wealthy sophisticates but are instead an ordinary middle-class couple experiencing routine problems and everyday tragedies. There are a few amusing moments in the film. Scenes of their courtship are played for gentle laughs, and when they are married and bring home an adopted child, their inexperience as parents is played in a delightfully light manner. On the whole, though, the film focuses on the disappointments in their marriage.

Told in flashback and from Julie's point of view, *Penny Serenade* begins with Julie announcing that she is leaving Roger, but then she pauses to listen to a collection of sentimental records ("You Were Meant For Me," "Poor Butterfly," "My Blue Heaven") that cue her memories of their courtship and marriage. The film thus contrasts the romantic idealism of the songs and the reality of their life together. Roger is a newspaperman, but unlike the dynamic Walter Burns of *His Girl Friday*, he fails in his profession. While working as an American correspondent in Japan, he and Julie are caught in an earthquake that destroys their home and causes her to have a miscarriage. They adopt a child, Trina, but the court nearly takes her away from them when they get into financial difficulties, and then, when Trina is school-aged, she dies from a sudden illness. Only the promise that Roger and Julie will adopt another child allows for a moderately happy ending. In the final shot, they walk into a dark room of their apartment, discussing how they will remodel it on behalf of the new arrival. The metaphor—of the couple heading into the darkness hopeful for the future—represents the film's ambivalent mood perfectly.

Unusually for a melodrama, there are no clear villains or mean-spirited deceptions in this story (no one akin to the vicious Maida Walker of *In Name Only*, for example). Roger and Julie are surrounded by benevolent people. Their friend Applejack (Edgar Buchanan) is kind and helpful, Miss Oliver (Beulah Bondi) from the adoption agency is sympathetic to them, and a judge (Wallis Clark) confirms their adoption of Trina even though Roger cannot prove that he can support her. Rather than duplicitous characters or sordid machinations, the story focuses on the unexpected twists of fate that can destroy and redeem lives. With the war looming, and threatening to break up families, this was a timely and powerful theme, and one that the film pursues in a remarkably quiet and restrained manner.[6]

The film's dramatic climax comes when Roger pleads with the judge to grant permanent custody of one-year-old Trina to him and Julie despite their financial woes. The scene required Cary to be helpless and weak in a way that he had never attempted before. As his character searches for the right words to convince the judge, his voice and his stance shift from angrily protesting against the injustice of it all to begging the judge not to take away his daughter. His voice finally trembles and breaks, as he tries not to cry and cannot stop himself. It was a remarkable risk for an actor in this era to take, and George Stevens was proud that he encouraged Cary to shed his "established aura" on-screen and play a character who is humiliated and vulnerable. Stevens recalled that "Cary didn't hold up on doing that [scene] at all."[7] It is notable, though, that Stevens chose to film the scene in medium shots and never to go in for a close-up of his face. Having Cary Grant cry in a medium shot was bold enough. A close-up may have been too unsettling for audiences who were more accustomed to seeing his loss of composure played for laughs.

Stevens filmed the scene over and over again, even though he was behind schedule on *Penny Serenade* and the studio was leaning on him to work faster. Dunne recalled that Cary "had given everything he had to the screen that day," and when they watched the rushes together, she was floored by his performance.[8] "There's your Oscar," Dunne told him in the screening room.[9] She was partly right. Having been overlooked so many times in the past, he was at least nominated for the Best Actor Academy Award for *Penny Serenade*. He went to the ceremony with Rosalind Russell at his side, joking with her to distract him during this tense, awkward event, but he did not win, and he could not have been too pleased to see Gary Cooper walk away with the Best Actor award (for the flag-waving *Sergeant York*).

His performance in *Penny Serenade* was widely praised. "Very few would believe that Cary Grant, our man about town, could lift a sob in your throat as big as a golf ball," the columnist Hedda Hopper observed, while the *Los Angeles Times* critic Edwin Schallert noted that a preview audience applauded Cary's "long, demanding speech."[10] Other critics took up a common theme of urging movie theaters to supply handkerchiefs for audiences to dry their tears while watching this "tear-jerker" or "weepie," as it was variously called.[11]

Penny Serenade was a solid box-office hit, but it also proved to be the last film that Cary and Irene Dunne made together.[12] They enjoyed working together, but they did not see much of each other socially. She was a devout Catholic, married to a dentist, and led a strait-laced lifestyle by Hollywood standards.[13] She recalled that they often had fun on the set, and that Cary became a joker once his initial jitters died down. "Between takes he was so amusing with his cockney stories," she said. "I was his best audience. I laughed and laughed and laughed. The more I laughed, the more he went on."[14] On the *Penny Serenade* set, they also talked in more intimate terms, as the storyline prompted Cary to confide to Dunne that he and Barbara Hutton hoped to marry and have children together.[15] A single issue ended his screen partnership with Dunne. She was top-billed in their three films together, and although Cary was by now the bigger star, she insisted that she should continue to have top billing in future. Cary regarded this in business-like terms and refused to be second-billed. "It's ladies first in the rowboats but not in the movies," he commented later.[16]

As his professional relationship with Dunne came to an end, he found a very different kind of collaborator. Alfred Hitchcock would do more than any other director to sustain Cary's career and his enduring reputation, and Cary in turn would add significantly to Hitchcock's *oeuvre*. At first glance, the director and the star were an unlikely match both professionally and personally. When Hitchcock arrived in Hollywood in March 1939, he was already known for his pacy British-made thrillers, such as *The 39 Steps* (1935) and *The Lady Vanishes* (1938), and his reputation soared with his first Hollywood film, the gothic melodrama *Rebecca* (1939). Few would have imagined that this director, soon to be known as "the master of suspense," would forge an important working relationship with a star known as the master of screwball comedy. They seemed light years apart in terms of lifestyle, and image too. The balding, plump Hitchcock led a quiet life with his wife Alma and his daughter Pat, and he wore dark suits more appropriate to foggy London than sunny Hollywood. Nevertheless, the star and the director had an immediate rapport when they met in 1939, and they began searching for ways to work together.[17]

Cary later attributed his bonhomie with "Hitch," as his friends called him, to the fact that they "both knew what liquorice allsorts were" (that is, a type of candy loved by British schoolchildren).[18] This was an oblique reference not just to their shared nationality but also to their class background. Back in London, Hitchcock grew up above his family's greengrocers shop and later above their fish and chips shop. The Hitchcocks were probably better off than the Leaches, but both families were working class. Both Archie and Alfred left school at the age of fourteen, and both overcame the limited prospects of British working-class men by pursuing a career in show business. When they met in Hollywood decades later, they were uniquely placed to recognize one another's success and the distance they had traveled to achieve it. Hitchcock could admire the extraordinary self-invention at work in Cary's screen persona, while Cary enjoyed Hitchcock's droll music hall humor. "It's Hitch," the director would say, explaining his nickname to new friends, "without the cock."[19]

It is telling that their relationship was forged in the winter of 1940–41, when Britain's survival in the war hung in the balance. The threat of invasion was high, and the Blitz was a terrifying ordeal that destroyed cities and killed tens of thousands of civilians. From the distance of California, these two expatriate Englishmen no doubt shared a sense of guilt and shame about living in a neutral country while friends and relatives faced the horror of the war. Hitchcock was so worried for his mother that he traveled back to Britain in June 1940, insisting that she move from her home in London's East End to a country cottage in Surrey. He had more success with her than Cary had a year earlier with Elsie, who moved only to the suburban fringe of Bristol.[20]

Elsie was a constant concern for Cary during the blitz. He contacted her more often than ever before, seeking reassurance—urgently by cablegram—that she was okay. On the morning of August 13, when he opened the *Los Angeles Times* to read the front-page headline "Nazis Begin War For England," Cary immediately wrote to Elsie saying, "Darling do let me know how you are. As always anxious. God bless. Love Archie Leach."[21] A month later, when newspaper headlines reported a terrible night of bombing in London, he sent another cablegram. "Don't forget darling to cable me now and then as would like to know all is well with you," he wrote, sending regards to his Aunt Rose as well as "all my love to you dearest."[22] A cablegram sent in October said, "Had letter thru from Aunt Rose so please give all there my love and God's good wishes and to yourself dear. Be of good heart always."[23] Elsie responded to each of his messages immediately and reassuringly. "Am alright at present," she wrote; "God keep us safe from enemies. You always darling Archie in my thoughts. Living for you. Wondering when meet again keeping cheerie love always."[24]

Bristol was high on the list of the Luftwaffe's targets because it was a port city and a manufacturing center. On one of the worst nights of the bombing, December 2–3, 1940, over one hundred enemy planes dropped 120 tons of high explosives on Bristol, destroying large parts of the city center and killing 156 people.[25] Among the dead were Cary's closest relatives in Bristol apart from Elsie: his uncle, John Leach, whom he listed as his next of kin after his father's death; his aunt, Rose Leach, who had been helpful with Elsie since her release from the asylum; their daughter Dorothy, her husband (Frances Marsh), and their son (Bruis Marsh). All were killed by a direct hit on their home at 9 Dean Street. Another uncle, Frederick Leach, was killed just around the corner, at 91 Bishop Street. The impact of the bombs was so intense that their bodies were never recovered.[26]

Cary's immediate response to this devastating news is not known, but in the months that followed he arranged for his salary from another film—this one to be made for Warner Bros. in the autumn of 1941—to be donated to British War Relief. Like the donation MGM made with his salary for *The Philadelphia Story*, Warner Bros. made the payment directly to the charity to avoid income-tax deductions. As before, Cary insisted that "not a cent" of his donation could be spent on "combative material." This time, he also added that all of the money must be spent "to buy materials for the relief of women and children suffering from bomb raids."[27] For the time being at least, this was the best and most effective response that he could make on behalf of his family and friends in Bristol.

Cary and Alfred Hitchcock, meanwhile, were already at work on their first film together. There had been a few missteps along the way. In May 1940, Hitchcock asked Cary to star alongside Carole Lombard in the director's one and only foray into screwball comedy, *Mr. and Mrs. Smith* (1941).[28] Weary of screwballs and worried that Hitchcock would not be at his best in this genre, Cary turned him down, making way for Robert Montgomery to play the role instead.[29] In July, Cary agreed that he would collaborate with Hitchcock on one of the episodes of *Forever and a Day* (1943), a portmanteau film being made by the Hollywood British community to aid British war charities. Then the production suffered a succession of delays that prevented their involvement.[30] In September, Columbia thought it might attract them with *Royal Mail*, an epic tribute to Britain's early marine mail service that would allow them to "fly the flag for Britain in Hollywood," but both the director and the star were wary of historical films, and they allowed *Royal Mail* to get lost in the shuffle of other projects.[31]

Hitchcock had a better idea for their first film. In September, he arranged to meet Cary on the RKO lot, and he told him the story of Francis Iles's 1932 novel, *Before the Fact*.[32] In Iles's story, Johnny Aysgarth is a dashingly handsome and charming Englishman who is also a liar, a cheat, a thief, and—ultimately—a murderer. His victim is his shy wife Lina, who finds him so irresistible that she allows him to kill her. Throughout the novel, there is little doubt that Johnny will kill Lina for her money. The suspense arises not from the question of whether he will kill her but how and when he will do it. The answer comes on the very last page, when he gives her a glass of milk laced with poison, and she knowingly drinks it.[33] RKO bought the rights to *Before the Fact* several years earlier, and a number of scriptwriters had stumbled while trying to adapt the novel for the screen.[34] Hitchcock thought that he could crack it by sticking more closely to the novel and casting Cary in the lead role.

Suspicion (1941), as the story was renamed, was a major gamble for Cary, but he signed on immediately and without his usual anxious prevaricating. He found Hitchcock's love of storytelling and his confidence as a director reassuring.[35] He also appreciated that Hitchcock had no interest in making "Cary Grant films" but instead wanted to use his star's appeal and familiarity to lure audiences into identifying with him before revealing that his debonair charm serves as a mask for much darker qualities.[36] *Suspicion* thus begins in the bright and cheery mode of a Cary Grant romantic comedy. There is a "meet cute" between Johnny and Lina, and some cheeky banter when he admires her "ucipital mapilary" (an invented term for the base of her neck) and nicknames her "monkey face." Lina, as expected, falls in love with him, but then the suspicions about him begin to build, and not least because he asks their mutual friend, a bestselling crime writer, so many questions about ways to poison people.

Gradually the film shifts from the bright mode of romantic comedy to the shadowy gothic mode of Hitchcock's earlier film, *Rebecca* (1940). Casting the star of *Rebecca*, Joan Fontaine, to play Lina enables this tonal change to happen almost imperceptibly. Like *Rebecca*, the story of *Suspicion* is motivated by her character's fascination with a man she is attracted to but finds dangerous and mysterious. So much of *Suspicion* centers on Lina looking at Johnny, initially with desire and later with trepidation, that it becomes difficult to discern how much of what we see is real or imagined. At the climax of the film, she is sitting up in bed, watching and waiting for Johnny, while he brings the glass of milk to her. As he climbs the dark, curved staircase, only his silhouette is visible—the familiar tall, well-tailored, and well-built frame—and the glass of milk he carries glows with poisonous intent. It remains unclear whether this malevolent image arises from her anxious mind (she has taken to her bed with nervous exhaustion) or if it represents Johnny's true character. *Suspicion* keeps the audience guessing until its very last scene.

Photograph 17.29 *Suspicion* (RKO Radio Pictures, 1941) begins as a light romantic comedy, with only a hint of shadow behind Joan Fontaine and Cary.
Source: author's screen capture

Many years after the film was made, Cary and Hitchcock recalled that they thought the film should end as the novel did, with Johnny poisoning Lina.[37] They also remembered the twist that Hitchcock wanted to add to the ending. Lina would write a letter to her mother, explaining that she has been murdered by Johnny and, just before she drinks the poisoned milk, she would ask Johnny to mail the letter. The very last shot of the film would show Johnny mailing the letter that would lead to his arrest. This would have been a clever ending, and one that would fulfill the censors' requirement that all crimes must be punished. Both Cary and Hitchcock remembered that this preferred ending was overruled by RKO. All that remains of it is an oblique reference to it in Hitchcock's cameo midway through the film. The director is seen, very briefly, posting a letter, as though he has decided to turn in Johnny himself.

"The studio insisted that they didn't want to have Cary Grant play a murderer," Cary said.[38] When filming began on February 10, 1941, the script was still being rewritten, and Hitchcock and his writers were struggling to find

Photograph 17.30 By the end of *Suspicion*, Johnny is in full shadow as he brings Lina a glass of milk.

Source: author's screen capture

a plausible happy ending for Johnny and Lina. Hitchcock shot the film in sequence, beginning with the opening scene (Johnny and Lina meeting on the train) and proceeding chronologically from there.[39] This suited the film's darkening mood and it also allowed the writers to continue wrestling with the story and its ending. Finally, on April 23, they shot an ending in which Lina drinks the milk, and then reveals to Johnny that she thinks it is poisoned. He is astonished that she thinks he would murder her, and he realizes that his errant ways have fueled her suspicions. As he promises to reform and asks her to forgive him, the film fades out as they embrace.[40]

This was the ending audiences saw at the film's first preview screening at a Pasadena theater in mid-June. RKO executives, on hand to gauge responses to the film, were alarmed to hear the audience laugh when Lina drank the milk. "What sane woman would act that way?" one audience member complained on a comment card. Another preview screening was quickly arranged, this time in Inglewood, but the ending met with a similarly disapproving response.[41] Having allowed the production costs to creep upward, rising above $1 million by this point, the studio was adamant that the ending must be changed.[42]

In late July, the writers and the stars were hastily recalled to film another ending in which Lina does not drink the milk.[43] Instead, she leaves the glass by her bedside and the next morning announces that she is going to stay with her mother. Johnny insists on driving her there, and Lina once again thinks that Johnny is trying to kill her—this time by pushing her out of the car as it swerves along a clifftop coastal road. It is another wonderfully ambiguous scene, as it appears equally plausible that Johnny could be trying to push her out of the car and that he could be trying to save her from falling out of it. When he pulls over to the side of the road and insists that he never meant her any harm, she suddenly—and inexplicably—becomes convinced that he never intended to kill her. As in the earlier ending, Johnny expresses remorse for making her suspicious and he insists that she would be better off without him. Their reconciliation is then handled in the quickest and subtlest of ways: they get back in the car, Johnny turns the car around to head back to their home, and as they drive away he places his arm around Lina.

Critics admired *Suspicion* for its suspense, but this ending was consistently cited as a let-down. *The Hollywood Reporter* headlined its review, "*Suspicion* can be a smash hit with change in ending."[44] *Variety* took a similar line: "Hitchcock and his scriptwriters devised a most inept and inconclusive windup that fails to measure up to the dramatic intensity of the preceding footage."[45] In the *New York Times*, Bosley Crowther complained that the ending "is not up to Mr. Hitchcock's usual style."[46] Decades later, Hitchcock discussed the ending as a kind of travesty; an example of studio hacks meddling with a director's artistic vision.[47] Yet it is hard to imagine any satisfactory ending for *Suspicion*. The essence of the film—its intrigue and its suspense—rests in Johnny's ambiguity, as well as the careful balance Cary strikes between the character's seductive charm and his chilly menace. Any attempt to prove that he is clearly one thing or another could only end in disappointment.

Critical complaints aside, *Suspicion* was a box-office hit, earning $1.3 million in North America and a further $900,000 abroad.[48] It was a hard-won success. The production had dragged on for months because of the problems with the ending, an outbreak of flu (which felled Cary, Hitchcock, and Fontaine in succession), and the tensions that developed on the set between Cary and Joan Fontaine. In her memoir, Fontaine recalled that "Cary was fascinating to work with" and she admired his mastery of the art of film acting:

He knew exactly where each light was, rightly insisted that his key and eye lights were positioned as he knew they should be. Actors who have made many films and watched their rushes after each day's work know more about their camera angles and lighting than anyone else. . . . His timing, his body movements were superb. Everything he did was in balance.

She also admitted that a "distance" opened up between them because, she claimed, Cary did not realize that "the part of Lina was the major role" until they were halfway through making the film. "She had all the sympathy," Fontaine insisted; "He was the villain."[49] This rather flat understanding of the film would have surprised not only Cary but also Hitchcock, who was so fascinated by the character that he and Cary had created that he suggested to RKO that the film's title should be changed to "Johnny."[50]

Cary seldom said anything negative or hostile about his co-workers, but thirty years after making *Suspicion*, he still resented Joan Fontaine. "It wasn't hard to play someone who looked as if he wanted to kill her," he told Maureen Donaldson. "All she had to do was look frightened all the way through the movie," he added. "But with my character, you never know whether he's a killer or not for almost the entire film. Try conveying *that* for an hour and a half."[51]

While the making of *Suspicion* dragged on, Cary was setting up the Warner Bros. deal that would allow him to donate his salary to war-related charities. Initially, this deal centered on *The Man Who Came to Dinner* (1942), a screen adaptation of George S. Kaufman and Moss Hart's hit Broadway comedy that would reunite the *His Girl Friday* team. Cary was set to star as Sheridan Whiteside, an acerbic New York drama critic who breaks his leg while traveling and finds himself stuck in a middle American home over Christmas. Everyone recognized that Cary was too young to play the imperious Whiteside, but Jack Warner was so keen on this set-up that he got Kaufman and Hart's permission to change the story, making Whiteside younger and introducing a romance between him and his secretary.[52] The production plans now looked very promising: Howard Hawks directing Cary as Whiteside and Rosalind Russell as his long-suffering secretary.[53] Then Cary hesitated a little bit too long before signing his contract.[54] Warner began looking at other casting options, and the alternatives he considered (among them Orson Welles, Clifton Webb, and Monty Woolley) prompted Rosalind Russell and Howard Hawks to drop out.[55] The opportunity to reunite the *His Girl Friday* team was lost, and *The Man Who Came to Dinner*—with William

Keighley directing and Monty Woolley and Bette Davis in the lead roles—was not quite as sharp as it might have been.

Eager not to let his Warner Bros. deal slip away, because of the arrangements made for tax-free charitable donations, Cary hastily agreed to make a different film for the studio. Jack Warner had purchased the rights to another Broadway hit, Joseph Kesselring's *Arsenic and Old Lace*, and he lined up Frank Capra to direct it. Capra thought Cary could be convinced to star in the film if he saw the play on Broadway, and in September 1941 he sought Warner's permission for an all-expenses-paid jaunt to New York. Warner, now all too familiar with Cary's anxieties, approved only if Cary would sign a contract to make the film before traveling. "He may want to stall after seeing the show," Warner warned Capra.[56] This proved to be prophetic. *Arsenic and Old Lace* is the film Cary most regretted making, the one he always cited as his least favorite of his own films.[57]

The play itself was not the problem. *Arsenic and Old Lace* works well as both a ghoulish farce and a sly commentary on how Americans view their country's history. Cary plays Mortimer Brewster, a drama critic whose sweet, elderly aunts claim that their ancestors came over on the *Mayflower*, and whose cousin Teddy believes so fervently that he is Teddy Roosevelt that he recreates the Battle of San Juan Hill every time he climbs the stairs (blowing a bugle and yelling "Charge!" as he ascends). On the day that he marries, Mortimer discovers that his aunts are murdering their lodgers with arsenic and Teddy is burying the bodies in the basement (under the delusion that he is digging the Panama Canal). To Mortimer's astonishment, these seemingly kind people refuse to acknowledge that they have ever harmed anyone, preferring to live in a bubble of their own innocence and virtue.

In most of his comedies, Cary plays the calmest and sanest character—the one who represents the audience's perspective on the story—and the other characters are the eccentrics. This is true of *Arsenic and Old Lace* until Mortimer realizes what his relatives have been up to, and then he appears to be madder than they are as he tries to cover up their crimes. He frantically runs from character to character, and up and down the stairs, as the revelations and complications pile up. His eyes pop open with disbelief, he whinnies with frustration, and he plays an entire scene tied to a chair and with a handkerchief stuffed in his mouth. It is the broadest and most frenzied comic performance that he ever gave. As Richard Schickel observed, Cary whinnied for Howard Hawks too, but Hawks's frenzied moments are brief and fleeting, whereas Capra seems to be trying to compensate for the set-bound staginess of *Arsenic and Old Lace* by placing Cary in constant, frantic motion.[58]

Capra claimed in his autobiography that he considered *Arsenic and Old Lace* to be a "muggers' ball" and he simply "let the scene stealers run wild."[59] It is true that he assembled a near-perfect cast of character actors to support Cary. Especially memorable are Jean Adair and Josephine Hull as the aunts who kill with kindness, and Raymond Massey and Peter Lorre as Mortimer's criminally insane brother and his alcoholic sidekick. But Capra was not a director who believed in improvisation or collaboration. He was the master of his set, and his status in Hollywood meant that he was one of the few directors powerful enough to lean on Cary, pushing him to give a performance that made him uncomfortable on the set and then embarrassed when watching it later.[60]

Cary's star status meant that, as ever, the story had to be at least partially rewritten to accommodate him. Just as Warner Bros. had earlier planned to rewrite *The Man Who Came to Dinner*, adding the romance audiences would

Photograph 17.31 Cary threw himself into the broad comedy of *Arsenic and Old Lace* (Warner Bros., 1944) but he was embarrassed by his performance.
Source: author's screen capture

expect of a Cary Grant film, the studio added scenes to *Arsenic and Old Lace* that beefed up his role and shaped it to his image. In the film, Mortimer Brewster became not just a drama critic but also the world's most famous bachelor and the author of the books *Marriage: A Fraud and a Failure* and *Mind Over Matrimony*. This was hardly an inside joke. At the time the film was made, there was continual speculation in the press about whether he would marry Barbara Hutton, or if he would resist marrying again, as he had with Mary Brian and Phyllis Brooks. Some authors claim to have spotted another "in joke" in the film. It is said that, in the graveyard outside the Brewster home, there is a headstone that bears the name Archie Leach.[61] However, this is not visible in the film, and it seems unlikely that, after the recent deaths of his Leach relatives, he would make this macabre joke. The film's references to mental illness hit close enough to home. "Insanity runs in my family. It practically gallops!" Mortimer tells his fiancée (Priscilla Lane). This line, and the many references to the asylum, were in the original play and could not be avoided.

Arsenic and Old Lace was filmed in a brisk eight weeks in the autumn of 1941.[62] The film could not be released until the play's Broadway run ended—a contractual obligation that delayed its appearance in theaters until 1944—but Cary was paid as soon as filming finished. His salary, at $160,000, was his highest yet, but only $50,000 of this went into his own pocket, because $50,000 went to British War Relief, $25,000 went to the American Red Cross, $25,000 went to the USO (a charity that supplied entertainment to the troops), and $10,000 went to his agent, Frank Vincent.[63] These very significant charitable donations offered him a reason not to regret the film, even if his own performance made him shudder. He was not reassured by the critics. *The Hollywood Reporter*, for example, avowed that "Cary Grant gives a grand performance, just about the best comedy effort of his career," while the *Los Angeles Times* called the film "a triumph for Cary Grant."[64] One suspects he was more attuned to the *New York Times* critic who complained that his energetic performance was "likely to wear down, eventually, the stoutest spectator."[65]

When he first arrived on the set, Capra introduced him to the cast, including Jean Adair, who was playing one of the Brewster aunts. "You don't remember, do you?" Cary asked her. "I've seen you on the screen many times," she replied, "but I don't recall having met you personally." Cary then reminded her that nearly twenty years earlier she looked after a teenage boy who was stuck in a boarding house in Rochester, New York, alone on his birthday and suffering from rheumatic fever. She did remember the "very nice" boy but she had no idea that he grew up to be Cary Grant.[66] He also ran into Orry-Kelly, who was Warner Bros.' leading costume designer. Kelly told him that he was about to volunteer for the army, and he touched a nerve when he asked Cary about his own plans for wartime service. According to Kelly, Cary cut him off "in a rather supercilious manner" and told him about his meeting with Lord Lothian. Kelly concluded that his old friend "had gone to the point of no return" in his transformation from Archie Leach to Cary Grant.[67]

This was true in ways that Kelly could not have known. *Arsenic and Old Lace* was nearly finished filming on December 7, 1941, when the Japanese attack on Pearl Harbor brought the United States into the war at last. In the wake of the devastating, surprise attack, many filmmakers put aside their careers and joined the military. For Cary, though, America's entry into the war would bring other changes. Finally, he could apply for US citizenship without being accused of being a coward or a traitor, and this in turn would enable him to volunteer for US military service. He would also change his name, legally, to Cary Grant. Hollywood's most sought-after star—known for being offered nearly every significant leading role and notorious for being unable to commit to films—was clear that he would take time away from his film career and serve his new country.

18

The attack on Pearl Harbor unleashed a frenzy of patriotism, anxiety, and prejudice across the United States, but its impact was especially acute in California. Los Angeles was gripped with the fear that a Japanese attack on the city was imminent. There were numerous false alarms—enemy planes sighted over the city and submarines seen off the coast. A blackout was imposed across the region, and Japanese Americans were rounded up and interned on the mistaken assumption that they were spies and saboteurs. In the fervor of the moment, everyone wanted to be seen to being doing his or her bit. Film stars rushed to join up, and those who could not join up devoted time to wartime charities and causes. The industry's first prominent casualty was Carole Lombard, who died in a plane crash while returning from a personal appearance at a war bonds rally in her home state, Indiana. Lombard's tragic death only reinforced the widespread determination to contribute to the war effort. Hollywood, long regarded as the home of glamour and excess, now wanted to be known for its sense of duty and commitment.[1]

With the United States in the war at last, Cary could apply for US citizenship without being accused of being a shirker back in Britain. He seized the opportunity in the week after Pearl Harbor, and looked forward to enlisting in the US Army Air Force when his citizenship papers came through. His friendship with Howard Hughes, not to mention his roles in *The Eagle and the Hawk*, *Wings in the Dark*, *Suzy*, and *Only Angels Have Wings*, ensured that he wanted to become a flier himself.[2] In the meantime, while he watched so many others join up, his war service had to be limited to civilian activities. He was on the board of directors of several charities: the Hollywood Victory Committee, and the Hollywood divisions of British War Relief and United Nations War Relief, and the Jesterate of Masquers (an actor's charity). He spent his evenings and weekends in committee meetings, at fundraisers on weekends, and making personal appearances in military hospitals and camps. Believing that serious times called for serious films, he also sought to make more significant and socially aware films.[3]

The first of these, George Stevens's *The Talk of the Town* (1942), began shooting at Columbia on January 19, 1942.[4] Stevens developed the film's original story with Cary in mind.[5] Like Hitchcock, Stevens understood that

Cary's presence in the film allowed him to take risks that would be impossible with a less familiar, less attractive star. The audience liked and trusted Cary enough to go along for a ride with him, even if the ride seemed to be heading in a very unusual direction, as it does in *The Talk of the Town*.[6] The film begins with a disturbing montage: a factory fire that results in the death of a man; the bellicose factory owner and a corrupt district attorney blaming the fire on a local radical named Leopold Dilg; the hasty trial of Dilg and the prospect that he will be executed for arson and murder; and Dilg's escape from jail by attacking a guard.

The montage sets the tone for a social problem film exploring the limits of democracy and the potential for fascism in the United States. There was a brief but prominent cycle of these films during the early war years—Orson Welles's *Citizen Kane* (1941), Capra's *Meet John Doe* (1941), Hitchcock's *Saboteur* (1942), and Cukor's *Keeper of the Flame* (1942)—and *The Talk of the Town* begins as darkly as any of them. Throughout the film, Dilg is in hiding in his own hometown, seeking refuge from the mob that wants to lynch him and a justice system that seeks to execute him. He hides in the attic of schoolteacher Nora Shelley (Jean Arthur) at the very moment she has rented her home to a legal scholar, Professor Lightcap (Ronald Colman), who has just been nominated to a seat on the US Supreme Court. A romantic triangle develops as Dilg and Lightcap debate the nature of justice—Lightcap arguing for the higher unwavering principles of the law and Dilg arguing the case for humanity in the interpretation of the law—while Shelley looks on nervously.

Dilg is in some respects a darker character than Johnny Aysgarth in *Suspicion*. He attacks a policeman and threatens both Shelley and Lightcap with violence. He is also scruffier: this was one film on which Cary did not supply his own wardrobe but instead allowed the studio to supply him with inexpensive "workingman's clothes."[7] Yet as the film progresses, the character emerges from the darkness, tidies himself up, and is allowed more than a measure of humanity. In parallel, the initially stiff Lightcap loses some of his hauteur (signaled in the shaving of his carefully manicured "Van Dyke beard") and comes to Dilg's aid, proving his innocence. The growing warmth and friendship between the two men is one of the film's most distinctive qualities. It is interesting to see Cary and Ronald Colman together on-screen. By 1942, Colman's career was past its prime (he took third billing in *The Talk of the Town*), but he had been Hollywood's premier British gentleman for more than a decade. Although he and Cary play American characters, British class hierarchies seem to persist in the film, with the upper-middle-class Colman playing an ivory tower elitist and the formerly working-class Cary playing a downtrodden factory worker.

If the film does not quite work, it is because it veers too widely between its darker social concerns and light romantic comedy. Stevens was apparently smitten with Jean Arthur. He allows her to have a few too many "madcap" moments, and he places too much emphasis on her character's dilemma— is she in love with Dilg or Lightcap?—which is really no dilemma at all. Columbia made much of the fact that Stevens filmed two different endings, one with Shelley choosing Dilg and the other with her choosing Lightcap, and then tested the endings on audiences.[8] However, it is hard to believe that these numerous and widely reported preview screenings were anything other than a publicity stunt. The preview audiences made the obvious choice, opting for the ending that has the two lead stars together.[9]

Once again Cary and Jean Arthur were at odds during the filming, each thinking the other was trying to upstage them. When they made *Only Angels Have Wings* together, Cary knew that he had Howard Hawks on his side, but on *The Talk of the Town*, he saw that there was a rapport between George Stevens and Jean Arthur, and he suspected that Stevens was favoring her.[10] Tensions came to the fore when they were filming the last scene. As in so many Cary Grant films, this ending has no grand romantic statement or passionate kiss. Rather, Dilg intends to walk away from Shelley, insisting that she would be better off with Lightcap than with him, but Shelley follows him, protesting that it is her decision to make. Finally, he pauses to kiss her and walks off again, and then in the very last shot, he hastily doubles back to grab her hand and take her with him.

Stevens filmed this finale over and over again, making the two stars very uncomfortable. "It was terrible," Arthur recalled, "I don't know why he did it."[11] Eventually, Cary suggested to Arthur that the problem was that she was "overplaying" the scene. He advised her to tone down her performance, and she responded, by his account, with "hysterics." Luckily, this was the last scene to be filmed, because it was also the end of the line for Cary and Jean Arthur. Cary turned down the lead in Stevens's next film, *The More the Merrier* (1942), which would have brought them together again, and several years later, when Frank Capra proposed reuniting them for *A Woman of Distinction* (1950), Arthur replied that she would make the film "with anybody but Cary."[12]

Stevens had become a slow director, filming scenes from every possible angle so that he would have the greatest leeway when editing. This caused delays on the set and in the editing room. His first cut of *The Talk of the Town* was nearly three hours long and it took him several weeks to pare it down to 118 minutes.[13] When it was released in August 1942, the critical consensus was that Stevens should have cut more. As *Variety* put it, "intelligent pruning" was needed.[14] Many critics also noted that Stevens was not as successful as Frank Capra in combining socially aware drama with light comedy. In New York's *Daily News*, Kate Cameron took an easy potshot at the film—"There's a lot of talk in *The Talk of the Town*"—while Philip K. Scheuer of the *Los Angeles Times* observed that at the premiere, held as a benefit for servicemen, many of the men in uniform grew restless and walked out of the film.[15] On release, *The Talk of the Town* was by no means a flop—the trio of stars ensured solid box-office returns—but it fell short of both critical and commercial expectations.[16]

As soon as *The Talk of the Town* was completed in April 1942, Cary embarked on the first of several wartime tours, appearing in live stage shows throughout the United States. It was the first time he had done anything like this since he toured with *A Wonderful Night* eleven years earlier. But this first wartime tour, "The Hollywood Victory Caravan," was on a much larger scale. It was a show business extravaganza that had its own specially chartered train, kitted out so that the dozens of stars and musicians taking part in the shows could rehearse en route from Los Angeles to Washington, DC. The first public appearance, on April 30, was the most sedate. The First Lady, Eleanor Roosevelt, hosted a tea for the company on the White House lawn. That evening, the first show was held at the city's Constitution Hall, and then the train took them to another dozen cities, as the company gradually worked its way back to the West Coast over two weeks.

In each city, the stars paraded through the central business district, beginning at the train station and proceeding to the arena where the show was held. Crowds numbering in the thousands lined the streets to greet them, enthusiastically waving and shouting to the stars they had seen so many times on-screen but never imagined they would see on their own main street. Cary, especially, met with roaring approval from the crowds. At an early stop in Boston, he was visibly moved by the public's response to him. When the crowd outside the train station greeted him with deafening enthusiasm, he wiped tears from his eyes. He was then astonished to find that crowds lined the 2 miles of streets between the station and the auditorium.[17] "I never saw anything like it," he commented afterward, but a similar reception awaited him in each of the other cities.

In St. Louis, which had claimed him as a local ever since his summer at Forest Park, there were shouts of "Hi, Archie!" and "Welcome back, Archie!" from the crowds lining the streets. During the show that evening, the crowd laughed so enthusiastically at his jokes that he asked, in a bewildered tone, "What am I doing?" several times. "Where did I get that laugh?" he asked, adding, "Is my slip showing?"[18]

Local newspapers were fascinated by him, and reported his every move in detail. His immaculate appearance was often noted, and his suits described in fine detail ("a gray half-striped English draped double-breasted suit, soft blue and white striped shirt, a small checked necktie and no hat" in St. Louis). The reporters who met him backstage, though, observed that he was "the jittery type" and "all over the place" while waiting to go on stage.[19] This surprised the reporters, but it would not have surprised anyone who had worked with him—on stage or on a film set.

The stage shows were reminiscent of vaudeville, with Cary and the comedian Bob Hope sharing the master of ceremonies role, introducing the other stars and "keeping the audience in stitches" between the skits and songs.[20] Cary performed a skit with Bert Lahr (best known for playing the Cowardly Lion in *The Wizard of Oz*) in which he was a wily income-tax collector and Lahr was a rich and spoiled movie star seeking a refund. James Cagney performed the title song from his recent hit film *Yankee Doodle Dandy*. Joan Blondell did what was described as an "eminently proper striptease" in a dress that would not unzip. Olivia de Havilland and Joan Bennett did a sketch about women working in defense factories. Bing Crosby, a top draw for audiences, sang at least a few songs. Comedians Groucho Marx and Laurel and Hardy revived their best-loved comic routines. Charles Boyer provided a more serious moment when he spoke about the Free French and proudly speculated that he was the youngest American in the arena because he had become a citizen only a few weeks earlier. Merle Oberon recited a somber poem written by a flier just before his death.[21]

All of the star turns were well received but it was the auction that excited audiences the most. The stars offered onstage kisses to the highest bidders. A kiss from Claudette Colbert proved to be the most valuable, with $1,000 paid for a single kiss on the lips. Cary raised more money than any of the other men, when a woman in Chicago paid $500 for a kiss from him. On stage, she was so excited that she pressed a wad of bills into his hand amounting to $1,200, and he was so nervous that he put the entire amount into his pocket without counting it. It was just one of many encounters he had with star-struck fans.[22] "Now I can die happy," women repeatedly said to him when they bought a kiss or simply caught his attention on the parade route. All of this would have seemed a rather vulgar business before Pearl Harbor, and there is no doubt that Cary would have preferred a more digni- fied form of war service. In the heat of the moment, however, the shows and even the auctions were celebrated for raising money (bringing in $600,000 for army and navy relief funds) and boosting morale.[23]

Back at home in Santa Monica, and with the roar of the crowds still ringing in his ears, he was finally in a position to make some far-reaching changes to his life. On May 23, 1942, Randolph Scott and Frank Horn accompanied him to the Los Angeles federal courthouse, where his best friend and his personal secretary were sworn in to affirm the facts of his citizenship application. As part of the American naturalization process, he was able to request that his name should change as well. Thus, when the application was approved, Archibald Alec Leach renounced his British citizenship and became Cary Grant, American citizen.[24] He took the oath of citizenship, along with three hundred other immigrants, at the same courthouse on June 26, 1942.

Aware that this would be headline news in the United States and in Britain, and always wary of the press, he issued a written statement to reporters to en- sure that his words were not misconstrued:

> I applied for citizenship when America entered the war so that I could be el-
> igible to volunteer my services to the country that has treated me so kindly
> and in which I have been privileged to live for many years. I am, now, grate-
> fully, an American.[25]

The next day, he applied for a commission in the US Air Force, and then, anticipating that he would soon leave for officer training school, he asked Barbara Hutton to marry him and she accepted.[26]

Many years later, when Cary spoke about his marriage to Barbara, he admitted that "I'm not sure that either one of us really wanted to marry the other by the time we got around to it."[27] It may be that, like so many other couples in 1942, they felt compelled to tie the knot before he went off to military service. Some sources also allege that they could not marry until 1942 because the divorce agreement between Barbara and Count Haugwitz- Reventlow (settled in March 1941) stipulated that if she remarried within a year, her custody of their six-year-old son, Lance, would be reduced from six to three months per year.[28] There may also have been a spirit of defiance in their decision to wed. Over the course of their two-year romance, gossip columnists had frequently speculated about their impending engagement or, alternatively, their impending break-up. More recently, the columnists delighted in referring to them as "Cash and Cary"—a joke that highlighted the improbable match between the "poor little rich girl" and the acrobat-turned-actor.[29]

Cary responded to this unwanted attention by fastidiously preventing reporters and photographers from ever getting a glimpse of them together. He and Barbara avoided nightclubs, where the paparazzi would spot them, and she did not accompany him to premieres and other public occasions. The press got a rare glimpse of them when Rosalind Russell and Freddie Brisson married in October 1941. Cary was Brisson's best man and Barbara was one of Russell's bridesmaids. When the wedding pictures were released to the press, Cary and Barbara could be seen in the same photograph, even if they were on different sides of the bride and groom.[30] Otherwise, they kept their relationship remarkably private. Cary would always chat with the reporters and gossip columnists who visited the set of his films as long as they never brought up his private life. If they did ask personal questions, his good humor ceased. "It's none of your business," he flatly responded if the conversation drifted away from filmmaking.[31]

For their own wedding, Cary and Barbara managed to catch the press completely off guard. The ceremony was planned as a top-secret event. They married at the secluded Lake Arrowhead vacation home of Frank Vincent, Cary's agent and friend. Vincent had arranged for a pastor from the local Lutheran church to conduct the six-minute ceremony, and even the pastor did not know the identity of the couple in advance. The ceremony, held at noon, took place on a patio overlooking the lake, and in the shade of an oak tree. They invited only a few guests. Madeline Hastletine, the wife of the sculptor Herbert Hastletine, was Barbara's matron of honor and the only guest who was not employed by the couple. William Robertson (Barbara's property manager), "Ticki" Tocquet (her former governess and current paid companion), and Frank Horn (Cary's secretary) were the other guests, and Frank Vincent was his best man.[32]

An RKO photographer was also on hand so that, when the story was reported on the front page of newspapers around the world, there would be a suitable photograph to accompany the news. The wedding photo reveals that they were smartly but not formally dressed. Cary, in a blue-gray pinstripe suit, grins happily at the camera, while Barbara, wearing a silk skirt and matching jacket, manages only a characteristically wan smile for the camera. This was all remarkably restrained for a Hollywood star and the richest woman in the world, but in the midst of the war, they were careful to avoid any signs of ostentation. In keeping with this, they let it be known that they would not have a honeymoon. Cary took a day off from filming for the wedding and returned to work the next day. The film he was making, as many newspapers wryly reported, was entitled *Once Upon a Honeymoon* (1942).[33]

The title was not a coincidence. The script was based on an original story by Leo McCarey, who had enjoyed toying with Cary's man-about-town image in *The Awful Truth* and *My Favorite Wife*, and now intended to make a film that had some broad parallels with his relationship with Barbara Hutton. Indeed, *Once Upon a Honeymoon* appears to be a form of explanation or apology for Barbara's marriage to Count Haugwitz-Reventlow in 1935. From the perspective of 1942, that marriage seemed like an indelible stain on her character. Haugwitz-Reventlow was a Prussian-born aristocrat who had served as an officer in the German army during the First World War, and Barbara had renounced her American citizenship to marry him. When they separated in 1939, their bitter divorce battle played out in the newspapers for the next two years. By the time she married Cary, her reputation was badly in need of rehabilitation, and McCarey thought that he could contribute toward this while also making a film that would educate American audiences about Nazi ideas and methods.[34]

Once Upon a Honeymoon does not refer to Hutton directly, but the story does illustrate how an American woman might find herself firstly married to a German aristocrat and secondly saved from that marriage by Cary Grant. It also pointedly allows for her to atone for her disloyalty. Ginger Rogers plays Katie O'Hara as a feisty Brooklyn showgirl and social climber who marries Baron Von Luber (Walter Slezak) without realizing that he is a Nazi operative who is laying the groundwork for the German invasion of neighboring countries. Cary is an American foreign correspondent, Pat O'Toole, investigating Von Luber and, in the process, falling in love with Katie. She leaves Von Luber as soon as she discovers the truth about him and, despite falling in love with Pat, she returns to him so that she can uncover his next moves. In the process, the story affords her the opportunity to recite the American "Pledge of Allegiance," to speak of her love of baseball and the Statue of Liberty, and ultimately to kill the baron—albeit in self-defense. By the end of the film, there is no doubt that a woman can have made the mistake of marrying a dubious European aristocrat and yet still be a loyal and patriotic American.

The parallels with Hutton aside, McCarey conceived of *Once Upon a Honeymoon* first and foremost as a film that would highlight Nazi barbarism.[35] The story includes scenes depicting the treachery of the *Anschluss*, the bombing of Warsaw, the persecution of the Jews, a U-boat sinking a neutral ship with civilian passengers, and even an explanation of Nazi policies of eugenics. McCarey aimed to temper the propaganda with comedy, keeping audiences entertained by ridiculing the Nazis in the manner of Charlie Chaplin's *The Great Dictator* (1940) and Ernst Lubitsch's *To Be or Not to Be* (1942).[36] Unfortunately, however, *Once Upon a Honeymoon* is nowhere near as assured as those films. It is an uneven film that fails both as a melodramatic exposé and as a black comedy. It reaches its nadir when Pat and Katie are mistaken for Jews, sent to a concentration camp, and then smile and laugh with relief when the US ambassador arranges for their release.

McCarey invented what scriptwriter Sheridan Gibney disparagingly termed the film's "comic gags" and "little vaudeville routines" during the filming. In an early scene, for example, when Pat and Katie meet for the first time, she mistakes him for her dress fitter and he plays along in order to get an interview with her. On the set, McCarey encouraged the stars to prolong the scene and make it funnier. He demonstrated to Cary how to take Rogers's measurements in an exaggerated and suggestive manner. The stars, Gibney recalled, were enthralled by McCarey. They thought he was "marvelous" and "They would do anything he told them to," but Gibney thought that the silliness "cheapened the picture" and "distracted" from its real drama.[37]

Gibney also recalled that McCarey was in the grip of alcoholism during the filming. He was not drunk on the set, but he stayed out all night drinking and sometimes never made it home.[38] This is the likely explanation for the production delays. Filming began on June 8, 1942, and it was scheduled to finish nine weeks later in early August, but, with many last-minute retakes, it extended into late September.[39] When it was rushed into release in November, it came under heavy fire from film critics. Bosley Crowther of the *New York Times* referred to *Once Upon a Honeymoon* as "callous," "downright offensive," and in "markedly dubious taste." Other critics were not quite as outspoken but they warned audiences that the film was awkward and unsatisfactory.[40] This did not prevent its success at the box office.[41] Having the names Cary Grant and Ginger Rogers on the marquee guaranteed healthy ticket sales, but the film did nothing to enhance the reputation of anyone involved in making it.

In August, as the filming of *Once Upon a Honeymoon* dragged on, Cary finally received a letter from the Air Force informing him that within a month he would be asked to report to officer training school in Miami.[42] This was news that Cary had been waiting for eagerly but that RKO had been dreading. All of the studios were reluctant to see their most bankable stars drafted. They delayed their departure by making an official case for deferring a star's enlistment until a film (or two) that was already in production, or nearing production, could be completed. Even though *Once Upon a Honeymoon* would be finished in September, RKO made the case that Cary should be allowed to make one more film after this, and then enlist in December. The studio promised that this next film, *Mr. Lucky* (1943), would have "definite propaganda value . . . in that its story deals with the regenerating effect of patriotism."[43]

In fact, the story of *Mr. Lucky* would have been a familiar one to anyone who had seen prominent war films such as *Foreign Correspondent* (1940), *Sergeant York* (1941), and *Casablanca* (1942). Its story is a "conversion narrative" that centers on an American man who is initially disinterested in the war but slowly realizes the moral imperative of fighting against fascism and for democracy. If *Mr. Lucky* has a few fresh twists, it is because the author of the original story, Milton Holmes, wrote it with Cary in mind. Holmes was not a professional writer but a caretaker at the Beverly Hills Tennis Club, where Cary often played a game or two on Sundays.[44] In January 1942, Holmes approached Cary at the club with a risky opening gambit. "I saw you in *Suspicion* and liked you—for the first time," he said, explaining that he admired Cary for playing a darker and more malevolent character.[45] He went on to tell him the story of *Mr. Lucky*, about a gangster who plans to swindle a wartime charity but ultimately realizes the error of his ways. Cary was intrigued enough to read the treatment, and he liked it so much that RKO jumped on it, quickly buying the rights for $30,000, and then assigning a succession of veteran scriptwriters (among them Charles Brackett, Adrian Scott, and Dudley Nichols) to develop a full screenplay.[46]

It is easy to see why Cary was intrigued. *Mr. Lucky* is infused with some of the most distinctive elements of his earlier films, including references to Cary's real life. His character is a New York gangster with an adopted name and an indeterminate nationality. "Joe" may or may not be his real name, and he may or may not be American, Australian, or Greek (the script leaves these points open), but he is irresistibly handsome, and he is pursued by a high-spirited heiress who is described in Holmes's treatment as "a dead ringer for

Katharine Hepburn." His feelings toward her are hard to gauge. He seems to be genuinely interested in her yet he is clearly out to steal from her war relief charity. Although she does not steal his clothes or make him wear a frilly negligee, she does put him to work knitting for the war effort, amid a circle of dowagers, and a crowd of men gathers to observe this very public, unmasculine spectacle. On the set, Cary added to the self-referential elements by improvising a rhyming slang in which he referred to his pistol as "a lady from Bristol."[47]

Mr. Lucky was another film on which Cary had no interest in supplying his own tax-deductible wardrobe; his gangster wears gaudy suits and loud ties.[48] Unlike the gangsters he played in his Paramount films, this one also has a genuine air of streetwise menace about him. When the heiress, Dorothy (Laraine Day), shows him around her family's home, pointing out the paintings of her ancestors, he turns on her. "You talk about this side of your family and that side of your family, as far as I know we only had one side and it was awful poor," he sneers. "Lots of times there wasn't what-for to eat. That's why I ran away from home when I was nine. I was tired of being hungry and seeing my old lady hungry until she died." The contempt with which he delivers these lines foreshadows the ending. He leaves her, sailing away on a ship while she pleads with him from the dock to stay. His response to her, shouted from the deck, is chilling: "You don't belong with a grifter like me. You just got some mud on your dress. Give it time, it will dry out and brush off!"

This would have been an admirably hard-hitting ending, but a coda ends the film on a much warmer note. The draft-dodging gangster atones for his sins by joining the merchant marine, and the heiress is waiting for him months later when he returns on shore leave. In this respect *Mr. Lucky* is a conventional war film, aiming to reassure and comfort audiences. The film is weakened by Laraine Day, who lacks the fire and wit that Katharine Hepburn brought to playing heiresses. Day was cast after filming began and only after other stars, including Olivia de Havilland, proved to be unavailable.[49] It is weakened too by the direction of H. C. "Hank" Potter, who cannot summon the spark that Howard Hawks might have brought to the film. Nevertheless, the story had the right combination of humor, cynicism, romance, and moral uplift for wartime audiences, as well as a title that highlighted its star's charm.[50] *Mr. Lucky* was by far RKO's biggest hit of 1943, earning $2.6 million in North America and $865,000 in foreign markets.[51]

The title proved to be ironic for Cary. He had agreed to allow RKO to seek a deferment for him so that he could complete this one last film before enlisting. But in December, as filming proceeded, the War Department halted all voluntary enlistments and lowered the age of eligibility for military service from 45 to 38. Cary, who would be 39 when *Mr. Lucky* finished filming in January, was no longer eligible to enlist. As a prominent personality, he was informed, he might be asked to perform "temporary services" for the government but only "from time to time" and not to an extent that would interfere with his filmmaking career. This was a bitter blow for him. The majority of his peers—Douglas Fairbanks Jr., Henry Fonda, Clark Gable, Robert Montgomery, Tyrone Power, James Stewart, and Robert Taylor—were already in uniform, and they were publicly celebrated for their service. Sitting out the war in Hollywood not only looked cowardly but also denied him the opportunity to serve his adopted country in a meaningful way.[52]

What the War Department really wanted him to do was visit the troops. He would be a morale booster for thousands of men and women stationed at remote training camps in the United States, far from their hometowns and awaiting orders to embark for the combat zones of Europe and the Far East. In March 1943, he toured sixteen military camps over three weeks, beginning at Camp Polk in Leesville, Louisiana, and ending at Camp Crowder in Neosho, Missouri. At each camp, he toured the facilities and talked with the men about their training and duties. He ate with them in the "mess tent," eschewing the officers' table to sit with the rank and file. He toured nearby hospitals, visiting with convalescing soldiers who had returned from overseas. And he went on stage for two shows nightly.[53]

Once again, as on the Hollywood Caravan tour, he performed vaudeville routines and hosted a revue show featuring a variety of other acts. This time, however, he had his old friend and partner Don Barclay with him on the tour, and they revived some of their old routines and created some new ones.[54] Cary also left time to talk with the audience. "I stand around, tell a few stories and answer questions," he told a reporter. "It's good fun."[55] It could turn sour. On at least one occasion, a man shouted, "Why aren't you in uniform?" He could only explain that he would like to be in uniform, but he was too old and the government preferred him to be on stage rather than in battle.[56]

Cary still held hopes of getting near the frontline. Together with Don Barclay and the actor George Murphy, he had condensed the rapid-fire Broadway comedy *Hellzapoppin'* into a 75-minute show that required minimal sets and support. In April and May 1943, the trio pressed the War Department to allow them to take the show overseas and entertain the troops in North Africa and Britain.[57] Then, while still waiting for a decision, Murphy accepted an offer to appear in the charity film *This Is the Army* (1943), and plans for an overseas tour with *Hellzapoppin'* fell apart.[58]

Apart from allowing him to serve in a more meaningful way, the overseas tour also would have allowed Cary to see his mother. It had been more than three years since Cary's last trip to Bristol. Elsie had made no secret of her disapproval when he became an American citizen, and she made no secret of her disappointment at missing Cary and Barbara's wedding. When a reporter came to her door in Bristol, seeking a comment, she admitted she had not sent her newlywed son any form of congratulations.[59] Cary, meanwhile,

Photograph 18.32 Elsie Leach with her "little doggy," circa 1942.
Source: The Cary Grant Papers, courtesy of the Margaret Herrick Library

could not help but notice that her letters became increasingly despairing as the war wore on. Although she had become a volunteer firewatcher in Bristol, she did not make friends easily and grew increasingly lonely. "Darling if you do not come over as soon as the war ends I shall come over to you," she wrote to him in the autumn of 1942. "I have no one only my little doggy. I think of you always darling. I hope you and your wife are living happily. I hope I shall have the privilege of meeting her."[60] But Elsie never did meet Barbara Hutton, and Cary—despite continuing efforts to arrange an overseas trip—did not manage to get back to Bristol during the war.

Instead, he spent much of the war in Hollywood, or, to be more exact, in the Pacific Palisades neighborhood of Los Angeles, where he had rented "Westridge," the estate (at 1515 North Amalfi Drive) that Douglas Fairbanks Jr. and his wife Mary Lee had recently renovated. Cary had hoped to continue living at Ocean Front, but Barbara "did not like the beach house or the people on the beach." Hence, when Fairbanks went into the army and his wife went East for the duration, Cary regretfully sold the beach house and rented Westridge from Fairbanks. Cary and Barbara had enjoyed one of their first dates at Westridge, at a party given by the Fairbankses, and it was much closer to the type of home that she was accustomed to. The vast mansion was situated on a high bluff and it had clear views to the ocean (5 miles away), 12 acres of grounds, a swimming pool, and a tennis court.

When Cary and Barbara moved to Westridge, she brought not only her son Lance but a staff of eleven servants to look after them.[61] For a man who wanted to serve his country in wartime, this degree of luxury was nothing short of embarrassing, but such were the contradictions of being Cary Grant. He found his life with Barbara at Westridge intolerable. Of course, he was having an easy war compared to just about everyone else, but he was not having a good war and it was not going to get any better.

"It's almost impossible to get a great story, a great director, and a great feminine star—all for the same film," Cary told a reporter in mid-1942. He went on to explain that proposed films generally fell into three categories. "One has an excellent script, with a fair director, and one or two good feminine stars; another has a medium script, with possibly a medium director and possibly one good feminine player, and the third has a good director, a very good leading lady and only a fair script." He preferred to make films that fell within the third category, he said, because they had the most scope for development on the set.[1] He spoke while filming *Once Upon a Honeymoon*, which certainly had a good director, a very good leading lady, and only a fair script. But his comments were made within the larger context of having a wealth of options. His relative freedom as a freelance star, together with a wartime shortage of leading men, meant that he was in greater demand than ever before, and this made choosing his films even more difficult.

He still had ongoing and non-exclusive deals with both RKO and Columbia. RKO was clearly eager to keep him happy. Over the years, his renegotiated contracts allowed his pay to rise from a flat $75,000 per film (in 1937) to $50,000 per film plus 2.5 percent of the box-office gross (in 1941), to $100,000 per film plus 10 percent of the box-office gross in excess of $1,500,000 (in 1942). This last arrangement proved to be especially lucrative. For the first film made under these arrangements, *Mr. Lucky*, his combined salary and earnings share reached $298,500 (and in later years there would be additional earnings from subsequent screenings and sales of the film). The 1942 contract also gave him approval of the script, the director, and the co-star of the films he made, a degree of power and control that few other stars achieved during the studio era.[2]

At Columbia, he remained tied to the far less attractive deal that he had signed in 1937. Columbia's studio boss, Harry Cohn, was only too happy to exercise the options that obligated Cary to make eight films for the studio. In 1943, he still owed Columbia two films at the comparatively low salary of $100,000 for each. The problem was that the studio's best filmmakers—including Frank Capra, Leo McCarey, Howard Hawks, and George Stevens—had by this time departed for war service or better deals at other studios, and there was no one of their caliber left at Columbia. Cary steered clear of his obligations at Columbia for as long as he could.[3]

After making two films in succession at RKO (*Once Upon a Honeymoon* and *Mr. Lucky*) he was expected to return to Columbia in May 1943, but instead he suddenly announced that his next film would be made for Warner Bros. Harry Cohn was livid, and he protested to both Cary and Warner Bros. that Cary's longstanding contractual obligation to Columbia took precedence over any new deal. [4] Ultimately, though, Cohn had to compromise. The Warner Bros. film was *Destination Tokyo*, a patriotic flag-waver made at the request of the US Navy, and in the heat of wartime this was enough to keep Harry Cohn at bay—at least for six weeks. The agreement reached between Columbia and Warner Bros. was that Cary would film all of his scenes for *Destination Tokyo* within six weeks—despite a production schedule that extended twice as long—so that he could return to Columbia in August.[5]

Destination Tokyo was not a film that Cary wanted to make for its director or its leading lady. In fact, this was Delmer Daves's first time directing and women scarcely feature in the story, which takes place almost entirely on a submarine out at sea. Instead, the appeal of *Destination Tokyo* for Cary can be found in a letter that the producer Jerry Wald wrote to him, pitching the film as one that Warner Bros. was making at the behest of the US Navy. The Navy, Wald informed him, needed volunteers for the submarine service, and *Destination Tokyo* was thus conceived as a recruitment film aiming to reassure potential volunteers (and their families) that serving on a submarine was like joining a family—a very well-trained, safety-conscious, dutiful, and kind family. They insisted that the captain of the submarine must not be a "grizzled veteran" but should be played by a young and good-humored man. Or, as Wald wrote in his letter, "they told us Cary Grant was the ideal type of sub captain."[6]

Wald's letter also explained that the film's story was based on a real, top-secret, treacherous mission undertaken by a US submarine crew, collecting data from Tokyo Bay in advance of the famous Doolittle Raid (the first US air attack on Tokyo). The film was ultimately promoted to the public on these terms too—as a true account of the raid—but the story is almost entirely fictional. It is not clear whether Cary realized this or not, but, even if he did, he was unlikely to resist Wald's appeal to his patriotism or the opportunity to play a character unlike any he had played so far.

He modeled his character, Captain Cassidy, on Noel Coward's portrayal of a British naval captain in the much-admired British war film *In Which*

We Serve (1942). Cassidy, like Coward's Captain Kinross, is a kind yet firm father figure, offering sage advice and supportive leadership to an assortment of younger men heading into battle. In *Destination Tokyo*, as in so many other Second World War combat films, the "crew" is characterized with broad brushstrokes. Tommy (Robert Hutton) is the wide-eyed newcomer to the submarine, "Wolf" (John Garfield) is a boastful ladies' man, "Sparks" (John Forsythe) is the jovial radio operator, "Pills" (William Prince) is a man of science who learns to pray, "Tin Can" (Dane Clark) is a Greek American fighting to avenge the murder of his relatives by Nazis, "Cookie" is the long-suffering cook who mothers the men, and Mike (Tom Tully) is an older veteran who is stabbed in the back while trying to save a downed Japanese pilot from icy waters.

In addition to Mike's death, there are several dramatic climaxes in the film's unusually long, 135-minute running time. Far out at sea, Tommy has an appendicitis and "Pills" must (very apprehensively) perform surgery to save him. A torpedo fails to launch and Tommy is the only man slim enough to crawl into the narrow launch space and defuse it. And a mission that takes the submarine into Tokyo Bay ends with the vessel under attack and being blasted by depth charges that nearly destroy it. As dramatic as these incidents are, the film is as interested in the submarine itself as it is in the action. Whole scenes are devoted to demonstrating operational procedures: taking the vessel underwater and bringing it to the surface again, loading and firing torpedoes, and revealing how the crew can eat, sleep, and shower in such a confined space.

If *Destination Tokyo* was designed to suit the propaganda needs of the military and the curiosity of wartime audiences, it nevertheless has some distinctive Cary Grant elements. The technique he had perfected as a screwball comedy performer—signaling an awareness of the chaos unfolding around him while also keeping his cool—serves him well in this dramatic role too. He uses a subtle dance of his eyes and a clenching of his jaw to show that he is registering the very real dangers that threaten the submarine, even though (for the sake of the less experienced crew) he projects an air of calm confidence. Through much of the film, he also looks to be the most sharply dressed officer ever to wear a uniform, and as in so many of his films, the drama climaxes with the removal or destruction of his clothes. In *Destination Tokyo*, it is in the heat of the Tokyo Bay battle, as depth charges pound the submarine and leaks threaten to flood the vessel, that his despair is expressed through his dishevelment. His sleeves are rolled up in the heat, his shirt is unbuttoned to reveal his bare chest, and his tousled hair drips with perspiration as he struggles to maintain a calm demeanor. Here, as in all of his films, these moments of disheveled despair prefigure a reassertion of his power. "Let's have a crack at those Japs!" he declares to the crew, rallying them to attack rather than hide from the enemy.

During his six weeks on the set of *Destination Tokyo*, Cary befriended some of the young cast members, including John Forsythe (now best known for playing the oil magnate Blake Carrington in the 1980s television series *Dynasty*) and Robert Hutton, who was a distant relative of Barbara Hutton. Cary had some fun at Hutton's expense. The novice actor was told not to attend the evening screenings of "rushes" because seeing himself on-screen for the first time was likely to make him self-conscious. But after filming his first big scene, when his character defuses the torpedo that failed to launch, he could not resist sneaking into the screening room. Cary, Delmer Daves, and Jerry Wald pretended not to notice him sitting at the back row, and when the

Photograph 19.33 In *Destination Tokyo* (Warner Bros., 1943), Cary initially looks very sharp in uniform, but, as in his comedies, circumstances conspire to undo his composure.

Source: author's screen capture

close-ups of Hutton came on the screen, Cary feigned a tantrum. "Why does that son of a bitch get all the close-ups and I get nothing?" he shouted at Daves and Wald. When they argued that the scene rightly belonged to Hutton, Cary stormed out of the room, shouting, "I quit! I'm walking off the movie!" and Daves and Wald hurried after him. Hutton, horrified to find himself at the center of this conflict, waited a moment before attempting to sneak out of the room, only to find the trio outside the door, "dying laughing" at the joke they had played on him.[7]

When *Destination Tokyo* was released on New Year's Eve, 1943, the young cast and the first-time director garnered much of the critics' attention. Surprisingly few newspaper critics commented on Cary's newly earnest and paternal demeanor.[8] The leading film industry trade papers praised him— he was "never better" according to *Variety*, while *The Hollywood Reporter* marked this as "one of his finest portrayals"—but they were more interested in predicting that the film would be a box-office "smash."[9] They were correct. *Destination Tokyo* turned out to be the biggest hit of Cary's career at that time, with earnings of $3.2 million in North America alone, making it Warner Bros.' most successful film of the year.[10] It was also successful, at least in one case, as a recruitment film. Bernard Schwartz, an eighteen-year-old from the Bronx who idolized Cary, volunteered for the navy after seeing the film. Schwartz happily revealed this to Cary years later, when he had changed his name to Tony Curtis and was co-starring with him in the submarine drama *Operation Petticoat* (1959).[11]

Finishing *Destination Tokyo* in August 1943 meant that Cary could no longer put off his return to Columbia. Harry Cohn had used the disagreement over *Destination Tokyo* to press Cary to return to Columbia and to make *Once Upon a Time* with the little-known Janet Blair as his co-star.[12] This was quite a come-down in his high-flying career. The director, Alexander Hall, was undistinguished and, although he had directed Cary in two earlier films, *Sinners in the Sun* and *The Toast of New York*, they had no particular rapport. The script was both a slight and bizarre tale, based on a radio play, that centers on a caterpillar named "Curly" who dances whenever the song "Yes, Sir, That's My Baby" is played.[13] Humphrey Bogart and Rita Hayworth had rejected it earlier in the year, with Hayworth preferring to go on suspension (without pay) rather than play the female lead.[14]

Cary may have found something appealing in the story's seedy show business setting. His character, Jerry Flynn, is a type of Broadway impresario that he would have encountered in his own stage days, and Cary plays him with a streetwise swagger that suggests he is equal parts showman and swindler. Down on his luck and facing bankruptcy, Jerry will do anything to revive his fortunes. In this case, he stoops to the sub-vaudeville level of publicizing the dancing caterpillar. When the initially skeptical press is won over, and Curly the caterpillar becomes a national celebrity, Walt Disney offers to buy Curly for a huge sum and make a film around him. But Curly's owner, a ten-year-old orphan named Pinky (Ted Donaldson), refuses to sell him no matter what the price. While they argue over this, Curly disappears only to emerge days later as a butterfly. In the ending, Jerry, Pinky, and Pinky's hitherto disapproving older sister, Jeannie (Janet Blair), watch in awe as Curly flies away.

Initially, *Once Upon a Time* resembles a Preston Sturges–style satire, ridiculing the mayhem and excitability of the media-driven American public, and of course the idea of a caterpillar dancing to "Yes, Sir, That's My Baby" owes more than a nod to the madcap world of *Bringing Up Baby* and a leopard that can only be soothed by hearing "I Can't Give You Anything But Love, Baby." As the title suggests, however, *Once Upon a Time* is a whimsical fairy tale rather than a screwball comedy. The caterpillar's dance and even the caterpillar itself are never revealed: Curly remains in the shoebox, seen by the characters but not by the camera. The friendship between Jerry and Pinky is the story's chief concern, and expectations of a romance between Jerry and Pinky's showgirl sister are not fulfilled. In the ending, when the materialistic Jerry learns a lesson from the sweet and trusting Pinky, the film becomes as moralistic and sentimental as *A Christmas Carol*.

Once Upon a Time is a children's film, and it relies heavily on the performance of Cary's ten-year-old co-star, Ted Donaldson. In later years, Donaldson thanked Cary for looking after him and he praised him for his generosity as an actor. "From the first day on the set," Donaldson reminded Cary many years later, "you made everything easy for me." Donaldson recalled the many ways that Cary demonstrated a "givingness" toward him. This included one afternoon when they waited hours for the cameraman, Franz Planer, to set up the lighting for a scene. When Cary discovered that the lighting was on him, he protested. "This should be a close-up of the *kid*," he insisted to Alexander Hall, and Planer had to re-light the scene to favor Donaldson.[15]

Cary's generosity extended to the publicity campaign for the film, when he told reporters that he was really secondary to Donaldson in the film. "The kid steals every scene," he told them.[16] Bosley Crowther, writing in the *New York Times*, was one of many critics to follow this lead, offering the opinion, "It is the youngster, little Ted Donaldson, who is most appealing in this film."[17] Yet it was Cary who sold the film to audiences. In the early summer of 1944, when the D-Day landings brought grim news and the rival film releases were earnest war dramas such as *Since You Went Away*, *Tender Comrade*, and *The White Cliffs of Dover*, the lightweight *Once Upon a Time* proved to be a big success with American audiences.[18]

Cary had a youngster of his own while making *Once Upon a Time*. His stepson, eight-year-old Lance Reventlow, lived with Cary and Barbara for six months of the year and spent the other six months with his father. Court Haugwitz-Reventlow had become an American citizen, and he lived at least part of the year in Pasadena in order to be near Lance. By all accounts, Lance had a difficult relationship with his father, but he adored his new stepfather. He called Cary "The General" and enjoyed playing tennis and swimming in the pool at Westridge with him. Barbara played upon her ex-husband's insecurities by telling the columnist Louella Parsons that Lance and Cary got along so well that Lance "would love to be called Lance Grant."[19] This mischief aside, it is clear that Cary took his first experience of fatherhood very seriously, and that he and Lance developed a lasting bond.[20]

Cary and Barbara found their married life to be a trial. They had no privacy at Westridge, and she apparently liked it that way. In addition to her staff of servants, Barbara's former governess, "Ticki" Tocquet, lived with them and continued to serve as her paid companion. Lance's governess, Margaret Latimer, also lived with them. There were house guests and formal dinner parties almost every night. When Cary came home from the studio, he never knew how many people she would have invited to their table, but he could be sure that they would be her "hangers-on," people who flattered and indulged her because she wined and dined them. Many of them were fading European aristocrats who had come to the United States for the duration of the war, and Barbara encouraged them to converse in French over dinner.[21]

Cary had no problem with wealthy people. He counted some of the richest Americans among his best friends, but they were all men who were driven in their work. He had no interest in the idle rich, or in Old World pretensions and formalities. During this period, he proudly told a reporter that on most days he was up at 7:00 a.m., at the studio from 9:00 a.m., and he returned home by 8:00 p.m. only on nights when he was not obligated to attend a committee meeting for one of his many wartime charities.[22] Increasingly, as he wearied of Barbara's dinner parties, he asked to have his dinner served in an upstairs room, where he could study his lines for the next day of filming. Barbara

Photograph 19.34 In wartime, Barbara Hutton and Cary Grant posed for this publicity photo, showing their quiet home life at Westridge. In fact, she entertained lavishly and often.

Source: The Cary Grant Papers, courtesy of the Margaret Herrick Library

was unaccustomed to such impudence. She had given each of her previous husbands a financial settlement when she married them, so that they could live in the style she favored without the need for work. Her life became their work. Cary, from her perspective, thought only of his career, and when they saw his friends socially she complained that "all they ever talked about was movies."[23] Worse, his idea of a relaxing evening was going to the Friday night boxing matches at Hollywood's Legion Stadium. Barbara refused to accompany him to "the fights." "They terrify me," she complained.[24]

In later years, Cary admitted that her spending habits also caused many petty arguments, including one over the cost of newspapers. He was aghast to discover, when he came home one evening, that she paid to have eleven copies of the same evening paper delivered to their door. "Why does *each* servant need their own *special* copy of the paper?" he demanded to know.[25] Like many other people who grew up poor and made their own money, he hated to see money wasted and he was on the lookout for people who might take advantage of him. She, on the other hand, had inherited a vast fortune, and she sought loyalty from everyone—her husbands, friends, and servants—by being extravagant with them.

The gulf between them over matters of money—and increasingly everything else—probably explains why Cary's fortieth birthday party, on January 18, 1944, was not hosted by Barbara. Instead, Johnny Maschio hosted a joint birthday party for Cary and his own wife, Constance Moore (who shared Cary's birthday). Maschio arranged a cocktail party with dozens of guests, including Hollywood royalty such as Jack Warner and his wife Ann, and the film star Norma Shearer.[26] Still, the evening was on a smaller scale than anything Barbara was likely to plan.

Turning forty, together with his troubled marriage, may also explain his decision to make the most unlikely of all Cary Grant films, *None but the Lonely Heart*. Richard Llewellyn's novel was not yet published when RKO purchased it at Cary's urging in July 1943, but the galleys were circulating in Hollywood because Llewellyn's previous novel, *How Green Was My Valley*, had been a huge Oscar-winning success for Twentieth Century-Fox in 1941. Most studios recognized that *None but the Lonely Heart* had much more limited box-office appeal and they passed on it.[27] Set in the 1930s, the story centers on an unemployed teenager, Ernie Mott, who lives in the East End of London with his "Ma" and scrapes by on pennies until he becomes involved with a small-time crime racket.

Cary was determined that this should be his next film and RKO, always eager to please him, quickly purchased the screen rights for the high sum of $60,000.[28] Cary knew that he could not play a nineteen-year-old, let alone one who worries about his acne and cannot find a girlfriend. He wanted to play an adult version of Ernie: an unemployed ne'er-do-well drifter who is frustrated by the confines of British working-class life.[29] Like Jimmy Monkley in *Sylvia Scarlett*, Ernie Mott is the kind of man young Archie Leach might have turned into had he not discovered the world of show business. As Cary turned forty, he was eager to explore and connect with this type of character. He also saw the film as opportunity to prove himself as an actor who could play a "serious" role in a realist drama.

RKO's decision to hire Clifford Odets to write the screenplay suggests that studio executives also conceived of the film as a likely *succès d'estime* and not as a popular hit. Odets, a left-wing playwright whose works were staged by

New York's experimental Group Theater, ensured that the script maintained the unsentimental grit of Llewellyn's novel. He did extensive research into working-class British life, including asking Cary about his own upbringing. The two men became close friends as Cary reminisced about his youth and family life.[30] Among the notes Odets made while researching the film was an observation, which Cary also made to the musician Quincy Jones many years later, that the British working classes were similar to African Americans in terms of the low status and the lack of opportunities they had in their respective countries. This idea—of a social system that offers few means of escaping poverty—informs the film's representation of Ernie Mott's frustrations and limitations.[31]

In October 1943, while Odets was working on the script, Alfred Hitchcock was announced as the film's director.[32] By background alone he was an obvious choice for *None but the Lonely Heart*. Hitchcock was a true cockney, and one who knew working-class life in London's East End better than Cary. But if he ever seriously considered directing the film, he was likely to have been put off by Odets's script, which describes the street that Ernie lives on as "a real slum" with "filth and squalor everywhere."[33] Hitchcock had no interest in this kind of realism.[34] He thought that films should not offer audiences "a slice of life" but should instead give them "a slice of cake."[35] *None but the Lonely Heart*, as written by Odets, was definitely not going to be a "slice of cake."

A month later, Odets himself was announced as the film's director even though he had never directed a film before.[36] It was unusual for a star of Cary's stature to work with first-time directors but, as with Delmer Daves and *Destination Tokyo*, Cary had faith in Odets's talent and convictions. His faith was rewarded when Odets rejected RKO's set designs for the street that Ernie Mott and his "Ma" live on, pointing out that the designs were "too pretty." He informed the studio that the street must be so dismal that it serves as "the villain of the story." At his urging, another Group Theater veteran, Mordecai Gorelik, was hired to create a new design for a vast set recreating a long stretch of an East End backstreet.[37] No less than $35,000 was spent on this one set and with the goal of making it convincingly dreary and depressing.[38] Other neighborhood settings—a fish and chips shop, a pawnshop, an amusement arcade, and a garage—were imagined in a similarly drab fashion. Even Ernie's faithful dog, Nipper, was chosen for his mean appearance. This was not a film for a cute and frisky crowd-pleaser like Asta (the canine scene-stealer of *The Awful Truth* and *Bringing Up Baby*). The bull terrier who plays

Nipper had a rather grand name, Mayor of Little Willows, but Odets chose this sad-looking dog "not for cuteness but [to represent] man's loneliness."[39]

RKO invested heavily in all aspects of the film. Most remarkably, for the role of "Ma," the studio secured the *grande dame* of Broadway, Ethel Barrymore, who had not made a film in over ten years. She was lured back to Hollywood by a salary of $50,000 as well as the studio's agreement to pay a further $66,000 to secure her release from the play she was touring with (*The Corn is Green*).[40] An actress of Barrymore's stature and gravitas was needed because the troubled relationship between Ernie and Ma had become the dramatic crux of the film. In an early scene, just after Ernie has unexpectedly returned home from his travels, he laughs off his long absence from home and tries to kiss Ma, but she slaps him hard across the face. "A bit of proper respect is what is needed," she tells him. "I get no more from you than I got from that father of yours." Gradually they reconcile, as Ernie realizes that she is dying of cancer and that she has been handling stolen goods in her pawnshop in order to make a better life for him. In the ending, when she is dying in a prison bed, they both break down in tears. Ma cries because she has "disgraced him," and Ernie responds by embracing her and saying, "Disgraced me? No, Ma, I'm the boy who loves you, needs you, wants you!"

This scene is in the novel, but it does not have as much emotion, particularly on Ernie's part. Llewellyn's teenaged Ernie—described in one book review as a "pathetic little twerp"—does not have the emotional intensity to declare his love for his mother or cry with her.[41] The reimagining of this scene for the film may have been informed by Cary's own recollections of his reunion with Elsie, or it may have represented an emotional outpouring he longed for but never had with her. Either way the scene points toward the extent to which *None but the Lonely Heart* was invested with his own memories of his childhood. Another indication of this is the framed photograph of Elias Leach that can be seen hanging on the wall of Ma's house. This was not done for the public, who would have no way of recognizing his father, but as a means of grounding Cary's performance in his own experience of working-class family life.

Odets asked Cary about cockney slang and expressions, and incorporated these into the dialogue. He convinced Cary to play the piano and sing cockney songs in the film (very briefly), and he even proposed having him perform acrobatics or walk on stilts, although these ideas were abandoned. At the same time that he wanted the film to represent the reality of Archie Leach's background, he was aware that he would have to be on guard to keep Cary's

Photograph 19.35 Cary's recollections of working-class life informed *None but the Lonely Heart* (RKO Radio Pictures, 1944). Here, Ernie Mott argues with his mother (Ethel Barrymore).
Source: author's screen capture

charm from seeping into the film. Odets warned himself in his notes to "beware of Grant's jocularity and playing for people's affections." He considered asking Cary to adopt some form of physical deformity. He also insisted that Cary must wear unattractive clothing, although they compromised on this last point.[42] Ernie initially is dressed in an ill-fitting cheap suit and looks disheveled and unshaven, but midway through the film, when he reconciles with Ma, she buys him a smart new suit and he straightens up his appearance. As Odets's own script describes it, he then "looks like Cary Grant."[43]

When the film was released in September 1944, most critics were impressed by Cary's willingness to depart from his established image and broaden his range as an actor. He must have been pleased—and relieved—to read a steady stream of reviews admiring his "exceptional characterization" (*New York Times*) and "his varied capacity as an actor" (*Los Angeles Times*), and proclaiming his performance to be "the finest thing he has ever done" (*Hollywood Reporter*) and proof of "his consummate acting skill" (*Variety*).[44]

But critics also complained that the cockney accents and expressions were difficult to understand. They considered the film too gloomy and thought that the romantic subplots, involving Ernie's flirtations with neighbors Ada (June Duprez) and Aggie (Jane Wyatt), were undeveloped. The film's political message, paying tribute to the "common man" of the 1930s who was destined to be the soldier of the Second World War, was deemed to be out of date at this point in the war.[45]

None but the Lonely Heart was hardly likely to be a box-office hit, and it earned only $1.3 million in the domestic market.[46] Coincidentally, it was released at the same time as Arsenic and Old Lace, which had been held back from release until the play's run on Broadway ended. The frantic comedy proved to be much more appealing to the public, earning $2.8 million domestically. It was useful for Cary to have this ready-made box-office hit on release while the None but the Lonely Heart fizzled out.[47] Nevertheless, it was disappointing for him to see his most ambitious and personal film make so little impact.

Another blow was delivered at the Academy Awards. None but the Lonely Heart was not nominated for Best Film of the year, and Clifford Odets did not receive a nomination for either the screenplay or his direction. Cary was nominated for the Best Actor award. This second nomination, after Penny Serenade, suggested that that the Academy could only appreciate his acting in dramatic roles, and dramatic roles that required him to cry no less. Even so, he lost once again—this time to Bing Crosby, who won for his role in Leo McCarey's Going My Way. Of the key players in None but the Lonely Heart, only Ethel Barrymore won an Academy Award—the Best Supporting Actress for her performance as Ma, and, given her status as an acting royalty, this was hardly an affirmation of the film. Years later, Cary spoke of the lesson that the film's failure had taught him. "The only time I ever played myself was in None but the Lonely Heart and nobody wanted to see the real me," he commented. "So I put away Archie Leach and went back to being Cary Grant."[48]

Going back to being Cary Grant entailed facing up to his unhappy home life. While filming None but the Lonely Heart in the spring of 1944, he and Barbara realized that they needed to separate. She could not understand why he insisted on working so hard. He made five films in their first two years of marriage, and when he was not filming, he often appeared on the radio (in Lux Radio Theatre versions of his films and also on comedy sketch shows). Then there was his continuing war work. After his tour of Southern military bases with Don Barclay in the spring of 1943, Cary continued to entertain the troops for the remainder of the war, although usually closer to home in California. At weekends, he visited hospitals and bases with Barclay or Bob Hope, who took Barclay's part in their long-standing, crowd-pleasing mindreading routine.[49] He and Randolph Scott also worked together, co-hosting revues for returning servicemen, nurses, and WACS through the auspices of the Masquers Club (a Los Angeles–based private club for actors).[50] Barbara, meanwhile, continued to pursue a "continental lifestyle"—of formal dinner parties and a parade of houseguests—and she was embarrassed by his absence.[51]

They decided to separate before Lance was due to return to Westridge on June 15, but then Lance's father discovered that Barbara and Lance had been writing letters to one another in code, including one from Lance that read (when decoded), "To hell with my father. I would like it if he died."[52] Count Haugwitz-Reventlow immediately filed suit against Barbara, accusing her of being an unfit mother, and he refused to allow Lance to return to her custody. A ten-month legal battle ensued, during which Lance was taken first to Canada and then to Boston by his father.

The custody battle played out in newspapers across the United States, where stories about the "poor little rich girl" were often front-page news.[53] Under these circumstances, Cary and Barbara decided to stay together, knowing that another separation and likely divorce would not help Barbara's chances of regaining custody of her son.[54] In early August they had an argument so heated that Cary stormed out of the house and went to stay with Rosalind Russell and Freddie Brisson. After a few nights, the Brissons invited Barbara for dinner, and by the end of the evening they assumed that the reunion was going well, because Cary and Barbara spent the night together in a guest bedroom. Then in the morning Freddie Brisson went into his dressing room and found Cary there, sleeping alone on the floor. "I think we've got trouble again," Brisson reported back to his wife.[55]

In mid-August, Cary and Barbara issued a statement announcing "a friendly separation" with "no thought of divorce." Barbara stayed on at Westridge, while Cary stayed at the Brissons'. A few weeks later, on September 9, they confounded even the most seasoned observers of Hollywood marriages when they both attended Elsa Maxwell's party celebrating the liberation of Paris. Maxwell, a socialite and a columnist, arranged a grand black-tie affair at a Beverly Hills mansion. The 135 guests spent the evening dining, dancing, and enjoying a stage show that included Judy Garland singing "The Last Time I Saw Paris," Frank Sinatra singing "I'll Be Seeing

You" (both accompanied by the composer Arthur Schwartz on piano), and Charles Boyer reciting the "Marseillaise." The guests were also intrigued to see Cary and Barbara arrive at the party separately, greet one another with a kiss, dance together and with others, and then kiss goodnight and leave separately.[56]

This dignified meeting masked Cary's unhappiness of the failure of his marriage, and his increasing desperation to win Barbara back. He could not hide his emotional turmoil from the executives who were so eager to keep him working. RKO's studio boss, Charlie Koerner, was so concerned that he arranged for Cary and Barbara to have a "romantic getaway" in a "special apartment" in San Francisco.[57] There, they were spotted trying to "patch things up" in a discreet corner of the Fairmont Hotel's "Top of the Mark" bar, famous for its spectacular views of the city.[58]

Jack Warner also had reason for concern. Warner was in the midst of negotiating with Harry Cohn to buy out the remainder of Cary's Columbia contract. Cary owed one more film to Columbia, and Warner arranged to loan Humphrey Bogart (a contract star at Warner Bros.) to Columbia in return for getting Cary released from the studio. Cary, in turn, would agree to star in the upcoming Warner Bros. musical *Night and Day*, a biopic of the Broadway composer Cole Porter.[59] He was reluctant to agree to this film because he knew Cole Porter socially, and he had happily left musicals behind when he came to Hollywood. However, he was also very keen to "clear out" of Columbia, and his manager, Frank Vincent, advised him to accept Warner's offer. Work was the distraction he needed from his personal problems, Vincent assured him.

Cary was not entirely convinced.[60] He told Vincent "his whole life's happiness [is] at stake," that he had to devote himself to reconciling with Barbara, and that "in his present state of mind" he would not be able to give a good performance. When Cary's feelings were relayed to Warner Bros., Jack Warner responded generously, agreeing to give him the time that he needed. Warner was taken aback when Cary replied that he needed "at least six months," but he agreed to this and rearranged the studio's production plans accordingly.[61]

The break allowed Cary and Barbara to come to terms for a reconciliation. For Barbara, it was pivotal that he should not work so much. For Cary, it was crucial that they move out of Westridge, which had come to seem more like a hotel than a home.[62] He bought a smaller home—still a mansion but not as vast as Westridge—at 10615 Bellagio Road in Bel Air.[63] This new house was built to an English Cotswolds design, which suited his nostalgia for the countryside near Bristol. The house also suited him because its comparatively small size meant that Barbara's paid companion, "Ticki," would not move with them, there was not room for so many houseguests, and there was no need for so many servants.[64]

In November 1944, they moved out of Westridge and into the new Bellagio Road home, and Barbara accompanied him to the San Francisco premiere of *None but the Lonely Heart*. This rare public appearance together signaled the importance he attached both to their reconciliation and the film.[65] By January 1945, it was clear that the new domestic arrangements would not solve their problems, and Cary became increasingly eager to get back to work. At the end of the month, he invited the director and screenwriters of the upcoming *Night and Day* to Bellagio Road for a full-day story conference, and on a Sunday no less. A few days later, in early February, he embarked on another two-week tour of military bases and hospitals, taking him through Florida, Georgia, and Louisiana.[66] When he returned to Los Angeles, he immediately went into rehearsals for the Lux Radio Theatre production of *Bedtime Story*, co-starring with Greer Garson in this light-hearted comedy. On February 26, the day this was broadcast, Cary and Barbara announced that they had separated once again.[67]

Four months later, Barbara appeared in a Los Angeles court, looking "chic and dainty as a Dresden doll," according to one sneering account of the proceedings. She was seeking a divorce on the grounds of "cruelty without provocation" and "grievous mental distress, suffering, and anguish," but she greeted Cary's manager, Frank Vincent, by throwing her arms around him and saying, "Hello, darling."[68] Cary did not attend the hearing. He was represented by his personal lawyer, Stanley Fox, who would come to play an increasingly important part in his professional and personal life.[69] Fox chose not to question Barbara during the hearing. The questioning was left to her own lawyer, who put Barbara and then "Ticki" on the stand to describe Cary's "cruelty." They both testified that on some evenings, Cary retired early from Barbara's dinner parties and on others he went upstairs and refused to join the table at all. This left Barbara so embarrassed and "nervous" that she had to seek "medical help."[70] On these grounds, the divorce was granted and Cary's second marriage came to end.

Eventually, Cary and Barbara would become friendly again. On holidays and special occasions, Cary would see Lance, and he would continue to serve as a father figure to the boy while Barbara married four more times.[71] Initially, though, the couple kept their distance from one another. Cary was eager to make it known that, unlike Barbara's other husbands, he had taken no money from her as part of the divorce. Barbara was eager to pin the blame for the divorce on him. She told a reporter that "He just isn't interested in anything but his career, and when you're married to a man, you've got to have something to talk about. You can't just sit solemnly and think about a career."[72] The irony was that this was exactly how she left Cary back in the early months of 1945—alone in the house on Bellagio Drive that he had bought for the two of them, and taking a long break from one thing in life that he found fulfilling, his career.

20

By April 1945, Cary was itching to return to the studio. It had been nearly a year since *None but the Lonely Heart* had finished filming. His self-imposed hiatus from filmmaking kept him away for the first six months, and then Warner Bros. repeatedly pushed back the start of his next film, the Cole Porter biopic *Night and Day*. Scripting problems and other delays meant that the studio did not need him until May 15, but he was so restless that he began turning up at the Warner Bros. lot early in April, asking to attend story conferences with the scriptwriters, and seeking wardrobe fittings and photographic tests. Studio executives were alarmed when they heard about this. His salary was $10,000 per week, and the executives wanted it made very clear that he was not yet on the payroll. It is a testament both to how often he turned up and his reputation for hard-nosed business dealings that Warner Bros. insisted on written reassurance that he was working for free. He was happy to oblige them and to get back to work.[1]

Jack Warner conceived of *Night and Day* as a big-budget extravaganza that would celebrate the twentieth anniversary of the studio's earliest, pioneering sound films. Warner paid Cole Porter $300,000 for the rights to his best-known songs.[2] To secure Cary for the film, Warner agreed to a relatively modest salary of $100,000 but also agreed to buy out Cary's remaining obligation to Columbia, a sum likely to be higher than his salary.[3] Warner approved a budget that allowed the film to be made in Technicolor, which was still rare enough to mark the film as a "prestige" release. And he assigned the studio's premier director, Michael Curtiz, to make the film.

Curtiz was at the top of his game in 1945, having recently made a succession of box-office hits, including *Casablanca* (1942), for which be won the Best Director Academy Award, and the musicals *Yankee Doodle Dandy* (1941) and *This Is the Army* (1943). He was a brilliant director—a master of both visual design and narrative pace—and this undoubtedly explains why Cary agreed to work with him despite his reputation as a tyrant on the set. He soon came to regret this decision, and for the rest of his life he marveled at Curtiz's displays of temper on the set of *Night and Day*. Curtiz spent so much time "blowing his top," Cary recalled, that the director would lose track of the task at hand. "What am I doing? What am I doing?" Curtiz would ask at the end of his tirades. "You're blowing your top, that's what you're doing," Cary replied.[4]

Timekeeping was an initial source of aggravation. Throughout his free-lance career, Cary insisted that he would only work from 9:00 a.m. to 6:00 p.m., taking a one-hour lunch break starting at 1:00 p.m. This was stipulated in all of his contracts, but Curtiz was not used to actors having so much power. He thought that lunch breaks made actors sluggish and he put them off as long as possible. At 6:00 p.m. he often pressed the cast and crew to get "one more shot." When Cary refused, other actors followed his lead and Curtiz blew up.[5]

There were also many creative battles on the set, and Cary never let Curtiz forget that he had the upper hand with Jack Warner. Curtiz spent hours lining up the shots for the scene set at Yale University, when the young Cole Porter leads a student pep rally. Curtiz used Cary's double on the set to get the lighting and the camera angles set up. Then they were ready to shoot and summoned the stars. Cary came on the set and realized that Curtiz was going to film him in close-ups while he played a man twenty-five years younger than himself. He refused to do it, and insisted that entirely new set-ups were required so that he could play the scene mainly with his back to the camera. On other occasions, Cary refused to film scenes with what he termed "weak dialogue" and "lousy characterization."[6] The script, still unfinished when filming began, was a major source of acrimony.

The scriptwriters for *Night and Day* knew that the film's story could not be a faithful account of Cole Porter's life.[7] Porter had been born into a wealthy family, married an even wealthier woman, and lived a life of luxury in Paris, Venice, and New York. His life story therefore lacked the rags-to-riches storyline of so many biopics, which emphasized their subjects' triumph over adversity. Porter had known some adversity. He suffered a terrible riding accident in 1937, when a horse fell on him and crushed his legs, but this occurred long after he was successful and it did not alter his career path. He was also primarily (if not entirely) gay.[8] This section of his life was entirely off limits to the scriptwriters. The censorship code, as well as the sexual mores of the time, prevented any mention of homosexuality. The scriptwriters instead developed a thin and an almost entirely fictional storyline in which Porter rejects his family's wealth, struggles to establish his career, and later resolves not to live off his wife's fortune.[9]

The film's emphasis would be on Porter's busy backstage life—writing, rehearsing, and watching performances of his shows. As Porter, Cary sings at least part of several songs, including "In the Still of the Night," "You're the Top," and "Night and Day." This was the closest he ever came, after his Broadway years, to making a musical, and the best that can be said is that he is a competent although not a very expressive singer. Most of the songs are performed by others, including Mary Martin ("My Heart Belongs to Daddy"), Monty Woolley ("Miss Otis Regrets"), Ginny Simms ("I've Got You Under My Skin"), and Jane Wyman ("You Do Something to Me").

Despite the emphasis on the songs, Cary found the dramatic storyline to be too sketchy. On some days, he insisted on changing the dialogue himself. On other days, the writers were called to the set for more significant revisions. Four weeks into filming, Cary agreed to stay past his 6:00 p.m. finishing time in order to meet with Curtiz, producer Arthur Schwartz, and the scriptwriters in order to address the story's weaknesses. The meeting lasted past midnight and resulted in major revisions to the second half of the story. Still, Cary was not satisfied.[10] A typical daily production report noted that "Mike [Curtiz] is just about frantic," because Cary was "picking at and criticizing the script" and calling the writers onto the set two or three times to "change things around."[11]

The story that emerged from these constant rewrites suggests that, in the absence of a credible storyline for Porter's personal life, the writers drew upon Cary's own recent life to make Porter a more vivid character. The Cole Porter of *Night and Day* is a man so fixated on his career that he devotes all of his time and energy to it, neglecting his wife Linda Lee (Alexis Smith). Cole and Linda Lee forgo their honeymoon so that Cole can begin rehearsals on a new show, just as Cary and Barbara Hutton missed their honeymoon so that Cary could return to work. Cole neglects Linda Lee so much and for so long that she finally leaves him, only returning after his riding accident.

In the film's last shot, Cole and Linda Lee are reunited in a clinch shot, but a close-up of his face reveals him to be resigned and humbled rather than happy. It is a strikingly downbeat ending to a film otherwise bubbling with catchy tunes. It has parallels in Cary's own sadness after his divorce from Barbara, and it suggests that he realized that finding fulfillment in work may preclude finding it at home. His Cole Porter only smiles when he is at rehearsals, shows, and after-show parties, and he basks in his success and the praise that it brings him. Away from work, a sad malaise overtakes him, and he can only pay attention to his wife momentarily and until work suddenly distracts him again. In keeping with this, Curtiz filmed each backstage scene as frenetically charged with energy and creativity, and he filmed the more personal scenes in a comparatively inert manner that suggests Porter's restlessness to get back to work.

The *Night and Day* shoot was plagued by wider problems during the summer of 1945. A strike by the Conference of Studio Workers nearly emptied the studio of set builders. To get around this, many scenes for *Night and Day* were filmed outside the studio gates: Los Angeles City College served as the Yale University campus, the Hill Grove mansion in Beverly Hills stood in for Cole Porter's Long Island estate, Busch Gardens in Pasadena was transformed into a London park, and a standing London street set built for Twentieth Century-Fox's *Hangover Square* (1945) became the London street of *Night and Day*. For other scenes, the studio tried to recycle some of its own sets, but Cary scrutinized these and found many of them wanting. "I don't think there has been a set in this picture that has not been changed by Cary," the production manager reported, "and it has cost this studio a terrific amount of money."[12]

Costumes also troubled him. As usual, Cary supplied his own modern clothing, but when he scrutinized the costumes of his co-stars, he insisted on changes, noting that military uniforms were incorrect and, in a later scene, that the color of the men's shirts was unflattering.[13] Technicolor was another issue. He was nervous about making his first Technicolor feature film, and when he saw the rushes for a scene in which Cole visits his dying grandfather, Cary complained that he "looks sicker than the grandfather" and insisted that the lighting must be changed.[14] The production manager reported that "These situations have been coming up all through the picture," with Cary "criticizing sets, costumes, actor, dialogue, and everything else." He added that "Mike [Curtiz] is nearly whipped on account of it."[15]

On and on it went. Cary fussed and niggled and protested throughout the making of *Night and Day*. Curtiz's temperament and the problems arising from the strike were partly to blame, but there is no doubt that, over the years, Cary had become a fussy perfectionist. The power that he wielded as a star, combined with his nervous anxiety about performing, combined to make him a meticulous and sometimes difficult presence on the set. The irony, of course, is that he made his name playing such charming, breezy, and seemingly easygoing characters. His Cole Porter is certainly a dashing and debonair figure, with a love of show business that brings an infectious pizzazz to the film. When the cameras were not rolling, however, Cary's eyes zeroed in on any imperfection he could find on the set or in the script, and he insisted that it was fixed.

Filming started on June 15 and by September 29 it was five weeks over schedule and still not finished, but Cary was due to return to RKO to start work on *Notorious*. *Night and Day* would have to be completed in the evenings, and on days that RKO could spare him. By the time the last re-take was finally taken on December 11, the production cost had spiraled to $4.4 million, which would normally signal a financial disaster for the studio.[16] But from the very first previews, everyone who saw *Night and Day* knew that it would be a runaway hit.[17] Some critics complained that the story was not true to Porter's life, and the New York critics in particular thought that the film did not capture the sophistication of Porter's music, but its popular appeal was never doubted. It was clearly "a box-office smash," as *Variety* predicted, and one that would "mop up from New England to New Zealand."[18]

Released in July 1946, *Night and Day* earned $5 million in North America and another $2.4 million in the rest of the world, making it the biggest box-office success of Cary's career at this time.[19] It is easy to see why post-war audiences found the film appealing. Its parade of popular songs made for a particularly light and easy form of escapism. It is notable too that, despite his concerns, Technicolor suited Cary, showing his tanned skin, his jet-black hair (so black that it takes on an almost blue sheen), and his fashionable attire all the more vividly. Cole Porter himself was flattered to be played by so handsome a star and to have such an attractive showcase for his music, but Cary was always embarrassed that he portrayed a man he knew personally, and portrayed him in a manner that was obviously contrived for the film. In later years, he could not mention the film without apologizing for it.[20]

If Michael Curtiz was Cary's nightmare director, Alfred Hitchcock was his dream. Although their first film together, *Suspicion*, had its share of production difficulties, Hitchcock was known for planning his films carefully before filming began, developing the script with the writers and using storyboard drawings to establish the visual effects he wanted. All of this planning enabled him to preside over a calm and orderly set. He was known never to lose his temper or raise his voice. He seldom gave elaborate instructions to actors (let alone orders), and he was always keen to take a lunch break. He also gave Cary a lift to the studio on many days. They both lived on Bellagio Road (albeit on opposite sides of the Bel Air Country Club's golf course), and so Hitchcock would pick Cary up and along the way he would tell him about the practical jokes he was plotting for that day.[21] Little wonder that Cary loved working with him. "Any film with Hitch was fun," he recalled.[22]

Cary was Hitchcock's ideal leading man, and the director often conceived of his films with Cary in mind, only to find that he was either unavailable or too expensive.[23] This very nearly happened with *Notorious*. The film was initiated by the independent producer David Selznick, who knew that Hitchcock and scriptwriter Ben Hecht had written the story expressly for Cary and Ingrid Bergman. Selznick was fine with Bergman. He had brought the Swedish actress to Hollywood in 1939 and still had her under contract. But Selznick balked at Cary's salary demands, and for a few days at least it appeared that Joseph Cotten would play the male lead instead. Finally, Selznick agreed to pay Cary a salary of $150,000, plus 10 percent of the film's earnings over $1,5 million and up to $3 million.[24] This allowed him to earn $300,000 for *Notorious*—an extraordinary salary for the time. Cary made more on this single film than the annual salary of studio bosses such as Harry Cohn, Darryl F. Zanuck, and Jack Warner.[25]

Selznick put together the "package" for *Notorious*—that is, he oversaw the development of the script and brought together the director and the stars—but then he sold it to RKO so that he could focus his full attention on another film, *Duel in the Sun* (1946).[26] *Notorious* went into production at RKO in October 1945, and with the often obsessive and meddling Selznick off the picture, everyone enjoyed the three-month shoot. Cary and Hitchcock had established their good working relationship on *Suspicion*, and Bergman and Hitchcock had just made *Spellbound* (1945) together. Although Bergman said that initially they had "some disagreements" on that first film together, they developed a good professional and personal relationship. Biographers of both director and the star say that Hitchcock was at least "exceptionally fond" and perhaps "deeply in love" with Bergman, while she in turn loved him as a father figure and mentor.[27]

Cary and Ingrid were acquaintances prior to making *Notorious* but they became good friends on the set.[28] He saw that she had trouble relaxing in front of the camera, and occasional difficulty with pronouncing words in English. Helping her distracted him from his own jitters.[29] He also admired her talent and her disinterest in glamour.[30] Selznick had pressed Bergman to become "the new Garbo"—that is, another glamorous screen siren from Sweden—but she resisted his attempts at a makeover. She convinced Selznick that "natural" beauty should be her trademark, and so she remained fair-haired without becoming a platinum blonde, and her makeup was, by Hollywood standards at least, kept to a minimum.[31] Cary was usually attracted to fair-haired women and he preferred the natural look, too, but somehow there was never even a suggestion of a romance between him and Bergman.

Cary, on the rebound from Barbara Hutton in the spring of 1945, had quickly become involved with Betty Hensel, an elegant, twenty-three-year-old blonde described in the press as a "socialite."[32] There was some scandal about the relationship. Back in her home town of St. Louis, Betty was already engaged to marry an army doctor, and just three days before the wedding, she jilted him, apparently at Cary's urging.[33] Cary and Betty then began an on-again off-again relationship that lasted for two years and was often the subject of speculation in the gossip columns. Bergman, meanwhile, was married to a Swedish dentist, Petter Lindstrom, and they had a daughter, Pia. But it was an unhappy marriage, and during the summer of 1945 she had affairs with both the photojournalist Robert Capa and the musician Larry Adler.[34]

She was best known for playing stoical, saintly women, but *Notorious* was a change of pace for Bergman. She plays Alicia Huberman, a hard-drinking and sexually promiscuous German exile in Miami, whose father is convicted of being a Nazi spy. Alicia is notorious for being "a Nazi tramp," as one early script put it, although it turns out that she neither shared her father's political beliefs nor took part in his espionage. Cary plays Devlin, the FBI agent who recruits Alicia to infiltrate a spy ring of Nazi exiles in Rio de Janeiro, using her family connections to gain the spies' trust.

They meet for the first time at a late-night party at Alicia's home in Miami. The scene is Cary's first appearance in the film, and Hitchcock filmed most of it in one unusually long shot, lasting 90 seconds, that shows Devlin, sitting in the foreground with his back to the camera, watching Alicia as she drinks and flirts with a forced gaiety. Only the back of Devlin's head and shoulders can be seen, but the carefully groomed, shiny black hair and the well-tailored dark suit unmistakably belong to Cary Grant. Even in silhouette, and filmed from behind, he is a strikingly handsome figure. Like the shot of Johnny Aysgarth as he climbs the stairs in *Suspicion*, this shot calls attention to his ambiguity, and, as in *Suspicion* more generally, doubts about him run throughout *Notorious*.

When the camera finally pivots around to reveal Devlin's face, he turns on the charm and flirts with her in a gentle, warm manner. This first scene sets up the dynamic of the story. The attraction between Alicia and "Dev," as she calls him, is palpable from their first exchange of looks, and it is the driving force of the story right through to the ending. Yet that dark, inscrutable first shot of Devlin, together with a name so close to "devil," serves to warn the audience. The film's suspense stems from waiting to see just how callously he will judge her, how much danger he will put her in, and whether or not he will let her die rather than admit that he loves her.

Cary never looked sharper or more handsome than he does in *Notorious*, yet Devlin is the coldest and most humorless character he ever played. When Devlin and Alicia go for a moonlit drive after meeting at her party, she discovers that he is "some kind of policeman" and drunkenly struggles to throw him out of her car. He responds by knocking her out with his fist. The next morning, she awakens sprawled in her bed, hungover and disheveled. As he walks into the room, the camera takes her vantage point as she rolls over in bed, and the image of him spins around in line with her point of view until he is upside down in the frame. This dramatic camerawork serves as another warning, from the director to the audience, that this is not the debonair, witty Cary Grant of screwball comedies. Indeed, shortly after Devlin and Alicia arrive in Rio de Janeiro, he watches as she infiltrates the Nazi spy ring so effectively that she marries one of the principal spies, Alexander Sebastian (Claude Rains).

The film allows for just one romantic scene between Devlin and Alicia, but it is a memorable one to say the least. Just after they have arrived in Rio, and on the terrace of her apartment overlooking beautiful Copacabana beach, they embrace, tentatively at first. The camera moves in for a tight close-up as they kiss passionately, nuzzle one another, banter affectionately, and then continue to embrace and kiss while moving from the balcony to the living room. They continue in this fashion even while he phones his hotel to check his messages, only breaking away from one another because he has a message from his boss, calling him back to the office. Filmed in one continuous, mobile close-up shot, this kissing scene lasts for a full two and a half minutes. According to Hitchcock, the actors "felt terribly uncomfortable" while performing it. On the set, they found it unnatural and contrived to cling together and kiss as they moved through the apartment. On the screen, however, the effect is overwhelmingly intimate. Hitchcock joked that the scene offers audiences "a kind of temporary *ménage à trois*" with the stars, giving them "the great privilege of kissing Cary Grant and Ingrid Bergman together."[35]

The scene also allows the audience to see a crack in Devlin's otherwise grim persona. He smiles at her when he leaves her apartment—his only genuine smile in the entire film—but this brief moment of happiness does not last. Devlin becomes bitterly jealous when he sees Alicia with Alexander Sebastian. Although she marries Sebastian only as part of her mission work,

Photograph 20.36 Awkward to film but perfect on screen: the long, intimate kissing scene in *Notorious* (RKO Radio Pictures, 1946)
Source: author's screen capture

he all but abandons her while she is undercover in the Sebastian household. With Alicia isolated in this vast mansion, and living under the cold, scrutinizing gaze of Sebastian's mother (terrifyingly played by the Austrian actress Leopoldine Konstantin), this tale of contemporary espionage takes on the mood and tone of a gothic thriller.

Hitchcock conveys Alicia's precarious situation in one of his most flamboyant shots. During a formal party at the Sebastian mansion, the camera sweeps downward from a long shot, looking down on the guests as the mingle, all the way to an extreme close-up of Alicia's hand as she nervously clutches a key she has purloined for Devlin. As she stands on a chessboard-patterned floor, there is no doubt that she is his pawn, willing to sacrifice herself to win, or reawaken, his love. His motivations remain unclear. When he finds out, via the key to the wine cellar, that the Nazis exiles are storing uranium in Burgundy bottles, he is fascinated. "Vintage sand," he says keenly as he inspects the contents of a broken bottle. Yet a moment later, when Sebastian finds them in the cellar, Devlin throws him off track by kissing Alicia as passionately as the most devoted lover. Hitchcock once again films the kiss in the tightest of close-ups, placing the audience at the center of this intense and tender moment between them. But then, as Sebastian approaches, Devlin reverts to form. "Push me away," he whispers to her, as though the kiss was only a strategy after all.

Sebastian is as ardent and needy in his love for Alicia as Devlin is cold and distant. But when Sebastian realizes that she is an American agent, he and his mother begin slowly poisoning her to death. The last 20 minutes of the film hinges on the question of whether Devlin will save Alicia, or whether his hard-hearted jealousy will distract him from her peril. The de-nouement is staged in fairy-tale fashion, with Devlin assuming the role of a Prince Charming saving the heroine from confinement in the evil palace. He arrives just in time, and as he carries the poisoned Alicia out of the house and professes his love to her, it is plain that he has nearly killed her. He may not have actually poisoned her, but his ego and jealousy led to her peril.

Hitchcock later commented that Sebastian's love for Alicia was "prob-ably deeper" than Devlin's, and his biographers have seen Sebastian as a form of surrogate for him. Sebastian, too, is an unattractive, middle-aged man who loves Bergman fervently and hopelessly, knowing that she will never return his love.[36] By extension, Cary's character is an envied, unde-serving rival, whose good looks mask his bad character. Cary, in the midst of his divorce from Barbara Hutton, must have realized that Devlin's emo-tional flaws mirrored at least some of his own. The star and the character shared a predilection for falling very quickly in love and then growing sud-denly jealous, distrustful, and cold. Once again, as in *Suspicion*, Hitchcock offered audiences a perspective on Cary Grant in *Notorious* that hit rather close to home.

Much more than that, *Notorious* represents a high point for its three prin-cipal talents. Hitchcock combined his two favorite types of story, the espio-nage thriller and the gothic melodrama, to make a film that is both fraught with suspense and torturously romantic. Bergman, playing a woman who believes she is unworthy of love, is captivatingly vulnerable and yet resolute in her mission. Cary, playing a "fat-headed guy full of pain" (as the character describes himself in the ending), offers a remarkably nuanced performance, perfectly conveying the toxic jealousy and callous egotism that lay beneath his cool demeanor. *Notorious* is a romantic tragedy, a film that believes in the sincerity of its lovers but shows that they are doomed by their psycho-logical weaknesses (doomed, that is, without a fairy-tale ending). The stylish direction, rich black-and-white cinematography, and lush settings also make the film a feast for the eyes.

Photographs of the director and the stars—some taken on the set, some staged for publicity—reveal their warmth and ease with one another. They would all work together again, although not as a threesome. Neither Cary nor Claude Rains commented on whether they got along better on this film than they had on *The Last Outpost*, ten years earlier, but there is no doubt that making *Notorious* lifted Cary's spirits. Oddly enough, this dark film brought him out of the depression that followed his break-up with Barbara Hutton, and the bonhomie on set banished the frustration he felt working with Michael Curtiz. He was sentimental enough about the shoot to purloin one of the most significant props—the key that Alicia stole for Dev—and treasure it as a keepsake.

When *Notorious* was released in August 1946, it became one of the biggest hits of the year. Earnings of $4.8 million in North America and $2.3 million in

Photograph 20.37 Friends and co-workers: Cary, Ingrid Bergman, and Alfred Hitchcock during the making of *Notorious*
Source: The Cary Grant Papers, courtesy of the Margaret Herrick Library

the wider world nearly matched those of *Night and Day*.[37] This was a banner year for Cary at the box office. The critics focused mainly on Hitchcock, admiring his bold direction first and foremost. At a time when screen kisses generally did not last for more than a few seconds, they were particularly impressed by the first kissing scene.[38] It "fairly ignites the celluloid with which it was filmed," *The Hollywood Reporter* commented.[39] *Notorious* got little recognition at the Academy Awards—Ben Hecht and Claude Rains were nominated but did not win—but it has intrigued and delighted audiences far longer than any of the year's award winners, and it still stands as a high point for the director, the stars, and the suspense-thriller genre.

Hitchcock pitched future projects to Cary as they made *Notorious*. One that they tentatively agreed on was a screen adaptation of Shakespeare's *Hamlet*. Hitchcock planned a "modernized version" of the story with Cary playing the conflicted, obsessive lead role.[40] Of all the films that fell by the wayside during Cary's career (and there were many), his starring role in Hitchcock's *Hamlet* is the most intriguing, but it fell almost as soon as it was announced to the press. A writer came forward insisting that he held the copyright to modern-day versions of *Hamlet*, and Hitchcock became embroiled in a lawsuit that dragged on for several years.[41] Other proposals came and went, as Cary and "Hitch" continued to see other socially. He occasionally had dinner with the Hitchcocks, including their teenage daughter, Pat. Other guests included Ingrid Bergman and Petter Lindstrom, the actress Teresa Wright, and Hitchcock's collaborator Joan Harrison, who sometimes brought her boyfriend, Clark Gable. By the standards of the Bel Air set, these were small, informal dinners, with dancing (to music on the radio) or board games after the meal.[42]

Cary had a much flashier social life as well. When Trans-World Airlines initiated a new, nonstop cross-country service from Los Angeles to New York, Howard Hughes (the owner of TWA) piloted the first flight on February 14, 1946. In order to garner the most publicity, Hughes filled the 38-seater plane with other Hollywood notables, including Paulette Godard, Veronica Lake, Walter Pidgeon, William Powell, Edward G. Robinson, Johnny Maschio, and Constance Moore. Cary was on board, too, traveling to join Betty Hensel, who was already in New York. Hughes treated all of his passengers to a weekend at the Sherry-Netherland Hotel before flying them back to Los Angeles in time for work on Monday morning.[43] It was a festive beginning for a service that became known as the "red-eye" flight in later years, when it was much more commonly made.

Cary and Betty Hensel were often seen in Sunset Boulevard hotspots such as Ciro's and the Mocambo. Together with other nightclubbing pals—James Stewart, the pianist Eddy Duchin, and the screenwriter John McClain—Cary threw a party at the Clover Club on March 30 that marked the end of wartime restraint. It was a black-tie affair, and the four hosts formed a reception line to greet their three hundred guests as they arrived for an evening of fine dining and dancing. Many of Hollywood's biggest names were there, and most of Cary's close friends, including Randolph Scott and his new wife, Patricia. The guest who made most heads turn was Virginia Cherrill. She was in the process of divorcing the Earl of Jersey, and when Cary heard that she was visiting Hollywood for the first time in many years, he invited her to the party. Observers noted that they had an amicable chat, but also that he was much more attentive to Betty Hensel.[44] Once again, speculation began about if and when Hollywood's most eligible bachelor would marry his latest elegant, blonde girlfriend.[45]

A few weeks later, and with a month's break before he was due on the set of his next film, Cary decided to try TWA's new transatlantic flight service from New York to Paris. He then took the short flight onward to London. It had been nearly seven years since he had last seen his mother. Elsie had written to him regularly during the war, telling him that she saw all of his films (*Mr. Lucky* was a particular favorite) but also that "it is not like seeing you personally."[46] As the years passed, her letters had grown more plaintive, asking him when he would visit her and also expressing her wish to visit him ("I should like to spend a holiday six months in America").[47] It is not clear how often he wrote back to her. It *is* clear that he often forgot her birthday, because she always wrote afterward to remind him. "My birthday came on the 8th of February," she wrote to him a few days after the occasion in 1946, also noting that, at sixty-nine, "I am getting old."[48] Cary apologized to her by cablegram, explaining that he had been "away from home on business trip" and expressing the hope that "within few weeks will be able make journey to see you dearest." As ever, he ended with, "all my love Archie."[49]

There is no doubt that his intentions were good. He came to London to meet with his friend Alexander Korda, a key player in reviving the British film industry after the war, and to discuss a joint production deal with him.[50] Simultaneously, he was in talks with Hitchcock and his business partner, Sidney Bernstein, about making "two or three films" in Britain with their new production company, Transatlantic Films.[51] The advent of transatlantic flights made these sorts of ventures much more feasible than they had been in the past, and they would enable Cary to spend more time in Britain and drop in on Elsie more often.

As good as his intentions were, there is also no doubt that he avoided spending prolonged periods of time with Elsie. Upon his arrival in London on April 23, a reporter asked her about her plans to see him. "I have spoken with my son on the phone but I do not know when he is coming [to Bristol]," she responded. "I know he won't be able to stay but I hope we shall be able to spend a day together in Bristol."[52] Then, when Cary drove down to Bristol on the morning of April 26, he did not go directly to his mother's house but instead toured the city with a local reporter.

He had not seen Bristol since the Blitz, and he was taken aback by the vast swathes of the city center that had been flattened by the bombs. There was virtually nothing left of the Castle Street shopping area—the thriving hub of the city before the war—except for the shell of St. Peter's Church, now surrounded by empty lots covered in weeds. At Old Market, the Empire Theatre was still standing, but many other buildings were gone. Cary looked around, perplexed, trying to find familiar shops and landmarks. Nearer to the Hippodrome, he found the statue of Edward Colston still standing. In the twenty-first century, this statue would be pulled from its plinth by crowds protesting the commemoration of a man who played a prominent role in the slave trade. In 1946, Cary had no interest in the statue or the man, but he was keen to see if the ornamental dolphins that decorated the plinth had survived. When he was a boy, they were one of his favorite sights as he walked to work at "the Hippo." He was relieved to see that they were intact but he was stunned by the wider damage. "It is a depressing sight to see so much of historic Bristol so badly battered," he observed sadly.[53]

He lunched at the Grand Hotel and toured the British Aeroplane works at Filton, where he saw the giant, ill-fated Brabazon plane that was being designed for transatlantic travel. Only then did he make his way to Howard Road in Westbury Park, where he surprised Elsie.[54] It was an odd way to manage a long-awaited homecoming, especially since he was in Bristol only for the day, but he planned another day trip later in the week, and he reassured her that he would spend more time in Britain in the future. As on earlier and later trips, she never visited with him in London.

He spent nine more days in London, flying back to Los Angeles on May 8 to prepare for his next film, tentatively titled *Suddenly It's Spring*. The original story was written by Sidney Sheldon. In later years he would have a very successful career in television and as a novelist, but at this time he was a struggling writer. Sheldon later said that he wrote *Suddenly It's Spring* with Cary in mind, but he also admitted that in this era almost all film comedies were written with Cary in mind. "There was no second choice," he commented, adding, "If you could not get Cary, you dropped down several levels."[55]

He got Cary because *Suddenly It's Spring* caught the eye of Dore Schary. An old friend from Cary's Broadway days, Schary was now producing for David Selznick, who also liked Sheldon's screenplay. Much to the dismay of both Schary and Sheldon, however, Selznick insisted on renaming the story *The Bachelor and the Bobby-Soxer*. Ever the showman, Selznick foresaw that the title, bringing together Cary's old Hollywood glamour and the post-war phenomenon of the teenager, would be a winner.[56]

Despite the novelty of the title, Sheldon's story was closely modeled on the screwball comedies Cary made with Leo McCarey and Howard Hawks, in which female desire opens up a chaotic world for the cool, contented bachelor. He is Dick Nugent, a nightclubbing man-about-town as well as an accomplished painter. When he gives a talk about painting at a local high school, he is wolf-whistled by many of the girls. The bobby-soxer of the title, Susan, also sees him as an object of desire, but her lust is expressed in a more chaste manner: she sees him dressed as a knight in shining armor. Nevertheless, she pursues him just as relentlessly as Katharine Hepburn did in *Bringing Up Baby*. She breaks into his apartment late at night and, although he is blameless, he is jailed when she is discovered there. He is released only on the condition that he will let Susan down gently by acting as her boyfriend until she gets over him. He is, in other words, stuck with her.

A succession of indignities ensues. He must escort her to a riotous high school basketball game and to a malt shop. He is made to drive a convertible jalopy and speak in teenage slang. At a school picnic he competes in a series of races, including a sack race, that leaves him face down on the ground—clothes stained, perspiring and humiliated. If the storyline is thin and improbable, it at least offers a vehicle for Cary's responses to these indignities: his double takes, his eyes wide with alarm, his absent-minded talking to himself, and his slight, understated whinnying at the absurdity of it all. His co-stars, on the other hand, are given little to do. The former child star Shirley Temple, playing Susan, is at least the source of his trials and tribulations, but Myrna Loy, playing Susan's older sister, is on the sideline until the ending, when she and Cary find themselves boarding the same flight and their simmering romance finally (but very briefly) comes to the fore.

Myrna Loy recalled that, more than a decade after *Wings in the Dark*, she was keen to work with Cary again, but she agreed to co-star in *The Bachelor and the Bobby-Soxer* mainly because of the paycheck.[57] Her salary of $150,000 matched Cary's, although he had 10 percent of the gross on top of his salary. Shirley Temple's salary, at $66,000, also added heavily to the budget. Dore Schary, producing at RKO (and making a cameo as Cary's driver in the airport scene), tried to compensate for the high star salaries by assigning one of the studio's "B" directors, Irving Reis, to shoot the film. Reis was put under pressure to shoot quickly and not exceed the budget of $1.7 million.[58] The set then became a pressure cooker. Everyone's nerves frayed, but the primary conflict was between Cary and Reis, and it brought filming to a halt.

Filming began on June 10, 1946, but it did not last long. In Myrna Loy's version of events, Cary "had the jitters" and was "very persnickety" when filming began. Thinking that Reis was favoring her, he stormed off the set.[59] Dore Schary, on the other hand, recalled that it was Reis who stormed off the set. The director had a "mercurial" temperament, while Cary was "easy to work with—demanding—but easy and malleable."[60] Shirley Temple, meanwhile, remembered that the trouble stemmed partly from Cary being "obsessively concerned with nuance and detail" but also from his many suggestions for "ad-libs" and "comic routines" that would liven up the comedy. Temple thought that his suggestions had merit, but she also saw that they prompted Loy to suggest changes to her own lines, and that Reis was caught in the middle of these two "warring contestants."[61]

Filming had to be suspended for days while Schary devised a compromise. He would direct the actors while Reis focused on the technical aspects of direction—the lighting and camerawork.[62] This got the production back on track, but it remained a tense and unhappy set. One day, during a lull in filming, Temple began to perform an impersonation of Cary for the crew, speaking in a broad cockney accent, imitating his double take, and insisting (as he was known to do) that his right side must always be favored by the camera. The crew laughed and egged her on until suddenly they went silent. Cary had appeared behind her and he was not amused. According to Temple, he "stalked away" and would not return until she went to his dressing room to apologize to him. He accepted her apology and then, as she was leaving, he mimicked her mimicry. "By the way," he said in his broadest cockney accent, "it was a pretty good imitation."[63]

Today, *The Bachelor and the Bobby-Soxer* seems both light as a feather and hopelessly dated. Its 90-minute running time is mostly a string of gags centered on a forty-two-year-old man dating a high school student. But on release in the summer of 1947 the film was greeted with nearly unanimous praise. It had been a long time since Cary had made what people called a "typical Cary Grant comedy," and critics and audiences had evidently missed them. Sidney Sheldon won the "best original screenplay" Academy Award for writing this highly formulaic film.[64] The box-office tally—$4.2 million in North America and another $1.35 million abroad—made it RKO's biggest hit of 1947, and Cary's third blockbuster in a row.[65] His percentage deal meant that he earned over $550,000 from this one film.[66]

He explained to a reporter that he understood that the film would not be regarded as significant. "Sometimes a comparatively unimportant motion picture comes my way," he said. "Yet I get a feeling that it is going to be something that will please my public. That is enough for me."[67] He clearly knew how to please his public. Ten years after striking out as a freelance star, he regularly featured in the top-ten rankings of the most popular stars, he had his choice of films, and he was amply rewarded for making them. Finding films that continued to challenge him and appeal to the public would be difficult, however, and, despite his ambitions for *Hamlet* and working with Korda in London, it would be all too easy to coast on his more predictable successes in Hollywood.

In 1946, Cary was still living in the Bellagio Road house that he bought two years earlier as part of his attempt to reconcile with Barbara Hutton. It was a mansion built for a Bel Air lifestyle that he had no interest in living. Now divorced and on his own, he left much of the house empty and unfurnished. Visitors were surprised to find that he used just a few downstairs rooms, mainly his living room and his den. The living room had a movie screen and a 16mm projector, as well as piles of scripts and stacks of recent novels, which were sent to him by agents and producers eager to interest him in adapting them for the screen. The den was decorated with his paintings (seascapes by Eugène Boudin prominent among them). The walls were lined with shelves holding his own, more permanent book collection, and there was a grand piano that he often played. The upstairs was largely deserted, and Cary admitted that rather than going up to his bedroom, on many nights he slept on a fold-out sofa in the den.[1]

This was the quiet lifestyle that he adopted in his forties. True, he was often seen with Betty Hensel at fashionable nightclubs and restaurants, and at the Santa Anita races, but henceforth he was known for *not* entertaining at home.[2] After all of the Sunday open houses on Ocean Front, and all of Barbara Hutton's formal dinners, he stopped hosting parties. He was not quite a recluse. The Bellagio Road house was large enough to serve as a second home to some of Cary's closest friends, who were also very successful and unusually itinerant men. Alexander Korda, now amicably divorced from Merle Oberon, stayed with Cary when he was in Hollywood on business. Cary described the Hungarian-born British filmmaker as "a man of Old World charm." The same could be said of another close friend, playwright Frederick Lonsdale, whose successful and much-filmed theatrical works include *Monsieur Beaucaire* (1919) and *The Last of Mrs Cheyney* (1925). "Freddie," was twenty years older than Cary, but they shared a similar background. Lonsdale, too, was a working-class Brit who had remade himself as a suave, modern, metropolitan gentleman. They met on the transatlantic show business circuit—Hollywood to New York to London and back again—that was often traveled by ship and train during the 1930s and 1940s.[3]

Cary's closest friend in this period of his life was not known for his Old World charm or for enjoying leisurely transatlantic crossings. Howard Hughes was, however, even more itinerant than the others. The millionaire aviator was unmarried and rootless apart from his dedication to his work. Cary always explained his friendship with Hughes in the same way. They enjoyed each other's company, he said, because they could sit together for hours without feeling obliged to make conversation. If this seems an odd basis for a friendship, it should be remembered that both men were so far at the top of their respective fields that most people they met sought to impress them, work with them, or interest them in an investment. They were free of that with one another. They had in common a penchant for privacy, a preoccupation with their careers, and a love of flying. In other respects, they were very different. Cary marveled that, when he and Hughes took a weekend trip together—flying off to New York or Catalina or Mexico—Hughes would bring along just a couple of shirts in a cardboard box. Cary, who planned his wardrobe carefully and traveled with monogrammed luggage, admired Hughes for not caring about his appearance or what people might think of him.[4]

Hughes never commented publicly on his friendship with Cary, but Cary's friend, Irene Mayer Selznick, observed that Hughes envied Cary's good looks, his social grace, and his ease with women. "The one thing that Howard Hughes couldn't be, to his sorrow, was Cary Grant," she recalled. She found it odd that when Hughes saw that she and Cary were close friends, he proposed that he should be her close friend, too. He did not have a "woman friend," he told her.[5] This was a key difference between Cary and Hughes. Cary enjoyed his friendships with women, among them Irene Selznick, Rosalind Russell, Dorothy di Frasso, and Constance Moore, and when he was romantically involved with a woman, he did not play the field. Hughes, by contrast, was interested in women primarily as sexual conquests, and he pursued sexual relationships with the actresses he employed—or promised to employ.[6]

Ingrid Bergman was wary of him. Shortly after making *Notorious*, Hughes flew Cary, Bergman, and Irene Mayer Selznick to New York for a weekend jaunt. On the return flight, Bergman was delighted when Hughes, flying the plane at a low level, gave her an aerial tour of the Grand Canyon at dawn, but she was otherwise ill at ease with him, suspecting that behind his professed shyness and loneliness, he was an arrogant and manipulative man. "He's just dying to see you again," Cary told her after the New York trip. She reprimanded Cary for interfering. She was determined not to be added to Hughes's list of conquests.[7]

For Hughes, Hollywood was a side interest. His life's work was developing new aircraft, and he could be reckless. On July 7, 1946, he nearly killed himself and others when testing a new plane. As he flew off the designated flight path and over residential areas of Los Angeles, he lost control of the plane. As it plummeted, he aimed for a crash landing on the Los Angeles Country Club golf course. He did not quite make it. His plane descended over the streets of Beverly Hills, clipping the rooftops of two houses and then crashing into another. Fortunately, no one was at home, and as the house burned to the ground, he managed to crawl out of the cockpit. A neighbor dragged him away from the flames, but he was so severely hurt, with broken bones and third-degree burns, that the emergency room doctors did not think he would survive the first night.[8] Cary was one of the few people allowed past the security guards posted outside Hughes's hospital room, and, when Hughes was well enough to leave the hospital, Cary invited him to recuperate at Bellagio Road. Cary was in the midst of filming *The Bachelor and the Bobby-Soxer*, and so Hughes was alone most days apart from visits from his latest girlfriend, the newly signed Fox star Jean Peters. She sat at his bedside while he was still bedridden, and later wheeled him into the living room, where they screened films using Cary's 16mm projector.[9]

In October 1946, when *The Bachelor and the Bobby-Soxer* was completed, Cary planned to embark on his first film with Alexander Korda in London. This was going to be *The Devil's Delight*, a comedy written by popular humorist Alan Melville and directed by Carol Reed. Cary would play the devil.[10] But Korda was having production problems on other films, and he had to put Cary off indefinitely. Left with a hole in his schedule, Cary agreed to make a film that he had previously turned down several times, *The Bishop's Wife*, in which he would play an angel rather than the devil. The connection between the two roles was of course his other-worldly qualities—grace, gravitas, and good looks were required for both.

The Bishop's Wife was produced by the film mogul Samuel Goldwyn who, like David Selznick, ran a boutique studio known for making only the highest-quality films. Goldwyn could not imagine anyone other than Cary playing the angel. He kept calling him, even after Cary turned him down several times. When the London trip was canceled, he finally got him.[11] Initially, Cary had no problems with the production set-up. The director, William A. Seiter, was accomplished if not distinguished. Cary's old friend David

Niven, recently returned to Hollywood after war service in Britain, would play the bishop, and Teresa Wright, a much-admired actress he had met over dinner at the Hitchcocks', was set to play the bishop's wife.[12]

It was the script that worried Cary. Before filming began, he was promised that his criticisms would be taken into account. He liked the premise: an angel, named Dudley, comes to earth during the Christmas season to help a beleaguered Episcopalian bishop, but a chaste romance develops between the angel and the bishop's wife. Cary's complaint was that the angel came across as "a rather conceited, impudent, highhanded magician." He was all tricks and gimmicks, and not the "self-effacing, generous human character" Cary thought he should be. Scriptwriter Robert E. Sherwood was charged with rewriting the script to address these concerns, but when Cary read the new script over the Christmas holiday in 1946, he was still not satisfied with it.[13]

He began trying to wriggle out of playing the angel. He was appalled when Niven told him that he wanted to play the angel, and Goldwyn had promised him that the role would make a great Hollywood comeback for him.[14] Then when Cary became available, he was pushed aside. "Cary Grant is big box office and you are not," Goldwyn told Niven, relegating him to the secondary role of the bishop.[15] Niven was under contract to Goldwyn and had no choice in the matter. Cary immediately offered to trade places with Niven, letting his friend have part of the angel that he was so keen to play.[16] This was not a bad idea. It would have made Niven happy and allowed Cary to breathe some life into the rather priggish role of the bishop, but Goldwyn did not agree.

Cary promised Goldwyn that he would make a different film with him— any film—if only he could be let out of playing the angel. Goldwyn refused his offer. He played it tough because the contract negotiations between Cary's agent, Frank Vincent, and Goldwyn's legal team had been so tough. Vincent set forth the same terms that David Selznick had agreed for Notorious. Cary would accept nothing less than a salary of $150,000 plus 10 percent of the film's earnings above $1.5 million and up to $3 million, allowing him to earn $300,000 from the film. Goldwyn could not believe his ears when he heard these terms, but he eventually had to admit to his own staff that he "wanted Grant so badly for this picture that there was nothing that could be done." The star was in a position "to write his own ticket," Goldwyn concluded when he agreed to Cary's terms.[17]

After Cary signed the contract in October 1946, Goldwyn was determined that his star would play the role he agreed to play.[18] Sadly, Frank Vincent died suddenly in October 1946, at the age of sixty-four.[19] Cary no longer had his manager and mentor wheeling and dealing on his behalf, and helping him to negotiate an escape from *The Bishop's Wife*. In early January 1947, with this stalemate lingering and production not due to start for another month, Cary left town for a holiday, traveling first to New York to see friends and the latest shows, and then to Mexico with Howard Hughes.[20] Hughes was visiting Jean Peters, who was making her first film, the Tyrone Power swashbuckler *Captain from Castile* (1947), on location in Guadalajara. Cary went along for the ride, which proved to be momentous.[21]

Hughes flew a twin-propeller DC3 plane with just two crew members and Cary aboard. They took off from New York at noon on Friday, January 10. Bad weather prompted Hughes to change his flight plan, but he did not inform anyone on the ground about this and, always eager for privacy, he kept the plane's radio switched off. Thus, when the plane did not arrive as planned for refueling in Amarillo, Texas, and it could not be reached by radio, the authorities concluded that it had crashed.[22] Search parties were dispatched to find the wreckage, and news bulletins and headlines announced that Howard Hughes and Cary Grant were "missing." For twelve hours, it was thought that the reckless aviator had finally managed to kill himself and that, much more tragically, he had taken the beloved movie star with him.[23] Actually, they had stopped in El Paso for refueling, and they did not realize all of the trouble they were causing until they refueled again in Nogales, Arizona, at midday on Saturday. All that they could do was apologize before heading onward, to Mexico City and Acapulco, to see their friends.[24]

A few weeks later, Cary returned to Los Angeles very much alive but unable to free himself from the commitment to play an angel. He reported for rehearsals on February 3, 1947, and filming started three weeks later. It was not a happy set. David Niven was miserable playing the bishop, and when he criticized the part, Goldwyn threatened to fire him.[25] Theresa Wright discovered that she was pregnant during the first week of rehearsals and dropped out of the film.[26] Her replacement, Loretta Young, sulked because she could not wear her customary gowns and elaborate makeup. "A bishop's wife is not a glamour girl," Goldwyn scolded her, insisting that she look the part.[27]

Three weeks into filming, Goldwyn watched the rushes and saw that his disgruntled stars were giving lifeless performances. On March 17, he halted filming and fired director William Seiter. He asked William Wyler and then Howard Hawks to step in, but both directors steered clear of the troubled set.[28] Instead, Seiter's replacement was Henry Koster, a less distinguished director but one who specialized in light, heartwarming comedy (he had directed many of the child star Deanna Durbin's films). All of the footage shot by Seiter was discarded, and Koster and Robert E. Sherwood spent three weeks revising the script before filming started again on April 11. Cary was stuck playing the angel for a further twelve weeks of filming, until July 9.[29]

It remained a tense set. Loretta Young had worked with Cary on *Born to Be Bad* more than a decade earlier. She was surprised to find that since then he had become such a perfectionist, and she found his meticulousness distracting. When he suddenly halted filming in the middle of a take because he realized that, although the scene was set in winter, the windows had not been frosted, she finally asked him not to make these criticisms. To her surprise, he apologized and ceased nit-picking—around her at least.[30] Henry Koster found him less compliant. Koster recalled that Cary was "never rude or anything," but he was "a very nervous man" and he was unhappy with the film. "The worst thing that can happen to a director," Koster said, "is to work with an actor who doesn't want to play a part [but] has to do it."[31]

Koster and Goldwyn tried to convince Cary to play the angel for light comedy rather than philosophical other-worldliness.[32] This may be why, in the finished film, the other characters are favored by the camera, and the expected reverse shots, showing Cary talking or his reactions, are few and far between. One of the few moments Cary's performance comes to life is when Dudley sees a harp and cannot resist playing it. Cary took pride in learning to play the instrument, at least well enough to handle it convincingly on-screen.[33] Otherwise, *The Bishop's Wife* did not offer him many opportunities to shine. The romance between the angel and the bishop's wife could not come to any interesting fruition because the censors would never allow such sacrilege. Similarly, the comic potential was limited because, as an angel, he had to maintain his dignity and not suffer the humiliations that were his specialty as a performer. Some humor arises from the angel's magical powers; for example, he slyly refills glasses with a wave of his finger. But the film is not quite a light-hearted supernatural comedy along the lines of *Topper* (1937), *I Married a Witch* (1942), and *Blithe Spirit* (1945), and it never manages to develop the Irish Catholic whimsy of *Going My Way* (1944) and *The Bells of St. Mary's* (1945).

Late in June, when Goldwyn previewed a rough cut of the film, he realized that it was still falling flat. He called in screenwriter Charles Brackett and writer-director Billy Wilder to help. Brackett judged Cary to be "wildly miscast" in this "fair, weak little picture." He and Wilder agreed with Goldwyn that more humour was needed, and they wrote some additional scenes for

Niven, notably a gentle slapstick routine that has the bishop stuck in a chair.[34] By this time, the production cost reached over \$3 million and Goldwyn feared the film would flop.[35] It was quite a coup, then, when *The Bishop's Wife* was selected for the second annual Royal Command Film Performance in London. It was there, before an audience that included King George VI and Queen Elizabeth, that the film was first screened in November 1947.[36]

The Bishop's Wife was released in the United States at the height of the holiday season. Many critics responded enthusiastically to it, regarding it as a charming holiday film. Some admired Cary's performance for its restraint and dignity.[37] Others thought he was an unlikely "heavenly messenger" (*Los Angeles Times*) and "the last person in the world I would suspect of being an angel" (New York's *Daily News*).[38] A key issue for many was the film's representation of religion. *Life* magazine made *The Bishop's Wife* its "film of the week" but nevertheless regarded the mere suggestion of a romance between the angel and the bishop's wife as a "lapse in taste."[39]

Despite the criticisms, *The Bishop's Wife* was a solid box-office success during the holidays. Once the festive season had passed, Goldwyn changed the title to *Cary and the Bishop's Wife*, and added a suggestive by-line to advertisements: "Have *you* heard about Cary and the bishop's wife?"[40] This gave the film new life at the box office.[41] Earnings climbed to \$3.5 million in North America, placing it among the top twenty films of the year.[42] Subsequently, it has not quite achieved the status of a classic film, but it has had a long afterlife, with frequent screenings in the holiday season. A high-profile remake, as *The Preacher's Wife* (1996), has Denzel Washington, Whitney Houston, and Courtney B. Vance in the lead roles. Back in 1947, it was a film that Cary was glad to be done with, and one that he regretted ever agreeing to make.[43]

Frank Vincent's death was a blow to Cary not only because he lost an old friend, but also because he lost a canny business advisor who had helped him carve out ever more powerful and lucrative deals. Along with two of Vincent's other clients, actors Joel McCrea and Edward G. Robinson, Cary was a pallbearer at Vincent's funeral and an executor of his estate.[44] This is how he came to purchase the house at 9966 Beverly Grove that he would own for the rest of his life. Vincent bought the house for \$82,500 just a few months before his death.[45] It was humble by the standards of Beverly Hills, and very different from the Westridge estate and the Bellagio Road mansion. Modeled on a French farmhouse, it had just one story and three bedrooms. The relatively high price reflected the property's spectacular southerly views, looking toward downtown Los Angeles (to the east) and Santa Monica and the Pacific Ocean (to the west), as well as its four acres of land in an as yet undeveloped area near the top of Benedict Canyon. Cary admired the views and the privacy but, not quite ready to move in himself, he initially rented it to Howard Hughes, who also admired its airy yet secluded position.[46]

While Vincent's estate was in probate, the trio of executors temporarily took over the running of the Frank Vincent Agency. They looked after their own business affairs as well as those of the agency's other clients, including Richard Dix, Brian Donlevy, Rita Hayworth, Rosalind Russell, and Claire Trevor.[47] This experience proved pivotal for Cary, who realized that he no longer needed an agent.[48] Vincent had taught him everything he needed to know about freelancing, and Cary did not need anyone else's advice about the direction of his career. What he did need was a lawyer to negotiate on his behalf, draw up contracts, and make sure that the terms (including the stream of income from the percentage deals) were met. He therefore decided not to hire a new agent but instead to assign the attorney Morton Garbus, who had worked for Vincent, to deal with all of his legal affairs.[49] Now that he earned $300,000 a film, paying Garbus only for his billable hours would be a huge saving on paying an agent 10 percent of his salary.

Garbus was a self-made man, of Russian-Jewish lineage, and he and Cary got along so well that in July 1947 they drove across the country together to New York. They took the northerly route, via Wyoming and Nebraska, stopping in small towns and admiring the scenery on this very long journey through small-town America. Cary loved "motoring," as he called it, and these extended journeys fed his nostalgia for his itinerant years in vaudeville and touring Broadway shows.[50] Garbus was heading to New York on business, while Cary was sailing on the *Queen Elizabeth* to Britain on August 1.[51]

The ocean crossing was made in luxury. Cary had a suite on the *Queen Elizabeth*, and he ate at the captain's table along with his friend Freddie Lonsdale, who was traveling with him. They were both delighted to meet another passenger, the fifteen-year-old Elizabeth Taylor, who had been a child star for several years but was star-struck to meet Cary Grant.[52] On arrival in London on August 6, it was Alexander Korda's turn to play host to Cary. Korda kept a suite of rooms at Claridge's Hotel in Mayfair and Cary took up residence there, and enjoyed the reception that Korda threw for him at the Dorchester Hotel on Friday night. Two hundred filmmakers and other notables greeted Cary like a returning hero. The free-flowing champagne raised a few eyebrows in the midst of Britain's post-war austerity crisis, but

Korda was a film mogul known for his excesses, and he was celebrating Cary's planned entry into British filmmaking, not just as a one-off but for a string of films.[53]

Their original project, *The Devil's Delight*, was put on hold. After playing an angel, it was too soon for Cary to play the devil. But he and Korda also had plans for a series of comedy films, in which Cary would play an American traveler visiting different countries and struggling with their customs and mores. Although played for humor, the series was conceived in the spirit of post-war internationalism, as one that would build understanding between the United States and the rest of the world. Cary spoke enthusiastically about these plans to the press, naming Istanbul as the location of the first film. If he realized the irony of his returning to Britain to play an archetypal American, he never commented on it.[54]

At the weekend he drove down to Bristol and checked into the Grand Hotel. In her letters, Elsie let him know that she enjoyed *Night and Day* and *The Bachelor and the Bobby-Soxer*.[55] She did not comment on *Notorious*, but Cary was likely to take some satisfaction from seeing the title on the marquee of three of the city's biggest cinemas when he arrived.[56] It was a beautifully dry, warm summer, and he and Elsie enjoyed going for long drives in the car. Once again, as on his last trip, they crossed the Clifton Suspension Bridge (spanning the Avon River Gorge) and toured the Somerset countryside. In the evening, Cary was spotted alone in a box seat at the Hippodrome. It was still a venue for music hall, and that evening, watching a female impersonator and ventriloquist named Bobbie Kimber, he may have been reminded of his youthful admiration for Vesta Tilley.[57]

He also visited Fairfield School. The students were on their summer holiday, but Cary toured the school and posed for photographers sitting at his old desk in one of the classrooms. The school's secretary showed him the registration book that recorded the dates of students starting and finishing their studies, and the qualification they achieved. He saw his own entry in the book—with "U. Remove" indicating both his unclassified certificate and his expulsion from the school. His also saw that another box on the page, labeled "Occupation taken up after leaving" had been filled in with "unknown."[58] On this visit, though, the secretary took the opportunity to write, "Film Star" and "now Cary Grant" in the book, lifting him from disgrace to distinction right before his eyes.[59]

In London, he saw the latest West End shows, including the newly opened musical *Annie Get Your Gun* and the drama *Deep Are the Roots*, about an

African American GI returning to the Deep South after the war.[60] Touring Shepperton Studios, he caught up with David Niven on the set of Korda's *Bonnie Prince Charlie* (1948), and attended a preview screening of Korda's *Anna Karenina* (1948), starring Vivien Leigh.[61] However, he waited in vain for Korda to offer him a viable script. When he finally departed from Southampton on September 4, the script still was not ready, but he planned to return in the new year to begin filming with Korda.[62] Then, en route to New York, fate intervened with those plans.

Cary settled in for a comfortable journey aboard the *Queen Mary*. Freddie Lonsdale, the film financier Jock Whitney, the producer Arthur Hornblow and his wife, and Merle Oberon (traveling with her new husband, cinematographer Lucien Ballard) were among the friends on board. But the woman who caught Cary's eye was twenty-three-year-old Betsy Drake. As Cary told it, their meeting was like a scene in a screwball comedy. He ran into her—literally collided with her—as he exited and she entered a phone booth on the ship. He initially suspected that "a bit of coquetry was going on" because he was used to people engineering situations in which they could meet him. But then he recognized her as the actress he had seen in *Deep Are the Roots*. He had admired her performance and also found her attractive. She was his type: slim, fair, blue-eyed, and well spoken.[63] Like Ingrid Bergman, Betsy did not dye her hair blonde, or wear high heels and heavy makeup, and like Katharine Hepburn, she had a tomboy-ish quality to her angular face.

He became so smitten, so quickly that he was too shy to ask Betsy for a date himself. He pleaded with Merle Oberon to act on his behalf and invite Betsy to join their table for dinner. They went together to her cabin door and, in another scenario straight from a screwball comedy, Cary hid around the corner while the softly spoken Oberon extended an invitation. Betsy joined them the next night. At the table, Cary was half amused and half annoyed to see Freddie Lonsdale flirting with her. Had Freddie been a bit younger, Cary later commented, "I probably would have lost her to him."[64]

Betsy came from a wealthy American family. They were the Drakes of the five-star Drake Hotel in Chicago, but she was born in Paris, where her bohemian parents lived an expatriate lifestyle until the Wall Street Crash brought them home in 1930. As the family's fortunes declined, her parents divorced and her mother had a nervous breakdown. Betsy was raised by nannies in the Drake Hotel, and later sent to live with various relatives on the East Coast. A nervous, stuttering child, she found confidence and approval when she began acting in high school plays. At seventeen, she quit high school to move to New York and work as a model while pursuing auditions, and a few years later she tried her luck in Hollywood without success. When she returned to New York, the director Elia Kazan cast her in the London production of *Deep Are the Roots*. She was on her way back to New York when she met Cary.[65]

Sitting down to dinner on the *Queen Mary* with Cary's circle of show business friends must have been daunting for Betsy. She had the manners and bearing to converse confidently with them, but she was also much younger and more liberal than this crowd. She lived in Greenwich Village and was interested in hypnotism and yoga. Professionally, she was interested in stage rather than film acting, and particularly the worthy, socially conscious drama and intense "method" acting style that Elia Kazan (a founder of the Actors Studio) espoused. While she rejected the commercialism and glamour of the older Hollywood generation, she could not quite bring herself to reject Cary Grant. He, in turn, was intrigued that someone so well mannered and refined could be so youthful and open-minded. He asked for her to dine with him every evening for the remainder of the journey.[66]

Now inescapably middle-aged at the age of forty-three, Cary was attracted not so much by her youth—there were plenty of young women eager to date him—but by her integrity and unconventional interests. He found common ground with her troubled family, including her mother's mental illness, and her struggle to establish her career. He saw her as a waif and stray in need of his support and expertise. At the same time, her inquisitive perspective on life seemed to offer him a new path, away from the staid interests of his wealthy friends, and toward something more authentic. They would be both teacher and pupil with one another.

By the time the *Queen Mary* docked in New York four nights later, they were in love. He stayed in New York until the end of September, trying to convince her to come back to Hollywood with him, and assuring her that he could get her work. She was wary of returning to the film industry on these terms, and in late September, Cary had to fly back to Los Angeles without her.[67]

He was starting work on *Mr. Blandings Builds His Dream House*, another film shepherded through pre-production by David Selznick and then produced at RKO, where Dore Schary was now head of production.[68] The set-up was similar to the one for *The Bachelor and the Bobby-Soxer*. Dore Schary was producing, Cary and Myrna Loy were starring, and the story was very much in the mold of established Cary Grant comedies, although this one had a timely theme about Americans leaving the city for the suburbs.

Cary plays Jim Blandings, a successful advertising executive trying to come up with a slogan for "Wham," a canned meat product that he loathes. Together with his wife Muriel (Loy), their two daughters (Sharyn Moffatt and Connie Marshall), and their ever-cheerful African American maid, Gussie (Louise Beavers), they live on Manhattan's Upper West Side as "modern cliff dwellers." That is, in a tall building and a tiny apartment, with stuffed closets, a shared bathroom, and an overflowing medicine cabinet. Their longing for more room leads them to the open spaces of Connecticut. They buy a Colonial-era home with the intention of renovating it, but ultimately realize that they must tear down the ramshackle property and build their dream house. A stream of complications and upsets ensues.

Filming began on October 6, 1947, and it was a happy set. The director, H. C. Potter, had worked with Cary on *Mr. Lucky*, and they understood each other's methods. On this third film together, Cary and Myrna Loy also worked well together. They did not have Shirley Temple to contend with and they both liked the script. Their co-star, Melvyn Douglas (playing the Blandings' lawyer and best friend, Bill), was another kindred spirit. Both Loy and Douglas understood that their characters functioned as foils for Cary.[69] Loy, who had long specialized in playing ideal wives, remains calm and unflappable as each mishap threatens to puncture Cary's cool demeanor. Similarly, Douglas blithely points out impending catastrophes while sitting back and casually puffing on his pipe. Cary is thus given ample room to shine as the increasingly exasperated Jim Blandings, who is, as Bill describes it, "fleeced, bilked, rooked, flimflammed and generally taken to the cleaners" as he tears down one house and builds another.

Cary's best comic moments come across on-screen as entirely spontaneous. Early in the film, when the shortcomings of the Manhattan apartment are established, he gets into the shower and is startled by the icy water. His initial anguished howl of "Oh!" quickly transforms into a bellowing rendition of "Home on the Range." The scene succinctly establishes two key aspects of his character: his desire for a perfect home and his urgent need to maintain an imperturbable manner. Yet it is funny especially because it seems so incidental and offhand. He worked hard to achieve this nonchalance. His copy of the shooting script reveals the meticulous care he took with dialogue. He took a pen to the page, cutting down dialogue to the bare essentials, changing a word here and there to make the phrasing more elegant, and, in some instances, changing whole sentences.[70]

In the climactic scene, once the house has been built and he has been subjected to a string of costly calamities, Jim finally loses his cool and declares that he hates the house because it has placed him on the "All-American sucker list." The script called for him to continue speaking in this vein, saying,

> Everywhere you turn they've got a hand in your pocket. If you take out their hands, they find more pockets. It's a conspiracy, I tell you, a conspiracy against every man and woman who wants a home of their own. Against every boy and girl who were ever in love!

Cary crossed out portions of the dialogue and, in the margins of the script, he penned the amended dialogue that he actually speaks in the film:

> You start out to build a home and wind up in the poor house. And if it can happen to me what about the fellows who aren't making $15,000 a year? What about the kids who just got married and want a home of their own? It's a conspiracy, I tell you, a conspiracy against every boy and girl who were ever in love![71]

His changes removed some of the more unpleasant elements of the dialogue (hands probing into pockets) and they also addressed one of the more awkward aspects of the story. Far from representing the ordinary Americans who dreamed of leaving the city for a ready-built suburban subdivision, the Blandings were a decidedly well-off family, building their own custom-designed home in the far reaches of rural (but still commutable) Connecticut. This was based on a true story. Eric Hodgins, a Manhattan executive, wrote the comical novel after over-spending so much on his own custom-built house that he had to sell it. Although the book-reading public enjoyed it, it was not clear that the mass movie audience, who made a fraction of Jim Blandings' annual salary, would find have much sympathy for his predicaments.[72] Importantly, then, the revised dialogue gives Jim a higher purpose than concern for his own wallet. He isn't just a rich man who is angry about the high cost of luxury; he has some concern for the less well-off and the young.

During the filming, the House Un-American Activities Committee (HUAC) opened hearings to investigate subversive, communist influences in Hollywood. The issue divided the film industry. The Motion Picture Alliance for the Preservation of American Ideals, a right-wing group, included filmmakers such as Gary Cooper, Walt Disney, Leo McCarey, and Robert Taylor, who were "friendly witnesses" in the HUAC hearings.[73] Lela Rogers, the mother of Ginger Rogers, was another friendly witness, and in her testimony she took particular aim at *None but the Lonely Heart*. She was working at RKO when the story arrived, she told the committee, and she advised against its purchase. She thought that a story about poverty "lent itself to communism" and she considered its screenwriter and director, Clifford Odets, to be a communist. Many other screenwriters and directors were accused of being "reds" and subpoenaed to appear before the committee.[74]

On the other side of the political divide, liberal filmmakers rallied to support the subpoenaed "unfriendly witnesses" (those accused of being or having once been communists) by forming the Committee for the First Amendment. Myrna Loy recalled in her memoir that directors John Huston and William Wyler came to the *Mr. Blandings* set, seeking support for the Committee for the First Amendment, but Cary avoided getting involved. As she remembered, "he wasn't unsupportive, but he didn't say, 'I want to belong to this thing.'" He did not donate money to the cause, as Loy and Melvyn Douglas did, and he did not travel to Washington, DC, along with stars such as Humphrey Bogart, Lauren Bacall, and Danny Kaye, to lend public support to the subpoenaed "unfriendly witnesses" (who later became known as the Hollywood Ten).[75]

His reluctance to get involved may have stemmed from his close personal and professional relationships with people on opposing sides of the argument—Leo McCarey on the right and Clifford Odets on the left—but he was also against stars using their fame as a soapbox. "I'm definitely opposed to actors taking sides in public and spouting spontaneously about love, religion, or politics," he told an interviewer three years earlier, explaining, "We aren't experts on those subjects."[76] In the short term, as Hollywood acquiesced to HUAC's agenda, he was probably glad he kept quiet. Even a star as powerful as Bogart was made to recant his liberal views, by writing an apologetic article for a fan magazine entitled "I'm No Communist."[77] A few years later, though, Cary was dismayed by the treatment of Charlie Chaplin, whose left-leaning politics led to him being driven out of the United States in 1952. He did speak out on Chaplin's behalf. "I want Charlie Chaplin back," he said publicly. "Personally, I don't think he is a communist. Whatever his political views, they are secondary to the fact that he is a great entertainer."[78]

Political tensions aside, production of *Mr. Blandings* proceeded smoothly during the autumn of 1947. The outdoor scenes were shot at RKO's ranch in

Encino, California, which was decorated with wintry trees to make it look more like New England.[79] A last-minute rush to complete the film meant working through the holidays, except Christmas Eve and Christmas Day, until it was completed on December 30, 1947.

At the time, *Mr. Blandings* was probably seen as a safer bet at the box-office than the quirky *Bishop's Wife*. It was the more conventional Cary Grant comedy. From the earliest reviews, however, it became apparent that all the talk about construction expenses drained some of the escapism and comedy from *Mr. Blandings. Variety*, for example found the film only "mildly amusing," and the reviewer wondered whether the "average filmgoer" would have any interest in the housing problems of a man "trying to make ends meet on $15,000 a year."[80] In her syndicated column, Hedda Hopper echoed this with a backhanded compliment, telling readers that the film would "tickle anyone who has ever attempted to build a dream house."[81] Other critics, including those closer to Jim Blandings's social set at the *New York Times* and the *New Yorker*, described the film only as "casual fun" and "amiable."[82]

The public seems to have agreed because *Mr. Blandings* was only a modest success. Its North American box-office take, $2.8 million, was a significant drop from Cary's previous films, and, because of the costly star salaries, it was not enough to turn a profit.[83] It was the first of his comedies to lose money in a decade, although at the time this may have been attributed to the sharp post-war decline in movie-going rather than changing audience tastes.

After completing *Mr. Blandings*, Cary was due to go back to Britain and start work with Korda. Meeting Betsy put those plans on hold. Instead of going to Britain, he became determined to kick-start her film career in Hollywood. She visited him in Hollywood for the holidays in 1947 and she did not return to New York. She took an apartment in Hollywood for appearance's sake, but she and Cary moved into the Beverly Grove house together (the Bellagio Road mansion was too grand for her tastes).[84] He arranged for her to make a screen test, and then he talked Dore Schary and David Selznick into offering her a contract. Cary and Betsy were seen together so often that no one was surprised when it was announced that she would be the co-star in his next film, or that the title, *Every Girl Should Be Married*, pointed so strongly in the direction that they were heading.[85]

22

During the Hollywood studio era, one of the first realities for a star of any stature was maintaining a good relationship with the press and especially its gossip columnists. Early in his freelancing career, Cary was so happy to be free of the Paramount publicity machine that he steered clear of journalists as much as possible and, when required to do interviews, he refused to answer personal questions. He quickly developed a reputation for being "difficult." Five years later, in 1942, the Hollywood Women's Press Club voted him the "most cooperative film player" of the year.[1] He had become adept at handling the press, and he was especially adept at handling the two most powerful gossip columnists in Hollywood, Hedda Hopper and Louella Parsons.[2]

Through their widely syndicated daily newspaper columns, their radio broadcasts, and the articles they wrote for the fan magazines, Hopper and Parsons wielded a huge influence over the reputations of stars and the fortunes of newly released films. They were rivals, personally and professionally, which meant that stars had to perform a delicate balancing act, making sure that each columnist thought that they were given equal, if not preferential, treatment over the other. Publicists gave them a steady stream of news, but they also reported idle gossip. They turned up at parties and premieres, and in their columns the next day they reported on the evening: who was together or apart, who looked well, who stayed late or left early. Stars were so intimidated by them that they took care to phone them with news of their career, and to send them birthday and Christmas gifts—anything to stay on their good side.[3]

Cary loathed both women but he was careful not to let them know it.[4] Louella Parsons was the less venomous of the two but she was tactlessly intrusive. When she saw Cary at a party, she had no qualms about asking him directly, "When are you going to marry Betty Hensel?," and then reporting to her readers that he was "flustered" by the question.[5] Hedda Hopper had to be treated with extra care. She had a particularly malign perspective— nativist, right-wing, Anglo-phobic, and homophobic—that she turned on anyone she disapproved of. Cary had known her in her earlier career as an actress. One of her last roles before her acting career petered out was a minor part in *Topper* in 1937. It is not clear whether this association explains why she alternated between writing sneering and fawning comments about him in her column. In the autumn of 1940, Noel Coward passed through Los Angeles twice while touring California, staying with Cary at Ocean Front on both occasions. Hopper's comments on this were thick with innuendo. "Noel Coward and Cary Grant took up where they left off about a month ago," she wrote in her column. "I mean Noel was Cary's house guest."[6] In 1944, however, when Barbara Hutton was fighting for custody of her son, Cary arranged for Hopper to write a glowing (and largely fictional) account of Barbara and Cary's home life at Westridge, portraying them as a model married couple with a happy home life.[7]

He learned that it was crucial to feed the columnists' egos. When *Life* magazine profiled Hopper in 1941 and photographed the stars who supposedly helped her to move to a new house, Cary was prominent among them, carrying a steep stack of hat boxes for her (elaborate headwear was her trademark).[8] In 1947, he invited Hopper to a party he gave at the Long Beach marina, where his guests were watching Howard Hughes test a new aircraft over the water. Hopper was able to hobnob with the other guests—James Stewart, Henry Fonda, and Randolph Scott—and write it up in her column.[9] When Betsy arrived in Hollywood, Cary accompanied her when she went to Hopper's house for an interview, and a few days later Cary and Betsy also "dropped by" Louella Parsons's home for an interview. Both columnists informed their readers about the visits, suggesting Cary was an old friend.[10] More routinely, he gave both Hopper and Parsons regular bits of information about his films and his travel plans as a means of keeping them happy and making sure that he had a hand in what they wrote about him.

The care he took to remain in their favor paid dividends for Betsy when she signed with RKO. Hopper and Parsons introduced Betsy to their readers with a number of flattering items about her long before the release of her first film, *Every Girl Should Be Married*. Parsons exaggerated Betsy's success on the Broadway and West End stage, and, claiming to have seen her screen test, declared her to be "the most promising newcomer I've seen in many a day."[11] Hopper was not as prone to gushing, but she did report from the set of *Every Girl Should Be Married* that Betsy is "intelligent and photogenic and has a natural quality all her own." She also referred to Betsy as "Cary's discovery" and speculated about a romance between them, but this was not part of the plan.[12] Betsy wanted to be seen as an actress in her own right, and not as one whose career was based on being Cary Grant's girlfriend.[13]

Nevertheless, Betsy needed building up. The public had never heard of her, and on the basis of Cary's enthusiasm for her, RKO cast her in the leading role—alongside him, of course—in *Every Girl Should Be Married*. To clinch the deal, Cary accepted lesser terms for this film. Costs were reigned in for a ten-week shoot that lasted from May 24 to July 21, 1948. The director was the little-known Don Hartman, who was an experienced screenwriter (notably of the *Road* comedies starring Bing Crosby and Bob Hope) but the director of only one film before this. Cary also took an upfront, guaranteed salary of just $50,000, although he would also earn 10 percent of the gross over $500,000. Beside Cary, the only significant name in the cast was Franchot Tone, whose salary was a flat $50,000. Betsy's salary was a mere $12,500. All of this ensured that the budget was kept down to $1.2 million—far lower than any of his other recent films.[14]

Don Hartman was a new arrival at RKO, where he took up a producer-director role (like those once held by Howard Hawks and Leo McCarey) and chose *Every Girl Should Be Married* as his first film for the studio. The RKO story department was not keen on the original short story by Eleanor Harris, which had been published in the *Ladies' Home Journal*. The reader described it as "a trite little romance" that was both "precocious and artificial."[15] Hartman, however, saw its potential as a Cary Grant film. The story of a headstrong woman who pursues an attractive yet elusive man fit well with Grant's image as Hollywood's most eligible bachelor. Hartman pitched it to Cary with Barbara Bel Geddes (then an up-and-coming RKO contract player) penciled in as the story's heroine. Cary signed to make the film only when it was agreed that Betsy would take Bel Geddes's place.[16]

The film is a remarkable debut for Betsy. From the very first scene of *Every Girl Should Be Married*, in which her character decries the double standard by which men pursue women but women cannot pursue men, she is the film's driving force and Cary is merely the object of her pursuit. In her performance, she emulates the clear-eyed, brisk manner of Katharine Hepburn in *Bringing Up Baby*, but the story does not offer her leopards to play with, or bacchanalian fun in the wilds of Connecticut, or even the confidence to stand on her own two feet. Betsy's Anabel Sims chases after Cary's Dr. Madison Brown because she wants a husband, children, and a suburban home. She does not seek to liberate him, as Hepburn did in *Bringing Up Baby*, but to confine them both in a conventional life.

Every Girl Should Be Married is as narrow-minded as its title suggests. It begins as a screwball comedy, with a "meet cute" between Anabel and

Photograph 22.38 Betsy Drake in *Every Girl Should Be Married* (RKO Radio Pictures, 1948) has the look and manner of Katharine Hepburn, but she is interested only in becoming a wife and mother.
Source: author's screen capture

Madison as they both reach for the same issue of *Better Babies* magazine at a newsstand. "How many have you?" Anabel asks him with interest. "None— fortunately—I'm not married," he says warily. This sets in motion Anabel's pursuit, which continues in a screwball vein as she stalks him relentlessly and uses another man (Franchot Tone's character) to make him jealous. Her singlemindedness is played for laughs but the film never laughs at her conventionality. In the ending, when he finally acquiesces, she tells him that "From the moment I first saw you, I knew that all I wanted was to cook little intimate dinners for you for the rest of my life." The scene is played for sentiment rather than humor.

Cary's best moment comes when he performs a full-bodied impersonation of her naïve, ingratiating manner. Apart from this very brief music hall turn, he has little to do other than look handsome in the mature, pipe-smoking manner of a doctor. It is Betsy's film through and through. Following a preview of the film in November 1948, *Daily Variety* reported that Betsy's career would be "hotter than a stove."[17] A month later, when the film was released, there was a chorus of approval for her performance. Critics praised her for being "foxily amusing and just a little bit poignant as well" (*New York Times*)[18] and "an electrifying young girl who generates enough energy to supply power for a municipal lighting plant" (New York's *Daily News*).[19] Hers was "the most auspicious movie debut in quite some time" (*Los Angeles Times*).[20] Both Louella Parsons and Hedda Hopper also took the opportunity to remind their readers that Betsy was now a major star.[21]

Every Girl Should Be Married became RKO's biggest hit of the year, but the film's earnings—$2.8 million in North America and a further $665,000 abroad—were not high by the standards of previous years.[22] The post-war decline in movie-going was hitting Hollywood hard by 1948, and it was hitting RKO especially hard.[23] Keen to promote a new star, RKO's publicity department encouraged the fan magazines to portray Drake as a Cinderella to Cary's Prince Charming.[24] This was hardly the image she wanted. According to the screenwriter Arthur Laurents, she was frustrated by Hollywood. Laurents occasionally dined with Cary and Betsy at the Hitchcocks', and he recalled that Betsy complained "often" and "at length" about being treated as a lightweight star rather than a serious actress. On one occasion, a tipsy Hitchcock responded to her complaints by saying, for all to hear, "Full of shit, isn't she?" Cary kept the peace, smiling as though Hitchcock's remark was intended as funny rather than cutting.[25]

Laurents was writing the screenplay for Hitchcock's *Rope* (1948), and he observed that Hitchcock was keen for Cary to star in this film, as the prep school teacher who slowly realizes, over the course of a dinner party, that two of his students have murdered another student missing from the party.[26] Laurents commented in his memoir that he assumed that Cary rejected *Rope* because the story's gay undertones made him nervous.[27] However, it hardly seems likely that a star of capable of wearing a negligee and screaming "I just went gay all of the sudden" (in *Bringing Up Baby*) would shy away from the subtextual references to homosexuality in *Rope*. It is more likely that Cary realized that the two students (played by Farley Granger and John Dahl) have more significant roles than the teacher. He may also have been wary of Hitchcock's experimental approach to this film. Hitchcock was planning to shoot *Rope* entirely on a single set and in a series of ten-minute takes that would create the illusion of an unedited play, and the technical challenges involved in this were likely to preoccupy him. When Cary turned it down, James Stewart seized the opportunity to make his first film with Hitchcock, but Cary's instincts proved to be correct. *Rope* did not ignite much interest among audiences.[28]

There were other interesting offers around the same time. William Wyler invited Cary to star alongside Olivia de Havilland in the costume drama *The Heiress* (1949), a part that went to Montgomery Clift.[29] Alexander Korda was still pressing Cary about their joint filmmaking venture. The British producer had a few proposals for him, including the delayed *The Devil's Delight* and an adaptation of George Bernard Shaw's *Arms and the Man*. Even more intriguingly, Korda wanted him to play Holly Martins in the thriller *The Third Man* (1950) with Noel Coward as Harry Lime (the parts taken taken by Joseph Cotten and Orson Welles in a revised production set-up).[30]

Cary chose instead to boost Betsy's career by making *Every Girl Should Be Married*. Betsy, in turn, put her own career on hold after that film was finished, so that she could travel with Cary when he went to Europe to make *I Was a Male War Bride*. This was not his long-awaited collaboration with Korda, but instead a welcome reunion with director Howard Hawks. They had not made a film together since *His Girl Friday* nine years earlier. Their reunion was prompted by Darryl F. Zanuck, the head of production at Twentieth Century-Fox, who had a story that he thought was perfect for Hawks, and which Hawks thought was perfect for Cary Grant.[31]

The original story, published under the drab title "Male War Bride Trial to Army," was a true account of a Belgian army officer stationed in Germany, who married an American nurse and then entered into a bureaucratic nightmare trying to return to the United States with her. The author, Henri Rochard, discovered that the US military had procedures in place for American male soldiers returning home with foreign brides, but it had no procedures for female soldiers returning with foreign husbands. Rochard could enter the United States only as a "war bride." He found himself referred to as "Mrs. Rochard" and he was sent to eat and sleep in spaces allotted for the brides. Once he had made it to the United States, he wrote an account of his experiences that was published in the *Baltimore Sun* newspaper.[32] It was amusing enough to warrant re-publication in the popular *Reader's Digest*, which gave the story the catchier title *I Was a Male War Bride*.[33]

Hawks and producer Sol C. Siegel worked with a variety of writers to shape this story into a screwball comedy. Prominent among them were Hagar Wilde (who wrote the short story and contributed to the screenplay of *Bringing Up Baby*) and Charles Lederer (co-author of the *His Girl Friday* screenplay). The screenwriters reimagined Rochard as a suave French army captain, and his wife Catherine became a spiky American army lieutenant rather than a nurse. From the outset, it was understood that this would be another story in which a seemingly confident man is led into ever more humiliating circumstances by his association with a forthright, modern woman. The ultimate humiliation, when he must wear women's clothes to pass as a "war bride," was the screenwriters' invention. It did not happen to the real Rochard, and in fact it happens only in the last ten minutes of the film, but it became the film's most memorable moment.[34]

Zanuck saw the story's potential not only as a comedy but also as an opportunity for filming in Europe, where Twentieth Century-Fox was looking for ways to spend its "frozen funds" (box-office earnings that, due to currency regulations, could not be repatriated to the United States). Hence, Cary and Betsy embarked for Europe in September 1948, planning to spend four months abroad. It was expected that half of the filming would be done in Germany, shooting outdoor scenes on location in and around Heidelberg, and then the other half would be done in Britain, where interior scenes would be filmed at Shepperton Studios.[35]

Cary signed for a flat fee of $100,000 plus 10 percent of the studio's earnings above $1 million and up to $2.5 million (a deal that would ultimately give him earnings of $250,000 from the film). In addition, Twentieth Century-Fox gave him an allowance of $50,000 to pay for his travel expenses, including accommodation, food, and the use of a new car in both Germany and Britain.[36] But Cary did not realize just how basic the accommodation and food would be. Germany was still in ruins, and the US Army was charged with feeding the cast and crew. Cary was not the only one to complain that army catering did not meet the usual Hollywood standards. The hotel and the dressing rooms were basic too. He was particularly astonished that he had to share a bathroom with his co-star Ann Sheridan, an indignity that would never happen in Hollywood. He and Betsy were so depressed by the conditions that they left Germany as often as they could, driving across the border to France or Switzerland at the weekends.[37]

Despite their close quarters, Cary and Ann Sheridan got on well.[38] Sheridan had spent most of her career at Warner Bros. co-starring in gritty crime films with tough guys such as James Cagney and George Raft. With *I Was a Male War Bride*, she was delighted to break free from her Warner career, and bring her spirited, tough gal persona to comedy. She admired Hawks's technique of allowing actors to work out their own scenes, ad-libbing and finding humor that was not in the script. "We'd sit and think and inevitably it was Cary who would tell you what to say," she recalled. "Howard is a very clever man. He picked brains. And he had a very clever brain to pick in Cary Grant, believe me."[39]

The story sends Henri Rochard and Catherine Gates on a three-day mission together across the German countryside. There is no explanation as to why a captain in the French army would be working with an American lieutenant, or why this particular French captain has a mid-Atlantic accent. There is also little emphasis on the mission itself, which involves seeking out a black marketeer. The film focuses instead on their combative relationship. At the outset, she is wary of his playboy tendencies and he is intimidated by her sharp tongue and professional competence. Everything she does seems to undermine him, and his efforts to reassert his authority are laughable. Taking charge of a rowboat, he leads them to the edge of a steep weir and she must save them. When trying to retrieve her dropped compact for her, he ends up astride a railway gate as it is raised, falling to the ground at her feet. While he follows a bad lead to find the black marketeer, she manages to complete their mission successfully.

The turning point in their relationship comes when he stops trying to dominate her and instead nurtures her, massaging her sore back with liniment as she falls asleep. It is a surprisingly tender scene: when she has drifted off to sleep, he opens the windows so that she will have fresh air, and adjusts the bedside lamp so that it will not disturb her. Then, when he finds he cannot get out of the room on his own, he sleeps in a hard chair rather than waking her. A day or so later, when a runaway motorcycle lands them in a haystack, he shouts, "Catherine! Darling! Are you all right?" with genuine, desperate affection. It may not be the most romantic speech ever committed to film, but it demonstrates more feeling than he showed in previous screwball comedies. In most of his other post-Paramount films, an admission of love, if there was one, was made in the final fade-out.

In *I Was a Male War Bride*, he reveals his feelings and marries Catherine only to be faced with the bureaucratic hurdles he must jump in order to enter the United States. This sets in motion a new string of humiliations, which peak with Catherine putting him in drag so that he can board the ship as a "bride." Catherine takes to this task with glee, cutting a wig for him from a horse's tail ("Can you at least cut it off the *mane*?" he asks her) and naming him Florence. Hawks later claimed that Cary intended to put on feminine airs when in drag, and that he convinced Cary that it would be far funnier to "just act like a man in woman's clothes."[40] That is the way he plays it. He has none of his usual grace when he dons the wig, skirt, and stockings, but instead lumbers in an ungainly manner that emphasizes his complete humiliation.

Filming in Germany was plagued by wet weather, which brought the production to a standstill many times. The location shooting yielded few of the spectacular landscapes and vistas the filmmakers were seeking.[41] When they finished in Germany in late November, Cary and Betsy had a week in Paris before filming resumed on December 8 at Shepperton Studies in Britain.[42] Everyone hoped that filming indoors, in a well-equipped studio near London, would make this second half of the shoot easier, but this was not the case. Conditions in Britain were far from ideal. Everyone suffered from the usually cold British winter, and from eating a diet severely restricted by the government's austerity program, which continued to curtail imports.[43] Then the illnesses began. Within two weeks of starting at Shepperton, Randy Stuart, who had a co-starring role as a WAC, developed hepatitis. Howard Hawks got a severe case of hives that was relieved only by long soaks in a tub of salt water. Ann Sheridan became ill with pleurisy, which turned

Photograph 22.39 Cary is a surprisingly lumbering and unattractive "war bride." With Ann Sheridan in *I Was a Male War Bride* (Twentieth Century-Fox, 1949).
Source: author's screen capture

into pneumonia. It was impossible to shoot around Sheridan, and in mid-December filming was suspended for five weeks.[44]

Cary and Betsy stayed in London and on Christmas Day Cary went alone to Bristol, where Elsie was no doubt pleased to host a family get-together at her house. Propriety prevented Cary from bringing his twenty-four-year-old girlfriend to Elsie's house overnight, but he did bring champagne, port, and presents for his mother and for his favorite cousin, Eric Leach, and Eric's wife Maggie. This was Cary's first Christmas in Bristol, and his first Christmas with Elsie, since 1914—thirty-four years earlier—but he left for London the very next day. He was eager to return to Betsy and never particularly keen to stay in Bristol for lengthy visits.[45]

Filming at Shepperton briefly resumed in late January, when Ann Sheridan recovered enough to struggle back to work. The last thing they had filmed in Germany was the exterior shot of Cary crashing into a haystack in a field outside Heidelberg. At Shepperton, they began filming the interior scene within the haystack late in the afternoon. Cary had worked out the scene with Hawks and Sheridan. It is quite a funny one, in which Catherine challenges Henri to prove the reputation Frenchmen have as great kissers. They were just about to shoot it when Cary suddenly complained that it was a "bloody awful" scene. "But Cary, you wrote it," Hawks reminded him. Rather than arguing with him about it, Hawks sensed something was wrong and dismissed the cast and crew for the day.[46] That night, at 2:00 a.m., Cary became so ill that he went to the hospital, where he was diagnosed with hepatitis. Over the next two weeks, as "yellow jaundice" set in and he rapidly lost weight, it became apparent that he would not be able to work for weeks.

Hawks suspended filming, and the cast and crew went back to California, where filming would resume when Cary recovered.[47] This proved to be a long time. He was in the hospital for several weeks, and by some accounts he came close to dying. When he was well enough to leave the hospital, Betsy leased a flat on Grosvenor Square from the socialite Pamela Churchill Harriman (a former daughter-in-law of Winston Churchill). There, for another month, he continued to recuperate with Betsy at his side, trying to keep his spirits up.[48] Friends rallied, sending yellow flowers and jokey cards about him having had "the best years of your liver," but his mood was low as he struggled through a very slow recovery.[49]

By early March, Betsy was overdue on the set of her second film, *Dancing in the Dark* (1949), back in Hollywood. Cary was not fully recovered but he was improving, and he was desperate to go home. Betsy departed without him on the *Queen Mary*, but not before she and Alexander Korda arranged for him to travel home in the most careful and private conditions.[50] On March 15, 1949, he boarded a Dutch cargo vessel, the *Dalerdijk*, that had a small number of first-class cabins. He was accompanied by Korda's personal physician, Dr. Tibor Csato, who took the adjoining cabin and kept a close and friendly watch over him. They made the journey from London to Los Angeles entirely by sea, with brief stops in the ports of Venezuela, Colombia, and Ecuador (by way of the Panama Canal), before sailing up to Long Beach harbor in Los Angeles.[51]

When the *Dalerdijk* arrived at Long Beach three weeks later, Betsy was on the dock waiting to greet him. Knowing there would be cameras present, Cary had sunbathed on the deck of the ship to the point that his skin appeared oaken brown rather than jaundiced yellow, but he could not hide the extent of his weight loss. The illness had taken 37 pounds from his already slim frame.[52] He was now so thin that shooting *I Was a Male War Bride* could not resume again until he had gained at least half of the weight back.[53] It was six weeks before he was able to begin filming again, and even then, as Howard Hawks said, in the film it looked as though "Cary ran into a haystack on a motorcycle and came out weighing twenty pounds less."[54] His recovery would be long and faltering over the next few years.

On April 28, filming resumed on the Twentieth Century-Fox studio lot, and *I Was a Male War Bride* was finally completed in late May—just eight months after it started.[55] By this time, the film had developed a reputation for being cursed by misfortune, and expectations for its success were low. This explains why, on release in August 1949, critics were skeptical, suggesting that it was overlong at 105 minutes and should be "trimmed" (*Variety*), referring to the plot and characterization as "flimsy" (*New York Times*), and expressing surprise "to see Cary Grant looking so poorly" (*Los Angeles Times*).[56]

Cary got a better sense of the film's potential when he attended a preview screening in New York a few weeks before its release. He was not having a good summer. Still not feeling well, he traveled in July to the Johns Hopkins Hospital in Baltimore, where, much to the surprise of other patients, he spent eight days having medical tests.[57] When he left the hospital, he went to New York to meet Hawks for the preview. He approached this with some trepidation, not knowing what to expect from a film produced in fragments and under such strained conditions, but he was delighted to find the audience roaring with laughter. The response inspired him to say that he thought *I Was a Male War Bride* might be "the best comedy I've ever made."[58]

This was certainly an exaggeration, but the film did prove to be one of his biggest box-office hits, earning an estimated $4.1 million in North America, which made it the third-biggest hit of the year.[59] It was a good way of closing the decade. His doctors were advising him to take several months off from work, and so he sat on the sidelines for the remainder of 1949, trying to decide on his next project, when his third decade in films began.[60]

He had long since decided that he wanted to marry Betsy, but Betsy wanted to establish her career first. "I must succeed on my own, and not even think of marriage until I have made at least two good pictures," she told Louella Parsons. "If people say, 'She made good because of Cary Grant,' that's bad for him and bad for me."[61] Yet Cary was too powerful in Hollywood for Betsy to have a career that was truly independent of his influence. At Fox, producer George Jessel found that Betsy had been cast in the backstage musical *Dancing in the Dark* even though the part called for a brassy showgirl such as Betty Grable or June Haver. When Jessel protested to his boss, Darryl Zanuck, that Betsy was too slight and demure for the role, Zanuck told him that Cary signed to make *I Was a Male War Bride* on the proviso that Zanuck would cast Betsy "in a film or two."[62] Jessel was stuck with her, and he could not hide his hostility toward her even when Louella Parsons visited the set.[63] It would not have helped Betsy that the film was directed by Irving Reis, Cary's old foe from *The Bachelor and the Bobby-Soxer*. Being Cary Grant's girlfriend was a mixed blessing for her career.

In December 1949, when *Dancing in the Dark* was finished and Betsy was due to start on her third film, the comedy *Pretty Baby* (1950), she finally agreed to marry Cary. They made no announcement and did not tell most of their friends. Like Cary's wedding to Barbara Hutton, the impending ceremony was kept top secret. The only friend who was told was Howard Hughes, and that was because, as Cary's best man, he was put in charge of making the arrangements. He flew the couple (piloting the plane himself of course) to Scottsdale, Arizona, where the real estate developer Sterling Hebbard and his wife hosted the wedding on their ranch on Christmas Day, 1949.[64] Hughes stumbled in his duties when he dropped the wedding ring in the middle of the ceremony, but Cary was forever grateful to his friend for arranging what he described as "an extraordinary day" that was "thoughtfully planned by an extraordinary mind."[65]

On December 26, they flew back to Los Angeles and embarked on a marriage that by all accounts was loving, mutually supportive, and full of adventures. "Betsy was good for me," Cary recalled. She brought him new

ideas, new books, new ways of thinking.[66] He was eager to help her in her
career, and a letter of congratulations from Ingrid Bergman suggests that he
also hoped to start a family. "I hope you too will soon have a baby in your
arms. . . . I know how absolutely crazy you are about children," she wrote.[67]
But if Cary and Betsy were planning to have children, it was not a plan for the
immediate future.[68] As 1949 gave way to 1950, she was making *Pretty Baby*
and he was going back to work for the first time in seven months.

He had been expected to return to RKO in January 1950, but Howard
Hughes had bought a controlling interest in the studio, and so his best man
became his boss. He was either displeased by this or he was unimpressed
by Hughes's handling of studio operations, because he never made another
film for RKO. He still owed the studio three films, but the creative control
he had over his films—approval of the script, cast, and director—meant that
he could delay fulfilling his contract as long as he wished. He simply made
demands that the studio could not meet. At his request, for example, RKO
bought the film rights to Terence Rattigan's 1944 play *Love in Idleness* (for the
considerable sum of $139,000) even though the story would cause problems
with censorship. Then he insisted that Greta Garbo should be his co-star
in the film, even though she had retired from films seven years earlier. He
insisted that Peter Glenville, a British actor and stage director, should be the
director, even though Glenville had never directed a film before. RKO paid
for Glenville to travel to Hollywood for ten days of talks, and afterward Cary
told the studio that he had lost interest in the story.[69]

While keeping RKO at bay, he quietly made a one-picture deal with his old
friend Dore Schary at MGM on January 3, 1950. Schary had fallen out with
Howard Hughes, and when he resigned from RKO, he became head of production at MGM.[70] Cary seemed to be choosing one friend over the other,
but it was more likely a strategic career decision on his part. He wanted to
break free of his close association with light comedy and glamour, which was
looking increasingly old-fashioned, and he wanted to try his hand with the
tougher and more realistic films that were now winning favor with critics and
audiences. Over the past few years, issue-oriented or "message films" such as
The Lost Weekend (about alcoholism), *The Best Years of Our Lives* (veterans
readjusting to civilian life), *The Snake Pit* (mental illness), and *Crossfire* and
Gentleman's Agreement (anti-Semitism) demonstrated the shift away from
escapism and toward social relevance.[71]

Schary was a key figure in this shift. At MGM, a studio once known
for its high-toned glamour, he gave the green light to the realist war film

Battleground, the gritty crime drama *The Asphalt Jungle*, and an exposé of Southern racism, *Intruder in the Dust* (all released in 1950).[72] Schary had already promised the young screenwriter Richard Brooks that he could direct his own screenplay, a tense political drama initially entitled "Ferguson" that Brooks wrote with the gruff Spencer Tracy in mind for the lead.[73] Tracy showed no particular interest in the script, though, and the script was sent out to other potential leads, including Cary. Coincidentally, Brooks and Cary then met through a mutual friend when they were both spending a day at the Santa Anita racetrack. "I know that name," Cary said, to Brooks's delight. Cary had read the script and liked it, and, to Brooks's surprise, he did not object when Brooks said that he wanted to direct the film.[74]

Schary assigned the production to the Arthur Freed unit—better known for its colorful musicals—and allowed Brooks to direct the film on a budget that, at just below $1.5 million, was modest by MGM standards. The story, although set in South America, would have to be filmed entirely on the studio's backlot. Cary's co-stars would be newcomers José Ferrer and Paula Raymond, and the shoot would be done in a brisk seven weeks in January and February of 1950. The relatively short filming time meant that Cary accepted a flat upfront salary of $200,000 rather than insisting on his standard percentage compensation deal that aimed to yield $300,000 for ten weeks of shooting.[75]

Crisis (1950), as "Ferguson" was renamed, ranks alongside *None but the Lonely Heart* as one of Cary's most unusual and riskiest films. Brooks altered the script slightly to suit Cary's image, giving Dr. Ferguson a young wife, Helen (Raymond), and thereby adding a romantic dimension to the story.[76] Otherwise, it is a determinedly bleak film. Dr. Ferguson is an American brain surgeon traveling through a South American country with his wife when they are kidnapped by Farrago (Ferrer), a ruthless dictator who desperately needs surgery to remove a brain tumor. Ferguson must decide whether to operate, and thus perpetuate the dictator's power over his volatile country, or yield to the opposition's wishes and allow Farrago to die. The (unspecified) South American locale is poor rather than picturesque. Farrago is a megalomaniac and his wife, Isabel (Signe Hasso), is equally ruthless and untrustworthy. Throughout, it is clear that Dr. Ferguson may be killed even if he does manage to save Farrago's life.

Cary appears appropriately grim and resentful about this predicament, and he adopts the confident, precise air of a surgeon quite convincingly, demonstrating both the intelligence and the arrogance of his character. He also brings some palpable tenderness to Ferguson's relationship with his wife. José Ferrer is compelling, too, as the dying megalomaniac. The problem with the film is that it is neither a realistic exposé of political corruption nor a *noir*-ish nightmare of entrapment. It veers between long-winded discussions of freedom and dictatorship, and a succession of melodramatic plot twists. It therefore pleased no one. The critics who were most likely to approve of a gritty political drama, such as Manny Farber in the *New Republic* and John McCarten in the *New Yorker*, complained instead that the story was too far-fetched, while the commercially-minded critics, such as those in *The Hollywood Reporter* and *Variety*, warned that it was too talkative to be entertaining.[77]

MGM's publicity department promoted the film as a typical Cary Grant light comedy. Press advertisements featured an image of Cary and Paula Raymond smiling beside palm trees, as though the film was a romantic comedy set in the tropics, with the tagline, "Here's devil-may-care Cary walking headlong into a *Crisis!*" The film's trailer similarly highlighted scenes that could seem—out of context—like they belonged to a romantic comedy.[78] This probably accounts for the film's reasonably good opening week in July 1950 and also its precipitous box-office fall-off thereafter.[79] MGM's studio ledger reveals that *Crisis* was a box-office disaster, earning a pitiful $895,000 in North America and $520,000 in foreign markets.[80] Since leaving Paramount thirteen years earlier, none of his films had failed so miserably to find an audience and none had met with such across-the-board critical indifference. Hedda Hopper was quick to draw attention to his misstep: "Cary Grant is worth everything in a comedy," she wrote in her column, "but not worth fifty cents of my dough in *Crisis*."[81]

Today, *Crisis* is remembered for initiating Richard Brooks's career as a director, which led on to notable films ranging from *Blackboard Jungle* (1955) to *Looking for Mr. Goodbar* (1977). Brooks was always quick to admit his debt to Cary and also to speak of how generous and supportive he was as a mentor and a friend.[82] In 1950, however, *Crisis* was a worrying sign that Cary's appeal was waning—that he was an old-fashioned star who belonged to an earlier era of Hollywood filmmaking. It was not a good start to the new decade and it must have appeared, to him and to others, to herald the beginning of the end of his career.

PART FOUR

TRUTH SEEKER, 1951 TO 1962

23

Cary and Betsy retreated into a very quiet, very private life during their first year of marriage. His preoccupation with his career had been a major factor in the failure of his previous marriages and he was not going to make the same mistake again. He did not make a film for a full year after completing *Crisis* at the end of February 1950. He and Betsy set up house on Beverly Grove and, in his third marriage, he enjoyed a stable married life for the first time. Betsy decided that she would learn to cook and although her initial efforts were often "dreadful," she recalled that Cary never complained. "He'd eat burnt steak without flinching." But they were not an entirely conventional couple. She talked with him about hypnosis, diets, religions, books she was reading, and artists she was studying, and she brought him a poem every morning to read with his breakfast, including rather highbrow, modernist poetry by the likes of Marianne Moore and Ezra Pound.[1] He loved her for her inquisitive intellect, and for making him look inward and seek truths beyond his career.

Hollywood's publicists complained that the Grants "have drawn an Iron Curtain around their marriage." Cary and Betsy did not go through any of the motions expected of Hollywood couples: posing for press photographers in their home, giving joint interviews, attending premieres and black-tie charity functions. Betsy did not like nightclubs, and so Cary was no longer seen at Ciro's, the Mocambo, or the Clover Club. In fact, they seldom went out in the evening at all, which led one fan magazine to declare in a headline that theirs was "Hollywood's Strangest Marriage."[2] They were occasionally spotted at the Santa Anita racetrack, though, and they enjoyed long weekend lunches with old and new friends. Among the new friends were director Richard Brooks, and actors Richard Anderson, Janet Gaynor, and Jean Simmons. Among the older friends were Katharine Hepburn and her close companion Spencer Tracy. Hepburn lived just up the road from Beverly Grove and she became a particularly good friend of Betsy's, admiring her intellectual interests and her unconventional approach to life.[3]

Betsy's career slowed to a near halt. After her debut in *Every Girl Should Be Married*, she starred in three films that sank without a trace: the musical *Dancing in the Dark* (1949), the comedy *Pretty Baby* (1950), and the melodrama *The Second Woman* (1950). If this was not enough to make producers wary of casting her, she did not fit with any of the feminine types that were current in Hollywood. She was too well-spoken and intelligent to play the kind of "girl next door" roles that made June Allyson a star, too wholesome to be a savvy woman of the world like Lauren Bacall, and not suited to—or interested in—being a blonde bombshell akin to Marilyn Monroe. In fact, Betsy had a clause in her contract stipulating that she would not pose in a bathing suit for the "pin-up" photographs that were commonplace in this era.[4]

She was out of place in Hollywood and better suited to the New York theater world.[5] It was perhaps to prevent her from returning there that Cary agreed to embark on a new project with her. Beginning in January 1951, he and Betsy co-starred in *Mr. and Mrs. Blandings*, a weekly 30-minute situation comedy series on NBC radio.[6] Howard Hughes bought the rights to use the Blandings characters from David Selznick, and then set up his Trans-World Airlines, or TWA, as the sponsor of the series.[7] Following in the footsteps of other popular husband-and-wife sitcoms such as *The Adventures of Ozzie and Harriet* (Nelson), *My Favorite Husband* (Lucille Ball's forerunner to *I Love Lucy*), and *Halls of Ivy* (starring husband and wife Ronald Colman and Benita Hume), *Mr. and Mrs. Blandings* continued the adventures of the Blandings family in their dream house.

Cary and Betsy recorded twenty-two episodes of *Mr. and Mrs. Blandings*, which aired on Sunday evenings. Cary was never happy with the series. He thought the writing was poor and fired the writers, who sued him for breach of contract.[8] Betsy wrote some of the later episodes herself, using the pseudonym of Matilda Winkle.[9] After a rocky initial reception, the reviews improved but the ratings were never top-notch.[10] Betsy had a slight stammer in her speech, which meant that re-takes were often needed and the taping sessions could drag on for hours.[11] The show was expensive to produce—with Cary's salary of $3,000 accounting for nearly a third of each episode's costs—and it was not renewed for a second season.[12]

While *Mr. and Mrs. Blandings* was still running, Cary returned to filming in March 1951. The previous month, he had an offer he did not want to refuse, a starring role in what promised to be the smartest, glossiest, and most sophisticated comedy of the year. In the years since Joseph L. Mankiewicz produced *The Philadelphia Story* at MGM, he had moved to Twentieth Century-Fox and become a writer and director of distinctively "adult" dramas such as *A Letter to Three Wives* (1949) and *All About Eve* (1950); literate, well-constructed films that open up a tight little world for scrutiny: suburban marriage in *A Letter to Three Wives*, and a backstage look at Broadway in *All About Eve*. In his next film, it would be the medical world, as seen through the eyes of a progressive, iconoclastic doctor.[13]

The extraordinary success of the Oscar-winning *All About Eve* meant that Mankiewicz had considerable freedom to develop his next film. Studio executives did not balk when he chose to film an obscure German play, *The Case of Dr. Praetorius* by Curt Goetz, and they did not balk at his first treatment, which stated that "From the very outset, our hero must be launched as a provocative and off-beam character."[14] The character, Dr. Praetorius, is a compassionate doctor, an admired professor at a medical school, and an outspoken challenger of any form of hypocrisy or orthodoxy. When his pupil, Deborah (Jeanne Crain), finds that she is pregnant and yet unmarried, he urges her to cherish the child and ultimately marries her so that he can cherish the child himself. He is a stalwart supporter of his friend, the intimidating and mysterious Shunderson (Finlay Currie), even though Shunderson seems to harbor dark secrets. And he stands up to a jealous colleague, Professor Elwell (Hume Cronyn), who launches a McCarthy-style witch hunt into his past.

When studio boss Darryl F. Zanuck read Mankiewicz's script, his immediate verdict was "the role is perfect for Cary Grant."[15] It is not difficult to see why he would want Cary to play this character. Dr. Praetorius is a man of many views, which he expounds upon at length, and if almost any other actor portrayed him, he was likely to come across as pompous and sanctimonious. Cary's characteristically understated and ingratiating manner would go some way in preventing this. Zanuck's other verdict was that the script had too much dialogue and not enough action. Mankiewicz, however, was unconcerned by the verbosity of his characters (each gets a lengthy speech), and he could point out that the emphasis on dialogue did not hold back *All About Eve*. Indeed, he decided to make a virtue of this by changing the title of *The Case of Dr. Praetorius* to *People Will Talk*.[16]

Cary's enthusiasm for *People Will Talk* was manifold. He welcomed the opportunity to work with Mankiewicz again, especially now that he was at a career high point, and he also appreciated the chance to play a very different sort of doctor from the grim, determined fellow he played in *Crisis*. It is likely, too, that he was attracted to the core concern of the story: that the medical profession had become more interested in prescribing pills than getting to the heart of what ails the mind and body. His own struggle to recover from hepatitis had led him to reflect on this. Nearly two years before he read the *People Will Talk* script, he described the doctor who accompanied him on the sea journey from London to Los Angeles, Dr. Tibor Csato, as "a man who has tremendous spiritual values as well as a knowledge of the human machine," adding, "You seldom find that in a medical man."[17] In *People Will Talk*, he got a chance to portray a similarly idealized doctor on-screen, and in a film that promised to explore the limitations of modern medicine.

The trouble with the film is that it does not stick with this idea, or follow it to an interesting conclusion. Instead, Mankiewicz pursued several distracting storylines. He was apparently eager to challenge Hollywood's censors (at the Breen office), by portraying an unwed mother in sympathetic terms. Unfortunately, though, Deborah is played by the blankly inexpressive Jeanne Crain (a major star at Fox at that time). Moreover, the film pursues her backstory all the way to her family's rural farm, where both her father and uncle give long-winded accounts of themselves. Another storyline, about the witch hunt, was informed by Mankiewicz's recent experience as president of the Screen Directors Guild, but it seems to belong in a different film.[18] The parallel storyline about Shunderson's past also adds a long-winded speech but little drama to the film.

Darryl Zanuck had enough faith in the film to give it a high-profile premiere at Grauman's Chinese Theater, in the heart of Hollywood, on July 19, 1951. It was for this occasion that Cary was afforded one of the industry's strangest honors, putting his hand and shoe prints into the cement in the theater's forecourt. He joined the pantheon of stars immortalized in this way, obliging with a smile (and a cloth at hand to wipe the wet cement from his hands and shoes). The preview itself was a major occasion with a star-studded audience and many of the industry's top executives.[19] Word of mouth was good enough for Zanuck to book the film for a four-week run at New York's vast Roxy Theater, and also to spark some buzz about Cary possibly winning an Academy Award.[20]

New York was not as kind to the film. When it opened at the Roxy in late August, the review in the *New Yorker* began by saying that Mankiewicz "has come a cropper," while others complained that it is overly long (at 110 minutes) and suffered from a "wordy, rambling script."[21] Cary himself received good notices. According to *Time*, he "plays to perfection" in *People Will Talk*, while the *New York Times* commented that he "is obviously having the time of his life playing Dr. Praetorius."[22] It is true that there is some zeal in his performance, particularly in the incidental scenes, such as when he conducts an amateur orchestra or when he plays with an elaborate toy train set, but his zeal could not save the film. *Variety* estimated that *People Will Talk* earned $2.1 million in North America, meaning that it was neither a hit nor an outright flop.[23] It was clear, though, that one of the year's most anticipated films had fallen flat, and today it quite rightly remains one of the lesser known of his films.

Between films in the summer of 1951, Cary and Betsy went on a "motoring holiday," as Cary liked to say. They drove through Arizona and New Mexico, seeing the Grand Canyon and meeting up with his former stepson, Lance Reventlow, who was now fifteen years old and living with a governess on a ranch near Sante Fe.[24] At the time, Barbara Hutton was divorcing her fourth husband, Prince Igor Troubetzkoy, and Lance was completely estranged from his father. Cary and Betsy were keen to step in and look after the son Hutton so often left behind. It was on this visit that Cary made his one and only Western. He and Lance starred in *The Killer of Fossil Gulch*, a short, silent film that Betsy shot on an 8mm camera. The surviving footage shows Cary hamming it up in his death scene, clutching his chest and staggering along the ground after being shot by a rival gunslinger played by Lance. "He needed parents," Betsy recalled. "I was devoted to him and so was Cary."[25]

They returned home in August to play parents in the family drama *Room for One More* (1952).[26] This screen family lived much more modestly than the Blandings. They struggle, not to build their dream house, but with the everyday expenses arising from their three children and a further two foster children, as well as a dog and a litter of kittens. Director Norman Taurog specialized in family films and he had worked with virtually every child actor in Hollywood. He learned that, to get the best performances from them, it was useful to get the cast acquainted prior to filming, and then to offer the kids presents and candy for good work during filming.[27] He insisted on two weeks of rehearsals before the cameras rolled, and the strategy clearly worked. Cary and Betsy, playing parents George and Anna Rose, are entirely at ease with their screen children. One of the foster children, twelve-year-old Jane (Iris Mann), is brought into the family when her abusive mother deserts her. The other, twelve-year-old Jimmy-John (Clifford Tatum Jr.), is an orphan with a bad attitude and his legs in braces (presumably a polio-related condition). Although the two newcomers provide most of the story's drama, the film is nearly stolen by the five-year-old actor George Winslow, who plays the Roses' youngest child, Teenie. In his very first film, Winslow's angelic appearance, deep "foghorn" voice, and deadpan delivery establish him as a screen natural.

Room for One More is that rarity among Hollywood's family films. The children are not precocious, their lives are affected by tragic circumstances that cannot be wished away, and the parents have day-to-day concerns apart from their children. The story's real-life basis partly explains the film's vitality. Author Anna Perrott Rose wrote about her own experiences with her husband George, their three children, and two foster children, publishing the tale first as a short story in the *Ladies' Home Journal* in 1949 and then expanding it to a book in 1950.[28] The film also benefits from Cary and Betsy's interplay as husband and wife. Whether they are being affectionate or bickering or simply looking after their extended clan, they have an easygoing on-screen intimacy that is understated and convincing.

Warner Bros. had purchased the story and put it into development independently of Cary and Betsy. It was not an obvious choice for either of them.[29] Betsy had played ingénue roles before this, not mothers, and Cary is neither debonair nor sophisticated as George Rose (called "Poppy" by his family). He is a city engineer struggling to make ends meet on a modest salary. His circumstances are not too far off those of the modest newspaper editor in *Penny Serenade*, but where that film leaned toward melodrama, *Room for One More* leans toward gentle comedy. Poppy has some comical long-suffering moments, especially when the children's demands prevent him from sleeping with his wife, but for the most part, the kids are front and center, and the film looks and feels like a 1950s television sitcom—albeit a rather good one.

The modest budget of just over $1 million allowed for few sets, black-and-white photography, and a swift seven-week shooting schedule. A bit of location filming in Malibu, for scenes of the family's holiday at the beach, was the only sign of largesse.[30] Filming went smoothly and it was completed on schedule in mid-October 1951. Six weeks later, Cary and Betsy attended a sneak preview at the Warner Bros. theater in Beverly Hills, taking Lance Reventlow with them.[31] They were not quite fostering Lance, but his mother's ongoing illnesses and travels meant that he often spent his holidays, including the Christmas of 1951, at Beverly Grove. Cary enjoyed kitting him out with new clothes and taking him on the rounds of Christmas parties, where he could introduce the teenager to some of his favorite film stars.[32]

Jack Warner was delighted with *Room for One More*, and he performed a small miracle when he convinced the Hollywood censors at the Breen Office (formerly the Hays Office) that a scene at the beach, in which Poppy explains "where babies come from" to Jimmy-John, was inoffensive and could remain in the film.[33] It *is* an inoffensive scene. Poppy's explanation is medical rather than sexual, and although he sketches illustrations in the sand, the sketches are not seen on-screen. Yet the Catholic film censorship organization, the Legion of Decency, insisted that both this scene and Poppy's expressions of "physical desire for his wife" should be cut. The Legion of Decency had millions of members who followed its ratings of new films, but Jack Warner stood firm and refused to cut the scenes. The Legion responded by giving the film a B rating, indicating that it was "morally objectionable in parts" and therefore not recommended viewing.[34]

Since it is a family film, the Legion of Decency rating probably hurt *Room for One More* at the box office. Takings were probably slighted, too, by reviews that were keen to warn audiences not to expect a sophisticated Cary Grant comedy. There were mixed opinions on the degree of sentiment. Some critics commended the film by saying that it is "fairly free of obvious tear-jerking" (*Time*) and likely to leave audiences with "a lump in the throat and a mist in the eyes" (*Chicago Tribune*) while others complained about its "mawkishness" (*New York Times*).[35] The box-office takings—approximately $2.4 million in North America and $1.1 million abroad—marked *Room for One More* as a modest success.[36] Warner Bros. was pleased enough to contemplate a sequel to the film and, when that did not work out, to create a television sitcom with the same name that ran for a single season in 1962.[37]

Cary had his own reasons to be pleased with the film's takings. To keep costs down, he had agreed to a salary of just $50,000 up front as an advance on 10 percent of the film's earnings, meaning that he ultimately pocketed $350,000 from the film's theatrical release.[38] This was significantly less than the windfall he received from a similar percentage deal on *The Bachelor and the Bobby Soxer*, but it was still an extraordinary star salary. At a time when movie attendances were in free fall, and belts were being tightened all over Hollywood, his income remained among the highest in the industry.[39]

With *Crisis*, *People Will Talk*, and *Room for One More*, Cary had branched out beyond his man-about-town image, taking risks and winning some critical praise but no great popular success along the way. For his next film, he returned to more familiar ground. At Twentieth Century-Fox, producer Sol C. Siegel was very keen on an original story, a comedy entitled "Fountain of Youth" and then "Darling, I Am Growing Younger," that was written by Harry Segall and then developed into a script by I. A. L. Diamond (who would later work with Billy Wilder on *Some Like It Hot*).[40] This script obviously was not written with Cary in mind. Its lead character, who takes a youth serum and finds himself growing younger, is described as a middle-aged man with a "receding hairline" and a physique that is "chunky in the wrong places."[41]

Darryl Zanuck saw the opportunity to take the comedy in a different direction.[42] The studio boss was on the lookout for a follow-up to the money-spinning *I Was a Male War Bride*, and he convinced Hawks that with some revisions, "Darling, I Am Growing Younger" could become another Cary Grant comedy. Hawks brought in his trusted screenwriters, Ben Hecht (who contributed to *Gunga Din*) and Charles Lederer (who contributed to *His Girl Friday* and *I Was a Male War Bride*), for this transformation. By the time they had turned "Darling, I Am Growing Younger" into *Monkey Business*, Cary was convinced too. He signed on for an eight-week shoot lasting from early March to late April of 1952.[43]

Hawks and his writers refashioned the story in a way that made *Monkey Business* a kind of sequel to *Bringing Up Baby*, which had grown in reputation through re-releases and repertory screenings. In *Monkey Business*, Cary plays Professor Barnaby Fulton, a middle-aged, graying-at-the-temples version of Dr. David Huxley, with similarly styled—but thicker—Harold Lloyd glasses accentuating his absent-minded intellectual nature.[44] His marriage to Edwina (Ginger Rogers) is a happy one, and Zanuck insisted that it must be clear that the Fultons are still attracted to one another. "We do not want the audience to get the impression that these people have no sex life," he said. After seven or eight years of marriage, he continued, their attraction to each other is "not as violent as the first fine rapture" and "their relationship is different now than it was when they were newlyweds."[45]

This situation is the starting point for the comedy that follows. Barnaby's work as a commercial scientist has him searching in vain for a "youth serum" in his commercial laboratory. A chimpanzee who is meant to test the serum escapes from his cage, and while loose in the lab and imitating Barnaby, the chimp concocts a serum that really does work and dumps it in the water cooler. Everyone who drinks the water gets a dose of this improvised yet effective youth serum, beginning with Barnaby. Thus, it is a chimpanzee rather than a leopard that sets the comedy in motion, but nevertheless both animals unleash a wilder and less inhibited side to the human characters. In *Monkey Business*, the middle-aged and staid Barnaby and Edwina are rejuvenated as hyperactive and hormonal youths.

Barnaby takes the serum first and becomes a college kid again. His glasses come off and he does a cartwheel of delight. He buys a loud new suit and a sports car, and he enjoys a day out with his boss's young and very attractive secretary, Miss Laurel (Marilyn Monroe). Eager to impress her, he takes her roller-skating but ends up flat on his back. He takes her swimming and does a high dive that ends up as a belly flop. He crashes his new sports car not once but twice. The serum thus comes to seem less like a fountain of youth and more like a potion for the kind of indignities so often heaped upon Cary in screwball comedies.

Cary takes to the slapstick proceedings eagerly. Once again, as in *Bringing Up Baby* and *His Girl Friday*, Hawks was happy to play upon the audience's affection for the star by including some playful references. Where the earlier films had oblique or in-the-know references (to "Jerry the Nipper" and Archie Leach), *Monkey Business* was much more direct. The film begins with Barnaby absent-mindedly walking out of the front door of his house while the credits are still rolling. "Not yet, Cary," a voiceover intones, and he backs into the doorway while the credits finish. From this point onward, the story moves along at a lightning pace and the early scenes of Barnaby rediscovering his youth are a fine showcase for Cary's talents as a physical comedian.

While Hawks had a good sense of *Money Business* as a star vehicle for Cary, he was less certain about the role of Edwina. The director later claimed that he originally thought that only Cary should take the serum, but then Ginger Rogers was cast and she insisted that she should have her own comic turn with the serum.[46] Hawks's claim is not entirely credible. Cary's turn with the serum takes only 30 minutes and it could not be extended to a full film. But Hawks was right to admit that the film's second and third acts are not as funny as the first. In the second act, Edwina takes the serum and insists that she and Barnaby go on a second honeymoon, and in the third act both Barnaby and Edwina unknowingly take a heavier dose of the serum and revert even further back into youth, allowing Barnaby to join forces with a group of unruly children, including one played by George "foghorn" Winslow.

Hawks's biographer, Todd McCarthy, observes that the director was disappointed to have the forty-one-year-old Ginger Rogers playing Edwina. She was the oldest woman ever to take a leading role in a Hawks film—and he did not warm to her on the set.[47] Like Jean Arthur and Rita Hayworth before her, Rogers was treated with icy condescension by the director. Marilyn Monroe was another actress who felt diminished by him. He recognized that Monroe had a strong presence on-screen, but thought that she was "goddamn dumb" and treated her accordingly. Her unease on the set was compounded by illness, and it was only at the end of the shoot that she discovered she needed to have an appendectomy.[48]

This was Cary's second film with Ginger Rogers, after the lamentable *Once Upon a Honeymoon* nearly ten years earlier, and they enjoyed working together.[49] He found Marilyn Monroe "rather shy and quiet" and he did not get to know her well. She was not yet a major star, and her role in *Monkey Business*, playing a "dumb blonde," did not give her much room to shine. Cary later admitted that he did not see her potential. He admitted, too, that he was not attracted to her because her overtly sexualized persona reminded him of Mae West. Yet he felt sorry for Marilyn when he saw the crew whistling at her and making crude remarks, observing that the attention was unwanted and embarrassing for her.[50] He also came to her defense when nude photographs, which she posed for in her hungry years before stardom, came to light during the making of *Monkey Business*. They were published in *Playboy*, causing a sensation as well as a scandal for the more puritanical guardians of the public. Pressed on the subject, Cary refused to give an inch to the puritans. "There wouldn't be any great art if girls hadn't posed in the nude," he told the press, comparing Marilyn to the models who posed for Dalí, Renoir, and Titian.[51]

Marilyn's rapidly ascending stardom gave the film additional prominence, and her figure dominated in some of the advertising when the film was released in September 1952.[52] Critics, however, took a surprisingly curmudgeonly perspective on *Monkey Business*. Sophisticated and mainstream critics alike commented disapprovingly on the "thin, familiar slapstick" (*Variety*), the "plain, ordinary slapstick" (*Chicago Tribune*), the "extended barrage of whooping childish behavior by a film full of grown-up clowns" (*New York Times*), and the "fleeting laughter" (*New Yorker*).[53] *Variety* speculated that these reviews, and many more like them, dampened the box-office takings.[54] *Monkey Business* earned just $2 million in North America, placing it at the bottom end of a ranking of the fifty top-earning films of the year.[55]

In the midst of filming *Monkey Business*, Cary received a call from Dore Schary at MGM. Schary had another typical Cary Grant comedy, or at least a script that Sidney Sheldon had written with Cary in mind.[56] Cary was naturally intrigued. Sheldon had written *The Bachelor and the Bobby-Soxer*, and this new script, *Dream Wife*, aimed to be the kind of sophisticated "battle of the sexes" comedy that scored so well for him in the past.[57] He read the script and told Schary that he was interested, subject—as always—to agreeing on his co-star and director. Schary proposed Deborah Kerr, who was under contract at MGM, as his co-star. The English actress, known for her ladylike poise and elegance, had become a major Hollywood star through roles in high-profile historical films such as *King Solomon's Mines* (1950), *Quo Vadis*

(1951), and *The Prisoner of Zenda* (1952), but she was eager for the change of pace that a contemporary comedy would offer.[58] Cary was delighted to work with Kerr, and *Dream Wife* turned out to be the first of three films that they made together. Schary gave Cary his choice of director, but when none of his choices were available, Cary suggested that Sheldon should direct his own script. Sheldon was both thrilled and daunted to direct his first film, and Schary agreed in order to keep Cary on board.[59]

Like Delmer Daves and Richard Brooks before him, Sheldon could not believe his luck, finding that one of Hollywood's biggest stars was willing to star in his first film as director. Sheldon then found what many other directors had found. Cary could be difficult on the set, especially at the beginning of the shoot. His combination of perfectionism and anxiety led him to complain about everything, and to tell Sheldon repeatedly that he "never would have agreed to do the film" if he had known that the set, the script, and the wardrobe would have the faults he found in them. But he loosened up as the film proceeded and made everyone laugh by clowning around between takes and keeping his co-stars in good humor.[60] The shoot lasted just six weeks, from September 17 to November 1, 1952, and when it was done Schary was so sure that it was a sparkling comedy that he began talking about a sequel.[61]

In *Dream Wife*, Sheldon aimed to take a light-hearted look at contemporary gender roles and marriage in modern America. Cary's character, the American businessman Clemson Reade, is ready to marry and has two choices of wife. One is his fiancée, Priscilla Effington (Kerr), an intelligent and dedicated State Department official. "Clem" and "Effie," as they call one another, are clearly in love but he is tired of taking second place to her career. He meets his other potential wife while on a business trip in the (fictional) oil-rich Middle Eastern kingdom of Bukistan. She is Princess Tarji (Betta St. John), a submissive young beauty who has been trained from birth to dedicate her life to pleasing her husband. Clem chooses Tarji over Effie, only to find that marrying Tarji means he must adhere to a myriad of traditions, including never being alone with her during their customary three-month engagement. Further complications ensue when Effie is assigned to look after Tarji and introduces her to the concept of women's liberation. In the ending, Tarji decides that she must choose her own husband, and Clem and Effie are reunited.

Sheldon knew how to write dialogue for Cary. When Clem returns from Bukistan, eager to see Effie, he finds her in a conference with three other officials. He is introduced to them and remains polite but says, with his perfectly cadenced, sardonic speech, "I *must* say I am delighted to meet you, *mustn't* I?" Sheldon also wrote some familiar slapstick sequences. Clem, returning from Bukistan burdened with luggage, opens the door for an American woman at the airport only to find that she lets it shut in his face, and when he sneaks into Tarji's hotel room at night, hoping to have a private moment with her, in the darkness he caresses not Tarji but her burly bodyguard.

What Sheldon and his fellow scriptwriters, Herbert Baker and Alfred Lewis Levitt, did not grasp is that a key factor in a Cary Grant comedy was offering the perspective of a sharp and confident woman. Effie is given little voice and few comic moments of her own, and Tarji's character is written as an Orientalist fantasy of sexy-yet-obedient femininity (a stereotype Sheldon reprised in his 1960s television series, *I Dream of Jeannie*). The masculine and misogynistic perspective marks *Dream Wife* as significantly different from Cary's other comedies and far less appealing. A spirited, intelligent woman—like those played by Irene Dunne, Katharine Hepburn, Rosalind Russell, and Ann Sheridan—is needed to expose some of the rough edges concealed beneath his debonair façade, but neither Deborah Kerr nor Betta St. John is given the importance and vigor that their predecessors enjoyed.

Cary may have realized this, because when he did interviews to support the film, he stressed that he had nothing against working women, adding that he looked forward to a woman taking the most powerful job in the country. "I am waiting for a woman president," he said. "Mark my words, if women were running the world today, there would be a vast improvement."[62]

Dore Schary still had high hopes for *Dream Wife* when he arranged for an early preview of the film in Hollywood in March 1953.[63] His expectations that MGM had a hit on the scale of *The Bachelor and the Bobby-Soxer* were crushed by the leading trade papers, which sneered at the film for being "pretty preposterous" (*Hollywood Reporter*) and a "highly contrived piece of nonsense" (*Variety*).[64] Unnerved, Schary pulled the plug on *Dream Wife*. Plans for its New York City premiere at the grand Radio City Music Hall were canceled, and it was moved instead to the much smaller Rivoli Theater. The advertising budget was slashed, and Sidney Sheldon lost his job at MGM.[65]

Schary wrote in his memoir that *Dream Wife* should have been made in Technicolor so that its exotic setting could be visualized in a more spectacular fashion.[66] It is true that the film has a dull, set-bound visual dynamic that was at least ten years out of date. In his own memoir, Sheldon blamed the film's failure on Schary, claiming that the studio boss lost his nerve when he saw those initial bad reviews.[67] Sheldon also might have admitted that the film suffered from his limitations as a director (he directed only one film after this). Both men felt compelled to write about *Dream Wife* because it was such a colossal, career-damaging failure for all concerned. Its earnings in North America amounted to a dismal $1.2 million, and with foreign earnings of $700,000, MGM was left with a loss of over $400,000.[68]

Dream Wife did not lose as much money as his other MGM film, *Crisis*, but its failure was probably more disturbing for Cary. *Crisis* had been an experiment that didn't work, but *Dream Wife* was a comedy designed to let him do what he did best. When critics sneered and audiences stayed away, it added to the impression given by the lackluster responses to *Monkey Business*, that his image and his style of comedy were going out of fashion. In 1953, after more than twenty years, it was easy to imagine that his career as a movie star had run its course. Many of his contemporaries retired or moved into television during this period, while others, such as Gary Cooper and Randolph Scott, sustained their careers by making Westerns, a genre that Cary was determined to avoid.

The most exciting stars of the early 1950s were the young "rebel males," Marlon Brando and Montgomery Clift, actors who had no interest in being urbane and charming.[69] They played losers, misfits, and neurotics, who came from the wrong side of the tracks and made no attempt to hide it. They popularized "method acting," an intense and emotional style of performance that was far removed from Cary's precise and controlled approach to acting for the camera. Cary had nothing against the younger generation. His friend Irene Mayer Selznick had produced the play that made Brando a star, Tennessee Williams's *A Streetcar Named Desire* in 1947, and Cary backed the production with $5,000 of his own money.[70] Although he had no regard for method acting, he always spoke well about Brando in particular, and when they sat together at a premiere a few years later, they amicably traded notes about acting.[71]

Nevertheless, the ascendance of the Brando generation seemed to mark the end of Cary's own reign in Hollywood. "It was the period of the blue jeans, the dope addicts, the method, and nobody cared about elegance or comedy at all," he recalled.[72] There were other factors slowing his career. His salary demands were so high that he was deemed too expensive for the romantic comedy *Roman Holiday* (1953) and the Hitchcock thriller *Dial M for Murder* (1954)—far better films than any he made in this period.[73] He also let some opportunities pass because he was apprehensive about working with "difficult" people, turning down *Sabrina* (1954) because of Billy Wilder's reputation for being rough on actors. "I'd already worked with enough of those kinds of directors to last a lifetime," he said in later years, noting that "Humphrey Bogart did the picture and he looks pretty unhappy all the way through."[74]

A Star is Born (1954) was more tempting for him. He had tremendous respect for the director, George Cukor. He agreed to run through some scenes from the script at Cukor's house, and Cukor was convinced that Cary was perfect for the role of the aging, alcoholic star Norman Maine, who falls in love with an ingénue played by Judy Garland.[75] Garland herself "wooed" Cary, trying to talk him into making the film, but he knew that her drug and alcohol problems made her erratic and unreliable on the set, and so, after months of dithering, he finally turned down the role.[76] "Jimmy Mason did a grand job," he reflected, adding that Mason told him it was "a chore waiting [on the set] day after day to see if Judy would appear."[77]

This is how it came to pass that, a full year after finishing *Dream Wife*, he still had no firm plans to make another film. When he spoke about the fleeting nature of fame, he often used an allegory, derived from one of Charlie Chaplin's comedies, that shows a streetcar getting ever more crowded until the newcomers push the other passengers out of the car. In Cary's telling, when he first boarded "a streetcar named Aspire," Ronald Colman was driving and Gary Cooper had his legs stretched out over several seats, but gradually he found a seat of his own. Then Cary saw Tyrone Power getting on and he said, "Don't let him in!" When Gregory Peck got on, he said, "Oh, no! That's the best looking guy I've ever seen! Don't let him on!"[78] As more and more new stars arrive, the old stars are pushed off. Cary was too humble to say that for over a decade he occupied the best seat on the streetcar, but in 1952 he was fairly certain that he was being pushed off. Perhaps the biggest surprise was that he did not mind. He had not found his place in the new Hollywood of the 1950s, but for the first time, he was happily married and ready to leave his career behind him—for a while at least.

24

Later in his life, when Cary looked back on the early 1950s, he said that he "retired" after completing *Dream Wife* in November 1952.[1] This has led some biographers to claim that he announced his retirement publicly at a press conference and retreated into a sulky seclusion, but there was no press conference, or even an announcement, and he did not entirely retreat from public life.[2] At the time, if he thought he was retired, he kept it to himself. When reporters asked him why he was not making a film, he said that he could not find "any good scripts," but he always added that he was looking forward to working with Hitchcock again on *To Catch a Thief*.[3] While filming did not begin until May 1954, his upcoming collaboration with Hitchcock was regularly reported in the trade papers during 1952 and 1953.[4]

His respite from filmmaking lasted for only 18 months, and he was never far out of the public eye. Just a month after finishing *Dream Wife*, he and Betsy sailed on a cargo freighter from Los Angeles to Manila, where they started a two-month tour of the Far East, visiting military bases and hospitals over the holidays and into the New Year. In the midst of the Korean War, this was a patriotic endeavor, and one that they embarked on for purely altruistic reasons. There was little publicity about the tour apart from wire reports that noted the couple's arrival in Hong Kong, Tokyo, and Singapore.[5] With Betsy at his side, Cary went on tours of the American bases in the region, meeting the troops by day and entertaining them informally in the evening, with Cary telling anecdotes about Hollywood and answering questions. They also toured military hospitals, going from bed to bed on the wards and meeting with injured soldiers.[6] He was characteristically self-deprecating when he spoke about the tour. The men he met were disappointed that he was not Marilyn Monroe, he said, but they made him "mighty welcome" nonetheless.[7]

Returning to Los Angeles in March 1953, Cary and Betsy soon visited the Hitchcocks at their weekend home in the hills above Santa Cruz, California.[8] Now that Cary was at home many days, he and Betsy were finding the Beverly Grove "farmhouse" too small. Betsy took up new hobbies and interests with such gusto that she would suddenly fill the living room with associated purchases—tripods, lenses, and cameras when she took up photography, easels and paints when she took up painting, and piles of books about everything. Cary preferred tidier and more organized surroundings. Rather than selling the property, they began to look for a larger second home, not as far away as Santa Cruz but in the resort town of Palm Springs, just two hours' drive from Beverly Grove.[9]

The house that they purchased, named Los Palomas, still stands at 928 North Avenida Palmas in the heart of Palm Springs, and it is said to have been modeled on "an Andalusian farmhouse," but this was a far grander house than the one on Beverly Grove. The six-bedroom, white-stucco mansion has vaulted ceilings, exposed wooden beams, and French doors opening up to one and a half acres of gardens with a swimming pool, tamarisk and palm trees, and bougainvillea covering the high, privacy-ensuring walls bordering the property.[10] Here, in this quiet enclave, Cary, Betsy, and their white poodle, named April, spent most of their time, going back to Beverly Hills only when Cary had business there.[11]

Betsy took up writing for television, but because she used pseudonyms it is difficult to trace her credits. She described their life in Palm Springs in leisurely terms. "I think I like best the days it rains in Palm Springs," she said. "We get up in the morning, put on blue jeans or shorts, and sit around drinking coffee, discussing everything from God to the garment industry." She wrote and painted. He swam and played the piano. They had frequent weekend guests. They occasionally went to Las Vegas, not to gamble but to see the shows. And despite his determination never to make a Western, he became a dedicated and skilled horseman, spending hours each day on the trails surrounding the town. "Anything he sets his mind on he does well," Betsy observed. "You'd think Cary was born in the saddle."[12] David Niven, an occasional weekend guest at Los Palomas, made a similar observation when he found Cary having swimming lessons in the pool early one morning. "Why lessons?" Niven asked. "You swim beautifully. I've seen you do it for years." Cary's reply, "I want to do it *perfectly*," struck Niven as typical of a man who was both a "restless soul" and a perfectionist.[13]

He had not given up work completely. He was often found in the garden reading the seemingly endless stream of movie scripts that were sent to him, and he continued to appear occasionally in Lux Radio Theatre adaptations of his own films, including *Room for One More* in 1952 and *The Bishop's Wife* in 1953. Sometimes, he also performed radio plays of films he had turned down, including Hitchcock's *I Confess* (1953), which was broadcast in September 1953.[14]

His fiftieth birthday on January 18, 1954, was overshadowed by the death of Dorothy di Frasso. Just before she died, she visited Los Angeles for the holidays, dining with Cary and Betsy, and accompanying Cary to Danny Kaye's New Year's Eve party.[15] A few days later, she took a side trip to Las Vegas to see Marlene Dietrich's show at the Sahara Hotel, and on the train back to Los Angeles she had a heart attack and died at the age of sixty-five. Cary took it upon himself to escort her body on the train journey back to New York, where he and Betsy attended her funeral and then stayed on in New York for somber birthday celebrations.[16] They went to the latest Broadway shows with Irene Mayer Selznick, and they joined Barbara Hutton and Lance Reventlow for dinner at the Pierre Hotel Grill. Cary was disappointed to learn that Hutton was going to marry another wayward playboy, Porfirio Rubirosa.[17] This marriage, Hutton's fifth, lasted less than three months.

The lifestyle of the idle rich was not for Cary. "It wasn't long before I discovered that work was important to my happiness," he said.[18] He might have added that Hitchcock made him an irresistible offer. *To Catch a Thief* would be filmed on location in the south of France, in and around Cannes, and making the film entailed spending a month on the Riviera. His co-star would be Grace Kelly, an actress as beautiful, elegant, and talented as any Cary had worked with. She was only twenty-five years old in 1954, but her career had skyrocketed over the previous two years. Already, she had co-starred with Gary Cooper (*High Noon*, 1952), Clark Gable (*Mogambo*, 1953), James Stewart (*Rear Window*, 1954), and Bing Crosby (*The Country Girl*, 1954), and just two months before filming began for *To Catch a Thief*, she won the Best Actress Academy Award for *The Country Girl*.

Cary was thrilled to be working with her and to be working again with Hitchcock. It had been eight years since they collaborated on *Notorious*, and Hitchcock was sure he had the perfect story for his favorite star. *To Catch a Thief* was based on a novel by David Dodge, and when Hitchcock read it in galley form, just before its publication in 1952, he leaped at it.[19] It is not hard to see why. The story centers on John Robie, an American acrobat turned jewel thief, who is known as "the Cat" for his ability to evade capture by climbing along the window ledges and across the roofs of the best hotels on the Riviera. His criminal career ended with the Second World War, when he joined the French Resistance, but then, as the story begins after the war, a copycat jewel thief is at work, stealing from the wealthiest visitors to the Riviera. Robie is suspected of the crimes, and he sets out to solve them in order to prove his innocence. The saying "It takes a thief to catch a thief" is the crux of the story.

Robie's moral ambiguity makes him an ideal Hitchcock villain, and his acrobatic past and transatlantic identity make him an ideal character for Cary. Hitchcock's cameo in *To Catch a Thief* plays upon his determination to lure and capture Cary for the film. In an early scene, Robie's own quiet retirement comes to an abrupt end when the police raid his home, believing him to be "the Cat." He escapes from them, catches a bus, and takes a seat. Sitting at the back, he glances to his right and sees a bird in a cage, and then he glances to his left and does a double take as he sees Hitchcock looking straight ahead nonchalantly.

If the director did manage to cage the star, it was a very gilded cage. Paramount offered Hitchcock an unusually high budget of $3 million, ensuring that the location shooting would be done in five-star style.[20] Cary received an advance of $300,000 against his 10 percent share of the film's earnings. One sign of how eager Hitchcock was to work with him again is the difference in their pay. Hitchcock, too, got 10 percent of the earnings, but his percentage would be calculated *after* Cary's earnings had been deducted from the gross.[21]

Hitchcock was also very keen to work again with Grace Kelly. In their two previous films together, *Dial M for Murder* and *Rear Window*, she had

Photograph 24.40 The gilded cage; Cary Grant and Alfred Hitchcock, making his cameo in *To Catch a Thief* (Paramount Pictures, 1955)
Source: author's screen capture

emerged as the quintessential "Hitchcock blonde," whose classical beauty and pristine manners mask a smoldering sensuality. In *To Catch a Thief*, she plays Francie Stevens, the finishing-school daughter of a *nouveau riche*, jewelry-laden American widow visiting the Riviera. Francie can scarcely conceal her attraction to Robie and, in the tradition of the best Cary Grant films, she unashamedly pursues and seduces him.

While *To Catch a Thief* riffed on some familiar story elements, it was also a strikingly modern film that finally freed Cary from studio-bound, black-and-white films such as *Monkey Business* and *Dream Wife* that now looked so old-fashioned. *To Catch a Thief* was filmed in Technicolor and in the new widescreen VistaVision format, allowing the Riviera to become another of the film's star attractions. Aerial shots establish the sunny setting, with villages clinging to mountainside peaks and the bright blue Mediterranean below. There are car chases along vertiginous cliffside roads, a pursuit on foot that upsets a local flower market, and scenes at the beach that allow both Cary and Grace Kelly to look sleekly athletic in their bathing suits. It is a dazzlingly bright, colorful, chic film.

Cary and Betsy traveled to the Riviera in mid-May, sailing from New York to Naples on the Italian liner the *Andrea Doria* and disembarking at Cannes. They checked in to a suite at the Carlton Hotel and had a few days at leisure before filming began on May 31, 1954. Cary told the screenwriter John Michael Hayes that he looked forward to being able to walk around Cannes without being bothered by fans. "This isn't like America," he told Hayes. "In Europe they don't worship stars." Hayes was then amused when he accompanied Cary to the men's clothing stores in the town. Word quickly spread that Cary Grant was in one of the boutiques in the shopping district, and crowds gathered so quickly on the street outside that Cary had to flee out the back door and dash back to the hotel.[22]

He did manage to find what he was shopping for: the blue-and-white striped pullover that Robie wears in the film's early scenes. As ever, he provided his own wardrobe for *To Catch a Thief*, and he wanted to buy something locally, as Robie would, to wear in the early scenes. For the later scenes, when he is with Grace Kelly and pretending to be an American businessman visiting Cannes (as a means of catching the new "Cat"), he consulted with the film's costume designer, Edith Head, about his wardrobe. Head was at the very top of her profession, yet she did not mind collaborating with Cary. "He has a discerning eye, a meticulous sense of detail," she wrote in her memoir. "When we were making *To Catch a Thief*, he planned a color scheme for his wardrobe throughout the picture. He found what Grace Kelly was wearing in each scene, then selected clothes to complement hers." Head was delighted when Cary approved of her designs: "That he admired the clothes I'd done for Grace was my best assurance and insurance."[23]

In an early scene, when Francie and Robie meet, Francie wears a light blue evening gown that is shoulder-less apart from a draped sash. This suits Kelly's regal, statuesque figure and also sets expectations of Francie's icy, aloof character. It is all the more surprising, then, when Cary escorts her back to her hotel room and, at the door, Francie pulls him forward for a long, languorous goodnight kiss, and eyes him seductively before gently closing the door. A close-up of Cary allows him to register a lengthy double take to the camera, conveying Robie's surprise, bemusement, and delight as some brassy horns on the soundtrack underline the comical playfulness of the scene. Francie is not a vamp but a debutante playing at being a seductress.

Where Cary's earlier films used slapstick to express desire and attraction, *To Catch a Thief* uses dialogue so laden with innuendo that it is as comical as it is sexy. When Francie takes Robie for a picnic high in the hills overlooking Monte Carlo, she asks him, "Would you like a leg or a breast?" before revealing that they are having chicken for lunch. "You make the choice," he replies, while stifling a grin. Later, in her hotel room, as a firework display lights up the night sky outside, she is at her most coyly seductive, playing upon his attraction to the diamonds around her neck as well as to her breasts. "You can't take your eyes off them," she teases. He tries to resist her, stating plainly that "I have about the same interest in jewelry that I have in politics, horseracing, modern poetry, and women who need weird excitement—none." But when she maneuvers him onto the sofa, gestures to a point somewhere between the necklace and the top of her shoulder-less gown, and invites him to "Look, John, hold them," he can resist no longer. The fade-out, as they kiss and recline on the sofa and the fireworks climax outside, was as suggestive as any film of this era could be.[24]

Cary was impressed by Grace Kelly's talent. He found her to be "perfectly natural" in front of the cameras—unselfconscious, unconcerned about her appearance—and able to interact with him spontaneously and confidently. "She made it so easy," he remembered. "I could say anything to her and she would have the perfect answer."[25] When he asked her, "How is it that you're so experienced at dialogue?," she attributed her skills and confidence to her early experience of acting in television soap operas, which were broadcast live.[26] In *To Catch a Thief*, the stars' ease with one another, and his obvious delight in her performance, is one of the film's many pleasures. The film benefits, too, from a fine array of character actors: Jessie Royce Landis as Francie's inordinately rich but down-to-earth mother, John Williams as an English insurance man (whose dry manner reinforces the idea that Cary could be American), and the French actress Brigitte Auber as the girl who turns out to be the real "Cat."

The location filming lasted for nearly four weeks. Although some delays were caused by bad weather—the sunny south of France was surprisingly rainy that June—it was a happy shoot.[27] John Michael Hayes was sensitive to Cary's interference with the script. He recalled that Cary would arrive in the mornings with annotated pages, suggesting improvements to Hayes's work. Cary would suggest they perform a scene twice, first as Hayes had written it and a second time as Cary had rewritten it. Then Cary would perform Hayes's version stiffly and his own version perfectly. Hayes circumvented this by priming the cast and crew to applaud the first version so enthusiastically that Cary had to admit, "I guess it is all right the way it is." Eventually, Cary caught on to the trick and "enjoyed the joke," according to Hayes.[28] Brigitte Auber remembered the script rewrites differently. "Every now and then, Hitchcock would say, 'Where is Cary? Let's change this scene,'" she said, "and sometimes Cary would say, 'I can't say this line' and he would change it on the spot."[29]

In the evenings, Hitchcock was keen to take his friends to dinner. Alfred and Alma, Cary and Betsy, and Grace Kelly, together with her lover, the fashion designer Oleg Cassini, enjoyed elaborate meals at the region's finest restaurants.[30] At the end of June, the location shooting was finished and the cast and crew left the Riviera and returned to the confines of a Hollywood studio for a further eight weeks of filming between July and September 1954.[31] The studio scenes were shot on the Paramount lot, and so Cary was back at his old studio, driving through the studio gates on Marathon Street each morning just as he had done twenty years earlier. He never commented on this, but he must have relished his change of status. Now he chose his own films, directors, and co-stars. He took a percentage of the earnings, and no one questioned his power to intervene on the script, his wardrobe, and the set design. When Robie's villa was recreated as a Paramount set, Cary was unhappy that reproductions of well-known paintings were hanging on the walls. He invited the set designer, Arthur Krams, to come to Beverly Grove for cocktails, and then he and Betsy invited Krams to use any of their

Photograph 24.41 Cary, Grace Kelly, and Alma and Alfred Hitchcock on the set of *To Catch a Thief*
Source: The Cary Grant Papers, courtesy of the Margaret Herrick Library

paintings on the set. Krams was astonished to be able to borrow paintings worth a fortune.[32]

Cary's identification with Robie, at least insofar as they would share the same taste in art, is not surprising. Once again, Hitchcock blended elements of Cary's real life with his character. Robie lives in a beautiful hilltop villa not unlike the Beverly Grove. He is happily retired but pressed back to work. His nationality is hard to pin down. As Francie tells him, when she rejects Robie's pretense that he is an American businessman visiting the Riviera, "You're like an American character in an English movie. You just don't talk the way an American tourist ought to talk. You're not American enough to carry it off." And he is, as she says, a "lone wolf" wary of becoming emotionally involved. In the film's ending, when they kiss on the terrace of Robie's villa, he finally surrenders to Francie. Her last line, "Oh, mother will love it up here," prompts a look of alarm from Robie that is comical but also signals that he will find fault in any romantic commitment.

To Catch a Thief was released in August 1955, nearly a year after it was completed. Cary, as a stakeholder in the film, agreed to go on a promotional tour, making personal appearances at local premieres and answering questions on stage afterward. Those who saw him backstage reported that his stage fright was nearly paralyzing before he went out and then dissolved when the warmth and enthusiasm of the audience's applause greeted him.[33] The first premiere took place in Grace Kelly's hometown of Philadelphia, where Cary got to know her family ("They all look like movie stars," he exclaimed) and also publicly paid tribute to her talent as an actress. He traveled on to seven more cities, relieved to see that the film was a big hit with audiences.[34]

Critics were surprisingly quick to find fault with *To Catch a Thief*—to dismiss it as a "slick" star vehicle with dialogue that was in questionable taste.[35] Cary and Grace Kelly got off lightly in these reviews. Hitchcock was the target of critics disappointed that he had emphasized "glib comedy" (as the review in *Variety* put it) over his trademark suspense.[36] The critics were in a minority, though, as the film's holdover engagements and box-office tallies indicated that it was a crowd-pleaser with audiences. Earnings in North America were estimated at $4.5 million, making it a very solid hit.[37] *To Catch a Thief* reaffirmed Cary's box-office status and also offered a formula for his future films. Henceforth, every film he made would be in color and in a widescreen format. They would include location shooting in tourist-trail settings, and they would have a knowing, adult humor that would upset the censors and amuse audiences.

Over the next ten years, this proved to be a fine formula, but it was not infallible, as Cary discovered with his next film. As ever, he was having trouble deciding which film to make. Billy Wilder wanted him to star in the romantic comedy *Love in the Afternoon* (1957), but Cary once again shied away from the director, and this was one of the few times that a part rejected by Cary Grant went to Gary Cooper.[38] It had been the other way around so often back in their Paramount days. Director David Lean was also seeking him for the war film *The Bridge on the River Kwai* (1957). Cary was keen enough on this film to meet with Lean to discuss whether his character, Shears (the part later taken by William Holden), should be played as either an American or an Englishman. He began "thinning down" for the role of a half-starved man in a Japanese prisoner-of-war camp. Then, much to Lean's dismay, Cary pulled out of the film before signing his contract, citing a scheduling conflict with another film he wanted to make.[39]

His preferred film was an epic tale of the Napoleonic Wars, grandly named *The Pride and the Passion*.[40] He had sworn off historical films since *The Howards of Virginia*, and he did not like the title of this one, but he was excited by producer Stanley Kramer's ambitions for the film.[41] Kramer envisaged *The Pride and the Passion* along the lines of the recent blockbusters *Quo Vadis* (1951), *The Greatest Show on Earth* (1952), and *The Robe* (1953), which had all passed the $10 million mark in box-office earnings—that is, films that told such large-scale stories, in such a spectacular fashion, that they would draw audiences away from their televisions and back into movie theaters.[42] Kramer planned to film on location in Spain, in Technicolor and VistaVision, and he hoped to have Cary and Marlon Brando as his stars.[43] This combination would be a spectacle in itself—the screen's most debonair and dignified star together with its most modern, torn-shirt rebel.

Brando did initially signal some interest in *The Pride and the Passion*, but he backed out before signing a contract. His replacement, Frank Sinatra, was one of Cary's favorite singers, but he was not in Brando's class as an actor, and he was hardly a reason to risk making a historical film. Despite this disappointment, Cary entered into the making of *The Pride and the Passion* enthusiastically. Once again, his salary was 10 percent of the earnings, which gave him a proprietorial interest in the film.[44] He arrived in Spain in early April 1956, a week early for the sixteen-week shoot.[45] Kramer had financing from United Artists and a $3.5 million budget, and this allowed him to bring hundreds of technicians and to hire thousands of extras to fulfill his grandiose ambitions for the film. Cary watched with fascination as the initial crowd scenes were filmed. He was also excited to visit a country that had been isolated since General Franco took control in the late 1930s.[46]

On the eve of the start of shooting, April 23, the stars assembled at a huge party staged at a Madrid hotel for a full contingent of the international press. For twenty-one-year-old Sophia Loren, the evening was terrifying. The Italian film star was making her first English-language film and she had never hobnobbed with Hollywood stars before. Meeting Sinatra was daunting enough, but she had heard that Cary was not keen on having her in the film. He had approval over his co-stars, and it had taken some time for Kramer to convince him that Loren could handle the role. When he finally arrived at the party, two hours late, she thought he "looked as though he had just stepped down from the screen, a dream come true." But when they were introduced he annoyed her by joking, "How do you do, Miss Lolloloren, or is it Miss Lorenigida?" He was playing upon the name of the most famous

Italian actress of the time, Gina Lollobrigida, but she was not amused. "I can't stand this guy," she thought. It was an inauspicious start to a relationship she came to describe as a "special partnership."[47]

When they started filming a few days later, they had plenty of time to get to know each other well. There were numerous logistical problems and production delays, and as they waited for filming to resume, they relaxed and got to know one another. They started going to dinner together in the evenings, driving through the countryside in a "flaming red MG" (supplied by the production company), and looking for out-of-the-way restaurants where they shared "confessional" talks. "I was fascinated by him," she said later, "with his warmth, affection, intelligence, and his wonderfully dry, mischievous sense of humor."[48] She observed that he tried to charm her by being funny and making light of serious things, and that this served as a mask for him to hide behind when he felt vulnerable. The more open she was with him, she noted, the more he let his mask fall and the more he revealed to her about his early life and his struggle, as an adult, to sustain romantic relationships.[49]

Loren was an olive-skinned, dark-haired, voluptuous beauty who, at this stage in her life, spoke in broken English. She could hardly have been more different from the other women Cary was attracted to—the lean, elegant, well-spoken blondes—but he quickly fell in love with her. She had quite the tale to tell about her own upbringing in war-torn Italy, sheltering from frequent bombing, and living with her unmarried mother, who had been abandoned by her father. Her openness set off a need in him to talk about his own upbringing—his older brother's death, his mother's disappearance, his loneliness as a child—and also a need to find out more about it himself.[50] Five weeks into filming, he wrote to the General Register Office in London, requesting copies of his father and mother's birth certificates, their marriage certificate, and his half-brother Eric's birth certificate.[51] Through talking with her, and through seeking these facts and dates, he was just beginning to come to terms with his family history and with the identity he had been so quick to leave behind twenty-five years earlier.

A month into the filming, Betsy arrived in Spain for a planned visit.[52] She could see what was happening between Cary and Sophia, but she also knew that she was powerless to stop their relationship so long as they were filming on remote locations across Spain.[53] Betsy stayed in Madrid, with her friend Judy Balaban and Judy's husband, Jay, and at weekends they saw Cary and other friends who visited Spain that summer. Grace Kelly—now married and known as Her Serene Highness, Princess Grace of Monaco—came to Madrid in May as part of her honeymoon tour with Prince Rainier. *The Pride and the Passion* had prevented Cary from attending their wedding, but he took a break from filming to spend time with the newlyweds in Madrid.[54] The Hitchcocks were also on a European tour that summer, and they came to Madrid to see Cary and Betsy a few weeks later.[55]

Betsy left Spain as planned in mid-July, once again sailing on the *Andrea Doria*. Late in the night of July 25, 1956, when the ship was passing Cape Cod en route to New York, the *Andrea Doria* hit another transatlantic passenger ship, the Swedish liner the *Stockholm*, and it began to sink. It was a terrifying accident. The screeching collision of the two ships, the panic of passengers as they raced to get out of their cabins and onto the deck, and the difficulty the crew had launching the lifeboats made for an ordeal few of the passengers would ever forget. Betsy found her way into a lifeboat and was picked up by the *Île de France*, which rescued many of the passengers that night.[56] She was barefoot, having run from her cabin without putting on her shoes, and she left behind her jewelry and her writing, but she survived (46 people out of the 1,709 people on board died).[57] Checking into the St. Regis Hotel in New York, she sent Cary a cable signed, "Your safe, sound and rescued wife," which reached him before he heard news of the accident.[58]

The location shoot for *The Pride and the Passion* continued for five more weeks, through August 1956, when Cary and Sophia had to part. Loren was in a long-term relationship with her mentor, the film producer Carlo Ponti, who was married and unwilling to divorce his wife. Yet Cary had fallen so deeply in love with Loren that he told her that he would divorce Betsy and marry her. Loren said that she needed time to think, and Cary replied, "Why don't we get married first and then think about it?"[59]

They parted with the promise that they would see each other again when she came to Hollywood. Cary was sure that she would be perfect in his up-coming film, *Houseboat* (1958).[60] In the meantime, Loren went back to Italy, and Cary headed home to New York. His journey did not begin well. On his way to Copenhagen airport, his car was involved in a minor collision with another car, but the accident made front-page news around the world.[61] This time, it was his turn to reassure Betsy, as well as his mother in Bristol, that he was not badly hurt.[62]

The Pride and the Passion, meanwhile, turned out to be as spectacular as promised but devoid of characterization and human interest. Loosely based on C. S. Forester's novel *The Gun* (1933), it is almost entirely preoccupied with the mechanics of hauling a huge cannon from one side of Spain to the other. Cary plays Captain Anthony Trumbell, a Royal Navy artillery officer in Spain, who helps a ragtag army of Spanish peasants move the cannon to Avila, a city the peasants hope to liberate from French occupation. The proud and practical Trumbell is contrasted with the passionate leader of the peasant army, Miguel (Frank Sinatra). Miguel tolerates Trumbell's help but grows jealous of his interest in the peasant girl Juana (Sophia Loren).

According to Stanley Kramer, there was some off-screen reality to the on-screen love triangle. Sinatra was "openly lusting" for Loren during the filming, and when he saw that she and Cary were having an affair he grew hostile toward her and bored with the production. He was so restless that he left Spain early without completing all of his scenes, and Cary was left "doing close-ups with coat hangers as the foreground because Sinatra wasn't there." But the much bigger problem, as Kramer admitted, was that midway through making the film he realized that "the cannon was and would remain the main character" of *The Pride and the Passion*.[63] There was no point in having three stars on the set, because what he really wanted to film was the spectacle of the massive cannon being pulled uphill, carefully lowered downhill, dragged through canyons and across rivers, and, finally, blowing holes into the walls of the city of Avila.

Kramer succeeded in the objective of making a film about a cannon, with Technicolor, widescreen, dramatic landscapes and a huge cast of extras giving a sense of grandeur to its journey across Spain. Yet with Cary under-used in a rare officer-and-gentleman role, Sinatra wearing an unflattering wig and speaking in a ridiculous accent, and Loren in a one-dimensional role, the film seems a waste of talent. On release in July 1957, the reviews were decidedly mixed, with some critics admiring the film's spectacle and others lamenting its lack of interest in its characters.[64] The North American box-office earnings, estimated at $5.6 million, were respectable but they were likely inflated by the high ticket prices for the film's "road show" release.[65] The film's popularity was also dwarfed by the three biggest hits of that year— *Around the World in 80 Days*, *The Ten Commandments*, and *Giant*—which were also spectacular epics, but films that did not lose sight of their stories and their stars.[66]

When Cary returned home from Spain in the autumn of 1956, he had made only two films over the previous four years, preferring to spend lei-surely days at home in Palm Springs with Betsy. But his summer with Sophia Loren upturned his life. Over the next 18 months, he committed to making four films. The first of these, the achingly romantic love story *An Affair to*

Remember (1957), suggests that Loren remained foremost in his mind. The story of a couple who meet abroad, fall in love, and promise to meet again in six months, when they have freed themselves of their commitments at home, could not have been more timely for him.

It is hard to imagine now that the much-loved *An Affair to Remember* could have had any stars other than Cary Grant and Deborah Kerr. In the autumn of 1956, however, when it was in development at Twentieth Century-Fox, producer Jerry Wald and director Leo McCarey were seeking Yul Brynner for the male lead and Ingrid Bergman had already turned down the female lead (she was committed to a play in London).[67] Brynner wavered because he was concerned about working with McCarey, who had fallen into a deep career rut. When Cary expressed an interest, Brynner was quickly pushed aside, apparently to his regret, and Wald rushed to sign Cary before he changed his mind.[68] Cary was happy to work with McCarey again, and so keen on this film that he settled for a salary of $300,000 without insisting on a percentage of the earnings (a decision he may have regretted in later years).[69] He did make two demands before signing. One was that Kerr must be his co-star (Lauren Bacall, Olivia de Havilland, Joan Fontaine, Rita Hayworth, and Jennifer Jones were above her on Wald's casting wish-list). The other, arising from Betsy's experience of the *Andrea Doria*, was that the scenes set on an ocean liner must not be set on an Italian liner.[70]

Cary knew the story of *An Affair to Remember* very well. It was a remake of McCarey's *Love Affair* (1939), which had starred Irene Dunne and Charles Boyer, and the story was little changed for this new version. The main characters, Terry McKay and Nickie Ferrante, are the strangers who fall in love while at sea, and then, upon reaching New York, agree that they will meet again in six months at the top of the Empire State Building. McCarey considered *Love Affair* his favorite love story, and Wald thought that it was ripe for a widescreen, color remake.[71] With Twentieth Century-Fox's backing, they had a hefty budget of $2 million, but Cary began to worry that he had committed himself to a "B" movie when he heard some of their plans for the film. He assumed that they would should shoot on location, firstly on a real ocean liner and secondly on Madeira, where the liner stops and the lovers visit Ferrante's grandmother. He also assumed that they would be filming on location in New York, but Wald told him that due to that city's inclement winter weather, in the new script the liner is on a journey ending in San Francisco, and the lovers would plan to meet at the Top of the Mark.[72]

Cary was unhappy with these plans, but he dropped the idea of filming on a real liner when his favorite cameraman, Milton Krasner, told him that this would be too difficult. Cary insisted that the New York setting and the climax at the Empire State Building were nonnegotiable, and a compromise was reached.[73] The New York settings would be reinstated but they would be filmed mostly in a Hollywood studio, with a second unit dispatched to New York for background footage and no expensive location shooting for the stars. There was considerable conflict over these points, and in later years both Wald and McCarey joked about how difficult it could be working with Cary. In their characterization, he was a fusspot who rang them up in the middle of the night worried that the buttons on the ship stewards' uniforms were wrong. "I call him the Lovable Irritant," McCarey said.[74] Yet his intervention in *An Affair to Remember* was rather more significant than they were ready to admit. The scene atop the Empire State Building has a central place in fans' memories of the film's heartaches and pleasures.

The wintry New York setting also served the story more broadly. This very middle-aged love story opens with an image of the snow-covered trees of Central Park, setting up the contrast between the warm, loving home that Nickie and Terry find at his grandmother's house in Madeira, and their own cold existence in New York, where Nickie has given up painting to become a gigolo, and Terry has given up singing to become the mistress of a wealthy executive. When they meet and fall in love, they offer each other a kind of redemption. They will not only leave their moneyed partners, but in their six months apart he will resume painting and she will resume singing. "Winter must be very cold for those who have no memories to keep them warm, and we have already missed the spring," Terry tells Nickie after the visit to Madeira.

The lovers miss the whole of the next year when Terry is hit by a car as she runs to join him at the Empire State Building. "It was my own fault," she finally tells him in the ending, "I was looking up! It was the nearest thing to heaven—you were there." This intensely romantic ending—with tears on the characters' faces and strings swirling on the soundtrack—is a marked change of tone from the film's lighter, funnier scenes. McCarey blamed Cary for bringing too much comedy to the film. "He could never really mask his sense of humor," McCarey said, insisting that his earlier film was better for being a melodrama through and through.[75] Yet Nickie's transition, from light-hearted gigolo to sentimental lover, is served well by Cary's initial breeziness and increasing solemnity. In the ending, when Nickie realizes that

Terry has loved him all along, he closes his eyes and allows a wave of relief, shame, and happiness to consume him, demonstrating his character's complete transformation.

On first release in July 1957, critics were quick to dismiss *An Affair to Remember* as "really awfully maudlin" (*New Yorker*), a "saccharine trifle" (*Time*), and not just a soap opera but "a bubble bath of bathos and banality" (*San Francisco Examiner*).[76] Audiences disagreed then—the film was a big hit, with North American box-office earnings reaching $3.9 million—and they have disagreed ever since.[77] A perennial favorite, *An Affair to Remember* was voted the fifth most romantic film ever made by the American Film Institute in 2000.[78] It has been revived and reissued innumerable times. Modern audiences may cringe at the scene of a children's choir (Terry McKay's pupils) singing cacophonously. Even Deborah Kerr lamented this in later years. "*An Affair to Remember* is a good film," she said, "but we certainly could have done without those wretched children. I like kids but for some reason they've always irritated me in this particular movie."[79] That scene aside, the film still makes audiences laugh and cry, and, decades after it was made, it inspired Nora Ephron's *Sleepless in Seattle* (1993) as well as a Warren Beatty remake, *Love Affair* (1994).

Back in 1957, the critic for *Variety* was one of the few to admire *An Affair to Remember* and to compliment Cary's performance, noting that he "is in top form in a made-to-order role."[80] In this fourth and last film with Leo McCarey, he once again played the debonair man-about-town to perfection. But there was also a new romantic intensity to his performance: a bitterness when he thinks that he has lost Terry and a vulnerability when he realizes that she loves him. It is not difficult to imagine that Cary channeled some of his feelings for Sophia Loren into this role, including his excitement toward the end of the shoot when she arrived in Hollywood, as well as his disappointment to find that Carlo Ponti had traveled with her.

Cary and Betsy continued living as husband and wife for two years after they returned from their fateful summer in Spain in 1956. This must have taken some considerable patience and understanding on Betsy's part. She stayed with Cary even as he waited for Sophia Loren to arrive in Hollywood, and as he lined up several films of his own to make in succession, with scarcely a break between them. One of his upcoming films, *Houseboat*, was from a script that Betsy had written and sold to Paramount just before she joined Cary in Spain. She sold it on the understanding that she and Cary would star in it together.[1] While Cary was in Spain, however, he informed Paramount that he had found "the new Garbo," and that Loren, rather than Betsy, should be his co-star in *Houseboat*.[2] At this point, Betsy refused any involvement in the film. She asked the studio to remove her name from the credits, but still she did not turn her back on Cary.[3]

Betsy went back to work as an actress. She had not made a film since *Room for One More* five years earlier, but in the spring of 1957, while Cary was filming *An Affair to Remember* at Twentieth Century-Fox, she was on a nearby soundstage at the same studio, filming *Will Success Spoil Rock Hunter?* She was third-billed, behind stars Tony Randall and Jayne Mansfield, in this very broad satire of Madison Avenue, playing a mousy fiancée who grows jealous when Randall begins working with the voluptuous Mansfield. Any parallels with her own personal life were presumably unfortunate coincidences, although in her funniest moment, when she sees Randall and Mansfield together, she looks very pleased to drop a plant pot on his head. The film was not a hit and her Hollywood career stalled again, but it was at least high-profile enough to enable her to line up a British film that would be shot in London over the summer of 1957.[4]

Cary had just ten days off between finishing *An Affair to Remember* in mid-April and starting rehearsals for his next film, *Kiss Them for Me*, at the beginning of May. Jerry Wald produced both films, and it was during the making of *An Affair to Remember* that he convinced Cary to make *Kiss Them for Me*. Wald had tried to sell studio executives on this story for nearly a decade, pitching it to Warner Bros. in the mid-1940s, to RKO in the late 1940s, and to Columbia in the early 1950s.[5] None of them wanted it, but by 1957, Wald was an independent producer at Twentieth Century-Fox, and with Cary Grant lined up as star, he was finally able to raise a $2 million budget for the film, with $450,000 designated as Cary's pay for nine weeks of work.[6]

Kiss Them for Me was based on a popular novel, *Shore Leave* by Frederic Wakeman, published in 1944. Centered on three navy fliers and their experience of four days of leave in San Francisco, the book explores the gulf between battle-weary soldiers and civilian war profiteers. A stage adaptation was retitled *Kiss Them for Me* and it ran on Broadway for a modest 110 performances in 1945. Ten years later, as Wald continued pushing for a screen adaptation, he was rebuffed on the grounds that the story was too much of its moment, an end-of-war tale that would no longer interest audiences in the post-war era.[7] Wald, however, was fascinated by the main character, Andy Crewson. He described him as "a handsome, brilliant, devil-may-care, conqueror of any woman and all women," as well as "an arrogant, humble, bitter, tender, sad, funny, brave young man." And he persevered in his efforts to bring a character he thought could be "one of the screen's most provocative heroes" to the screen.[8]

Crewson can be seen as the flip side of the navy captain portrayed by Cary in *Destination Tokyo*, produced by Wald fourteen years earlier. The wartime captain was custom-made for propaganda purposes: an uncomplicated, upstanding hero and dedicated family man. By contrast, the post-war Captain Crewson is still a war hero but he hates civilians, loathes wartime red tape, avoids phone calls from his ex-wife, and declares his only interest on leave is to "get drunk and chase girls." This being a Cary Grant film, the "girls" chase him. The fun-loving Alice, played with peroxide-blonde glee by Jayne Mansfield, interests him until he meets the cool, elegant Gwynneth, played by Suzy Parker. Crewson's romance with Gwynneth, and his leave more generally, is interrupted by a succession of requests for him to give speeches to war workers and interviews to the press, but he is too jaded for these duties and spends most of his leave on the run from responsibility.

Wald recognized that there were some problems with casting Cary in this role. Crewson is meant to be a twenty-three-year-old roughneck who was unemployed before the war and speaks in slangy "bad English" (according to the script notes). "We're not going to make Cary Grant look like a kid," he observed, cautioning against mentioning the character's age or explaining his background in the film.[9] The slang was dropped, and Cary was allowed to bring some gentlemanly charm to his role. Wald decided that this would make for a good contrast with his two companions on leave, a high-spirited hick nicknamed "Mississip" (Larry Blydon) and the shrewd aspiring politician "Mac" (Ray Walston). For good measure, he also had Crewson mock some of his own good manners. Pulling out a chair for Gwynneth to sit in, for example, he comments that "I once saw a man do this in an English movie."

Julius Epstein, a screenwriter known for bringing light humor to serious drama, not least in *Casablanca*, wrote the screenplay, emphasizing the men's jokey banter over the original story's concerns about war profiteers. A long list of directors was drawn up for Cary's approval, including George Cukor, Leo McCarey, and John Ford, but Cary settled on a younger director. Stanley Donen was only thirty-three years old but he had already co-directed *On the Town* (1949), collaborating with Gene Kelly on the hit musical about three soldiers on shore leave.[10] This made him an obvious choice for *Kiss Them for Me* except that Donen did not like the story and he was not keen to work with Jayne Mansfield, who was widely considered to be a second-rate version of Marilyn Monroe. Yet Donen "found it impossible to refuse" when Cary personally asked him to direct the film, and he did his best to open out the stage-bound story.[11] Shooting on location in San Francisco, together with color and widescreen, was crucial to this.

On release in November 1957, *Kiss Them for Me* drew very mixed reviews. Some critics found the humor "hilarious, smart and ribald" (*San Francisco Examiner*) and enjoyed "solid chuckles" (*Variety*), but others thought it little more than "a tiresome lot of manly jokes and drinking bouts" (*New Yorker*).[12] Nearly all agreed that Jayne Mansfield was "an inane caricature of a dumb blonde" and that the fashion model-turned-actress Suzy Parker "needs a lot more tutoring in speaking her lines" (New York's *Daily News*).[13] Cary's performance drew praise for being amusing "in a fashion which he makes look effortless" (*Chicago Daily Tribune*), but there was a sting to the observation in the *New York Times* that "Mr. Grant is a little creaky for this kind of navy-flier jazz."[14] Finding roles appropriate to his age was an increasing challenge in the latter part of his career.

The mixed reviews were mirrored in weak box-office returns. *Variety* estimated that North American box-office earnings reached only $1.8 million, placing the film just outside a ranking of the top fifty films of the year.[15] It was a rare misstep in Cary's post–*To Catch a Thief* career. The silver lining was that *Kiss Them for Me* established his personal and professional relationship with Stanley Donen. Donen was the last of the great directors who helped to shape Cary's career and screen image with some unusually smart, stylish, sophisticated comedies. They became life-long, close friends and, although their working relationship was rocky at times, they made three further films together—*Indiscreet* (1958), *The Grass is Greener* (1960), and *Charade* (1963)—each of them better than this first one.[16]

While *Kiss Them for Me* was still in production in the spring of 1957, Sophia Loren arrived in Hollywood for the first time. She was accompanied by Carlo Ponti and, although he was still married, she was pleased that leaving Italy gave her and Ponti their first chance to live together. Then, over the next few months, Ponti traveled back and forth between Los Angeles and Rome on business, and she and Cary began seeing each other again. By Loren's account, she could scarcely resist Cary as he sent her a bouquet of roses every day, wrote intimate notes for her, and phoned her frequently.[17] According to Ray Walston, who plays Mac in *Kiss Them for Me*, Loren then "started showing up" at the studio in the evenings to watch the rushes and "you could tell she and Cary were very fond of one another."[18] But by the time they attended the premiere of *The Pride and the Passion* together in July, their affair had cooled to the point that they could not hide their discomfort at being together. The press noticed that, when posing together for photographers, she looked nervous and he was "unusually grim."[19]

The day after the premiere, Cary flew to London to see Betsy, who was filming the comedy *Next to No Time* (1958) there.[20] He also traveled down to Bristol. Elsie, now eighty years old, was still in good health and living on her own. They had a lot of catching up to do; he had not visited Bristol in five years.[21] As usual, Cary kept the local press on his side by giving interviews to journalists who were only too eager to take him on a tour of his hometown, encouraging him to reminisce about the Bristol he knew as a child and to comment on the newly rebuilt post-war Bristol. This time, however, one reporter noted the "gray flecks" in his hair and his disappointment to see the city's redevelopment. "So much of what I remember is gone," he lamented, before quickly adding, "It's still a fine old city and I love every bit of it."[22]

He returned to Los Angeles to begin work on *Houseboat* in August 1957. Betsy's original script told the story of a Midwestern married couple with three children, and the family's comical adventures when they move out of rented accommodation and onto a dilapidated houseboat.[23] When Paramount agreed to replace Betsy with Sophia Loren, the studio assigned the *Room for One More* scriptwriters, Melville Shavelson and Jack Rose, to revise the script. Rose also produced the film, while Shavelson directed. They kept the premise of the young family moving onto a dilapidated houseboat, but in the new story the married couple divorced and the mother died before the film begins. This brings the father back into the children's lives. He is a government lawyer working in Washington, DC, who struggles to look after the children and to find a suitable home for them after their mother's death. Their problems are solved when a young Italian woman comes into their lives and they all go to live on the broken-down houseboat.[24]

Loren plays the hot-tempered yet soft-hearted Cinzia Zaccardi, who takes up employment with the Winston family because she is eager to escape from her stuffy father (an Italian orchestra leader touring the United States). The Winstons refer to her as a maid, but she is more a nanny in the mode of Mary Poppins, arriving in the nick of time to save the family, caring for the children, and helping their bewildered father learn how to relate to them. She dances exuberantly at a street festival, sings peppy ditties with gusto ("Presto, presto, do your very best-o"), and looks chic and shapely in a colorful wardrobe designed by Edith Head.

Once Betsy walked away from the film, *Houseboat* became, unmistakably, a star vehicle for Loren. Cary's Tom Winston is so uptight and humorless that even his own children find him tedious. It is only in the second half of the film that some tried-and-tested Cary Grant humor emerges. He gets sprayed in the face with water by an errant hose, the family slathers him in paint while fixing up the houseboat, and its gangplank sinks beneath him while he is fully dressed. The story does not contrive a situation in which he must wear women's clothing, but in one wry scene, set in a laundromat, he finds himself submerged within the conversation of the gossiping housewives around him.

These moments aside, *Houseboat* gives audiences little of the smooth, light-hearted Cary that they might expect to see in a romantic comedy. Instead, the film veers into a family melodrama, as the children—a distinctly troublesome trio—bring the 1950s preoccupation with bad parenting to the fore. *Houseboat* is not quite a melodrama on a par with *Rebel Without a Cause* (1955), but there are some similarly heated moments between the wayward children and the weak father. Cary's suave bachelor reveals himself to be a shallow fellow. "In certain circles, I'm considered quite charming and debonair," Tom tells Cinzia, "but children can look right through me as though there were nothing there. Maybe there isn't." This reflective, pointed comment marks a turning point in Tom and Cinzia's romance. Here art was imitating life. As Loren commented in her memoir, during the making of *The Pride and the Passion*, she fell in love with Cary only after he dropped his charm and humor and revealed the more vulnerable side of his personality.[25]

The three-month shoot was difficult for both stars. "The magic of our period in Spain had ended," Loren wrote about the filming of *Houseboat*; "We were at a standstill."[26] When the cast and crew went to Washington, DC, to shoot on location for ten days, she and Cary traveled separately and stayed in different hotels, but Cary had not given up on trying to convince Loren to marry him.[27] Hedda Hopper, writing privately, revealed that Cary's phone was bugged, and that she listened in on a conversation between Cary and Loren in which he pleaded with her to marry him. When Loren told him that Carlo Ponti was finally seeking a divorce from his wife, "Cary went out of his mind." He began promising Loren that he would divorce Betsy, and that they could go to Mexico and marry within a matter of weeks. Loren simply said, "No, no, no" as he spoke.[28]

Loren could not imagine living in Hollywood and, by extension, she could not imagine marrying Cary.[29] She had been romantically involved with Ponti for years, and she longed for him to divorce his wife so that she could marry him and return to Italy. She got her wish near the end of the making of *Houseboat*. She opened the newspaper one morning and read in Louella Parsons's column that Ponti's divorce had come through and that she and Ponti would be "married by proxy" in Mexico immediately.[30] Cary, she wrote in her memoir, was "slightly dazed" when she saw him at the studio that day, but he was "gentlemanly" and said only, "All the best, Sophia. I hope you'll be happy."[31] The problem was that they still had to shoot one last scene, the film's happy ending, in which Tom and Cinzi marry on the deck of the houseboat. For Cary, seeing Sophia in the character's white-lace wedding gown, and exchanging vows with her, could only have been devastating, but he was a veteran trouper. He performed the scene with just the right amount of emotion and solemnity. Then *Houseboat*, and his relationship with Loren, were finished.

The public remained in the dark about the stars' affair, and so when *Houseboat* was released in November 1958, there was no public commentary on their relationship or the strikingly somber wedding scene. Mainstream critics were divided between those who thought the film was an "agreeable light comedy" (*Los Angeles Times*) and "lots of fun" (*Chicago Daily Tribune*), and those who objected to the combination of romantic comedy and family melodrama.[32] This was "clumsy" (*Time*), "in bad taste" (*New York Times*), and "rather tedious" (*New Yorker*). *Variety* noted that the film was an especially strong showcase for Sophia Loren and correctly predicted that it would be a popular hit.[33] The North American box-office tally reached

Photograph 25.42 Cary Grant and Sophia Loren felt awkward filming the appropriately solemn wedding scene of *Houseboat* (Paramount Pictures, 1958). *Source*: author's screen capture

$3.5 million, placing it just inside the ranking of the top twenty films of the year.[34]

Back in the autumn of 1957, when *Houseboat* had just finished shooting, the cure for Cary's heartache was to make a much more elegant romantic comedy, to have Ingrid Bergman as his co-star, and to film in London rather than Hollywood. *Indiscreet* was based on a play, Norman Krasna's *Kind Sir*, that had been a flop on Broadway in 1953, but Stanley Donen thought that its failure on stage was the fault of the production rather than the play itself, and he hired Krasna to adapt his own play for the screen.[35] Donen recognized that this light yet sophisticated romantic comedy might have been custom-made for Cary. The lovers are two middle-aged but strikingly glamorous people, the dashing diplomat Philip Adams and the acclaimed actress Anna Kalman. The meet and fall in love, and Philip tells her that he is already married so that she will not expect to marry him. He is in fact a bachelor who uses this ruse with women in order to evade marriage. Anna feels guilty about what she believes to be their adulterous relationship until she finds out that he is actually single. She plots to make him jealous and, in the ending, he proposes to her.

Donen gave the brief story treatment to Cary, who immediately agreed to make the film without seeing a full script. Unlike the other directors Cary worked with, Donen said that Cary never prevaricated but made up his mind very quickly about films, giving him a decision within a day.[36] There was just one proviso: Cary insisted that Donen must sell Ingrid Bergman on the film as well. This was not a difficult task. Bergman, too, readily agreed to the film without reading a full script. "Cary, obviously, wants to work with you, and that's enough for me," she told Donen when he traveled to Rome to pitch the film to her. Cary and Donen then consulted Cary's lawyer and close friend, Stanley Fox, about setting up their own production company, named Grandon Productions, to produce the film themselves. This was a first for Cary. After arguing with studio bosses, producers, and directors for so many years, he would finally be in charge, and after demanding 10 percent of the earnings for so long, he would now own the film outright.[37]

Grandon proved to be the first of several companies that Fox helped Cary to establish. The purpose was not only to have greater authority over the making of the film; Cary already had a great deal of authority built into his contracts. There was also a tax advantage. As the film's owner, Cary's earnings would be considered capital gains, which were taxed at a lower rate than normal income. Another advantage was that Grandon would own the film. Warner Bros. would advance the film's production funds, and in return Warner would distribute the film for seven years, after which ownership reverted to Grandon. This was an important point in the era of television, and one Cary was perhaps particularly aware of. Now that the RKO film catalogue had been sold to television, his old films were regularly on television.

Grandon was set up as a British company, and the setting of *Kind Sir* was changed from New York to London. This suited a number of purposes. The play's setting might have seemed too familiar just a year after *An Affair to Remember*, with its memorable New York scenes. It is notable, too, that Donen seized the opportunity to film on location, capturing the grandeur and glamour of the real London in Technicolor, and avoiding the phony backlot London of so many Hollywood films. Filming at Elstree Studios (on the northern edge of London) also suited Cary's preferred co-star, Ingrid Bergman.[38]

It had been more than a decade since Cary and Ingrid made *Notorious* together, and in this time Bergman herself became notorious. In 1949, while she was still married to Petter Lindstrom, she had an affair with the Italian director Roberto Rossellini and became pregnant. When this became publicly known, the backlash against her was fierce. American moralists felt betrayed that a woman they venerated for playing nuns and saints did not live up to her screen image. She was denounced far and wide, including on the floor of the US Senate, where a senator demanded that she should be barred from the United States.[39]

Bergman had already fled the country to join Rossellini in Rome. Soon after she arrived in December 1949, she received a message from Cary that read, "Ingrid dearest, it would not be possible in a single cablegram to tell you of all your friends who send you love and affection."[40] In the midst of the scandal surrounding her, she was touched by this gesture. She responded by thanking him for being a steadfast friend. "I shall never forget that you were the first one to give me a kind word of encouragement," she wrote to him.[41] They continued to write to one another over the ensuing years, and occasionally to talk on the telephone by long distance, while Bergman raised the three children that she had with Rossellini and made several films with him.

She made a kind of comeback with American audiences in 1956, when she starred in *Anastasia*, a Hollywood-financed film shot in Britain. She won the Academy Award for Best Actress for her performance, but she was appearing in a play in Paris at the time and did not return to the United States for the ceremony. Cary attended on her behalf. When her name was announced, he raced up to the stage to collect her award, beaming with pride that she had won. "Dear Ingrid," he said, speaking directly to her on television and radio, "if you can hear me now, or if you can see this, I want you to know that each of the other nominees, and all of the people with whom you worked on *Anastasia*, and dear 'Hitch,' and Leo McCarey, and everyone here tonight, send you our congratulations, our love, our admiration, and every affectionate thought." The next day, Bergman wrote to Cary, thanking him and telling him that she could hear his speech. She had been taking a bath in Paris when her seven-year-old son ran into the bathroom with the radio in his hands. "Mama, they're talking about you!" he said. She heard Cary say, "Wherever you are now," and she yelled back, "I am here, Cary! In the bathroom!"[42]

In the years since her departure from Hollywood, they pondered when they could work together again, with Bergman joking with him that "I would like to work with you again before I have to play your mother."[43] *Kind Sir* was their chance and they took it. Bergman flew to London to start rehearsals on November 11, 1957, and her arrival caused a sensation. In the previous two weeks, the papers had been filled with the news that Roberto Rossellini was having an affair, that his mistress was pregnant, and that he and Bergman had separated. The press was therefore waiting for her at the airport, eager to question her about her marriage.[44]

Cary was also waiting for her at the airport, and he did his best to protect her. As journalists surrounded her, firing questions, he interrupted them by joking, "Ingrid, wait until you hear about my problems!" The reporters laughed but continued to question her. "Come on, fellas, you can't ask a lady that," Cary reprimanded them. "Ask me the same question and I'll give you an answer," he said as they made their way out of the airport and into a waiting car. "So, you're not interested in *my* life? It is twice as colorful as Ingrid's," he insisted.[45]

In the week before filming began, everyone agreed that they did not like the title *Kind Sir*, and not least because it was associated with a Broadway flop, but they still had not decided what the new title should be. Donen suggested "They're Not Married" but Jack Warner advised against it. "With Bergman in the picture," Warner wrote, "it would be extremely dangerous to use the word 'married' or anything pertaining to 'marriage' in the title."[46] Warner proposed "Irresistible" and the studio's sales department proposed "Indiscreet." Cary did not like either title, but on the day of the press party that launched the film, he had to choose, and so *Kind Sir* became *Indiscreet*.[47]

Indiscreet proved to be a suitable title for a romantic comedy in which the characters are preoccupied with appearing to behave by the norms of conventional morality but have no intention of actually following those norms. Bergman's character is immediately attracted to Cary. His entrance in the room stops her speech and the camera lingers on him, and then lingers on her looking at him, making her desire for him unmistakable. Throughout the romance that develops between them, they go through the motions of observing propriety—leaving the door open while they are in her flat alone, pretending after a date that he is only coming into her flat for a coffee, and, on several occasions, saying goodnight in front of others before he returns to her flat for the evening.

The film leaves little doubt that they are sleeping together, and Donen plays upon this coyness with a wonderfully inventive use of split screen. When Philip and Anna speak over the telephone—he is in Paris and she is in London—they are both in bed and in their pajamas, and their pillows and bodies are aligned within the frame. The split screen makes it clear that they are not in the same bed, but the intimate way that they speak and shift positions conveys that they are accustomed to being in bed together. This

Photograph 25.43 In *Indiscreet* (Warner Bros., 1958), a split screen allows Cary Grant and Ingrid Bergman to perform a love scene together but in different beds.

Source: author's screen capture

contrivance may have been designed to confound the censors, but it is also entirely in keeping with Philip and Anna's insistence on being seen to observe "the rules" (their term for the customs governing romantic relationships) while also breaking the rules. In the ending, when she discovers that he has lied to her, that he is actually a bachelor, she finally turns the rules upside down. "How dare he make love to me and *not* be a married man!" she bellows.

In keeping with the film's preoccupation with both traditional and progressive mores, the London setting is treated in a fresh and modern manner. The sights of "landmark London," such as Big Ben and Piccadilly Circus, were well known to filmgoers. These and other location settings—the Garrick Club, the Covent Garden Opera House, and the gates outside Buckingham Palace—represent a stuffy, old-fashioned London, but in *Indiscreet* they are seen in newly playful ways. Philip and Anna don't belong to the Garrick Club, for example, but they bend the rules in order to dine in this gentleman's club. At the opera house, they give their prime seats to a young couple being denied "standing room." One of London's less well-known sights, Cleopatra's Needle (an Egyptian obelisk on the Embankment), is used as the backdrop to a kiss, and this piece of exotica adds to the impression of a reimagined city. So, too, does a scene set in the Blitzed area around what is now the Barbican, where the bomb damage, seen on a bright and sunny morning, suggests that something new and better may rise from the ashes of the old.

In *Indiscreet*, London is not the familiar city of costume dramas or realist war films, and it is not yet the youthful "swinging London" of the 1960s. It is a city made modern through an affluent, open-minded outlook and a particularly vivid Technicolor palette. Much of the film is set in Anna's flat, which is established as being in a rather grand building that is within earshot of Big Ben. Any expectation of the traditionally formal and stuffy décor associated with Mayfair or Knightsbridge is quickly dashed. Her bright and airy flat is strikingly contemporary, with colorful furnishings and modern paintings by Picasso, Dufy, and Piper on the walls. There is not an antique in sight. The setting is one that suits a cosmopolitan couple—Philip is from San Francisco while Anna refers to London as her "adopted city"—and a couple who defy conventions without abandoning them altogether.

Cary has a particularly memorable scene at a formal dinner. After the meal, the assembled guests rise to dance a Scottish reel, and Philip is the first on his feet. Although he does not know the steps, he improvises—hesitantly at first and then with increasing vigor—until he is dancing a jig and kicking his heels in the air gleefully. It is a delightfully exuberant moment—reminiscent of a similarly high-kicking dance scene in *Sylvia Scarlett*—and it adds a winning dimension to this character's suave, smooth personality. He also has one not-so-suave moment. When he is out and about with Anna, and her fans ask her for her autograph, the fans are portrayed as intrusive pests, and Cary, in the guise of Philip, glowers at them with disdain. This, it seems, was his revenge for being plagued by autograph hunters for decades.

Filming at Elstree lasted for nearly three months, but it was interrupted by an unusually lengthy Christmas break that allowed Bergman to spend the holidays at home with her children in Rome.[48] Cary and Betsy got together for the holidays too. She joined Cary in London in December, and they spent the holidays on a yacht owned by the Greek shipping tycoon Aristotle Onassis, sailing in the Mediterranean and going ashore in Monaco to dine at the palace with Princess Grace and Prince Rainier.[49] Cary was embracing his wealth and status wholeheartedly. His income in 1957 was a staggering $950,000 (from his new films alone).[50] He had already purchased a Rolls-Royce at home in Beverly Hills, but while making *Indiscreet*, he decided to buy the "Silver Cloud" Rolls-Royce seen in the film and keep it in London to use whenever he visited Britain.[51]

In January 1958, filming resumed for another five weeks, and Cary spent his fifty-fourth birthday in London. He was filming on location in the West End that day and in the evening he was photographed in the Salisbury Arms pub, in the heart of the theater district on St. Martin's Lane, celebrating with Ingrid Bergman.[52] Filming in the studio continued for another three weeks, until early February, when they did the remaining location shooting over the course of three nights of dusk-to-dawn shoots amid the city's bright lights.[53]

Cary was pleased with *Indiscreet* for many different reasons. He and Donen planned a film that had a sheen of luxury and sophistication yet a relatively modest budget of $1.6 million. Despite the star salaries, the Technicolor, and the location filming, few sets were needed and the cast was small (besides Philip and Anna, the only other significant roles were Anna's sister and brother-in-law, and her maid and chauffeur). He was pleased, too, that they managed to bring it in slightly under budget, a very rare occurrence in his career.[54] He was also proud to make a film that was, as he put it, "about two mature people falling in love, nothing more" at a time when contemporary films were perceived as issue-oriented and violent. And he was thrilled to work again with Bergman, noting that she "just glows" in the film.[55]

When *Indiscreet* was released in the summer of 1958, critics were quick to welcome the re-teaming of the stars of *Notorious*. Some admired the film as a "very elegant and stylish picture" (*Detroit Free Press*) and as one made in "the high old style" (*Time*), but others regarded it as "light, airy and weightless as a soufflé" (*New York Times*), "a handsomely mounted piece of fluff" (*New Yorker*), and "in the featherweight class" (*Chicago Tribune*).[56] The star power alone ensured the film's commercial success. North American earnings of $3.4 million and foreign earnings of $2.6 million combined to make the film a money-spinner for Grandon and for Bergman, who was paid $75,000 and 10 percent of the gross.[57]

Cary stayed on in London during February and March of 1958 because Betsy was making another film there, the thriller *Intent to Kill*. He enjoyed traveling around Britain and Europe while she worked, and in late February he visited Moscow as a tourist. At the height of the Cold War, this was an unusual trip to make, but he accepted an invitation from the American film producer Sam Spiegel, who was traveling there to urge the Soviet authorities to allow *The Bridge on the River Kwai* to be released in Russia, which seldom imported American films. Cary was delighted by the city—not only because he had never been there before, but also because no one recognized him. He was not a star to Russians, and he could roam the streets of Moscow without being stared at, pointed at, and asked for his autograph, as he so often was elsewhere.[58]

He found the experience so refreshing that he lowered his guard while speaking to Western reporters in Moscow. "I am so happy," he told them. "For the first time in my life I feel free." He meant that he was delighted to be free of the trappings of stardom, but he took some flak in the press back home, where any favorable comment about Russia was regarded as un-American.[59] When he returned to the United States, Bob Hope helped him to diffuse some of the criticism by making light of it. They were presenting the Best Actor award at the Academy Awards in late March, and Hope introduced Cary to the audience as "my good friend from Moscow" and then turned to him to say, "Comrade, why haven't I seen you at the meetings?" The laughter—their own and the audience's—effectively ridiculed those who had taken issue with him.[60]

He was back in London for the UK release of *Indiscreet* in July 1958. He decided to do for *Indiscreet* in the United Kingdom what he had done for *To Catch a Thief* in the United States: accompany the film on a city-by-city tour, appearing at preview screenings and taking questions after the film was shown. This set him on a tour that took in nine cities over thirteen days. It was a faster pace than any tour he did with the Pender Troupe forty years earlier, but also a considerably more luxurious one. He traveled in his new Rolls-Royce and he was welcomed in the manner of visiting royalty. In Hammersmith, for example, the local mayor and mayoress greeted him at the cinema wearing their ceremonial robes.[61] Bristol, interestingly, was one of the few major cities he did not appear in, presumably because he wanted to keep his private life there, and especially his mother, out of the spotlight.

He returned to Beverly Grove in late July, preparing for another film that would involve lengthy location shooting. Before filming started, he and Betsy finally had a reckoning. Their marriage was described in fan magazines and press profiles in idyllic terms, and Betsy received letters from women asking her how she did it, marrying the perfect man *and* keeping him happy.[62] In truth, since Cary met Sophia Loren two years earlier, their marriage had not been the same. He was perpetually restless and kept himself busy with nearly continuous filmmaking, location shooting, and promotional tours. At home, Betsy was miserable and also disappointed in herself for having turned into a "subservient wife" and for "swallowing all of the myths" about marriage that prevailed in the 1950s.[63] She went into therapy, seeking some insight into her life and the direction it had taken since she met Cary.

It wasn't until September 1958, two years after Cary's affair with Sophia Loren, that Betsy finally decided she could not live with him any longer. Her breaking point came unexpectedly as they were having breakfast in bed. As he chatted to her, she realized that she could no longer contain her anger. "Go fuck yourself!" she suddenly told him. He went into the bathroom, "buttoning the top of his pyjamas with his bare bottom showing" and slammed the door. That, she recalled later, was "the beginning of the end" of their marriage.[64] Eleven years after their first meeting, and nine years into their marriage, she wanted to get away from both her husband and show business. They would not finalize their divorce for nearly four years, but she immediately moved out of the Beverly Grove and Palm Springs houses and into her own new home in the Mandeville Canyon neighborhood of Los Angeles. There, she sought a new life for herself writing fiction and studying psychiatry.[65] Cary, meanwhile, remained as preoccupied with his career as ever. A week after Betsy's departure, he left home to begin several weeks of location shooting on his next film. *North by Northwest* would be his sixty-sixth film and, in the opinion of many, the very best film of his career.

"I don't even know what the story is," Cary told a reporter in July 1958, a month before filming began for *North by Northwest*. "If Hitch is going to make it, that's enough for me."[1] His confidence was well placed. His fourth film with Hitchcock was their best yet: a tense thriller, with sophisticated humor and romance, shot on spectacular locations in VistaVision and Technicolor, and with a strikingly modern musical score by Bernard Herrmann. On its initial release in 1959, *North by Northwest* proved to be a big commercial and critical hit, but more importantly, over the next several decades, it gradually became *the* Cary Grant film—that is, his most frequently revived film, the film that receives the highest rankings in critical and audience surveys, and a film that seems like a summation of his entire career. It has its own distinctive pleasures, too, and not least among them is the enthralling crop-dusting scene. The sight of Cary in his sharply tailored gray suit, looking like an affluent American businessman and yet running for his life from a marauding airplane, has become an iconic image, representing not only his career but cinema itself.

It can be surprising, therefore, to learn that Hitchcock initially considered James Stewart for the lead in *North by Northwest*.[2] There is no doubt that Hitchcock and Stewart enjoyed working together, and because they were filming *Vertigo* in the autumn of 1957, while the *North by Northwest* script was in development, it is likely that they discussed the new story and its possibilities. As the script took shape, however, both Hitchcock and the scriptwriter, Ernest Lehman, realized that Stewart was not right for the role of Roger O. Thornhill, the Madison Avenue advertising executive of *North by Northwest*. Stewart was too down-to-earth and sincere to play such a slick and superficial man, and, as Lehman later commented, Stewart's laconic manner and Midwestern drawl would have slowed the fast pace of the film. "If Jimmy Stewart played that role," Lehman said, "the picture would be six hours long."[3]

Lehman recalled that his aim when writing *North by Northwest* was to create "the Hitchcock picture to end all Hitchcock pictures," a film with "wit, glamour, sophistication, action, and lots of changes of locale."[4] His earliest surviving script, from November 1957, suggests that from the beginning,

CHAPTER 26   359

he imagined Cary at the center of this most Hitchcockian film. Thornhill is described as "tall, lean, [and] faultlessly dressed."[5] Stewart was tall and lean too, but no one ever described him as "faultlessly dressed." The script's description of the character points to Cary. So, too, does the story's interest in scratching the surface of the character's handsome façade, looking to find what might lie behind so much charm and good tailoring. This was a longstanding interest of Hitchcock's and one that was not focused on Cary alone. Indeed, Hitchcock's first high-profile film, *The Lodger* in 1926, was adapted from a stage play entitled *Who Is He?*, a suspense-thriller about a handsome young man who may or may not be a serial killer. In *The Lodger*, Ivor Novello plays the intriguingly mysterious lead, and in Hitchcock's later films many more leading men—including Robert Donat, Laurence Olivier, Joseph Cotten, Gregory Peck, Farley Granger, James Stewart, and Anthony Perkins—played characters whose good looks mask a range of moral ambiguities, from mere complacency to murderous psychosis.

Yet Cary was the most compelling of Hitchcock's leading men. This was not only because he was the best-looking and most debonair of stars, but also because as an actor he was able to convey ambiguity so subtly. As David Thomson observed of Cary, "there is a light and a dark side to him, but whichever is dominant, the other creeps into view."[6] This is why each of the four films that Cary made with Hitchcock could have been titled *Who Is He?* and why the question could never be answered with any finality. In *Suspicion*, Johnny's handsome charm masks a ne'er-do-well embezzler and also, just possibly, a murderer. In both *Notorious* and *To Catch a Thief*, he is revealed to be a hard-hearted "lone wolf" who, without the *deus ex machina* of the plot, would remain irretrievably damaged and inaccessible. *North by Northwest* is even more remarkable for suggesting that there may be nothing beneath his character's façade; that the façade has been so carefully constructed, and maintained with such attentive polish, that any substance beneath it has long since been subsumed and forgotten.

On one level, *North by Northwest* is *about* Cary Grant. Where his earlier films occasionally made sly references to Archie Leach, this one draws more striking parallels between the character and the star. The story is set in motion when a foreign spy ring mistakes Roger O. Thornhill for a CIA spy named George Kaplan, not realizing that Kaplan is a fictitious identity invented to distract attention from a real spy. Like Cary, then, the character has two names: Thornhill is a real person that no one is particularly interested in, while Kaplan is an invented person that everyone is chasing.

Thornhill is twice-divorced, as Cary was at this point. He is recognized wherever he goes. "I know. I look vaguely familiar," he says while trying to hide, in movie-star style, behind sunglasses. Women fawn over him, including the beautiful Eve (Eva Marie Saint), but they also abandon him rather quickly. His relationship with his mother is rather intense for a middle-aged man, a situation heightened by casting the actress Jessie Royce Landis, who was only seven years older than Cary, as his mother. The leader of the foreign spy ring, Vandamm (James Mason), tells him that he is unconvincing playing an "outraged Madison Avenue man" and suggests that he needs "training from the Actors Studio"—a barb that plays upon the idea that Cary was not a serious actor but a star who simply played himself on-screen.

Of course, the film is not *just* about Cary Grant. Thornhill's quest to prove that he is not Kaplan entails an odyssey that begins amid the sleek glass façades of Madison Avenue, where advertising campaigns are created to fuel modern American capitalism, and ends with a struggle atop the stony, unsmiling façade of that monument to American patriotism, Mount Rushmore. Along the way, Thornhill is revealed to be the personification of the consumerism he peddles: an utterly superficial fellow who is defined only by his image and appetites: having cocktails, going to the theater, keeping his many girlfriends sweet. As his attachment to his mother suggests, he has never had to grow up or take responsibility for anything—until, that is, midway through the film, when a solemn and earnest government agent, known as the Professor (Leo G. Carroll), explains why the spies have mistaken him for Thornhill and asks him to continue with the ruse for the sake of his country. "I'm an advertising man, not a red herring," he indignantly replies, without realizing that being an advertising man might be just as vapid and insignificant as a red herring. Even when trying to underscore his life's significance, he can only be glib. "I've got a job, a secretary, a mother, two ex-wives, and several bartenders dependent on me," he tells the Professor, "and I don't intend to disappoint them all by getting myself *slightly* killed!"

Thornhill's north by northwest journey takes him away from the soft, sheltering comforts of civilization and challenges him firstly to survive and secondly to save Eve using only his own wits and strength. This odyssey unfolds over five acts. At the beginning of each act, Thornhill thinks that he is in control, or that he knows how to take control of the events that continue to spiral into chaos and turmoil. After each act's denouement, he straightens his suit and tie and begins the next act afresh. On the set and on location, this was made possible by having six identical suits to work through; the original by the Savile Row tailor Kilgour and five copies made by the Beverly Hills tailor Quintino.[7] On screen, the illusion of the indefatigable suit allows for him to be repeatedly set up as a perfectly groomed, perfectly controlled, and perfectly confident character who is then shaken to the core and stripped of his control and dignity. Thus, like so many Cary Grant films, *North by Northwest* tests just how long his character can maintain his breezy nonchalance. The difference is that this one film has the narrative arc of five films, and, together with its knowing dialogue and witty repartee, its excessive storyline means that it walks a fine line between being a genuine, very suspenseful thriller, and being a self-referential pastiche of just about everything that Cary and Hitchcock had done before (together and separately).

"In the films I made with Hitchcock," Cary recalled many years later, "the humor relieved the suspense. People laugh in the theater because what's on-screen is not happening to them. I played my role as though it wasn't happening to me. And I think that's how I got the audience on my side."[8] This "formula," as Cary described it, is certainly apparent in *North by Northwest*, but it does not fit quite as well with the other three films he made with Hitchcock (*Notorious*, in particular, is moodier than the description allows). Moreover, the strategy did not originate entirely with the films he made with Hitchcock. As early as *Topper*, Cary's wry performance signaled to the audience that they should not take the fatal car crash or the supernatural ghost story too seriously, that this was a starting point for a comedy. Nevertheless, he and Hitchcock had honed and perfected the "formula" to the point that, in *North by Northwest*, the humor could be sustained through far greater violence and menace than anything seem in *Topper*.

North by Northwest begins as a light comedy set in the kind of smart Manhattan locales familiar from *Topper* and *The Awful Truth*, and Cary portrays Thornhill in a similar man-about-town mode. He looks strikingly youthful for a man of his age (fifty-four at the time of filming) and also quite distinguished. The gray of his suit brings out the flecks of gray in his hair, while his trademark tan suggests a life of leisurely affluence. As familiar and captivating as this character is, it is apparent from the start that in this particular guise he is just a little too cynical and pleased with himself. He leaves his office building with his secretary in tow, and maneuvers through the crowded streets with a confidence bordering on arrogance. He dictates a corny message to accompany the chocolates he is sending to his girlfriend ("something for your sweet tooth, baby, and all your other sweet parts"). He steals a taxi from a man on the street ("I have a sick woman here. You don't

Photograph 26.44 Cary as Roger Thornhill, one of the "Mad Men," dictating to his secretary (Doreen Lang) as he walks up Madison Avenue in *North by Northwest* (MGM, 1959)

Source: author's screen capture

mind, do you?"). He asks his secretary to remind him to "think thin" so that he won't gain weight. And he strides through the lobby of the swanky Plaza Hotel and into its famed Oak Bar with such casual ease that it is clear that he is due for some sort of comeuppance.

It is in the Oak Bar that Thornhill is mistaken for Kaplan, manhandled by thugs into a car, and taken to a Long Island mansion, where the leader of a foreign spy ring, Philip Vandamm (James Mason), interrogates him. Thornhill and Vandamm meet in the mansion's oak-paneled library, a setting so redolent of English manor houses—with landscape paintings, oriental rugs, and book-lined shelves—that it could serve as the set for one of Noel Coward's drawing-room comedies. Vandamm highlights the theatricality by closing the curtains, adjusting the lighting, and commenting on Kaplan's disguise. "Not what I expected," he says, "a little taller, a little more polished than the others." James Mason's English hauteur draws attention to Cary's vaguely transatlantic accent and indefinite origins.[9] Cary never seemed more American, in manner and in accent, than when being sneered at by Mason. As Thornhill, he protests over and over again that he is not Kaplan and that he must leave because he has tickets for the theater. "With such expert play acting," Vandamm says wearily, "you make this very room a theater."

Thornhill has been abducted and is being held against his will, but Cary plays the scene in his most casual Noel Coward style, placing his hands in his pockets and delivering his dialogue in a flippant but not an angry tone. He cannot remain unflappable forever, though, and especially not when Vandamm's men pin him to a chair, force-feed him whiskey, and put him behind the wheel of a car that they push down a cliffside road. His drunken ride of terror—spinning around hair-pin turns and nearly over a cliff—has a parallel in each of the previous films he made with Hitchcock. In *Suspicion*, his character is at the wheel for the clifftop drive in which Lina almost falls from the car. In *Notorious*, a drunken Alicia drives erratically while he looks on warily, and in *To Catch a Thief*, it is Francie who takes him on a white-knuckle clifftop ride. These harrowing drives are the suspense-thriller equivalent of the screwball comedy scenes in which Cary loses his clothing. That is, they serve to strip him of his polite demeanor and allow all of his hitherto repressed feelings to come to the fore. The panic that he does not express in the drawing room becomes fully apparent as the car careers wildly out of his control.

Thornhill survives the drive, only to be intercepted by the police and arrested. Having been abducted, terrorized, and humiliated, the first act of the film ends with this grown man phoning his mother from the police station.

The second act begins with him seeking a rational explanation for his ordeal. He explains what happened to a disbelieving judge who fines him for drunk driving. He returns to the Long Island mansion with the police, but finds that the spies have covered their tracks. Together with his skeptical mother, he searches for clues in Kaplan's room at the Plaza Hotel. "They've mistaken me for a much shorter man!" he says indignantly when inspecting Kaplan's suit. He moves on to the United Nations to interview the delegate who owns the Long Island mansion. Before he can get past the initial pleasantries, however, the delegate is swiftly knifed in the back and dies at Thornhill's feet. No one sees the spy throw the knife, but everyone sees a stunned Thornhill, pulling the knife from the delegate's body as it falls to the floor. A photographer instantly takes a picture of Thornhill, knife in hand, standing over the body, and so the second act ends by giving him another identity. Thornhill is, as newspaper headlines declare, "the United Nations Killer."

The third act begins with him fleeing from New York to Chicago aboard the Twentieth Century Limited train, and it is in this sleek, modern setting that he dons sunglasses as a disguise and meets Eve Kendall. She certainly treats him more like a movie star than an advertising executive, a spy, or a killer: she tips the maitre d' to seat him at her table in the dining car, flirts with him over a cocktail, and invites him back to her compartment for the evening. Eva Marie Saint was an unlikely choice to play this cool, elegant temptress. Previously, she was best known for her role in *On the Waterfront* (1954), playing a convent girl on the mean streets of Hoboken, New Jersey, who falls in love with Marlon Brando's doomed character. "You don't have to cry in this picture—we're gonna have fun with this one," Cary joked with her when they first met, and he did everything he could to put her at ease.[10] Hitchcock gave her little direction but what he said was crucial. "He told me not to use my hands, and to lower my voice, and always, in my scenes with Cary Grant, to look directly into his eyes."[11] She followed his advice, and became one of the most memorable of Hitchcock's blondes.

The love scene in her compartment, shot in intimate close-ups, echoes the long kissing scene in *Notorious* (a "ménage à trois," as Hitchcock described it, involving the audience and the two stars).[12] This time the intimacy is all the more remarkable given that these two people have only just met, and their rolling movements as they kiss, although motivated by the train's motion, seem so close to lovemaking.

The arrival of Eve brings some warmth and feeling to the story and, by pursuing Cary's character in the romantic comedy mode of so many of his previous leading ladies, she provides a kind of reassurance that this is, after all, a Cary Grant film, and so there must be an easy way out of his predicament. The next morning, her benevolence is underscored when the train arrives in Chicago, and he evades the police by disguising himself as a porter carrying her luggage through the station. The sight of Cary wearing the uniform of a "red cap" (as the porters were known), and laden with her suitcases ("What have you got in these *bags*?" he asks), is so incongruous that it comes across as a bit of mild fun rather than a humiliation for him, a playful moment between them that gives little sense of the betrayal to come.

The tension begins to build again when Eve passes a message to him, instructing him to meet the real George Kaplan at "Prairie Stop," a bus stop on a remote highway one hour outside of Chicago. The audience is aware at this point that Eve is somehow in league with the spies and that the message places Thornhill in some peril, but the scene at "Prairie Stop" initially appears harmless. A wide establishing shot shows Thornhill as a tiny figure amid the flat, empty landscape. There is no dialogue for a full four minutes, and it is only as he waits expectantly that the vast space begins to seem as though it leaves him exposed and vulnerable. A note of alarm is raised when another man arrives to catch a bus, and he observes, in a local accent that underlines just how far from home Thornhill has traveled, that the plane is "dustin' crops where there ain't no crops."

The bus arrives and the man departs. Alone again, Thornhill looks impatient until he realizes that the plane is now heading directly for him. Hitchcock shows much of the ensuing action from Thornhill's point of view, so that when the plane descends, barreling down on him, it threatens to break through the screen and decapitate the audience as well. On a second dive, it not only lunges at him but also rains bullets around him. He evades injury by throwing himself to the ground as the plane swoops over. With his pristine suit now covered in the dry, dusty dirt of the prairie, he tries to hail a lone car coming down the highway, but this is not Madison Avenue, and the car is not a taxi, and so his city skills are of no use here. With the plane descending on him again, he runs toward a small cornfield where he assumes the crops will offer some shelter. This time, the plane lunges down, shoots at him, *and* drops insecticide on him. Running to the road, he forcibly stops an oil tanker-truck by standing in its path as it barrels down the highway at him. Hitchcock again shows much of this from Thornhill's point of view, so that the grille of the

Photograph 26.45 In one of the most famous scenes in film history, Roger Thornhill is attacked in fields far from Madison Avenue.
Source: author's screen capture

truck fills the screen as it screeches to a halt and comes within an inch of killing him. Reverse shots from the truck's point of view reveal Thornhill's alarm but also, as his face fills the screen, his underlying unflappability. Even as the plane hits the tanker, igniting an explosion, he has the wherewithal to pull himself up from under the truck and flee from the carnage.

If it is possible to laugh at or at least enjoy the crop-dusting scene—hesitantly and amid gasps—it is because the Hitchcock-Grant "formula" is in peak form here. This story turn is so absurdly implausible—why would the spies choose to murder Thornhill by sending him to a remote bus stop and attacking him from a plane?—that it cannot be taken entirely seriously. Moreover, Cary's performance is so agile that it is hard to imagine that he is in any real mortal danger. Whether throwing himself to the ground or running for his life, his movements are spectacularly graceful and athletic—more than worthy of a well-trained Pender "tumbler." His stride is so swift as he runs, first toward and then across the screen, that his tie flaps in the wind over his shoulder, marking his speed and power. Once he is set in motion like this, he seems capable of defying anything that chases him, and because the pilot is never seen, the predatory plane takes on an existential quality. It is anything and everything that threatens him.

The crop-dusting scene can summon very specific meanings for those familiar with Cary Grant's life story (and, as we shall see, he was keen to tell his life story to the press during this period). The demonic plane may represent everything that this most polished of gentleman distanced himself from: the messiness of his childhood, his marriages, and his depression and anxiety. All of the secrets that he kept, and all of the lies and half-truths that he told to the press over the years, might be embodied in the plane that seems to be both careering out of control and determinedly bearing down on him. On a broader level, and for those who have no knowledge of this star, the power of the scene may derive from the contrast between this most modern of men—the smartly tailored urban executive—and a more rugged past represented by the bleak prairie and the primitive machinery of the single-engine propeller plane. He belongs to the coddled lifestyle of the city and the suburbs, and he appears utterly lost and defenseless on this frontier landscape. Yet his dominance in the frame, and the determination seen in his face, also suggest his vitality and his will to survive. The white-collar worker who seemed so complacent is now endowed with a dynamic masculinity. From this point onward, Thornhill is newly energized and aggressive in his quest.

In the fourth act of his odyssey, he dusts the prairie dirt from his suit and heads straight back to Chicago to confront Eve about her treachery; firstly in her hotel room, where she placates him with a drink and an offer to have his suit pressed, and secondly in an auction room, where he sees for the first time that she is with Vandamm. In both scenes, he is eager to cast her as a *femme fatale*. "She puts her heart into her work, in fact, her whole *body*," he tells Vandamm. Cornered by Vandamm's henchmen in the auction room, he escapes by being so obnoxious and disruptive that the police are called to arrest him. This enables the Professor to make contact with him and explain the story to him at last. Hitchcock wisely buries most of the expository dialogue beneath the roar of an airplane engine, but the dialogue comes to the fore again when the Professor tells him that Eve is a double agent and his spiteful accusations may have alerted Vandamm to this. "I'm sure you didn't mean it," the Professor tells him, "but I'm afraid you've put her in an extremely dangerous situation." As he says this, the camera moves in for a close-up of Thornhill, whose remorseful look registers, for the first time in the film, that he cares about someone other than himself.

Just as his remorse registers, there is a dissolve to Mount Rushmore so that, just for a few seconds, Cary's face is superimposed on the patriotic figures carved into the mountainside. This is perhaps Hitchcock's greatest tribute to his favorite star: the suggestion that he is as admired and iconic as any of the figures carved into the mountain. Yet where Washington, Jefferson, Roosevelt, and Lincoln appear stern, distant, and immobile, Cary-as-Thornhill is pressed into action on behalf of his country, and as an actor too. Back in the auction rooms, when Vandamm suggested that he was a bad actor, Thornhill replied, "Apparently the only performance that will satisfy you is when I play dead," and this is exactly what he does in the next scene. A meeting with Vandamm in the Visitor's Center below the monument culminates in Eve pulling out a pistol and shooting Thornhill not once but twice. He crumbles as the bullets hit him, then twists, turns, and staggers to the floor with his eyes registering shock and disbelief as he goes down. It is a performance worthy of any method actor, and one that convinces Vandamm, who watches as Thornhill is pronounced dead and his inert body is carried away on a stretcher.

North by Northwest is such a roller-coaster ride that it comes as no real surprise when the car that carried Thornhill's body away from the Visitor's Center pulls into a discreet wooded glade and Thornhill emerges, unharmed and looking as sharp as ever. The killing was staged to provide an opportunity

Photograph 26.46 Thornhill "puts his body into his work" when Eve (Eva Marie Saint) shoots him with blanks.
Source: author's screen capture

for him to meet with Eve, and in the protected covering of the wood they exchange apologies and explain their actions to one another. Thornhill assumes that Eve will be free when Vandamm leaves the country that night, and he is outraged to find that her government minders expect her to accompany Vandamm on a journey overseas. "Perhaps you ought to try learning how to lose a few cold wars!" Thornhill says angrily to the Professor. This is one of the film's only references to any contemporary reality for this spy story. Otherwise, there is little sense that the film is concerned with anything other than finding moral fiber in Thornhill, but in this instance his outburst results in him being knocked out by a park ranger and therefore prevented from stopping Eve's departure.

Thornhill's newly chivalrous nature is signaled in the fifth act of the film by a change of clothes. It is unclear why the park ranger's punch deprives him of the gray suit that remained intact through all of the other calamities, but when Thornhill awakens in a hospital, he has no clothing. Like a newborn baby, he is clad only in a towel, but he looks as muscular and tanned as any Hollywood star. The Professor brings him new clothes—an off-the-peg combination of dark trousers and a plain white shirt, which costumes him more democratically as a middle American everyman.[13] Yet there is no diminishing Cary Grant's star aura. When he escapes the Professor by climbing out of the hospital window, and then in through the window of the neighboring room, the woman occupying the room cries out, "Stop!," and then, putting on her glasses, says more invitingly, "*Stop*." But there is no stopping Thornhill now.

As in the finale of *Notorious*, when Devlin saves Alicia from the clutches of Sebastian and his wicked mother, Thornhill is transformed into a Prince Charming intent on saving the imperiled princess from the evil palace. In *North by Northwest* the palace is not a gothic mansion but a stunningly modern Frank Lloyd Wright–style house. Thornhill scales the exterior so that he can spy on the spies, and learns that Vandamm intends to kill Eve by throwing her from an airplane over open water. The ensuing denouement is one of Hitchcock's most spectacular chase sequences. After running from the house, Thornhill and Eve find themselves pursued by Vandamm's henchmen across the steep façade of Mount Rushmore itself.

As they cling precariously to the rock face, hiding from the henchmen, Thornhill proposes marriage to Eve. She accepts, but as soon as she does, she slips from her perch, and tears a strip from his trousers as she falls. It is always this way in Cary Grant films: romantic commitment entails disorder, humiliation, and chaos. Thornhill is then pounced upon and must wrestle with one of the henchmen on a cliff face. Surviving that, he prevents Eve from a vertiginous fall by holding her with one hand, while his other hand is stepped on by another henchman. A gunshot brings the ordeal to an end. The henchmen are dead, Vandamm is in handcuffs, and, in the finale, Thornhill lifts Eve up to safety. The scene echoes the ending of *Bringing Up Baby*, when David lifted Susan on the platform as the brontosaurus collapsed beneath her. This time, however, there is an additional, concluding scene. The shot of him lifting Eve up from the cliff-face jumps to a shot of him lifting her onto the upper berth of a train bed as he says, "Come on, Mrs. Thornhill." The next and last shot, of a train rushing into a tunnel, is a visual joke and yet it also represents, as Robin Wood has observed, "the 'phallic symbol' toward which the whole film has moved."[14] At last, Thornhill had proven himself to be more than a "red herring." He has found strength, moral fiber, and purpose in his journey, and, as in so many Cary Grant films, the "bachelor" character finally accepts the commitment and maturity that comes with marriage. Of course, he accepts this only in the last 30 seconds of the film; the pleasure of the film is the long path to acceptance rather than whatever follows it. After five acts spread over 130 minutes, he accepts it with a smile at the end of *North by Northwest*.

It was a long shoot and, for Cary, an unusually arduous one. His character is in every scene except a single one in which government spies meet to discuss his plight. Otherwise, he is called upon not only to carry the film but also to keep the audience apprised of its twists and turns. According to the scriptwriter Ernest Lehman, Cary's initial enthusiasm for the film quickly dissipated. "Suddenly, all Cary could think about and talk about was how desperately he wanted out of the movie," Lehman recalled. "The role was all wrong for him. The picture would be a disaster, etcetera, etcetera." Cary resented being laden with expository dialogue, and he did not understand some of the specific plot details. "What's all this got to do with Mount Rushmore?" he asked Lehman, and "What *is* on the microfilm?" When Lehman could not answer, he grew wary of the film.[15]

He had some understandable concerns. Lehman developed the script from two initially unrelated story ideas that he and Hitchcock relished. One was the murder of a UN delegate within the General Assembly itself. The other was the idea of a pursuit across the faces of Mount Rushmore. The writer and director realized that these two ideas could be combined to create a chase story beginning in New York and ending on Mount Rushmore. An early title, "The Man on Lincoln's Nose," gave way to "Breathless!" and then to "In a Northwesterly Direction," but the emphasis was always on a long chase full of unexpected twists and turns.[16] The title *North by Northwest*, as many have noted, is derived from Shakespeare, and Hamlet's assertion that "I am but mad north-north-west: when the wind is southerly I know a hawk from a handsaw."[17] In parallel, Roger Thornhill can be seen as a complacent, feckless, pampered city slicker, but when fate turns against him, he sharpens into a chivalrous, determined, and committed protagonist.

As tempting as it is to think that Cary and Hitch were finally making their modern-day *Hamlet* when they embarked on *North by Northwest*, the script was not finished when filming began, and during the filming Lehman was still writing and rewriting scenes.[18] Cary was never one to object to rewrites or improvisation during filming—in fact he often insisted on it—but in this case he struggled to grasp the broader tone and purpose of the unfinished script. Lehman and Hitchcock were loosely remaking Hitchcock's *The 39 Steps* (1935), a story defined by its original author, John Buchan, as a "shocker" in which the "incidents defy the probabilities and march just inside the borders of the possible."[19] The trouble for Cary was that, while the script remained incomplete, it appeared too improbable. "It's a terrible script," he complained to Hitchcock midway through the shoot, "I still can't make head or tail of it."[20] Nevertheless, there is no doubt that his performance is a master class in screen acting, demonstrating his grace and athleticism on-screen, his unrivaled comic timing, and his carefully nuanced gestures and facial expressions.[21] Indeed, the story of *North by Northwest* is told through his performance rather than exposition. It is always clear what he is thinking, and what he will do next, by watching his eyes in particular. They convey his thoughts with seemingly effortless transparency and efficiency.

Photograph 26.47 Despite some tensions while making *North by Northwest*, Cary and "Hitch" appear amicable.

Source: The Cary Grant Papers, courtesy of the Margaret Herrick Library

Filming began with location shooting at the United Nations building in New York on August 27, 1958.[22] Hitchcock could not get permission to film inside the building or on its grounds, and so the exterior shots were done covertly, with a camera hidden in a truck across the street. In the film, when Cary emerges from a taxi and strides quickly up to the plaza in front of the building, he is walking among members of the public rather than "extras," and at least one of them does a double take as he passes. There were "extras" for the scenes filmed at Grand Central Station, which were filmed in the middle of the night when the station was closed.[23] A short stretch of Madison Avenue was blocked off to shoot the film's first scene, and, like George Kaplan, Cary stayed at the Plaza during the shoot, and so he could simply take the elevator down to the lobby when they were ready to film his scene there. A journalist watching Hitchcock film the scene was surprised to see that director and star did not confer before filming Cary striding across the lobby. "He's been walking across this lobby for years," Hitchcock explained. "I don't need to tell him how."[24]

The cast and crew then moved on to Chicago where they stayed at the Ambassador East Hotel as they filmed scenes in the hotel and at Union Station.[25] Cary had one of the hotel's penthouse suites, and his neighbor was Judy Garland, who was in the midst of a seven-night run of concerts at the Orchestra Hall. He and Eva Marie Saint went to her final show, trying to be discreet by arriving just as the lights dimmed but still causing a stir.[26] Then it was on to Rapid City, South Dakota, for two days of filming at nearby Mount Rushmore National Park. The park officials would not let the cameras get near the monument itself.[27] Hitchcock had spoken too flippantly about filming "The Man on Lincoln's Nose" and they were not amused by his lack of "reverence" for this "national shrine."[28] They allowed filming only in the parking lot and the Visitor's Center, and even this caused a bit of a stir. One local commentator asked, "I wonder how Hitchcock and Grant, both born in England, would feel if a grown man were to play hide and seek on a statue of Queen Victoria?"[29]

The refusal to film on the monument was hardly a blow to Hitchcock. All along, from New York to South Dakota, the plan was to film key establishing shots on location, and then return to the studio to film the majority of scenes. This included the scenes on Mount Rushmore itself. The vertiginous scenes of Thornhill and Eve clinging to the mountain were actually filmed in the relative comfort and safety of an MGM soundstage, where a replica of the monument was built.[30] The crop-dusting scene was shot on an isolated stretch of road near Blackwells Corner, California, in the San Joaquin Valley, which stood in for the Midwest.[31] They filmed there for five days in October, with Cary taking refuge from the sweltering heat in his air-conditioned limousine.[32] Only the long shots were filmed there, however; the closer shots of him ducking and diving into the dirt were filmed in the studio, with the airplane back-projected on a screen behind him.[33] The artful matching of these shots and the careful editing, together with the extraordinary spectacle, make this one of the most convincing scenes ever to be faked in a studio.

There were some tensions during the shoot. When Cary first saw the sets built for the train scenes, he immediately pointed out their deficiencies, and without flinching at the time or expense involved, Hitchcock ordered them to be rebuilt to a higher standard.[34] It is unclear whether the director actually agreed with his star or simply knew it was better to give in to his exacting standards. There was also a very awkward moment during the filming of the elevator scene, when Thornhill's skeptical mother asks the henchmen, "You gentlemen aren't *really* trying to kill my son, are you?" Cary fretted over the scene, and between takes he commented to Ernest Lehman that Hitchcock did not have a sure hand with light comedy. Hitchcock, unfortunately, overheard him, and he was "furiously offended" by his friend's disloyal and disrespectful comment, although he kept quiet about it and pressed on with the scene.[35]

The tensions were exacerbated by delays in filming that sent production costs, budgeted at $3.6 million, climbing to $4.3 million.[36] Hitchcock was once again earning less than Cary—he had a salary of $250,000 while Cary's salary was $300,000—and both men would also get 10 percent of the earnings once the production costs were returned twice over. Cary's salary, though, covered only twelve weeks of shooting, ending on November 7, and after that date his contract stipulated that he would be paid the sum of $5,000 per day.[37] Hence, as production entered its thirteenth week, and then its fourteenth, fifteenth, and finally its sixteenth week of production, his salary spiraled upward to $465,000.[38] This inflated sum ate into the film's profit margin, diminishing the additional income that Hitchcock eventually hoped to receive. Hitchcock must have wondered, at some point before filming finished on December 18, if Cary's star power was really powerful enough to warrant the extraordinary cost he brought to a film. It is notable that in his next films, *Psycho* (1960) and *The Birds* (1963), he avoided using major stars, and let his own name serve as the star attraction.

Critics certainly regarded *North by Northwest* as a Hitchcock film first and foremost. "*North by Northwest* upholds Hitchcock suspense genius" was the headline of Philip K. Scheuer's review in the *Los Angeles Times*. Like many other critics, Scheuer mentions the film's stars, its wonderful musical score, and its screenwriter only briefly and in passing.[39] Worse, from Cary's point of view, was the faint praise of critics such A. H. Weiler, who observed in the *New York Times* that "Cary Grant was never more at home than in this role as the advertising-man-on-the-lam."[40] The assumption that he was "playing himself" on-screen, and this was somehow an easy thing to do, had long annoyed him.[41] There was careful "technique" involved in appearing "natural" on-screen, he often commented, although critics seldom recognized it.[42]

Cary did not join Hitchcock and Eva Marie Saint at the *North by Northwest* premiere in Chicago on July 2, 1959, but a few weeks later he went into the MGM commissary for lunch and he saw Hitchcock seated at a table across the room. With everyone in the dining room watching, Cary crossed the room, got down on his knees, and "salaamed the director exaggeratedly."[43] After the tensions on the set, this was a public display of humility. It was also a display of gratitude, because as soon as *North by Northwest* was released, it was clear that it would become the biggest hit of Cary's career (at that time). Its box-office earnings climbed to $5.7 million in North America and $4.1 million in foreign markets. The profit from this first theatrical release (after production, publicity, and distribution costs were taken into account) was a rather slim $837,000, but the film's frequent revivals and re-releases would add considerably to that figure.[44]

In 1959, and despite its popularity, there are few signs that *North by Northwest* was regarded as a film that would fascinate audiences for decades to come. The critical favorites that year were *Ben Hur*, *The Nun's Story*, and *The Diary of Anne Frank*, and it was these rather solemn and earnest films that were recognized by the Academy Awards, the Golden Globe Awards, and the New York Critics Awards. By contrast, *North by Northwest* is funnier and more flippant, and therein lies a large part of both its influence and its enduring appeal. Its influence is seen most immediately in the decision to bring Ian Fleming's James Bond novels to the screen, beginning with *Dr. No* in 1963. The similarly dapper, debonair, and ironically detached Bond would also fend off every plot contrivance that a spy story could throw at him.[45] Over a longer term, *North by Northwest* also became emblematic of 1950s America, and particularly the unquestioning affluence, consumerism, and complacency of the Eisenhower era. The acclaimed television series *Mad*

Men (2007–2015) is a far darker exploration of that era, but its creators were clearly eager to acknowledge the inspiration they drew from *North by Northwest*. The series' opening credits borrow imagery directly from the film, and although its tall, dark, and handsome main character, the advertising executive Don Draper (Jon Hamm), is a more toxic incarnation of Roger Thornhill, he too combines beguilingly debonair and morally vapid traits.

The beauty of *North by Northwest* is that, amid the breathlessly exhilarating ride that it takes us on, it lays bare Thornhill's superficial nature while also reassuring us that there is some substance to this most modern of men. This is the narrative arc common not only to many of Cary Grant's films but also to much of Cary Grant's publicity, which aims to explain his transition from Archie Leach to Cary Grant in terms of an American success story rather than a show-business conjuring act. In *North by Northwest*, it is also plain to see that his reinvention has provided him with some form of the fountain of youth. He is as athletic and glamorous as ever in his mid-fifties. Roger O. Thornhill's initials may spell out "rot," as Eve points out, but ultimately Cary-as-Thornhill promises agelessness as well as virtue behind the glamour. It is the ultimate Cary Grant film because it allows the audience to believe that someone as fabricated as Cary Grant could exist; that the star's reinvention of himself was as seamless and authentic as Thornhill's transition from selfish playboy to ardent savior.

By the late 1950s, Cary himself had finally come to realize how troublesome his own reinvention of himself had been, how much he had buried and denied in order to live his new life. As a means of grappling with this revelation, and dealing with the breakdown of his third marriage, he had gone into a form of therapy based on the hallucinogenic drug LSD. He soon declared that LSD was a wonder drug, and told reporters that he was a new and saved man. Over time, however, he would find that personal transformations are not as swift and seamless as the movies suggest, and that inner demons are not so quickly or easily evaded as crop-dusting assassins.

27

In October 1958, while Cary was filming *North by Northwest*, he and Betsy announced their separation in a press release:

> After careful consideration and long discussion, we have decided to live apart. We have had, and shall always have, the deepest respect for each other. But, alas, our marriage has not brought us the happiness we fully expected and mutually desired. So, since we have no children needful of our affections, it is consequently best that we separate for a while. There are no plans for divorce and we ask only that our statement be respected as being complete. We ask our friends to be patient with, and understanding of, our decision.[1]

Their respect for one another was real. He and Betsy would remain in close contact for several years and on friendly terms for the rest of their lives. But the statement's measured tone masks the upheaval and soul searching that they had been through in recent years. It was Betsy who first turned to LSD as a form of therapy. She had been miserable in their marriage ever since Cary spent the summer of 1956 in Spain with Sophia Loren. In 1957, Betsy confided her unhappiness to a close friend, the television actress Sally Brophy, who told her about a psychotherapist who was treating her for depression, using "a wonder drug." The sessions took place at the recently opened (and rather grandly named) Psychiatric Institute of Beverly Hills. Betsy, eager to try anything that might ease her despair and save her marriage, made an appointment at the institute. This was the first of her many sessions with LSD.[2]

In the 1950s, very few people had heard of lysergic acid diethylamide.[3] The drug had been discovered in 1938 by the Swiss chemist Albert Hoffman while he was working as a researcher for the pharmaceutical company Sandoz. Several years later he stumbled upon the drug's hallucinogenic qualities when he accidentally ingested a tiny amount in his laboratory; a scenario not unlike the starting point of *Monkey Business*, except that LSD filled Hoffman with "fear and despair" rather than youthful energy. The intense hallucinations he experienced, together with the sense that his ego had vanished and he had gained access to his unconscious mind, led Hoffman to believe that the drug could have potential as a psychiatric medicine. Sandoz released the drug to university researchers, with the aim of exploring its potential as a treatment for psychosis and schizophrenia. By the mid-1950s, it had been adopted by a small number of adventurous psychotherapists. They noted that the drug has the capacity to unlock forgotten or repressed experiences and traumas, allowing patients not only to recollect but to relive such experiences.[4]

In 1957, LSD was still so little known that when Betsy told a dinner party gathering (including Cary, Clifford Odets, and the violinist Jascha Heifetz) that she was going to try it, they showed little interest or alarm.[5] LSD was not yet associated with hippies or psychedelics (terms not yet in common use), it was not considered a recreational or inebriating drug, and it was not illegal. It was a rare and experimental form of psychotherapy, available only to well-connected and wealthy patients. At the Psychiatric Institute of Beverly Hills, it was on offer at $100 a session. The "institute" was set up by just two doctors, radiologist Mortimer Hartman and psychiatrist Arthur Chandler, who saw the drug as offering a kind of fast-tracked Freudian therapy, allowing patients direct access to their unconscious. The patients, they assured the Sandoz company, were mere "garden variety neurotics."[6]

Betsy found that LSD helped her come to terms with her harrowing experience on the ill-fated *Andrea Doria*, and eventually, it also gave her the courage and clarity to realize that she needed to separate from Cary. Before then, at some point in 1957, Cary became so intrigued by Betsy's accounts of her experiences that he booked an appointment for himself. This would be the first of many Saturdays that he spent at the institute. The days began at eight in the morning, when he went into a small, private room and took two tiny blue pills with a glass of water. He chose his own background music—jazz—for the record player, and he lay down on a psychiatrist's couch, wearing an eye mask to keep out the light. Dr. Hartman monitored his progress over the eight to ten hours that the drug affected him, sometimes sitting at his side and listening to him describe what he was experiencing, sometimes prompting him with a word or suggestion to help him along, and sometimes leaving him alone and asking afterward what had transpired.[7]

For Cary, the drug was revelatory because, nearly forty years after leaving home, it allowed him to peer into his own past. He could see how far he had traveled from being Archie Leach, and he could acknowledge how difficult it was to live up to the image of Cary Grant. He described one session spent "turning and turning" around on the couch. He could not understand why, and he could not stop himself from turning, until Dr. Hartman made him realize that he was trying to "unscrew" himself because he now realized how "screwed-up" he was.[8] "I've been going around in a fog," he concluded. "You are just a bunch of molecules until you know who you are. You spend your time getting to be a big Hollywood actor, but then what?" While LSD allowed the fog to lift, the question of "then what?" would prove harder to solve.[9]

Cary's truth-seeking, mystical quest did not begin with LSD but had been developing, with the encouragement of Betsy, for several years. Five years earlier, she had learned hypnosis and used this to help Cary stop smoking. He woke up the next day astonished that he no longer wanted to smoke, and he eagerly related this to the press. He soon embraced "self-hypnosis" and insisted that this had enabled him to heal a cut on his back suffered while filming the duel scene in *The Pride and the Passion*. He told a reporter, "Every morning and every night, I said to myself, 'pure oxygen, being breathed into my body, go directly to my wounds and cleanse them, while all poisons and disease leave me as I exhale.' It worked. In four days there was no sign that I had ever been hurt." Similarly, when he had a lipoma excised from his forehead in 1957, he insisted that the same technique resulted in his facial scar healing in just a few days (in the short break he had between finishing *An Affair to Remember* and starting *Kiss Them for Me*).[10] And when he was asked how he maintained his youthful physique, he insisted that he merely had to remind himself to "think thin."[11] Alfred Hitchcock, who battled against obesity all his adult life, was surely poking fun at this philosophy when he put the same words into the mouth of the glib Roger O. Thornhill in *North by Northwest*.

Yet taking LSD was more than a matter of hypnosis and "thinking thin." Cary thought that the drug had allowed him to be "born again," not in a religious sense but as a man liberated from his neuroses and hang-ups, and he was eager to proselytize about it. As David Niven recalled, Cary started by announcing to his "spellbound friends" that LSD had made him a new man, freeing him from his inhibitions. "All actors long to be loved, that's why we become actors," he told them, "but I don't give a damn anymore. I'm self-sufficient at last!" Niven and the others were startled. "It seemed to the rest of us a most hazardous trip for Cary to have taken to find out what we could have told him anyway: that he had always been self-sufficient, that he had always been loved, and that he would continue to give a damn about himself—and particularly about others."[12]

Eventually, he could not resist proselytizing to reporters. In February 1959, he was on location in Key West, filming *Operation Petticoat* and also doing interviews for the completed but not-yet-released *North by Northwest*. Two of the leading film correspondents, Lionel Crane of Britain's *Sunday Pictorial* newspaper and the American syndicated columnist Joe Hyams, interviewed him separately, expecting to hear the usual fluff about his enthusiasm for his latest film. Hyams was initially taken aback when Cary revealed that he wore women's nylon panties rather than men's cotton underwear while on location. Nylon, he explained, was easier to wash and dry in his hotel room sink. Not realizing that Cary had already revealed this to other reporters, Hyams considered it too odd to print.[13]

When Cary began telling Hyams about his LSD treatments, it was not an incidental anecdote. He spoke of re-experiencing his own birth. He spoke of the "insecurities" of his youth casting a long shadow over his adult life ("the things that are done to us when we are young affect us all our lives"). He spoke about his parents and the realization that he needed to forgive them for their shortcomings and love them for "the most useful, the best, the wisest of their teachings." He spoke about seeking love and approval through acting, and revealed that his marriages failed because of his inability to love. He concluded that he had been "an utter fake, a self-opinionated bore, a know-all who knew very little" until LSD opened his eyes and allowed him to find his real self.[14]

"May I publish this?" Hyams asked incredulously. "Not yet, but the time's coming and I'll let you know when I'm ready," Cary responded. Hyams respected Cary's wishes until he discovered that Cary had given Lionel Crane much the same interview without asking Crane to withhold publication. The revelations had already been printed in the British *Sunday Pictorial*.[15] Hyams therefore decided to proceed with publication in the *New York Herald Tribune*, and his interview was picked up for national syndication. On the eve of publication, Cary got wind of what was coming and demanded that Hyams stop the presses, but it was too late. Headlines such as "Reborn Star Says He's Happy, No Longer a Fake" were splashed across the front pages of newspapers across the United States in April 1959.[16]

Cary, reeling from this exposé, issued a hasty press release. "I've never had an interview with Hyams," he claimed. "The interview is completely erroneous."[17] Yet Hyams had taped the interview, and he and Cary had been photographed together.[18] This public relations disaster was entirely uncharacteristic of Cary, who always played the press so skillfully. His enthusiasm for LSD led him to lower his guard and, in a changing Hollywood, he and other stars no longer had the protection of the studio system. Power within the industry was increasingly decentralized, and journalists did not have to tread as carefully as they had in the past. It is telling that the longest-serving columnist, Louella Parsons, was the first to come to Cary's defense, pouring scorn on Hyams in her column.[19] But Hyams understood that the rules had changed and he did not have to be as solicitous of stars as his predecessors were. He sued Cary for libel, as well as damages of $500,000, and Cary was forced to seek an out-of-court settlement with him.

It is telling that Cary allowed Lionel Crane to print his interview in a British tabloid newspaper, but he did not want Hyams's similar interview appearing in American newspapers. The British tabloids would not be taken seriously by powerful or influential people, but American newspapers were another matter. The idea that he was undergoing "psychiatric treatment," and that he now realized he had been a "fake" for most of his life, could potentially harm his reputation in the industry and with audiences. He was not willing to give up on being "a big Hollywood actor" just yet. He quickly lined up another, more sympathetic interview in the popular *Look* magazine.

In the *Look* profile, LSD figured as the key to the happiness that "the new Cary Grant" had found, but it was not the sole focus of the article. His success, his fine physique, and his amicable separation from Betsy were also discussed. He revealed his mother's mental illness for the first time in public, telling the interviewer that Elsie had suffered a "severe mental breakdown" when he was a child. He acknowledged that his LSD therapy made him realize that, ever since her disappearance, he felt rejected by his mother and he had avoided women with her dark-haired, olive-skinned looks. He admitted, obliquely, that he had fallen in love with Sophia Loren, and that, more recently, he had become romantically involved with Loren's on-set "double," Ljubica Otavesic.[20] She was a former basketball player, who left Yugoslavia for London to pursue her ambitions to become an actress. He and the twenty-six-year-old "Luba," as he called her, had an on-again, off-again romance during his visits to London.[21]

Cary's revelations appalled at least one reader. Hedda Hopper had become more caustic as movie-going declined and her own status and relevance diminished.[22] When she read the *Look* article, she immediately wrote (privately) to the magazine's editor, Mike Cowles, complaining that it was "the damnest [sic] mish-mash I have ever read" and suggesting that Cowles should let her write about Hollywood stars. "This may surprise you," she wrote about Cary; "He started with boys and now he has gone back to them." She alleged that Cary was having an affair with his (male) chauffeur, "and he's using a lot of pretty girls to cover up."[23] If this was true, it was a very elaborate cover-up. After his separation from Betsy, Cary was involved not only with Luba Otavesic but with the actress Kim Novak, the fashion model Aurora Moore, and the British pop singer Alma Cogan.[24]

LSD may have turned Cary into a truth seeker and a mystic (he called Dr. Hartman "my wise Mahatma"), but he also remained, rather incongruously, a playboy and a remarkably savvy businessman.[25] When he finished *North by Northwest*, his last four films had been made for four different studios. His next deal demonstrated that he understood how significantly the industry was changing, and how he could take advantage of the changes. He took advice from the powerful Hollywood agent Lew Wasserman, but he refused to sign with Wasserman's MCA talent agency.[26] Instead, he continued to represent himself with Stanley Fox on retainer to handle legal matters. When MCA took over Universal-International Pictures, Universal's new priority was to sign high-profile filmmakers to produce independently on the studio lot and then allow Universal to release the films.[27] Alfred Hitchcock had already signed at Universal. Cary would, too, but not before he demanded—and held out for—an historic deal.

Universal was the only one of the eight leading Hollywood studios that Cary had yet to work with, and the studio finally signed him by allowing him the most favorable terms. It agreed to front the production money for his films, with budgets up to $3 million, even though the films would be made without studio supervision and by Cary's own production companies (set up with each film's director and/or co-star participating). Cary would take an advance salary of $300,000 and his production company would take 75 percent of the film's profits or 10 percent of its gross rental earnings (whichever was higher). Significantly, in the age of television, ownership of each film would revert to his companies seven years after its release. Universal's take was a distributor's fee (30 percent of the box-office gross) plus 25 percent of the profits. The deal was lined up in December 1958, and for just one film, *Operation Petticoat*, but when that film proved to be a runaway hit, it was extended for four more films. In the midst of this, *Variety* estimated that Cary was making $3 million per film, and, on its front page, it dubbed him the industry's "richest actor" and "one of the most astute businessmen now operating in the industry."[28]

Operation Petticoat was initially conceived as a comedy for Tony Curtis, one centered, like so many other 1950s films, on Second World War service. It was directed by the thirty-seven-year-old Blake Edwards, who had a few directing credits behind him but many more to come. The comedy writers Stanley Shapiro and Maurice Richlin were developing the original story. The expectation was that it would be made in black and white for $1 million, with Curtis top-billed, and a second-billed actor playing his older, commanding officer.[29] Jeff Chandler, Henry Fonda, and Robert Taylor were among those considered. Then Curtis read the script and saw that it was set on a submarine during the Second World War. Recalling *Destination Tokyo*, Curtis insisted that Universal should at least ask Cary if he would consider the role. Much to everyone's surprise, Cary wanted to play it.[30]

Curtis had long regarded Cary as his screen idol. *Destination Tokyo* inspired him to volunteer for the navy, and during a long tour of duty, *Gunga Din* was one of the few films on board his ship. Curtis and his shipmates watched it so many times that they began screening it without the sound, voicing the roles themselves.[31] Fifteen years later, when Curtis had become a film star, his impersonation of Cary was so fine-tuned that he volunteered to perform it in Billy Wilder's cross-dressing comedy, *Some Like It Hot* (1959). Playing a down-on-his-luck saxophonist, he adopts Cary's accent when pretending to be a high-society millionaire as a means of impressing Marilyn Monroe. When his friend, played by Jack Lemmon, overhears him, he says, "Where did you get that *phony* accent? Nobody talks like that!" The joke is, of course, that everyone knows Cary talks like that. When they met on the set of *Operation Petticoat*, Curtis was relieved that Cary did not take offense at this. He told Curtis that he was amused and flattered by his impersonation.[32]

Bringing Cary into *Operation Petticoat* entailed a major overhaul of just about every aspect of the production, but Universal jumped at the chance to work with him. The script was revised for him, his company (Granart Films) took over the production, and the film was financed on his terms. With Cary on board, *Operation Petticoat* became a $3 million production made in color and widescreen, and with extensive location shooting in and around a naval base in Key West (standing in for the Philippines). Cary flew to Key West on January 18, 1959, his fifty-fifth birthday, to start six weeks of filming there followed by a further six weeks of filming on the Universal studio lot back in California.[33]

Operation Petticoat opens in the present day of 1959, as Lieutenant Commander Matt Sherman (Cary), arrives at the USS *Sea Tiger*, a docked submarine that is about to be retired, and goes on board to recall his days as captain. A flashback begins as he wistfully reads the log he kept in December 1941, when the submarine came under attack from the Japanese while stationed in the Philippines. The opening thus allows Cary to demonstrate that he can play both the gray-haired senior officer of 1959 and the much younger captain of 1941. The opening scenes also echo *Destination Tokyo*, which begins with his arrival on the submarine and uses the captain's writings as a narrational device. Yet *Operation Petticoat* is not a remake of *Destination Tokyo* so much as a revisioning of it as a sex comedy. The *Sea Tiger* does not go on a perilous mission to Tokyo, but instead ends up involved in a series of shenanigans that are played for laughs even as the men struggle to find a safe harbor in Japanese-controlled waters.

Initially, the comedy arises from the clash between Cary's strict, ship-shape-and-Bristol-fashion Captain Sherman and the new arrival on board, the louche Lieutenant Nick Holden (Tony Curtis). Holden is the kind of character Cary sometimes played at Paramount in the early 1930s: a strikingly handsome sophisticate, who wears his pristine white uniform as though he is prepared for a catwalk rather than naval duty. Holden's polish, like Cary's, belies a rough-and-tough upbringing, and he proves tougher and more resourceful than he looks. As the supply officer, he stocks the submarine with much-needed supplies by pilfering them rather than waiting on the navy bureaucracy to provide them. The more sustained humor arises when Captain Sherman is compelled to transport five stranded American nurses on the *Sea Tiger*, living in very close quarters with the men. At first, the women are merely in the way, but gradually they are integrated into the submarine's day-to-day life to the point that the vessel itself is painted pink, its engine is fixed by using a girdle to replace a broken valve, and, when an American war ship mistakenly attacks the submarine, the vessel is saved by releasing the women's brassieres into the water around the ship. The captain of the war ship recognizes that the pink submarine must be American when he fishes one of the brassieres from the water. Holding it up to admire its shape and size, he declares, "The Japanese have nothing like *this*."

The film follows a familiar comic path of pushing Cary's cool, calm character to breaking point, not least when he is showing one of the nurses the shower cubicle, and she inadvertently turns on the tap and douses him in water. But there was one indignity he refused to perform. There is a scene in the film in which Lieutenant Holden and another sailor (played by Gavin MacLeod) steal a pig from a local farmer, taking it back to the submarine for

Christmas dinner. The scene is played as slapstick, as they struggle to capture the pig and get it into their vehicle, and then when they are stopped at a road-block and disguise the pig as a sailor (putting a coat and hat on it) to evade detection. Just before the scene was filmed, director Blake Edwards suddenly had the idea that it would be much funnier if it was played by Lieutenant Holden and Captain Sherman; that is, if Cary was seen wrestling with the pig (echoing his encounter with the leopards in *Bringing Up Baby*). Edwards and the writers pleaded with Cary to try this. "We got down on our knees and said, 'You own the film; you can get rid of the scene if you don't think it's any good, but let us show you what we're talking about it!'" But Cary thought it would be an indignity too far, and he refused to do it.[34]

"It ended up being a rather unpleasant experience," Edwards said about the making of *Operation Petticoat*, adding, "There was great personal conflict between Cary and myself." This was partly due to a power struggle between Cary and the young Edwards, who wanted to assert his authority as director. It was also due to two quite different senses of humor. When Cary tried to improvise on set, with additional bits of dialogue or routines, Edwards rejected his suggestions just as strongly as Cary rejected playing a scene with a pig.[35] Cary got on much better with Tony Curtis, who loved working with his idol. "Cary became a kind and committed friend to me," Curtis said. "He represented the best of what a father would be, the best of what a brother would be, and the best of what a fellow worker would be."[36]

One of the chief pleasures of *Operation Petticoat* is watching these two stars together, and enjoying the balance they achieve between Cary's restraint and Curtis's more frenetic approach to comedy. If the film does not stand among Cary's best today, it is because the story is built around sexist jokes. Edwards's sense of humor is risqué in the manner of a 1950s *Playboy* magazine cartoon. He had little interest in the women characters beyond making them the butt of jokes. In the film's ending, it is revealed that both Matt and Nick have married two of the nurses (played by Joan O'Brien and Dina Merrill), but the nurses's characters are so thinly drawn that these relationships are scarcely developed.

When *Operation Petticoat* was released in time for Christmas in 1959, many critics pointed out that no one who experienced the difficult times of December 1941 would have expected to see them treated so lightly, so soon. Yet this was surely a key part of the film's appeal. It allows the contemporary audience to look back to the darkest days of the war, obliterating painful memories and emphasizing self-assured good times. As the critics put it, the film treats the war as a "jolly sailor's romp" (New York's *Daily News*). It is "a lightweight piece of nonsense" (*Los Angeles Times*) and "as light as a sack full of feathers" (*Variety*).[37] It was not a film for the smarter set of critics—the reviews in the *New York Times* and the *New Yorker* were especially dismissive—but this did not stop it from becoming the biggest box-office hit of Cary's career.[38] Earnings of $9.3 million in North American and $3.5 million in foreign markets also made it the top-earning film in Universal's long history.[39]

In 1959, the success of both *North by Northwest* and *Operation Petticoat* propelled Cary to second place in the film industry's annual poll of "money-making stars." It was his first time in the top five, where he would remain for the next five years.[40] The only other star of Cary's generation to enjoy this level of success in the early 1960s was John Wayne, but Wayne's films cast him as an aging and often embittered throwback to an earlier age; he was the last of the true cowboys. Cary, by contrast, cut a far more dashing and contemporary figure, and his perpetually youthful appearance had become a cornerstone of his image.

In this, his fourth decade of filming, he enjoyed working with a younger generation of stars at his new studio, Universal. Stars on this vast studio lot did not have mere dressing rooms but their own bungalows, complete with front porches, which they used for socializing at lunchtime and at the end of the day. Marlon Brando, Tony Curtis, Rock Hudson, Shirley MacLaine, and Elizabeth Taylor were among Cary's new neighbors, and old friends Alfred Hitchcock and James Stewart were also nearby.[41]

Now that he made films for his own production companies, Cary was even more involved in pre- and post-production duties. His first task when *Operation Petticoat* finished filming in April 1959 was to fly to London to secure the screen rights to his next film, *The Grass is Greener*, from playwrights Hugh and Margaret Williams.[42] He had seen the play while visiting London over the previous Christmas holiday (during the short break between filming *North by Northwest* and *Operation Petticoat*).[43] Since then it had become a solid West End hit, and Cary and director Stanley Donen planned to revive their Grandon production company to adapt it for the screen. Like Grandon's *Indiscreet*, they envisaged a sophisticated romantic comedy, with a small cast and some location shooting to overcome the staginess of the play. Ingrid Bergman was not available, but just before leaving Hollywood, Cary introduced her as a presenter at the 1959 Academy Awards ceremony. Now that her marriage to Roberto Rosellini was over, her appearance at the ceremony was like a homecoming in which she was welcomed back to the fold. Cary, who had been a loyal friend to her throughout her exile, was with her on stage, holding her hand and beaming at her side.[44] They would continue to search for another film they could make together, but sadly without success.

Cary lined up Rex Harrison and his wife Kay Kendall as his co-stars in *The Grass is Greener*.[45] They would play Victor and Hilary, the Earl and Countess of Rhyall, a happily married couple whose fading fortunes have led them to open their very grand stately home for public tours. Cary was set to play the American "oil millionaire" Charles Delacro, who strays off the tour and into the family quarters, where he meets Hilary and sweeps her off her feet. The staid Victor must find a way of winning his wife's affections again, and his strategy entails asking Charles to join them for a weekend and ultimately challenging him to a duel.

The casting plans changed when Kay Kendall died suddenly at the age of thirty-two, and Rex Harrison did not want to make the film without her. Cary and Stanley Donen then made two unfortunate decisions. The first was that Cary would take Rex Harrison's role and play the stuffy Victor—Cary's first time playing an aristocrat and the first time in decades that he would play a man *not* chased by the leading lady. The second decision was to cast the laconic, slightly portly Robert Mitchum as the dazzlingly irresistible Charles. The other roles were cast more appropriately. Deborah Kerr, co-starring with Cary for the third time, plays the coolly aristocratic Hilary. Jean Simmons plays Hilary's flighty friend, Hattie, and Moray Watson is the dry, calm-headed butler, Sellers.

Cary may have been attracted to *The Grass is Greener* at least in part for its unconventional views on marriage. When Hilary assumes that Victor intends to divorce her, he says, "Who said anything about divorce? I don't like divorce and I don't think adultery is sufficient grounds for it." This appears to have been his personal philosophy as well as his character's. He and Betsy were both openly dating others, and so it confounded observers when Betsy joined him in London for the filming, which began at Shepperton Studios in April 1960. They spent a happy Easter weekend in Monaco with Princess Grace, Prince Rainier, and their two young children.[46] They were spotted in Bristol at weekends too, visiting Elsie, and they had a holiday in Monaco with Princess Grace when filming finished, but they would not confirm or deny rumors of a reconciliation. "We're happily separated-married," Cary told reporters.[47]

The filming lasted for an unusually long sixteen weeks, from April through July 1960. Some delays were caused by Cary. As the film's producer, he was no less exacting about sets and costumes than he was when the money at stake was not his own. The art director had produced stately home interiors as faithfully as possible without realizing that authenticity was not the primary objective. When Cary arrived, he took one look at the high-ceilinged, cavernous sets and ordered them rebuilt in proportions that would not dwarf the actors. As the film's star, he also expected time and care to be taken with his appearance on screen. The cameraman Christopher Challis was taken aback to realize that Cary "had decided ideas about how he should be photographed" and he was offended when Cary proceeded to give him detailed instructions about lighting and camera angles. British studio workers were not accustomed to stars wielding so much power.[48] Stanley Donen, meanwhile, was disappointed to find that the Eastman color stock manufactured in Britain did not work well with the widescreen Technirama format. When viewing the rushes, he recognized that the film's grainy, blue-ish hue was unattractive, but he found that there was little he could do about it.[49]

Location filming was done at Osterley House, the former home of the ninth Earl of Jersey and his wife, who just happened to be Virginia Cherrill. They had long since divorced, and the house—like the fictional house in the film—was taken over by National Trust as a tourist attraction. Donen filmed the building and grounds in a suitably spectacular fashion, with aerial shots displaying its grandeur, and some scenes spilling out from the living areas to the sunny gardens. He also filmed another clever split-screen sequence, as he had in *Indiscreet*. This one depicts a telephone conversation with Victor and Hattie at one end of the line (at home) and Charles and Hilary at the other (at the Savoy in London). The joke is that their responses mirror each other's perfectly, and to achieve this Donen had the two sets built side by side, so that the actors could orchestrate their mimicry in perfect unison.[50]

Yet no matter how inventive Donen was, there is no getting around the fact that the story is a stagey drawing-room comedy, and Cary and Robert Mitchum are miscast as romantic rivals. When *The Grass is Greener* was released in December 1960, critics were quick to highlight these deficiencies. *Variety* praised Cary, but not the film: "It is a tribute to his once-a-generation flair for light comedy that every time he wanders out of eye-and-ear range, the comedy sputters, stammers and stalls."[51] Many critics praised the opening credits, which match the star names with images of toddlers playing on a lawn, more than the film itself. The Noel Coward song that plays over the credits, "The Stately Homes of England" also drew more praise than the story, which was deemed to be "watered-down Noel Coward" (*New York Times*), "a bit more static and talkative than the average film" (*Chicago Tribune*), and "much too conversational" (*Boston Globe*).[52] The mixed reviews hurt at the box office, although North American earnings of $3 million were just enough to place *The Grass is Greener* among the top forty films of the year.[53]

Cary had a striking array of choices for his next film. For more than a year, he had been pursued again by director David Lean, this time to play General Allenby in the epic *Lawrence of Arabia* (1962). He was genuinely intrigued by this, but he prevaricated too long and Lean lost patience with him.[54] "Bugger and blast to the star system!" Lean wrote to his producers before casting the lesser-known Jack Hawkins in the role.[55] Around the same time, producer "Cubby" Broccoli asked Cary to star in the first film of the James Bond series, *Dr. No* (1963). Broccoli was an old friend. They had mutual friends in Howard Hughes and Randolph Scott, and Cary had been the best man at Broccoli's wedding in 1959. But Broccoli was probably relieved when Cary refused to commit to making the envisaged series of films, if only because the still little-known Sean Connery was so much less expensive.[56] Another offer came from Jack Warner, who wanted Cary to play the lead in a screen adaptation of the Broadway hit *The Music Man* (1962). Cary had seen Robert Preston play the role on stage, and he told Warner "nobody can play that role as well as Bob." [57] He might have added that he had no interest in returning to musicals at this point in his career.

Instead, his next film put him on the familiar ground of screwball comedy. *That Touch of Mink* (1962), like *Operation Petticoat*, began as an in-house Universal production co-written by Sidney Shapiro, who had co-authored two money-spinning comedies for Doris Day and Rock Hudson, *Pillow Talk* (1959) and *Lover Come Back* (1961). On the strengths of those films, Shapiro stepped up to a production role on *That Touch of Mink*, but he did not have Day or Hudson in mind for the leading roles.[58] He hoped that Marilyn Monroe would star as Cathy Timberlake, the "small town Cinderella" in New York who meets her Prince Charming when he rides past her in a limousine and inadvertently splatters her dress with muddy water.[59] But *Pillow Talk* and *Lover Come Back* made Doris Day the number-one movie star in the United States.[60] She was at the zenith of her career, and, with Cary on hand to play Prince Charming, in the guise of a millionaire executive Philip Shayne, the story was revised as a vehicle to bring the two stars together for the first time. Cary's production company, this time named Granley Films, co-produced with Doris Day's Arwin Productions and Sidney Shapiro's Nob Hill Productions.

In June 1961, Cary accompanied Doris Day to New York on a shopping trip, picking out the wardrobe that his millionaire executive would buy her unemployed office worker when he whisks her off to Bermuda for a romantic getaway. A tie-in with the department store Bergdorf Goodman was arranged, along with a fashion show set at the store that would feature prominently in the film.[61] The New York trip went smoothly, but when filming began on the Universal lot the following month, there were "touchy moments on the set," when Cary and Doris Day disagreed over set designs and camera angles.[62] "Of all the people I performed with," Day wrote in her memoir, "I got to know Cary least of all. Our relationship was amicable but devoid of give-and-take." He was "very distant."[63] Director Delbert Mann also noted that Cary was reserved on the set, but he recalled that Day, at the age of thirty-eight, was preoccupied by masking her age on the screen.[64] Cary, benefiting from the double standard that deems older men to be "distinguished," embraced a notably more mature look in *That Touch of Mink*, wearing cardigans and allowing more gray hair to show.

On the screen, Doris Day's perky, wholesome persona is not a good match for Cary's more restrained sophisticate. They do not spark off one another in the way that they did with their previous co-stars, and the film seems like a compilation of familiar vignettes, mainly from her films with Rock Hudson. Tamar Jeffers McDonald has pointed out a key difference between *That Touch of Mink* and the Rock Hudson–Doris Day comedies. Although Day consistently plays a woman determined to remain a virgin until she is married, in the films with Rock Hudson his characters employ various forms of subterfuge and manipulation to try to seduce her. This was not the approach of the more mature, dignified Cary Grant. In *That Touch of Mink*, he is straightforward with her, quite plainly offering her a life of luxury as his mistress, but not offering to marry her. She struggles to turn him down because she finds him so attractive.[65]

He is the object of desire, and the central dilemma is whether or not she will give in to her desire for him. This allows her to be the focus of most of the film's comical sequences. When they go to Bermuda, for example, she imagines that everyone on the street and in the hotel sees them in a double bed together. His best moment comes when, in the midst of a taking a shower, he hears that Cathy has gone to a motel with another man. With only a towel covering his body, he runs from the shower and into the street to hail a cab.

This brings some overdue energy to the film, but it scarcely matches the comical shower scenes from so many of his previous films.

As in the Rock Hudson–Doris Day comedies, each character has a sidekick. Gig Young plays Philip's frustrated friend in much the same manner that Tony Randall did in the earlier films, and Audrey Meadows plays Connie's wise-cracking roommate along lines earlier perfected by Thelma Ritter. The film's overly familiar qualities are also not helped by its studio-bound sensibility. Unlike Cary's other recent films, there was no spectacular location shooting for *That Touch of Mink*. Even the exterior New York scenes were filmed on the Warner Bros. backlot in Burbank, and a second unit was dispatched to Bermuda to film with doubles standing in for the stars.[66]

No matter how routine the film feels, and how outdated its jokes about sexuality now seem, it was a huge success when it was released in June 1962. *Variety* acknowledged that the story was so familiar that it was "essentially threadbare," but also asserted that the film's stars and its "jollity" compensated for this.[67] Other reviewers noted that Rock Hudson had been playing Cary Grant parts for years, and so it was good to see Cary Grant taking one himself.[68] The film's North American earnings reached $8.5 million, placing it among the top five films of the year.[69]

That Touch of Mink ends with Philip and Cathy on honeymoon in Bermuda. On their earlier trip, the consummation of their affair was prevented when she broke out in a rash. This time, it is his anxiety about giving up his long-cherished bachelordom that causes him to break out in a rash. Even at the age of fifty-seven, Cary could still play the reluctant, highly desirable bachelor. This was true off the screen as well. Over the previous year, he had an affair with Greta Thyssen, a former Miss Denmark (in the Miss Universe contest).[70] Thyssen told an interviewer that Cary was very frank with her about the terms of their affair. "He told me many times that even if he loved me, he could also love someone else he might meet," and he urged her to be as open-minded as he was. "I might love you today, but I can make no promises if I find someone as pretty as you tomorrow," he stated plainly. They enjoyed dining in fine restaurants, by candlelight, and with violins serenading them, and so she was not surprised, the first time she was invited to dinner at Beverly Grove, to find a similarly romantic atmosphere. However, she was surprised when he announced that dinner would be served in the bedroom and that they would be eating off trays on the bed. This was not a seduction technique, but a means for them to watch television together as they ate. "The housekeeper being there makes it okay," Greta insisted in an interview.[71]

Hollywood's most debonair star, its most-sought after bachelor, was a huge fan of television. He wanted nothing to do with it professionally. Suspecting that big-screen stars diminished themselves by appearing on small screens in people's living rooms, he declined requests to guest-star on programs such as *Alfred Hitchcock Presents* (1955–1965) and *The Judy Garland Show* (1963–1964).[72] Nevertheless, he loved watching TV. It was in the summer of 1961, while filming *That Touch of Mink*, that he first saw the actress Dyan Cannon on a program called *Malibu Run* (1960–1961). He was so attracted to her that he used his contacts to arrange a meeting. She was wary of this sort of set-up and initially she resisted, but eventually curiosity got the better of her. They met and soon began dating. With Dyan, Cary did not insist that his affections might wander at will, or that his love for her today might be forgotten tomorrow.[73] Betsy, watching the relationship develop from afar, realized in July 1962 that, after four years of separation, it was time to file for divorce.[74] Cary, believing that LSD had freed him from his demons, thought that he was now ready to love unconditionally, to marry, and to start a family. And so, at the very peak of his popularity, he began to contemplate retiring from films altogether.[75]

PART FIVE

LEGEND, 1962 TO 1986

28

"Do you know what's wrong with you?" Audrey Hepburn asks Cary Grant in *Charade* (1963) before answering her own question with a wistful, "*nothing.*" The scene has become one of the best known in his career because it sums up, so succinctly, the enormous public admiration and affection that he enjoyed in the years before his retirement. The revelations about his use of LSD did little, if anything, to dent his reputation. His latest films were more popular than ever before, and his old films were frequently on television, finding new audiences and admirers. He regularly appeared on lists of the best-dressed men. His distinctive voice made him a favorite of impressionists, in nightclubs and on television. Even President John F. Kennedy and his brother, the Attorney General Robert F. Kennedy, were fans. They would phone Cary from the White House and laughingly demand, "Let's hear your voice!" To which he could only respond, "I'm trying to eat my lunch and you fellows are *fooling* around."[1]

There were downsides to this level of fame. He could not go out in public without being mobbed. He stopped traveling by ocean liners to Britain because his fellow passengers would not allow him any privacy on the journey (a situation he made light of in the shipboard scenes of *An Affair to Remember*). He couldn't go shopping for the same reason. "I seem to cause a disturbance," he commented dryly.[2] To his continuing despair, people felt free to approach him in public whatever the circumstance—in the midst of a baseball game, at the theater, and even while eating a meal in a restaurant—to ask for his autograph. If he consented to give it, he would immediately be surrounded by more autograph seekers. He tried various methods of putting people off, including charging 25 cents (claiming that the money would go to charity), but nothing worked.[3]

There were of course many more upsides to his fame, including being able to meet just about anyone who took his fancy. In the summer of 1961, the person he most wanted to meet was Dyan Cannon. Born Diane Friesen in Tacoma, Washington, and to middle-class parents, Dyan was a twenty-four-year-old aspiring actress when Cary saw her on television. She was strikingly attractive, and—with her petite figure, blonde hair, and hazel eyes—she was similar in appearance to his previous wives and long-term girlfriends. She was exuberant and high-spirited, with a bright smile and a rollicking laugh, but the prospect of meeting Cary initially brought out a more reticent side to her. As a star, he was a larger-than-life figure to her, and, as a man, he was three years older than her father. She put off meeting him for weeks. Finally, she agreed to meet him at his bungalow on the Universal lot. "Standing in front of me," she recalled, "was the most arrestingly handsome man I have ever laid eyes on. I hadn't, and still haven't, seen anyone who radiated such godlike masculine beauty." He was dressed simply in a white linen shirt, white trousers, and leather sandals, but she found him even more attractive in person than he was on-screen. "He held me with his gaze and broke into an absolutely enchanting smile," she recalled. She was left "breathless."[4]

In her account of the early days of their relationship, he emerges as an unpretentious man who lived a rarefied life. On her first visit to Beverly Grove, he met her as her car pulled into the driveway. Barefoot and accompanied by his dog, an easygoing German Shepherd named Gumper, he gave her a tour of the house, and she noted that this was not the mansion one might expect. Only the spectacular views and the Impressionist paintings on the walls signaled his wealth. Otherwise, the furnishings were informal and chosen for comfort. There was "nothing for show," as she put it. He joked that his decorating scheme was "French country meets English old codger," and he sat down at the grand piano and began serenading her with Cole Porter's "You're the Top." Then, like his previous girlfriend, Greta Thyssen, she was surprised to learn that dinner would be served in the bedroom, and on trays, so that they could sit on the bed and watch *Dr. Kildare* on television as they ate.[5]

The more glamorous aspects of his life were daunting to this young, little-known actress from Tacoma. They dined in one of Beverly Hills's most exclusive restaurants, Romanoff's, where Cary was treated like royalty. They went to a party at Clifford Odets's house, where other guests included Frank Sinatra, Danny Kaye, and Howard Hughes. A sighting of the increasingly reclusive Hughes was especially rare, but he was not a hermit, Cary joked to Dyan. "He just generally prefers to keep as much distance between himself and the human race as possible." As the months passed, she met a wider circle of his friends. They went to Alfred and Alma Hitchcock's home for dinner and she noted the affectionate, bantering relationship between the star and his director, not least when "Hitch" greeted them at the front door with the deadpan comment, "I hope you'll forgive me, Cary, but we are out of LSD."[6]

By the spring of 1962, their relationship had progressed to the point that Cary wanted Dyan to accompany him on a trip to London and Bristol, so that he could introduce her to Elsie. Dyan observed, on this and later trips, that he looked forward to visiting Bristol until he actually embarked on the journey from London. Then, as they drove, he would grow anxious and gloomy about seeing his mother. Elsie's letters to him were warm and affectionate, but in person she could be cool and spiky, and she was underwhelmed when he tried to appeal to her with extravagant gifts. On this trip—perhaps with reference to the soon-to-be-released *That Touch of Mink*—he brought her a full-length mink coat. She would not accept it. "What would I do with that silly old thing?" she asked him. She had a point—mink coats were more Beverly Hills than Bristol—but her rejection of the gift hurt him.[7]

Apprehensive about his mother's mood, Cary did not introduce Dyan to her on this trip, but he did introduce Dyan to his cousin Eric Leach and his wife Maggie. (Cary had little contact with his half-brother Eric since Elsie's release from the asylum twenty-five years earlier.) His *cousin* Eric was just a year older than Cary. He worked as a car salesman, and he and Maggie lived just a few streets away from Cary's Hughenden Road birthplace. Dyan was charmed by their warmth and down-to-earth outlook. Then the next day she was star-struck when meeting Noel Coward and Elaine Stritch, who were rehearsing Coward's new musical, *Sail Away*, at the Hippodrome.[8] These were the disparate threads of Cary's life: he would always be a Bristol boy, but he was show business royalty too, and he was living a life his mother and cousins could scarcely imagine.

Cary was in Britain to see Stanley Donen, who had moved to London after filming *Indiscreet* there. Cary had finally agreed to star in Donen's *Charade* after months of prevaricating between it and Howard Hawks's *Man's Favorite Sport* (1964). He was keen to work again with Hawks. It had been ten years since *Monkey Business*, but he was not happy with the script for *Man's Favorite Sport* and eventually he backed out, allowing Rock Hudson to take his place.[9] His reluctance about *Charade* had nothing to do with Donen (with whom he'd made three films over the past five years). The sticking point was the age difference between him and his proposed co-star, Audrey Hepburn. He thought the public would be turned off by seeing him, at the age of fifty-eight, falling in love with Hepburn, who had a youthful, ingenue quality that made her seem younger than her thirty-three years.[10] The irony of this was not lost on Dyan, who pointed out that she was eight years *younger* than Audrey Hepburn. Cary was not fazed. Ever alert to his public image, he told her that on-screen he was "bound by the shackles of social convention," but what he did in his private life was his own business.[11]

Photograph 28.48 Audrey Hepburn flirts with Cary Grant in *Charade* (Universal, 1963).
Source: author's screen capture

Cary signed for *Charade* only when Donen's young scriptwriter, Peter Stone, agreed to work with him, revising his own original story to make it clear that Hepburn was chasing after him.[12] Cary's co-stars had been chasing him for decades, but in *Charade* Hepburn's attraction to him is more pronounced. The build-up to the scene in which she asks, "Do you know what's wrong with you?" begins when they ride in a tiny elevator up to their hotel rooms. "A good place for making friends," she says to him as they squeeze into the elevator. She touches the dimple in his cheek and asks, "How do you shave in there?" Originally, he was going to respond, "Like porcupines make love—very carefully," but they decided that the line was too risqué.[13] He simply resists her advances, protesting that "I could already be arrested for transporting a minor above the first floor!"

On another occasion, when he wants to take a shower in his hotel room, she locks him in her room. He responds by taking a shower in her room, fully dressed and for her amusement. It is not the first (or even the second or third) screwball shower scene of his career, but he performs it with glee, pretending to scrub himself while still wearing his suit. Her response makes it clear that she finds him all the more attractive for his sense of humor. Although they made just this one film together, Audrey Hepburn easily stands among Cary's most sympathetic co-stars. Like Katharine Hepburn (to whom she was not related), she maintains an air of intelligence and elegance while also being playful, mischievous, and love-struck. A key difference, though, is that there is more sexual chemistry between Cary and Audrey Hepburn. In a scene in a nightclub, for example, they play a game in which he must pass an orange to her without either of them using their hands. The ripple of desire that registers between them is quite different from his chaste hijinks with Katharine Hepburn.

Hepburn plays Regina "Reggie" Lambert, a wealthy Parisian whose husband is murdered at the outset of the film. She discovers that he was a part of a wartime gang that stole a shipment of gold and its four other members are now convinced that Reggie knows where the gold is hidden. Cary's character tells her that he wants to help her, but his true identity is one of the charades of the title. He introduces himself first as Peter Joshua, and then he is said to be Alex Dyle, and then Adam Canfield, all characters who may or may not pose a threat to Reggie. This is a set-up so Hitchcockian that *Charade* has developed the reputation as "the best movie Hitchcock never made."[14] Like Johnny Aysgarth in *Suspicion*, Cary's mystery character is seen in shadowy silhouette, and in the climactic chase scene Reggie is as terrified of him as Lina was of Johnny. It is only in the very last scene that Cary's character is revealed to be a harmless bureaucrat, Brian Cruikshank, who has been investigating the lost gold on behalf of the American Embassy. When Brian finally reveals this to Reggie, he screws his face up and crosses his eyes for her. For all the mystery about his identity, the scene suggests, he is simply a rather handsome but quite silly man.

Charade is lighter and more frivolous than the films Cary made with Hitchcock, but it is also more violent, beginning with the body of Reggie's husband being thrown from the train, and then proceeding one by one through the killings of each of the four members of the gang. Some of the violence—including a rooftop fight scene that leaves Cary clinging to a tall building in much the same manner he was left clinging to Mount Rushmore in *North by Northwest*—is directly inspired by Hitchcock, but it is rendered more brutally by Donen. The location shooting, at the Alpine ski resort Megève and on the streets of Paris, ensures that that the film also has the spectacular, escapist qualities typical of Cary's films since *To Catch a Thief* in 1955.

Filming began on October 22, 1962, in the Studios de Boulogne in Paris.[15] Audrey Hepburn and Stanley Donen had worked together before, on the musical *Funny Face* (1957), but Cary and Audrey had never met, and so just before filming began, Donen arranged to introduce them over dinner in a smart restaurant. "I'm so nervous," she admitted to Cary when he arrived. He tried to put her at ease, suggesting that she use a yoga technique to relax. As he instructed, she placed her hands on the table with her palms upward, closed her eyes and took deep breaths, but then, with her eyes closed, she accidentally knocked over a bottle of red wine, spilling it all over his white shirt. "I wanted to crawl into a hole," Hepburn recalled. "I felt terrible and kept apologizing." She assumed that he would be irate and leave, but of course he had been suffering such indignities in his films for years. He took it in his stride, staying on for the meal despite his stained shirt and sending her a reassuring note the next day. Later, on the set, the accident became the inspiration for a scene in which she spills ice cream on his suit.[16]

The two stars worked well together. Hepburn was touched that Cary recognized her feelings of vulnerability on set and tried to put her at ease. She recalled that on a day when she was "twitching" and "nervous" while waiting to film a scene, he took her hands and said, "You've got to learn to like yourself a bit more."[17] Their other co-stars—among them Walter Matthau, James Coburn, and George Kennedy—recalled an easygoing set with a lot of joking and laughter. They were intrigued to work with Cary and eager to learn from him. Coburn observed that on the set Cary would try every scene three different ways. "Every shot, every scene, he would do big, small, and right in-between. He would find a dynamic that seemed to work, but he explored all of the possibilities first."[18]

Dyan was able to join Cary for the holidays, staying with him at the Hôtel Raphael in Paris. On New Year's Eve, Audrey Hepburn and her husband, the actor Mel Ferrar, hosted a party at the rather grand chateau they were renting on the outskirts of Paris. It was a small affair. The only guests were Cary and Dyan, Stanley Donen and his wife, and Peter Stone and his wife. Stone recalled that despite plenty of champagne and caviar, the party fell a bit flat because none of the couples were very happy with one another.[19] For Cary and Dyan, the tension arose because she had just told him that she intended to spend a full year touring with the stage comedy *How to Succeed in Business Without Really Trying*, and he could not talk her out of it.[20] Hence, when *Charade* was completed in February 1963, Cary returned to Los Angeles, alone and resigned himself to traveling at weekends to wherever the tour took her, including Chicago, San Francisco, St. Louis, and Toronto. One of Dyan's co-stars commented, "We saw more of Cary in the wings than we did the stage manager. It was easy to see he was in love, and so was Dyan."[21]

While making *Charade*, Cary finally settled the lawsuit that Joe Hyams had brought against him. When Cary denied talking with Hyams about LSD, Hyams had accused him of libel and sought $500,000 in damages. They settled out of court by agreeing to collaborate on another article, telling Cary's life story, that Hyams could sell to the highest-bidding publication. Hyams was surprised to find Cary friendly and keen to get to work. Before Cary departed for Paris, they met daily for several weeks in Cary's bungalow on the Universal lot. Cary sat at his desk, wearing horn-rimmed glasses as he pored over old photographs and family documents, telling the story of his early life candidly for the first time.[22] He recollected his parent's unhappy marriage, their financial struggles, Elsie's illness and disappearance, and his own tough, early years in show business. It was by far the frankest account of his youth he had given to date.

Hyams wrote "The Life Story of Cary Grant as told to Joe Hyams" and sent the article to Cary in Paris. Ever the perfectionist, Cary could not resist asking if he could re-write a few pages. Hyams agreed and found that Cary's own writing "captured the full flavor of his personality." Flattered, Cary asked to rewrite a few more pages, and then a few more, and on and on until he had written an entirely new article by himself. It was renamed "Archie Leach by Cary Grant," and Hyams took no credit for it, although he still collected the $125,000 that the *Ladies' Home Journal* paid to publish it over the first three issues of 1963.[23] Cary, astonished at the price Hyams received from the magazine, requested a commission of 15 percent. He had, after all, written the articles. Hyams, more than happy with the windfall he received from the articles, readily agreed.[24]

If Elsie read "Archie Leach by Cary Grant" (published in *Woman's Own* magazine in Britain), she did not mention it in her letters to him. She was now in her mid-eighties, and her letters had become increasingly rambling and downbeat. For the first time, she began writing to him about her marriage. "You see Archie darling . . . your father deceived me," she wrote in one letter. In another letter, she regretted "not having a second man in my life. . . . only your father and not much of him."[25] In her most disturbing letter, she informed him that, "Your Dad did not want you." She did not elaborate on this blunt revelation but turned instead to her own frustration with Elias Leach. "He should have enlighten[ed] me about marriage life. Not all those years. And now I am too old to have another man in my life."[26]

Rather than being hurt by her revelations, he was pleased that his usually buttoned-up mother was opening up to him. He immediately responded to her with a cablegram, saying, "A wonderful letter from you today, darling. Thank you, thank you. Wanted you to know how very happy it made me feel. Love always, Archie."[27] He also recognized that old age was catching up with her. For many years, Eric and Maggie Leach had been checking on her. More recently, Cary arranged to have a nearby doctor visit her regularly.[28] Now, he recognized that it was time for Elsie to move into a care home, but this was a difficult subject to raise with her given the years she spent institutionalized. He visited Bristol in June and in October of 1963, touring care homes with her and assuring her that she could move out if she was unhappy. Eventually, she agreed to move into the small, private Chesterfield nursing home in Clifton.[29] She would spend her last years there, living in the neighborhood she was born in, although in far better material circumstances than her parents had been able to provide.

In between his trips to Bristol, Cary went to New York to do publicity for *Charade* and then on to Washington, DC. Robert F. Kennedy had phoned him—this time not as a joke—inviting him to support the Stay-in-School Fund Committee, a charity that Kennedy backed along with his wife Ethel Kennedy and the First Lady, Jackie Kennedy.[30] Cary agreed to come to Washington in September to support the charity on condition that he did not have to make any speeches. Yet when he arrived at the Justice Department to meet Robert Kennedy, throngs of employees were there to greet him. Temporarily back-footed, he nervously joked, "I'm a mess. I didn't finish school!" He was more confident touring a junior high school, greeting students in classrooms as he had once done at Fairfield on a trip back to Bristol. The students gave him such a rapturous reception that Kennedy, trailing behind him, was heard asking, "Maybe some of you would like to shake hands with the Attorney General?"[31]

The climax of his Washington trip was the premiere of *Charade* at the city's largest and most lavish movie theater, the Loew's Palace, on September 24, 1963. The president and the first lady had seen the film privately, a week earlier, when a print was sent to the Kennedy family retreat in Hyannis Port, Massachusetts, so that they could watch it during a weekend break. Nevertheless, Jackie took the lead in organizing the black-tie event at the Loew's Palace, which was attended by Robert and Ethel Kennedy, and Vice-President Lyndon Johnson and his wife, Ladybird. To Cary's delight, Ella Fitzgerald performed a few songs. "She is one of the greatest singers of all time," he raved; "She is like an entire orchestra in one person."[32]

This was the hottest ticket in town, costing as much as $100 (at a time when the average ticket price was less than one dollar), with proceeds going to the Stay-in-School charity.[33] There was absolutely no discernible link between the story of *Charade* and this charitable cause. Rather, the event brought Hollywood's most glamorous star to the nation's capital at a time when the city was enjoying its most glamorous era, later dubbed "Camelot." The assassination of President Kennedy on November 22, 1963, brought this era to an end and sent the country, and much of the world, into mourning.

The wider release of *Charade*, on December 5, 1963, was timed to fill theaters through the holiday season. In the weeks between Kennedy's assassination and the film's release, Peter Stone woke up in the night with a panicked realization. In one of the film's lighter moments, when Cary and Audrey Hepburn are walking along the Seine, they joke about "assassination," using the very word that was now so laden with tragedy and despair. A rapid bit of dubbing, replacing that word with "elimination," solved that specific problem.[34] At this moment of heightened sensitivities, the film's violence still made critics uncomfortable.[35] Audiences were warned that "violence and murder are treated as occasions of great hilarity, which they are not" (*Los Angeles Times*), and that the film is "full of bloody violence" (*New York Times*), "a bloody awful farce" (*Time*), and "farfetched and bloody" (*Chicago Tribune*).[36] Audiences proved more robust than the critics. *Charade* was another huge hit, with earnings of $6.15 million in North America making it one of the top ten films of the year.[37] It has since proven to be a perennial favorite, and ranks among the most admired and frequently revived of Cary's films.[38]

Only one person complained to Cary about the age difference between him and Audrey Hepburn. "She's too *old* for you," Ingrid Bergman chided him, joking that his next co-star should be (the even younger) Jane Fonda.[39] In fact, Cary wanted Hepburn to co-star in his next film, *Father Goose* (1964), playing a schoolteacher adrift in the South Pacific during the Second World War, with seven young schoolgirls in her care. Hepburn, however, was already set to play Eliza Doolittle in the musical *My Fair Lady* (1964).[40] Jack Warner asked Cary to play Professor Henry Higgins, the linguist who teaches Doolittle how to speak "propah." But Cary had seen the show on Broadway, with Rex Harrison playing Higgins, and refused Warner outright. "You don't understand," Cary explained to him, "I speak Cockney. I sound like Eliza does at the beginning of the story!" He would not make the film, he told Warner; in fact, he would not even go to see it if Rex Harrison did not play Higgins.[41]

The stuffy Professor Higgins could not have been more different from the lead character of *Father Goose*. Walter Eckland is a slovenly, aging, alcoholic American. This was a bold choice for Cary to make as he approached his sixtieth birthday. His youthful appearance was now a cornerstone of his image, and he was continually asked about how he managed to defy the aging process. He liked to make light of this by telling a story about a telegram from the *Encyclopaedia Britannica* that arrived at his Universal offices. "How old Cary Grant?" it asked, and he replied with a telegram that read, "Old Cary Grant fine. How you?"[42] Jokes aside, ageing was a serious subject for a movie star, and he clearly gave it more thought than he was willing to admit. Over the prior ten years, he had quit smoking, cut back on drinking, kept his trim shape, maintained the tan that disguised the age spots on his face, and allowed only flecks of gray to appear in his thick, dark hair.

It is remarkable, then, that in *Father Goose* he chose to play a disheveled old man. Walter's hair is completely gray and he has a half-grown, scruffy gray beard. His clothes are unkempt. His walk is stiff and lumbering, and he is rude to just about everyone who approaches him. Cary always insisted that, in appearance if not in manners, this character was more like him than any other he played; that when he was not working, he often wore sloppy clothing and did not shave.[43] But *Father Goose* was not written as an autobiographical study. It was a determined change of pace for him, an acting challenge that allowed him to break away from his suave-and-handsome image. He embraced it eagerly.

The script, "A Place of Dragons" by S. W. Barnett and Frank Tarloff, had been sent to him by Universal. The story intrigued him, but he wanted Peter Stone to rewrite it.[44] Stone had proven to be an ideal collaborator on *Charade*—willing to transform his own original story to suit Cary's image—and Cary trusted to him to work similar magic with this story. They worked closely together on the script. Cary went through Stone's scripts line by line, editing the dialogue to make it tighter and more succinct, and also toughening it. As "A Place of Dragons" was transformed into *Father Goose*, Cary was determined that Walter would remain gruff and unpleasant. No sophistication was allowed to seep into the script.[45]

Cary and Stanley Fox set up a production company, Granox, to produce the film. More than ever before, Cary became "deeply involved" in every aspect of the production.[46] One aspect of this was casting. Having admired the

French actress Leslie Caron in the recent film *The L-Shaped Room* (1962), he offered her the role turned down by Audrey Hepburn, as the strait-laced schoolteacher, Catherine Freneau, protecting seven young pupils. Caron happily accepted, not least because her pay would be a generous $250,000.[47] Cary had wanted to work with the British actor Trevor Howard ever since he had seen him in Carol Reed's *Outcast of the Islands* (1951)—a title that would also fit this film—and he offered Howard $60,000 to join the *Father Goose* cast.[48] Howard played Commander Houghton, the Australian naval officer who gives Walter the code name "Father Goose" when he presses him into wartime service, spotting Japanese planes over the skies of the deserted island. Cary also auditioned and selected the seven young actresses who play Catherine's pupils, choosing children with little or no prior acting experience in order to avoid the precociousness so typical of Hollywood screen kids.[49]

Another key creative decision was selecting Broadway composer Cy Coleman to write the film's music. Cary invited Coleman to Los Angeles to discuss the film, and over lunch in the Universal commissary, he sang Coleman's own songs to him in order to demonstrate his admiration. Coleman took the job. Cary explained that he wanted the score to have the flavor of the jaunty English music hall tunes he remembered from his childhood, singing (the more recent) "I've Got a Lovely Bunch of Coconuts" as an example. It was an eccentric instruction but it allowed Coleman to hear what Cary had in mind. He created a score sprightly enough to ensure that the wartime scenario does not become too frightening, and that Walter's misanthropy makes him ridiculous rather than threatening.[50]

Director David Miller came to resent Cary's all-controlling approach to the film. By the time filming began on April 8, 1964, Miller had resigned and another Universal director, Ralph Nelson, replaced him for the twelve-week shoot.[51] Leslie Caron recalled that Cary was "simply the grandest partner that anyone could dream of, and very sweet when in a good mood." Like others before her, she noted that between takes he liked to sing old music hall songs in his broadest cockney accent. She also remembered that he grew increasingly frustrated as production delays took the film two weeks over schedule. "This film is ruining me!" he would cry out on the set.[52] He had reason to despair. As the production costs mounted from a budgeted $3.5 million to nearly $4 million, he knew that the excess would come out of his own company's profits.

Costs were also driven upward by location shooting in Jamaica, which stood in for the South Seas setting. Everyone enjoyed the three weeks spent on a beautiful stretch of beach between Ocho Rios and St. Anne's Bay on Jamaica's north coast.[53] Dyan joined Cary, and Leslie Caron was joined by her boyfriend, Warren Beatty, for what she termed a "brief season in heaven."[54] The bright, sunny, palm-fringed atmosphere was an essential ingredient in the film's easygoing escapism.

Father Goose is rather like *The African Queen* (1951) reimagined as a family film. Walter and Catherine follow a similar path to that taken by the unshaven Charlie and the prim Rose in *The African Queen*, falling in love in a remote war-threatened locale despite their initial distrust of one another. With seven schoolgirls in the cast, not to mention a pelican that follows Walter like a mascot, *Father Goose* is a lighter, frothier film. There are some familiar Cary Grant elements, too. When Catherine and the girls arrive on Walter's desert island, the island becomes a maelstrom of femininity, and Walter is left whinnying with frustration at their intrusion into his hitherto exclusively masculine world. The new twist is that he is surprised and a little bewildered when Catherine stirs some long-lost feelings of desire, and the girls awaken a parental protectiveness in him. This last part of the story, culminating in Walter and Catherine's marriage, unfolds swiftly and with remarkably little sentiment.

When *Father Goose* opened at New York's Radio City Music Hall on December 10, 1964, it was Cary's twenty-seventh film to debut in this stylish, vast, and very lucrative venue. He had long since established a record for having more films play Radio City than any other star, and his recent films—*Operation Petticoat*, *That Touch of Mink*, and *Charade*—had broken records for ticket sales. He visited Radio City so often that he knew the staff by name. He did not like seeing his face in close-up on the hall's vast screen, but he loved standing behind the curtain as his films played, listening to the audience responses, keen to hear the timing and pitch of their laughter.[55] At Radio City and elsewhere, *Father Goose* was another big hit.[56] *Variety* estimated its North American earnings to be $6 million, placing it among the top ten films of the year.[57]

Critics liked it, too. Many warned readers that the star was not so debonair in this film, but they also assured them that the film is "a cozy comedy" (*New York Times*), "polished, persuasive and consistently amusing" (*Chicago Tribune*), and "hilarious" (*Los Angeles Times*).[58] By this time, it had become a tradition for the Academy Awards to overlook Cary. *Father Goose* was nominated for only one major award, Best Original Screenplay, and it won. Accepting the award, Peter Stone referred to the many instances in which

Cary's films, but not Cary himself, were recognized by the Academy. "I want to thank Cary Grant, who keeps winning these things for other people," he told the audience.[59]

Cary left longer and longer gaps between his films as he pondered retirement.[60] Dyan was back in Los Angeles now, getting some television jobs but also spending a lot of time with him. She regularly joined him for two of his favorite outings, to the Santa Anita racetrack and the Los Angeles Dodgers baseball games.[61] They enjoyed weekends in Palm Springs, Las Vegas, and San Francisco, and they took longer trips to New York, London, and Paris. Jet travel fed Cary's wanderlust, and he was always on the move. They also visited Elsie, who boasted to the staff at the Chesterfield that her son would soon retire to Bristol, buying a bungalow there to share with her.[62] When Dyan finally met Elsie, she found her to be rather cold and distant toward both of them. Over lunch, she observed that Cary's attempts to make small talk with her were "like trying to push a boulder uphill." On this and later visits, Elsie called Dyan "Betsy," but no one was sure if she was being forgetful or mischievous.[63]

Nearly four years into their relationship, Cary and Dyan were going strong but for two recurrent points of conflict. One was that Cary wanted Dyan to try LSD and experience the kind of personal enlightenment that he found with the drug. She reluctantly gave in once, but found that the drug sent her into a nightmare of unpleasant hallucinations.[64] To her dismay, he urged her over and over again to give it another try. The other issue was marriage. Dyan was eager to marry and Cary was not. LSD had led him to understand the lasting influence that Elsie's disappearance had on his relationships with women. His three previous marriages failed, he realized, because he felt compelled to drive women away before they disappeared like his mother had. He was not confident that this realization would allow him to break the pattern, and he delayed making a commitment to her. Then Dyan discovered that she was pregnant, and he immediately put his apprehensions aside, thrilled that his long-held dream of having a child would at last come true.[65]

They married on July 22, 1965, at the Dunes Hotel in Las Vegas. Like his previous weddings, this was another top-secret occasion, with few guests and little fanfare. The Dunes was chosen because Cary had become friendly with its owner, Charlie Rich, and Rich offered the couple the hotel's most private rooms for the ceremony and celebration. Dyan's only guests were her parents, her agent, and her agent's husband. Cary's only guests were Stanley Fox, Charlie Rich, and his wife.[66] Cary and Dyan then honeymooned in

County Galway, Ireland, staying at the remote country estate of film director John Huston. After a week there they broke the news to the press and went to Bristol to tell Elsie, who had not been invited to any of her son's four weddings. "Congratulations, *Betsy*," was her response. "It's Dyan!" they replied in unison.[67]

Now that he was going to be a parent, Cary resolved to retire from the screen, but he could not resist squeezing in one more film before the baby arrived. He turned down Hitchcock, who pitched *Torn Curtain* (1966) to him, and he turned down Stanley Donen, who pitched *Arabesque* (1966) to him, roles that went to Paul Newman and Gregory Peck, respectively.[68] He chose instead to star in a remake of a film he had turned down decades earlier, *The More the Merrier* (1943). George Stevens had directed, and Jean Arthur and Joel McCrea starred in, this screwball comedy about an office worker and a soldier forced to share an apartment during the wartime housing shortage in Washington, DC. The elderly character actor Charles Coburn co-starred as the third roommate, a cigar-chomping businessman who encourages the young couple's romance. The remake, entitled *Walk, Don't Run*, would be set in Tokyo during the 1964 Summer Olympics. Up-and-coming stars Jim Hutton and Samantha Eggar would play the young couple and, remarkably, Cary chose the Charles Coburn role, a character who has no love interest but plays Cupid for others.

It was a remarkably low-key choice for his final film, but this appears to have been one of the main attractions of *Walk, Don't Run* for him. Sol C. Siegel, who produced *I Was a Male War Bride* and *Monkey Business* at Fox, initiated this project at Columbia and with Spencer Tracy in mind for the role of the older man. When Cary got wind of the film, he approached Siegel, who was only too happy to accommodate him. Cary and Stanley Fox, working together again as the Granley Company, co-produced the film with Sol C. Siegel Productions. The director, Charles Walters, had a distinguished list of credits, including popular musicals and comedies such as *High Society* (1956) and *Please Don't Eat the Daisies* (1960). Walters worked for months with Cary and screenwriter Sol Saks to turn the *Walk, Don't Run* script into a Cary Grant film.[69] "He has a unique personality," Saks said, "and almost every line has to be fitted to it."[70]

In October 1965, Cary flew to Tokyo and checked in to the Imperial Suite at the Okura Hotel for five weeks of location filming, followed by ten weeks on the Columbia studio lot in Hollywood. It was a happy shoot. Cary insisted that Jim Hutton should play Steve, an athlete in Tokyo for the Olympics.[71]

Hutton was floored to discover that Cary admired his earlier comedies, and he was keen to learn from "the master." "He is the most generous actor I've ever worked with," Hutton said during the shoot. "He is corroborating for me hunches, notions and blind instincts about acting, and it feels just great to get that affirmation."[72] Samantha Eggar was a late addition to the cast, playing Christine, the prim office worker who finds herself with two unwanted roommates in her tiny apartment. Eggar had never played comedy before, and she was initially daunted by the prospect of working with Cary, but on the set she found him eager to help her develop her comic timing and gestures.[73] She also found him friendly. "He bounces out on the set early in the morning, has a cheery greeting for everybody and keeps up the pace all day long," she commented. She, too, valued his generosity as a performer. "If it's your scene, Cary makes sure it is played to the best advantage for you."[74]

Cary knew that *Walk, Don't Run* would not be a masterpiece but he saw the script as "a good romp" that would allow him some fine moments of light comedy.[75] For this last screen role, he chose to play a transatlantic character, Sir William Rutland, who was knighted for his wartime services to industry but often points out that he is "half American." On a business trip to Tokyo amid the Olympics, he finds himself sharing Christine's cramped flat. Much of the comedy arises from the misunderstandings and mishaps he encounters within this feminine space: sharing a bathroom, staining a tablecloth, losing his trousers, and getting locked out of the apartment. Cary performs the tight little comic vignettes with the timing and nuance of the best silent film comedians. When he must climb up the side of the house and across a precarious bit of roofing, he performs with the athleticism of his boyhood hero, Douglas Fairbanks. He also has one last scene in which he loses his clothes. At the climax of the film, when he needs to speak with Steve urgently, he joins Steve's Olympic walking marathon, by stripping off his street clothes and posing as an athlete in his undershirt and boxer shorts. In this guise, he strides through the streets of Tokyo, to the dismay of onlookers.

Walk, Don't Run allowed him one more turn at all the things he did best on-screen, as well as a victory lap of self-referential moments. Cary's reputation as a penny pincher is referenced when Steve haggles with him over the rent and taxi fares, and Sir William says, "You remind me of *me*." When Christine's co-worker says that it never occurred to her that he might be her boyfriend, he looks in the mirror, pinching the skin on his neck to confirm that he is now too old to be the film's love interest (a point he reiterated to the press on many occasions).[76] He absentmindedly whistles

Photograph 28.49 In *Walk, Don't Run* (Columbia Pictures, 1966), Cary waves a misty-eyed farewell in the last scene of his last film.
Source: author's screen capture

the theme music from *Charade* while making coffee, and sings the theme song from *An Affair to Remember* while in the shower. More poignantly, he placed photographs of his parents on Sir William's desk, in plain view of the camera, so that Elias and Elsie Leach could appear with him in his last film (the second time, after *None but the Lonely Heart*, that this photo of his father adorned the set).

At the end of the film, he pauses to wave goodbye to two children who have observed the comings and goings in the flat throughout the film. This wistful, misty-eyed farewell is also Cary's last moment on-screen before walking away from his career after thirty-four years and seventy-two films. He never commented on how he felt on the last day of filming, February 12, 1966, but it is likely that any sadness was tempered by the impending arrival of his first child. Jennifer Diane Grant was born two weeks later, on February 26. She was a month premature, and weighed just 4 pounds and 8 ounces, but she was healthy, and her parents were ecstatic. Dyan fondly remembered Cary telling the reporters outside the hospital, "She's my best production. She's the most beautiful baby in the world." Later, when Jennifer came home from the hospital, Cary greeted them outside the house. Showering Dyan with kisses, he took the baby in his arms and said, "This is the moment I have been waiting for my whole life."[77]

There was still post-production work to be done on *Walk, Don't Run*. For the musical score, Cary called on the jazz musician and pop producer Quincy Jones. Cary had met Jones through their mutual friend, the singer Peggy Lee, and he knew that Jones could give the film an upbeat, playful score befitting a film with so much silent comedy.[78] Their work together and their shared love of jazz sparked a friendship that lasted for the rest of Cary's life.

Quincy Jones was pleased to find that Cary was a jazz fan and listened to Dave Brubeck, Count Basie, Oscar Peterson, and Bill Evans, among others. In later years, they sometimes went to jazz clubs around the city, and Cary invited Jones to join him on days at the Hollywood Park racetrack. Jones, an African American from the tough south side of Chicago, was surprised to find himself at the races with Cary and other British actors, including Michael Caine and Roger Moore. He was not surprised to find that Cary, always careful with his money, never put more than two dollars on a single bet.[79]

When *Walk, Don't Run* was released in June 1966, the critics were quick to recognize a remake of *The More the Merrier* and to label the story old-fashioned. The same critics, though, were quite reverential toward Cary. As the critic for *Time* put it, *Walk, Don't Run* has "a wheezy plot that must be older than Cary Grant," but the film also has "the ageless advantage of Cary Grant himself . . . perfectly cast as the anything-but-tired tycoon."[80] The critic for the *New Yorker* agreed that "the gags are so old one responds to them with piety rather than amusement" but added that "Mr. Grant has never looked handsomer or in finer fettle."[81] The *New York Times* put it more dramatically on the day after the film's local premiere. "Yesterday, Grant took Tokyo."[82] The box-office returns, estimated to be $4.5 million in North America, were good but not great, falling significantly below the $6 million threshold of Cary's other recent films.[83]

In January 1967, Cary and Dyan took Jennifer to meet Elsie in Bristol. At the age of 89, Elsie had her first grandchild, and Dyan could see the tenderness that came over her when holding Jennifer. But Elsie was never far from sadness. "I don't want to see too much of this baby," she told Cary and Dyan when they were leaving Bristol. "I'll fall in love with her and then you'll take her away again."[84] Dyan saw that Cary, too, doted on Jennifer and that he was very happy to be a full-time father, but she thought that his attitude toward her had changed since they married. At a dinner with Aristotle Onassis and Maria Callas a few years earlier, Callas had advised Dyan, "If you want to know how a man is going to treat his wife, look at how he treats his mother."[85] Now she saw this coming true in her own marriage, as Cary became increasingly distant toward her.

Dyan thought he was overly protective of Jennifer and overly controlling toward her. She felt trapped by him.[86] She was eager to go back to work, but he was entirely against this. At a press conference to publicize the opening of *Walk, Don't Run* in London, there was an awkward moment when a journalist asked Cary if he and Dyan would make a film together. "No," he replied, quickly and decisively, but Dyan, sitting beside him, contradicted him by nodding her head affirmatively.[87] He wanted his daughter to have the perfect childhood—the childhood he did not have—and he could not see that he was driving his wife away in pursuit of this. In August 1967, when Jennifer was just eighteen months old, Dyan filed for divorce.[88]

A long, bitter, and very public legal battle ensued, fighting over the financial settlement and custody of Jennifer. In the heat of this courtroom battle, Dyan made much of his LSD use, casting him as an unfit father and an irrational and at times violent husband.[89] In the memoir that she wrote some forty years later, entitled *Dear Cary*, she painted a much more affectionate portrait of him. She was still dismayed by the LSD, but she had come to realize that she expected too much of him during their marriage. She had expected him to be *the* Cary Grant, and she then found that "he was only human, with feet of clay like all of us."[90] This was the pattern to Cary's relationships as well as the blind spot in his own self-image. In his "Archie Leach by Cary Grant" article, he reflected that for more than half his life he had "cautiously peered out from behind the façade of a man known as Cary Grant," aware that "If I could not see clearly out, how could anyone else see in?"[91] This self-knowledge did not save his fourth marriage, but fatherhood gave him a reason to leave his image behind and embark on a new, more private life. It was a decision he would never regret.

29

No one thought that Cary Grant should retire from the screen. Old collaborators such as George Cukor and Alfred Hitchcock, who would make and plan films until their dying days, found it baffling that he would turn his back on his talent when he was still a popular star, able to get the green light for any film that might interest him.[1] The younger filmmakers who wanted to work with Cary continued to pitch projects to him, promising him the moon if he would come out of retirement.[2] Audiences simply wanted more of his films. When he met fans in public, they often put the question to him, "Why won't you make another film?" He was quite clear in his thinking. He had made seventy-two feature films over thirty-four years, and when he made his last in 1966, he was sixty-two years old. "I got tired of getting up at six o'clock and tripping over all those cables and drinking coffee out of Styrofoam cups," he said, adding, "It's not as glamorous as you might think."[3]

He had outlived many of his generation. Humphrey Bogart, Gary Cooper, Errol Flynn, Clark Gable, and Tyrone Power died in the decade before Cary retired, and Spencer Tracy would die in the following year. Orry-Kelly had also died. Cary had contacted him several years earlier, when Kelly was designing the costumes for their mutual friend Rosalind Russell in *Auntie Mame* (1958). This was during Cary's LSD phase, when he was reflecting on his past, and so it is likely that he wanted to make amends with his estranged friend. Kelly remained bitter toward him. "I felt he was a bit magnanimous when he asked me to fall over at the thought of lunch with the Great Grant," he wrote in his autobiography. Cary was more sentimental about his old friend, serving as a pallbearer at Kelly's funeral in 1964.[4]

The death of one's peers leads inevitably to thoughts about the time that is left and what to do with it, and here too Cary was very clear. From the time Jennifer was born in 1966, he was adamant that he wanted to be a full-time father. He did not want to be filming long hours, and away on location, when he could be spending time with her. His divorce from Dyan Cannon intensified his resolve. Dyan was awarded custody of Jennifer, with Cary entitled to visitation rights sixty days of the year and overnight visits "at reasonable times." She moved to the Malibu Colony (a gated neighborhood in the ocean-front town) and for a few years Cary rented a house a few doors down so that he could be near Jennifer. Dyan, however, was reviving her career, traveling wherever work took her, and taking Jennifer with her.[5] Arranging to spend sixty days a year with Jennifer was going to be a challenge.[6]

He found a solution of sorts when Fabergé, the luxury fragrance company, asked him to join their board of directors. He leaped at the opportunity, not for the money but for access to a private jet. This enabled him to travel at will, coming home readily from trips if Dyan offered him time with Jennifer, or flying out to meet Jennifer wherever Dyan might be filming. His duties for Fabergé were not demanding. The company required him only to attend board meetings and occasionally appear at events such as trade shows, where his mere presence would generate excitement.[7] He and the company's founder, George Barrie, had an immediate rapport. Barrie had spent many years in show business as a musician before becoming a businessman. Like so many of Cary's friends, he was a self-made man who did not flaunt his wealth.[8] So, too, was Stanley Fox, his long-term lawyer and business partner, and so too was the tycoon Kirk Kerkorian, a former boxer who now owned Western Airlines and MGM. Cary took seats on the board of directors of both companies. Later, he would also join the board of the Hollywood Park racecourse. Going to the races had long been one of his favorite days out.[9]

He was four years into his retirement—long enough for others to realize that he really had retired—when the Board of Governors of the Academy of Motion Picture Arts and Sciences decided to award him an Honorary Academy Award for lifetime achievement. The Academy's new president, Gregory Peck, is likely to have prompted this long-overdue honor. Everyone thought it would be a lovely idea if Cary's favorite co-star, Grace Kelly, presented the award at the ceremony on April 7, 1970, and she happily agreed to do this. She was about to set off from Monaco when Cary advised her against it. He was suddenly faced with a scandal. A thirty-year-old Los Angeles woman was claiming that Cary was the father of her newborn child. He denied this, and the case went to court in October 1970, only to be dismissed when the woman refused to take a blood test. Back in April, however, Cary did not want Princess Grace to be mixed up in any scandal. He urged her to stay home.[10]

It was Frank Sinatra who presented Cary with the Oscar that night. Sinatra spoke of his "sheer brilliance" as an actor, and also his "skill, finesse, subtlety, and charm." To demonstrate the point, an eight-minute compilation of film clips was shown. Taken from a wide range of his most popular films, the clips of him kissing a succession of leading ladies and then being slapped or abused by them delighted the audience. When the compilation ended and the lights came up, Cary walked out on stage, and everyone in the audience of the Dorothy Chandler Pavilion rose to their feet and gave him a standing ovation.[11]

Sinatra saw him fighting back tears and stayed with him at the podium for a moment, ribbing him about the film clips. "Do you realize I'm the only girl you ever went with who never slapped you?" Sinatra joked. After a few more, similar lines of banter from Sinatra, Cary was together enough to speak. He thanked the directors (Howard Hawks, Alfred Hitchcock, Leo McCarey, George Cukor, George Stevens, and Stanley Donen) and also the writers (Philip Barry, Dore Schary, Bob Sherwood, Ben Hecht, Charles Lederer, Clifford Odets, Sidney Sheldon, Stanley Shapiro, and Peter Stone) he valued most. He said that he felt privileged to be "a part of Hollywood's most glorious era" and expressed hope for Hollywood's future. He promised to cherish the award until he died, and he did.[12] It took pride of place on the bookshelf in his bedroom on Beverly Grove, where he could see it without having it on display to guests.[13]

If he knew, deep down, that he really was a brilliant actor, he never spoke about it. When he discussed screen acting, he discussed technique, and often gave drinking a glass of water as an example. When the director called "Action!," he said, the glass had to be lifted at just the right angle so that the ice doesn't clink and it is not caught by the lights. He had to remember to hold his head so that his double chin would not show and at the same time drink the water without spilling it. He must not put down the glass while speaking, or it would distract from the dialogue. And he must say his lines with feeling even though his co-star, who would be in the reverse shot, may not even be on the set.[14] It is this idea of acting, as a very precise craft, that made him so happy to work with Hitchcock, who storyboarded his films in a similarly fastidious and carefully planned manner.

When asked his opinion about great actors, Cary often mentioned Laurence Olivier, an actor who played classical roles and transformed himself into characters of different centuries and countries. In 1979, Cary presented Olivier with an Honorary Academy Award, and he spoke about Olivier's talent and his status as "the most admired actor" in these terms.[15] This was not the way he thought about his own talent. In the 1970s, he often said that "light comedy" actors such as Burt Reynolds and James Garner had a glint in their eyes similar to his own. "They have a wonderful ability to put the audience on, and make fun of themselves a bit, and not take it too seriously," he said, adding that this was the "common thread" linking all three of them.[16] He had a point, and yet it is hard to imagine either Reynolds or Garner portraying the desperate father of *Penny Serenade*, the cold-as-ice Devlin of *Notorious*, the heartbroken Nickie of *An Affair to Remember*, or even the bedraggled Walter of *Father Goose*. Cary's range, both as an actor and as a personality, makes him incomparable. This is why the frequent declarations that an up-and-coming star is "the new Cary Grant"—whether applied to Jeff Daniels (too middle-American), Hugh Grant (too upper-middle-class), or George Clooney (too somber)—never quite stick.[17]

In retirement, Cary was often asked about contemporary films, too, and he usually expressed polite disinterest, insisting that his new life was so consuming that he did not have time for films or novels. Jennifer came first in his life now.[18] When she came to stay at his house on Beverly Grove, he spent the day with her, making up songs and dances, playing cards and other games, swimming in the pool, and having TV dinners in the evenings. He often taped their time together on cassette, or filmed on a Super-8 camera. He saved the drawings that she made and other mementoes of her childhood, and placed all of them in the fire-proof vault. As Jennifer later described it, in her affectionate memoir of her childhood, *Good Stuff*, his careful archiving provided her with a "time machine" that allowed her to relive the everyday activities of her childhood. Cary knew he would not be there for much of her adult life, and he wanted her to have these memories of the good times and love that they shared. In her later life, she was very grateful for this.[19]

He often traveled when Jennifer was staying with her mother, going to Europe several times each year. He saw much more of Elsie, who was still at the Chesterfield nursing home in Clifton. He would stay nearby at the Avon Gorge Hotel, visiting her as well as his cousin Eric and his wife Maggie, and, as in the past, enjoying English fish and chips and beer. He took Elsie out for drives—she loved to cross the Severn Bridge and drive through South Wales—and he taped her speaking so that her voice could be added to Jennifer's tapes. She died on the afternoon of January 22, 1973, when she was just two weeks shy of her 96th birthday. She went peacefully or, as Cary put it, "in a perfect way." She had been served a cup of tea in her room, and when the server came back to collect the cup, she had passed away. Cary's good relations with the local papers meant that he was able to arrive in Bristol quietly, hold a small, very private funeral for Elsie, and then leave the city before her death was reported to the public.[20]

He kept up with Grace Kelly more than any of his other co-stars. They wrote to each other regularly, acknowledging birthday presents or planning to rendezvous in cities such as Paris and London if they were both traveling. He visited Monaco many times, especially for the Monte Carlo International Circus Festival, held annually in November. He was so keen on this that Prince Rainier appointed him as a festival judge. Jennifer accompanied him to the festival on a few occasions, and she observed his delight in the trapeze artists especially.[21] He showed her how acrobats grip their partner— "It's wrist to wrist, darling, hands can slip"—just as he had shown Katharine Hepburn on the set of *Bringing Up Baby* forty years earlier.[22]

He also kept in close contact with his friend and favorite director, Alfred Hitchcock, and his wife Alma. They had dinners together, sometimes at the Hitchcocks' and sometimes at Hitch's favorite restaurant, Chasen's in West Hollywood, and they sent each other short but very affectionate notes on birthdays and anniversaries. Cary attended the director's seventy-fifth birthday party and found himself seated next to his *Mr. Lucky* co-star, Laraine Day. On Hitchcock's eightieth birthday, Cary jokingly sent him a ham as a present, and "Hitch" thanked him "from one ham to another."[23]

When Cary introduced the director to George Barrie, Hitchcock told Barrie that Cary was "the only actor I ever loved."[24] Their close friendship was apparent when the American Film Institute (AFI) paid tribute to Hitchcock in March 1979. The occasion was a formal banquet attended by dozens of producers, actors, and writers who had worked with the director over the years. At the head table, Hitchcock was seated with Alma on one side and Cary on the other. Ingrid Bergman hosted the evening and, after testimonials and good wishes all round, she went to Hitchcock's table and presented him with the key from *Notorious*. Cary had taken the prop from the set in 1946, and he gave it to Bergman a decade later, telling her that it had been a good luck charm for him and that he wanted her to have it now. At the ceremony, she gave it to Hitchcock with the same good wishes, and the three old friends hugged one another as the evening came to an end.[25]

Hitchcock thanked Cary for attending the tribute. "I can hardly write this without a tear in my eye, because of our fondness for each other. How wonderful for you to be present," he wrote in a brief note, adding, "May I have the privilege of photographing you again one day, because you can be, you know."[26] Even at the age of eighty, Hitchcock wanted to continue making films and he was still pressing Cary to be his star. Cary was there, too, when Hitchcock was knighted in January 1980, in a ceremony held at Universal

Studios because the director was too frail to travel to London. Cary took the opportunity to tell the press, "It's nonsense about 'Hitch' calling actors cattle. He's an incredible dear and we had a marvelous association over the years."[27] A few months later, in April 1980, Hitchcock died.

The AFI had approached Cary earlier, in 1976, asking to honor him, but Cary was very shy about these occasions. He got nervous about any kind of public appearance, and he hated giving speeches in particular. "Even worse," he told a friend, "I can't stand to be there when people get up and say all those things about me. It's difficult to take."[28] He turned down the AFI, but five years later he accepted the Kennedy Center Honors for "lifetime contributions to the performing arts in America and the nation's culture." The event was televised but, crucially, he did not have to make a speech. He only had to attend the ceremony, and he was happy to have Barbara and Jennifer at his side. Because it was a shared tribute—with Count Basie, Helen Hayes, Jerome Robbins, and Rudolf Serke also being honored—there was little time for others to make speeches. When Rex Harrison and Audrey Hepburn spoke at the podium about their admiration for him, he he had to wipe the tears from his face. The audience, including President Reagan and his wife Nancy, rose to their feet and applauded him.[29]

He rarely appeared on television. Unlike many of his contemporaries, he turned down offers from talk shows and he refused to appear in documentaries about the old days. Although he looked at least ten years younger than his age, he wanted audiences to remember him as he was, and not see him with his silver hair and glasses. He did agree to give interviews to major newspapers from time to time. He was keen to talk about his happiness in retirement and also set the record straight on a few points about the past (he was always eager to point out that Mae West did not discover him, and to say that working with Hitchcock was a joy).[30]

As long as he was able to, he wanted to correct the falsehoods and half-truths about his career, and to give his own account of it. He was furious when he heard that the comedian Chevy Chase said that he was gay on television. Chase had appeared on the late-night talk show *Tomorrow* on September 25, 1980, and when host Tom Snyder referred to Cary, Chase affected a limp wrist and a lisp as he said, "I understand he is a homo. What a gal!" Cary's response was a $10 million lawsuit.[31] "I don't have anything against homosexuals," he told his friend, the filmmaker Peter Bogdanovich. "I just don't happen to be one." Chase apologized and the suit was settled out of court.[32]

In the late 1970s, Cary fell in love with Barbara Harris, a public relations executive at the Lancaster Hotel in London. They met in 1976, when the hotel was hosting a Fabergé trade show, and he was immediately attracted to her. Barbara was born to British parents in Tanganyika (now Tanzania) and she spent her childhood in East Africa until she was sent to a boarding school in Britain. She was very much Cary's type—smart, elegant, stylish, and disinclined to wear makeup—but at the age of twenty-six she was forty-six years younger than him. They became good friends at first. He had decided long before not to marry again, and he was wary of starting another romance with a younger woman. Within two years, however, their relationship deepened into a romance.[33]

As Jennifer Grant comments in her memoir, many people who hear about the relationship between Cary and Barbara assume that it could not be genuine. They see the age disparity as too wide. Yet those who knew them personally saw that their feelings were genuine; that they had a strong emotional bond and enjoyed each other's company in an unmistakably romantic and committed way.[34] Jennifer was only twelve when she met Barbara, and from their very first meeting, they got along well. Three years later, Jennifer was there, and smiling, on April 11, 1981, when Cary and Barbara married on the terrace of the Beverly Grove house. For Cary, it was a characteristically low-key wedding, with Jennifer, Stanley Fox, and his wife as the only guests.[35]

This fifth marriage was a very happy one. The house had been in a state of perpetual and incomplete renovations for years before Barbara arrived in the late 1970s, but she oversaw their completion, turning the house into a home that they could enjoy. They became homebodies, with Cary looking after his business interests (including following the income streams from his frequently revived films) and Barbara lending a hand as his publicist and personal assistant. She loved the garden, and cooking and entertaining at Beverly Grove. They traveled, including trips to Britain to see Barbara's mother, but for the most part Cary's wanderlust was sated, and he happily settled into a contented domestic routine.[36]

Then, he got a bit restless. He was being pursued by an agent who had booked Ginger Rogers on the lecture circuit. Rogers had toured the country, speaking about her career, showing film clips, and answering audience questions in medium-sized theaters. The agent, Nancy Nelson, knew that Cary would draw sell-out crowds if he agreed to do something along these lines, but Cary, with his dislike of public speaking, initially resisted. Then they hit upon a formula tailored especially for him. They would show the eight-minute compilation of film clips put together for the Academy Awards show in 1970, and then Cary would not give a speech, or even a brief talk, but he would simply take questions from the audience for 80 minutes.[37] He knew from his wartime experiences touring army camps, and later promoting *To Catch in Thief* in the United States and *Indiscreet* in the UK, that this kind of give-and-take could be fun for him and for the audience.

He had a few provisos before he signed on to do a show. Some were routine: first-class travel and hotel expenses would be covered, he would not become involved with publicity before the show, and during the show no audio or video recording would be made and no cameras would be allowed. More unusually, he insisted that ticket prices should be kept low; he was not doing this for the money. Most unusually, he wanted to do the show only in smaller, "out of the way" cities. He did not aspire to fill Lincoln Center in Manhattan or the Dorothy Chandler Pavilion in Los Angeles. He asked for bookings in places like Saginaw, Michigan, and Youngstown, Ohio. Initially, these were discussed as places to "try out the format" with less fallout if it didn't work. Once it became clear that the format did work, he decided to stick with the smaller cities.[38]

On October 21, 1982, he made his debut at the 2,000-seat Flint Center for the Performing Arts in Cupertino, California, a city that was not quite as well known then as it is now (as the headquarters of Apple, Inc.). Cary filled in for the scheduled speaker, entertainer Steve Allen, who had to cancel at the last moment. He was announced only as a "mystery guest" replacement, and audiences were of course delighted to discover that they were going to have *A Conversation with Cary Grant*, as the show was called. They laughed at the film clips, asked questions, and listened as he told anecdotes about his life and career. He often laughed heartily himself, and audiences were charmed to see this robust gentleman, with thick, white hair and big, black-rimmed glasses, full of mirth and quick quips.

In this first show, as in later shows, most of his stories were funny and nostalgic, but some were bittersweet. When he was asked who his favorite leading lady was, he always said that his favorite was Grace Kelly, and he talked about the tragedy of her death in a car accident in September 1982. He was asked about his childhood and his parents ("We were not very happy"), about Mae West, about Hitchcock and how they filmed the crop-dusting scene in *North by Northwest*, and about why he became an actor ("I think I became an actor because I needed as much love as I could get"). When he was asked about his current life, he proudly pointed out Barbara in the audience and said, "My marriage is the greatest pleasure in my life."[39]

A Conversation with Cary Grant carried on, sporadically, for two years. He never hit the road on tour, but traveled to individual engagements in cities such as Texarkana (Arkansas), Claremont and Stockton (California), Clearwater and Sarasota (Florida), Baltimore (Maryland), Kingston and Schenectady (New York), Cleveland (Ohio), Oklahoma City (Oklahoma), Memphis and Nashville (Tennessee), and Austin and San Antonio (Texas). He was keen to show Barbara this side of the United States, far from Manhattan and Beverly Hills, and to return to it himself. He had developed an affection for American towns and small cities while touring with the Pender Troupe, the Lomas Troupe, and the company of the vaudeville playlet *The Woman Pays*. Indeed, he spent most of the 1920s on tour, criss-crossing the United States, and he wanted to revisit some of those places, and relive those days, in his final years.[40]

Cary and Barbara were always at home to see Jennifer over the holidays and other breaks. She was now a student at Stanford University, and when she came home with her boyfriend for Thanksgiving in late November 1986, they all enjoyed a quiet dinner and a game of Trivial Pursuit. Jennifer also recalled that her "big bear of a Dad" gave her a huge hug when she left the next morning.[41] Cary and Barbara then traveled to Davenport, Iowa, in the very middle of America, for another *Conversation with Cary Grant*. *The Woman Pays* had played in Davenport sixty-one years earlier. Now, he enjoyed strolling through the city with Barbara and admiring the views of the Mississippi River. When they saw a restaurant named Archie's, they knew that was where they should have lunch. Then they went to the Adler Theater for the afternoon routine, checking ticket sales, settling into the dressing room, and doing sound and light checks. Cary felt well until the technicians were finishing up, and then he developed a headache and slight nausea. He and Barbara retreated first to the dressing room and then, with the help of a wheelchair, to the hotel. He did not want to go to the hospital because he thought if he rested he could still do the show. He would not let Barbara cancel the show until 6:30 p.m. (two hours before its start). Then, as his condition worsened, he reluctantly agreed to go to a local hospital. Shortly before 11:30 p.m., on November 29, 1986, he died of a massive stroke.[42]

Ten years earlier he had joked about death, "You know, when I was young, I thought they'd have the thing licked by the time I got to this age." He also made the more somber point, "I think the thing you think about at my age

Photograph 29.50 Barbara and Cary on their wedding day, with Jennifer, on the terrace of their Beverly Grove home.
Source: The Cary Grant Papers, courtesy of the Margaret Herrick Library

is how you're going to do it and whether you'll behave well."[43] In the end, he went in a way that characterized his life. He was a trouper, worrying about putting on the next show, in a theater far from home, just as he had worried about doing the next scene or shot on innumerable sound stages and locations for so many years of his life. It was characteristic, too, that he did not want a funeral or any sort of service. Always a very private man in life, he wanted to die privately as well. He was cremated, and his ashes were scattered over the Pacific Ocean and in the long, steep backyard of Beverly Grove, the home where he had been so happy in the later years of his life.[44]

Two years later, Barbara and Jennifer allowed one tribute, a black-tie dinner at the Beverly Hills Hilton, costing $1,000 per ticket, and with proceeds going to the Princess Grace Foundation. Prince Rainier hosted 940 guests, including many friends and filmmakers Cary had worked with over the years, who told stories celebrating his life. The emphasis that night was on "happy thoughts" and "good stuff," to use two of his favorite expressions, and remembering a man who began life with so little, and created so much, to the delight of so many.[45]

There would be many more celebrations of his achievements, in the form of film seasons at major cultural institutions, as well as countless re-releases of his films and screenings on television. More than any other Hollywood star of his generation, Cary Grant has continued to delight and fascinate audiences long after his retirement and death. An icon of the twentieth century, he embodied its aspirations. He was classless, and able to rise from poverty to affluence while remaining down-to-earth and unpretentious. He dressed impeccably, demonstrating that a man could look after his appearance without being a dandy. He related to women in a way that few men of his generation did, finding intelligent women interesting rather than threatening. He was the very model of dignity, and yet the most extraordinarily playful man. In all of these ways, he broke out of the confines of class, nationality, and gender, and held out the promise that anyone could do the same if they wanted to. He did this across a body of work that still thrills, amuses, and delights audiences. Becoming Cary Grant was his life's work, and even as he strived to achieve it, he made it look like the most natural, desirable thing anyone could do.

Notes

Introduction

1. Clipping from *The News-American* (February 15, 1984), file 616, Cary Grant Papers, Margaret Herrick Library, Academy of Motion Picture Arts and Sciences, Beverly Hills, California (hereafter CGP/AMPAS).
2. Judith Michaelson, "An Intimate Chat with Cary Grant," *LAT Calendar* (March 18, 1985), 1 and 4; Jean Reed, "Cary Grant a Charmer," *Variety* (hereafter *V*) (December 7, 1983), 103.
3. Maeve Druesne, "Mr. Grant Comes to Town," *Films in Review* (January 1987), 30–31.
4. Nancy Nelson, *Evenings with Cary Grant: Recollections in His Own Words and by Those Who Knew Him Best* (New York: Citadel Press, 1991), 316.
5. Maureen Donaldson and William Royce, *An Affair to Remember: My Life with Cary Grant* (London: Macdonald, 1989), 93–94; Jennifer Grant, *Good Stuff: A Reminiscence of My Father* (New York: Alfred A. Knopf, 2011), 9.
6. "Personal Notes: Articles," file 662, CGP/AMPAS.
7. CGP/AMPAS, https://collections.new.oscars.org/Details/Collection/617
8. Pauline Kael, "Profiles: The Man From Dream City," *New Yorker* (July 14, 1975), 40–68; David Thomson, *The Biographical Dictionary of Film* (London: Little Brown, 2002 [1975]), 351–52.
9. Interview with Betsy Drake in Graham McCann, *Cary Grant: A Class Apart* (London: Fourth Estate, 1996).

Chapter 1

1. Cary Grant, "Archie Leach," *Ladies' Home Journal* (hereafter *LHJ*) (January–February 1963), 133.
2. Madge Dresser and Philip Ollerenshaw (eds.), *The Making of Modern Bristol* (Tiverton: Redcliffe Press, 1996).
3. "Know Your Place: 1880s and 1900," Bristol City Council, http://maps.bristol.gov.uk/pinpoint/
4. Ibid., 51.
5. "Certified Entry of Birth: Archibald Alec Leach" (January 18, 1904). Entry number 80. General Register Office, Bristol Registration District.
6. "Certificate of Marriage: Elias James Leach and Elsie Maria Kingdon," file 614, CGP/AMPAS.
7. Nelson, *Evenings with Cary Grant*, 33–34.

8. "Certified Entry of Death: John William Elias Leach" (February 7, 1900). Entry Number 79. General Register Office, Bristol Registration District.

9. Grant, "Archie Leach," *LHJ* (January–February 1963), 136.

10. "Certified Entry of Birth: Elsie Maria Kingdon" (February 8, 1877), file 614, CGP/ AMPAS.

11. "William Kingdon" (1881), England census return for 3 Poor House Steps, Hotwells Road, Clifton, Bristol; class: RG11; piece: 2481; folio: 60; page: 24; GSU roll: 1341597.

12. "Certified Entry of Death: William Kingdon" (October 11, 1887). Entry Number 434. General Register Office, Barton Regis Registration District.

13. "Alice Kingdon" (January 2, 1892), entry 18684, Lunacy Patients Admission Registers; class: MH94; piece 31; National Archives of the UK; Kew, Surrey, England.

14. "Charles Llewellyn Kingdon" (1891), England census return for *Formidable*, off Portishead, Bristol; class: RG12; piece: 1959; folio: 128; page: 14; GSU roll: 6097069.

15. "E. Kingdon" (1891), England census return for 7 Raglan Place, Horfield, Bristol; class: RG12; piece: 1973; folio: 72; page: 25; GSU roll: 6097083.

16. "Elias Leach," Bristol Church of England Parish Registers; Reference: P/St.Ju/R/1/b; Bristol Archives, Bristol, England.

17. "John Leach Bristow" (1861), England census return for 3 Carlisle Court, Redcliffe, Bristol; class: *RG 9*; piece: *1713*; folio: *75*; page: *4*; GSU roll: *542855*.

18. "Elizabeth Leaf" (1861), England census return for 1 Weares Building, Bedminster, Bristol; class: RG 9; piece: 1705; folio: 29; page: 6; GSU roll: 542854.

19. "Elizabeth Leach" (1891), England census return for 29 Ellbroad Street, St. Philip, Bristol; class: RG12; piece: 1960; folio: 50; page: 26; GSU roll: 6097070. "Elizabeth Leach" (1901), England census return for 42 Argyle Road, Bristol; class: RG13; piece: 2375; folio: 52; page: 27.

20. Laura Bergquist, "The Curious Story Behind the New Cary Grant," *Look* (September 1, 1959), 58; Grant, "Archie Leach," *LHJ* (January–February 1963), 134.

21. Grant, "Archie Leach," *LHJ* (January–February 1963), 133; "Certificate of Baptism: Archibald Alec Leach" (February 8, 1904), file 614, CGP/AMPAS.

22. Grant, "Archie Leach," *LHJ* (January–February 1963), 133–34.

23. Cleveland Amory, "That Touch of Class," *Parade* (September 22, 1985), 6; Dyan Cannon, *Dear Cary: My Life with Cary Grant* (New York: HarperCollins, 2011), 109–10; Donaldson and Royce, *An Affair to Remember*, 156

24. Bergquist, "The Curious Story Behind the New Cary Grant," 58; Grant, *LHJ* (January–February 1963), 134.

25. Grant, "Archie Leach," *LHJ* (January–February 1963), 133–34.

26. Ibid.

27. Ibid., 133; *Wright's Bristol Directory* (London and Bristol: Kelly's Directories, 1907), 495.

28. Ibid.

29. "Archibald Leach" (March 21, 1910), *Admission Register, 1907–1923*, North Street Wesleyan School, Bristol Archives, Bristol, UK.

30. "Certified Entry of Death: Charlotte Monk" (October 26, 1910). Entry Number 176. General Register Office, Bristol Registration District; *Western Daily Press* (October 27, 1910), 10.

31. "Archibald Leach" (1911), England census return for 5 Seymour Avenue, Bishopston, Bristol; class: RG14; piece: 15056; schedule number: 304.

32. "Archie Leach" (May 2, 1913), Examination Report, Bishop Road Boys' School, file 614, CGP/AMPAS.

33. Grant, "Archie Leach," *LHJ* (January–February 1963), 134.

34. Ibid., 136.

35. Ibid., 134–36.

36. Ibid., 134.

37. Ibid., 136.

38. Cannon, *Dear Cary*, 111.

Chapter 2

1. Grant, "Archie Leach," *LHJ* (January–February 1963), 133.

2. Cannon, *Dear Cary*, 108; Donaldson and Royce, *An Affair to Remember*, 153–54.

3. Grant, "Archie Leach," *LHJ* (January–February 1963), 136.

4. *Female Casebook: Volume 28* [entry 8696], Bristol Lunatic Asylum, ref 40513/C/3/21, Bristol Archives, Bristol, UK.

5. Ibid.

6. Paul Tobia, "The Patients of the Bristol Lunatic Asylum in the Nineteenth Century, 1861–1900" (PhD diss., University of the West of England, 2017), 154–57.

7. Donal F. Early, *The Lunatic Pauper Palace: Glenside Hospital Bristol, 1861–1994* (Bristol: Friends of the Glenside Museum, 2003), 33–34.

8. "Alice Kingdon" (January 2, 1892), Admissions Warrants, Bristol Lunatic Asylum, Reference 50413/Med/PR/AW/23, Bristol Archives, Bristol, England.

9. *Female Casebook: Volume 28* [entry 8696].

10. Tobia, "The Patients of the Bristol Lunatic Asylum," 104–18.

11. Early, *The Lunatic Pauper Palace*, 35; *Western Daily Press* (April 30, 1915), 5.

12. Lionel Godfrey, *Cary Grant: The Light Touch* (London: Book Club Associates, 1981), 24.

13. "John Leach" (1911), England census return for 9 Dean Street, St. Paul's, Bristol; class: RG14; piece: 14869; schedule number: 99. "Alfred Leach" (1911), England census return for 3 Brighton Street, St. Paul's, Bristol; class: RG14; piece: 15063; schedule number: 38.

14. Grant, "Archie Leach," *LHJ* (January–February 1963), 138.

15. "Elizabeth Palmer" (1911), England census return for 42 Argyle Road, St. Paul's, Bristol; class RG14; piece 14867; schedule number 337.

16. Donaldson and Royce, *An Affair to Remember*, 148; Nelson, *Evenings with Cary Grant*, 36.

17. *Admissions Register: Fairfield School, 1914–1917*, p. 993; ref. 21131/SC/FAI/A/4, Bristol Archives, Bristol, UK.

18. Ibid.; Godfrey, *Cary Grant*, 24–26.

19. Roderick Mann, "Cary Grant: The Last of the Super Stars," *Sunday Express* (October 11, 1964), 2.

20. Amory, "Touch of Class," 6; Grant, "Archie Leach," *LHJ* (January–February 1963), 138.

21. Amory, "Touch of Class," 6; Donaldson and Royce, *An Affair to Remember*, 149; Grant, "Archie Leach," *LHJ* (January–February 1963), 138; Nelson, *Evenings with Cary Grant*, 36.

22. Grant, "Archie Leach," *LHJ* (January–February 1963), 138.

23. *Western Daily Press* (March 22, 1916), 3.

24. Grant, "Archie Leach," *LHJ* (January–February 1963), 138.

25. Tony Faramus, "Cary Grant, by the Man Who Ran His Life," *Daily Mail* (December 9, 1986), 18–19.

26. Grant, "Archie Leach," *LHJ* (January–February 1963), 138.

27. Ibid.

28. Ibid., 138–39.

29. Ibid., 140.

30. John Major, *My Old Man: A Personal History of Music Hall* (London: HarperPress, 2012), 1–5.

31. Grant, "Archie Leach," *LHJ* (January–February 1963), 140; Gordon Irving, "What a Cary On: Cary Grant's Early Years as a Variety Perfomer," *The Stage* (April 24, 1997), 11.

32. Grant, "Archie Leach," *LHJ* (January–February 1963), 140.

33. *Boy Scout Diary and Notebook*, folder 528, CGP/AMPAS; Max Barnes, "Hollywood to Bristol: I Tour the City with the Ghost of Archie Leach," *Bristol Evening World* (hereafter *BEW*) (July 30, 1957), 7.

34. Ibid.; Grant, "Archie Leach," *LHJ* (March 1963), 40.

35. *Boy Scout Diary and Notebook*.

36. Ibid.

37. Ibid.

38. Ibid.

39. *Bristol Evening Post* (hereafter *BEP*) (November 28, 1933), 13.

40. Fairfield School, *Admissions Register*, 1914–17.

41. Grant, "Archie Leach," *LHJ* (March 1963), 140.

42. Robin Young, "Rivals Clash on Cary Grant's Guilty Secret," *The Times* (August 22, 1996), Cary Grant Clippings File, Theatre and Performance Biographical Files, National Art Library, Victoria and Albert Museum, London, UK.

43. Grant, "Archie Leach," *LHJ* (March 1963), 140–42.

Chapter 3

1. Letter from Elias Leach to Elsie Leach (May 5, 1918), file 252, CGP/AMPAS.

2. "Mabel Johnson," 1911 England Census, class: RG14; piece: 15002; schedule number: 121, https://www.ancestry.co.uk; Certified Entry of Death: Mabel Alice Bass otherwise Leach. Informant: Elias Leach. Registered January 29, 1932. Entry 144, General Register Office, Bristol Registration District.

3. Certified Entry of Birth: Eric Leslie Leach. Parents: Elias Leach and Mabel Alice Leach late Bass formerly Johnson. Registered: September 26, 1921. Entry: 313. General Register Office, Bristol Registration District.

4. Cary Grant, "Archie Leach," *LHJ* (January–February 1963), 140.

5. Ibid.; *The Era* (May 15, 1918), 21.

6. Grant, "Archie Leach," *LHJ* (January–February 1963), 140.

7. *New York Tribune* (March 13, 1921), 42.

8. *Western Daily Press* (July 14, 1917), 3.

9. *The Era* (April 24, 1918), 12; *Aberdeen Evening Express* (August 27, 1918), 4.

10. *New York Tribune* (March 13, 1921), 42.

11. Grant, "Archie Leach," *LHJ* (January–February 1963), 140; *Birmingham Daily Mail* (April 21, 1917), 8.

12. *The Era* (April 24, 1918), 12.

13. *The Era* (May 22, 1918), 6.

14. Maxine Arnold, "Portrait in Quicksilver," *Photoplay* (November 1947), 70, 126–27; Pete Martin, "How Grant Took Hollywood," *Saturday Evening Post* (February 19, 1949), 23–24; *V* (March 3, 1943), 1 and 47.

15. Grant, "Archie Leach," *LHJ* (January–February 1963), 140.

16. Ibid.; Walter Ramsey, "The Life Story of Cary Grant," *Modern Screen* (October 1933), 29–30, 103.

17. "Memorandum of Agreement between Robert Pender and Elias Leach" (August 9, 1918), file 661, CGP/AMPAS.

18. Grant, "Archie Leach," *LHJ* (January–February 1963), 140.

19. "Bob Pender Company Tour, 1918," file 661, CGP/AMPAS.

20. Grant, "Archie Leach," *LHJ* (January–February 1963), 141.

21. Ibid.; *New York Tribune* (March 13, 1921), 42.

22. Ibid.

23. Barbara Grant Jaynes, interview with the author, April 10, 2016.

24. Grant, "Archie Leach," *LHJ* (January–February 1963), 140–42.

25. Grant, "Archie Leach," *LHJ* (January–February 1963), 140.

26. Ibid., 142; *Lancashire Daily Post* (November 11, 1918), 4; *Preston Herald* (November 16, 1918), 5.

27. *Glasgow Daily Record and Mail* (December 14, 1918), 16.

28. *The Stage* (November 13, 1919), 26; *The Stage* (April 1, 1920), 26.

29. Ibid.

30. Grant, "Archie Leach," *LHJ* (January–February 1963), 142.

31. Ibid.

32. Ibid.

33. *The Stage* (May 6, 1920), 10.

34. Jerry White, *The Worst Street in North London: Campbell Bunk, Islington, Between the Wars* (London: Routledge and Kegan Paul, 1986), 67.

35. *Olympic* (July 21, 1920), UK and Ireland, Outward Passenger Lists, 1890–1960, https://www.ancestry.co.uk/search/categories/img_passlists/

36. Grant, "Archie Leach," *LHJ* (January–February 1963), 142; Ramsey, "Life Story of Cary Grant," 30.

37. Grant, "Archie Leach," *LHJ* (March 1963), 23; *New York Times* (hereafter *NYT*) (July 28, 1920), 23.

38. *Olympic* (July 28, 1920), New York, Passenger and Crew Lists, 1820–1957, https://www.ancestry.co.uk/search/categories/img_passlists/

39. Grant, "Archie Leach," *LHJ* (March 1963), 24.

40. *New York Hippodrome Theater, Souvenir Booklet* (1922), file 650, CGP/AMPAS.

41. *V* (August 13, 1920), 15.

42. *Billboard* (hereafter *B*) (August 13, 1920), 39 and 53; *Central New Jersey Home News* (September 19, 1920), 2.

43. *V* (April 29, 1921), 16.

44. Grant, "Archie Leach," *LHJ* (March 1963), 35.

45. Ibid.

46. Ibid., 35–38.

47. Ibid., 38; *Wilkes-Barre Times Leader* (June 27, 1921), 2.

48. Ibid.; *Washington Times* (September 27, 1921), 12.

49. Anthony Slide, *New York City Vaudeville* (Charleston, SC: Arcadia Publishing, 2006), 34.

50. *V* (October 21, 1921), 17.

51. *V* (December 16, 1921), 31.

52. *Rochester Democrat and Chronicle* (January 8, 1922), 21; Elizabeth Wilson, "Cary's a Capra Man Now!," *Screenland* (April 1942), 28–29; [New York, NY] *Daily Mirror* (September 11, 1944), 18.

53. Letter from Bob Pender to Mr. Leach (May 21, 1922), file 661, CGP/AMPAS.

54. Ibid.

55. *V* (April 28, 1922), 6.

56. An *Evening Standard* Reporter, "Bob Pender Tells How Stilts Led Cary Grant to Fame," [London] *Evening Standard* (c.1938), "Cary Grant," Billy Rose Clippings Files, Billy Rose Theater Collection, New York Public Library, New York, NY (hereafter BRCF/NYPL).

57. Grant, "Archie Leach," *LHJ* (March 1963), 38.

Chapter 4

1. Grant, "Archie Leach," *LHJ* (March 1963), 38; Ed Sullivan, "Ascending!," *Silver Screen* (April 1938), 26–27.

2. Grant, "Archie Leach," *LHJ* (March 1963), 38.

3. Ibid., Cannon, *Dear Cary*, 81; Eleanor Harris, "The Riddle of Cary Grant," *McCall's* (September 1958), 75.

4. Grant, "Archie Leach," *LHJ* (March 1963), 38; Pete Martin, "How Grant Took Hollywood," *Saturday Evening Post* (February 19, 1949), 57.

5. Cary Grant, "Archie Leach," *LHJ* (April 1963), 87; Frederic James Smith, "He Stepped Up From Stilts," *Los Angeles Times* (hereafter *LAT*) (June 18, 1939), H7.

6. Ibid.; Harris, "The Riddle of Cary Grant," 75; Sullivan, "Ascending!," 27.

7. Grant, "Archie Leach," *LHJ* (April 1963), 148.

8. Alexander Woollcott, "The Play," *NYT* (September 4, 1922), 11; *B* (September 22, 1922), 1 and 107; *V* (September 8, 1922), 18–19.

9. *Better Times, New York Hippodrome Souvenir Booklet*, file 650, CGP/AMPAS; *B* (April 7, 1923), 8.

10. *V* (December 10, 1924), 4.

11. Letter from Elias Leach to Archie Leach (April 17, 1923), file 252, CGP/AMPAS.

12. *V* (August 2, 1923), 27; Harris, "The Riddle of Cary Grant," 75.

13. *B* (August 4, 1923), 17; *V* (August 2, 1923), 28.

14. Frank Cullen with Florence Hackman and Donald McNeilly, *Vaudeville Old and New: An Encyclopedia of Variety Performers in America*, Volume 1 (London: Routledge, 2006), 864–65.

15. Grant, "Archie Leach," *LHJ* (April 1963), 148.

16. Ibid.

17. *LAT* (October 28, 1923), 29.

18. Amory, "Touch of Class," 4–9 [annotated copy in file 700, CGP/AMPAS]; C. Ray Hall, "Sports, etc.," *Louisville Courier-Journal* (September 16, 1984), 51.

19. *Philadelphia Inquirer* (hereafter *PI*) I (July 27, 1924), 6S.

20. *V* (September 10, 1924), 29.

21. James Bawden and Ron Miller, *Conversations with Classic Film Stars: Interviews from Hollywood's Golden Era* (Lexington: University of Kentucky Press, 2016), 118.

22. *V* (March 7, 1933), 39.

23. *V* (December 10, 1924), 4.

24. Jean Dalrymple, *September Child: The Story of Jean Dalrymple* (New York: Dodd, Mead and Company, 1963), 87; Nelson, *Evenings with Cary Grant*, 54–55.

25. Ibid., 87–88.

26. *V* (October 28, 1925), 65.

27. *B* (January 10, 1925), 16.

28. *Detroit Free Press* (hereafter *DFP*) (December 7, 1925), 14.

29. Grant, "Archie Leach," 149; *B* (May 28, 1927), 15; *Brooklyn Daily Eagle* (December 26, 1926), 4E; *New York Daily News* (hereafter *NYDN*) (January 2, 1927), 16F.

30. Ibid.; George Stevens Jr., "Interview with Cary Grant," file 25, George Stevens: A Filmmaker's Journey collection, Margaret Herrick Library, Academy of Motion Picture Arts and Sciences (hereafter A Filmmaker's Journey/AMPAS).

31. Orry-Kelly, *Women I've Undressed: The Fabulous Life and Times of a Legendary Hollywood Designer* (London: Allen and Unwin, 2016), 88–90.

32. Marc Eliot, *Cary Grant* (New York: Three Rivers Press, 2004) 46; Charles Higham and Roy Moseley, *Cary Grant: The Lonely Heart* (San Diego, New York, and London: Harcourt Brace Jovanovich, 1989), 26.

33. Natasha Inchley, "Orry-Kelly: The Australian Designer Who Dressed Hollywood in its Golden Age," *The Guardian* (August 21, 2015), https://www.theguardian.com/artanddesign/2015/aug/21/orry-kelly-the-australian-designer-who-dressed-hollywood-in-its-golden-age

34. Orry-Kelly, *Women I've Undressed*, 93 and 102.

35. Ibid., 90–93.

36. Ibid., 141.

37. Ibid., 88–93; Dean Van Dun, "A Flyer in Neck-ties: A Hectic Hidden Chapter in the Life of Cary Grant, filled with paint, stencils and . . . Hunger," Publication and date not indicated, Scrapbook 3, CGP/AMPAS.

38. Orry-Kelly, *Women I've Undressed*, 88–93.

39. Michael A. Lerner, *Dry Manhattan: Prohibition in New York City* (Cambridge, MA: Harvard University Press, 2009), 142–44; George Chauncey, *Gay New York: Gender, Urban Culture, and the Making of the Gay Male World, 1890–1940* (New York: Basic Books, 1994), 301.

40. *B* (May 14, 1927), 10.

41. Grant, "Archie Leach," 149.

Chapter 5

1. Chauncey, *Gay New York*, 305.

2. Grant, "Archie Leach," *LHJ* (April 1963), 149; Letter from Arthur Hammerstein to Archie Leach (January 12, 1928), file 108, CGP/AMPAS.

3. Nelson, *Evenings with Cary Grant*, 55.

4. *NYT* (August 22, 1927), 21.

5. George Stevens Jr., "Interview with Cary Grant," file 25, A Filmmaker's Journey/ AMPAS.

6. *V* (October 12, 1927), 51; [Wilmington, DE] *Morning News* (September 21, 1927), 13; [Wilmington, DE] *Evening Journal* (September 23, 1927), 26.

7. Gordon M. Leland, "Hammerstein's Golden Dawn," *B* (December 10, 1927), 10; J. Brooks Atkinson, "The Play," *NYT* (December 1, 1927), 32; *V* (December 7, 1927), 48.

8. *NYT* (February 19, 1928), 2.

9. *DFP* (June 3, 1928), D6; *V* (March 28, 1928), 50; *V* (April 25, 1928), 52.

10. Grant, "Archie Leach," *LHJ* (April 1963), 149.

11. Letter from Arthur Hammerstein to Archie Leach (February 21, 1928), file 112, CGP/ AMPAS.

12. Grant, "Archie Leach," *LHJ* (April 1963), 150; Nelson, *Evenings with Cary Grant*, 150.

13. *Indianapolis News* (June 18, 1928), 19.

14. Harris, "Riddle of Cary Grant," 75; Pete Martin, "How Grant Took Hollywood," *Saturday Evening Post* (February 19, 1949), 57; *V* (March 3, 1943), 47.

15. Ibid.

16. Grant, "Archie Leach," *LHJ* (April 1963), 149–50; *B* (October 6, 1928), 8.

17. [Wilmington, DE] *Evening Journal* (October 17, 1928), 28.

18. [Wilmington, DE] *Evening Journal* (November 1, 1928), 7.

19. [Wilmington, DE] *Morning News* (November 1, 1928), 2.

20. [Wilmington, DE] *News Journal* (November 1, 1928), 16.

21. *PI* (November 6, 1928), 10.

22. *V* (November 14, 1928), 51; *V* (November 21, 1928), 52.
23. Grant, "Archie Leach," *LHJ* (April 1963), 150.
24. Edward Baron Turk, *Hollywood Diva: A Biography of Jeanette MacDonald* (Berkeley: University of California Press, 2000), 63.
25. *V* (February 6, 1929), 64.
26. [Wilmington, DE] *Morning News* (December 13, 1928), 2.
27. Charles Brackett, "The Theater," *New Yorker* (February 9, 1929), 23.
28. J. Brooks Atkinson, "The Play," *NYT* (January 29, 1929), 12.
29. Turk, *Hollywood Diva*, 63.
30. [Detroit, MI] *Evening Journal* (April 15, 1929), Scrapbook 1, CGP/AMPAS; *V* (May 29, 1929), 53.
31. Harris, "Riddle of Cary Grant," 79; Turk, *Hollywood Diva*, 62.
32. Contract between the Shubert Theater Corporation and Archie Leach (July 12, 1929), file 521, CGP/AMPAS.
33. Orry-Kelly, *Women I've Undressed*, 149.
34. *Adriatic* (July 21, 1929), UK and Ireland, Incoming Passenger Lists, 1878–1960, https://www.ancestry.co.uk/search/categories/img_passlists/
35. Orry-Kelly, *Women I've Undressed*, 149.
36. *Arabic* (August 17, 1920), UK and Ireland, Outward Passenger Lists, 1890–1960, https://www.ancestry.co.uk/search/categories/img_passlists/
37. Donaldson and Royce, *An Affair to Remember*, 256.
38. Ibid.; Tex McCrary and Jinx Falkenberg, "New York Close Up," *New York Herald Tribune* (September 13, 1949), Scrapbook 1, CGP/AMPAS.
39. *V* (November 6, 1929), 62; *NYT* (November 1, 1929), 31.
40. *B* (November 9, 1929), 7.
41. *Brooklyn Daily Times* (November 1, 1929); *New York Sun* (November 1, 1929); *Brooklyn Eagle* (November 1, 1929); all in Scrapbook 1, CGP/AMPAS.
42. *PI* (February 25, 1930), 8; Gail Borden, "'Wonderful Night' Lives Up To Its Name," *Chicago Daily News*, Scrapbook 1, CGP/AMPAS.
43. Letter from J. J. Shubert to Archie Leach (November 6, 1930), file 116, CGP/AMPAS.
44. Ibid.
45. *V* (September 1930), 51.
46. *Detroit News* (October 27, 1930), Scrapbook 1, CGP/AMPAS.
47. *Philadelphia Record* (September 23, 1930); *Philadelphia Public Ledger* (September 23, 1930); both Scrapbook 1, CGP/AMPAS.
48. *LHJ* (March 1963), 40.
49. *Boston Globe* (hereafter *BG*) (December 21, 1930), 56.
50. Archie Leach, "From the Ring to Muny Opera," *St. Louis Post-Dispatch* (June 7, 1931), 17.
51. [Camden, NJ] *Evening Courier* (February 22, 1931), 7; *Windsor Star* (March 24, 1930), 19.
52. *New York Mirror* (March 15, 1930), Scrapbook 1, CGP/AMPAS;
53. *B* (December 21, 1929), 5.
54. [Boston, MA] *Sunday Globe* (December 14, 1930), Scrapbook 1, CGP/AMPAS.

55. Ibid.

56. *PI* (October 12, 1930), 77.

57. Graham McCann, *Cary Grant: A Class Apart* (London: Fourth Estate, 1996), 11–12.

58. John Paddy Carstairs, "He's Grand and He's Grant," *Film Pictorial* (December 17, 1932), 20.

59. Orry-Kelly, *Women I've Undressed*, 147–48; *Pittsburgh Post-Gazette* (March 11, 1931), 28.

60. Contract between Paramount Publix Corp. and Archie Leach (May 8, 1931), file 76, CGP/AMPAS.

61. *V* (August 2, 1932), 15.

62. Nelson, *Evenings with Cary Grant*, 61.

63. Orry-Kelly, *Women I've Undressed*, 151.

64. *St. Louis Post-Dispatch* (August 18, 1931), 19.

65. Myles Standish, "Man of Aplomb—Cary Grant on the Phone," *St. Louis Post-Dispatch* (July 26, 1959), 105.

66. Nelson, *Evenings with Cary Grant*, 59.

67. Contract between Harrison Hall, Inc., and Archie Leach (August 31, 1931), file 112, CGP/AMPAS.

68. Fay Wray, *On the Other Hand: A Life Story* (London: Weidenfeld and Nicholson, 1990), 115–16.

69. Ibid., 118.

70. *B* (October 10, 1931), 17; *V* (October 6, 1931), 61; *NYT* (September 30, 1931), 34; *V* (October 13, 1931), 55.

71. Ibid.

Chapter 6

1. Donovan Pedelty, "A Ladder to Film Fame," *Film Weekly* (April 15, 1932), 14; Grant, "Archie Leach," *LHJ* (April 1963), 154.

2. *V* (November 3, 1931), 49.

3. *V* (December 8, 1931), 51.

4. Bawden and Miller, *Conversations with Classic Film Stars*, 118.

5. Grant, "Archie Leach," *LHJ* (April 1963), 154.

6. Wray, *On the Other Hand*, 119.

7. Ibid., 119–20; *V* (November 10, 1931), 51.

8. Wray, *On the Other Hand*, 120.

9. Nelson, *Evenings with Cary Grant*, 64.

10. Grant, "Archie Leach," *LHJ* (April 1963), 154.

11. Orry-Kelly, *Women I've Undressed*, 160.

12. Orry-Kelly, *Women I've Undressed*, 170; Dore Schary, *Heyday: An Autobiography* (Boston and Toronto: Little, Brown and Company, 1979), 64.

13. Orry-Kelly, *Women I've Undressed*, 173–74.

14. Bawden and Miller, *Conversations with Classic Film Stars*, 118–19; Grant, "Archie Leach," *LHJ* (April 1963), 49; Orry-Kelly, *Women I've Undressed*, 170.

15. Orry-Kelly, *Women I've Undressed*, 170.

16. *LAT* (December 14, 1931), 7; *V* (December 15, 1931), 6; "Production Cost Estimates" (January 26, 1932), *This Is the Night*, Paramount Pictures production records, Margaret Herrick Library, Academy of Motion Picture Arts and Sciences, Beverly Hills (hereafter PPR/AMPAS).

17. Tino Balio, *Grand Design: Hollywood as a Modern Business Enterprise, 1930–1939* (New York: Charles Scribner's Sons, 1993), 145–46.

18. Bawden and Miller, *Conversations with Classic Film Stars*, 118–19; Grant, "Archie Leach," *LHJ* (April 1963), 154; Wray, *On the Other Hand*, 128.

19. Walter Ramsay, "The Life Story of Cary Grant," *Modern Screen* (October 1933), 28–30.

20. E. J. Stephens, Michael Christaldi, and Marc Wanamaker, *Images of America: Early Paramount Studios* (Charleston, SC: Arcadia, 2013), 73–127; Douglas Gomery, *The Hollywood Studio System* (London: BFI, 1986), 26–50.

21. Joel W. Finler, *The Hollywood Story* (London: Octopus, 1988), 155–59.

22. Jeffrey Meyers, *Gary Cooper: American Hero* (London: Rowman and Littlefield, 2001), 73–75.

23. Jack Jamison, "Cary Versus Gary," *Photoplay* (June 1933), 33.

24. Frances Farmer, *Will There Really Be a Morning? An Autobiography* (New York: Putnam, 1972), 112–14.

25. *LAT* (July 31, 1932), B8; Rosalind Shaffer, "Bodyguard Is Accepted Rule in Hollywood," *Chicago Tribune* (hereafter *CT*) (July 17, 1932), F5; and Dan Thomas, "Hollywood Hunts for New Faces to Develop Star Material," *State-Journal* [Lansing, MI], April 23, 1932, 5.

26. *This Is the Night*, files 211-f.1 and 211-f.2, PPR/AMPAS.

27. *V* (April 19, 1932), 15.

28. Nelson, *Evenings with Cary Grant*, 68.

29. Bawden and Miller, *Conversations with Classic Film Stars*, 119.

30. *V* (May 10, 1932), 8–10; *V* (May 17, 1932), 8–10; *V* (May 24, 1932), 25–27; *V* (May 31, 1932), 8–9.

31. Scrapbook 1, CGP/AMPAS.

32. *V* (April 19, 1932), 15.

33. Orry-Kelly, *Women I've Undressed*, 173.

34. Bawden and Miller, *Conversations with Classic Film Stars*, 119.

35. Letter from Lester Neale to Cary Grant (July 29, 1932) and Report by Thomas and Moore Certified Public Accountants (August 2, 1932); file 588, CGP/AMPAS.

36. "Estimated Costs," *Hot Saturday*, file 103-f.1, PPR/AMPAS.

Chapter 7

1. Orry-Kelly, *Women I've Undressed*, 173–74.

2. Ibid., 174–75.

3. Robert Nott, *The Films of Randolph Scott* (Jefferson, NC: McFarland, 2014); C. H. Scott, *Whatever Happened to Randolph Scott?* (Madison, NC: Empire, 1994).

4. Ben Maddox, "They Keep Bachelor's Hall," *Silver Screen* (March 1933), 20–21.

5. "Estimating Costs," *Hot Saturday*, 103-f.1, PPR/AMPAS.

6. The addresses are indicated in his annual income tax returns; "Income Tax," file 582, CGP/AMPAS.

7. Miranda Seymour, *Chaplin's Girl: The Life and Loves of Virginia Cherrill* (London: Simon and Schuster, 2009), 122.

8. Wray, *On the Other Hand*, 153.

9. Seymour, *Chaplin's Girl*, 122–23.

10. Nelson, *Evenings with Cary Grant*, 102–3.

11. *LAT* (April 27, 1932), 1; *The Hollywood Reporter* (hereafter *THR*) (April 26, 1932), 1; *THR* (April 27, 1932), 1.

12. *LAT* (June 18, 1932), 14.

13. Edwin Schallert, "Extra Players All Hand-Picked," *LAT* (June 27, 1932), II:8.

14. John Baxter, *Von Sternberg* (Lexington: University of Kentucky Press, 2010), 152–56; Peter Bogdanovich, *Who the Devil Made It: Conversations with Legendary Film Directors* (New York: Knopf, 1997), 373–77; Maria Riva, *Marlene Dietrich: The Life* (New York: Knopf, 1992), 131–32; Karin Wieland, *Dietrich and Riefenstahl: Hollywood, Berlin, and a Century in Two Lives* (London: W. W. Norton, 2011), 188 and 204–8.

15. Higham and Moseley, *Lonely Heart*, 56–57.

16. Peter Bogdanovich, *Who the Hell Is In It: Portraits and Conversations* (London: Faber and Faber, 2004), 100–1.

17. Bawden and Miller, *Conversations with Classic Film Stars*, 120.

18. *THR* (July 13, 1932), 1–2.

19. Cary Grant, "Archie Leach," *LHJ* (March 1963), 40.

20. Riva, *Marlene Dietrich*, 152.

21. Grant, "Archie Leach," *LHJ* (March 1963), 40.

22. "Revised Costs," November 11, 1932, *Madame Butterfly*, file 131-f.3, PPR/AMPAS.

23. *Motion Picture Herald* (hereafter *MPH*) (May 7, 1932), 20.

24. *CT* (June 26, 1932), 7:10; Lynn Norris, "Will He Follow in Valentino's Footsteps?," *Movie Classic* (August 1932), 52.

25. Mark Glancy, *Hollywood and the Americanization of Britain, from the 1920s to the Present* (London: Tauris, 2014), 60–65.

26. John Paddy Carstairs, "He's Grand and He's Grant," *Film Pictorial* (December 17, 1932), 20.

27. Louella O. Parsons, "Hollywood Gossip News," *Honolulu Advertiser* (June 7, 1932), 4; *LAT* (May 8, 1932), 2.

28. Bawden and Miller, *Conversations with Classic Film Stars*, 119.

29. "Detailed Estimated Costs," *Hot Saturday*, file 103-f.1, PPR/AMPAS.

30. *V* (November 8, 1932), 16.

31. "Revised Costs," November 11, 1932, *Madame Butterfly*, file 131-f.3, PPR/AMPAS.

32. Mollie Merrick, "Hollywood in Person," *Boston Globe* (July 28, 1932), 22; *V* (July 5, 1932), 37.

33. Letter from B. P. Schulberg to Sam Katz (October 5, 1932), *Madame Butterfly*, file 131-f.4, PPR/AMPAS.

34. Author uncredited, "Sylvia Sidney," *Interview* (January 1990), 104.

35. *Motion Picture* (February 1933), 68; *V* (December 27, 1932), 14.

36. Philip K. Sheuer, "Romantic Story Screened," *LAT* (November 27, 1932), 9; *CT* (December 29, 1932), 9; *NYDN* (December 24, 1932), 21.

37. *V* (January 24, 1933), 11, 21, and 25.

38. *V* (November 1, 1932), 10, 21, and 23.

39. *NYT* (September 25, 1932), X3; *V* (September 20, 1932), 4.

40. *LAT* (October 8, 1932), A7; *NYT* (September 24, 1932), 18; *V* (September 27, 1932), 12.

41. Seymour, *Chaplin's Girl*, 115.

Chapter 8

1. Richard Carr, *Charlie Chaplin: A Political Biography from Victorian Britain to Modern America* (London and New York: Routledge, 2017), 23.

2. Kael, "Profiles: The Man From Dream City," 45.

3. Seymour, *Chaplin's Girl*, 9–54.

4. Ibid.

5. Ibid., 83–84, 128–30; Nelson, *Evenings with Cary Grant*, 92–94.

6. Seymour, *Chaplin's Girl*, 113–14.

7. *LAT* (December 23, 1932), A7; *NYDN* (January 2, 1933), 21.

8. Marybeth Hamilton, *The Queen of Camp: Mae West, Sex and Popular Culture* (London: Pandora, 1995), 157–76.

9. Nelson, *Evenings with Cary Grant*, 71–72.

10. Mae Tinee, "Westward Ho!," *CT* (December 24, 1933), D6.

11. Bawden and Miller, *Conversations with Classic Film Stars*, 119.

12. Edith Head, *The Dress Doctor* (New York: Little, Brown and Company, 1959), 60.

13. *V* (January 2, 1934), 1 and 27.

14. *THR* (January 10, 1933), 3.

15. Hamilton, *The Queen of Camp*, 169.

16. Balio, *Grand Design*, 265.

17. Mortimer Franklin, "The Two Women in His Life," *Screenland* (February 1934), 25.

18. Bawden and Miller, *Conversations with Classic Film Stars*, 119.

19. Nelson, *Evenings with Cary Grant*, 72.

20. Orry-Kelly, *Women I've Undressed*, 180.

21. Seymour, *Chaplin's Girl*, 126.

22. Ibid., 117.

23. Ibid., 130–31.

24. Ibid., 121.

25. *THR* (December 19, 1932), 1.

26. *LAT* (February 19, 1933), 7.

27. *V* (February 3, 1933), 3; *THR* (January 28, 1933), 3; Philip K. Scheuer, "Sea Melodrama Screened," *LAT* (February 21, 1933), 7; *V* (March 21, 1933), 11, 21, and 23.

28. *V* (January 17, 1933), 6; *THR* (February 23, 1933), 1.

29. *THR* (March 16, 1933), 2; *V* (March 21, 1933), 50; *V* (April 11, 1933), 4.
30. *THR* (February 11, 1933), 1; *THR* (March 20, 1933), 3.
31. *THR* (April 8, 1933), 3.
32. *THR* (May 23, 1933), 6.
33. *THR* (June 3, 1933), 3.
34. *V* (July 18, 1933), 37; *V* (August 15, 1933), 11, 21, and 50.
35. *THR* (September 15, 1933), 1.
36. *V* (October 17, 1933), 14.
37. Balio, *Grand Design*, 265.
38. *THR* (September 29, 1933), 3.
39. Nelson, *Evenings with Cary Grant*, 72.

Chapter 9

1. J. Eugene Chrisman, "We Can't Afford a Hollywood Marriage!," *Hollywood* (October 1933), 42 and 55.
2. Anthony Slide, *Inside the Hollywood Fan Magazine: A History of Star Makers, Fabricators, and Gossip Mongers* (Jackson: University of Mississippi State Press, 2010), 122–43.
3. Brett Abrams, *Hollywood Bohemians: Transgressive Sexuality and the Selling of the Movieland Dream* (Jefferson, NC, and London: McFarland and Company, 2008), 3–12.
4. Maddox, "They Keep Bachelor's Hall," 20–21.
5. *Modern Screen* (October 1933), 12–13.
6. *V* (October 24, 1933), 41.
7. Eliot, *Cary Grant*, 79–80; Higham and Moseley, *The Lonely Heart*, 60.
8. Eliot, *Cary Grant*, 80.
9. Abrams, *Hollywood Bohemians*, 150–54; William J. Mann, *Behind the Scenes: How Gays and Lesbians Shaped Hollywood, 1910–1969* (New York: Viking, 2001), 151.
10. Cary Grant and Randolph Scott photographs, folders 11 and 12, box 2, Paramount Pictures photographs, Margaret Herrick Library, Academy of Motion Picture Arts and Sciences, Beverly Hills, CA (herafter PPP/AMPAS).
11. Scrapbooks 3, 4, 5, and 6, CGP/AMPAS.
12. Eliot, *Cary Grant*, 102–4; Higham and Moseley, *The Lonely Heart*, 68–73; Mann, *Behind the Scenes*, 159.
13. *V* (May 16, 1933), 25.
14. Seymour, *Chaplin's Girl*, 132.
15. Grace Kingsley, "Hobnobbing in Hollywood," *LAT* (December 23, 1932), 7.
16. Seymour, *Chaplin's Girl*, 123 and 132.
17. Ibid., 134.
18. *V* (August 15, 1933), 7.
19. *LAT* (October 8, 1933), 10.
20. *THR* (October 24, 1933), 2.
21. *Daily Variety* (hereafter *DV*) (October 27, 1933), 1; *LAT* (October 28, 1933), 3; *THR* (October 26, 1933), 2.

22. *V* (September 12, 1933), 60.

23. *THR* (October 5, 1933), 2.

24. *THR* (November 10, 1933), 3.

25. *LAT* (November 12, 1933), 1.

26. Cannon, *Dear Cary*, 113–14.

27. *V* (September 12, 1933), 60.

28. Aubrey Solomon, *Twentieth Century-Fox: A Corporate and Financial History* (Metuchen, NJ, and London: Scarecrow Press, 1988), 21.

29. Nelson, *Evenings with Cary Grant*, 75–77.

30. Bawden and Miller, *Conversations with Classic Film Stars*, 120.

31. Gary Giddins, *Bing Crosby: A Pocketful of Dreams, The Early Years, 1903–1940* (New York: Little, Brown and Company, 2001), 347; *THR* (November 3, 1933), 1.

32. *NYT* (December 23, 1933), 12; *V* (December 22, 1933), 10; *V* (January 16, 1934), 10, 23, 25, and 27.

33. *Daily Mail* [Hagerstown, MD] (November 14, 1933), 3.

34. *Gloucestershire Echo* (December 23, 1933), 4.

35. Eliot, *Cary Grant*, 97.

36. "Special Menu," folder 733, box 50, CGP/AMPAS.

37. *The Sphere* (December 2, 1933), 5; *LAT* (December 7, 1933), 3.

38. *London Evening News* (November 26, 1933), 6.

39. Ibid.; *THR* (November 24, 1933), 1.

40. *BEW* (November 24, 1933), 1; *The Citizen* [Gloucester, UK] (November 25, 1933), 4.

41. *Western Daily Press* (November 27, 1940), 7.

42. Godfrey, *Cary Grant*, 60–61.

43. Ibid.

44. Donaldson and Royce, *An Affair to Remember*, 150; Nelson, *Evenings with Cary Grant*, 266.

45. Godfrey, *Cary Grant*, 175.

46. *BEP* (November 28, 1933), 1 and 8.

47. *Western Daily Press* (November 29, 1933), 8.

48. Certified Entry of Death: Mabel Alice Bass otherwise Leach. Informant: Elias Leach, 1 Broad's Court, Rosemary Street, Bristol. Registered January 29, 1932. Entry 144, General Register Office, Bristol Registration District.

49. Cannon, *Dear Cary*, 114.

50. Cannon, *Dear Cary*, 112–14; Donaldson and Royce, *An Affair to Remember*, 158–59; Seymour, *Chaplin's Girl*, 138–39.

51. Cannon, *Dear Cary*, 114–15.

52. *THR* (December 19, 1933), 6.

53. *THR* (January 4, 1934), 2.

54. *BEW* (December 14, 1933), 1; *THR* (December 16, 1933), 1.

55. *Daily Mirror* (January 9, 1934), 2; *Western Daily Press* (December 15, 1933), 7.

56. Higham and Moseley, *The Lonely Heart*, 67.

57. Eliot, *Cary Grant*, 102–3.

58. Donaldson and Royce, *An Affair to Remember*, 159.

59. *St. Louis Dispatch* (January 8, 1934), 1.
60. *Edinburgh Evening News* (January 9, 1934), 9.
61. *THR* (January 8, 1934), 2.
62. Kenneth Green, "Virginia Cherrill's Quiet Little Quota Film," *The Era* (January 31, 1934), 14.
63. *BEW* (February 9, 1934), 14.
64. Seymour, *Chaplin's Girl*, 139.
65. *BEP* (January 23, 1934), 8.
66. *THR* (January 16, 1934), 9.
67. *THR* (March 2, 1934), 5.
68. Cannon, *Dear Cary*, 115; Seymour, *Chaplin's Girl*, 141.
69. The photograph appears in the documentary film *Becoming Cary Grant*, Yuzu Productions, 2017.
70. Cannon, *Dear Cary*, 115; Donaldson and Royce, *An Affair to Remember*, 154.
71. Letter from Elsie Leach to Cary Grant, December 12, 1938, box 17, CGP/AMPAS.
72. Grant, "Archie Leach" (April 1963), 151; Seymour, *Chaplin's Girl*, 141–43.
73. *BEW* (February 9, 1934), 1; *Los Angeles Times* (February 10, 1934), 3.
74. *Boston Globe* (February 17, 1934), 20.

Chapter 10

1. Seymour, *Chaplin's Girl*, 143.
2. *THR* (February 17, 1934), 2.
3. *Pittsburgh Press* (February 26, 1934), 9.
4. Helen Harrison, "The Grant That Took Virginia," *Silver Screen* (May 1934), 47 and 70–73.
5. Nelson, *Evenings with Cary Grant*, 75.
6. Rian James, "Hollywood," *Brooklyn Daily Eagle* (April 10, 1934), 23; George Shaffer, "Bachelor Pal Keeps Quarters at Grant Home," *CT* (March 2, 1934), 15.
7. *THR* (March 15, 1934), 2; *Pittsburgh Post-Gazette* (July 19, 1934), 17.
8. *NYDN* (January 3, 1934), 36; *DV* (January 13, 1934), 1.
9. Seymour, *Chaplin's Girl*, 146; *THR* (March 5, 1934), 6.
10. Sandy Sturges (ed.), *Preston Sturges by Preston Sturges* (New York: Touchstone, 1991), 277.
11. Bawden and Miller, *Conversations with Classic Film Stars*, 120.
12. *THR* (May 14, 1934), 6; *MPH* (May 5, 1934), 46; *NYT* (May 12, 1934), 12; *V* (May 15, 1934), 14.
13. *V* (May 29, 1934), 10 and 19; *V* (July 10, 1934), 10 and 25.
14. Drew Todd, "Decadent Heroes: Dandyism and Masculinity in Art Deco Hollywood," *Journal of Popular Film and Television* 32, no. 4 (2005): 168–81.
15. *THR* (March 20, 1934), 8.
16. *DV* (April 20, 1934), 3.
17. *MPH* (May 12, 1934), 42; *THR* (May 25, 1934), 3.

18. *MPH* (July 14, 1934), 50; *MPH* (July 21, 1934), 56; *MPH* (July 28, 1934), 59 and 62; *MPH* (August 4, 1934), 36–37; *MPH* (August 11, 1934), 41–42; *MPH* (August 18, 1934), 44 and 48; *MPH* (August 25, 1934), 44.

19. Seymour, *Chaplin's Girl*, 146.

20. *THR* (June 9, 1934), 4; *MPH* (June 18, 1934), 16.

21. *LAT* (June 18, 1934), II:7; *THR* (June 16, 1934), 2; Marguerite Martyn, "Archie Leach Comes Back," *St. Louis Post-Dispatch* (June 23, 1934), 14.

22. *THR* (June 20, 1934), 4; Martyn, "Archie Leach Comes Back."

23. Seymour, *Chaplin's Girl*, 148; *NYDN* (July 12, 1934), 47.

24. Seymour, *Chaplin's Girl*, 150.

25. Ibid., 150–51.

26. Louella O. Parsons, "Miss Cherrill Leaves Grant after Quarrel," *San Francisco Examiner* (hereafter *SFE*) (October 1, 1934), 3.

27. Seymour, *Chaplin's Girl*, 152.

28. Louella O. Parsons, "Today in Hollywood," *Reading Times* (October 8, 1934), 11.

29. Seymour, *Chaplin's Girl*, 152–53; *LAT* (October 6, 1934), 3.

30. Ibid.

31. *Akron Beacon-Journal* (October 5, 1934), 1; *Capital Journal* [Salem, OR] (October 5, 1935), 1; *Daily Democrat* [Tallahassee, FL] (October 4, 1934), 1.

32. *Evening Post* [New York, NY] (October 5, 1934), 1.

33. *LAT* (October 16, 1934), 2.

34. *NYDN* (December 12, 1934), 4.

35. *LAT* (December 4, 1932), 2.

36. *LAT* (December 12, 1934), 1.

37. *Washington Post* (December 12, 1934), 2.

38. Letter from Hedda Hopper to Lloyd Wendt [editor, *Chicago Tribune* magazine] (August 25, 1958); file 7.f148, Hedda Hopper Papers, Margaret Herrick Library, Academy of Motion Picture Arts and Sciences, Beverly Hills, CA (hereafter HHP/AMPAS).

39. *CT* (March 27, 1935), 16.

40. Seymour, *Chaplin's Girl*, 158.

41. Grant, "Archie Leach," *LHJ* (April 1963), 151.

42. Scrapbook 5, CGP/AMPAS.

Chapter 11

1. *V* (May 1, 1934), 2.

2. *THR* (June 6, 1934), 2.

3. *V* (June 5, 1934), 12.

4. *MPH* (August 18, 1934), 55.

5. *The Sun* [Baltimore] (August 12, 1934), T6.

6. *DV* (October 1, 1934), 4; *THR* (October 12, 1934), 6.

7. James Kotsilibas-Davis and Myrna Loy, *Myrna Loy: Being and Becoming* (London: Bloomsbury, 1987), 96–97.

8. *DV* (October 4, 1934), 2; *THR* (December 20, 1934), 2.

9. Sidney Skolsky, "Hollywood," *NYDN* (February 2, 1935), 26.

10. Kotsilibas-Davis and Loy, *Myrna Loy*, 97.

11. *V* (February 5, 1934), 14.

12. *THR* (January 10, 1935), 3.

13. *MPH* (February 16, 1935), 64–65; *MPH* (March 2, 1935), 66 and 68–69; *MPH* (March 16, 1935), 51 and 53; *MPH* (March 30, 1935), 64; *MPH* (April 6, 1935), 72; *MPH* (April 13, 1935), 65; *MPH* (April 20, 1935), 70; *MPH* (May 4, 1935), 66; *MPH* (May 11, 1935), 72; *MPH* (May 18, 1935) 70; *MPH* (May 25, 1935), 63; *MPH* (June 8, 1935), 108; *MPH* (June 15, 1935), 99.

14. "Contracts and Agreements," file f.521, CGP/AMPAS; *THR* (November 3, 1934), 1.

15. Irene Thirer, "Handsome Mr. Grant Happy in Wicked Roles," *New York Post* (November 11, 1935) [BRCF/NYPL].

16. *Pittsburgh Post-Gazette* (January 31, 1935), 8; *Oakland Tribune* (January 31, 1935), 10.

17. *Brooklyn Daily Eagle* (May 7, 1935), 25; *PI* (May 5, 1935), 22.

18. Sara Day, "Hollywood," *Screen and Radio Weekly* (April 28, 1935), 10.

19. Nelson, *Evenings with Cary Grant*, 74–75.

20. *DV* (May 16, 1935), 4; *THR* (May 27, 1935), 2.

21. Nelson, *Evenings with Cary Grant*, 75.

22. Thirer, "Handsome Mr. Grant."

23. *New York Evening Journal* (June 19, 1935) [BRCF/NYPL].

24. W. H. Mooring, "Talk, Dark and Handsome," *Film Weekly* (August 14, 1937), 9–10.

25. Gomery, *The Hollywood Studio System*, 38–39; Scott Eyman, *Ernst Lubitsch, Laughter in Paradise* (Baltimore: Johns Hopkins University Press, 2000), 225–27.

26. "Contracts and Agreements," file f.521, CGP/AMPAS.

27. "Costs," *The Last Outpost*, file 123-f.1, PPR/AMPAS.

28. "Assistant Director's Reports," *The Last Outpost*, file 123-f.1, PPR/AMPAS.

29. "Costs," *The Last Outpost*, file 123-f.2, PPR/AMPAS; Herbert Coleman, *The Man Who Knew Hitchcock: A Hollywood Memoir* (Lanham, MD: Scarecrow Press, 2003), 61–62.

30. "The Cutting Room: *The Last Outpost*," *MPH* (July 13, 1935), 68.

31. Memo from Dick Johnston to Mr. Herzbrun (August 29, 1935), *The Last Outpost*, file 124-f.6, PPR/AMPAS.

32. Bawden and Miller, *Conversations with Classic Film Stars*, 120.

33. David J. Skal with Jessica Rains, *Claude Rains: An Actor's Voice* (Lexington: University of Kentucky Press, 2008), 92–93.

34. William J. Mann, *Kate: The Woman Who Was Katharine Hepburn* (London: Faber and Faber, 2006), 235; Patrick McGilligan, *George Cukor: A Double Life* (New York: St. Martin's Press, 1991), 126.

35. A. Scott Berg, *Kate Remembered* (London: Simon and Schuster, 2003), 107

36. Thomson, *The Biographical Dictionary of Film*, 194–95.

37. Budget of Production Cost (August 14, 1935), *Sylvia Scarlett*, box 60P, Subseries 2620, RKO Radio Pictures Studio Records (Collection PASC 3), UCLA Library Special Collections, Charles E. Young Research Library, University of California, Los Angeles (hereafter RKO/UCLA).

38. Bogdanovich, *Who the Devil Made It*, 448–49; Gavin Lambert, *On Cukor* (New York: Rizzoli, 2000 [1972]), 80.

39. Bawden and Miller, *Conversations with Classic Film Stars*, 120.

40. Robert Emmet Long (ed.), *George Cukor: Interviews* (Jackson: University of Mississippi Press, 2001), 21.

41. Katharine Hepburn, *Me: Stories of My Life* (New York: Knopf, 1991), 193; Lambert, *On Cukor*, 78–79; *THR* (October 26, 1935), 2.

42. Hepburn, *Me: Stories of My Life*, 193–95.

43. Long, *George Cukor*, 21.

44. Andrea Weiss, "A Queer Feeling When I Look at You: Stars and Lesbian Spectatorship in the 1930s," in Christine Gledhill (ed.), *Stardom: Industry of Desire* (London: Routledge, 1991), 287–304.

45. Richard B. Jewell, "RKO Film Grosses, 1929–1951: The C. J. Tevlin Ledger," *Historical Journal of Film, Radio, and Television* 14, no. 1 (1994): 44.

46. *Illustrated Daily News* [Los Angeles, CA] (October 7, 1935) [BRCF/NYPL].

47. *THR* (December 9, 1935), 3.

48. *V* (January 15, 1936), 18; *LAT* (January 19, 1936), 63; *NYT* (January 10, 1936), 12.

49. Louella O. Parsons, "Today in Hollywood," *SFE* (December 5, 1935), 14.

50. Thirer, "Handsome Mr. Grant."

51. *DV* (September 13, 1935), 3; *V* (January 1, 1936), 132.

52. *THR* (September 13, 1935), 1.

53. *V* (August 19, 1936), 17.

54. *THR* (March 23, 1937), p. 3.

55. Michaelson, "An Intimate Chat with Cary Grant," 1 and 4.

56. *BEW* (November 16, 1935), 1.

57. Paul Holt, "Cary Grant Works On as Father Dies," *Daily Express* [UK] (December 3, 1935, 19), 6.

58. "Certified Entry of Death: Elias Leach" (December 1, 1935). Entry Number 80. General Register Office, Bristol Registration District.

59. Nelson, *Evenings with Cary Grant*, 81–82.

60. Grant, "Archie Leach" *LHJ* (January–February 1963), 134.

61. Read Kendall, "Odd and Interesting," *LAT* (January 24, 1937), 48.

62. Godfrey, *Cary Grant*, 78.

63. "Elsie Leach" (July 26, 1936), Entry in the *Register of Departures, Discharges and Transfers of Voluntary, Temporary and Certified Patients*, Bristol Lunatic Asylum, Bristol City Records Office, Bristol, UK.

64. *THR* (February 4, 1936), 2.

Chapter 12

1. *V* (January 15, 1936), 6; *V* (February 12, 1936), 7; *THR* (January 4, 1936), 8.

2. *MPH* (January 9, 1937), 14–15.

3. Arthur Ungar, "Top Players and Money Directors," *V* (December 23, 1936), 1, 6–7.

4. Louise B. Gabriel, *Images of America: Early Santa Monica* (Charleston, SC: Arcadia Publishing, 2006), 111–17; Nelson, *Evenings with Cary Grant*, 79; David Niven, *The Moon's a Balloon* (New York: Dell, 1972), 220.

5. Nelson, *Evenings with Cary Grant*, 89–91.

6. Sheet 2A, Santa Monica, California (April 22, 1940), Department of Commerce, Bureau of the Census, Sixteenth Census of the United States.

7. Nelson, *Evenings with Cary Grant*, 91.

8. Ibid., 79.

9. Esther Meade, "Still Pals: Not Even a Wife Could Separate Cary and Randy—But Then Virginia Wouldn't Want To," *Modern Screen* (September 1934), 48 and 102.

10. Brendan Gill and Jerome Zerbe, *Happy Times* (New York: Harcourt Brace Jovanovich, 1973), 9–28.

11. Ibid., 43.

12. Cary Grant and Randolph Scott photographs, folders 11 and 12, box 2, PPP/AMPAS.

13. Maude Cheatham, "Movie Bachelors at Home," *Screenland* (January 1936), 30–31 and 87; "Batching It," *Modern Screen* (September 1937), 50–51.

14. *V* (February 5, 1936), 12.

15. Julie Lang Hunt, "We Will Never Understand Cary Grant in Hollywood," *Photoplay* (August 1935), 46–47, 84.

16. *Greenville News* [South Carolina] (March 5, 1936), 1.

17. Jerry Asher, "The Real Story of Randy Scott's Secret Marriage," *Screenland* (November 1936), 24–25, 72; Nott, *The Films of Randolph Scott*, 24–26.

18. *DV* (February 13, 1936), 3; *THR* (February 14, 1936), 2.

19. Patrick McGilligan, *Film Crazy: Interviews With Hollywood Legends* (New York: St. Martin's Griffin, 2000), 25.

20. *NYT* (May 2, 1936), 11.

21. Matthew Bernstein, *Walter Wanger: Hollywood Independent* (Berkeley and Los Angeles: University of California Press, 1994), 436.

22. Lenore Coffee, *Storyline: Recollections of a Hollywood Screenwriter* (London: Cassell and Company, 1973), 116–18.

23. Dialogue Continuity [script] by Herman Mankiewicz (July 30, 1935), *Suzy*, file 2994, Turner/MGM Scripts, Margaret Herrick Library, Academy of Motion Picture Arts and Sciences (hereafter MGM Scripts/AMPAS).

24. Treatment by Lenore Coffee and C. G. Sullivan (August 30, 1935), *Suzy*, file 2995, MGM Scripts/AMPAS.

25. Script by Ernest Vajda, Dorothy Parker and Alan Campbell, October 10, 1935, *Suzy*, file 2996, MGM Scripts/AMPAS.

26. *Illustrated Daily News* [Los Angeles, CA] (October 7, 1935), Scrapbook 6, CGP/Herrick; Thirer, "Handsome Mr. Grant," [BRCF/NYPL]; Alma Whitaker, "Romance Still Interests Screen Romeo, Cary Grant," *LAT* (July 25, 1936), 7.

27. "Advertising," *Suzy*, file 3007, MGM Scripts/AMPAS.

28. *THR* (July 30, 1936), 1.

29. E. J. Mannix Ledger, Howard Strickling Papers, Margaret Herrick Library, Academy of Motion Picture Arts and Sciences (hereafter Mannix/Herrick).

30. *MPH* (July 18, 1936), 52; Frank S. Nugent, "The Screen," *NYT* (July 25, 1936), 16; *V* (July 29, 1936), 14.

31. *LAT* (June 16, 1936), 9; *V* (July 1, 1936), 13.

32. *CT* (December 9, 1936), 24; *NYDN* (November 19, 1936), 68.

33. *V* (November 25, 1936), 14.

34. *V* (December 9, 1936), 10, 16, and 21.

35. "Cary Grant, Actor" (July 16, 1936), file 976, Paramount Pictures Contract Summaries, Margaret Herrick Library, Academy of Motion Pictures Arts and Sciences (hereafter Paramount Contracts/Herrick).

36. Nelson, *Evenings with Cary Grant*, 84.

37. *THR* (January 14, 1937), 1; *THR* (January 18, 1937), 4.

38. Tom Kemper, *Hidden Talent: The Emergence of Hollywood Agents* (Berkeley: University of California Press, 2010), 72.

39. Eliot, *Cary Grant*, 11–12; Lee Guthrie, *The Life and Loves of Cary Grant* (New York and London: Drake, 1977), 95; McCann, *A Class Apart*, 79.

40. Emily Carman, *Independent Stardom: Freelance Women in the Hollywood Studio System* (Austin: University of Texas Press, 2016), 150–61; Kemper, *Hidden Talent*, 124–32.

41. Carman, *Independent Stardom*, 69–70; Gomery, *The Hollywood Studio System*, 33; Meyers, *Gary Cooper*, 126.

42. *DV* (September 23, 1936), 5; "Cary Grant, Actor" (September 18, 1936), file 976, Paramount Contracts/Herrick.

43. *V* (March 10, 1937), 10 and 27; *V* (April 14, 1937), 10 and 34.

44. Nelson, *Evenings with Cary Grant*, 77.

45. "Cary Grant, Actor" (December 8, 1936), file 976, Paramount Contracts/Herrick.

46. *THR* (March 3, 1937), 7.

47. Farmer, *Will There Really Be a Morning?*, 21–22.

48. Jewell, "RKO Film Grosses, 1929–1951," 44.

49. *Photoplay* (February 1937), 76–77; *Hollywood* (February 1937), 57.

Chapter 13

1. Wray, *On the Other Hand*, 108; Bernard F. Dick, *Columbia Pictures: Portrait of a Studio* (Lexington: University of Kentucky Press, 2015).

2. George Stevens Jr., "Interview with Cary Grant," file 25, A Filmmaker's Journey/ AMPAS.

3. Contract between Cary Grant and Columbia Pictures (February 4, 1937), Cary Grant, Personnel Files, Warner Bros. Archives, Cinematic Arts Library, University of Southern California, Los Angeles (hereafter WB/USC).

4. Ibid.

5. *NYT* (March 17, 1937), 31.

6. Nelson, *Evenings with Cary Grant*, 79.

7. Richard Lewis Ward, *A History of the Hal Roach Studios* (Carbondale: Southern Illinois University Press, 2005), 96.

8. Harris, "The Riddle of Cary Grant," 80.

9. "Final Cast and Time Schedule" (March 19, 1937), *Topper*, box 1:104, Hal Roach Papers, Hollywood Museum Collection, Cinematic Arts Library, University of Southern California, Los Angeles (hereafter Roach/AMPAS).

10. Author uncredited, *Topper* script (February 12, 1937), p. 20, box 1:92, Topper, Roach/USC.

11. *NYT* (August 20, 1937), p. 21; *V* (July 14, 1937), p. 20; Philip K. Scheuer, "'Topper,' Novel Fantasy Offered in Screen Form," *LAT* (August 12, 1937), 11.

12. *V* (January 19, 1938), 8.

13. *NYT* (November 4, 1937), 8.

14. *DV* (June 19, 1937), 5; *THR* (July 1, 1937), 1.

15. *DV* (June 22, 1937), 2.

16. Jane M. Greene, "The Road to Reno: *The Awful Truth* and Hollywood Comedy of Remarriage," *Film History* 13, no. 4 (2001), 337–58.

17. Viña Delmar, "*The Awful Truth*: Final Draft" (undated), collection 073, Film Scripts, Charles E. Young Research Library, University of California, Los Angeles .

18. Wes D. Gehring, *Leo McCarey, From Marx to McCarthy* (Lanham, MD: Scarecrow Press, 2005), 156–61.

19. James Mason, *Before I Forget* (London: Sphere Books, 1982 [1981]), 408.

20. Bogdanovich, *Who the Devil Made It*, 413–14; Harris, "Riddle of Cary Grant," 80.

21. Ralph Bellamy, *When the Smoke Hits the Fan* (New York: Doubleday and Co., 1979), 130; Wes D. Gehring, *Irene Dunne: First Lady of Hollywood* (Lanham, MD: Scarecrow Press, 2006), 82.

22. Bogdanovich, *Who the Devil Made It*, 413–14; Harris, "Riddle of Cary Grant," 80.

23. Gehring, *Irene Dunne*, 84–85; Gehring, *Leo McCarey*, 152; Bogdanovich, *Who the Devil Made It*, 379.

24. *DV* (October 6, 1937), 5.

25. Edwin Schallert, "Hollywood Sets Cap for Bigger Film Grosses," *LAT* (December 26, 1937), C1; *V* (January 5, 1938), 54.

26. "Cary Grant" (September 14, 1937), Payroll Records, RKO/UCLA; Gerald Mast, "'Everything's Gonna Be All Right': The Making of *Bringing Up Baby*," in *Bringing Up Baby*, ed. Gerald Mast (New Brunswick, NJ: Rutgers University Press, 1988), 7.

27. Berg, *Kate Remembered*, 95.

28. Richard B. Jewell, *RKO Radio Pictures: A Titan is Born* (Berkeley: University of California Press, 2012), 136.

29. Todd McCarthy, *Howard Hawks: The Grey Fox of Hollywood* (New York: Grove Press, 1997), 247; Linda Rosenkrantz, "The Role That Got Away," *Film Comment* 14, no. 1 (January–February 1978), 42.

30. George Stevens Jr., *Conversations with the Great Moviemakers of Hollywood's Golden Age at the American Film Institute* (New York: Vintage Books, 1997), 123.

31. Bawden and Miller, *Conversations with Classic Film Stars*, 122.

32. Hepburn, *Me: Stories of My Life*, 238.

33. Nelson, *Evenings with Cary Grant*, 100.

34. Stevens Jr., *Conversations with the Great Moviemakers*, 119.

35. Mast, "Making of *Bringing Up Baby*," 8–9.

36. "*Bringing Up Baby*, Final Script" (September 16, 1937), file S589, *Bringing Up Baby*, RKO/UCLA.

37. Ronald R. Butters, "Cary Grant and the Emergence of Gay 'Homosexual,'" *Dictionaries: Journal of the Dictionary Society of North America* 19 (1998): 188–204.

38. Patrick McGilligan, *George Cukor: A Double Life* (New York: St. Martin's Press, 1991), 126.

39. Bogdanovich, *Who the Devil Made It*, 487.

40. Assistant Director's Reports, file P81, *Bringing Up Baby*, RKO/UCLA.

41. Nelson, *Evenings with Cary Grant*, 100.

42. Jewell, *RKO Radio Pictures*, 136–37.

43. Assistant Director's Reports.

44. "Daily Budget Reconciliation" (May 6, 1939), *Bringing Up Baby*, file P81, *Bringing Up Baby*, RKO/UCLA.

45. Mast, "The Making of *Bringing Up Baby*," 13.

46. McCarthy, *Howard Hawks*, 254.

47. *V* (February 16, 1938), 15; *THR* (February 10, 1038), 3; *MPH* (February 19, 1938), 39.

48. *V* (February 23, 1938), 8–10.

49. Frank S. Nugent, "The Screen," *NYT* (March 4, 1938), 17.

50. John Mosher, "The Current Cinema," *New Yorker* (March 5, 1938), 61–62.

51. See, for example, Ed Sullivan's syndicated column, *CT* (February 27, 1938), G2; and Norbert Lusk, "Star Held Miscast in Goofy Farce," *LAT* (March 21, 1938), p. 10.

52. *V* (March 16, 1938), 8–10.

53. *MPH* (June 4, 1938), 81; *MPH* (June 11, 1938), 58.

54. Jewell, "RKO Film Grosses, 1929–1951," Appendix 1.

55. McCarthy, *Howard Hawks*, 256.

56. Berg, *Kate Remembered*, 115–16; Jewell, *RKO Radio Pictures*, 162–63; McCarthy, *Howard Hawks*, 256–57.

57. *MPH* (January 16, 1937), 22.

58. Grant, "Archie Leach," *LHJ* (March 1963), 42.

59. Sullivan, "Ascending!," 26–27.

Chapter 14

1. Letter from Elsie Leach to Archie Leach (September 30, 1937), file 253, box 17, CGP/AMPAS.

2. Letter from Elsie Leach to Archie Leach (November 10, 1937), file 253, box 17, CGP/AMPAS.

3. Letter from Elsie Leach to Archie Leach (September 30, 1937).

4. Amory, "Touch of Class," 4–9.

5. Letter from Elsie Leach to Archie Leach (December 12, 1938), file 253, box 17, CGP/ AMPAS.

6. Letter from Elsie Leach to Archie Leach (January 10, 1939), file 253, box 17, CGP/ AMPAS.

7. Cablegram from Archie Leach to Elsie Leach (August 6, 1938), file 253, box 17, CGP/ AMPAS.

8. Edwin Davis (Kerly, Sons and Karuth) to Cary Grant (January 2, 1942), file 253, box 17, CGP/AMPAS.

9. *DV* (July 1, 1940), 7; *MPH* (January 16, 1937), 22.

10. Wray, *On the Other Hand*, 191.

11. Bosley Crowther, "Modesty and Mr. Grant," *NYT* (December 4, 1938), X9.

12. Nelson, *Evenings with Cary Grant*, 92.

13. Grant, "Archie Leach," 34.

14. Barry Day (ed.), *The Letters of Noël Coward* (London: Methuen, 2007), 363.

15. Nelson, *Evenings with Cary Grant*, 93.

16. *Pittsburgh Post-Gazette* (May 4, 1937), 10; Nancy E. Loe, *William Randolph Hearst: An Illustrated Biography* (Santa Barbara, CA: Albion, 1988), 82.

17. Caroline S. Hoyt, "Man About Town," *Modern Screen* (July 1937), 32–33; Vivian Howard, "Bachelor at Large," *Modern Screen* (April 1936), 38–39.

18. Nelson, *Evenings with Cary Grant*, 82.

19. *Hollywood* (October 1937), 10; *THR* (June 16, 1937), 2.

20. *Motion Picture* (April 1937), 62; *Screenland* (April 1937), 99.

21. Nelson, *Evenings with Cary Grant*, 89; Ginger Rogers, *Ginger: My Story* (London: Headline, 1991), 227–29.

22. *Screenland* (April 1937), 64.

23. Nelson, *Evenings with Cary Grant*, 89.

24. Ibid., 91.

25. Ibid., 102.

26. Louella Parsons, "Cary Grant Billed to Star in *Holiday*," *PI* (December 24, 1937), 9.

27. *THR* (January 11, 1937), 3.

28. Gehring, *Irene Dunne*, 98.

29. Mann, *Kate*, 144–45.

30. McGilligan, *George Cukor*, 141.

31. Schickel, *Cary Grant*, 86.

32. Nelson, *Evenings with Cary Grant*, 51.

33. *DV* (March 9, 1938), 2; Schickel, *Cary Grant*, 86.

34. *THR* (February 5, 1938), 1.

35. *NYDN* (June 24, 1938), 42; *LAT* (May 16, 1938), 32; *THR* (May 16, 1938), 3; *V* (May 18, 1938), 12.

36. *NYT* (June 24, 1938), 15.

37. *LAT* (May 4, 1938), 10.

38. *MPH* (August 6, 1938), 37; and *V* (June 1, 1938), 10; *V* (June 8, 1938), 8; *V* (June 15, 1938), 8; *V* (July 6, 1938), 7.

39. *MPH* (August 13, 1938), 79; *MPH* (August 20, 1938), 58; *MPH* (September 17, 1938), 48.

40. *LAT* (May 22, 1938), IV: 6.

41. *Honolulu Star-Bulletin* (May 14, 1938), 1.

42. "Assistant Director Reports," *Gunga Din*, file 88P, subseries 1072, RKO/UCLA.

43. George Stevens Jr., "Interview with Cary Grant," file 25, George Stevens: A Filmmaker's Journey collection, Margaret Herrick Library, Academy of Motion Picture Arts and Sciences.

44. Susan Winslow, "Interview with Sam Jaffe," file 33, A Filmmaker's Journey/AMPAS.

45. Stevens Jr., "Interview with Cary Grant."

46. Marilyn Ann Moss, *Giant: George Stevens, A Life on Film* (Madison: University of Wisconsin Press, 2004), 3–26.

47. Ibid.

48. Susan Winslow, "Interview with Douglas Fairbanks Jr.," file 22, A Filmmaker's Journey/AMPAS.

49. George Stevens Jr., "Interview with Pandro Berman," file 10, A Filmmaker's Journey/AMPAS.

50. "Estimated and Actual Costs," March 11, 1939, *Gunga Din*, file 88P, subseries 1072, RKO/UCLA; Jewell, *RKO Radio Pictures*, 170.

51. Winslow, "Interview with Douglas Fairbanks Jr."; Jewell, *RKO Radio Pictures*, 169.

52. George Stevens Jr., "Interview with Cary Grant."

53. George Stevens Jr., "Interview with Pandro Berman."

54. "*Gunga Din* screenplay by Ben Hecht and Charles MacArthur added to by Dudley Nichols and Howard Hawks" (June 17, 1937), file 2609, George Stevens Papers, Margaret Herrick Library, Academy of Motion Picture Arts and Sciences (hereafter GSP/AMPAS).

55. Rudy Behlmer, *Behind the Scenes: The Making of . . .* (Hollywood: Samuel French, 1990), 89–92.

56. Douglas Fairbanks Jr., *The Salad Days: An Autobiography* (London: Fontana, 1989), 407–8; Susan Winslow, "Interview with Douglas Fairbanks Jr."

57. George Stevens Jr., "Interview with Pandro Berman."

58. "*Gunga Din* screenplay," 34, 42, 51, 55–56, 63–65, 80, 95.

59. Frederic Cople Jaher and Blair B. King, "Hollywood's India: The Meaning of RKO's *Gunga Din*," *Film and History* 38, no. 2 (2008): 38.

60. *Gunga Din* script (October 26, 1938), file 2612, GSP/AMPAS.

61. James Chapman and Nicholas J. Cull, *Projecting Empire: Imperialism and Popular Cinema* (London: I. B. Tauris, 2009), 43.

62. Jaher and King, "Hollywood's India," 44.

63. *LAT* (January 25, 1938), 8; *NYT* (January 27, 1938), 17; *New Yorker* (February 4, 1939), 60–61; *V* (January 25, 1939), 11.

64. "*Gunga Din* Preview Comments," file 2616, GSP/AMPAS.

65. *V* (February, 1, 1939), 7–8; *V* (February 8, 1939), 8–10; *V* (February 15, 1939), 8–11; *V* (February 22, 1939), 7–9; *V* (March 1, 1939), 9–11; *V* (March 8, 1939), 7–10; *V* (March 15, 1939), 9–11.

66. Jewell, "RKO Film Grosses, 1929–1951," 171.
67. Behlmer, *Behind the Scenes*, 100–1.
68. *THR* (January 25, 1939), 3.
69. Irene Thirer, "Cary Grant Speaks Well of Free-lancing via Contract," *New York Post* (December 1, 1938), 11.
70. Nelson, *Evenings with Cary Grant*, 91–92.
71. Bland Johnson, "Package Must Create Public Demand," clipping dated December 2, 1939, newspaper not indicated, BRCF/NYPL.
72. Cablegram from Cary Grant to John Leach (November 1, 1938), file 253, box 17, CGP/AMPAS.
73. Letter from Elsie Leach to Archie Leach (November 10, 1937).
74. Letter from Elsie Leach to Archie Leach (December 12, 1938).

Chapter 15

1. *Montreal Gazette* (November 24, 1938), 23.
2. *DV* (November 19, 1938), 3; Louella Parsons, "Cary Grant Starts Work on Andes Aviation Film," *PI* (November 25, 1938), 20.
3. Nelson, *Evenings with Cary Grant*, 105–6.
4. *NYDN* (December 12, 1938), 3.
5. Nelson, *Evenings with Cary Grant*, 106; *LAT* (December 15, 1938), 2.
6. Nelson, *Evenings with Cary Grant*, 109–10.
7. *DV* (December 28, 1938), 3.
8. Irene Thirer, "Cary Grant Speaks Well of Free-lancing via Contract," publication and date not indicated, BRCF/NYPL.
9. John Offner, *Jean Arthur: The Actress Nobody Knew* (New York: Limelight Editions, 1997), 86.
10. Bawden and Miller, *Conversations with Classic Film Stars*, 122.
11. McBride, *Hawks on Hawks*, 118.
12. Ibid., 42–43.
13. McCarthy, *Howard Hawks*, 273.
14. Nelson, *Evenings with Cary Grant*, 107.
15. *THR* (May 11, 1939), 3; *NYT* (May 12, 1939), 25; *New Yorker* (May 20, 1939), 89; *V* (May 17, 1939), 12; *Wall Street Journal* (May 12, 1939), 9.
16. *V* (May 24, 1939), 7 and 10; *V* (May 31, 1939), 9–11; *V* (June 7, 1939), 7, 9–10; *V* (June 14, 1939), 9–11.
17. Bogdanovich, *Who the Devil Made It*, 314.
18. Lucie Neville, "Monotonous Parts Fatal for Careers," *Washington Post* (August 14, 1938), TT1.
19. "Estimated and Actual Costs" (August 12, 1939), *In Name Only*, file 95P, subseries 1293, RKO/UCLA.
20. *DV* (January 28, 1939), 3.
21. *DV* (March 27, 1939), 1.
22. Larry Swindell, *Screwball: The Life of Carole Lombard* (Brattleboro, VT: Echo Point, 1976), 252–53.

23. *DV* (December 1, 1938), 1.
24. *Boston Globe* (August 31, 1939), 21; *THR* (August 2, 1939), 3; *LAT* (August 2, 1939), 13; *New Yorker* (August 12, 1939), 49.
25. *NYT* (August 4, 1939), 11.
26. Jewell, "RKO Film Grosses," Appendix 1.
27. *DV* (April 17, 1939), 3.
28. *DV* (April 21, 1939), 3; Louella Parsons, "Close_Ups and Long Shots of the Motion Picture Scene," *SFE* (April 21, 1939), 17.
29. *The Constitution* [Atlanta] (June 10, 1939), 4.
30. Letters from Elsie Leach to Archie Leach (December 12, 1938), (January 10, 1939), (March 28, 1939); and cablegrams (January 17, 1939), (February 8, 1939), (February 17, 1939), box 17, CGP/AMPAS.
31. Letter from Elsie Leach to Archie Leach (March 28, 1939), box 17, CGP/AMPAS.
32. *BEW* (June 26, 1939), 1.
33. *BEP* (June 29, 1939), 6.
34. Letter from Elsie Leach to Archie Leach (October 12, 1943), box 17, CGP/AMPAS.
35. Nelson, *Evenings with Cary Grant*, 109.
36. *CT* (July 30, 1939), SW4.
37. *LAT* (August 8, 1939), 1.
38. *DV* (September 13, 1939), 5.
39. McCarthy, *Howard Hawks*, 282.
40. *THR* (August 2, 1939), 1; *V* (September 6, 1939), 3.
41. *THR* (September 14, 1939), 1; *Washington Post* (September 9, 1939), 11.
42. *DV* (September 18, 1939), 7.
43. Mike Steen, *Hollywood Speaks: An Oral History* (New York: G. P. Putnam's Sons, 1974), 91–92.
44. Ibid.
45. Rosalind Russell and Chris Chase, *Life Is a Banquet* (New York: Random House, 1977), 88–91.
46. Bellamy, *When the Smoke Hits the Fan*, 132–33; Bogdanovich, *Who the Devil Made It*, 316; Nelson, *Evenings with Cary Grant*, 112–13.
47. McCarthy, *Howard Hawks*, 283.
48. Ibid., 256; Russell and Chase, *Life Is a Banquet*, 89; *MPH* (March 29, 1940), 35.
49. *THR* (November 1939, 3); *Detroit Free Press* (hereafter *DFP*) (January 20, 1940), 16; *LAT* (January 27, 1940), 9; *NYT* (January 12, 1940, 13); *V* (January 10, 1940), 14.
50. "AFI's 100 Funniest Movies of All Time." Accessed online: https://www.afi.com/100years/laughs.aspx
51. *SFE* (October 16, 1939), 21.
52. Nelson, *Evenings with Cary Grant*, 109–10.
53. Ibid., 111.

Chapter 16

1. Cary Grant, "A Film Star's Life Is Not So Easy," *BEP* (July 1, 1939), 5.
2. Niven, *The Moon's a Balloon*, 214.

3. Norman Payne, "Should the Boys Be Embarrassed?," *Picturegoer and Film Weekly* (March 2, 1940), 6–7.

4. Scrapbook 10, CGP/AMPAS.

5. H. Mark Glancy, *When Hollywood Loved Britain: The Hollywood "British" Film* (Manchester: Manchester University Press, 1999), 168.

6. *LAT* (October 3, 1939), 12; *New York Herald Tribune* (October 9, 1939), BRCF/NYPL.

7. *DV* (May 20, 1940), 9.

8. *LAT* (November 29, 1940), 3.

9. "Production Schedule" (December 1, 1940), *My Favorite Wife*, box 104P, subseries 1819, RKO/UCLA.

10. "*My Favorite Wife* script" (November 25, 1939), subseries 1819, box 687, RKO/UCLA.

11. James Bawden, "Gail Patrick [interview]," *Films in Review* 32, no. 54 (May 1981): 286–94.

12. Bogdanovich, *Who the Hell Made It*, 664–68.

13. Eliot, *Cary Grant*, 204; Higham and Moseley, *The Lonely Heart*, 107–8.

14. Bogdanovich *Who the Hell Made It*, 664–68.

15. Nelson, *Evenings with Cary Grant*, 115.

16. Louella O. Parsons, "Close-Ups and Long Shots of the Motion Picture Scene," *SFE* (October 21, 1939), 32.

17. *DV* (January 15, 1940), 1; *DV* (March 12, 1940), 1; "*My Favorite Wife* script" (March 13, 1940), subseries 1819, box 687s, RKO/UCLA.

18. Bogdanovich *Who the Hell Made It*, 664–68.

19. "Final Cost report" (December 28, 1940), *My Favorite Wife*, box 104P, subseries 1819, RKO/UCLA.

20. Bogdanovich *Who the Hell Made It*, 664–68.

21. Jewell, "RKO Film Grosses, 1929–1951," Appendix 1.

22. "Cary Grant," *My Favorite Wife*, box PRC-51, Payroll Records, RKO/UCLA.

23. *NYT* (May 31, 1940), 15.

24. *THR* (April 30, 1940), 3; *LAT* (June 29, 1940), 9; *PI* (May 30, 1940), 9; *V* (May 1, 1940), 18.

25. *THR* (February 15, 1939), 11.

26. *DV* (July 15, 1940), 6.

27. *V* (November 13, 1940), 56.

28. James Reid, "Cary Plays the Game His Own Way," *Silver Screen* (October 1940), 24–25, 76–78.

29. Ibid., 76.

30. Mark Glancy, *Hollywood and the Americanization of Britain, from the 1920s to the Present* (London: Tauris, 2014), 255–56.

31. *LAT* (March 27, 1940), 15; *DV* (October 20, 1941), 1 and 11.

32. Nelson, *Evenings with Cary Grant*, 117–18.

33. *LAT* (April 4, 1940), 6; *DV* (June 28, 1940), 8.

34. *NYT* (September 27, 1940), 27; *LAT* (August 19, 1940), 7; *V* (September 4, 1940), 18.

35. *DV* (May 13, 1940), 2; Sheilah Graham, "Hays Says Man Can Take Bath on Screen, but Not in 'Still,'" *The Sun* [Baltimore] (June 9, 1940), 6.

36. *V* (September 18, 1940), 9–10; *V* (September 25, 1940), 9–10; *V* (October 2, 1940), 9–11; *V* (October 9, 1940), 9–11.

37. *V* (November 13, 1940), 56.

38. *LAT* (May 31, 1940), 13; *SFE* (June 2, 1940), 36; *PI* (June 4, 1940), 20.

39. Grant, "Archie Leach," *LHJ* (March 1963), 40.

40. Marcia Kramer, "Only 10 Show Up for Burial of Barbara Hutton," *NYDN* (May 26, 1979), 4C; Enid Nemy, "Barbara Hutton Dies on Coast at 66," *NYT* (May 13, 1979), 1 and 28.

41. Nemy, "Barbara Hutton Dies on Coast," 28.

42. Cary Grant, "Archie Leach," *LHJ* (April 1963), 151; Mayme Ober Peak, "Barbara's Millions Too Much for Cary," *Boston Sunday Globe* (September 3, 1944), 6.

43. Nemy, "Barbara Hutton Dies on Coast," 28.

44. Fairbanks, *The Salad Days*, 494–95; Nelson, *Evenings with Cary Grant*, 116–17; Louella O. Parsons, "What Next for Cary Grant?," *Photoplay* (August 1945), 32–33.

45. Katherine Clarke, "Cary Grant's History-Steeped Former Home to Hit the Market," *Wall Street Journal* (February 13, 2018). Available online: https://www.mansionglobal. com/articles/cary-grant-s-history-steeped-former-home-to-hit-the-market-88619

46. Louella O. Parsons, "The Married Life of the Cary Grants," *Photoplay* (February 1944), 28–29; Patricia O'Brien, "Love, Money and Barbara Hutton," *CT* (May 27, 1979), 12: 9.

47. Joseph Henry Steele, "How Cary Grant Lives," *Photoplay* (September 1940), 20–23, 84; Harris, "The Riddle of Cary Grant," 80.

48. Eliot, *Cary Grant*, 200–1.

49. Fairbanks, *The Salad Days*, 572; Nelson, *Evenings with Cary Grant*, 155; Parsons, "Married Life of the Cary Grants," 28–29.

50. *SFE* (September 17, 1940), 19.

51. Berg, *Kate Remembered*, 134–36.

52. Hepburn, *Me*, 216–19.

53. "Cary Grant," *Passport to Life*, box PRC-51, Payroll Records, RKO/UCLA; Kanin, *Great Hollywood Teams*, 148.

54. Bawden and Miller, *Conversations with Classic Film Stars*, 122.

55. *DV* (July 5, 1940), 3.

56. Hepburn, *Me*, 217.

57. Cary Grant, "The Role I Liked Best," *Saturday Evening Post* (January 10, 1948), 94.

58. "Synopsis of a screenplay dated June 27, 1940, with changes to July 2, 1940, by Waldo Salt and Donald Ogden Stewart," *The Philadelphia Story*, MGM Script Files, University of Southern California (hereafter MGM/USC).

59. "Dialogue treatment from Waldo Salt and Robert Metzler" (March 8, 1940), *The Philadelphia Story*, MGM/USC.

60. Bawden and Miller, *Conversations with Classic Film Stars*, 122.

61. Kael, "Cary Grant," 321–22.

62. McGilligan, *George Cukor*, 162–63.

63. *LAT* (September 16, 1940), 10.

64. Eddie Mannix Ledger, Strickling/Herrick; *V* (December 31, 1941), 1.

65. *NYT* (December 27, 1940), 22; *V* (November 27, 1940), 16.

66. *LAT* (December 5, 1940), 11.

67. Letter from Joseph Mankiewicz to Cary Grant (January 16, 1941), file 272, CGP/AMPAS.

68. Grant, "The Role I Liked Best."

69. *DV* (July 3, 1940), 1; Nelson, *Evenings with Cary Grant*, 120.

70. Higham and Moseley, *The Lonely Heart*, 176–77; McCann, *A Class Apart*, 134–35.

71. "King's Medal for Service in the Cause of Freedom: United States of America, F to J," file KMS 35, T339/36, Public Record Office, Kew, National Archives of the United Kingdom.

Chapter 17

1. Roger Carroll, "Catching Up with Cary," *Motion Picture* (February 1941), 21–23.

2. Edwin Schallert, "Grant Likely Lead in 'Reap the Wild Wind,'" *LAT* (December 17, 1940), 11.

3. *DV* (March 21, 1940), 2; *DV* (January 22, 1940), 3; *SFE* (September 17, 1940), 19.

4. George Cooper Stevens, *George Stevens: Interviews* (Jackson: University of Mississippi Press, 2004), 111.

5. Carroll, "Catching Up with Cary," 21.

6. Moss, *Giant*, 76.

7. Stevens, *George Stevens: Interviews*, 111.

8. Susan Winslow, "Interview with Irene Dunne" (April 26, 1982), file 21, *A Filmmaker's Journey*, AMPAS.

9. Bawden and Miller, *Conversations with Classic Film Stars*, 172.

10. Hedda Hopper, "Baby Scenes to Make 'Penny Serenade' Popular," *LAT* (April 19, 1941), 9; Edwin Schallert, "Sentiment Appeals in 'Penny Serenade,'" *LAT* (April 17, 1941), 2:11.

11. *NYT* (May 23, 1941), 25; *V* (April 16, 1941), 16.

12. *V* (May 15, 1941), 9; *V* (September 3, 1941), 24.

13. Gehring, *Irene Dunne*, 61–63.

14. Nelson, *Evenings with Cary Grant*, 115.

15. Ibid., 121.

16. Bawden and Miller, *Conversations with Classic Film Stars*, 123.

17. *SFE* (September 17, 1940), 19.

18. John Russell Taylor, *Hitch: The Life and Work of Alfred Hitchcock* (London: Abacus, 1981), 155.

19. Patrick McGilligan, *Alfred Hitchcock: A Life in Darkness and in Light* (New York: HarperCollins, 2003), 4.

20. Ibid., 263.

21. Cablegram from Archie Leach to Elsie Leach (August 13, 1940), file 253, box 17, CGP/AMPAS.

22. Cablegram from Archie Leach to Elsie Leach (September 14, 1940), file 253, box 17, CGP/AMPAS.

23. Cablegram from Archie Leach to Elsie Leach (October 28, 1940), file 253, box 17, CGP/AMPAS.

24. Cablegram from Elsie Leach to Archie Leach (October 15, 1940), file 253, box 17, CGP/AMPAS.

25. Helen Reid, *Bristol Under Siege: Surviving the Wartime Blitz* (Bristol: Redcliffe Press, 2005), 48.

26. Commonwealth War Graves Commission. *UK, WWII Civilian Deaths, 1939–1945* [Ancestry.com database online]; Letter from Cary Grant to Mrs. Robert L. Pierce (July 5, 1984), file 301, CGP/AMPAS; Grant, "Archie Leach," *LHJ* (January–February 1963), 138.

27. *DV* (March 31, 1941), 2.

28. *LAT* (May 13, 1940), 11

29. George Stevens Jr., "Interview with Cary Grant," file 25, *A Filmmaker's Journey*, AMPAS.

30. Glancy, *When Hollywood Loved Britain*, 170.

31. *DV* (September 23, 1940), 10; McGilligan, *Alfred Hitchcock*, 267–68.

32. *Box Office* (September 21, 1940), 15; James Monaco, "Cary on Hitch," *Take One* (May 1976), 20; Taylor, *Hitch*, 155.

33. Frances Iles, *Before the Fact* (London: Gollancz, 1932).

34. Paul Trivers, "*Before the Fact*: story treatment" (January 14, 1936), box 431; Boris Ingster and Arnaud d'Isseau, "*Before the Fact*: step plot" (November 16, 1939), box 430; Boris Ingster and Nathanael West, "*Before the Fact*: screenplay" (January 16, 1940), box 431, *Suspicion* script files, RKO/UCLA.

35. Taylor, *Hitch*, 155.

36. McGilligan, *Alfred Hitchcock*, 286.

37. François Truffaut with Helen G. Scott, *Hitchcock*, revised edition (London: Paladin, 1984), 198–200; Bawden and Miller, *Conversations with Classic Film Stars*, 121.

38. Ibid.; Nelson, *Evenings with Cary Grant*, 124.

39. "Daily Progress Reports" (January 31, 1941 to April 23, 1941), *Suspicion* production files, box 116, RKO/UCLA.

40. Joan Harrison and Alma Reville, "*Before the Fact*: first draft script" (November 28, 1940); Joan Harrison, Alma Reville, and Samson Raphelson, "*Before the Fact*: screenplay" (December 28, 1940 with changes through June 23, 1941); Samson Raphelson, "*Before the Fact*: notes on structural ideas" (February 18, 1941); box 431, *Suspicion* script files, RKO/UCLA.

41. "*Before the Fact* previews," folder 657, Alfred Hitchcock Papers, Margaret Herrick Library, Academy of Motion Picture Arts and Sciences (hereafter Hitchcock/AMPAS).

42. "*Before the Fact*: budget" (February 4, 1941); "*Suspicion*: negative cost" (August 23, 1941); *Suspicion* production files, box 116, RKO/UCLA.

43. Author uncredited, "*Before the Fact*: new ending" (July 18, 1941), folder 655, Hitchcock/AMPAS.

44. *THR* (September 18, 1941), 3.

45. *V* (September 24, 1941), 8.

46. *NYT* (November 21, 1941), 23.

47. Truffaut with Scott, *Hitchcock*, 198; Sidney Gottlieb (ed.), *Alfred Hitchcock Interviews* (Jackson: University of Mississippi, 2003), 92; Rick Worland, "Before and After the Fact: Writing and Reading Hitchcock's 'Suspicion,'" *Cinema Journal* 41, no. 4 (Summer 2002): 3–26.

48. Jewell, "RKO Film Grosses," Appendix 1, 31.

49. Joan Fontaine, *No Bed of Roses: An Autobiography* (New York: William Morrow, 1978), 133–34.

50. Telegram from Alfred Hitchcock to George Schaefer (August 18, 1941), *Suspicion* production files, folder 657, RKO/UCLA.

51. Donaldson and Royce, *An Affair to Remember*, 230.

52. Letter from Jack Warner to Hal Wallis (March 5, 1941); Inter-office memo from Paul Nathan to Hal Wallis (March 8, 1941); *The Man Who Came to Dinner* production files, WB/USC.

53. Memo from Jack Warner (January 27, 1941); Memo: Proposed Cary Grant deal (unsigned, undated); *The Man Who Came to Dinner* production files, WB/USC.

54. Notes of a phone conversation between Jack Warner and Sam Briskin (April 9, 1941), *The Man Who Came to Dinner* production files, WB/USC.

55. Inter-office memo from Howard Hawks to Hal Wallis (April 4, 1941); Inter-office memo from Steve Trilling to Hal Wallis (May 16, 1941); *The Man Who Came to Dinner* production files, WB/USC.

56. Telegram from Jack Warner to Frank Capra (September 26, 1941), *Arsenic and Old Lace* production files, WB/USC.

57. Amory, "Touch of Class," 5; Nelson, *Evenings with Cary Grant*, 125–26.

58. Richard Schickel, *Cary Grant: A Celebration* (London: Bloomsbury Books, 1995 [1983]) 126.

59. Frank Capra, *The Name Above the Title: An Autobiography* (New York: Da Capo Press, 1997), 311.

60. Nelson, *Evenings with Cary Grant*, 125–26.

61. Harris, *Cary Grant*, 122; Wansell, *Cary Grant*, 79.

62. "Contract: Warner Bros. and Cary Grant" (September 25, 1941), *Arsenic and Old Lace* production files, WB/USC.

63. Inter-office memo from Roy Obringer to [illegible] (December 13, 1941), *Arsenic and Old Lace* production files, WB/USC.

64. *THR* (September 1, 1944), 3; Edwin Schallert, "Arsenic Gay Grim Screen Excursion," *LAT* (September 23, 1944), 7.

65. *NYT* (September 2, 1944), 17.

66. *Daily Mirror* [New York, NY] (September 11, 1944), 18.

67. Orry-Kelly, *Women I've Undressed*, 262.

Chapter 18

1. Roy Hoopes, *When the Stars Went to War: Hollywood and World War II* (New York: Random House, 1994), 73–98.

2. *LAT* (June 27, 1942), 1.

3. Mary Morris, "Meet Cary Grant," *PM* (April 30, 1944), 10.

4. *DV* (January 9, 1942), 6.

5. *DV* (August 20, 1941), 2.

6. George Stevens Jr., "Interview with Cary Grant," file 25, *A Filmmaker's Journey*, AMPAS.

7. *DFP* (July 7, 1942), 4.

8. *DV* (June 23, 1942), 7; *LAT* (June 25, 1942), 2:10; *SFE* (August 16, 1942), 89.

9. Moss, *Giant*, 96–97.

10. Stevens Jr., "Interview with Cary Grant."

11. Susan Winslow, "Interview with Jean Arthur," file 4, *A Filmmaker's Journey*, AMPAS.

12. Bawden and Miller, *Conversations with Classic Film Stars*, 122.

13. *THR* (May 28, 1942), 3.

14. *V* (July 29, 1942), 8.

15. *NYDN* (August 28, 1942), 44; *LAT* (August 31, 1942), 8.

16. *V* (January 6, 1943), 58.

17. Joseph F. Dinneen, "Man Pays $1000 for Autographs of Stars," *Boston Daily Globe* (May 2, 1942), 1 and 5; Martha Jackson, "The Hollywood Victory Caravan," *St. Louis Star-Times* (May 7, 1942), 22.

18. *St. Louis Post-Dispatch* (May 8, 1942), 3.

19. Hazel Holly, "Backstage with the Victory Caravan!," *SFE* (May 20, 1942), 17.

20. *St. Louis Post-Dispatch* (May 2, 1942), 5.

21. Fred G. Hyde, "16,000 Hail Show of Film Caravan," *PI* (May 3, 1942), 16.

22. William Moore, "Film Stars Sell Kisses," *CT* (May 7, 1942), 3.

23. *DV* (May 15, 1942), 1; *DV* (May 20, 1942), 1.

24. "Archibald Alexander Leach," Petition 98061, Petitions (1942), California, Federal Naturalization Records, 1843–1999. Online database: https://www.ancestry.co.uk

25. *LAT* (June 27, 1942), 1.

26. *LAT* (July 10, 1942), 36; *Sunday Pictorial* (July 12, 1942), 2.

27. Harris, "The Riddle of Cary Grant," 81.

28. Barbara Boston and Warren Hall, "Barbara Hutton is Back in Circulation," *NYDN* (March 6, 1941), 10.

29. Jimmie Fidler, "In Hollywood," *St. Louis Star-Times* (March 6, 1942), 11; Hedda Hopper, "Hollywood," *LAT* (June 9, 1942), 2:9; Louella O. Parsons, "Glamour Queens Without Escorts," *SFE* (January 12, 1941), 28; Ed Sullivan, "Little Old New York," *NYDN* (December 8, 1941), 51; Walter Winchell, "On Broadway," *NYDN* (October 9, 1941), 48.

30. *St. Louis Post-Dispatch* (October 27, 1941), 4:1.

31. John Franchey, "Blondes Preferred," *Modern Screen* (June 1941), 28–29.

32. *NYT* (July 9, 1942), 23; Cynthia Miller, "I, Cary, Take Thee, Barbara," *Modern Screen* (October 1942), 36–37, 66; Sally Jefferson, "Matrimony Deferred," *Photoplay* (October 1942), 64–65.

33. *LAT* (July 10, 1942), 38.

34. Robbin Cross, "Director Takes Bow" [uncredited newspaper clipping], BRCF/ NYPL.

35. Ibid.

36. Gehring, *Leo McCarey*, 183–85.

37. Patrick McGilligan, *Film Crazy: Interviews with Hollywood Legends* (New York: St. Martin's Griffin, 2000), 161.

38. Ibid.

39. *DV* (June 8, 1942), 2.

40. Kate Cameron, "Ginger Rogers–Cary Grant, New Comedy Team," *NYDN* (November 13, 1942), 52; Edwin Schallert, "'Once Upon a Honeymoon' Ekes Fun Out of Tragedy," *LAT* (December 26, 1942), 8.

41. Jewell, "RKO Film Grosses," Appendix 1.

42. Nelson, *Evenings with Cary Grant*, 130; *NYT* (October 6, 1942), 19.

43. "Affidavit to Support Claim for Occupational Deferment" dated June 26, 1942, file 758, CGP/AMPAS.

44. *V* (February 11, 1942), 5.

45. *SFE* (February 5, 1942), 16.

46. Budget (November 17, 1942), *Mr. Lucky* production files, file 133P, RKO/UCLA.

47. Milton Holmes, "Bundles for Freedom" (January 30, 1942), *Mr. Lucky* script files, file S889, RKO/UCLA.

48. "Budget" (November 17, 1942), *Mr. Lucky*, production files, file 133P, RKO/UCLA.

49. Hedda Hopper, "Hollywood," *NYDN* (July 7, 1942), 34; *V* (November 4, 1942), 3.

50. *LAT* (August 18, 1943), 12; *NYT* (July 23, 1943), 21; *SFE* (July 9, 1943), 11.

51. Jewell, "RKO Film Grosses," Appendix 1.

52. Nelson, *Evenings with Cary Grant*, 130–32; Hoopes, *When the Stars Went to War*, 220–39.

53. *The Times* [Shreveport, LA] (March 17, 1943), 8; *Town Talk* [Alexandria, LA] (March 18, 1943), 11; *Sheboygan Press* [Sheboygan, WI] (March 20, 1943), 3.

54. *V* (March 3, 1943), 1 and 47.

55. Mary Morris, "Meet Cary Grant," *PM Sunday Magazine* (April 30, 1944), 10.

56. *DV* (April 14, 1943), 4.

57. Letter from Cary Grant to H. H. Bolds, US Department of State (May 5, 1943), file 657, CGP/AMPAS.

58. Julia McCarthy, "The Near Riot Was Dimpled Devil Cary," *NYDN* (March 3, 1943), 43; Hedda Hopper, "Hollywood," *NYDN* (March 21, 1943), 72.

59. *Sunday Pictorial* (July 12, 1942), 2.

60. Letter from Elsie Leach to Archie Leach (November 1, 1942), box 17, CGP/AMPAS.

61. Harris, "The Riddle of Cary Grant," 80–81; Fairbanks, *The Salad Days*, 494, 505, 772–73.

Chapter 19

1. *Washington Post* (July 26, 1942), 2 and 4.

2. "Cary Grant," *Mr. Lucky*, box PRC-51, Payroll Records, RKO/UCLA; Memo from Morton Garbus (undated), Contracts and Agreements, file 521, CGP/AMPAS.

3. Contract between Cary Grant and Columbia Pictures (February 4, 1937), Cary Grant personnel file, WB/USC.

4. Letter from Harry Cohn to Cary Grant (May 29, 1943), Cary Grant personnel file, WB/USC.

5. Letter from B. B. Kahane (Columbia Pictures) to Cary Grant (June 16, 1943), Cary Grant personnel file, WB/USC.

6. Letter from Jerry Wald (Warner Bros.) to Cary Grant (June 2, 1943), file 17, box 2, CGP/AMPAS.

7. Nelson, *Evenings with Cary Grant*, 135–38.

8. Kate Cameron, "*Destination Tokyo*: Whale of a Thriller," *NYDN* (January 1, 1944), 15C; Bosley Crowther, "*Destination Tokyo*," *NYT* (January 1, 1944), 9; Philip K. Scheuer, "Inside Story of Tokyo Raid Thriller," *LAT* (January 1, 1944), 5.

9. *V* (December 22, 1943), 12; *THR* (December 21, 1943), 3.

10. William Schaefer Ledger, WB/USC.

11. Lillian Ross, "Isn't It Wonderful," *New Yorker* (June 3, 2002), 76.

12. Letter from B. B. Kahane (Columbia Pictures) to Cary Grant (undated), Cary Grant personnel file, WB/USC.

13. *V* (April 16, 1941), 33.

14. *DV* (December 22, 1942), 4; *DV* (January 18, 1943), 6; *DV* (January 22, 1943), 1.

15. Letter from Ted Donaldson to Cary Grant (June 20, 1979), file 181, CGP/AMPAS.

16. Louella O. Parsons, "In Hollywood," *SFE* (March 21, 1944), 16.

17. Bosley Crowther, "Pleasant Fantasy," *NYT* (June 30, 1944), 17; Wanda Hale, "*Once Upon a Time*: Happy Innovation," *NYDN* (June 30, 1944), 30; *V* (April 26, 1944), 12.

18. *V* (July 5, 1944), 16–17; *V* (July 12, 1944), 14–15; *V* (July 19, 1944), 15–16.

19. Parsons, "The Married Life of the Cary Grants," 28–29, 76–79.

20. Nelson, *Evenings with Cary Grant*, 148–49.

21. Harris, "The Riddle of Cary Grant," 80–81; *NYT* (August 31, 1945), 19.

22. Mary Morris, "An Interview with Cary Grant," *PM Sunday Picture News* (April 30, 1944), Scrapbook 15, CGP/AMPAS.

23. Author uncredited, "The New Barbara Hutton," *American Weekly* (August 18, 1946), 4–5.

24. Hedda Hopper, "The Fighting Grants," *Modern Screen* (October 1944), 56, 102–3.

25. Harris, "The Riddle of Cary Grant," 81.

26. Louella O. Parsons, "In Hollywood," *SFE* (January 21, 1944), 23.

27. Hedda Hopper, "Looking at Hollywood," *LAT* (July 21, 1943), 12; Pete Martin, "How Grant Took Hollywood," *Saturday Evening Post* (February 19, 1949), 22; *V* (June 30, 1943), 24.

28. "Final Cost Summary" (October 18, 1944), *None but the Lonely Heart*, box 140P, RKO/UCLA.

29. Clifford Odets, "None but the Lonely Heart" (screenplay dated August 20, 1943), box 988S, *None but the Lonely Heart*, RKO/UCLA.

30. Nelson, *Evenings with Cary Grant*, 141–44.

31. Ibid., 29; Clifford Odets, "Notes: Ernie," *None but the Lonely Heart*, box 19, subseries 2, Clifford Odets Papers, Billy Rose Theatre Division, New York Public Library for the Performing Arts (hereafter COP/NYPL).

32. *THR* (October 15, 1943), 1.

33. Clifford Odets, "None but the Lonely Heart" (screenplay dated August 20, 1943), box 988S, *None but the Lonely Heart*, RKO/UCLA, 11.

34. Truffaut with Scott, *Hitchcock*, 171–72.

35. Ibid., 135–36.

36. *NYT* (December 24, 1943), 17.

37. Mordecai Gorelik, "Hollywood's Art Machinery," *Sight and Sound* (Autumn 1946), 90–91.

38. "Final Cost Summary" (October 18, 1944), *None but the Lonely Heart* production files, box 140P, RKO/UCLA.

39. Clifford Odets, "Research for the Film," box 18, COP/NYPL; *Boston Sunday Globe Pictorial* (November 5, 1944), 2.

40. Ibid.

41. Author uncredited, "None but the Lonely Heart," *Kirkus Reviews* (September 28, 1943), https://www.kirkusreviews.com/book-reviews/richard-llewellyn-2/none-but-the-lonely-heart/.

42. Clifford Odets, "Notes: Ernie," *None but the Lonely Heart*, COP/NYPL.

43. Clifford Odets, "None but the Lonely Heart" (screenplay dated December 18, 1943), *None but the Lonely Heart* story files, box 988S, RKO/UCLA, 66.

44. Bosley Crowther, "*None but the Lonely Heart*," *NYT* (November 18, 1944), 12; Edwin Schallert, "Grant, Barrymore Star in Murky Story," *LAT* (October 21, 1944), 5; *THR* (October 2, 1944), 3; *V* (October 4, 1944), 8.

45. James Agee, "*None but the Lonely Heart*," *The Nation* (December 2, 1944), 21; John Lardner, "The Current Cinema," *New Yorker* (November 24, 1944), 78.

46. Richard B. Jewell, "RKO Film Grosses," Appendix 1.

47. William Schaefer Ledger, WB/USC.

48. Bawden and Miller, *Conversations with Classic Film Stars*, 125.

49. *LAT* (October 29, 1943), 14; *NYDN* (January 16, 1944), 6.

50. *DV* (January 22, 1945), 3; Office of Talent Reports 20-31 (1944), Hollywood Victory Committee, Special Collections, Cinematic Arts Library, University of Southern California, Los Angeles (hereafter HVC/USC).

51. Parsons, "What Next for Cary Grant?," 32–36, 106.

52. *LAT* (May 26, 1944), 1; *SFE* (March 1, 1945), 1.

53. *SFE* (July 25, 1944), 1.

54. Louella O. Parsons, "Barbara Hutton and Cary Grant Parted; Will Delay Divorce," *SFE* (August 15, 1944), 1.

55. Russell and Chase, *Life Is a Banquet*, 143.

56. Hedda Hopper, "Looking at Hollywood," *LAT* (September 13, 1944), 12; Elsa Maxwell, "Elsa Maxwell's Party Line," *Pittsburgh Post-Gazette* (September 22, 1944), 19; *Life Magazine* (October 9, 1944), 91–95.

57. Richard B. Jewell, *Slow Fade to Black: The Decline of RKO Radio Pictures* (Oakland: University of California Press, 2016), 23.

58. Phyllis Battelle, "Sentimental View of San Francisco," *Pittsburgh Sun-Telegraph* (April 1, 1944), 19.

59. Memo from Jack Warner to Steve Trilling (August 17, 1944), Cary Grant personnel file, WB/USC.

60. Memo from Trilling to Warner (August 8, 1944), Cary Grant personnel file, WB/USC.

61. Memo from Trilling to Warner (September 28, 1944), Cary Grant personnel file, WM/USC.

62. Harris, "The Riddle of Cary Grant," 80–81.

63. *LAT* (November 19, 1944), C9.

64. Harris, "The Riddle of Cary Grant," 81; Amory, "Touch of Class," 4–9.

65. Hortense Morton, "Close-Up of Cary Grant Given Press by Golden Gate Theater," *SFE* (November 4, 1944), 16.

66. Office of Talent Reports 32-39 (1945), HVC/USC.

67. Hedda Hopper, "Dime Store Heiress, Cary Grant, Part Again," *LAT* (February 27, 1945), B1.

68. *Time* (September 10, 1945), 24.

69. Nelson, *Evenings with Cary Grant*, 147–48.

70. *NYT* (August 31, 1945), 19.

71. Ibid.

72. "The New Barbara Hutton," 4–5.

Chapter 20

1. Arthur Schwartz to Steve Trilling (April 2, 1945); Arthur Schwartz to Roy Obringer (April 12, 1945); Cary Grant to Warner Bros. (May 2, 1945), Cary Grant personnel file, WB/USC.

2. Cole Porter contract (August 6, 1943); Letter from Jack Warner to Cole Porter (August 14, 1943), *Night and Day* legal file, WB/USC.

3. Memo from Mr. Obringer to Mary Lou Mitchell (February 23, 1945), Cary Grant personnel file, WB/USC.

4. George Stevens Jr., "Interview with Cary Grant," file 25, A Filmmaker's Journey/AMPAS.

5. Daily Progress Reports (June 29, 1945, and June 30, 1945), *Night and Day* production file, WB/USC.

6. Daily Progress Reports (June 16, 1945, and July 11, 1945), *Night and Day* production file, WB/USC.

7. Memo from Jack Moffit to Hal Wallis (July 14, 1943), *Night and Day* story file, WB/USC.

8. William McBrien, *Cole Porter* (New York: Alfred A. Knopf, 1998), 103.

9. Memo from Arthur Schwartz to Jack Warner (April 13, 1944), *Night and Day* legal file, WB/USC.

10. Daily Progress Report (July 14, 1945), *Night and Day* production file, WB/USC.

11. Daily Progress Report (August 22, 1945), *Night and Day* production file WB/USC.

12. Daily Progress Report (September 5, 1945), *Night and Day* production file, WB/USC.

13. Daily Progress Reports (July 21, 1945, and August 28, 1945), *Night and Day* production file, WB/USC.

14. Daily Progress Report (July 6, 1945), *Night and Day* production file, WB/USC.

15. Daily Progress Report (August 18, 1945), *Night and Day* production file, WB/USC.

16. William Schaefer Ledger, WB/USC.

17. Letter from Jack Warner to Cole Porter (February 11, 1946), *Night and Day* story file, WB/USC.

18. *Life* (August 5, 1946), 101–7; Kate Cameron, "Cole Porter's Tunes Highlight Film Biog," *NYDN* (July 26, 1946), 42; John McCarten, "The Current Cinema," *New Yorker* (July 27, 1946), 48; T. M. P., "Night and Day, Warner Version of Cole Porter's Life," *NYT* (July 26, 1946), 16; *V* (July 7, 1946), 8.

19. William Schaefer Ledger, WB/USC.

20. Cary Grant, "Archie Leach," *LHJ* (March 1963), 40.

21. Tex McCrary and Jinx Falkenberg, "A Suspenseful Postcard for Cary," *St. Louis Post-Dispatch* (August 21, 1951), 2D.

22. James Monaco, "Cary on Hitch," *Take One* (May 1976), 20.

23. McGilligan, *Alfred Hitchcock*, 401.

24. Letter from Morton Garbus to Cary Grant (October 5, 1949), file 521, CGP/AMPAS.

25. *V* (March 31, 1948), 3 and 17.

26. Leonard Leff, *Hitchcock and Selznick: The Rich and Strange Collaboration of Alfred Hitchcock and David O. Selznick in Hollywood* (Berkeley: University of California Press, 1999), 207; McGilligan, *Alfred Hitchcock*, 357.

27. McGilligan, *Alfred Hitchcock*, 379–80; Donald Spoto, *Notorious: The Life of Ingrid Bergman* (New York: HarperCollins, 1997), 165–66, 192.

28. Ingrid Bergman and Alan Burgess, *Ingrid Bergman: My Story* (London: Michael Joseph, 1980), 77

29. McGilligan, *Alfred Hitchcock*, 380; Spoto, *Notorious*, 198.

30. Nelson, *Evenings with Cary Grant*, 149–51.

31. Bergman and Burgess, *Ingrid Bergman: My Story*, 76–77.

32. *SFE* (February 2, 1946), 13.

33. *St. Louis Post-Dispatch* (March 15, 1945), 3; *St. Louis Star-Times* (March 15, 1945), 3.

34. Spoto, *Notorious*, 182–84.

35. Truffaut with Scott, *Hitchcock*, 400.

36. McGilligan, *Alfred Hitchcock*, 380–81; Donald Spoto, *The Dark Side of Genius: The Life of Alfred Hitchcock* (New York: Ballantine, 1983), 304.

37. Jewell, "RKO Film Grosses, 1929–1951," Appendix 1.

38. Bosley Crowther, "The Screen in Review," *NYT* (August 16, 1946), 19; John McNulty, "The Current Cinema," *New Yorker* (August 24, 1946), 42; Philip K. Scheuer, "'Notorious' Fascinating to Watch," *LAT* (August 23, 1946), 2:7; *Time* (August 19, 1946), 98–100; *V* (July 24, 1946), 6.

39. *THR* (July 24, 1946), 3.

40. Samuel Taylor, "Preliminary Memorandum on 'Hamlet'" (November 2, 1945), folder 1124, Hitchcock/AMPAS.

41. Letter from Alfred Hitchcock to Cyrus Friedman (October 3, 1945), folder 1124, Hitchcock/AMPAS; *V* (October 27, 1954), 5.

42. McGilligan, *Alfred Hitchcock*, 371; Spoto, *The Dark Side of Genius*, 303.

43. *DV* (February 13, 1946), 2; *DV* (February 18, 1946), 7; *LAT* (March 5, 1946), 2:1; *V* (February 20, 1946), 2

44. Louella Parsons, "Hollywood," *SFE* (April 2, 1946), 9.

45. *Modern Screen* (March 1946), 77; *LAT* (January 17, 1947), 2.

46. Letter from Elsie Leach to Archie Leach (December 10, 1943), box 17, CGP/AMPAS.

47. Letter from Elsie Leach to Archie Leach (December 4, 1944), box 17, CGP/AMPAS.

48. Letter from Elsie Leach to Archie Leach (February 10, 1946), box 17, CGP/AMPAS.

49. Cablegram from Archie Leach to Elsie Leach (March 14, 1946), box 17, CGP/AMPAS.

50. Edwin Schallert, "Partnership Announced by Cary Grant, Korda," *LAT* (April 2, 1946), 11; *V* (April 3, 1946), 4.

51. Taylor, "Preliminary Memorandum on 'Hamlet.'"

52. *BEP* (April 25, 1946), 1; Scrapbook 15, CGP/AMPAS.

53. Selwyn Valters, "'World' Has a Visitor—Cary Grant," *BEW* (April 26, 1946), 1 and 6.

54. Ibid.

55. Sidney Sheldon, *The Other Side of Me* (London: HarperCollins, 2005), 154.

56. Ibid., 159–60; Schary, *Heyday*, 140.

57. Kotsilibas-Davis and Loy, *Myrna Loy*, 204.

58. "Budget of Production Cost" (July 22, 1946), *The Bachelor and the Bobby-Soxer*, file 159P, subseries 155, RKO/UCLA.

59. Kotsilibas-Davis and Loy, *Myrna Loy*, 204–5.

60. Schary, *Heyday*, 140.

61. Shirley Temple Black, *Child Star: An Autobiography* (New York: McGraw-Hill, 1989), 400.

62. Schary, *Heyday*, 140.

63. Black, *Child Star*, 401–2.

64. Bosley Crowther, "The Screen," *NYT* (July 25, 1947), 12; John McCarten, "Fair Enough," *New Yorker* (August 2, 1947), 47; Edwin Schallert, "'Bachelor, Bobby-Soxer' Comedy Hit," *LAT* (August 15, 1947), 2:2; *V* (June 4, 1947), 16.

65. Jewell, "RKO Film Grosses, 1929–1951," Appendix 1.

66. Ibid.

67. Florence Fisher Parry, "I Dare Say—Cary Grant," *Pittsburgh Press* (August 21, 1946), Scrapbook 15, CGP/AMPAS.

Chapter 21

1. Hedda Hopper, "Cary Grant Picks Roles," *LAT* (June 29, 1947), 3:1; Elsa Maxwell, "That Angel, Cary," *Photoplay* (April 1948), 44 and 79–80.

2. *LAT* (January 17, 1947), 2; *Time* (July 27, 1962), 55.

3. Grant, "Archie Leach," *LHJ* (March 1963), 40.

4. Amory, "Touch of Class," 4–9; Hedda Hopper, "Hollywood," *LAT* (September 18, 1949), 4:1.

5. Irene Mayer Selznick, *A Private View* (London: Weidenfeld and Nicolson, 1987), 290–91.

6. Karina Longworth, *Seduction: Sex, Lies, and Stardom in Howard Hughes's Hollywood* (New York: Custom House, 2018).

7. Bergman and Burgess, *Ingrid Bergman: My Story*, 196–97.

8. Donald L. Bartlett and James B. Steele, *Howard Hughes: His Life and Madness* (New York: W. W. Norton, 1979), 138–41.

9. Ibid., 142; Longworth, *Seduction*, 270–71.

10. *BEP* (August 7, 1947), 5; *V* (January 14, 1948), 9.

11. A. Scott Berg, *Goldwyn* (London: Sphere Books, 1990), 424–25.

12. Production Memos, *The Bishop's Wife*, file 246, The Samuel Goldwyn papers, Margaret Herrick Library, Academy of Motion Picture Arts and Sciences, Beverly Hills, CA (hereafter Goldwyn/AMPAS).

13. Telegram from Pat Duggan to Sam Goldwyn (January 2, 1947), file 243, Goldwyn/AMPAS.

14. Ibid.

15. Letter from David Niven to Sam Goldwyn (September 14, 1945), file 3678; and letter from Leland Hayward to Sam Goldwyn (July 8, 1946), file 3479; both Goldwyn/AMPAS.

16. Telegram from Pat Duggan to Sam Goldwyn (January 2, 1947), file 243, Goldwyn/AMPAS; *DV* (January 17, 1947), 10.

17. Memo from George Slaff to files, "Cary Grant Contract" (October 11, 1946), file 5172, Goldwyn/AMPAS.

18. Henry Koster, *Henry Koster Interviewed by Irene Kahn Atkins* (Methuen, NJ: Directors Guild of America and Scarecrow Press, 1987), 86.

19. *DV* (October 30, 1946), 2; *THR* (October 28, 1946), 1.

20. *NYDN* (January 9, 1947), 52.

21. Longworth, *Seduction*, 271–72.

22. Hopper, "Cary Grant Picks Roles," 3:1; *LAT* (January 12, 1947), 3.

23. *NYDN* (January 12, 1947), C4.

24. Hopper, "Cary Grant Picks Roles."

25. Letter from Leland Hayward to Sam Goldwyn (July 16, 1946), file 3479, Goldwyn/AMPAS.

26. Production Reports (February 3–7, 1947), *The Bishop's Wife*, file 248, Goldwyn/AMPAS.

27. Berg, *Goldwyn*, 424.

28. *DV* (March 20, 1947), 1; *DV* (March 21, 1947), 4.

29. "Production Reports," *The Bishop's Wife*, file 248, Goldwyn/AMPAS.

30. Nelson, *Evenings with Cary Grant*, 161.

31. Koster, *Henry Koster Interviewed by Irene Kahn Atkins*, 86.

32. Berg, *Goldwyn*, 425.

33. *DV* (February 20, 1947), 4.

34. Anthony Slide (ed.), *"It's the Pictures That Got Small": Charles Brackett on Billy Wilder and Hollywood's Golden Age* (New York: Columbia University Press, 2015), 316–18.

35. "Picture Costs" (October 1, 1949), *The Bishop's Wife*, file 15, Goldwyn/AMPAS.

36. *V* (November 25, 1947), 1 and 63.

37. Bosley Crowther, "Christmas Picture," *NYT* (December 10, 1947), 2:3; *V* (November 19, 1947), 8.

38. Philip K. Scheuer, "Angel Grant Helps Spread Holiday Glow," *LAT* (December 26, 1947), 6; Kate Cameron, "Astor Shows Film Full of Christmas Spirit," *NYDN* (December 10, 1947), C13.

39. *Life* (January 12, 1948), 71–72.

40. "Publicity" (March 15, 1948), *The Bishop's Wife*, file 253, Goldwyn/AMPAS.

41. *V* (March 3, 1948), 3; *V* (January 5, 1949), 47.

42. Jewell, "RKO Film Grosses, 1929–1951"; *V* (January 5, 1949), 46.

43. Koster, *Henry Koster Interviewed by Irene Kahn Atkins*, 86.

44. *DV* (October 30, 1946), 2; *LAT* (October 31, 1946), 4; *THR* (November 1, 1946), 10.

45. *LAT* (June 16, 1946), 23.

46. Nelson, *Evenings with Cary Grant*, 158.

47. "Frank W. Vincent Agency" (October 1, 1946), file 545, CGP/AMPAS.

48. Tom Kemper, *Hidden Talent*, 72.

49. Memorandum from Morton Garbus to Cary Grant (May 6, 1947), file 8, CGP/AMPAS.

50. Florabel Muir, "Just for Variety," *DV* (July 23, 1947), 4; *DV* (November 22, 1948), 4.

51. Ibid.

52. Nelson, *Evenings with Cary Grant*, 164.

53. John Carpenter, "Talk of the Day," *London Evening News* (August 6, 1947), 2; Noel Whitcomb, "Under the Counter," *Daily Mirror* (August 9, 1947), 4; *BEWorld* (August 8, 1947), 1.

54. *DV* (June 11, 1947), 4; *DV* (June 16, 1947), 4.

55. Letters from Elsie Leach to Archie Leach (January 8, 1947, and January 18, 1947), file 254; CGP/AMPAS.

56. *BEW* (August 11, 1947), 2.

57. Vincent Moseley, "Cary Grant's Plans," *BEP* (August 12, 1947), 3 and 5.

58. "Archibald Alec Leach," Entry 993, *Admissions Register, Fairfield School, 1914–17*, Bristol Archives, Bristol, UK.

59. *BEW* (August 12, 1947), 1 and 4.

60. Ed Sullivan, "Their Finest Hour," *Modern Screen* (December 1947), 32–33 and 62.

61. *Coventry Evening Telegraph* (September 2, 1947), 1.

62. Hedda Hopper, "Hollywood," *NYDN* (September 25, 1947), 32.

63. Harris, "The Riddle of Cary Grant," 81.

64. Ibid.; Grant, "Archie Leach," *LHJ* (March 1963), 40; Nelson, *Evenings with Cary Grant*, 164–66.

65. Cari Beauchamp and Judy Balaban, "Cary in the Sky with Diamonds," *Vanity Fair* (August 2010), 146; Nelson, *Evenings with Cary Grant*, 166.

66. Harris, "The Riddle of Cary Grant," 81; Sam Roberts, "Betsy Drake, 92, Actress Who Starred with (and wed) Cary Grant, Dies," *NYT* (November 11, 2015). Accessed online: https://www.nytimes.com/2015/11/12/movies/betsy-drake-movie-and-stage-actress-dies-at-92.html

67. Ibid.

68. *DV* (September 30, 1947), 2.

69. Kotsilibas-Davis and Loy, *Being and Becoming*, 214.

70. Screenplay by Norman Panama and Melvin Frank, *Mr. Blandings Builds His Dream House* (September 8, 1947), *Mr. Blandings Builds His Dream House*, file 1307S, subseries 1783, RKO/UCLA.

71. Ibid., 127.

72. Robert Van Gelder, "Interview with a Best-Selling Author: Eric Hodgins," *Cosmopolitan* (May 1947), 18 and 122.

73. Herman Lowe, "Hollywood Red Blues Sung by Congressional Probe Witnesses," *V* (October 22, 1947), 1 and 4; Ruth Montgomery, "Film Stars at Probe Cast Reds in Role of Outlaws," *NYDN* (October 24, 1947), 1, 2, and 32.

74. Ruth Montgomery, "Mickey Mouse's Boss Says Commies Tried to Take Over," *NYDN* (October 25, 1947), 31.

75. Kotsilibas-Davis and Loy, *Being and Becoming*, 216.

76. PM's *Sunday Picture News* (April 30, 1944), Scrapbook 10, CGP/AMPAS.

77. Humphrey Bogart, "I'm No Communist," *Photoplay* (March 1948), 52–53.

78. *LAT* (February 14, 1953), 8.

79. Eric Hodgins, "Mr. Blandings Goes to Hollywood," *Life* (April 12, 1948), 110–24.

80. *V* (March 31, 1948), 11.

81. Hedda Hopper, "Hollywood," *LAT* (March 29, 1948), 15.

82. Bosley Crowther, "The Screen," *NYT* (March 26, 1948), 26; John McCarten, "The Current Cinema," *New Yorker* (April 3, 1948), 58.

83. Jewell, "RKO Film Grosses," Appendix 1; *V* (January 5, 1949), 46.

84. Harris, "The Riddle of Cary Grant," 81.

85. Louella O. Parsons, "Betsy Drake Off to Bright Start in Role Opposite Cary Grant," *SFE* (April 27, 1948), 13; John L. Scott, "Betsy Drake Is Newest Hollywood Discovery," *LAT* (May 30, 1948), 43.

Chapter 22

1. *LAT* (December 24, 1942), 18.

2. Nelson, *Evenings with Cary Grant*, 222–23.

3. Bergman and Burgess, *Ingrid Bergman: My Story*, 131; Sophia Loren, *Yesterday, Today and Tomorrow: My Life* (New York: Simon and Schuster, 2014), 89.

4. Donaldson and Royce, *An Affair to Remember*, 75–76.

5. Louella O. Parsons, "What Next for Cary Grant?," *Photoplay* (August, 1945), 32–34.

6. Hedda Hopper, "Hollywood," *LAT* (October 19, 1940), 10.

7. Hedda Hopper, "The Fighting Grants," *Modern Screen* (October 1944), 56, 102–4.

8. *Life* (July 14, 1941), 82–85.

9. Hedda Hopper, "Hollywood," *NYDN* (November 7, 1947), 71.

10. Hedda Hopper, "Hollywood," *LAT* (September 18, 1949), 4:3; Louella O. Parsons, "Betsy Drake Slated to Co-star with Robert Young," *SFE* (September 22, 1949), 15.

11. Parsons, "Betsy Drake Off to Bright Start," 13.

12. Hedda Hopper, "Hollywood," *LAT* (June 21, 1948), 21.

13. Louella O. Parsons, "In Hollywood," *SFE* (December 18, 1949), 18.

14. "Budget of Production Cost" (May 6, 1948), *Every Girl Should Be Married*, file P173, subseries 774, RKO/UCLA.

15. Frances Davis, "Reader's Report" (October 14, 1947), *Every Girl Should Be Married*, file 1336S, subseries 774, RKO/UCLA.

16. *DV* (October 22, 1947), 24; Parsons, "Betsy Drake Off to Bright Start," 13.

17. *DV* (November 10, 1948), 4.

18. Bosley Crowther, "The Screen In Review," *NYT* (December 24, 1948), 14.

19. Wanda Hale, "Grant is Capital's Offering for the Holiday," *NYDN* (December 24, 1948), 33.

20. Edwin Schallert, "New Star's Debut Wins Attention," *LAT* (February 2, 1949), 14.

21. Hedda Hopper, "Hopper's List of New 1949 Stars," *LAT* (January 2, 1949), 4:1; Louella O. Parsons, "Hollywood," *SFE* (November 15, 1948), 15.

22. Jewell, "RKO Film Grosses, 1929–1951," Appendix 1.

23. Richard B. Jewell, *Slow Fade to Black: The Decline of RKO Radio Pictures*, 77–79.

24. Wynn Roberts, "Cinderella is a Girl Named Betsy," *Photoplay* (November 1948), 42–43, 98; Sheilah Graham, "The Girl He Can't Forget," *Modern Screen* (February 1949), 40–41, 98; Mary McSkimming, "Let's Not Talk About Love," *Modern Screen* (September 1949), 54–55, 97.

25. Arthur Laurents, *Original Story by Arthur Laurents: A Memoir of Broadway and Hollywood* (New York: Alfred A. Knopf, 2000), 125–26.

26. Ibid., 131; McGilligan, *Alfred Hitchcock*, 399–400.

27. Laurents, *Original Story*, 131.

28. McGilligan, *Alfred Hitchcock*, 420.

29. *DV* (April 29, 1948), 1.

30. Charles Drazin, *In Search of the Third Man* (London: Methuen, 1999), 29–30; Rob White, *The Third Man* (London: BFI Publishing, 2003), 11.

31. McCarthy, *Howard Hawks*, 452.

32. Henri Rochard, "Male War Bride Trial to Army," *Baltimore Sun* (September 28, 1947), A5.

33. Henri Rochard, "I Was a Male War Bride," *Reader's Digest* (undated), *I Was a Male War Bride*, Twentieth Century-Fox Script Collection, Cinematic Arts Library, University of Southern California, Los Angeles, CA (hereafter TCF/USC).

34. Charles Lederer and Hagar Wilde, "*I Was A Male War Bride*: First Draft Continuity" (August 14, 1948), *I Was a Male War Bride*, TCF/USC.

35. McCarthy, *Howard Hawks*, 453–54.

36. *"I Was a Male War Bride*—Agreements" (July 23, 1948), file 39, CGP/AMPAS.

37. Hedda Hopper, "Hollywood," *LAT* (September 18, 1949), 4:3; McCarthy, *Howard Hawks*, 455.

38. John Kobal, *People Will Talk: Personal Conversations with the Legends of Hollywood* (London: Aurum Press, 1986), 238–39.

39. McCarthy, *Howard Hawks*, 457.

40. Joseph McBride, *Hawks on Hawks*, 80.

41. McCarthy, *Howard Hawks*, 457–58.

42. *BEW* (December 6, 1948), 1; *The People* (December 5, 1948), 3.

43. McCarthy, *Howard Hawks*, 458.

44. Ibid., 458–59; *DV* (December 31, 1949), 7.

45. *BEW* (December 28, 1948), 5.

46. McCarthy, *Howard Hawks*, 460–61; Kobal, *People Will Talk*, 238–39.

47. *BEP* (February 10, 1949), 1; *DV* (February 28, 1949), 15; P. L. Mannock, "Cary's Jaundice Shuts His Film," *Daily Herald* (February 10, 1949), 1.

48. Harris, "The Riddle of Cary Grant," 81.

49. Hedda Hopper, "Hollywood," *LAT* (September 18, 1949), 4:3.

50. Louella O. Parsons, "In Hollywood," *SFE* (March 3, 1949), 19.

51. Hedda Hopper, "Hollywood," *LAT* (March 15, 1949), 2:6; Louella O. Parsons, "In Hollywood" *SFE* (March 15, 1949), 2:6.

52. *LAT* (April 8, 1949), 14.

53. Louella O. Parsons, "In Hollywood," *SFE* (April 18, 1949), 13.

54. McBride, *Hawks on Hawks*, 82.

55. McCarthy, *Howard Hawks*, 461–62.

56. Bosley Crowther, "The Screen in Review," *NYT* (August 27, 1949), 7; Philip K. Scheuer, "Cary Grant Arch Male War Bride," *LAT* (August 20, 1949) 6; *V* (August 10, 1949), 8.

57. *Baltimore Sun* (August 2, 1949), 9.

58. A. H. Weiler, "By Way of Report," *NYT* (August 7, 1949), X3.

59. *V* (January 4, 1950), 59.

60. *DV* (May 5, 1949), 4.

61. Louella O. Parsons, "In Hollywood," *SFE Pictorial Review* (December 18, 1949), 18.

62. George Jessel with John Austin, *The World I Lived In* (Chicago: Henry Regnery Company, 1975), 156.

63. Parsons, "In Hollywood."

64. Harris, "The Riddle of Cary Grant," 81; *SFE* (December 26, 1949), 1; *DV* (December 28, 1949), 2.

65. Grant, "Archie Leach," *LHJ* (April 1963), 151.

66. Ibid.; Hedda Hopper, "Betsy's Back and 'Lion's' Got Her," *LAT Calendar* (January 1, 1965), 8.

67. Letter from Ingrid Bergman to Cary Grant (March 16, 1950), file 130, CGP/AMPAS.

68. Nelson, *Evenings with Cary Grant*, 121.

69. Memorandum from G. E. Youngman (Vice-President, RKO Radio Pictures) to Cary Grant (June 5, 1950), "Contracts," file 521, CGP/AMPAS.

70. Jewell, *Slow Fade to Black*, 79–80.

71. Thomas Schatz, *Boom and Bust: American Cinema in the 1940s* (Berkeley: University of California, 1997), 381–82.

72. Ibid., 337.

73. *DV* (July 26, 1949), 3.

74. Douglass K. Daniel, *Tough as Nails: The Life and Films of Richard Brooks* (Madison: University of Wisconsin Press, 2011), 7; Nelson, *Evenings with Cary Grant*, 168–69.

75. Memorandum from F. L. Hendrickson to Arthur Freed, "Cary Grant" (January 4, 1950), *Crisis*, box 8.21, Arthur Freed Papers, Cinematic Arts Library, University of Southern California (hereafter Freed/USC).

76. Daniel, *Tough as Nails*, 8.

77. John McCarten, "The Current Cinema," *New Yorker* (July 15, 1950), 63; Robert Polito (ed.), *Farber on Film: The Complete Film Writings of Manny Farber* (New York: Library of America, 2009), 335; *THR* (June 16, 1950), 3; *V* (June 21, 1950), 8.

78. Daniel, *Tough as Nails*, 62–63; Schary, *Heyday*, 210–11; Memorandum from Frank Whitbeck, "Trailer" (July 3, 1950), *Crisis*, box 820, Freed/USC.

79. *V* (July 5, 1950), 9.

80. Eddie Mannix Ledger, Howard Strickling Papers, Margaret Herrick Library, Academy of Motion Picture Arts and Sciences, Beverly Hills, CA (hereafter Strickling/AMPAS).

81. Hedda Hopper, "Hollywood," *NYDN* (June 11, 1951), 36.

82. Daniel, *Tough as Nails*, 11; Nelson, *Evenings with Cary Grant*, 169.

Chapter 23

1. Hopper, "Betsy's Back and 'Lion's' Got Her," 8; Nelson, *Evenings with Cary Grant*, 174–75.

2. Pamela Morgan, "Hollywood's Strangest Marriage," *Modern Screen* (April 1953), 64–65, 74–77.

3. Nelson, *Evenings with Cary Grant*, 180.

4. "Memo: Summary of Betsy Drake's Contract" (September 17, 1949), Betsy Drake personnel file, WB/USC.

5. Nelson, *Evenings with Cary Grant*, 167.

6. *DV* (November 9, 1950), 8; *V* (October 18, 1950), 23.

7. *V* (May 9, 1951), 24.

8. *THR* (December 5, 1952), 8.

9. *V* (March 7, 1951), 42.

10. Magee Adams, "Look and Listen," *Cincinnati Enquirer* (February 9, 1951), 10; John Crosby, "Mr. and Mrs. Blandings Ought to Be Better," *Minnesota Morning Tribune* (February 9, 1951), 31; Anton Remenih, "It Ain't Funny Blandings, but It's Good Radio," *CT* (January 24, 1951), 28.

11. William Frye, "Gentleman's Agreement," *Vanity Fair* (April 2003), 429–40.

12. *V* (January 24, 1951), 22; *V* (August 29, 1951), 25.

13. Cheryl Bray Lower and R. Barton Palmer, *Joseph L. Mankiewicz: Critical Essays with an Annotated Bibliography and a Filmography* (Jefferson, NC: McFarland and Co., 2001), 94–95.

14. Joseph L. Mankiewicz, "Screen Treatment: *Dr. Praetorius*" (December 8, 1950), *People Will Talk*, TCF/USC.

15. Darryl F. Zanuck, "Script Notes" (February 18, 1951), *People Will Talk*, TCF/USC.

16. Memo from Michael Abel to Darryl F. Zanuck, "Final Script Notes" (February 27, 1951), *People Will Talk*, TCF/USC.

17. Hedda Hopper, "Grant Guy," *CT* (September 18, 1949), 7 and 17.

18. Peter Lev, *The Fifties: Transforming the Screen, 1950-1959* (Berkeley: University of California Press, 2006), 69; Lower and Palmer, *Joseph L. Mankiewicz*, 97.

19. *LAT* (July 20, 1951), 3.

20. Mike Connolly, "Just for Variety," *DV* (July 24, 1951), 2; *THR* (August 17, 1951), 3.

21. Philip Hamburger, "The Current Cinema," *New Yorker* (September 1, 1951), 46–47; *V* (October 3, 1951), 4.

22. A. W., "The Screen," *NYT* (August 30, 1951), 20.

23. *V* (January 2, 1952), 70.

24. *The Mercury* (June 15, 1951), 4; Nelson, *Evenings with Cary Grant*, 148.

25. Betsy Drake interview in *Cary Grant: A Class Apart* (Turner Entertainment, 2004).

26. Telegram from Jack Warner to Cary Grant (July 14, 1951), file 2199B, *Room for One More*, WB/USC; *LAT* (July 26, 1951), 58.

27. [Baltimore] *Evening Sun* (September 5, 1951), 44.

28. "Literary Rights," file 12756A, box 1754B, *Room for One More*, WB/USC.

29. "Modification of the Employment Agreement and Share of Gross Receipts" (July 18, 1951), file 2701A

30. "Budgets" (September 19, 1951), file 1457B, *Room for One More*, WB/USC.

31. Telegram from Jack Warner to Norman Taurog (December 7, 1951), file 2199B, *Room for One More*, WB/USC.

32. Harris, "The Riddle of Cary Grant," 81; Leonard Lyons, "Gossip of the Nation," *PI* (February 1, 1952), 27; Louella Parsons, "Hollywood," *SFE* (January 2, 1952), 17.

33. Memorandum from Albert Howson to Jack Warner (January 17, 1952), file 2199B, *Room for One More*, WB/USC.

34. Memorandum from Jack Warner to Ben Kalmenson (January 19, 1952), file 2199B, *Room for One More*, WB/USC.

35. *Time* (January 28, 1952), 97–98; *CT* (February 26, 1952), 36; *NYT* (January 16, 1952), 21.

36. William Schaefer Ledger, Schaefer/USC.

37. *DV* (March 27, 1953), 2.

38. Memorandum from R. J. Obringer to Harold Bareford (August 19, 1952), Cary Grant personnel file, WB/USC.

39. *DV* (December 23, 1952), 1.

40. Harry Segall, "Fountain of Youth: Story Outline" (June 25, 1951); Harry Segall, "Darling, I Am Growing Younger: Writer's Working Script" (July 2, 1951); I. A. L. Diamond, "Darling, I Am Growing Younger: Writer's Working Script" (October 9, 1951); *Monkey Business*, TCF/USC.

41. Memorandum from Sol C. Siegel to Darryl F. Zanuck (October 9, 1951), *Monkey Business*, TCF/USC.

42. Memorandum from Sol C. Siegel to Darryl F. Zanuck (December 11, 1951), *Monkey Business*, TCF/USC.

43. McCarthy, *Howard Hawks*, 497–99.

44. Ibid., 496.

45. "Conference with Mr. Zanuck on typed screenplay of 12/11/51" (December 20, 1951), *Monkey Business*, TCF/USC.

46. McCarthy, *Howard Hawks*, 496.

47. Ibid., 496–97.

48. Ibid., 499.

49. Rogers, *My Story*, 401–2.

50. Nelson, *Evenings with Cary Grant*, 175.

51. Earl Wilson, "It Happened Last Night," [Camden, NJ] *Courier-Post* (July 28, 1952), 5.

52. *CT* (October 1, 1952), 37.

53. *V* (September 10, 1952), 6; Bosley Crother, "The Screen in Review," *NYT* (September 6, 1952), 12; Mae Tinee, "Slapstick Film is Long on the Funny Stuff," *CT* (October 6, 1952), 60; John McCarten, "The Current Cinema," *New Yorker* (September 13, 1952), 136–37.

54. *V* (November 5, 1952), 12.

55. *V* (January 7, 1953), 61.

56. Ruth Waterbury, "Cary Grant is Hollywood Phenomenon Because He's 'Just a Very Simple Man,'" [Lubbock, Texas] *Avalanche-Journal* (October 12, 1952), 5:8.

57. Schary, *Heyday*, 258; Sheldon, *The Other Side of Me*, 224–25.

58. Sarah Street, *Deborah Kerr, BFI Film Stars Series* (London: British Film Institute, 2018), 69.

59. Sheldon, *The Other Side of Me*, 226.

60. Ibid., 228–30.

61. Edwin Schallert, "'Marriage is a Very Public Affair' Named for Grant," *LAT* (January 29, 1953), 33.

62. Arlene Dahl, "Cary Grant Finds Women Are Wonderful," *CT* (December 8, 1952), 42.

63. Sheldon, *The Other Side of Me*, 246–47.

64. *THR* (March 9, 1953), 3; *V* (March 11, 1953), 6.

65. Sheldon, *The Other Side of Me*, 248–49.

66. Schary, *Heyday*, 258–59.

67. Sheldon, *The Other Side of Me*, 247–48.

68. Eddie Mannix Ledger, Strickling/AMPAS.

69. Graham McCann, *Rebel Males: Clift, Brando and Dean* (New Brunswick, NJ: Rutgers University Press, 1993).

70. Irene Mayer Selznick, *A Private View*, 306; *V* (December 3, 1947), 50.

71. *Sunday Graphic* (November 10, 1957), Cary Grant Clippings, British Film Institute Clippings File.

72. Harris, "The Riddle of Cary Grant," 81.

73. Edith Head and Paddy Calistro, *Edith Head's Hollywood* (New York: Dutton, 1983), 101; McGilligan, *Alfred Hitchcock*, 469.

74. Bawden and Miller, *Conversations with Classic Film Stars*, 117.

75. McGilligan, *George Cukor*, 219.

76. *THR* (October 14, 1952), 2; *THR* (July 10, 1953), 2; *THR* (August 5, 1953), 1.

77. Bawden and Miller, *Conversations with Classic Film Stars*, 117.

78. Charles Desmond, "He'll Never Win An Oscar," *Photoplay* (March 1957), 52–53, 75–76; George Stevens Jr., "Interview with Cary Grant," A Filmmaker's Journey/ AMPAS.

Chapter 24

1. Bawden and Miller, *Conversations with Classic Film Stars*, 124; James Monaco, "Cary on Hitch," *Take One* (May 1976), 20; Harris, "The Riddle of Cary Grant," 81.

2. Eliot, *Cary Grant*, 284–85; Harris, *Cary Grant*, 175; Nelson, *Evenings with Cary Grant*, 177.

3. *THR* (October 6, 1952), 2; Sheilah Graham, "Hollywood Camera," *Boston Daily Globe* (January 3, 1953), 5; Hedda Hopper, "Cary Grant on Law's Side in Next Film 'Catch That Thief,'" *LAT* (September 25, 1953), 3; Dorothy Manners, "Cary Grant Picks Role After Year," *PI* (December 2, 1953), 55.

4. "Cary Grant" (January 8, 1954), file 976, Paramount Contract Summaries, PPR/ AMPAS; *V* (August 28, 1952), 7; *DV* (October 1, 1952), 7; *V* (December 29, 1952), 2.

5. *DFP* (December 24, 1952), 12; *St. Louis Post-Dispatch* (January 5, 1953), 15; *Miami News* (February 26, 1953), 12.

6. Nelson, *Evenings with Cary Grant*, 178.

7. Hopper, "Cary Grant on Law's Side in Next Film 'Catch That Thief.'"

8. Harrison Carroll, "Behind the Scenes in Hollywood," [Lancaster, OH] *Eagle-Gazette* (April 4, 1953), 6.

9. Betsy Drake, "My Life with Cary Grant," *American Weekly* (August 4, 1957), 22 and 24; Harris, "The Riddle of Cary Grant," 83.

10. Linda Hardie, "Movie Colony Makeover," *Palm Springs Life* (October 29, 2010), https://www.palmspringslife.com/Movie-Colony-Makeover/

11. Drake, "My Life with Cary Grant," 22; Harris, "The Riddle of Cary Grant," 83.

12. Drake, "My Life with Cary Grant," 24.

13. David Niven, *Bring on the Empty Horses* (London: Hamish Hamilton, 1975), 301–2.

14. Ibid.; *LAT* (September 21, 1953), 30; McGilligan, *Alfred Hitchcock*, 401–2.

15. Louella Parsons, "Hollywood" (December 29, 1953), 21; Louella Parsons, "Hollywood," *SFE* (January 2, 1954), 7; *THR* (January 5, 1954), 4.

16. Grant, "Archie Leach," *LHJ* (March 1963), 40.

17. Dorothy Kilgallen, "On Broadway" [Pittsburgh, PA] *Post-Gazette* (January 15, 1954), 27; Ed Sullivan, "Little Old New York," *NYDN* (January 27, 1954), 49.

18. Harris, "The Riddle of Cary Grant," 81.

19. Steven DeRosa, *Writing with Hitchcock: The Collaboration of Alfred Hitchcock and John Michael Hayes* (London: Faber and Faber, 2001), 87–88; McGilligan, *Alfred Hitchcock*, 490–91.

20. McGilligan, *Alfred Hitchcock*, 493.

21. "Notes Pertaining to the Hitchcock Contract" (March 30, 1954), *To Catch a Thief*, file 5.15, PPR/AMPAS.

22. Rosa, *Writing with Hitchcock*, 109.

23. Edith Head, *The Dress Doctor* (New York: Little, Brown and Company, 1959), 156.

24. McGilligan, *Alfred Hitchcock*, 500-1.

25. John McClintock, "A Conversation with Cary Grant," [Palo Alto, CA] *The Peninsula Times-Tribune* (October 22, 1982), Lecture Clippings, file 616, CGP/AMPAS.

26. Nelson, *Evenings with Cary Grant*, 184-85.

27. McGilligan, *Alfred Hitchcock*, 500.

28. DeRosa, *Writing with Hitchcock*, 113-14.

29. McGilligan, *Alfred Hitchcock*, 499.

30. DeRosa, *Writing with Hitchcock*, 109-10; McGilligan, *Alfred Hitchcock*, 497.

31. McGilligan, *Alfred Hitchcock*, 500.

32. Harris, "The Riddle of Cary Grant," 75; Mike Steen, *Hollywood Speaks: An Oral History* (New York: G. P. Putnam's Sons, 1974), 246.

33. Nelson, *Evenings with Cary Grant*, 189-90.

34. *DV* (August 4, 1955), 5; Hedda Hopper, "In Hollywood," *LAT* (August 5, 1955), 22.

35. Bosley Crowther, "Screen: Cat Man Out 'To Catch a Thief,'" *NYT* (August 5, 1955), 14; *Time* (August 15, 1955), 58; John McCarten, "The Current Cinema," *New Yorker* (August 13, 1955), 48-49.

36. *V* (July 20, 1955), 6.

37. *V* (January 4, 1956), 88.

38. Cameron Crowe, *Conversations with Wilder* (London: Faber and Faber, 1999), 90-91.

39. Kevin Brownlow, *David Lean* (London: Faber and Faber, 1997), 352; Glenn Lovell, "A Conversation with Cary Grant," *San Jose Mercury News* (October 23, 1982), Lecture Clippings, file 616, CGP/AMPAS.

40. Bawden and Miller, *Conversations with Classic Film Stars*, 117.

41. *DFP* (August 10, 1955), 11.

42. *V* (June 12, 1957), 3 and 26.

43. *LAT* (June 28, 1955), 12.

44. *LAT* (June 15, 1956), 3:6.

45. Louella O. Parsons, "In Hollywood," *SFE* (April 10, 1956), 2:5.

46. *DV* (October 18, 1956), 1 and 4; Jane Cianfarra, "On the Road with 'Pride and the Passion,'" *NYT* (May 13, 1957), X5.

47. Loren, *Yesterday, Today, and Tomorrow*, 78-79.

48. A. E. Hotchner, *Sophia: Living and Loving, Her Own Story* (London: Michael Joseph, 1979), 92.

49. Ibid., 92-93; Loren, *Yesterday, Today, and Tomorrow*, 80-82.

50. Loren, *Yesterday, Today and Tomorrow*, 81.

51. Documents issued May 31, 1956, file 614, CGP/Herrick.

52. Nelson, *Evenings with Cary Grant*, 194; Louella Parsons, "Hollywood," *SFE* (April 23, 1956), 2:5.

53. Beauchamp and Balaban, "Cary in the Sky with Diamonds," 144.

54. Nelson, *Evenings with Cary Grant*, 194–95; Louella Parsons, "Hollywood," *SFE* (May 26, 1956), 11.

55. *V* (July 11, 1956), 62.

56. *LAT* (July 27, 1956), 1 and 6.

57. Nelson, *Evenings with Cary Grant*, 195–96.

58. Drake, "My Life with Cary Grant," 24.

59. Loren, *Yesterday, Today and Tomorrow*, 82.

60. *DV* (September 10, 1956), 2.

61. *SFE* (September 9, 1956), 1.

62. *LAT* (September 11, 1956), 3:1; Cablegram from Archie Leach to Elsie Leach (September 12, 1956), file 255, CGP/AMPAS.

63. Stanley Kramer with Thomas M. Coffey, *A Mad, Mad, Mad, Mad World: A Life in Hollywood* (New York: Harcourt, Brace and Co., 1997), 137–40.

64. Bosley Crowther, "Screen: Mighty Canvas," *NYT* (June 29, 1957), 10; John McCarten, "The Current Cinema," *New Yorker* (July 13, 1957), 48–49; Hortense Morten, "Kramer Spectacle Worth Its Value," *SFE* (July 19, 1957), 21; *V* (June 26, 1957), 6.

65. *V* (July 3, 1957), 3 and 11.

66. *V* (January 8, 1958), 30.

67. "Casting Ideas for 'Love Affair'" (October 31, 1956), *An Affair to Remember*: Project Book One, Jerry Wald Collection, Cinematic Arts Library, University of Southern California, Los Angeles, CA (hereafter Wald/USC).

68. Memo from Jerry Wald to Lew Schreiber (December 20, 1956), *An Affair to Remember*: Project Book Two, Wald/USC.

69. "Preliminary Production Cost Estimate" (January 18, 1958), *An Affair to Remember*: Project Book One, Wald/USC.

70. Memo from Jerry Wald to Buddy Adler (January 26, 1957), *An Affair to Remember*: Project Book Two, Wald/USC.

71. Bogdanovich, *Who the Devil Made It*, 430.

72. Letter from Jerry Wald to Buddy Adler and Leo McCarey (January 25, 1957), *An Affair to Remember*: Project Book Two, Wald/USC.

73. Ibid.

74. Harris, "The Riddle of Cary Grant," 74–75; Nelson, *Evenings with Cary Grant*, 161–62.

75. Bogdanovich, *Who the Devil Made It*, 430.

76. John McCarten, "The Current Cinema," *New Yorker* (August 3, 1957), 48; *Time* (August 5, 1957), 76; Hortense Morten, "'Affair to Remember' Now on Fox Screen," *SFE* (July 22, 1957), 2:3.

77. *V* (January 8, 1958), 30.

78. "AFI's 100 Greatest Love Stories of All Time," American Film Institute, https://www.afi.com/100Years/passions.aspx

79. Victor Davis, "In Those Few Brief Moments, Cary and I Loved Each Other," *Mail on Sunday* (August 8, 1993), 33–34.

80. *V* (July 17, 1957), 6.

Chapter 25

1. Carlotta Dyer, "*Houseboat*: Synopsis of a Screenplay" (March 12, 1956), file 462.f-H-921, *Houseboat*, Scripts, PP/AMPAS.

2. Army Acherd, "Just for Variety," *DV* (September 10, 1956), 2; Melville Shavelson, *How to Succeed in Hollywood Without Really Trying: P.S.—You Can't* (Albany, GA: BearManor Media, 2007), 70.

3. Memo from Michael H. Franklin to Teet Carle (October 2, 1957), "Billing 1957–1958," file 106-1, *Houseboat*, Production Records, PP/AMPAS.

4. *V* (January 8, 1958), 30.

5. Letter from Daniel M. Winkler to Jerry Wald (December 16, 1948); letter from William Fadiman to Jerry Wald (November 3, 1950); letter from Judith Bailey to Arthur Kramer (March 16, 1955); *Kiss Them for Me*, Wald/USC.

6. "Estimated Production Budget" (April 27, 1957), *Kiss Them for Me*, Wald/USC.

7. Bailey to Kramer (March 16, 1955), Wald/USC.

8. Letter from Jerry Wald to Arthur Kramer (August 14, 1956), *Kiss Them for Me*, Wald/USC.

9. Script notes by Jerry Wald (undated), *Kiss Them for Me*, Wald/USC.

10. Memo from Jerry Wald to Buddy Adler (February 20, 1957), *Kiss Them for Me*, USC/Wald.

11. Stephen M. Silverman, *Dancing on the Ceiling: Stanley Donen and His Movies* (New York: Alfred A. Knopf, 1996), 261–62.

12. Hortense Morton, "'Kiss Them for Me' Opens at Fox," *SFE* (November 7, 1957), 2:5; *V* (November 6, 1957), 6; John McCarten, "The Current Cinema," *New Yorker* (November 16, 1957), 109.

13. Dorothy Masters, "'Kiss Them For Me' Presented at Roxy," *NYDN* (November 9, 1957), C13.

14. Mae Tinnee, "Cary Expert, Jayne Dull in War Film," *CDT* (December 19, 1957), 4:8; Bosley Crowther, "Screen: Wartime Froth," *NYT* (November 9, 1957), 31.

15. *V* (January 8, 1958), 30.

16. Silverman, *Dancing on the Ceiling*, 263–65.

17. Loren, *Yesterday, Today and Tomorrow*, 87–89.

18. Nelson, *Evenings with Cary Grant*, 205.

19. Florabel Muir, "Behind Hollywood's Silken Curtain," *NYDN* (July 28, 1957), 24.

20. *The* [London] *Evening News* (July 16, 1957), 1.

21. *BEP* (July 26, 1957), 1 and 14.

22. *BEW* (July 26, 1957), 1, 9 and 12.

23. Carlotta Dyer, "*Houseboat*: Synopsis of a Screenplay" (March 12, 1956), file 462.f-H-921, *Houseboat*, Production Records, PP/AMPAS.

24. Melville Shavelson and Jack Rose, "*Houseboat* [script]" (May 15, 1957), file 462.f-H-922, *Houseboat*, Script Files, PP/AMPAS.

25. Loren, *Yesterday, Today, and Tomorrow*, 82.

26. Ibid., 91.

27. "Movements," file 106a-f.8, *Houseboat*, Production Records, PP/AMPAS.

28. Letter from Hedda Hopper to Mike Cowles (August 31, 1959), file 984, Hedda Hopper Papers, Margaret Herrick Library, Academy of Motion Picture Arts and Sciences, Beverly Hills, California (hereafter HH/AMPAS).

29. Loren, *Yesterday, Today, and Tomorrow*, 82.

30. Louella Parsons, "Hollywood," *SFE* (September 28, 1957), 2:20.

31. Loren, *Yesterday, Today, and Tomorrow*, 91.

32. John L. Scott, "'Houseboat' Diverting on Agreeable Voyage," *LAT* (November 20, 1958), 11; Mae Tinee, "'Houseboat' with Grant Lots of Fun," *CDT* (November 11, 1958), 35; *Time* (December 1, 1958), 82; Bosley Crowther, "The Screen," *NYT* (November 14, 1958), 24; John McCarten, "The Current Cinema," *New Yorker* (November 22, 1958), 138.

33. *V* (October 9, 1958), 6.

34. *V* (January 7, 1959), 48.

35. Silverman, *Dancing on the Ceiling*, 265–67.

36. Ibid., 267.

37. "Agreement with Grandon Productions" (November 15, 1957), *Indiscreet*, Legal Files, WB/USC.

38. Silverman, *Dancing on the Ceiling*, 267; Stephen Watts, "'Indiscreet' Before the Camera in Britain," *NYT* (January 26, 1958), X5.

39. Spoto, *Notorious*, 278–80 and 295–96.

40. Ibid., 285.

41. Letter from Ingrid Bergman to Cary Grant (March 16, 1950), file 130, CGP/AMPAS.

42. Letter from Bergman to Grant (March 29, 1957), file 130, CGP/AMPAS.

43. Letter from Bergman to Grant (February 24, 1954), file 130, CGP/AMPAS.

44. *LAT* (November 11, 1957), 2.

45. Bergman and Burgess, *Ingrid Bergman: My Story*, 341; *SFE* (December 12, 1957), 5.

46. Letter from Jack Warner to Stanley Donen (November 8, 1957), *Indiscreet*, Production Files, WB/USC.

47. Telegram from Stanley Donen and Cary Grant to Jack Warner (November 12, 1957), and Letter from Stanley Donen to Jack Warner (November 14, 1957); *Indiscreet*, Production Files, WB/USC.

48. Daily Progress Reports, *Indiscreet*, Production Files, WB/USC.

49. Harris, "The Riddle of Cary Grant," 74.

50. Ibid., 75.

51. Memorandum from Warner Bros. to Grandon Productions (May 15, 1958), *Indiscreet*, Legal Files, WB/USC.

52. "Birthday Toast," Unattributed Clipping, BRCF/NYPL.

53. Daily Progress Reports, *Indiscreet*.

54. Letter from G. L. Blattner to D. W. Cherry (January 6, 1958), Production Files, *Indiscreet*, WB/USC.

55. Nelson, *Evenings with Cary Grant*, 210–11; Bawden and Miller, *Conversations with Classic Film Stars*, 125.

56. *DFP* (August 15, 1958), 17; *Time* (July 21, 1958), 78; John McCarten, "The Current Cinema," *New Yorker* (July 12, 1958), 99; A. H. Weiler, "The Screen," *NYT* (June 27, 1958), 18; Mae Tinee, "Indiscreet," *CT* (August 7, 1958), D5.

57. William Schaefer Ledger, Schaefer/USC.

58. *LAT* (February 24, 1958), 2; *NYDN* (February 24, 1958), 3.

59. Louella Parsons, "Hollywood," *SFE* (February 28, 1958), 2:7; Louella Parsons, "Moscow Asks, Is George Raft No. 1 Star in US," *SFE* (March 8, 1958), 2:16.

60. "Alec Guinness Wins Best Actor: 1958 Academy Awards," YouTube, https://www.youtube.com/watch?v=SNoUul_7CZo

61. *V* (July 30, 1958), 5.

62. Beauchamp and Balaban, "Cary in the Sky with Diamonds," 146.

63. Susan Smith, "Betsy Drake Returns to Movies," *LAT* (October 16, 1978), 4:10.

64. Beauchamp and Balaban, "Cary in the Sky with Diamonds," 176.

65. Hopper, "Betsy's Back and 'Lion's' Got Her," 9; Smith, "Betsy Drake Returns to Movies."

Chapter 26

1. Jympson Harmon, "Cary Grant Faces the Music," [London] *Evening Standard* (July 28, 1958), *North by Northwest*, BFI Clippings File.

2. McGilligan, *Alfred Hitchcock*, 559; John Russell Taylor, *Hitch: The Life and Work of Alfred Hitchcock; The Authorised Biography* (London: Abacus, 1981), 227.

3. Writers Guild Foundation, "The Writer Speaks: Ernest Lehman [part 2]." Interview filmed in 1997. YouTube, https://www.youtube.com/watch?v=b-G-fH9SRbQ

4. Ibid.

5. Ernest Lehman, "Breathless!" (November 22, 1957), folder 506, *North by Northwest*, script files, AHP/AMPAS.

6. David Thomson, *The New Biographical Dictionary of Film*, Fourth Edition, 351–52.

7. Brendan Gallagher, "Cary Grant's 'North by Northwest' Suit is the Greatest in Film History" (January 28, 2019), *Grailed*, https://www.grailed.com/drycleanonly/cary-grant-north-by-northwest-style; Nelson, *Evenings with Cary Grant*, 366.

8. Nelson, *Evenings with Cary Grant*, 124.

9. Adrian Garvey, "'Steely Velvet': The Voice of James Mason," *Journal of British Cinema and Television* 12, no. 1 (2015): 85–86.

10. Kristine McKenna, *Talk to Her: Interviews* (Seattle: Fantagraphic Books, 2004), 210–11.

11. Jordon Riefe, "Living Legends," *Vanity Fair* (September 2, 2014), https://www.vanityfair.com/hollywood/2014/09/eva-marie-saint-cary-grant.

12. Truffaut with Scott, *Hitchcock*, 400.

13. Todd McEwen, "Cary Grant's Suit," *Granta* 94 (Summer 2006), 124.

14. Robin Wood, *Hitchcock's Films* (New York: Castle Books, 1965), 111.

15. Nelson, *Evenings with Cary Grant*, 215.

16. McGilligan, *Alfred Hitchcock*, 549; Lehman, "Breathless!" (November 22, 1957), folder 506; Lehman, "The Man on Lincoln's Nose" (July 21, 1958), folder 512; *North by Northwest*, Scripts, AHP/AMPAS.

17. Stanley Cavell, "North by Northwest," *Critical Inquiry* 7, no. 4 (Summer 1981), 761–76; McGilligan, *Alfred Hitchcock*, 574–75.

18. *NYT* (November 17, 1959), X5.

19. John Buchan, *The Thirty-Nine Steps* (London: Vintage Books, 2011 [1915]), 7.

20. Truffaut with Scott, *Hitchcock*, 380.

21. James Naremore, *Acting in the Cinema* (Berkeley: University of California Press, 1988), 213–35.

22. "Daily Reports," folder 530, *North by Northwest*, AHP/AMPAS.

23. *NYDN* (September 7, 1958), 61.

24. McGilligan, *Alfred Hitchcock*, 570.

25. Eleanor Page, "Hitchcock to Turn Chicago Hotel into Set for Movie," *CDT* (September 6, 1958), 1.

26. Herb Lyon, "Tower Ticker," *CDT* (September 11, 1958), 4:6.

27. Memo from Charles Coleman to Ruby Rosenberg (August 27, 1958), *North by Northwest*, Production Files, MGM/USC.

28. *Rapid City Daily Journal* (September 5, 1958), 1.

29. *CDT* (September 10, 1958), 20.

30. Bawden and Miller, *Conversations with Classic Film Stars*, 125.

31. Coleman, *The Man Who Knew Hitchcock*, 311.

32. McGilligan, *Alfred Hitchcock*, 571.

33. "Daily Reports," folder 531, *North by Northwest*, AHP/AMPAS.

34. Taylor, *Hitch*, 230.

35. Ibid.; McGilligan, *Alfred Hitchcock*, 570–71.

36. "Estimated Final Cost of Picture" (August 27, 1958), Daily Reports, *North by Northwest*, file 530, AHP/AMPAS.

37. Memo from F. L. Henderson to Messrs. Thau, et.al., "Cary Grant Contract" (August 18, 1959), *North by Northwest*, Production Files, MGM/USC.

38. Memo from Walter Strohm to Alfred Hitchcock, "Costs" (November 5, 1958), *North by Northwest*, Production Files, MGM/USC.

39. *LAT* (July 12, 1959), 5:3; *New Republic* (August 10, 1959), 23; *New Yorker* (August 15, 1959), 80; *Time* (August 17, 1959), 78–80; *V* (July 1, 1959), 7.

40. *NYT* (August 7, 1959), 28.

41. [Author uncredited], "Anyone Can't Do It," Press Release (1957), BRCF/NYPL; "Cary Grant on Acting," *Hollywood Reporter* (November 14, 1955), 28.

42. Naremore, *Acting in the Cinema*, 234–35.

43. McGilligan, *Alfred Hitchcock*, 575–76.

44. Eddie Mannix Ledger, Strickling/AMPAS.

45. James Chapman, *Hitchcock and the Spy Film* (London: Tauris, 2018), 236–38.

Chapter 27

1. Hedda Hopper, "Cary Grant and Wife Decide on Separation," *LAT* (October 18, 1958), 3:1.

2. Beauchamp and Balaban, "Cary in the Sky with Diamonds," 146.

3. Ibid., 144.

4. Albert Hoffman, *LSD: My Problem Child* (Oxford: Oxford University Press, 2013), 15–24.

5. Beauchamp and Balaban, "Cary in the Sky," 148.

6. Ibid., 173.

7. Ibid., 173–74.

8. Warren Hoge, "The Other Cary Grant," *NYT Magazine* (July 3, 1977), 14–15.

9. Laura Bergquist, "The Curious Story Behind the New Cary Grant," *Look* (September 1, 1959), 50–58 [58].

10. Harris, "The Riddle of Cary Grant," 74.

11. Bergquist, "The Curious Story," 55.

12. Niven, *Bring on the Empty Horses*, 303.

13. Donald Zec, "Cary's Little Sput-Knicks," *Daily Mirror* (January 12, 1959), 9.

14. Joe Hyams, *Mislaid in Hollywood* (London and New York: W. H. Allen, 1973), 87–98.

15. Lionel Crane, "'I Was Born Again' . . . Says Cary Grant in the Frankest Talk of His Life," *Sunday Pictorial* (March 8, 1959), 22–23.

16. Joe Hyams, "'Reborn' Star Says He's No Longer a Fake," *PI* (April 20, 1959), 1 and 15; Joe Hyams, "Betsy Remains Adorable," *PI* (April 21, 1959), 28; Joe Hyams, "Oh, Those Wasted Years," *PI* (April 22, 1959), 25.

17. *LAT* (April 20, 1959), 2.

18. Hyams, *Mislaid in Hollywood*, 91–92.

19. Louella Parsons, "Interview Upsets Cary," *SFE* (April 21, 1959), 15.

20. Bergquist, "The Curious Story," 50–58.

21. Letters from Cary Grant to "Luba" Otavesic (March 1958 to January 1959), Christie's, http://www.christies.com/lotfinder/Lot/cary-grant-5154360-details.aspx

22. Jennifer Frost, *Hedda Hopper's Hollywood: Celebrity Gossip and American Conservatism* (New York and London: New York University Press, 2011), 193–94.

23. Letter from Hedda Hopper to Mike Cowles (August 31, 1959), file 984, HH/AMPAS.

24. *NYDN* (May 16, 1959), 30; *SFE* (September 17, 1959), 21; *PI* (October 23, 1959), 17.

25. Beauchamp and Balaban, "Cary in the Sky," 174.

26. Dennis McDougal, *The Last Mogul: Lew Wasserman, MCA, and the Hidden History of Hollywood* (Boston: Da Capo Press, 2001), 260.

27. *V* (November 26, 1958), 3.

28. Eddie Kalish, "Richest Actor: Cary Grant," *V* (November 20, 1963), 1 and 14.

29. Sam Wasson, *A Splurch in the Kisser: The Movies of Blake Edwards* (Middleton, CT: Wesleyan University Press, 2009), 45.

30. Tony Curtis and Barry Paris, *Tony Curtis: The Autobiography* (London: Heinemann, 1994), 172.

31. Lillian Ross, "Isn't it Wonderful?," *New Yorker* (June 3, 2002), 76.

32. Curtis and Paris, *Tony Curtis*, 160.

33. *SFE* (January 21, 1959), 2:5.

34. Patrick McGilligan, *Backstory 4: Interviews with Screenwriters of the 1970s and 1980s* (Berkeley: University of California Press, 2006), 96–97.

35. Ibid.; Gabriella Oldham (ed.), *Blake Edwards: Interviews* (Jackson: University of Mississippi Press, 2017), 43–44.

36. "Tony Curtis on Cary Grant," YouTube, https://www.youtube.com/watch?v=pq0XMHKGOGc

37. Kate Cameron, "A Jolly Sailor's Romp on Music Hall Screen," *NYDN* (December 4, 1959), C16; John L. Scott, "'Petticoat' Amusing Naval Diversion," *LAT* (December 25, 1959), 3:13; *V* (September 30, 1959), 6.

38. Bosley Crowther, "The Screen," *NYT* (December 4, 1959), 38; John McCarten, "The Current Cinema," *New Yorker* (December 12, 1959), 96.

39. Kalish, "Richest Actor: Cary Grant," 14.

40. Peter Lev, *The Fifties: Transforming the Screen* (Berkeley: University of California Press, 2003), 306.

41. Nelson, *Evenings with Cary Grant*, 232.

42. John L. Scott, "Comedy Projected for Grant and Kerr," *LAT* (May 15, 1959), 2:9.

43. *LAT* (January 12, 1959), 4:9; Louella Parsons, "Cary, Ingrid Pledge Secrecy on Picture," *SFE* (January 15, 1959), 2:5.

44. "Gigi Wins Best Picture: 1959 Oscars," YouTube, https://www.youtube.com/watch?v=EhhZRGY1fU0

45. *Los Angeles Mirror* (January 24, 1961), 4.

46. Grant, "Archie Leach," 42.

47. *SFE* (May 1, 1960), 18; Army Acherd, "Just for Variety," *DV* (August 15, 1960), 2.

48. Christopher Challis, *Are They Really So Awful? A Cameraman's Chronicles* (London: Janus Publishing, 1995), 170–75.

49. *DV* (May 5, 1960), 3; *DV* (June 28, 1960), 6.

50. Stephen Watts, "Focus on Amour in Stately Home," *NYT* (June 26, 1960), X7.

51. *V* (November 30, 1960), 6.

52. Bosley Crowther, "The Screen," *NYT* (December 24, 1960), 8; Mae Tinee, "'Grass' Has a Chuckle in Every Line," *CT* (December 28, 1960), 26; M. L. A., "Cary Grant and Deborah Kerr Titled Triflers in New Film," *BG* (December 24, 1960), 10.

53. *V* (January 10, 1962), 13 and 58.

54. A. H. Weiler, "By Way of Report," *NYT* (October 16, 1960), X9; Howard Thompson, "Irish Actor Wins Major Film Role," *NYT* (November 19, 1960), 12.

55. Kevin Brownlow, *David Lean: A Biography* (London: Faber and Faber, 1997), 425.

56. Cubby Broccoli with Donald Zec, *When the Snow Melts: The Autobiography of Cubby Broccoli* (London: Boxtree, 1998), 164.

57. Nelson, *Evenings with Cary Grant*, 270.

58. Army Archerd, "Just for Variety," *DV* (January 29, 1960), 2.

59. Stanley Shapiro and Nate Monaster, First Draft Screenplay: *That Touch of Mink* (June 12, 1961), file 79, CGP/AMPAS.

60. Lev, *The Fifties*, 306.

61. *NYDN* (June 7, 1961), 72; *DV* (July 14, 1961), 9.

62. Army Archerd, "Just for Variety," *DV* (July 27, 1961), 2.

63. Doris Day, *Her Own Story* (London: W. H. Allen, 1975), 234.

64. Garry McGee, *Doris Day: A Sentimental Journey* (Jefferson, NC: McFarland, 2015), 38–39.

65. Tamar Jeffers McDonald, *Doris Day Confidential: Hollywood, Sex and Stardom* (London: Tauris, 2013), 194–95.

66. *DV* (August 3, 1961), 3.

67. *V* (May 9, 1962), 6.

68. Bosley Crowther, "The Screen," *NYT* (June 15, 1962), 16; Brendan Gill, "The Current Cinema," *New Yorker* (June 23, 1962), 90; John L. Scott, "'Touch of Mink' is Glossy Comedy," *LAT* (July 20, 1962), 4:13.

69. *V* (January 9, 1963), 13.

70. *DFP* (December 20, 1961), 7.

71. Marilyn Beck, "Greta Thyssen: 'I Dated Another Woman's Husband,'" *TV and Movie Screen* (August 1963), 43–44; Roderick Mann, "'I'll Never Marry Again' He Said at Thirty," *Sunday Express* (October 18, 1964), 2.

72. Army Archerd, "Just for Variety," *DV* (July 26, 1955), 10; Herb Lyon, "Tower Ticker," *CT* (January 2, 1964), 18.

73. Cannon, *Dear Cary*, 11–34.

74. *LAT* (July 19, 1962), 4:8.

75. Bergquist, "The Curious Story," 58.

Chapter 28

1. Nelson, *Evenings with Cary Grant*, 55–56.

2. Roberta Ostroff, "Mr. Grant is Out of Town," Clippings, file 695, CGP/AMPAS.

3. Ibid., 224–25.

4. Cannon, *Dear Cary*, 17–18.

5. Ibid., 52–54.

6. Ibid., 60–61, 178–79.

7. Ibid., 103, 107–8.

8. Ibid., 115–16.

9. McCarthy, *Howard Hawks*, 596–97; Silverman, *Dancing on the Ceiling*, 287.

10. Silverman, *Dancing on the Ceiling*, 288; Nelson, *Evenings with Cary Grant*, 243–44.

11. Cannon, *Dear Cary*, 79.

12. *Charade*: Screenplay by Peter Stone (August 21, 1962), file 11, CGP/AMPAS.

13. Gene Siskel, "Cary Grant: Hollywood's Debonair and Durable Screen Idol," *CT* (February 15, 1976), 6:2–3.

14. Anthony Lane, "The Current Cinema," *New Yorker* (November 4, 2002), 110–11.

15. *LAT* (November 13, 1962), 4:13; *DV* (January 8, 1963), 3.

16. Nelson, *Evenings with Cary Grant*, 244; Barry Paris, *Audrey Hepburn* (New York: Berkeley Books, 2001), 183.

17. Nelson, *Evenings with Cary Grant*, 244–45; Paris, *Audrey Hepburn*, 183.

18. Nelson, *Evenings with Cary Grant*, 245; Paris, *Audrey Hepburn*, 186–87.

19. Nelson, *Evenings with Cary Grant*, 247–48; Paris, *Audrey Hepburn*, 187; Silverman, *Dancing on the Ceiling*, 291.

20. Cannon, *Dear Cary*, 136–38.

21. James Bacon, "Cary Grant Answers Girl's Ad for Job, Marries Her," *St. Louis Post-Dispatch* (August 12, 1965), 58; Dorothy Kilgallen, "The Voice of Broadway," *NYDN* (November 29, 1963), 16.

22. Joe Hyams, *Mislaid in Hollywood*, 94–95.

23. Grant, "Archie Leach," *LHJ* (January–February 1963), 50–53, 133–40; *LHJ* (March 1963), 23–24, 35–42; *LHJ* (April 1963), 86–87, 148–54.

24. Ibid., 96–98.

25. Letter from Elsie Leach to Archie Leach (June 25, 1961), file 256, CGP/AMPAS.

26. Letter from Elsie Leach to Archie Leach (April 3, 1963), file 256, CGP/AMPAS.

27. Cablegram from Archie Leach to Elsie Leach (April 9, 1963), file 256, CGP/AMPAS.

28. Letter from Dr. Greville Elliott to Cary Grant (March 18, 1962), file 256, CGP/AMPAS.

29. *SFE* (June 13, 1963), 29; *LAT* (August 16, 1963), 4:12; letter from Dr. Francis Page to Cary Grant (November 14, 1964), file 302, CGP/AMPAS.

30. Louella Parsons, "Cary Grant, Traveler," *SFE* (September 2, 1963), 33.

31. *LAT* (September 21, 1963), 20; *Washington Post* (September 21, 1963), C3.

32. Dorothy McCardle, "Stay in School, Says Cary Grant," *Washington Post* (September 20, 1963), D2.

33. *V* (September 11, 1963), 2.

34. Nelson, *Evenings with Cary Grant*, 251; Silverman, *Dancing on the Ceiling*, 293.

35. Silverman, *Dancing on the Ceiling*, 292.

36. Philip K. Scheuer, "Hollywood Dons Whiskers – Santa or Freud?," *LAT Calendar* (December 22, 1963), 3; Bosley Crowther, "The Screen," *NYT* (December 6, 1963), 40; *Time* (December 20, 1963), 63; Mae Tinnee, "A Hitch is Needed to Make a Film Like This," *CT* (December 26, 1963), 2:11.

37. *V* (January 5, 1966), 36.

38. Michael Newton, "*Charade*: The Last Sparkle of Hollywood," *The Guardian* (December 13, 2013), https://www.theguardian.com/film/2013/dec/13/charade-audrey-hepburn-cary-grant

39. Bawden and Miller, *Conversations with Classic Film Stars*, 125.

40. Paris, *Audrey Hepburn*, 187.

41. Bawden and Miller, *Conversations with Classic Film Stars*, 117; Nelson, *Evenings with Cary Grant*, 270.

42. Bawden and Miller, *Conversations with Classic Film Stars*, 117; Roderick Mann, "Yes, Rich Old Cary Grant Is Just Fine," *SFE Show Time* (January 26, 1964), 2; *Time* (July 27, 1962), 40–41.

43. *Father Goose*: Publicity Release (undated), file 28, CGP/AMPAS; Nelson, *Evenings with Cary Grant*, 255; Siskel, "Cary Grant," 76.

44. Murray Schumach, "Hollywood 'Father Goose' Saga," *NYT* (May 17, 1964), X9.

45. *Father Goose*: Revised First Draft Screenplay (February 11, 1964), file 21; and *Father Goose* final screenplay (March 17, 1964 with changes through July 11, 1964), file 22, CGP/AMPAS.

46. Schumach, "Hollywood 'Father Goose' Saga."

47. Leslie Caron, *Thank Heaven: A Memoir* (New York: Viking, 2009), 164–65; *Father Goose*: Budgets (August 14, 1964), file 24, CGP/AMPAS.

48. Crosby Day, "A Wild, Woolly 'Goose' Chase," *Orlando Sentinel* (March 24, 2002), X9; *Father Goose*: Budgets.

49. *DV* (April 10, 1964), 3; Schumach, "Hollywood 'Father Goose' Saga."

50. Nelson, *Evenings with Cary Grant*, 257–59.

51. Day, "A Wild, Woolly 'Goose' Chase"; *Father Goose*: Budgets.

52. Caron, *Thank Heaven*, 166–68; Nelson, *Evenings with Cary Grant*, 257–58.

53. *Father Goose*: Budgets.

54. Cannon, *Dear Cary*, 167; Caron, *Thank Heaven*, 166.

55. James Bacon, "Cary Grant Tells Secret of His Undying Popularity," *SFE* (January 24, 1960), C3.

56. *NYT* (January 4, 1965), 35; *DV* (January 22, 1965), 3.

57. *V* (January 5, 1966), 6.

58. Bosley Crowther, "The Screen," *NYT* (December 11, 1964), 55; Mae Tinee, "'Father Goose' is Fine Family Fare for the Entire Family," *CT* (December 27, 1964), 5:13; Philip K. Scheuer, "How the West and the South Pacific Wars Were Won," *LAT Calendar* (December 20, 1964), 3.

59. Nelson, *Evenings with Cary Grant*, 259.

60. Cannon, *Dear Cary*, 197–98.

61. Ibid., 169.

62. Letter from Dr. Francis Page to Cary Grant (July 7, 1965), file 302, CGP/AMPAS.

63. Cannon, *Dear Cary*, 159.

64. Ibid., 166.

65. Ibid., 184, 218–19.

66. Ibid., 200; Nelson, *Evenings with Cary Grant*, 266.

67. Cannon, *Dear Cary*, 210–12.

68. McGilligan, *Alfred Hitchcock*, 663; Silverman, *Dancing on the Ceiling*, 294.

69. Brent Phillips, *Charles Walters: The Director Who Made Hollywood Dance* (Lexington: University Press of Kentucky, 2014), 166–68.

70. Philip K. Scheuer, "'Walk, Don't Run' Sets Fast Pace," *LAT* (January 11, 1966), 4:7.

71. Scheuer, "'Walk, Don't Run' Sets Fast Pace."

72. Dave Jampel, "Young Star Praises Veteran, Cary Grant," [Lafayette, IN] *Journal and Courier* (December 4, 1965), 29.

73. Abe Greenberg, "Samantha Eggar: A Cary Grant Fan," [Hollywood, CA] *Valley Times* (December 9, 1965), 9; Dick Kleiner, "Samantha Eggar Leans on Cary Grant," *Philadelphia Daily News* (December 28, 1965), 38.

74. Kleiner, "Samantha Eggar Leans on Cary Grant."

75. Cannon, *Dear Cary*, 223.

76. Scheuer, "'Walk, Don't Run' Sets Fast Pace."

77. Cannon, *Dear Cary*, 237–38.

78. Nelson, *Evenings with Cary Grant*, 268–69.

79. Ibid., 296 and 347.

80. *Time* (July 15, 1966), 81.

81. Brendan Gill, "The Current Cinema," *New Yorker* (September 3, 1966), 71.

82. Howard Thompson, "The Screen," *NYT* (August 25, 1966), 42.

83. *V* (January 4, 1967), 8.

84. Cannon, *Dear Cary*, 247–48; Nelson, *Evenings with Cary Grant*, 266–67.

85. Cannon, *Dear Cary*, 130.

86. Ibid., 227–29; 254–56.

87. Harold Myers, "London's Press, Gossip Types Try to Hotfoot Cary Grant, But Flop," *V* (August 10, 1966), 7.

88. *LAT* (August 23, 1967), 2:1.

89. Rudy Villasenor, "LSD Long Used by Grant, Wife Asserts," *LAT* (March 21, 1968), 3.

90. Cannon, *Dear Cary*, 262.

91. Grant, "Archie Leach," *LHJ* (January–February 1963), 51.

Chapter 29

1. McGilligan, *George Cukor: A Double Life*, 282.

2. Nelson, *Evenings with Cary Grant*, 271.

3. Gene Siskel, "Cary Grant: Hollywood's Debonair and Durable Screen Idol . . . with Feet of Clay," *CT* (February 15, 1976), F2.

4. Orry-Kelly, *Women I've Undressed*, 395.

5. J. Grant, *Good Stuff*, 86–87.

6. Rudy Villasenor, "Cary Grant Divorced; Wins Right to Visit Daughter, 2," *LAT* (March 22, 1968), 3.

7. Nelson, *Evenings with Cary Grant*, 285–86.

8. Ibid., 280.

9. Ibid., 291; J. Grant, *Good Stuff*, 91.

10. Nelson, *Evenings with Cary Grant*, 302; *LAT* (March 25, 1970), D18.

11. Nelson, *Evenings with Cary Grant*, 302–3.

12. "Cary Grant Receiving an Honorary Oscar," YouTube, https://www.youtube.com/watch?v=R0Zijgn-c9w/

13. Siskel, "Cary Grant," F3.

14. Cary Grant, "On Acting," *THR* (November 14, 1955), 25.

15. "Sir Laurence Olivier Receiving an Honorary Oscar," Youtube, https://www.youtube.com/watch?v=TSgvp0l1n2s/

16. Transcript, "Interview with Cary Grant by Diane de Dubovay" [circa 1982], file 636, CGP/AMPAS.

17. "Jeff Daniels Conversation: The New Cary Grant," YouTube, https://www.youtube.com/watch?v=OHXRSeiml-E&list=PL2omgtZEd1hCWFlA2pEmE6F5SsatfZs0b&index=3&t=0s; Christopher Tookey, "Is Hugh the New Cary Grant?," *Mail Online*, 2018, https://www.dailymail.co.uk/tvshowbiz/article-111654/Is-Hugh-new-Cary-Grant.html; David Thomson, "Is George Clooney the New Cary Grant?," *The Age*,

https://www.theage.com.au/entertainment/movies/is-george-clooney-the-new-cary-grant-20070603-ge510t.html

18. Siskel, "Cary Grant," F2.

19. J. Grant, *Good Stuff*, 9–23.

20. Guy Flatley, "Cary—From Mae to September," *NYT* (July 22, 1973), B1; *Western Daily Press* (January 29, 1973), 1.

21. Correspondence between Cary Grant and Grace Kelly, file 209, CGP/AMPAS.

22. J. Grant, *Good Stuff*, 53.

23. Letter from Alfred Hitchcock to Cary Grant (August 29, 1979), file 225, CGP/AMPAS.

24. Nelson, *Evenings with Cary Grant*, 280.

25. "Cary Grant and Friends Salute Alfred Hitchcock," YouTube, https://www.youtube.com/watch?v=LazJJK7AxVQ/

26. Letter from Alfred Hitchcock to Cary Grant (March 13, 1979), file 225, CGP/AMPAS.

27. McGilligan, *George Cukor*, 745; *SFE* (January 4, 1980), 24.

28. Nelson, *Evenings with Cary Grant*, 203–4.

29. Ibid., 204; Tom Shales, "Grant: From Out of the Shadows," *LAT* (December 25, 1981), D17.

30. Amory, "Touch of Class," 4–9; Warren Hoge, "The Other Cary Grant," *NYT Magazine* (July 3, 1977), 14–15; Siskel, "Cary Grant," F2–3.

31. *LAT* (November 14, 1980), 2; *V* (November 19, 1980), 5.

32. Bogdanovich, *Who the Hell's In It*, 117.

33. Nelson, *Evenings with Cary Grant*, 322–23.

34. Grant, *Good Stuff*, 109–11.

35. Nelson, *Evenings with Cary Grant*, 333.

36. Ibid., 331–37.

37. Correspondence between Cary Grant and Nancy Nelson, file 620, CGP/AMPAS.

38. Letter from Nancy Nelson to Cary Grant (August 27, 1981), file 620, CGP/AMPAS.

39. *A Conversation with Cary Grant*, Clippings, file 616, CGP/AMPAS.

40. Correspondence between Cary Grant and Nancy Nelson, file 620, CGP/AMPAS.

41. J. Grant, *Good Stuff*, 166–67.

42. Nelson, *Evenings with Cary Grant*, 371–75.

43. Hoge, "The Other Cary Grant," 15.

44. Ibid., 376.

45. Ibid., 377.

Sources

Abbreviations

AMPAS	The Academy of Motion Picture Arts and Sciences
B	*Billboard*
BEP	*Bristol Evening Post*
BEW	*Bristol Evening World*
BG	*Boston Globe*
BRCF	Billy Rose Clippings Files
CGP	The Cary Grant Papers
CT	*Chicago Tribune*
DFP	*Detroit Free Press*
DV	*Daily Variety*
HVC	Hollywood Victory Committee
LAT	*Los Angeles Times*
LHJ	*Ladies' Home Journal*
MPH	*Motion Picture Herald*
NYDN	*Daily News* [New York, NY]
NYPL	New York Public Library
NYT	*New York Times*
PI	*Philadelphia Inquirer*
SFE	*San Francisco Examiner*
THR	*The Hollywood Reporter*
V	*Variety*

Select Bibliography

Archival Sources

Bristol Lunatic Asylum. Casebooks. Bristol Archives, Bristol, UK.

Fairfield School. Records. Bristol Archives, Bristol, UK.

Freed, Arthur. Papers. Cinematic Arts Library, University of Southern California, Los Angeles, USA.

Goldwyn, Samuel. Papers. Margaret Herrick Library. Academy of Motion Picture Arts and Sciences. Beverly Hills, California, USA.

Grant, Cary. Papers. Margaret Herrick Library. Academy of Motion Picture Arts and Sciences. Beverly Hills, California, USA.

Hepburn, Katharine. Papers. Margaret Herrick Library. Academy of Motion Picture Arts and Sciences. Beverly Hills, California, USA.

Hitchcock, Alfred. Papers. Margaret Herrick Library. Academy of Motion Picture Arts and Sciences. Beverly Hills, California, USA.

Hollywood Victory Committee, Office of Talent Reports. Cinematic Arts Library, University of Southern California, Los Angeles, USA

Hopper, Hedda. Papers. Margaret Herrick Library. Academy of Motion Picture Arts and Sciences. Beverly Hills, California, USA.

Metro-Goldwyn-Mayer. Script Collection and Production Department Collection. Cinematic Arts Library, University of Southern California, Los Angeles, USA.

Motion Picture Association of America. Production Code Administration records and World War II records. Academy of Motion Picture Arts and Sciences. Beverly Hills, California, USA.

Motion Picture Association of America. World War II records. Academy of Motion Picture Arts and Sciences. Beverly Hills, California, USA.

National Art Library. Theatre and Performance Biographical Files. Victoria and Albert Museum. London, UK.

North Street School. Records. Bristol Records Office, Bristol, United Kingdom.

Paramount Pictures. Contract summaries, photographs, production records, and scripts. Margaret Herrick Library. Academy of Motion Picture Arts and Sciences. Beverly Hills, California, USA.

Public Record Office, National Archives of the United Kingdom, Kew, UK.

RKO Radio Pictures. Studio Records. UCLA Library Special Collections, Charles E. Young Research Library, University of California, Los Angeles, USA.

Roach, Hal. Production and script files. Hollywood Museum Collection. Cinematic Arts Library, University of Southern California, Los Angeles, USA.

Rose, Billy. Clippings. Billy Rose Theater Collection. New York Public Library. New York, New York, USA.

Schaefer, William and Margaret. Papers. Cinematic Arts Library, University of Southern California, Los Angeles, USA.

Stevens, George. *George Stevens: A Filmmaker's Journey*, interview transcripts. Academy of Motion Picture Arts and Sciences. Beverly Hills, California, USA.

Stevens, George. Papers. Margaret Herrick Library. Academy of Motion Picture Arts and Sciences. Beverly Hills, California, USA.

Strickling, Howard. Papers. Margaret Herrick Library. Academy of Motion Picture Arts and Sciences. Beverly Hills, California, USA.

Turner/MGM Script Collection. Margaret Herrick Library. Academy of Motion Picture Arts and Sciences. Beverly Hills, California, USA.

Twentieth Century-Fox Script Collection. Cinematic Arts Library, University of Southern California, Los Angeles, USA.

Wald, Jerry. Papers. Cinematic Arts Library, University of Southern California, Los Angeles, USA.

Warner Bros. Archives. Studio Records. Cinematic Arts Library, University of Southern California, Los Angeles, USA.

Articles and Chapters in Books

Bawden, James. "Gail Patrick [interview]." *Films in Review* 32, no. 54 (May 1981): 286–94.

Belton, John. "I Was a Male War Bride." *Velvet Light Trap* 3 (Winter 1971): 26–28.

Britton, Andrew. "Cary Grant: Comedy and Male Desire." *CineAction* 7 (1986): 36–51.

Butters, Ronald R. "Cary Grant and the Emergence of Gay 'Homosexual.'" *Dictionaries: Journal of the Dictionary Society of North America* 19 (1998): 188–204.

Cavell, Stanley. "*North by Northwest*." *Critical Inquiry* 7, no. 4 (Summer 1981): 761–76.

Druesne, Maeve. "Mr. Grant Comes to Town." *Films in Review* 28, no. 1 (January 1987): 30–1.

Garvey, Adrian. "'Steely Velvet': The Voice of James Mason." *Journal of British Cinema and Television* 12, no. 1 (2015): 83–100.

Glancy, Mark. "A Relic of the Bad Old Days: Hollywood's London in *None But the Lonely Heart* (1944)." In *London on Film*, edited by Pam Hirsch and Chris O'Rourke, 57–72. Switzerland: Palgrave Macmillan, 2017.

Glancy, Mark. "Don't Fence Me In: The Making of *Night and Day*." In *The Many Cinemas of Michael Curtiz*, edited by R. Barton Palmer and Murray Pomerance, 55–67. Austin: University of Texas Press, 2018.

Glancy, Mark. "The 'Awful Truth' About Cary Grant." In *Hollywood and the Great Depression: American Film, Politics and Society in the 1930s*, edited by Iwan Morgan and John Philip Davies, 139–58. Edinburgh: Edinburgh University Press, 2016.

Glitre, Kathrina. "Cary Grant: Acting Style and Genre in Classical Hollywood Cinema." In *Acting and Performance in Moving Image Culture: Bodies, Screens, Renderings*, edited by Jörg Sternagel, Deborah Levitt, Dieter Mersch, 71–86. New Brunswick, NJ: Transcript-Verlag, 2012.

Grant, Cary. "Archie Leach [part 1]." *Ladies, Home Journal* (January–February, 1963): 50–53, 133–42.

Grant, Cary. "Archie Leach [part 2]." *Ladies, Home Journal* (March 1963): 23–24, 35–42.

Grant, Cary. "Archie Leach [part 3]." *Ladies, Home Journal* (April 1963): 86–87, 148–54.

Greene, Jane M. "The Road to Reno: *The Awful Truth* and the Hollywood Comedy of Remarriage." *Film History* 13, no. 4 (2001): 337–58.

Harvey, Stephen. "Stanley Donen Interview." *Film Comment* 9, no. 4 (July–August 1973): 4–9.

Jaher, Frederic Cople, and Blair B. King. "Hollywood's India: The Meaning of RKO's *Gunga Din*." *Film and History: An Interdisciplinary Journal of Film and Television* 38, no. 2 (2008): 33–44.

Jewell, Richard B. "How Howard Hawks Brought *Baby* Up: An Apologia for the Studio System." *Journal of Popular Film and Television* 11, no. 4 (1984): 158–65.

Jewell, Richard B. "RKO Film Grosses, 1929–1951: The C. J. Tevlin Ledger." *Historical Journal of Film, Radio and Television* 14, no. 1 (1994): 37–49.

Jurca, Catherine. "Hollywood, the Dream House Factory." *Cinema Journal* 37, no. 4 (1998): 19–37.

Kael, Pauline. "Profiles: The Man From Dream City." *New Yorker* (July 14, 1975): 40–68.

Keil, Charlie. "Cary Grant and Katharine Hepburn: Domesticated Mavericks." In *What Dreams Were Made Of: Movie Stars of the 1940s*, edited by Sean Griffin, 192–216. New Brunswick, NJ: Rutgers University Press, 2011.

Krohn, Bill. "Ambivalence (*Suspicion*)." *Hitchcock Annual* 11 (2002–2003): 67–116.

Lehmann, Ulrich. "Language of the PurSuit: Cary Grant's Clothes in Alfred Hitchcock's *North by Northwest*." *Fashion Theory* 4, no. 4 (November 2000): 467–85.

McEwen, Todd. "Cary Grant's Suit." *Granta* 94 (Summer 2006): 117–26.

Monaco, James. "Cary on Hitch." *Take One* 5, no. 2 (May 1976): 20.

Schuelke, Kent. "Cary Grant." *Interview* (January 1987).

Schwarz, Benjamin. "Becoming Cary Grant." *Atlantic* (January–February 2007): 132–36.

Smith, Ian. "'My Name's Not Chaplin': *North by Northwest* and the Screen Persona of Cary Grant." *Film Studies* 2 (Spring 2000): 29–43.

Todd, Drew. "Dandyism and Masculinity in Art Deco Hollywood." *Journal of Popular Film and Television* 32, no. 4 (January 2005): 168–81.

Weiss, Andrea. "A Queer Feeling When I Look at You: Stars and Lesbian Spectatorship in the 1930s." In *Stardom: Industry of Desire*, edited by Christine Gledhill, 287–304. London: Routledge, 1991.

Worland, Rick. "Before and After the Fact: Writing and Reading Hitchcock's *Suspicion*." *Cinema Journal* 41, no. 4 (August 2002): 3–26.

Books

Abrams, Brett. *Hollywood Bohemians: Transgressive Sexuality and the Selling of the Movieland Dream*. Jefferson, NC: McFarland and Company, 2008.

Babington, Bruce, and Peter Evans, *Affairs to Remember: The Hollywood Comedy of the Sexes*. Manchester: Manchester University Press, 1989.

Bach, Steven. *Dazzler: The Life and Times of Moss Hart*. New York: Alfred A. Knopf, 2001.

Balio, Tino. *Grand Design: Hollywood as a Modern Business Enterprise, 1930–1939*. New York: Charles Scribner's Sons, 1993.

Barlett, Donald L., and James B. Steele. *Howard Hughes: His Life and His Madness*. New York: W. W. Norton, 1979.

Basinger, Jeanine. *The Star Machine*. New York: Alfred A. Knopf, 2007.

Bawden, James, and Ron Miller. *Conversations with Classic Film Stars: Interviews from Hollywood's Golden Era.* Lexington: University of Kentucky Press, 2016.

Baxter, John. *Von Sternberg.* Lexington: University of Kentucky Press: 2010.

Behlmer, Rudy. *Behind the Scenes: The Making of . . .* Hollywood: Samuel French, 1990.

Behlmer, Rudy. *Memo From David O. Selznick.* Hollywood: Samuel French, 1989.

Bellamy, Ralph. *When the Smoke Hits the Fan: A Reminiscence of Theater, Movies and TV.* New York: Doubleday, 1979.

Berg, A. Scott. *Goldwyn: A Biography.* London: Hamish Hamilton, 1989.

Berg, A. Scott. *Kate Remembered.* London: Simon and Schuster, 2003.

Bergman, Ingrid, and Alan Burgess. *Ingrid Bergman: My Story.* London: Michael Joseph, 1980.

Bernstein, Matthew. *Walter Wanger: Hollywood Independent.* Berkeley and Los Angeles: University of California Press, 1994.

Black, Shirley Temple. *Child Star: An Autobiography.* New York: McGraw-Hill, 1989.

Bogdanovich, Peter. *Who the Devil Made It: Conversations with Legendary Film Directors.* New York: Knopf, 1997.

Bogdanovich, Peter. *Who the Hell Is In It: Portraits and Conversations.* London: Faber and Faber, 2004.

Bowers, Scotty. *Full Service: My Adventures in Hollywood and the Secret Sex Lives of the Stars.* New York: Grove Press, 2012.

Broccoli, Cubby, with Donald Zec. *When the Snow Melts: The Autobiography of Cubby Broccoli.* London: Boxtree, 1998.

Brown, Peter Harry, and Pat H. Broeske. *Howard Hughes: The Untold Story.* London: Little, Brown and Company, 1996.

Buehrer, Beverly Bare. *Cary Grant: A Bio-Bibliography.* Westport, CT: Greenwood Press, 1990.

Cannon, Dyan. *Dear Cary: My Life with Cary Grant.* New York: HarperCollins, 2011.

Capra, Frank. *The Name above the Title: An Autobiography.* New York: Da Capo Press, 1997 [1971].

Carman, Emily. *Independent Stardom: Freelance Women in the Hollywood Studio System.* Austin: University of Texas Press, 2016.

Caron, Leslie. *Thank Heaven: A Memoir.* New York: Viking, 2009.

Carr, Richard. *Charlie Chaplin: A Political Biography from Victorian Britain to Modern America.* London and New York: Routledge, 2017.

Cavell, Stanley. *Pursuits of Happiness: The Hollywood Comedy of Remarriage.* Cambridge: MA, and London: Harvard University Press, 1981.

Challis, Christopher. *Are They Really So Awful? A Cameraman's Chronicles.* London: Janus Publishing, 1995.

Chaplin, Charles. *My Autobiography.* New York: Simon and Schuster, 1964.

Chapman, James. *Hitchcock and the Spy Film.* London and New York: I. B. Tauris, 2018.

Chapman, James, and Nicholas J. Cull. *Projecting Empire: Imperialism and Popular Cinema.* London: I. B. Tauris, 2009.

Chauncey, George. *Gay New York: Gender, Urban Culture and the Making of the Gay Male World, 1890–1940.* New York: Basic Books, 1994.

Coffee, Lenore. *Storyline: Recollections of a Hollywood Screenwriter.* London: Cassell and Company, 1973.

Cohan, Steven. *Masked Men: Masculinity and the Movies in the Fifties.* Bloomington: Indiana University Press, 1997.

Coleman, Herbert. *The Man Who Knew Hitchcock: A Memoir*. Lanham, MD: Scarecrow Press, 2003.

Cronin, Paul (ed.). *George Stevens: Interviews*. Jackson: University of Mississippi Press, 2004.

Crowe, Cameron. *Conversations with Wilder*. London: Faber and Faber, 1999.

Cullen, Frank, with Florence Hackman and Donald McNeilly. *Vaudeville Old and New: An Encyclopedia of Variety Performers in America*, Volume 1. London: Routledge, 2006.

Curtis, James. *Spencer Tracy: A Biography*. London: Hutchinson, 2011.

Curtis, Tony, and Barry Paris. *Tony Curtis: The Autobiography*. London: Heinemann, 1994.

Dalrymple, Jean. *September Child: The Story of Jean Dalrymple*. New York: Dodd, Mead and Company, 1963.

Daniel, Douglass K. *Tough as Nails: The Life and Films of Richard Brooks*. Madison: University of Wisconsin Press, 2011.

Dauth, Brian (ed.). *Joseph L. Mankiewicz: Interviews*. Jackson: University of Mississippi Press, 2008.

Day, Barry (ed.). *The Letters of Noël Coward*. London: Methuen, 2007.

Dherbier, Yann-Brice. *Cary Grant: A Life in Pictures*. London: Pavilion Books, 2011.

Dick, Bernard F. *Forever Mame: The Life of Rosalind Russell*. Jackson: University of Mississippi, 2006.

Dick, Bernard F. *Joseph L. Mankiewicz*. Boston: G. K. Hall, 1983.

Dick, Bernard F. *The Merchant of Poverty Row: Harry Cohn of Columbia Pictures*. Lexington: University of Kentucky Press, 1993.

Donaldson, Frances. *Freddy Lonsdale*. London: Bloomsbury, 2011 [1957].

Donaldson, Maureen, and William Royce. *An Affair to Remember: My Life with Cary Grant*. London and Sydney: Macdonald and Co., 1989.

Drazin, Charles. *In Search of the Third Man*. London: Methuen, 1999.

Dyer, Richard. *Heavenly Bodies: Film Stars and Society*. New York: Macmillan, 1986.

Dyer, Richard. *Stars*. London: British Film Institute, 1979.

Early, Donal F. *"The Lunatic Pauper Palace": Glenside Hospital, 1861–1994*. Bristol, UK: Friends of the Glenside Museum, 2003.

Eberwein, Robert. *The Hollywood War Film*. West Sussex, UK: John Wiley and Sons, 2010.

Eldridge, Mona. *In Search of a Prince: My Life with Barbara Hutton*. London: Sidgwick and Jackson, 1988.

Eliot, Marc. *Cary Grant: A Biography*. New York: Three Rivers Press, 2004.

Eyman, Scott. *Ernst Lubitsch: Laughter in Paradise*. Baltimore: Johns Hopkins University Press, 2000.

Eyman, Scott. *Hank and Jim: The Fifty-Year Friendship of Henry Fonda and James Stewart*. New York: Simon and Schuster, 2017.

Fairbanks Jr., Douglas. *A Hell of a War*. New York: St. Martin's Press, 1993.

Fairbanks Jr., Douglas. *The Salad Days: An Autobiography*. London: Fontana, 1989.

Farmer, Frances. *Will There Really Be a Morning? An Autobiography*. New York: Putnam, 1972.

Finler, Joel W. *The Hollywood Story*. London: Octopus, 1988.

Flynn, Errol. *My Wicked, Wicked Ways*. New York: Cooper Square Press, 2003 [1959].

Fontaine, Joan. *No Bed of Roses: An Autobiography*. New York: William Morrow, 1978.

Forbes, Bryan. *Notes for a Life*. London: Collins, 1974.

Frost, Jennifer. *Hedda Hopper's Hollywood: Celebrity Gossip and American Conservatism*. New York and London: New York University Press, 2011.

Gabriel, Louise B. *Images of America: Early Santa Monica*. Charleston, SC: Arcadia Publishing, 2006.

Gehring, Wes D. *Irene Dunne: First Lady of Hollywood*. Lanham, MD, and Oxford: Scarecrow Press, 2006.

Gehring, Wes D. *Leo McCarey: From Marx to McCarthy*. Lanham, MD, and Oxford: Scarecrow Press, 2005.

Geist, Kenneth L. *Pictures Will Talk: The Life and Films of Joseph L. Mankiewicz*. New York: Charles Scribner's Sons, 1978.

Getty, J. Paul. *As I See It: The Autobiography of John Paul Getty*. New York: Prentice Hall, 1976.

Giddins, Gary. *Bing Crosby: A Pocketful of Dreams, The Early Years, 1903–1940*. New York: Little, Brown and Company, 2001.

Gill, Brendan, and Jerome Zerbe. *Happy Times*. New York: Harcourt Brace Jovanovich, 1973.

Girelli, Elisabetta. *Montgomery Clift: Queer Star*. Detroit: Wayne State University Press, 2014.

Glancy, Mark. *The 39 Steps: A British Film Guide*. London: I. B. Tauris, 2003.

Glancy, Mark. *Hollywood and the Americanization of Britain, from the 1920s to the Present*. London: I. B. Tauris, 2014.

Glancy, Mark. *When Hollywood Loved Britain: The Hollywood "British" Film*. Manchester, UK: Manchester University Press, 1999.

Glitre, Kathrina. *Hollywood Romantic Comedy: States of the Union, 1934–65*. Manchester, UK: Manchester University Press, 2006.

Godfrey, Lionel. *Cary Grant: The Light Touch*. London: Book Club Associates, 1981.

Gomery, Douglas. *The Hollywood Studio System*. London: BFI, 1986.

Gottlieb, Sidney (ed.). *Alfred Hitchcock: Interviews*. Jackson: University of Mississippi, 2003.

Govoni, Albert. *Cary Grant: An Unauthorized Biography*. London: Robert Hale and Company, 1971.

Grant, Barry Keith (ed.). *Britton on Film: The Complete Film Criticism of Andrew Britton*. Detroit: Wayne State University Press, 2009.

Grant, Jennifer. *Good Stuff: A Reminiscence of My Father, Cary Grant*. New York: Alfred A. Knopf, 2011.

Gundle, Stephen. *Glamour: A History*. Oxford: Oxford University Press, 2008.

Guthrie, Lee. *The Life and Loves of Cary Grant*. New York and London: Drake Publishers, 1977.

Hadleigh, Boze. *Hollywood Gays*. New York: Barricade Books, 1996.

Hamilton, Marybeth. *The Queen of Camp: Mae West, Sex and Popular Culture*. London: Pandora, 1995.

Hanson, Helen. *Hollywood Heroines: Women in Film Noir and the Female Gothic Film*. London: I. B. Tauris, 2007.

Harris, Mark. *Five Came Back: A Story of Hollywood and the Second World War*. Edinburgh: Canongate, 2014.

Harris, Warren G. *Cary Grant: A Touch of Elegance*. New York: Doubleday, 1987.

Harvey, James. *Romantic Comedy in Hollywood: From Lubitsch to Sturges*. New York: Da Capo Press, 1998 [1987].

Head, Edith. *The Dress Doctor*. New York: Little, Brown and Company, 1959.

Hepburn, Katharine. *Me: Stories of My Life*. New York: Knopf, 1991.

Heymann, C. David. *Poor Little Rich Girl: The Life and Legend of Barbara Hutton*. London: Arrow Books, 1984.

Higham, Charles, and Roy Moseley. *Cary Grant: The Lonely Heart*. San Diego, New York, and London: Harcourt Brace Jovanovich, 1989.

Hoey, Michael A. *Elvis' Favorite Director: The Amazing 52-Year Career of Norman Taurog*. Albany, GA: BearManor Media, 2013.

Hofmann, Albert. *LSD: My Problem Child and Insights/Outlooks*. Translated by Jonathan Ott. Oxford: Oxford University Press, 2013 [1983].

Hoopes, Roy. *When the Stars Went to War: Hollywood and World War II*. New York: Random House, 1994.

Hotchner, A. E. *Doris Day: Her Own Story*. London: W. H. Allen, 1985.

Hotchner, A. E. *Sophia: Living and Loving: Her Own Story*. London: Michael Joseph, 1979.

Hyams, Joe. *Mislaid in Hollywood*. London: W. H. Allen, 1973.

Ibson, John. *Picturing Men: A Century of Male Relationships in Everyday American Photography*. Chicago: University of Chicago Press, 2002.

Jessel, George, with John Austin. *The World I Lived In*. Chicago: Henry Regnery Company, 1975.

Jewell, Richard B. *RKO Radio Pictures: A Titan is Born*. Berkeley: University of California Press, 2012.

Jewell, Richard B. *Slow Fade to Black: The Decline of RKO Radio Pictures*. Berkeley: University of California Press, 2016.

Kanin, Garson. *Great Hollywood Teams*. London and New York: Angus and Robertson Publishers, 1983.

Kanin, Garson. *Hollywood, and the People Who Made It*. St. Albans, UK: Granada Publishing, 1977.

Kelly, Gillian. *Robert Taylor: Male Beauty, Masculinity and Stardom in Hollywood*. Jackson: University of Mississippi, 2019.

Kemper, Tom. *Hidden Talent: The Emergence of Hollywood Agents*. Berkeley: University of California Press, 2010.

Klevan, Andrew. *Film Performance: From Achievement to Appreciation*. London and New York: Wallflower, 2005.

Kobal, John. *People Will Talk: Personal Conversations with the Legends of Hollywood*. London: Aurum Press, 1986.

Koster, Henry. *Henry Koster Interviewed by Irene Kahn Atkins*. Metuchen, NJ: Directors Guild of America and Scarecrow Press, 1987.

Kotsilibas-Davis, James, and Myrna Loy, *Myrna Loy: Being and Becoming*. London: Bloomsbury, 1987.

Kramer, Stanley, with Thomas M. Coffey. *A Mad, Mad, Mad, Mad World: A Life in Hollywood*. New York, San Diego, and London: Harcourt, Brace and Company, 1997.

Lambert, Gavin. *On Cukor*. New York: Rizzoli, 2000 [1972].

Lasalle, Mick. *Dangerous Men: Pre-Code Hollywood and the Birth of the Modern Man*. New York: Thomas Dunne/St. Martin's Press, 2002.

Lasky, Jesse L., with Don Weldon. *I Blow My Own Horn*. London: Victor Gollancz Limited, 1957.

Laurents, Arthur. *Original Story: A Memoir of Broadway and Hollywood*. New York: Alfred A. Knopf, 2000.

Leff, Leonard J. *Hitchcock and Selznick: The Rich and Strange Collaboration of Alfred Hitchcock and David O. Selznick in Hollywood*. Berkeley: University of California Press, 1987.

Leider, Emily W. *Myrna Loy: The Only Good Girl in Hollywood*. Berkeley: University of California Press, 2011.

Loe, Nancy E. *William Randolph Hearst: An Illustrated Biography*. Santa Barbara, CA: Albion Publishing, 1998 [1988].

Long, Robert Emmet (ed.). *George Cukor: Interviews*. Jackson: University of Mississippi Press, 2001.

Longworth, Karina. *Seduction: Sex, Lies, and Stardom in Howard Hughes's Hollywood*. New York: Custom House, 2018.

Loren, Sophia. *Yesterday, Today, and Tomorrow: My Life*. New York: Simon and Schuster, 2014.

Lower, Cheryl Bray, and R. Barton Palmer. *Joseph L. Mankiewicz: Critical Essays with an Annotated Bibliography and a Filmography*. Jefferson, NC, and London: McFarland and Company, 2001.

Mann, William J. *Behind the Scenes: How Gays and Lesbians Shaped Hollywood, 1910–1969*. New York: Viking, 2001.

Mann, William J. *Kate: The Woman Who Was Katharine Hepburn*. London: Faber and Faber, 2006.

Mast, Gerald (ed.). *Bringing Up Baby*. Rutgers Films in Print Series. New Brunswick, NJ: Rutgers University Press, 1988.

McBride, Joseph. *Hawks on Hawks*. London and Boston: Faber and Faber, 1996.

McBrien, William. *Cole Porter*. New York: Alfred A. Knopf, 1998.

McCann, Graham. *Cary Grant: A Class Apart*. London: Fourth Estate, 1996.

McCarthy, Todd. *Howard Hawks: The Grey Fox of Hollywood*. New York: Grove Press, 1997.

McDonald, Paul. *The Star System: Hollywood's Production of Popular Identities*. London: Wallflower, 2000.

McDonald, Tamars Jeffers. *Doris Day Confidential*. London: I. B. Tauris, 2013.

McDougal, Dennis. *The Last Mogul: Lew Wasserman, MCA, and the Hidden History of Hollywood*. Boston: Da Capo Press, 2001.

McGilligan, Patrick. *Alfred Hitchcock: A Life in Darkness and in Light*. New York: HarperCollins, 2003.

McGilligan, Patrick. *Film Crazy: Interviews With Hollywood Legends*. New York: St. Martin's Griffin, 2000.

McGilligan, Patrick. *George Cukor: A Double Life*. New York: St. Martin's Press, 1991.

McGilligan, Patrick (ed.). *Backstory 4: Interviews with Screenwriters of the 1970s and 1980s*. Berkeley: University of California Press, 2006.

McIntosh, William Currie, and William Weaver. *The Private Cary Grant*. London: Sidgwick and Jackson, 1983.

McKibbin, Ross. *Classes and Cultures: England, 1918–1951*. Oxford: Oxford University Press, 2000.

Meyers, Jeffrey. *Gary Cooper: American Hero*. London: Rowman and Littlefield, 2001.

Morecambe, Gary, and Martin Sterling. *Cary Grant: In Name Only*. London: Robson Books, 2001.

Moss, Marilyn Ann. *Giant: George Stevens, A Life on Film*. Madison: University of Wisconsin Press, 2004.

Naremore, James. *Acting in the Cinema*. Berkeley: University of California Press, 1988.

Naremore, James (ed.). *North by Northwest*. Rutgers Films in Print Series. New Brunswick, NJ: Rutgers University Press, 1993.

Nelson, Nancy. *Evenings with Cary Grant: Recollections in His Own Words and by Those Who Knew Him Best*. New York: Citadel Press, 1991.

Niven, David. *Bring on the Empty Horses*. London: Hamish Hamilton, 1975.

Niven, David. *The Moon's a Balloon*. New York: Dell, 1972.

Nott, Robert. *The Films of Randolph Scott*. Jefferson, NC: McFarland, 2014.

Offner, John. *Jean Arthur: The Actress Nobody Knew*. New York: Limelight Editions, 1997.

Oldham, Gabriela (ed.). *Blake Edwards*. Conversations with Filmmakers Series. Jackson: University of Mississippi Press, 2017.

Orry-Kelly. *Women I've Undressed: The Fabulous Life and Times of a Legendary Hollywood Designer*. London: Allen and Unwin, 2016.

Paris, Barry. *Audrey Hepburn*. New York: Berkeley Books, 2001.

Phillips, Alastair, and Ginette Vincendeau. *Journeys of Desire: European Actors in Hollywood, A Critical Companion*. London: British Film Institute, 2006.

Phillips, Brent. *Charles Walters: The Director Who Made Hollywood Dance*. Lexington: University of Kentucky Press, 2014.

Polito, Robert (ed.). *Farber on Film: The Complete Film Writings of Manny Farber*. New York: Library of America, 2009.

Reid, Helen. *Bristol Under Siege: Surviving the Wartime Blitz*. Bristol: Redcliffe Press, 2005.

Rempel, William C. *The Gambler*. New York: HarperCollins, 2018.

Richards, Jeffrey. *Cinema and Radio in Britain and America, 1920–1960*. Manchester, UK: Manchester University Press, 2010.

Richards, Jeffrey. *The Golden Age of Pantomime: Slapstick, Spectacle and Subversion in Victorian England*. London: I. B. Tauris, 2015.

Riva, Maria. *Marlene Dietrich: The Life*. New York: Knopf, 1992.

Rogers, Ginger. *Ginger: My Story*. London: Headline, 1991.

Royce, Bill. *Cary Grant: The Wizard of Beverly Grove*. Beverly Hills: Cool Titles, 2006.

Russell, Rosalind, and Chris Chase. *Life Is a Banquet*. New York: Random House, 1977.

Schary, Dore. *Heyday: An Autobiography*. Boston and Toronto: Little, Brown and Company, 1979.

Schatz, Thomas. *Boom and Bust: American Cinema in the 1940s*. Berkeley: University of California, 1997.

Schatz, Thomas. *The Genius of the System: Hollywood Filmmaking in the Studio Era*. New York: Pantheon Books, 1988.

Scheide, Frank, and Hooman Mehran (eds.). *Chaplin's* Limelight *and the Music Hall Tradition*. Jefferson, NC: McFarland, 2006.

Schickel, Richard. *Cary Grant: A Celebration*. London: Pavilion Books, 1983.

Schickel, Richard. *Cary Grant: A Celebration*. London: Bloomsbury Books, 1995 [1983].

Scott, C. H. *Whatever Happened to Randolph Scott?* Madison, NC: Empire, 1994.

Selznick, Irene Mayer. *A Private View*. London: Weidenfeld and Nicolson, 1987.

Seymour, Miranda. *Chaplin's Girl: The Life and Loves of Virginia Cherrill*. London: Simon and Schuster, 2009.

Shavelson, Melville. *How to Succeed in Hollywood Without Really Trying: P.S.—You Can't*. Albany, GA: Bear Manor Media, 2007.

Sheldon, Sidney. *The Other Side of Me*. London: HarperCollins, 2005.

Sherman, Vincent. *Studio Affairs: My Life as a Film Director*. Lexington: University of Kentucky Press, 1996.

Shingler, Martin. *Star Studies: A Critical Guide*. London: Bloomsbury Academic, 2012.

Shipman, David. *The Great Movie Stars: The Golden Years*. London: Hamlyn, 1970.

Silverman, Stephen M. *Dancing on the Ceiling: Stanley Donen and His Movies*. New York: Alfred A. Knopf, 1996.

Skal, David J., and Jessica Rains, *Claude Rains: An Actor's Voice*. Lexington: University of Kentucky Press, 2008.

Slide, Anthony. *Inside the Hollywood Fan Magazine: A History of Star Makers, Fabricators and Gossip Mongers*. Jackson: University Press of Mississippi, 2010.

Slide, Anthony (ed.). *It's the Pictures that Got Small: Charles Brackett on Billy Wilder and Hollywood's Golden Age*. New York: Columbia University Press, 2015.

Slide, Anthony. *New York City Vaudeville*. Charleston, SC: Arcadia Publishing, 2006.

Small, Pauline. *Sophia Loren: Moulding the Star*. Bristol, UK: Intellect Books, 2009.

Smyth, J. E. *Nobody's Girl Friday: The Women Who Ran Hollywood*. Oxford: Oxford University Press, 2018.

Solomon, Aubrey. *Twentieth Century-Fox: A Corporate and Financial History*. Metuchen, NJ: Scarecrow Press, 1988.

Spoto, Donald. *The Dark Side of Genius: The Life of Alfred Hitchcock*. New York: Little, Brown and Company, 1983.

Spoto, Donald. *Notorious: The Life of Ingrid Bergman*. New York: HarperCollins, 1997.

Steen, Mike. *Hollywood Speaks: An Oral History*. New York: G. P. Putnam's Sons, 1974.

Stephens, E. J., Michael Christaldi, and Marc Wanamaker. *Images of America: Early Paramount Studios*. Charleston, SC: Arcadia, 2013.

Stevens Jr., George. *Conversations with the Great Moviemakers of Hollywood's Golden Age*. New York: Vintage Books, 2006.

Sturges, Sandy (ed.). *Preston Sturges by Preston Sturges*. New York: Touchstone, 1991.

Swaab, Peter. *Bringing Up Baby*. BFI Film Classics Series. London: Palgrave Macmillan, 2010.

Swindell, Larry. *Screwball: The Life of Carole Lombard*. Brattleboro, VT: Echo Point, 1976.

Taylor, John Russell. *Hitch: The Life and Work of Alfred Hitchcock; The Authorised Biography*. London: Abacus, 1981.

Thomson, David. *Have You Seen . . .?* London: Penguin Books, 2008.

Thomson, David. *The New Biographical Dictionary of Film*. Fourth Edition. London: Little Brown, 2002 [1975].

Thomson, David. *Showman: The Life of David O. Selznick*. New York: Knopf, 1992.

Truffaut, François, with Helen G. Scott. *Hitchcock*. Revised Edition. London: Paladin, 1984.

Turk, Edward Baron. *Hollywood Diva: A Biography of Jeanette MacDonald*. Berkeley: University of California Press, 1998.

Vermilye, Jerry. *Cary Grant*. New York: Galahad Books, 1973.

Walker, Alexander. *"It's Only a Movie, Ingrid": Encounters On and Off Screen*. London: Headline, 1988.

Wansall, Geoffrey. *Cary Grant: Dark Angel*. New York: Arcade Publishing, 1996.

Wansall, Geoffrey. *Cary Grant: Haunted Idol*. London: William Collins, 1983.

Wasson, Sam. *A Splurch in the Kisser: The Movies of Blake Edwards*. Middletown, CT: Wesleyan University Press, 2009.

Watson, Moray. *Looking Back and Dropping Names: A Memoir*. Norwich, UK: Erskine Press, 2016.

Wieland, Karin. *Dietrich and Riefenstahl: Hollywood, Berlin and a Century in Two Lives*. London: W. W. Norton, 2011.

Williams, Esther, with Digby Diehl. *The Million Dollar Mermaid*. New York: Simon and Schuster, 1999.

Wood, Robin. *Hitchcock's Films*. New York: Castle Books, 1965.

Wood, Robin. *Howard Hawks*. London: British Film Institute, 1968.

Wray, Fay. *On the Other Hand: A Life Story*. London: Weidenfeld and Nicolson, 1989.

PhD Thesis

Tobia, Paul. "The Patients of the Bristol Lunatic Asylum in the Nineteenth Century." PhD diss., University of the West of England, 2017.

Filmography

Cary Grant's feature films are listed below in the order that they were produced, and the year of release is indicated in parentheses after the title. The credits reproduce those seen in the film. For further details, including uncredited names, see the text. Filming dates refer to the shooting days (and not rehearsals, re-takes, or post-production work). The release date is the date the film was first released in the United States. Unless marked with an asterisk, the budget, production costs, earnings, and profit or loss figures are taken from studio documents. The earnings figures are the distributor's share of the box-office gross. Those marked with an asterisk are estimates reported in the film industry trade press. Note that the production costs do not include the subsequent costs of distribution and publicity, which factor into the profit or loss figures. See the references within the text for the source of all dates and figures. "N/A" indicates that figures are not available.

1. *This Is the Night* (1932)
Production Company: Paramount
Produced by Paramount
Screenplay by George Marion Jr., and Benjamin Glazer
Based on a play by Rene Peter and Henri Falk, adapted for the stage by Avery Hopwood
Directed by Frank Tuttle
Cast: Lily Damita (*Germaine*), Charlie Ruggles (*Bunny West*), Roland Young (*Gerald Gray*), Thelma Todd (*Claire*), Cary Grant (*Stephen*), Irving Bacon (*Sparks*)
Filming Dates: January 19 to February 12, 1932
Release Date: April 8, 1932
Budget: $328,000
Production Cost: N/A
North American Earnings: N/A
Foreign Earnings: N/A
Total Earnings: N/A
Profit/(Loss): N/A

2. *Sinners in the Sun* (1932)
Production Company: Paramount
Produced by Paramount
Screenplay by Vincent Lawrence, Waldemar Young, Samuel Hoffenstein
Based on a story by Mildred Cram
Directed by Alexander Hall
Cast: Carole Lombard (*Doris Blake*), Chester Morris (*Jimmie Martin*), Adrienne Ames (*Claire Kinkaid*), Alison Skipworth (*Mrs. Blake*), Cary Grant (*Ridgeway*), Walter Byron (*Eric Nelson*), Rita La Roy (*Lil*)
Filming Dates: February 2 to March 26, 1932
Release Date: May 13, 1932
Budget: N/A
Production Cost: N/A
North American Earnings: N/A
Foreign Earnings: N/A
Total Earnings: N/A
Profit/(Loss): N/A

3. *Merrily We Go to Hell* (1932)
Production Company: Paramount
Produced by Paramount
Screenplay by Edwin Justus Mayer
Based on a novel by Cleo Lucas
Directed by Dorothy Arzner
Cast: Sylvia Sidney (*Joan*), Fredric March (*Jerry*), Adrienne Allen (*Claire*), Skeets Gallagher (*Buck*), George Irving (*Prentice*), Esther Howard (*Vi*), Florence Britton (*Charlie*), Charles Coleman (*Damery*), Cary Grant (*Charlie Baxter*), Kent Taylor (*Greg*)
Filming Dates: March 28 to April 30, 1932
Release Date: June 10, 1932
Budget: N/A
Production Cost: N/A
North American Earnings: N/A
Foreign Earnings: N/A
Total Earnings: N/A
Profit/(Loss): N/A

4. *Devil and the Deep* (1932)
Production Company: Paramount
Produced by Paramount

Screenplay by Benn W. Levy

Based on a story by Harry Hervey

Directed by Marion Gering

Cast: Tallulah Bankhead (*Diana Sturm*), Gary Cooper (*Lieutenant Sempter*), Charles Laughton (*Commander Sturm*), Cary Grant (*Lieutenant Jaeckel*), Paul Porcasi (*Hassan*), Juliette Compton (*Mrs. Planet*), Henry Kolker (*Commander Hutton*), Dorothy Christy (*Mrs. Crimp*), Arthur Hoyt (*Mr. Planet*), Gordon Westcott (*Lieutenant Toll*), Jimmie Dugan (*Condover*)

Filming Dates: May 30 to July 9, 1932

Release Date: August 12, 1932

Budget: N/A

Production Cost: N/A

North American Earnings: N/A

Foreign Earnings: N/A

Total Earnings: N/A

Profit/(Loss): N/A

5. *Blonde Venus* (1932)

Production Company: Paramount

Produced by Paramount

Screenplay by Jules Furthman and S. K. Lauren

Directed by Josef von Sternberg

Cast: Marlene Dietrich (*Helen Faraday*), Herbert Marshall (*Edward Faraday*), Cary Grant (*Nick Townsend*), Dickie Moore (*Johnny Faraday*), Gene Morgan (*Ben Smith*), Rita La Roy (*"Taxi Belle" Hooper*), Robert Emmett O'Connor (*O'Connor*), Sidney Toler (*Detective Wilson*), Morgan Wallace (*Dr. Pierce*)

Filming Dates: May 30 to August 27, 1932

Release Date: September 23, 1932

Budget: N/A

Production Cost: N/A

North American Earnings: N/A

Foreign Earnings: N/A

Total Earnings: N/A

Profit/(Loss): N/A

6. *Hot Saturday* (1932)

Production Company: Paramount

Produced by Paramount

Screenplay by Seton I. Miller, Josephine Lovett, and Joseph Moncure March

Based on a novel by Harvey Fergusson

Directed by William Seiter

Cast: Cary Grant (*Romer Sheffield*), Nancy Carroll (*Ruth Brock*), Randolph Scott (*Bill Fadden*), Edward Woods (*Connie Billop*), Lillian Bond (*Eva Randolph*), William Collier Sr. (*Mr. Brock*), Jane Darwell (*Mrs. Brock*), Stanley Smith (*Joe*), Rita La Roy (*Camille*), Rose Coghlan (*Annie Brock*), Oscar Apfel (*Mr. Randolph*), Jessie Arnold (*Aunt Minnie*), Grady Sutton (*Archie*)

Filming Dates: August 23 to September 15, 1932

Release Date: October 28, 1932

Budget: $248,000

Budget: N/A

Production Cost: N/A

North American Earnings: N/A

Foreign Earnings: N/A

Total Earnings: N/A

Profit/(Loss): N/A

7. *Madame Butterfly* (1932)

Production Company: Paramount

Produced by B. P. Schulberg

Screenplay by Josephine Lovett and Joseph Moncure March

Based on a story by John Luther Long and a play by David Belasco

Directed by Marion Gering

Cast: Sylvia Sidney (*Cho-cho San*), Cary Grant (*Lieutenant B. F. Pinkerton*), Charles Ruggles (*Lieutenant Barton*), Irving Pichel (*Yamadori*), Helen Jerome Eddy (*Cho-cho San's Mother*), Edmund Breese (*Cho-cho San's Grandfather*), Louise Carter (*Suzuki*), Sandor Kallay (*Goro*), Judith Vosselli (*Madame Goro*), Sheila Terry (*Adelaide*), Dorothy Libaire (*Peach Blossom*), Berton Churchill (*Mr. Sharpless*), Philip Horomato (*"Trouble"*)

Filming Dates: October 17 to November 25, 1932

Release Date: December 30, 1932

Budget: $350,000

Production Cost: $390,425

North American Earnings: N/A

Foreign Earnings: N/A

Total Earnings: N/A

Profit/(Loss): N/A

8. *She Done Him Wrong* (1933)
Production Company: Paramount
Produced by Paramount
Screenplay by Henry Thew and John Bright
Based on a story by Mae West
Directed by Lowell Sherman
Cast: Mae West (*Lady Lou*), Cary Grant (*Captain Cummings*), Owen Moore (*Chick Clark*), Gilbert Roland (*Serge Stanieff*), Noah Beery Sr. (*Gus Jordan*), David Landau (*Dan Flynn*), Rafaela Ottiano (*Russian Rita*), Dewey Robinson (*Spider Kane*), Rochelle Hudson (*Sally*), Tammany Young (*Chuck Connors*), Fuzzy Knight (*Rag Time Kelly*), Grace La Rue (*Frances*), Robert E. Homans (*Doheny*), Louise Beavers (*Pearl*)
Filming Dates: November 28 to December 17, 1932
Release Date: January 20, 1933
Budget: N/A
Production Cost: $200,000*
North American Earnings: $2,300,000*
Foreign Earnings: N/A
Total Earnings: N/A
Profit/(Loss): N/A

9. *The Woman Accused* (1933)
Production Company: Paramount
Produced by Paramount
Screenplay by Bayard Veiller
Based on a story by Rupert Hughes, Vicki Baum, Viña Delmar, Irvin S. Cobb, Gertrude Atherton, J. P. McEvoy, Zane Grey, Ursula Parrott, Polan Banks, Sophie Kerr
Directed by Paul Sloane
Cast: Nancy Caroll (*Glenda O'Brien*), Cary Grant (*Jeffrey Baxter*), John Halliday (*Stephen Bessemer*), Louis Calhern (*Leo Young*), Irving Pichel (*District Attorney Clarke*), Norma Mitchell (*Martha*), Jack La Rue (*Little Maxie*), Frank Sheridan (*Police Inspector*), John Lodge (*Dr. Simpson*), Lona André (*Cora Mathews*), Harry Holman (*Judge Osgood*)
Filming Dates: December 19, 1932, to January 16, 1933
Release Date: February 17, 1933
Budget: N/A

Production Cost: N/A
North American Earnings: N/A
Foreign Earnings: N/A
Total Earnings: N/A
Profit/(Loss): N/A

10. *The Eagle and the Hawk* (1933)
Production Company: Paramount
Produced by Paramount
Screenplay by Bogart Rogers and Seton I. Miller
Based on a story by John Monk Saunders
Directed by Stuart Walker
Cast: Fredric March (*Jerry Young*), Cary Grant (*Henry Crocker*), Jack Oakie (*Mike Richards*), Carole Lombard (*The Beautiful Lady*), Sir Guy Standing (*Major Dunham*), Forrester Harvey (*Hogan*), Kenneth Howell (*John Stevens*), Leyland Hodgson (*Kingsford*), Virginia Hammond (*Lady Erskine*), Douglas Scott (*Tommy*), Robert Manning (*Voss*), Adrienne d'Ambricourt (*Fifi*)
Filming Dates: March 1 to April 10, 1933
Release Date: May 19, 1933
Budget: N/A
Production Cost: N/A
North American Earnings: N/A
Foreign Earnings: N/A
Total Earnings: N/A
Profit/(Loss): N/A

11. *Gambling Ship* (1933)
Production Company: Paramount
Produced by Paramount
Screenplay by Max Marcin and Seton I. Miller
Based on stories by Peter Ruric, adapted by Claude Binyon
Directed by Louis Gasnier and Max Marcin
Cast: Cary Grant (*Ace Corbin*), Benita Hume (*Eleanor La Velle*), Jack La Rue (*Pete Manning*), Glenda Farrell (*Jeanne Sands*), Roscoe Karns (*Blooey*), Arthur Vinton (*Joe Burke*), Charles Williams (*Baby Face*), Edwin Maxwell (*District Attorney*), Spencer Charters (*First Detective*), Kate Campbell (*Woman Detective*), Edward Gargan (*First Deputy*), Sid Saylor (*The Sailor*)
Filming Dates: April 21 to May 23, 1933

Release Date: June 30, 1933
Budget: N/A
Production Cost: N/A
North American Earnings: N/A
Foreign Earnings: N/A
Total Earnings: N/A
Profit/(Loss): N/A

12. *I'm No Angel* (1933)
Production Company: Paramount
Produced by Paramount
Screenplay by Mae West, Lowell Brentano, and Harlan Thompson
Based on a story by Mae West
Directed by Wesley Ruggles
Cast: Mae West (*Tira*), Cary Grant (*Jack Clayton*), Gregory Ratoff (*Benny Pinkowitz*), Edward Arnold (*Big Bill Barton*), Ralf Harolde (*Slick Wiley*), Kent Taylor (*Kirk Lawrence*), Gertrude Michael (*Alicia Hatton*), Russell Hopton (*The Barker*), Dorothy Peterson (*Thelma*), Wm. B. Davidson (*The Chump*), Gertrude Howard (*Beulah*), Libby Taylor (*Maid*)
Filming Dates: July 10 to September 11, 1933
Release Date: October 7, 1933
Budget: N/A
Production Cost: N/A
North American Earnings: $2,200,000*
Foreign Earnings: N/A
Total Earnings: N/A
Profit/(Loss): N/A

13. *Born to Be Bad* (1934)
Production Company: Twentieth Century Pictures
Produced by Darryl F. Zanuck
Screenplay by Ralph Graves
Based on an original story by Ralph Graves
Directed by Lowell Sherman
Cast: Loretta Young (*Letty Strong*), Cary Grant (*Malcolm Trevor*), Jackie Kelk (*Mickey*), Marion Burns (*Mrs. Trevor*), Henry Travers (*Fuzzy*), Paul Harvey (*Attorney Brian*), Russell Hopton (*Steve Karns*), Harry Green (*Adolph*)
Filming Dates: October 21 to November 21, 1933

Release Date: May 18, 1934
Budget: N/A
Production Cost: $250,000*
North American Earnings: N/A
Foreign Earnings: N/A
Total Earnings: N/A
Profit/(Loss): N/A

14. *Alice in Wonderland* (1933)
Production Company: Paramount
Produced by
Screenplay by Joseph L. Mankiewicz and William Cameron Menzies
Based on a story by Lewis Carroll
Directed by Norman McLeod
Cast: Charlotte Henry (*Alice*), Richard Arlen (*Cheshire Cat*), Roscoe Ates (*Fish*), William Austin (*Gryphon*), Gary Cooper (*White Knight*), Leon Errol (*Uncle Gilbert*), Louise Fazenda (*White Queen*), W. C. Fields (*Humpty-Dumpty*), Alec B. Francis (*King of Hearts*), Skeets Gallagher (*Rabbit*), Cary Grant (*Mock Turtle*), Lillian Harmer (*Cook*), Raymond Hatton (*Mouse*), Sterling Holloway (*Frog*), Edward Everett Horton (*Mad Hatter*), Roscoe Karns (*Tweedledee*), Baby Le Roy (*Joker*), Mae Marsh (*Sheep*), Polly Moran (*Dodo Bird*), Jack Oakie (*Tweedledum*), Edna May Oliver (*Red Queen*), May Robson (*Queen of Hearts*), Charlie Ruggles (*March Hare*), Jackie Searl (*Dormouse*), Alison Skipworth (*Duchess*), Ned Sparks (*Caterpillar*), Ford Sterling (*White King*)
Filming Dates: September 18 to November 18, 1933
Release Date: December 22, 1933
Budget: N/A
Production Cost: N/A
North American Earnings: N/A
Foreign Earnings: N/A
Total Earnings: N/A
Profit/(Loss): N/A

15. *Thirty Day Princess* (1934)
Production Company:
Produced by B. P. Schulberg
Screenplay by Preston Sturges and Frank Partos
Based on a novel by Clarence Budington Kelland, adapted by Sam Hellman and Edwin Justus Mayer

Directed by Marion Gering

Cast: Sylvia Sidney (*Nancy Lane* and *Princess Catterina*), Cary Grant (*Porter Madison III*), Richard M. Gresham (*Edward Arnold*), Henry Stephenson (*King Anatol XII*), Vincent Barnett (*Count Nicholaus*), Edgar Norton (*Baron Passeria*), Ray Walker (*Dan Kirk*), Lucien Littlefield (*Parker*), Robert McWade (*Managing Editor*), George Baxter (*Donald Spottswood*), Marguerite Namara (*Lady in Waiting*)

Filming Dates: March 1 to April 14, 1934

Release Date: May 18, 1934

Budget: N/A

Production Cost: N/A

North American Earnings: N/A

Foreign Earnings: N/A

Total Earnings: N/A

Profit/(Loss): N/A

16. *Kiss and Make-Up* (1934)

Production Company: Paramount

Produced by B. P. Schulberg

Screenplay by Harlan Thompson and George Marion Jr.

Based on a play by Stephen Bekeffi, adapted by Jane Hinton

Directed by Harlan Thompson

Cast: Cary Grant (*Dr. Maurice Lamar*), Genevieve Tobin (*Eve Caron*), Helen Mack (*Annie*), Edward Everett Horton (*Marcel Caron*), Lucien Littlefield (*Max Pascal*), Mona Maris (*Countess Rita*), Rafael Storm (*Rolando*), Toby Wing (*Consuelo Claghorne*) Dorothy Christy (*Greta*)

Filming Dates: April 9 to May 11, 1934

Release Date: July 6, 1934

Budget: N/A

Production Cost: N/A

North American Earnings: N/A

Foreign Earnings: N/A

Total Earnings: N/A

Profit/(Loss): N/A

17. *Ladies Should Listen* (1934)

Production Company: Paramount

Produced by Douglas MacLean

Screenplay by Claude Binyon and Frank Butler

Based on a play by Alfred Savoir and Guy Bolton
Directed by Frank Tuttle
Cast: Cary Grant (*Julian de Lussac*), Frances Drake (*Anna Mirelle*), Edward Everett Horton (*Paul Vernet*), Nydia Westman (*Susi Flamberg*), Rafael Corio (*Ramon Cintos*), Rosita Moreno (*Marguerite Cintos*), George Barbier (*Joseph Flamberg*), Charles Ray (*Henri*), Charles E. Arnt (*Albert*), Clara Lou Sheriden (*Adele*), Henrietta Burnside (*Operator*), Joe North (*Butler*)
Filming Dates: May 21 to June 14, 1934
Release Date: August 3, 1933
Budget: N/A
Production Cost: N/A
North American Earnings: N/A
Foreign Earnings: N/A
Total Earnings: N/A
Profit/(Loss): N/A

18. *Enter Madame!* (1934)
Production Company: Paramount
Produced by Benjamin Glazer
Screenplay by Gladys Lehman and Charles Brackett
Based on a play by Gila Varesi Archibald and Dorothea Donn-Byrne
Directed by Elliott Nugent
Cast: Elissa Landi (*Lisa Della Robbia*), Cary Grant (*Gerald Fitzgerald*), Sharon Lynne (*Flora Preston*), Lynne Overman (*Mr. Farham*), Frank Albertson (*John*), Cecilia Parker (*Aline Chalmers*), Adrian Rosley (*The Doctor*), Michelette Burani (*Bice*), Paul Porcasi (*Archimede*), Adrian Rosley (*The Doctor*), Cecilia Parker (*Aline Chalmers*), Frank Albertson (*John*)
Filming Dates: August 6 to September 15, 1934
Release Date: November 2, 1934
Budget: N/A
Production Cost: N/A
North American Earnings: N/A
Foreign Earnings: N/A
Total Earnings: N/A
Profit/(Loss): N/A

19. *Wings in the Dark* (1935)
Production Company: Paramount
Produced by Arthur Hornblow Jr.
Screenplay by Jack Kirkland and Frank Partos
Based on a story by Nell Shipman and Philip D. Hurn, adaptation by Dale
Van Every and E. H. Robinson
Directed by James Flood
Cast: Myrna Loy (*Sheila Mason*), Cary Grant (*Ken Gordon*), Roscoe Karns
(*Nick Williams*), Hobart Cavanaugh (*Mac*), Dean Jagger (*Top Harmon*),
Russell Hopton (*Jake Brashear*), Matt McHugh (*1ˢᵗ Mechanic*), Graham
McNamee (*Radio Announcer*)
Filming Dates: November 5 to December 17, 1934
Release Date: February 9, 1935
Budget: N/A
Production Cost: N/A
North American Earnings: N/A
Foreign Earnings: N/A
Total Earnings: N/A
Profit/(Loss): N/A

20. *The Last Outpost* (1935)
Production Company: Paramount
Produced by E. Lloyd Sheldon
Screenplay by Philip MacDonald
Based on a story by F. Britten Austin, adaptation by Frank Partos and Charles
Brackett
Directed by Louis Gasnier and Charles Barton
Cast: Cary Grant (*Michael Andrews*), Claude Rains (*John Stevenson*),
Gertrude Michael (*Rosemary*), Kathleen Burke (*Ilya*), Colin Tapley
(*Lieutenant Prescott*), Margaret Swope (*Nurse Rowland*), Jameson Thomas
(*Cullen*), Nick Shaid (*Haidar*), Billy Bevan (*Private Foster*), Claude King
(*General*)
Filming Dates: May 20 to September 9, 1935
Release Date: October 4, 1935
Budget: N/A
Production Cost: N/A
North American Earnings: N/A

Foreign Earnings: N/A
Total Earnings: N/A
Profit/(Loss): N/A

21. *Sylvia Scarlett* (1935)
Production Company: RKO Radio Pictures
Produced by Pandro S. Berman
Screenplay by Gladys Unger, John Collier, Mortimer Offner
Based on a novel by Compton MacKenzie
Directed by George Cukor
Cast: Katharine Hepburn (*Sylvia Scarlett*), Cary Grant (*Monkley*), Brian Aherne (*Michael Fane*), Edmund Gwenn (*Henry Scarlett*), Natalie Paley (*Lily*), Dennie Moore (*Maude Tilt*), Lennox Pawle (*Drunk*)
Filming Dates: August 12 to October 22, 1935
Release Date: December 25, 1935
Budget: $656,930
Production Cost: $641,000
North American Earnings: $321,000
Foreign Earnings: $176,000
Total Earnings: $497,000
Profit/(Loss): ($363,000)

22. *The Amazing Quest* (UK, 1936), also known as *Romances and Riches* (US, 1937)
Production Company: Garrett-Klement Pictures
Produced by Alfred Zeisler
Screenplay by John L. Balderston
Based on a novel by E. Phillips Oppenheim
Directed by Alfred Zeisler
Cast: Cary Grant (*Ernest Bliss*), Mary Brian (*Frances*), Peter Gawthorne (*Sir James Aldroyd*), Henry Kendall (*Lord Honiton*), Leon M. Lion (*Dorrington*), John Turnbull (*Masters*), Arthur Hardy (*Crawley*), Iris Ashley (*Clare*), Garry Marsh (*The Buyer*), Andrea Malandrinos (*Guiseppi*), Alfred Wellesley (*Montague*), Marie Wright (*Mrs. Heath*), Buena Ben (*Mrs. Mott*), Charles Farrell (*Scales*), Quinton MacPherson (*Clowes*), Hal Garden (*Bill Bronson*)
Filming Dates: November 23, 1935, to January 30, 1936
Release Date (UK): August 6, 1936
Release Date (US): March 22, 1937

Budget: N/A
Production Cost: N/A
North American Earnings: N/A
Foreign Earnings: N/A
Total Earnings: N/A
Profit/(Loss): N/A

23. *Big Brown Eyes* (1936)
Production Company: Paramount
Produced by Walter Wanger
Screenplay by Raoul Walsh and Bert Hanlon
Based on stories by James Edward Grant
Directed by Raoul Walsh
Cast: Cary Grant (*Danny Barr*), Joan Bennett (*Eve Fallon*), Walter Pidgeon (*Richard Morey*), Lloyd Nolan (*Russ Cortig*), Alan Baxter (*Carey Butler*), Marjorie Gateson (*Mrs. Cole*), Isabel Jewell (*Bessie Blair*), Douglas Fowley (*Benny Battle*), Henry Kleinbach (*Don Butler*), Joseph Sawyer (*Jack Sully*), Dolores Casey (*Cashier*), Doris Canfield (*Myrtle*), Edwin Maxwell (*Editor*)
Filming Dates: February 17 to March 26, 1936
Release Date: May 2, 1936
Budget: N/A
Production Cost: $289,696
North American Earnings: N/A
Foreign Earnings: N/A
Total Earnings: $359,009
Profit/(Loss): ($14,645)

24. *Suzy* (1936)
Production Company: Metro-Goldwyn-Mayer
Produced by Maurice Revnes
Screenplay by Dorothy Parker, Alan Campbell, Horace Jackson, and Lenore Coffee
Based on a novel by Herbert Gorman
Directed by George Fitzmaurice
Cast: Jean Harlow (*Suzy*), Franchot Tone (*Terry*), Cary Grant (*Andre*), Lewis Stone (*Baron*), Benita Hume (*Madame Eyrelle*), Reginald Mason (*Captain Barsanges*), Inez Courtney (*Maisie*), Greta Meyer (*Mrs. Schmidt*), David Clyde (*"Knobby"*), Christian Rub (*"Pop" Gaspard*), George Spelvin (*Gaston*),

Una O'Connor (*Landlady*), Theodore Von Eltz (*Revue Producer*), Stanley
Morner (*Officer*)
Filming Dates: April 6 to May 29, 1936
Release Date: July 24, 1936
Budget: N/A
Production Cost: $614,000
North American Earnings: $1,223,000
Foreign Earnings: $580,000
Total Earnings: $1,803,000
Profit/(Loss): $498,000

25. *Wedding Present* (1936)
Production Company: Paramount
Produced by B. P. Schulberg
Screenplay by Joseph Anthony
Based on a story by Paul Gallico
Directed by Richard Wallace
Cast: Joan Bennett (*"Rusty" Fleming*), Cary Grant (*Charlie Mason*), George
Bancroft (*Pete Stagg*), Conrad Nagel (*Roger Dodacker*), Gene Lockhart
(*Archduke Gustave Ernest*), William Demarest (*"Smiles" Benson*), Inez
Courtney (*Mary Lawson*), Edward Brophy (*"Squinty"*), Purnell Pratt
(*Howard Van Dorn*), Douglas Wood (*Willett*), George Meeker (*Gordon
Blaker*), Damon Ford (*Mike Haley*), Lois Wilson (*Laura Dodacker*), Mary
Forbes (*Mrs. Dodacker*), George Offerman Jr. (*Sammy Smith*), John Henry
Allen (*Jonathan*)
Filming Dates: July 20 to September 14, 1936
Release Date: October 9, 1936
Budget: N/A
Production Cost: N/A
North American Earnings: N/A
Foreign Earnings: N/A
Total Earnings: N/A
Profit/(Loss): N/A

26. *When You're in Love* (1937)
Production Company: Columbia
Produced by Everett Riskin
Screenplay by Robert Riskin

Directed by Robert Riskin

Cast: Miss Grace Moore (*Louise Fuller*), Cary Grant (*Jimmy Hudson*), Aline MacMahon (*Marianne Woods*), Henry Stephenson (*Walter Mitchell*), Thomas Mitchell (*Hank Miller*), Catharine Doucet (*Jane Summers*), Luis Alberni (*Luis Perugini*), Gerald Oliver Smith (*Gerald Meeker*), Emma Dunn (*Mrs. Hamilton*), George Pearce (*Mr. Hamilton*), Frank Puglia (*Carlos*)

Filming Dates: October 5 to November 28, 1936

Release Date: February 27, 1937

Budget: N/A

Production Cost: N/A

North American Earnings: N/A

Foreign Earnings: N/A

Total Earnings: N/A

Profit/(Loss): N/A

27. *The Toast of New York* (1937)

Production Company: RKO Radio Pictures

Produced by Edward Small

Screenplay by Dudley Nichols, John Twist, and Joel Sayre

Based on books by Bouck White and Matthew Josephson

Directed by Rowland V. Lee

Cast: Edward Arnold (*Jim Fisk*), Cary Grant (*Nick Boyd*), Frances Farmer (*Josie Mansfield*), Jack Oakie (*Luke*), Donald Meek (*Daniel Drew*), Thelma Leeds (*Fleurique*), Clarence Kolb (*Vanderbilt*), Billy Gilbert (*Photographer*), George Irving (*Broker*), Frank M. Thomas (*Lawyer*), Russell Hicks (*Lawyer*), Oscar Apfel (*Wallack*), Lionel Belmore (*President of the Board*), Robert McClung (*Bellhop*), Robert Dudley (*Janitor*), Dewey Robinson (*Beef Dooley*), Stanley Fields (*Top Sergeant*), Gavin Gordon (*Major*), Joyce Compton (*Mary Lou*), Virginia Carroll (*Virginia Lee*)

Filming Dates: December 14, 1936, to April 15, 1937

Release Date: July 28, 1937

Budget: N/A

Production Cost: $1,072,000

North American Earnings: $846,000

Foreign Earnings: $202,000

Total Earnings: $1,048,000

Profit/(Loss): (530,000)

28. *Topper* (1937)
Production Company: Hal Roach Studios
Produced by Hal Roach
Screenplay by Jack Jevne, Eric Hatch, Eddie Moran
Based on a novel by Thorne Smith
Directed by Norman Z. McLeod
Cast: Constance Bennett (*Marion Kerby*), Cary Grant (*George Kerby*), Roland Young (*Mr. Topper*), Billie Burke (*Mrs. Topper*), Alan Mowbray (*Wilkins*), Eugene Pallette (*Casey*), Arthur Lake (*Elevator Boy*), Hedda Hopper (*Mrs. Stuyvesant*), Virginia Sale (*Miss Johnson*), Theodore von Eltz (*Hotel Manager*), J. Farrell McDonald (*Policeman*), Elaine Shepard (*Secretary*)
Filming Dates: March 25 to May 5, 1937
Release Date: July 16, 1937
Budget: N/A
Production Cost: $500,000
North American Earnings: N/A
Foreign Earnings: N/A
Total Earnings: N/A
Profit/(Loss): N/A

29. *The Awful Truth* (1937)
Production Company: Columbia Pictures
Produced by Leo McCarey
Screenplay by Viña Delmar
Based on a play by Arthur Richman
Directed by Leo McCarey
Cast: Irene Dunne (*Lucy Warriner*), Cary Grant (*Jerry Warriner*), Ralph Bellamy (*Daniel Leeson*), Alexander D'Arcy (*Armand Duvalle*), Cecil Cunningham (*Aunt Patsy*), Molly Lamont (*Barbara Vance*), Esther Dale (*Mrs. Leeson*), Joyce Compton (*Dixie Belle Lee*), Robert Allen (*Frank Randall*), Robert Warwick (*Mr. Vance*), Mary Forbes (*Mrs. Vance*)
Filming Dates: June 21 to August 17, 1937
Release Date: October 21, 1937
Budget: N/A
Production Cost: N/A
North American Earnings: N/A
Foreign Earnings: N/A
Total Earnings: N/A
Profit/(Loss): N/A

30. *Bringing Up Baby* (1938)
Production Company: RKO Radio Pictures
Produced by Howard Hawks
Screenplay by Dudley Nichols and Hagar Wilde
Based on a story by Hagar Wilde
Directed by Howard Hawks
Cast: Katharine Hepburn (*Susan*), Cary Grant (*David*), Charlie Ruggles (*Major Applegate*), Walter Catlett (*Slocum*), Barry Fitzgerald (*Mr. Gogarty*), May Robson (*Aunt Elizabeth*), Fritz Feld (*Dr. Lehman*), Leona Roberts (*Mrs. Gogarty*), George Irving (*Mr. Peabody*), Tala Birell (*Mrs. Lehman*), Virginia Walker (*Alice Swallow*), John Kelly (*Elmer*)
Filming Dates: September 23, 1937, to January 6, 1938
Release Date: February 16, 1938
Budget: $768,000
Production Cost: $1,073,000
North American Earnings: $811,000
Foreign Earnings: $459,000
Total Earnings: $1,270,000
Profit/(Loss): ($250,000)

31. *Holiday* (1938)
Production Company: Columbia Pictures
Produced by Everett Riskin
Screenplay by Donald Ogden Stewart and Sidney Buchman
Based on the play by Philip Barry
Directed by George Cukor
Cast: Katharine Hepburn (*Linda Seton*), Cary Grant (*Johnny Case*), Doris Nolan (*Julia Seton*), Lew Ayres (*Ned Seton*), Edward Everett Horton (*Nick Potter*), Henry Kolker (*Edward Seton*), Binnie Barnes (*Laura Cram*), Jean Dixon (*Susan Potter*), Henry Daniell (*Seton Cram*)
Filming Dates: February 22 to April 23, 1938
Release Date: June 15, 1938
Budget: N/A
Production Cost: N/A
North American Earnings: N/A
Foreign Earnings: N/A
Total Earnings: N/A
Profit/(Loss): N/A

32. *Gunga Din* (1939)
Production Company: RKO Radio Pictures
Produced by Pandro S. Berman and George Stevens
Screenplay by Joel Sayre and Fred Guiol
Based on a story by Ben Hecht and Charles MacArthur from Rudyard Kipling's poem
Directed by George Stevens
Cast: Cary Grant (*Cutter*), Victor McLaglen (*MacChesney*), Douglas Fairbanks Jr. (*Ballantine*), Sam Jaffe (*Gunga Din*), Eduardo Ciannelli (*Guru*), Joan Fontaine (*Emmy*), Montagu Love (*Colonel Weed*), Robert Coote (*Higginbotham*), Abner Biberman (*Chota*), Lumsden Hare (*Major Mitchell*)
Filming Dates: June 24 to October 19, 1938
Release Date: January 24, 1939
Budget: $1,332,025
Production Cost: $1,915,000
North American Earnings: $2,012,000
Foreign Earnings: $2,225,000
Total Earnings: $4,237,000
Profit/(Loss): $702,000

33. *Only Angels Have Wings* (1939)
Production Company: Columbia Pictures
Produced by Howard Hawks
Original screenplay by Jules Furthman
Directed by Howard Hawks
Cast: Cary Grant (*Geoff Carter*), Jean Arthur (*Bonnie Lee*), Richard Barthelmess (*Bat MacPherson*) Rita Hayworth (*Judy*), Thomas Mitchell (*Kid Dabb*), Allyn Joslyn (*Les Peters*), Sig Rumann (*Les Peters*), Victor Kilian (*Sparks*), John Carroll (*Gent Shelton*), Donald Barry (*Tex*), Noah Berry Jr. (*Joe Souther*), Maciste (*The Singer*)
Filming Dates: December 20, 1938, to March 24, 1939
Release Date: May 12, 1939
Budget: N/A
Production Cost: N/A
North American Earnings: N/A
Foreign Earnings: N/A
Total Earnings: N/A
Profit/(Loss): N/A

34. *In Name Only* (1939)
Production Company: RKO Radio Pictures
Produced by Pandro S. Berman and George Haight
Screenplay by Richard Sherman
Based on a novel by Bessie Breuer
Directed by John Cromwell
Cast: Carole Lombard (*Julie Eden*), Cary Grant (*Alec Walker*), Kay Francis (*Maida Walker*), Charles Coburn (*Mr. Walker*), Helen Vinson (*Suzanne*), Katharine Alexander (*Laura*), Jonathan Hale (*Dr. Gateson*), Nella Walker (*Mrs. Walker*), Alan Baxter (*Charley*), Maurice Moscovich (*Dr. Muller*), Peggy Ann Garner (*Ellen*), Spencer Charters (*Gardener*)
Filming Dates: April 10 to June 5, 1939
Release Date: August 18, 1939
Budget: $730,000
Production Cost: $722,000
North American Earnings: $926,000
Foreign Earnings: $395,000
Total Earnings: $1,321,000
Profit/(Loss): $155,000

35. *His Girl Friday* (1940)
Production Company: Columbia Pictures
Produced by Howard Hawks
Screenplay by Charles Lederer
Based on a play by Ben Hecht and Charles MacArthur
Directed by Howard Hawks
Cast: Cary Grant (*Walter Burns*), Rosalind Russell (*Hildy Johnson*), Ralph Bellamy (*Bruce Baldwin*), Gene Lockhart (*Sheriff Hartwell*), Helen Mack (*Mollie Malloy*), Porter Hall (*Murphy*), Ernest Truex (*Bensinger*), Cliff Edwards (*Endicott*), Clarence Kolb (*Mayor*), Roscoe Karns (*McCue*), Frank Jenks (*Wilson*), Regis Toomey (*Sanders*), Abner Biberman (*Louie*), Frank Orth (*Duffy*), John Qualen (*Earl Williams*), Alma Kruger (*Mrs. Baldwin*), Billy Gilbert (*Joe Pettibone*), Pat West (*Warden Cooley*), Edwin Maxwell (*Dr. Egelhoffer*)
Filming Dates: September 27 to November 21, 1939
Release Date: January 12, 1940
Budget: N/A
Production Cost: N/A

North American Earnings: N/A
Foreign Earnings: N/A
Total Earnings: N/A
Profit/(Loss): N/A

36. *My Favorite Wife* (1940)
Production Company: RKO Radio Pictures
Produced by Leo McCarey
Screenplay by Bella and Samuel Spewack
Based on a story by Bella and Samuel Spewack, and Leo McCarey
Directed by Garson Kanin
Cast: Irene Dunne (*Ellen*), Cary Grant (*Nick*), Gail Patrick (*Bianca*), Randolph Scott (*Burkett*), Ann Shoemaker (*Ma*), Scotty Beckett (*Tim*), Mary Lou Harrington (*Chinch*), Donald McBride (*Hotel Clerk*), Hugh O'Connell (*Johnson*), Granville Bates (*Judge*), Pedro de Cordoba (*Dr. Kohlmar*)
Filming Dates: December 6, 1940, to February 15, 1941, and March 8 to March 14, 1941
Release Date: May 17, 1940
Budget: $768,492
Production Cost: $921,532
North American Earnings: $1,452,000
Foreign Earnings: $605,000
Total Earnings: $2,057,000
Profit/(Loss): $505,000

37. *The Howards of Virginia* (1940)
Production Company: Frank Lloyd Pictures and Columbia Pictures
Produced by Frank Lloyd
Screenplay by Sidney Buchman
Based on a novel by Elizabeth Page
Directed by Frank Lloyd
Cast: Cary Grant (*Matt Howard*), Martha Scott (*Jane Peyton-Howard*), Sir Cedric Hardwicke (*Fleetwood Peyton*), Alan Marshal (*Roger Peyton*), Richard Carlson (*Thomas Jefferson*), Paul Kelly (*Captain Jabez Allen*), Irving Bacon (*Tom Norton*), Elizabeth Risdon (*Aunt Clarissa*), Anna Revere (*Mrs. Norton*), Richard Alden (*James Howard at 16*), Phil Taylor (*Peyton Taylor at 18*), Rita Quigley (*Mary Howard at 17*), Libby Taylor (*Dicey*), Richard Gaines (*Patrick Henry*), George Houston (*George Washington*)

Filming Dates: April 4 to July 6, 1940
Release Date: September 19, 1940
Budget: $1,300,000*
Production Cost: N/A
North American Earnings: N/A
Foreign Earnings: N/A
Total Earnings: N/A
Profit/(Loss): N/A

38. *The Philadelphia Story* (1940)
Production Company: Metro-Goldwyn-Mayer
Produced by Joseph L. Mankiewicz
Screenplay by Donald Ogden Stewart
Based on a play by Philip Barry
Directed by George Cukor
Cast: Cary Grant (*C. K. Dexter Haven*), Katharine Hepburn (*Tracy Lord*), James Stewart (*Macauley Connor*), Ruth Hussey (*Elizabeth Imbrie*), John Howard (*George Kittredge*), Roland Young (*Uncle Willie*), John Halliday (*Seth Lord*), Mary Nash (*Margaret Lord*), Virginia Weidler (*Dinah Lord*), Henry Daniell (*Sidney Kidd*), Lionel Pape (*Edward*), Rex Evans (*Thomas*)
Filming Dates: July 8 to August 14, 1940
Release Date: December 26, 1940
Budget: N/A
Production Cost: $914,000
North American Earnings: $2,374,000
Foreign Earnings: $885,000
Total Earnings: $3,259,000
Profit/(Loss): $1,272,000

39. *Penny Serenade* (1941)
Production Company: Columbia Pictures
Produced by George Stevens
Screenplay by Morrie Ryskind
Based on a short story by Martha Cheavens
Directed by George Stevens
Cast: Irene Dunne (*Julie Gardiner*), Cary Grant (*Roger Adams*), Beulah Bondi (*Miss Oliver*), Edgar Buchanan (*Applejack*), Ann Doran (*Dotty*), Eva Lee Kuney (*Trina at the age of six years*), Leonard Willey (*Dorothy Hartley*),

Wallis Clark (*Judge*), Walter Soderling (*Billings*), Baby Biffle (*Trina at the age of one year*)
Filming Dates: October 14, 1940, to January 14, 1941
Release Date: April 16, 1941
Budget: $839,229
Production Cost: N/A
North American Earnings: $1,250,000*
Foreign Earnings: N/A
Profit/(Loss): N/A

40. *Suspicion* (1941)
Production Company: RKO Radio Pictures
Produced by [N/A]
Screenplay by Samson Raphaelson, Joan Harrison, Alma Reville
Based a novel by Francis Iles
Directed by Alfred Hitchcock
Cast: Cary Grant (*Johnnie*), Joan Fontaine (*Lina*), Sir Cedric Hardwicke (*General McLaidlaw*), Nigel Bruce (*Beaky*), Dame May Whitty (*Mrs. McLaidlaw*), Isabel Jeans (*Mrs. Newsham*), Heather Angel (*Ethel [Maid]*), Auriol Lee (*Isobel Sedbusk*), Reginald Sheffield (*Reggie Wetherby*), Leo G. Carroll (*Captain Melbeck*)
Filming Dates: February 10 to April 23, 1941, and July 23 to 24, 1941
Release Date: November 14, 1941
Budget: $842,582
Production Cost: $1,102,074
North American Earnings: $1,306,000
Foreign Earnings: $919,000
Total Earnings: $2,225,000
Profit/(Loss): $440,000

41. *Arsenic and Old Lace* (1944)
Production Company: Warner Bros. Pictures
Produced by Frank Capra
Screenplay by Julius J. and Philip G. Epstein
Based on a play by Joseph Kesselring
Directed by Frank Capra
Cast: Cary Grant (*Mortimer Brewster*), Priscilla Lane (*Elaine Harper*), Raymond Massey (*Jonathan Brewster*), Jack Carson (*O'Hara*), Edward Everett

Horton (*Mr. Witherspoon*), Peter Lorre (*Dr. Einstein*), James Gleason (*Lt. Rooney*), Josephine Hull (*Abby Brewster*), Jean Adair (*Martha Brewster*), John Alexander ("*Teddy Roosevelt" Brewster*), Grant Mitchell (*Reverend Harper*)
Filming Dates: October 21 to December 17, 1941
Release Date: September 1, 1944
Budget: $1,220,000
Production Cost: $1,164,000
North American Earnings: $2,836,000
Foreign Earnings: $1,948,000
Total Earnings: $4,784,000
Profit/(Loss): N/A

42. *The Talk of the Town* (1942)
Production Company: Columbia Pictures
Produced by George Stevens
Screenplay by Irwin Shaw, Sidney Buchman
Based on a story by Sidney Harmon, adapted by Dale Van Every
Directed by George Stevens
Cast: Cary Grant (*Leopold Dilg*), Jean Arthur (*Nora Shelley*), Ronald Colman (*Michael Lightcap*), Edgar Buchanan (*Sam Yates*), Glenda Farrell (*Regina Bush*), Charles Dingle (*Andrew Holmes*), Emma Dunn (*Mrs. Shelley*), Rex Ingram (*Tilney*), Leonid Kinskey (*Jan Pulaski*), Tom Tyler (*Clyde Bracken*), Don Beddoe (*Chief of Police*)
Filming Dates: January 19 to April 8, 1942; April 18, 1942; April 20, 1942; and April 25, 1942
Release Date: August 20, 1942
Budget: N/A
Production Cost: N/A
North American Earnings: $1,100,000*
Foreign Earnings: N/A
Total Earnings: N/A
Profit/(Loss): N/A

43. *Once Upon a Honeymoon* (1942)
Production Company: RKO Radio Pictures
Produced by Leo McCarey
Screenplay by Sheridan Gibney
Based on a story by Sheridan Gibney and Leo McCarey

Directed by Leo McCarey
Cast: Cary Grant (*Pat O'Toole*), Ginger Rogers (*Katie O'Hara*), Walter Slezak (*Baron Von Luber*), Albert Dekker (*Le Blanc*), Albert Basserman (*General Borelski*), Ferike Boros (*Elsa*), Harry Shannon (*Ed Cumberland*), Natasha Lytess (*Anna*)
Filming Dates: June 8 to August 21, 1942; September 2 to September 29, 1942
Release Date: November 12, 1942
Budget: N/A
Production Cost: $1,441,000
North American Earnings: $1,805,000
Foreign Earnings: $720,000
Total Earnings: $2,525,000
Profit/(Loss): $282,000

44. *Mr. Lucky* (1943)
Production Company: RKO Radio Pictures
Produced by David Hempstead
Screenplay by Milton Holmes and Adrian Scott
Based on a story by Milton Holmes
Directed by H. C. Potter
Cast: Cary Grant (*Joe Adams/Joe Bascopolous*), Loraine Day (*Dorothy Bryant*), Charles Bickford (*Hard Swede*), Gladys Cooper (*Captain Steadman*), Alan Carney (*Crunk*), Henry Stephenson (*Mr. Bryant*), Paul Stewart (*Zepp*), Kay Johnson (*Mrs. Ostrander*), Erford Gage (*Gaffer*), Walter Kingsford (*Commissioner Hargraves*), Florence Bates (*Mrs. Van Every*)
Filming Dates: October 28, 1942, to January 5, 1943
Release Date: May 28, 1943
Budget: $769,543
Production Cost: $842,000
North American Earnings: $2,770,000
Foreign Earnings: $865,000
Total Earnings: $3,635,000
Profit/(Loss): $1,673,000

45. *Destination Tokyo* (1943)
Production Company: Warner Bros. Pictures
Produced by Jerry Wald
Screenplay by Delmer Daves and Albert Maltz
Based on an original story by Steve Fisher

Directed by Delmer Daves

Cast: Cary Grant (*Captain Cassidy*), John Garfield (*Wolf*), Alan Hale (*Cookie*), John Ridgely (*Reserve Officer Raymond*), Dane Clark (*Tin Can*), Warner Anderson (*Executive Officer*), William Prince (*Pills*), Robert Hutton (*Tommy Adams*), Tom Tully (*Mike*), Faye Emerson (*Mrs. Cassidy*), John Forsythe (*Sparks*)

Filming Dates: June 21, 1943, to October 11, 1943

Release Date: December 31, 1943

Budget: N/A

Production Cost: $1,516,000

North American Earnings: $3,237,000

Foreign Earnings: $1,307,000

Total Earnings: $4,544,000

Profit/(Loss): N/A

46. *Once Upon a Time* (1944)

Production Company: Columbia

Produced by Louis F. Edelman

Screenplay by Lewis Meltzer and Oscar Saul

Based on a story by Norman Corwin and Lucille Fletcher Herrmann

Directed by Alexander Hall

Cast: Cary Grant (*Jerry Flynn*), Janet Blair (*Jeannie Thompson*), James Gleason (*The Moke*), Ted Donaldson (*Arthur "Pinky" Thompson*), William Demarest (*Brandt*), Howard Freeman (*McKenzie*), Art Baker (*Gabriel Heatter*), Paul Stanton (*Dunhill*), Erwin Kalser (*Professor Van Dorn*), Vaughan Glaser (*Professor Draper*), John Abbott (*Reporter*), Lloyd Bridges (*Captain*)

Filming Dates: September 13, 1944, to December 17, 1944

Release Date: May 11, 1944

Budget: N/A

Production Cost: N/A

North American Earnings: N/A

Foreign Earnings: N/A

Total Earnings: N/A

Profit/(Loss): N/A

47. *None but the Lonely Heart* (1944)

Production Company: RKO Radio Pictures

Produced by David Hempstead

Screenplay by Clifford Odets

Based on a novel by Richard Llewellyn

Directed by Clifford Odets

Cast: Cary Grant (*Ernie Mott*), Miss Ethel Barrymore (*Ma*), Barry Fitzgerald (*Twite*), June Duprez (*Ada*), Janet Wyatt (*Aggie*), George Coulouris (*Jim Mordinoy*), Dan Duryea (*Lew Tate*), Roman Bohnen (*Did Pettyjohn*), Konstantin Shayne (*Ike Weber*)

Filming Dates: March 6 to May 20, 1944

Release Date: September 22, 1944

Budget: $1,266,914

Production Cost: $1,343,000

North American Earnings: $1,336,000

Foreign Earnings: $636,000

Total Earnings: $1,972,000

Profit/(Loss): ($72,000)

48. *Night and Day* (1946)

Production Company: Warner Bros. Pictures

Produced by Arthur Schwartz

Screenplay by Charles Hoffman, Leo Townsend, and William Bowers

Based on the career of Cole Porter, adaptation by Jack Moffitt

Directed by Michael Curtiz

Cast: Cary Grant (*Cole Porter*), Alexis Smith (*Linda Lee Porter*), Monty Woolley (*Himself*), Ginny Simms (*Carnie Hill*), Jane Wyman (*Gracie Harris*), Eve Arden (*Gabrielle*), Victor Francen (*Anatole Giron*), Alan Hale (*Leon Dowling*), Dorothy Malone (*Nancy*), Tom D'Andrea (*Bernie*), Selena Royle (*Kate Porter*), Donald Woods (*Ward Blackburn*), Henry Stephenson (*Omer Porter*), Paul Cavanagh (*Bart McCleiland*), Sig Ruman (*Wilowsky*), Carlos Ramirez (*Singer*), Milada Mladova (*Dancer*), George Zoritch (*Dancer*), Adam and Jane Di Gatano (*Dancers*), Estelle Sloan (*Dancer*), Mary Martin (*Herself*)

Filming Dates: June 16, to December 11, 1945

Release Date: July 25, 1946

Budget: N/A

Production Cost: $4,445,000

North American Earnings: $4,990,000

Foreign Earnings: $2,428,000

Total Earnings: $7,418,000

Profit/(Loss): N/A

49. *Notorious* (1946)
Production Company: RKO Radio Pictures
Produced by Alfred Hitchcock
Original screenplay by Ben Hecht
Directed by Alfred Hitchcock
Cast: Cary Grant (*Devlin*), Ingrid Bergman (*Alicia Huberman*), Claude Rains (*Alex Sebastian*), Louis Calhern (*Paul Prescott*), Madame Konstantin (*Madame Sebastian*), Reinhold Schunzel (*Dr. Anderson*), Moroni Olsen (*Walter Beardsley*), Ivan Triesault (*Eric Mathis*), Alex Minotis (*Joseph*), Wally Brown (*Mr. Hopkins*), Sir Charles Mendl (*Commodore*), Ricardo Costa (*Dr. Barbosa*), Eberhard Krumschmidt (*Hupka*), Fay Baker (*Ethel*)
Filming Dates: October 15, 1945, to January 23, 1946
Release Date: August 15, 1946
Budget: N/A
Production Cost: $2,376,000
North American Earnings: $4,850,000
Foreign Earnings: $2,300,000
Total Earnings: $7,100,000
Profit/(Loss): $1,010,000

50. *The Bachelor and the Bobby-Soxer* (1947)
Production Company: RKO Radio Pictures
Produced by Dore Schary
Original screenplay by Sidney Sheldon
Directed by Irving Reis
Cast: Cary Grant (*Dick*), Myrna Loy (*Margaret*), Shirley Temple (*Susan*), Rudy Vallee (*Tommy*), Ray Collins (*Beemish*), Harry Davenport (*Thaddeus*), Johnny Sands (*Jerry*), Don Beddoe (*Joey*), Lillian Randolph (*Bessie*), Veda Ann Borg (*Agnes Prescott*), Dan Tobin (*Walters*), Ransom Sherman (*Judge Treadwell*), William Bakewell (*Winters*), Irving Bacon (*Melvin*), Ian Bernard (*Perry*), Carol Hughes (*Florence*), William Hall (*Anthony Herman*), Gregory Gay (*Maitre d'Hotel*)
Filming Dates: July 15 to October 19, 1946
Release Date: July 24, 1947
Budget: $1,732,046
Production Cost: $1,961,000
North American Earnings: $4,200,000

Foreign Earnings: $1,350,000
Total Earnings: $5,550,000
Profit/(Loss): $700,000

51. *The Bishop's Wife* (1947)
Production Company: Samuel Goldwyn Productions
Produced by Samuel Goldwyn
Screenplay by Robert E. Sherwood and Leonardo Bercovici
Based on the novel by Robert Nathan
Directed by Henry Koster
Cast: Cary Grant (*Dudley*), Loretta Young (*Julia Brougham*), David Niven (*Henry Brougham*), Monty Woolley (*Professor Wutheridge*), James Gleason (*Sylvester*), Gladys Cooper (*Mrs. Hamilton*), Elsa Lanchester (*Matilda*), Sara Haden (*Mildred Cassaway*), Karolyn Grimes (*Debby Brougham*), Tito Vuolo (*Maggenti*), Regis Toomey (*Mr. Miller*), the Mitchell Boychoir
Filming Dates: February 24 to March 17, 1947, and April 16 to July 9, 1947
Release Date: December 9, 1947
Budget: $3,001,350
Production Cost: $3,050,056
North American Earnings: $3,460,000
Foreign Earnings: $1,150,000
Total Earnings: $4,610,000
Profit/(Loss): ($255,000)

52. *Mr. Blandings Builds His Dream House* (1948)
Production Company: RKO Radio Pictures
Produced by Norman Panama and Melvin Frank
Screenplay by Norman Panama and Melvin Frank
Based on a novel by Eric Hodgins
Directed by H. C. Potter
Cast: Cary Grant (*Jim Blandings*), Myrna Loy (*Muriel Blandings*), Melvyn Douglas (*Bill Cole*), Reginald Denny (*Simms*), Sharyn Moffett (*Joan Blandings*), Connie Marshall (*Betsy Blandings*), Louis Beavers (*Gussie*), Ian Wolfe (*Smith*), Harry Shannon (*Tesander*), Tito Vuolo (*Mr. Zucco*), Nestor Paiva (*Joe Apollonio*), Jason Robards (*John Retch*), Lurene Tuttle (*Mary*), Lex Barker (*Carpenter Foreman*), Emory Parnell (*Mr. PeDelford*)
Filming Dates: October 6 to December 30, 1947
Release Date: March 25, 1948

Budget: $1,915,000
Production Cost: $2,052,000
North American Earnings: $2,740,000
Foreign Earnings: $800,000
Total Earnings: $3,540,000
Profit/(Loss): ($225,000)

53. *Every Girl Should Be Married* (1948)
Production Company: RKO Radio Pictures
Produced by Don Hartman
Screenplay by Don Hartman and Stephen Morehouse Avery
Based on a story by Eleanor Harris
Directed by Don Hartman
Cast: Cary Grant (*Dr. Madison Brown*), Franchot Tone (*Roger Sanford*), Diana Lynn (*Julie Howard*), Betsy Drake (*Anabel Sims*), Alan Mowbray (*Mr. Spitzer*), Elisabeth Risdon (*Mary Nolan*), Richard Gaines (*Sam McNutt*), Harry Hayden (*Gogarty*), Chick Chandler (*Soda Clerk*), Leon Belasco (*Violinist*), Fred Essler (*Pierre*), Anna Q. Nilsson (*Saleslady*)
Filming Dates: May 24 to July 21, 1948
Release Date: December 23, 1948
Budget: $1,230,000
Production Cost: $1,263,000
North American Earnings: $2,850,000
Foreign Earnings: $665,000
Total Earnings: $3,515,000
Profit/(Loss): $775,000

54. *I Was a Male War Bride* (1949)
Production Company: Twentieth Century-Fox
Produced by Sol C. Siegel
Screenplay by Charles Lederer, Leonard Spigelgass and Hagar Wilde
Based on a story by Henri Rochard
Directed by Howard Hawks
Cast: Cary Grant (*Capt. Henri Rochard*), Ann Sheridan (*Lt. Catherine Gates*), Marion Marshall (*WAC*), Randy Stuart (*WAC*), William Neff (*Capt. Jack Rumsey*)
Filming Dates: September 28 to December 15, 1948, and April 28 to May 27, 1949

Release Date: August 9, 1949
Budget: N/A
Production Cost: $3,300,000
North American Earnings: $4,100,000
Foreign Earnings: N/A
Total Earnings: N/A
Profit/(Loss): N/A

55. *Crisis* (1950)
Production Company: Metro Goldwyn Mayer
Produced by Arthur Freed
Screenplay by Richard Brooks
Based on a story by George Tabori
Directed by Richard Brooks
Cast: Cary Grant (*Dr. Eugene Ferguson*), Jose Ferrer (*Raoul Farrago*), Paula Raymon (*Helen Ferguson*), Signe Hasso (*Senora Isabel Farrago*), Ramon Novarro (*Col. Adragon*), Gilbert Roland (*Roland Gonzales*), Leon Ames (*Sam Proctor*)
Filming Dates: January 4 to February 23, 1950
Release Date: July 3, 1950
Budget: N/A
Production Cost: $1,581,000
North American Earnings: $895,000
Foreign Earnings: $520,000
Total Earnings: $1,415,000
Profit/(Loss): ($713,000)

56. *People Will Talk* (1951)
Production Company: Twentieth Century-Fox
Produced by Darryl F. Zanuck
Screenplay by Joseph L. Mankiewicz
Based on a play by Curt Goetz
Directed by Joseph L. Mankiewicz
Cast: Cary Grant (*Dr. Noah Praetorius*), Jeanne Crain (*Deborah Higgins*), Finlay Currie (*Shunderson*), Hume Cronyn (*Prof. Rodney Elwell*), Walter Slezak (*Prof. Lionel Barker*), Sidney Blackmer (*Arthur Higgins*), Basil Ruysdael (*Dean Lyman Brockwell*), Katherine Locke (*Miss James*)
Filming Dates: March 20 to May 18, 1951

Release Date: July 19, 1951
Budget: N/A
Production Cost: $1,480,000*
North American Earnings: $2,100,000*
Foreign Earnings: N/A
Total Earnings: N/A
Profit/(Loss): N/A

57. *Room for One More* (1952)
Production Company: Warner Bros. Pictures
Produced by Henry Blanke
Screenplay by Jack Rose and Melville Shavelson
Based on a book by Anna Perrott Rose
Directed by Norman Taurog
Cast: Cary Grant (*George Rose*), Betsy Drake (*Anna Rose*), Lurene Tuttle (*Miss Kenyon*), Randy Stuart (*Mrs. Foreman*), John Ridgely (*Harry Foreman*), Irving Bacon (*Mayor*), Mary Lou Treen (*Mrs. Roberts*), Iris Mann (*Jane*), George Winslow (*Teenie*), Clifford Tatum Jr. (*Jimmy-John*), Gay Gordon (*Trot*), Malcolm Cassell (*Tim*), Larry Olsen (*Ben*)
Filming Dates: August 20 to October 12, 1951
Release Date: January 14, 1952
Budget: $1,079,000
Production Cost: $1,307,000
North American Earnings: $2,372,000
Foreign Earnings: $1,099,000
Total Earnings: $3,471,000
Profit/(Loss): N/A

58. *Monkey Business* (1952)
Production Company: Twentieth Century-Fox
Produced by Sol C. Siegel
Screenplay by Ben Hecht, Charles Lederer, I. A. L. Diamond
Based on a story by Harry Segall
Directed by Howard Hawks
Cast: Cary Grant (*Dr. Barnaby Fulton*), Ginger Rogers (*Edwina Fulton*), Charles Coburn (*Oliver Oxly*), Marilyn Monroe (*Lois Laurel*), Hugh Marlowe (*Hank Entwhistle*), Henri Letondal (*Dr. Jerome Lenton*), Robert Cornthwaite

(*Dr. Zoldeck*), Larry Keating (*Mr. Culverly*), Douglas Spencer (*Dr. Brunner*), Esther Dale (*Mrs. Rhinelander*) George Winslow (*Little Indian*)
Filming Dates: March 5 to April 30, 1952
Release Date: September 3, 1952
Budget: N/A
Production Cost: N/A
North American Earnings: $2,000,000*
Foreign Earnings: N/A
Total Earnings: N/A
Profit/(Loss): N/A

59. *Dream Wife* (1953)
Production Company: Metro Goldwyn Mayer
Produced by Dore Schary
Original screenplay by Sidney Sheldon, Herbert Baker, and Alfred Lewis Levitt
Directed by Sidney Sheldon
Cast: Cary Grant (*Clemson Reade), Deborah Kerr (*Effie*), Walter Pidgeon (*Walter McBride*), Betta St. John (*Tarji*), Eduard Franz (*Khan*), Buddy Baer (*Vizier*), Les Tremayne (*Ken Landwell*), Donald Randolph (*Ali*), Bruce Bennett (*Charlie Elkwood*), Richard Anderson (*Henry Malvine*), Dan Tobin (*Mr. Brown*), Movita (*Rima*), Gloria Holden (*Mrs. Landwell*), June Clayworth (*Mrs. Elkwood*), Dean Miller (*George*), Steve Forrest (*Louis*), Jonathan Cott (*Marine*), Patricia Tiernan (*Pat*)
Filming Dates: September 15 to November 1, 1952
Release Date: June 19, 1953
Budget: N/A
Production Cost: $1,565,000
North American Earnings: $1,215,000
Foreign Earnings: $700,000
Total Earnings: $1,915,000
Profit/(Loss): ($431,000)

60. *To Catch a Thief* (1955)
Production Company: Paramount
Produced by Alfred Hitchcock
Screenplay by John Michael Hayes
Based on a novel by David Dodge
Directed by Alfred Hitchcock

Cast: Cary Grant (*John Robie*), Grace Kelly (*Frances Stevens*), Jessie Royce Landis (*Mrs. Jessie Stevens*), John Williams (*H. H. Hughson*), Charles Vanel (*Bertani*), Brigitte Auber (*Danielle Foussard*), Jean Martinelli (*Foussard*), Georgette Anys (*Germaine*)
Filming Dates: May 31 to September 15, 1954
Release Date: August 3, 1955
Budget: $3,000,000
Production Cost: N/A
North American Earnings: $4,500,000*
Foreign Earnings: N/A
Total Earnings: N/A
Profit/(Loss): N/A

61. *The Pride and the Passion* (1957)
Production Company: Metro Goldwyn Mayer
Produced by Stanley Kramer
Screenplay by Edna and Edward Anhalt
Based on a novel by C. S. Forester
Directed by Stanley Kramer
Cast: Cary Grant (*Anthony*), Frank Sinatra (*Miguel*), Sophia Loren (*Juana*), Theodore Bikel (*General Jouvet*), John Wengraf (*Sermaine*), Jay Novello (*Ballinger*), Jose Nieto (*Carlos*), Carlos Larranaga (*Jose*), Philip Van Zandt (*Vidal*), Paco el Laberinto (*Manolo*), Julian Ugarte (*Enrique*), Felix de Pomes (*Bishop*), Carlos Casaravilla (*Leonardo*), Juan Olaguivel (*Ramon*), Nana de Herrera (*Maria*), Carlose de Mendoza (*Francisco*), Luis Guedes (*French Soldier*)
Filming Dates: April 23 to August 31, 1956, and January 28 to February 1, 1957
Release Date: July 10, 1957
Budget: $3,500,000*
Production Cost: N/A
North American Earnings: $5,500,000*
Foreign Earnings: N/A
Total Earnings: N/A
Profit/(Loss): N/A

62. *An Affair to Remember* (1957)
Production Company: Twentieth Century-Fox
Produced by Jerry Wald

Screenplay by Delmer Daves and Leo McCarey
Based on a story by Leo McCarey and Mildred Cram
Directed by Leo McCarey
Cast: Cary Grant (*Nickie Ferrante*), Deborah Kerr (*Terry McKay*), Richard Denning (*Kenneth*), Neva Patterson (*Lois Clark*), Cathleen Nesbitt (*Grandmother*), Robert Q. Lewis (*Announcer*), Charles Watts (*Ned Hathaway*), Fortunio Bonanova (*Courbet*)
Filming Dates: February 11 to April 10, 1957
Release Date: July 2, 1957
Budget: $2,048,700
Production Cost: N/A
North American Earnings: $3,900,000*
Foreign Earnings: N/A
Total Earnings: N/A
Profit/(Loss): N/A

63. *Kiss Them for Me* (1957)
Production Company: Twentieth Century-Fox
Produced by Jerry Wald
Screenplay by Julius Epstein
Based on a play by Luther Davis and a novel by Frederic Wakeman
Directed by Stanley Donen
Cast: Cary Grant (*Andrew Crewson*), Janye Mansfield (*Alice Cratchner*), Leif Erickson (*Eddie Turnbill*), Suzy Parker (*Gwenneth Livingston*), Ray Walston (*Lt. Howard McCann*), Larry Blyden (*Mississip Hardy*), Nathaniel Frey (*C. P. O. Ruddle*), Werner Klemperer (*Commander Walter Wallace*), Jack Mullaney (*Ensign Lewis*)
Filming Dates: May 2 to July 3, 1957
Release Date: November 6, 1957
Budget: $2,006,800
Production Cost: N/A
North American Earnings: $1,800,000*
Foreign Earnings: N/A
Total Earnings: N/A
Profit/(Loss): N/A

64. *Houseboat* (1958)
Production Company: Paramount
Produced by Jack Rose

Original screenplay by Melville Shavelson and Jack Rose
Directed by Melville Shavelson
Cast: Cary Grant (*Tom Winston*), Sophia Loren (*Cinzia Zaccardi*), Martha Hyer (*Carolyn Gibson*), Harry Guardino (*Angelo Donatello*), Eduardo Ciannelli (*Arturo Zaccardi*), Murray Hamilton (*Alan Wilson*), Mimi Gibson (*Elizabeth Winston*), Paul Peterson (*David Winston*), Charles Herbert (*Robert Winston*), Madge Kennedy (*Mrs. Farnsworth*), John Litel (*Mr. Farnsworth*), Werner Klemperer (*Harold Messner*)
Filming Dates: August 12 to October 21, 1957
Release Date: November 13, 1958
Budget: $1,988,000
Production Cost: $2,226,064
North American Earnings: $3,500,000*
Foreign Earnings: N/A
Total Earnings: N/A
Profit/(Loss): N/A

65. *Indiscreet* (1958)
Production Company: Grandon Productions
Produced by Stanley Donen
Screenplay by Norman Krasna
Based on a play by Norman Krasna
Directed by Stanley Donen
Cast: Cary Grant (*Philip Adams*), Ingrid Bergman (*Anna Kalman*), Cecil Parker (*Alfred Munson*), Phyllis Calvert (*Margaret Munson*), David Kossoff (*Carl Banks*), Megs Jenkins (*Doris Banks*)
Filming Dates: November 18, 1957, to February 7, 1958
Release Date: June 21, 1958
Budget: $1,597,817
Production Cost: $1,568,000
North American Earnings: $3,429,000
Foreign Earnings: $2,625,000
Total Earnings: $6,054,000
Profit/(Loss): N/A

66. *North by Northwest* (1959)
Production Company: Metro Goldwyn Mayer
Produced by Alfred Hitchcock
Screenplay by Ernest Lehman

Directed by Alfred Hitchcock

Cast: Cary Grant (*Roger Thornhill*), Eva Marie Saint (*Eve Kendall*), James Mason (*Phillip Vandamm*), Jessie Royce Landis (*Clara Thornhill*), Leo G. Carroll (*Professor*), Josephine Hutchinson (*Mrs. Townsend*), Philip Ober (*Lester Townsend*), Martin Landau (*Leonard*), Adam Williams (*Valerian*), Edward Platt (*Victor Larrabee*), Robert Ellenstein (*Licht*), Les Tremayne (*Auctioneer*), Philip Coolidge (*Dr. Cross*), Patrick McVey (*Chicago policeman*), Edward Binns (*Capt. Junket*), Ken Lynch (*Chicago Policeman*)

Filming Dates: August 27 to December 18, 1958

Release Date: July 2, 1959

Budget: $3,630,281

Production Cost: $4,326,000

North American Earnings: $5,740,000

Foreign Earnings: $4,100,000

Total Earnings: $9,840,000

Profit/(Loss): $837,000

67. *Operation Petticoat* (1959)

Production Company: Granart Company

Produced by Robert Arthur

Screenplay by Stanley Shapiro and Maurice Richlin

Based on a story by Paul King and Joseph Stone

Directed by Blake Edwards

Cast: Cary Grant (*Matt T. Sherman*), Tony Curtis (*Nick Holden*), Joan O'Brien (*Lt. Dolores Crandall*), Dina Merrill (*Lt. Barbara Duran*), Gene Evans (*Molumphry*), Richard Sargent (*Stovall*), Virginia Gregg (*Maj. Edna Hayward*), Robert F. Simon (*Capt. J. P. Henderson*), Robert Gist (*Watson*), Gavin MacLeod (*Ernest Hunkle*), George Dunn (*The Prophet*), Dick Crockett (*Harmon*), Madlyn Rhue (*Lt. Claire Reid*), Marion Ross (*Lt. Ruth Colfax*), Clarence E. Lung (*Ramon*), Frankie Darro (*Dooley*), Tony Pastor Jr. (*Seaman Fox*), Robert Hoy (*Reiner*), Nicky Blair (*Kraus*), John W. Morley (*Williams*), Arthur O'Connell (*Sam Tostin*)

Filming Dates: January 24 to April 18, 1959

Release Date: December 2, 1959

Budget: $3,000,000

Production Cost: N/A

North American Earnings: $9,300,000

Foreign Earnings: $3,500,000
Total Earnings: 12,800,000
Profit/(Loss): N/A

68. *The Grass Is Greener* (1960)
Production Company: Grandon
Produced by Stanley Donen
Screenplay by Hugh and Margaret Williams
Based on a play by Hugh and Margaret Williams
Directed by Stanley Donen
Cast: Cary Grant (*Victor, Earl of Rhyall*), Deborah Kerr (*Countess Hilary Rhyall*), Robert Mitchum (*Charles Delacro*), Jean Simmons (*Hattie Durrant*), Moray Watson (*Sellers*),
Filming Dates: April 2 to July 20, 1960
Release Date: December 23, 1960
Budget: $3,000,000*
Production Cost: N/A
North American Earnings: $3,000,000*
Foreign Earnings: N/A
Total Earnings: N/A
Profit/(Loss): N/A

69. *That Touch of Mink* (1962)
Production Company: Granley Company, Arwin Productions, Nob Hill Productions
Produced by Stanley Shapiro and Martin Melcher
Original screenplay by Stanley Shapiro and Nate Monaster
Directed by Delbert Mann
Cast: Cary Grant (*Philip Shayne*), Doris Day (*Cathy Timberlake*), Gig Young (*Roger*), Audrey Meadows (*Connie*), Alan Hewitt (*Dr. Gruber*), John Astin (*Beasley*), Richard Sargent (*Young Man*), Joey Faye (*Short Man*), Laurie Mitchell (*Showgirl*), John Fielder (*Mr. Smith*), Willard Sage (*Hodges*), Jack Livesey (*Dr. Richardson*)
Filming Dates: began July 10, 1961
Release Date: June 14, 1962
Budget: $3,000,000*
Production Cost: N/A

North American Earnings: $8,500,000
Foreign Earnings: N/A
Total Earnings: N/A
Profit/(Loss): N/A

70. *Charade* (1963)
Production Company: Universal
Produced by Stanley Donen
Screenplay by Peter Stone
Based on a story by Peter Stone and Marc Behm
Directed by Stanley Donen
Cast: Cary Grant (*Peter Joshua/Alexander Dyle/Adam Canfield/Brian Cruikshank*), Audrey Hepburn (*Reggie Lambert*), Walter Matthau (*Hamilton Bartholomew/Carson Dyle*), James Coburn (*Tex Panthollow*), George Kennedy (*Herman Scobie*), Dominique Minot (*Sylvie Gaudet*), Ned Glass (*Leopold Gideon*), Jacques Marin (*Inspector Grandpierre*), Paul Bonifas (*Félix*), Thomas Chelimsky (*Jean-Louis Gaudet*),
Filming Dates: began October 22, 1962, to February 8, 1963
Release Date: December 5, 1963
Budget: $3,000,000*
Production Cost: N/A
North American Earnings: $6,150,000*
Foreign Earnings: N/A
Total Earnings: N/A
Profit/(Loss): N/A

71. *Father Goose* (1964)
Production Company: Granox Company
Produced by Robert Arthur
Screenplay by Peter Stone and Frank Tarloff
Based on a story by S. H. Barnett
Directed by Ralph Nelson
Cast: Cary Grant (*Walter*), Leslie Caron (*Catherine*), Trevor Howard (*Houghton*), Jack Good (*Stebbings*), Sharyl Locke (*Jenny*), Pip Sparke (*Anne*), Verina Greenlaw (*Christine*), Stephanie Berrington (*Elizabeth*), Jennifer Berrington (*Harriet*), Laurelle Felsette (*Angelique*), Nicole Felsette (*Dominique*)
Filming Dates: April 8 to June 24, 1964

Release Date: December 10, 1964
Budget: $3,493,375
Production Cost: $3,873,250
North American Earnings: $6,000,000*
Foreign Earnings: N/A
Total Earnings: N/A
Profit/(Loss): N/A

72. *Walk, Don't Run* (1966)
Production Company: Granley Company and Sol C. Siegel Productions
Produced by Sol C. Siegel
Screenplay by Sol Saks
Based on a story by Robert Russell and Frank Ross
Directed by Charles Walters
Cast: Cary Grant (*William Rutland*), Samantha Eggar (*Christine Easton*), Jim Hutton (*Steve Davis*), John Standing (*Julius D. Haversack*), Miiko Taka (*Aiko Kurawa*), Ted Hartley (*Yuri Andreyovitch*), Ben Astar (*Dimitri*)
Filming Dates: October 11, 1965, to February 12, 1966
Release Date: June 29, 1966
Budget: N/A
Production Cost: N/A
North American Earnings: 4,500,000*
Foreign Earnings: N/A
Total Earnings: N/A
Profit/(Loss): N/A

Index

Page numbers in italic indicate illustrations.

Academy Awards, 68, 164, 219, 258, 351, 374, 407
Adair, Jean, 42, 229, 230
Affair to Remember, An, 3, 339–42, 343, 350, 378, 395, 410, 416, 533–34,
Alice in Wonderland, 111, 508
Allen, Fred, 59, 63
Amazing Quest, The, 137–38, 140, 512–13
Andrea Doria (ship), 331, 338, 340, 377
Arsenic and Old Lace, 42, 216, 228–31, 258, 522–23
Arthur, Jean, 150, 155, 188–89, 191, 195, 234, 321, 408
Astaire, Fred, 76, 121–22, 140
Awful Truth, The, 3, 81, 158–64, 166, 171, 177, 197, 202–3, 217, 361, 516

Bachelor and the Bobby-Soxer, The, 276–79, 282, 288, 290, 306, 322, 324, 527–28
Bankhead, Tallulah, 83, 90
Barclay, Don, 33, 46, 59, 69, 243, 258–59
Barry, Philip, 177, 212, 415
Barrymore, Ethel, 256, *257*, 258
Barthelmess, Richard, 76, 188, 190
Bass, Mabel Johnson. *See* Leach, Elias James
Becoming Cary Grant, 3
Bellamy, Ralph, 81, 160, 162, 164, 197, 198
Bennett, Constance, 149, 157
Bennett, Joan, 145, 147–48, 236
Bergman, Ingrid, 1, 159, *271*, *273*, 289, 340, 385, 404
    friendship with Cary Grant, 268, 273, 274, 281, 307, 351–52, 355, 417
    Indiscreet, 349–50, 351, *353*
    Notorious, 269–70, 272
    Rossellini scandal, 350–52
Berman, Pandro, 182, 183
Big Brown Eyes (1936), 48, 145, 513

Birds, The, 373
Bishop's Wife, The (1947), 282–86, 294, 328, 528
Blonde Venus, 83, 86–90, 93, 98, 503
Blood and Sand, 90
Bogart, Humphrey, 190, 250, 260, 293, 326
Born to Be Bad, 110, 128, 507–8
Brackett, Charles, 61, 241, 285
Brando, Marlon, 325, 336, 364, 385
Brian, Mary, 137, 138–39, 141–42, 150, 175, 193, 230
Bridge on the River Kwai, The, 335, 355
Bringing Up Baby, 3, 164–71, 179, 182, 188, 198, 204–5, 208, 213, 215, 251, 277, 299, 320, 369, 384, 517
Brisson, Freddie, 211
Bristol, England, 9–10, 111,
    bomb damage, 276
    cinemas, 16, 17, 19, 95, 194
    and Second World War, 193–94, 221–22
    theaters, 26, 27–30, 32, 36, 37, 114, 276, 397
Bristol Lunatic Asylum, 21–24, *23*, 115, 117–18
Brooks, Phyllis, *176*, 185, 191, 194–95, 211, 230
    breakup with Cary Grant, 199–200
    career, 176, 192–93
    relationship with Cary Grant, 176–77, 180, 181, 187–88,
Brooks, Richard, 308–9, 313, 323
Buchanan, Jack, 28, 65

Cagney, James, 145, 236, 301
Cannon, Dyan, 115, 391, 395
    dating Cary Grant, 396–97, 401, 407–8
    divorce from Cary Grant, 412, 413–14
    marriage to Cary Grant, 408, 411–12
Capra, Frank, 150, 155, 189, 228–29, 230, 233, 234, 235, 246

Captain Blood, 131
Caron, Leslie, 405, 406
Carroll, Nancy, 91, 102
Casablanca, 190, 241, 263, 345
Chang, Anna, *68*
Chaplin, Charlie, 19, 36, 93, 95, 96, 212,
    240, 293, 326
Charade, 3, 346, 395, 397–401, 402–4, 407,
    410, 538
Charig, Phil, 73, 74, 84
Cherrill, Blanche, 95–96, 125, 188
Cherrill, Virginia, 93–94, 95, 130, 137, 387
    childhood and family
        background, 95–96
    dating Cary Grant, 96–97, 101, 107–9
    divorces Cary Grant, 126–27, 128–29
    film career, 96, 108, 116, 150, 193
    marriage to Cary Grant, 118, 119–20,
        123, 124–27
    trip to London and Bristol, 111, 112,
        116–17, 118
Citizen Kane, 233
City Lights, 93, 94, 96, 108
Coffee, Lenore, 145–46
Cohen, Manny, 86, 97, 102, 131
Cohn, Harry, 155, 160, 177, 195, 198, 207,
    246–47, 250, 260, 267, 268
Colbert, Claudette, 145, 149, 194, 236
Colman, Ronald, 133, 149, 164,
    201, 233–34
Columbia Pictures, 150, 250
    contract with, 155–56, 246–47, 260
Cooper, Gary, 76, 87, 111, 155, 219, 329,
    335, 413
    career and status, 78, 102, 123, 129, 149,
        325, 326
    refuses film roles, 91–92, 103, 217
    rivalry with Cary Grant, 78, 83
Coward, Noel, 119, 138, 185, 187, 300,
    362, 397
    as role model, 65–66, 80, 138, 146,
        247–48, 363
    "The Stately Homes of England"
        (song), 387–88
    visits Hollywood, 105, 175, 296
    wartime spy activities, 216
Crawford, Joan, 195
Crisis, 308–10, 313, 315, 319, 325, 530

Crosby, Bing, 111, 236, 258
Cukor, George, 3, 4, 133–36, 177–79, 212–
    15, 233, 326, 345, 413, 415
Curtis, Tony, 250, 382, 383, 384, 385
Curtiz, Michael, 263–64, 265–66, 273

Dalrymple, Jean, 49–50
Daves, Delmer, 247, 249, 255, 323
Davies, Marion, 96, 124, 140, 141, 175, 176
Day, Doris, 388–90
Day, Laraine, 242, 417
Destination Tokyo, 3, 247–50, 255, 344,
    382, 383, 524–25
Devil and the Deep, 82, 502–3
di Frasso, Dorothy, 174–75, 194, 209,
    281, 329
Dial M for Murder, 325–26.
Dietrich, Marlene, 1, 78, 83, 86–89, 93,
    187, 211
Donaldson, Ted, 251–52
Donen, Stanley, 345–46, 401, 408, 415
    and *Charade*, 397–98, 400
    and *The Grass Is Always Greener*,
        385, 387
    and *Indiscreet*, 349–50, 352–53, 355, 397
    and *Kiss Them for Me*, 345
Douglas, Melvyn, 121, 185, 217, 291, 293
Drake, Betsy, 5, *298*, 340, 407, 408
    on the *Andrea Doria* (ship), 338
    career, 294, 296–97, 298–99, 306, 313–
        14, 318, 343, 346, 355
    in *Every Girl Should Be Married*, 296–98
    LSD use, 376–77
    married life, 307, 313, 317, 327–29, 339,
        343, 354, 356–57, 378
    first meeting with Cary
        Grant, 289–90
    in *Room for One More*, 317–18
    separation and divorce, 348, 357, 376,
        380, 381, 386, 391
    trip to Europe in 1948, 301, 303–6
    trip to Europe in 1954, 331, 333
    trip to the Far East in 1952–53, 327
    trip to Spain in 1956, 337–38
    as a writer, 314, 328, 343, 357
Dream Wife, 322–25, 326, 327, 331, 532
Dunne, Irene, 1, 149, *162*, 175, 177–78,
    213, 340

in *The Awful Truth*, 160–64,
as co-star with Cary Grant, 159,
    217–18, 324
in *My Favorite Wife*, 202–3
in *Penny Serenade*, 217–18
relationship with Cary Grant, 219–20

Eagle and the Hawk, The, 103, 116, 191,
    232, 506
Edwards, Blake, 382, 384
Enter Madame!, 123–24, 128,
    150–51, 510
Every Girl Should Be Married, 294, 296–99,
    300, 529

Fairbanks, Douglas, Jr., 141–42, 181–82,
    183, 210, 211, 243, 245
Fairbanks, Douglas, Sr., 38, 48, 119,
    141, 410
Farmer, Frances, 151
Father Goose, 404–7, 416, 538–39
Ferrer, José, 309–10
    film fan magazines, 106–7, 142–44, 175
Flynn, Errol, 131, 144, 413
Fonda, Henry, 140, 147, 158, 243, 296, 382
Fontaine, Joan, 181, 208, 223, *224*,
    226–27, 340
Fox, Stanley, 261, 350, 381, 404, 408, 409,
    414, 419
Freed, Arthur, 1, 308
Front Page, The (play), 182, 195
Furness, Betty, 130–31

Gable, Clark, 102, 131, 155, 212, 213, 243,
    329, 413
    role model for Cary Grant, 75, 76,
        90, 150
    social occasions with Cary Grant, 175,
        191, 274
Gambling Ship, 103, 132, 506
Garbo, Greta, 185, 268, 307, 343
Garbus, Morton, 287
Garland, Judy, 259–60, 326, 372, 391
Gaye, Vivian, 109, 111, 120
Gering, Marion, 75–76, 83, 92, 120
Goldwyn, Samuel, 282, 283–84, 285–86
Grant, Barbara (wife), 1, 2, 418–19, 420,
    421–22, *422*

Grant, Cary,
    accent, development of, 35, 57, 58, 68,
        81, 85,
    accent imitated, 382, 395
    acting and performance
        accents (on stage and screen), 50, 64–
            65, 121, 133, 137, 162, 183, 208
        anxieties about, 59, 62, 79, 81, 160,
            228, 278, 370
        comic skills, 36, 51, 122–23, 124, 158,
            183, 203, 229–30, 248, 371, 409
        difficulties and limitations, 63–64,
            67–68, 80–81, 89, 121
        generosity toward other actors, 71,
            190, 208, 251–52, 400, 409
        improvisation on set, 135, 157–58,
            160, 167–68, 171, 181–82, 196,
            198, 240, 301–2, 333, 370–71
        method acting, 290, 325, 360, 367
        music hall training, 34–36
        "playing himself" on screen, 4, 163–
            64, 360, 374
        perfectionism on film sets, 5, 266,
            285, 341, 373
        singing, 59–60, 65, 92, 111, 122, 256
        "tumbler" (gymnastic skills), 36, 101,
            123, 167, 178, 366
        technique, 152, 371, 374, 415
        training at Paramount, 79, 152
    appearance, 15, 24–25, 39, 45, 50, 60, 68,
        75, 103
        aging, 344, 375, 389, 397, 404,
            410, 418
    clothing and fashion sense, 45–46, 52,
        100, 121, 156, 248, 331–32, 381
    dimple, 75, 398
    hair, 87–88, 269, 346, 361, 404, 420
    height, 32, 39, 45, 75, 84, 92
    tanned, 38, 100, 180
    in Technicolor, 266, 267
    teeth, 25
    art collection, 210–11, 280, 333–34, 396
    attraction to women, 52, 100–1, 175–76,
        210–11, 289, 391, 395, 418–19
    autobiographical articles ("Archie Leach
        by Cary Grant"), 401–2, 412
    and autograph-seekers, 38, 180, 354,
        356, 395

Grant, Cary (*cont.*)
  Boy Scout diary, 28–30
  Boy Scouts, member of, 25, *26*
  Bristol, visits after leaving home, 36, 37,
    62, 111, 113–18, 137–39, 185, 193–
    95, 275–76, 288, 304, 346, 386,
    396–97, 402, 407, 408, 411, 416
  in Broadway shows
    Boom Boom (1928–29), 60–61
    Golden Dawn (1927–28), 57
    Nikki (1931), 69–71, 72, 73
    Polly (1928), 59–60, 73
    The Street Singer (1930–31), 65, 67, 69
    A Wonderful Night (1929–30),
      62–65, 69
  citizenship, 201, 216, 232, 237
  clothing store, 83, 85, 88
  daughter. *See* Grant, Jennifer
  death of, 421
  drinking, 124, 125–26, 404
  education and schooling,
    Bishop Road elementary school, 16,
      17–18, 19, 24
    Fairfield secondary school, 24–26,
      29–30, 31, 114, 194, 288
    North Street Wesleyan school, 17
  father. *See* Leach, Elias James
  film career
    "a streetcar named Aspire"
      (anecdote), 326
    agents, 73, 75, 148, 286–87, 381
    decision to go to Hollywood, 72–74
    difficulty choosing films, 156, 213,
      227–28, 350, 388
    films turned down, 185, 217, 234, 299–
      300, 325–26, 335, 388, 403, 408
    freelance star, 5, 148–50, 155, 171, 191
    House Un-American Activities
      Committee, 292–93
    name change, 76–77, 174
    production companies owned, 350,
      381, 385, 388–89, 404
    retirement, 1, 2, 4, 327, 407, 408, 413
    screen tests, early, 52, 61, 75
  films. *See* individual titles
  home movies, 3, 142, 177, 180, 194, 205
  homes
    in Bristol, 9–11, 17, 18, 24

    in Brixton (London), 34
    in the Los Angeles area, 74–75,
      85, 140–41, 199, 211, 245, 261,
      286, 419
    in New York City, 41, 45, 51, 58
    in Palm Springs, 328
  homosexuality, speculation about, 5,
    52, 87, 107–8, 142–43, 168, 205,
    380–81, 418
  illness, 42, 304–5, 315–16
  Korean War tour, 327
  lecture circuit tour with *A Conversation
    with Cary Grant, A*, 1, 419–21
  LSD, use of. *See* LSD
  marriages. *See* Cannon, Dyan; Cherrill,
    Virginia; Drake, Betsy; Grant,
    Barbara; Hutton,
    Barbara;
  mother. *See* Leach, Elsie
  music hall, early experiences
    in, 26–30
  music hall shows performed in
    After the Show (1919), 37
    Getting Ready for Pantomime
      (1918–20), 33–37
  pantomimes performed in
    Dick Whittington (1919–20), 37
    Jack and the Beanstalk (1918–19), 37
  performance. *See* acting
  radio performances, 130, 185, 258, 261,
    314, 328
  Second World War service,
    charities, 232, 252
    conscription in Britain, 201–2
    Hollywood Victory Caravan, 235–37
    King's Medal for Service in the Cause
      of Freedom, 216
    salary donations, 216, 222,
      227–28, 230
    seeks military commission, 231, 232,
      241, 242–43
    camp and hospital tours, 243–44,
      258–59, 261
  stinginess, reputation for, 126–27, 253–
    54, 409, 411
  star image
    as bachelor, 106–7, 143–44, 175, 230,
      275, 277, 297, 347, 349, 369, 390

clothing stolen or damaged in films, 9, 165–66, 248–49, 360–61, 368, 383, 389–90, 398, 409
as "art deco dandy", 121–22, 124
publicity, 66–67, 78, 90, 100, 106–7, 108, 142–44, 156, 175, 205, 251, 295–96, 327, 375, 379–380
as "mannequin", 89–80, 82, 98
references to himself on screen, 146–47, 178, 183, 198, 230, 242, 256–57, 321, 359–60
as "tough guy", 86–87, 90, 95, 103, 120
stilt-walking, 32, 35, 37, 39–40, 41, 42, 45, 46, 47, 52, 256
suicide staged, 125–26
in vaudeville shows, 40–51, 59, 236, 243
    Better Times (1922–23), 46–47
    From the Bottom to the Top (1923–24), 47–49
    Good Times (1920–21), 40–41
    Oh! I Did Not (1928), 59
    The Woman Pays (1924–25), 49–51, 148
Grant, Jennifer, 1, 410, 411–12, 413–14, 416–17, 419, 421–22, *422*
Grass is Greener, The, 346, 385–88, 537
Great Gatsby, The (book), 67
Gunga Din, 180–85, 191, 195, 202, 217, 320, 382, 518

Hammerstein, Arthur, 53, 57–58, 60, 67, 72
Hammerstein, Reginald, 53, 57
Harlow, Jean, 110, 145–47
Harris, Barbara. *See* Grant, Barbara
Harrison, Rex, 386, 403–4, 418
Hartman, Mortimer, 377, 378, 381
Hawks, Howard, 4, 227–28, 229, 242, 246, 284, 397, 415
    and *Bringing Up Baby*, 165–70, 198
    on Cary Grant as performer, 171, 190
    and *Gunga Din*, 182
    and *His Girl Friday*, 195–96, 198
    and *I Was a Male War Bride*, 300, 302–3, 304, 305
    influence on screen image of Cary Grant, 165–66, 204, 277

and *Monkey Business*, 320–21
and *Only Angels Have Wings*, 188–91
and women stars, 189–90, 195–96, 321–22
working methods, 167–69, 196, 301–2
Hayes, John Michael, 331, 333
Hays Office, the, 98–99, 128, 136, 318–19
Hayworth, Rita, 189–90, 191, 195, 250, 287, 321, 340
Head, Edith, 99, 331–32
Hearst, William Randolph, Sr., 96, 175
Hecht, Ben, 182, 184, 195, 268, 274, 320, 415
Hellzapoppin', 187, 243–44
Hensel, Betty, 269, 274–75, 280, 295
Hepburn, Audrey, 1, 395, 397–400, *398*, 403, 418
Hepburn, Katharine, 1, 133, 164, 170, 171, 215, 241–42, 289, 297, 313, 324, 398–99
    in *Bringing Up Baby*, 164, 167–68, *169*, 277
    "box-office poison" label, 179–80, 212
    in *Holiday*, 177–79
    in *The Philadelphia Story*, 212–15
    in *Sylvia Scarlett*, 133–36, *136*
His Girl Friday, 3, 81, 121, 148, 195–99, *197*, 218, 227–28, 300, 320, 321, 519–20
Hitchcock, Alfred, 1, 3, 4, 59, 137, 214, 232, 233, *273*, 330, *334*, 351, *371*
    and actors, 364, 372, 417–18
    Alfred Hitchcock Presents (television series), 391
    characters' similarities with Cary Grant, 272, 330, 334, 359–60, 366
    favorite actor is Cary Grant, 268, 359, 367, 417
    films considered but not made together, 222, 255, 275, 299–300, 326, 328, 408
    friendship with Cary Grant, 220–21, 273, 267, 274, 299, 327, 333, 338, 385, 396, 417–18
    Hamlet planned, 274, 279, 370
    influence on Cary Grant's career, 131, 331, 220, 335, 358–59, 361, 399

Hitchcock, Alfred (*cont.*)
  and *North by Northwest*, 358–59, 361,
    364, 365–66, 367, 370–74
  and *Notorious*, 267–74, 359, 361,
    364, 369,
  and *Suspicion*, 222–27, 359
  and *To Catch a Thief*, 327, 329–35, 359
  working relationship, 267, 268,
    333, 373–74
Holiday, 177–80, 212, 214, 215, 517
Hope, Bob, 236, 259, 297, 356
Hopper, Hedda, 127, 215, 219, 294, 295–
  96, 299, 309, 348, 380–81
Horn, Frank, 141, 168, 237, 238
Hot Saturday, 90–91, 97, 503–4
Houseboat, 338, 343, 346–49, *349*, 534–35
Howards of Virginia, The, 206–9, 210,
  336, 520–21
Hudson, Rock, 385, 388, 389, 390, 397
Hughes, Howard, 124, 130, 232, 287, 296,
  306, 388, 396
  friendship with Cary Grant, 86,
    174, 280–81
  plane crash, 281–82
  plane missing, 283–84
  relationship with Katharine Hepburn,
    134–35, 177
  and RKO, 307
  and Trans-World Airlines, 274, 275, 314
Hutton, Barbara, 39, *253*,
  divorce from Cary Grant, 261–62, 265
  early relationship with Cary Grant,
    209–12, 220, 230, 237–38
  marriage to Cary Grant, 238–39, 245,
    252–54, 258–61
  marriages to others, 209, 239, 261,
    317, 329
Hyams, Joe, 379–80, 401–2

"I Can't Give You Anything but Love,
  Baby" (song), 167, 251
I Was a Male War Bride, 300–6, 320,
  409, 530
I'm No Angel, 104–5, 113, 115, 120, 507
In Name Only, 191–93, 218, 519
In Which We Serve, 247–48
Indiscreet, 3, 346, 349–55, *353*, 356, 385,
  387, 397, 535

Jaffe, Sam, 181, 184
James Bond (films), 374, 388
Jones, Quincy, 255, 411

Kael, Pauline, 4, 95, 214
Kanin, Garson, 202–3, 205, 213
Kelly, Grace, 1, 159, *334*, 414
  admired by Cary Grant, 329, 332–33,
    335, 420
  career of, 329, 332
  death of, 420
  friendship with Cary Grant, 333, 417
  as Princess Grace, 337–38, 386,
    354, 422
  in *To Catch a Thief*, 330–31, 331–32
Kelly, Jack, 231, 413
  in Hollywood, 73, 74–75, 83, 84, 101
  in New York, 51–53, 62, 67, 69
  Women I've Undressed
    (autobiography), 52
Kennedy Center Honors, 418
Kennedy, President John F., 395, 403
Kennedy, Robert F., 395, 402–3
Kerr, Deborah, 1, 159, 322–23, 324, 340,
  342, 386
Kingdon, Alice (aunt), 12, 22, 24
Kingdon, Charles (uncle), 12–13,
  139, 172
Kingdon, Charlotte (aunt). *See* Monk,
  Charlotte
Kingdon, David (cousin), 113
Kingdon, David (uncle), 139
Kingdon, Elsie Maria (mother). *See*
  Leach, Elsie
Kingdon, Ernest (cousin), 24, 113
Kiss and Make-Up, 121–22, 125, 128,
  179, 509
Kiss Them for Me, 343–45, 346, 378, 534
Korda, Alexander, 137, 212, 275, 280, 282,
  287–88, 289, 294, 300, 305
Koster, Henry, 284–85
Kramer, Stanley, 336, 339

Ladies Should Listen, 121–23, 125, 128,
  179, 509–10
Lamour, Dorothy, 147, 177
Landi, Elissa, 123–24
Landis, Jesse Royce, 333, 360

Last Outpost, The, 132–33, 273, 511–12
Laughton, Charles, 83, 117, 131
Laurel and Hardy, 156, 159, 181, 236
Lawrence of Arabia, 388
Leach, Alfred (uncle), 24
Leach, Archie. *See* Grant, Cary
Leach, Elias James (father), 11, *63*,
    66, 256
  appearance and dress sense, 13–14,
    19, 24, 45
  death of, 138
  drinking, 17, 115
  employment, 15–16, 17, 19, 31
  family background, 13
  marriage to Elsie Maria Kingdon, 15,
    17–18, 19, 21–22, 31
  relationship with Archie Leach, 17, 19,
    24, 33–34, 36, 43, 47, 62
  relationship with Cary Grant, 109–10,
    113–15, 138–39
  relationship with Mabel Johnson Bass,
    31, 62, 114–15
Leach, Elizabeth Leaf (grandmother),
    13, 24, 29
Leach, Elsie (mother), 3–4, 9, 11–12, *15*,
    100, *173*, 222, *244*, 356, 410, 411
  appearance and dress sense, 13–14,
    117, 172
  aspirations, 13, 15–17, 172
  death of, 416
  family background, 12–13
  letters from, 172–73, 185–86, 193, 221,
    244–45, 275, 288, 401–2
  marriage to Elias James Leach, 15, 17–
    18, 19–20, 21–22, 31, 172
  mental illness, 12, 19, 20, 21–24,
    139, 380
  relationship with Archie Leach, 3–4, 16,
    18, 19–20, 25
  relationship with Cary Grant, 115, 117–
    18, 193–94, 256, 276, 304, 346, 386,
    396–97, 407, 408
  release from the asylum, 139, 172
Leach, Eric (brother), 31, *63*, 115, 137,
    139, 397
Leach, Eric (cousin), 397, 402, 416
Leach, Frederick (uncle), 222
Leach, John (uncle), 24, 185, 221–22

Leach, Percival (invented grandfather),
    66–67, 144
Leach, Rose (aunt), 185, 194, 221–22
Lean, David, 335, 388
Lederer, Charles, 300, 320, 415
Lehman, Ernest, 358–59, 370, 373
Lives of a Bengal Lancer, The, 123, 132, 182
Lloyd, Harold, 156, 165, 320
Lodger, The, 59, 359
Lomas, Robert. *See* Pender, Bob
Lomas, Tommy, 32, 47, 104
Lomas Troupe, the, 47–49, 101, 104
Lombard, Carole, 76, 141, 147, 175,
    222, 232
  at Paramount, 78, 82, 122, 145, 147
  contracts as freelance star, 149, 191
  In Name Only, 191–92
Lonsdale, Frederick, 280, 287, 289
Loren, Sophia, 343, *349*, 356–57, 376
  in *Houseboat*, 346–47,
  in *The Pride and the Passion*, 339
  relationship with Cary Grant, 336–38,
    339–40, 342, 346, 347–48, 380
Loy, Myrna, 128–29, 277–78, 290–91, 293
LSD, 375, 376–81, 391, 395, 407–8,
    412, 413
Lubitsch, Ernst, 79, 131–32, 185, 240

MacDonald, Jeanette, 60–61
MacMurray, Fred, 140, 145, 149
Mad Men (television series), 374–75
Madame Butterfly, 91–93, 103, 120, 504
Man Who Came to Dinner, The, 227–28
Mankiewicz, Joseph, 215, 314–16
Mansfield, Jayne, 343, 344, 345
March, Fredric, 78, 82, 164
Marx Brothers, The, 78, 158–59
Mason, James, 160, 326, 360, 362
McCarey, Leo, 4, 164, 177, 181, 246, 258,
    341, 345, 351
  and *An Affair to Remember*, 340–42
  and *Awful Truth, The*, 158–61
  and *My Favorite Wife*, 202–6
  and *Once Upon a Honeymoon*, 239–40
  and screen image of Cary Grant, 160–
    61, 171, 277, 342
McLaglen, Victor, 181, 183
Merrily We Go to Hell, 82, 97, 502

Metro-Goldwyn-Mayer (MGM), 3, 131, 144, 145–47, 212–13, 307–8, 414
Michael, Gertrude, 126, 132–33
Milland, Ray, 164, 217
Monk, Charlotte (aunt), 18
Monk family (cousins Dora, Josephine and Lillian), 18–20
Monkey Business, 319–22, 325, 331, 376, 409, 531–32
Monroe, Marilyn, 314, 321, 322, 327, 382, 388, 397
Montgomery, Robert, 121–22, 131, 164
Moore, Constance, 211, 254, 274, 281
Moore, Grace, 150
More the Merrier, The, 234, 408, 411
Morocco, 78, 87
Mr. and Mrs. Blandings (radio series), 314
Mr. Blandings Builds His Dream House, 290–292, 293–94, 314, 528–29
Mr. Lucky, 241–43, 275, 417, 524
Mutiny on the Bounty, 131, 145, 207
My Favorite Wife, 202–6, 217–18, 239, 520

National Vaudeville Artists Club (NVA), 45, 51
Netcher, Townsend, 142, 175
Night and Day, 260, 261, 263–67, 288, 526
Night Must Fall (play), 131
Ninotchka, 185
Niven, David, 141, 201, 217, 283, 284, 285–86, 289, 328, 378
None but the Lonely Heart, 254–58, *257*, 261, 293, 308, 410, 525–26
North by Northwest, 3, 357, 358–75, 376, 378, 379, 385, 400, 535–36
  crop-dusting scene, 358, 364–66, 372–73, 420
  filming, 160, 372–373
  Hitchcock-Grant "formula", 361, 366
  influence, 374–75
  reception, 374
  script and story development, 358–59, 370–71
  suit worn by Cary Grant, 358, 360–61, 365, 368

Notorious, 3, 133, 267–74, *271*, 283, 350, 355, 359, 363, 364, 369, 416, 417, 527

Oberon, Merle, 141, 212, 236, 280, 289
Odets, Clifford, 254–58, 293, 377, 398, 415
Olivier, Laurence, 201
Once Upon a Honeymoon, 239–41, 246, 322, 523–24
Once Upon a Time, 250–52, 525
Only Angels Have Wings, 188–91, 232, 518
Operation Petticoat, 250, 379, 381–85, 388, 407, 536–37
Orry-Kelly. *See* Kelly, Jack

Palm Beach Story, The, 120
Paramount Pictures, 3, 67–68
  contract with, 75–76, 83, 148–49, 151–52
  dramatic training school, 79, 85
  financial problems, 86, 97, 100
  loan-outs from, 102–3, 110, 133, 145–46, 150, 151
  programmers produced, 77, 91, 103, 120, 140
  Cary returns in 1954, 333
  salary earnings from, 75, 89, 129, 131
  studio culture, 77–78
Parsons, Louella, 90, 125, 130, 252, 295–96, 299, 306, 348, 380
Patrick, Gail, 204
Peck, Gregory, 326, 359, 408, 414
Pender, Bob, 31–44, 45, 47
Pender Troupe, the, 31–44, 45, 46, 48, 66, 101
Penny Serenade, 3, 217–20, 258, 318, 416, 521–22
People Will Talk (1951), 315–17, 319, 530–31
Philadelphia Story, The, 3, 170, 212–16, 217, 222, 521
Pickford, Mary, 38, 119, 141
Pirate Party on Catalina Island (1936), 144
Porter, Cole, 260, 263, 264, 267, 396
Powell, William, 103, 274, 325
Power, Tyrone, 175, 194, 243, 284, 326, 413
Pride and the Passion, The, 336–39, 346, 347, 378, 533
Psycho, 373

Raft, George, 79, 97, 103, 147, 301
Rains, Claude, 132–33, 270, 273, 274
Rebecca, 220, 222, 223
Reventlow, Lance, 209–10, 237, 252, 259, 317, 318, 329
RKO Radio Pictures, 3, 133–34, 151, 254, 290, 307, 350
   contracts with, 158, 164, 206, 246
   production costs, 151, 169, 182, 206, 256
Roach, Hal, 3, 156, 175, 176, 181
Rogers, Ginger, 176, 179, 195, 202, 239–40, 293, 321–22, 419
Roman Holiday, 325–26
Romance and Riches. See *The Amazing Quest*
Room for One More, 317–19, 328, 343, 346, 531
Rope, 299–300
Ruggles, Charles, 79, *80*
Russell, Rosalind, 238, 287, 324, 413
   friendship with Cary Grant, 196, 211, 219, 259, 281
   in *His Girl Friday*, 195–97
   plans to work together again, 217, 227–28

Saint, Eva Marie, 1, 360, 364, *368*, 372, 374
Saunders, John Monk, 69–71, 76, 103
Schary, Dore, 277, 278, 290, 294, 307–8, 322–23, 324–25, 415
Scott, Randolph, 79, 140, 175, 296, 325, 388
   friendship with Cary Grant, 84–86, 108, 124, 125, 174, 177, 211, 237, 275, 325
   girlfriends, 94, 109, 120, 177
   in *Hot Saturday*, 91
   house sharing with Cary Grant, 85, 119–20, 140–44, 199, 205, 211
   marriages, 144, 177, 211, 275
   in *My Favorite Wife*, 204–5
   publicity about, 106–7, 142–44, 156
   trip to England with Cary Grant, 111–13, 116
   wartime activities, 211, 259
Selznick, David, 268, 277, 290, 294, 314,
Selznick, Irene Mayer, 74, 281, 325, 329
Shapiro, Stanley, 382, 388–89, 415

She Done Him Wrong (1932), 97–101, *99*, 104, 120, 505
Sheldon, Sidney, 276–77, 279, 322–25, 415
Sheridan, Ann, 301–2, *303*, 304, 324
Sherwood, Robert E., 283, 284–85, 415
Shubert Organization, 60, 65, 69, 72
Schulberg, B.P., 75–76, 92, 120, 147
Shearer, Norma, 141, 254
Sidney, Sylvia, 78, 82, 91–93, 120–21
Simmons, Jean, 313, 386
Sinatra, Frank, 259, 336, 339, 396, 414–15
Singapore Sue (1931), 67–69, *68*, 73, 75, 80
Sinners in the Sun (1932), 82, 97, 191, 502
Sleepless in Seattle, 342
Some Like It Hot, 382
Star is Born, A, 326
Stevens, George, 3, 4,
   and *Gunga Din*, 181–84
   and *Penny Serenade*, 217–19
   and *The Talk of the Town*, 232, 234–35
Stewart, James, 211, 243, 275, 296, 385
   and Hitchcock, 214, 299–300, 358–59
   in *The Philadelphia Story*, 212–13, 214, 215–16
Stone, Peter, 398, 400, 404, 406, 415
Streetcar Named Desire, A (play), 325
Sturges, Preston, 120, 251
Suspicion, 222–27, 233, 363, 399, 522
Suzy, 145–47, 201, 232, 513–14
Sylvia Scarlett, 133–37, 140, 155, 171, 183, 202, 254, 512

Talk of the Town, The, 232–35, 523
Talmadge, Constance, 141, 142, 199
Talmadge, Norma, 199
Taylor, Elizabeth, 287, 385
Temple, Shirley, 177, 277, 278, 291
That Touch of Mink, 388–90, 391, 397, 407, 537–38
Thief of Bagdad, The, 48, 145
Third Man, The, 300
Thirty Day Princess, 120–21, 508–9
This is the Night, 79–81, *80*, 89, 121, 501
Thomson, David, 4, 359
Thyssen, Greta, 390, 396
Tillie, Vesta, 29, 34
To Be on Not to Be, 240

To Catch a Thief (1955), 327, 329–35, 359, 363, 400, 532–33
Toast of New York, The, 151, 171, 515
Topper, 28, 156–58, 171, 175, 176, 285, 295, 361, 516
Tracy, Spencer, 212, 213, 214, 308, 313, 409, 413
Twentieth Century–Fox Pictures, 3, 301, 314–15, 319

United Artists, 336
Universal-International Pictures, 380–81, 385, 388,

Valentino, Rudolph, 76, 90
Vincent, Frank W., 148, 230, 238, 260, 261, 283, 286–87
von Sternberg, Josef, 78, 86–89, 93

Wald, Jerry, 3, 247, 249–50, 340, 341, 343–44
Walk, Don't Run, 409–11, 412, 539
Walsh, Raoul, 48, 145
Wanger, Walter, 145
Warner, Jack, 187, 212, 227, 228, 254, 260, 263, 264, 268, 318–19, 352, 388, 403–4

Warner Bros. Pictures, 3, 52, 73, 158, 222, 227–28, 247, 318, 350
Wayne, John, 76, 190, 385
Wedding Present, 147–48, 514
West, Mae, 99, 129, 140, 145, 155, 322, 418, 420
  in *I'm No Angel*, 104–5
  in *She Done Him Wrong*, 97–101
When You're in Love, 150–51, 155, 514–15
Who Is He? (play), 359
Wilder, Billy, 285, 326, 335, 382
Wings in the Dark, 128–30, 185, 232, 278, 511
Winslow, George, 317, 321
Woman Accused, The, 102, 505
Wray, Fay, 70–71, 73–74, 76, 85–86, 114, 174
Wyler, William, 284, 293, 300

Young, Loretta, 110, 284, 285
Young, Roland, 79, 157

Zanuck, Darryl F., 110, 268, 300–1, 306, 315, 316, 320
Zerbe, Jerome, 142–43
Zukor, Adolph, 148, 151–52